PETER LOMBARD

BRILL'S STUDIES IN INTELLECTUAL HISTORY

General Editor

A.J. VANDERJAGT, University of Groningen

Editorial Board
M. COLISH, Oberlin College
J.I. ISRAEL, University College, London
J.D. NORTH, University of Groningen
H.A. OBERMAN, University of Arizona, Tucson
R.H. POPKIN, Washington University, St. Louis-UCLA

VOLUME 41/2

PETER LOMBARD

BY

MARCIA L. COLISH

VOLUME TWO

E.J. BRILL
LEIDEN · NEW YORK · KÖLN
1994

The paper in this book meets the guidelines for permanence and durability of the Committee on Production Guidelines for Book Longevity of the Council on Library Resources.

Library of Congress Cataloging-in-Publication Data

Colish, Marcia L.
    Peter Lombard / by Marcia L. Colish.
      p.   cm. — (Brill's studies in intellectual history, ISSN 0920-8607 ; v. 41)
    Includes bibliographical references and indexes.
    ISBN 9004098615 (set : alk. paper). — ISBN 9004098593 (v. 1 : alk. paper). — ISBN 9004098607 (v. 2 : alk. paper)
    1. Peter Lombard, Bishop of Paris, ca. 1100-1160. 2. Theology, Doctrinal—History—Middle Ages, 600-1500.   I. Title. II. Series.
BX1749.P4C64   1993
230'.2'092—dc20   93-8757
                                                          CIP

Die Deutsche Bibliothek - CIP-Einheitsaufnahme

Colish, Marcia L.:
Peter Lombard / by Marcia L. Colish. – Leiden ; New York ; Köln : Brill.
  (Brill's studies in intellectual history ; Vol. 41)
  ISBN 90–04–09861–5
NE: GT
Vol. 2 (1993)
  ISBN 90–04–09860–7

ISSN 0920-8607
ISBN 90 04 09860 7 (Vol. 2)
ISBN 90 04 09861 5 (Set)

PRINTED IN THE NETHERLANDS

CONTENTS

AUTHOR'S NOTE

I include this author's note in order to clarify some technical stylistic decisions made in this book which entail apparent inconsistencies, inconsistencies which medievalists have long since come to live with, if not to love, but which may trouble readers coming to this book from another part of the landscape.

First, there was no agreement on Latin spelling in the Middle Ages, a fact reflected in the policies of editors of medieval texts and the houses that publish them. Some editors and publishers systematically classicize the spelling of medieval Latin, however the language may be used in the manuscripts on which the texts depend. For example, they substitute "i" for "j" or "u" for "v" on this basis. On the other hand, some editors and publishers retain the spellings found in the manuscripts. I have followed the practice, when quoting from editions of medieval Latin texts, of preserving whichever decision regarding the spelling is followed by the edition in question.

Another discrepancy concerns the Anglicization, or not, of the Latin names of medieval personages, and the titles of well known works. There are names, such as John of Salisbury, Gilbert of Poitiers, and Peter Lombard, whose English form is in common use among Anglophone readers. It would be an affectation to refer to these people in Latin or in another language. On the other hand, there are figures, such as Ordericus Vitalis and Jacques de Vitry, for whom this is not the case. My practice has been to use whichever version of the name has the greatest immediate recognition value, regardless of the lack of symmetry that any result. Similarly, while the titles of works written in Latin will usually be cited in that language in the text, others, such as Abelard's *Ethics* and Augustine's *City of God* or *Eighty-Three Diverse Questions*, will be given in English as more familiar or as less cumbersome than their Latin originals.

I will have occasion to cite repeatedly in this book the works of scholastic theologians and canonists, not only by the page or column number in the texts in which their works are printed, but according to the more specific, and traditional, finding tools indicated by the subdivisions within their texts. This practice, too, is quite standard for medievalists, who will readily recognize abbreviations such as "d" for *distinctio*, "c" for *capitulum* or *causa*, "q" for *quaestio,* and *dictum* for a canonist's summation of a point. This system of abbreviations should serve as a guide for any readers unfamiliar with this standard scheme of citation for medieval texts.

Let me note as well that no effort has been made here to regularize the spelling of "mediaeval" to "medieval" or vice versa. When these adjectives occur in titles or in the house style of publishers, the spelling given by the author or by the publisher is the spelling that will be followed.

I will have occasion to cite female scholars, both in the bibliography and in footnotes organized alphabetically, who began to publish under one surname but who have changed their surnames thanks to a change in their marital status. I will cite their works alphabetized according to the first surnames under which they began to publish, with their subsequent surnames indicated in square brackets following their original names. I trust that this practice will not be confusing to readers who may initially seek citations to the writings of these scholars in locations where they will not be found.

ABBREVIATIONS

AHDLMA	*Archives d'histoire doctrinale et littéraire du moyen âge*
Beiträge	Beiträge zur Geschichte der Philosophie [und Theologie] des Mittelalters
CCCM	Corpus Christianorum, continuatio medievalis
CCSL	Corpus Christianorum, series latina
CIMAGEL	*Cahiers de l'Institut du moyen âge grec et latin de l'Université de Copenhague*
CSEL	Corpus scriptorum ecclesiasticorum latinorum
DTC	*Dictionnaire de théologie catholique*
ETL	*Ephemerides Theologicae Lovanienses*
FS	*Franciscan Studies*
Landgraf, *Dogmengeschichte*	Artur Michael Landgraf, *Dogmengeschichte der Frühscholastik*, 4 vols. (Regensburg: Friedrich Pustet, 1952–56)
MGH, Scriptores	Monumenta Germaniae Historica, Scriptores
Misc. Lomb.	*Miscellanea Lombardiana* (Novara: Istituto Geografico de Agostini, 1957)
PL	*Patrologia latina, cursus completus*, ed. J. P. Migne
RHE	*Revue d'histoire ecclésiastique*
Rolls Series	Rerum Brittanicarum medii aevi, Scriptores
RSPT	*Revue des sciences philosophiques et théologiques*
RSR	*Revue des sciences religieuses*
RTAM	*Recherches de théologie ancienne et médiévale*
ZkT	*Zeitschrift für katholische Theologie*

CHAPTER EIGHT

ETHICS, SACRAMENTS, AND LAST THINGS

The topics to be treated in this chapter, with the exception of ethics, are all found in the fourth and final book of Peter Lombard's *Sentences*. They received widely varying degrees of attention in the first half of the twelfth century. Some of them were regarded as meriting sustained and systematic investigation and were treated as subjects that warranted a clear and well-rationalized location in any *summa* or sentence collection. Others were taken up in a more random manner, without the sense that they needed discussion at some specifically chosen place in a theologian's writings, or were omitted altogether. Some aspects of these questions elicited a striking degree of consensus among contemporaries, while in other areas they were sharply divided. Controversy was particularly acute in the field of sacramental theology, both in response to the need to define and defend these rites of the church against heretics of an anti-sacramental persuasion and as an expression of the desire to work out practical and theoretical problems attached to their administration and reception. Peter Lombard plays a range of roles in his address to the subjects dealt with in this chapter. On some topics he takes a strongly partisan stand, and makes a critical contribution in helping to undermine the countervailing view. In some parallel areas, his equally partisan position does not have the same kind of effect. There are some fields in which he argues for caution and reticence over against what he regards as groundless speculation that has gotten out of hand. Finally, there are areas where his goal, a goal successfully attained, is to sum up and to expand upon the contemporary consensus, incorporating the insights of its bolder articulations while moderating their extremes.

ETHICS

This last-mentioned orientation is definitely the one that Peter takes in the field of ethics. From a schematic point of view, ethics is the major subject on which his gift for lucid organization deserts him. He does not take up all the points relevant to this topic in one place. There is some analysis of the psychology of ethical decision-making in his Pauline exegesis, and this theme recurs in his consideration of the fall in Book 2 of the *Sentences*. It is there, as well, under the heading of human nature, that he considers the vices, and the relationship between man's free will and divine grace in the moral life both before and after the fall. Ethical intentionality and sin reappear, in detail, in his analysis of the sacraments, typically penance and marriage, in Book 4. While Peter discusses the gifts of the Holy Spirit and the virtues which they help mankind to develop as an extension of his treatment of grace and free will in Book 2, his principal analysis of virtue, both the theological virtues, the cardinal virtues, and the gifts of the Holy Spirit occurs in Book 3, in connection with the moral aptitudes of the human Christ. Notwithstanding the schematic disjunctions which this plan of attack involves, Philippe Delhaye, our leading guide on Peter's ethical doctrine to date, is quite right in pointing out that his ideas do manage to cohere, on the whole, even though they are not presented synthetically.[1]

In general, Peter's ethics is marked by two notes, both of which are clear hallmarks of the theology of his time. On the one hand, he is deeply committed to the view that all meritorious acts require the collaboration of man's free will and God's grace. While he is resolutely opposed to the idea that grace is irresistible or that man, in his fallen state, is unable to desire the good, Peter is only marginally interested in what might be called a purely natural ethics. We recall here that, in his treatment of the nature of man as such, before the fall, he holds that grace must interact with man's free will if man is to acquire virtue. At the same time, Peter shares the view, widespread in his time, that the psychic ground on which man makes ethical decisions and on which he acts, reacts, and develops, is a subject that requires extended and sympathetic consideration. The systematic interiorizing of ethics, the analysis of what ethical behavior means in the inner life of the moral subject, and the consequent stress on intentionality in ethics that mark this period are equally compelling themes for Peter. He gives lucid articulation to these concerns. While seeking to preserve a sense that some acts are objectively wrong and while arguing that good intentions should normally be expressed in appropriate good actions, he retains the common view of the period that intentionality is the essence of the moral act and that, absent the act, it defines the moral status of the moral agent.[2]

---

[1] Philippe Delhaye, *Pierre Lombard: Sa vie, ses oeuvres, sa morale* (Montreal: Institut d'Études Médiévales, 1961), pp. 24–25, 28–100.
[2] The best overall study of this theme in our period is Robert Blomme, *La*

INTENTIONALISM IN ETHICS: THE CONSENSUS AND THE DISAGREEMENTS WITHIN IT

The analysis of the psychology of moral choice on which Peter draws is ultimately Stoic in provenance and was mediated to the twelfth century by patristic authorities such as Jerome and Augustine. This position was held widely during the period. The theory is based on the principle that sin, or virtue, lies in a fixed intentionality toward evil, or good, respectively. These moral states are controlled by the mind, not by the body. Temptations to sin or inclinations to virtue may, to be sure, arise in any part of the human constitution. But it is not the inclination itself, but a rational and deliberate assent to it, the mind having judged it to be morally desirable, that constitutes the moral agent's ethical commitment and that makes him vicious or virtuous. In Hieronymian language, the process involves, with respect to sin, a *passio* or temptation, a *propassio* or hospitable contemplation of the temptation, and a *consensus*, or conscious capitulation to it. Language also found in this period which embodies precisely the same analysis substitutes *suggestio*, *delectatio*, and *consensus*, the first term including the idea that the temptation may be internal or external. The school of Laon uses both of these vocabularies, repeating the point frequently, and their lead is followed widely. Peter follows suit.[3]

---

doctrine du péché dans les écoles théologiques de la première moitié du XIIᵉ siècle (Louvain: Publications Universitaires de Louvain, 1958). See also Artur Michael Landgraf, "Die Bestimmung des Verdienstgrades in der Frühscholastik," *Scholastik* 8 (1933): 1–40; *Dogmengeschichte* 1 part 2: 210–61; Odon Lottin, *Psychologie et morale aux XIIᵉ et XIIIᵉ siècles*, vols. 1–5 (Louvain: Abbaye de Mont-César, 1948–59), 2: 421–22, 4 part 1: 310–19.
   [3] *Sentences of Anselm of Laon*, no. 10, 85–86; *Sentences of Plausible Authenticity*, no. 218; *Sentences of William of Champeaux*, no. 277–78; *Sentences of the School of Laon*, no. 422, 423, 447, 449, 450–54, ed. Lottin in *Psych. et morale*, 5: 22, 73–74, 138–39, 221–22, 292, 302–03, 303–05; *Sententie Anselmi* 2, ed. Franz P. Bliemetzrieder in *Anselms von Laon systematische Sentenzen*, Beiträge, 18:2–3 (Münster: Aschendorff, 1919), p. 71; *Biblia latina cum Glossa ordinaria*, 4: *In Mattheum* 5:27; *In Epistolam ad Romanos* 6:12; *In Epistolam II ad Corinthios* 12:7, editio princeps (Strassburg: Adolph Rusch?, c. 1481); repr. with intro. by Karlfried Froelich and Margaret T. Gibson (Turnhout: Brepols, 1992); also *PL* 114: 94D, 488D–489A, 568C; Gratian, *Decretum* pars 1. d. 6. c. 1–c. 3; pars 2. c. 15. q. 1. pars 1 prologus, d. 2. c. 21, ed. Aemilius Friedberg, Corpus Iuris Canonici, 1 (Leipzig: Tauchnitz, 1879), cols. 9–11, 744–45, 1197; Roland of Bologna, *Die Sentenzen Rolands*, ed. Ambrosius M. Gietl (Amsterdam: Editions Rodopi, 1969 [repr. of Freiburg im Breisgau: Herder, 1891 ed.]), p. 255; Peter Abelard, *Ethics*, ed. and trans. David E. Luscombe (Oxford: Clarendon Press, 1971), p. 32; *Commentarius in I Corinthios* 10 in *Commentarius Cantabridgensis in Epistolas Pauli e schola Petri Abaelardi*, ed. Artur Michael Landgraf, 4 vols. (Notre Dame: University of Notre Dame Press, 1937–45), 2: 256–57; Hugh of St. Victor, *De sacramentis fidei christianae* 1.5.25, 2.13.1, *PL* 176: 257B–258D, 525C; *Sententiae divinitatis* 2.2.3, ed. Bernhard Geyer, *Die Sententiae*

Whether or not the theologians make express use of either of
these vocabularies, there is a broad consensus among them on the
point that intentionality is of the essence in the moral life.[4] Yet,
within that consensus, a number of related questions emerged on
which there was a wider play of opinions. One, which focused on
the sin of lying, involved a critique of Augustine's position in his
Contra mendacium, where he defines lying as involving both an objective untruth and the intention to deceive. Twelfth-century theolo-

---

divinitatis: Ein Sentenzenbuch der Gilbertischen Schule, Beiträge 7:2–3 (Münster Aschendorff, 1909), pp. 24*–26*, 28*–29*; Robert Pullen, *Sententiarum libri octo* 5.33, *PL*
186: 854D–856A; Peter Lombard, *In Epistolam Pauli ad Romanos* 6:12–14, 7:7–8, *PL*
191: 1407C–D 1416D. Scholars who have noted this vocabulary and this analysis
of the psychogenesis of ethical decisions in one or more of these figures include
Ermenegildo Bertola, "La dottrina morale di Pietro Abelardo," *RTAM* 55 (1988):
53–71; Blomme, *La doctrine du péché*, pp. 21–87; Scott Davis, "The Unity of the
Virtues in Abelard's *Dialogues*," *Proceedings of the PMR Conference*, 11, ed. Phillip
Pulsiano (Villanova: Augustinian Historical Institute, 1986), pp. 71–82; Lottin,
Psych. et morale, 2: 494–96; David E. Luscombe, "The *Ethics* of Abelard: Some
Further Considerations," in *Peter Abelard*, ed. Eligius M. Buytaert (Leuven:
Leuven University Press, 1974), p. 71.
[4] *Sentences of Anselm of Laon*, no. 68, 78; *Sentences of William of Champeaux*, no.
277–78; *Sentences of the School of Laon*, no. 422, 423, 447, 449, 5: 59, 67, 221–22, 292,
302–03, 303–05; *Biblia latina cum Glossa ordinaria*, 4: *In Matt.* 6:22–23, also *PL* 114:
104 C–D; Honorius Augustodunensis, *Elucidarium* 2.2–5, ed. Yves Lefèvre, *L'Elucidarium et les lucidaires: Contribution, par l'histoire d'un texte, à l'histoire des croyances
religieuses en France au moyen âge* (Paris: É. de Boccard, 1954), pp. 405–07; Alger of
Liège, *De misericordia et iustitia* 1.74, ed. Robert Kretzschmer, *Alger von Lüttichs
Traktat 'De misericordia et iustitia'; Ein kanonistischer Konkordanzversuch aus der Zeit des
Investiturstreits* (Sigmaringen: Jan Thorbecke Verlag, 1985), p. 244; Gratian, *Decretum* d. 6. c. 1–c. 3, pars 2. c. 32. q. 5, col. 9–11, 1132–36; Nikolaus M. Häring, ed.,
"Die *Sententiae magistri Gisleberti Pictavensis episcopi* I" 10.15, *AHDLMA* 45 (1978):
157; Peter Abelard, *Ethics*, pp. 4–14, 16–20, 22–26; *In Epistolam Pauli ad Romanos*
1:16–17, ed. Eligius M. Buytaert in *Opera theologica*, ed. Eligius M. Buytaert and
Constant J. Mews, CCCM 11–13 (Turnhout: Brepols, 1969–87), 11: 65; Hermannus, *Sentente magistri Petri Abaelardi (Sententie Hermanni)*, ed. Sandro Buzzetti,
Pubblicazioni della facoltà di lettere e filosofia dell'Università di Milano, 101,
sezione a cura di storia della filosofia, 31 (Florence: La Nuova Italia, 1983), pp.
141–55; *Ysagoge in theologiam*, ed. Artur Michael Landgraf in *Écrits théologiques de
l'école d' Abélard* (Louvain: Spicilegium Sacrum Lovaniense, 1934), pp. 76, 91–93;
Sent. div. 2.2.3, pp. 24*–26*, 28*–29*; Hugh of St. Victor, *De sac.* 1.4.15, *PL* 176:
240C–241A; *Summa sententiarum* 3.14–15, 4.4–5, *PL* 176: 111A–113B, 122B–124B;
Robert Pullen, *Sent.* 5.33, 6.2–11, 6.18–23, *PL* 186: 854D–856A, 865C–871A,
876C–880D; Roland of Bologna, *Sent.*, pp. 150, 255–61; *Summa magistri Rolandi* c.
15. q. 1, ed. Friedrich Thaner (Aalen: Scientia Verlag, 1962 [repr. of Innsbruck,
1874 ed.]), pp. 31–33. On this point, see Blomme, *La doctrine du péché*, passim; John
F. Benton, "Consciousness of Self and Perception of Individuality," in *Renaissance
and Renewal in the Twelfth Century*, ed. Robert L. Benson and Giles Constable
(Cambridge, MA: Harvard University Press, 1982), p. 274; Lottin, *Psych. et morale*,
3: 99–104; Luscombe, "The *Ethics* of Abelard," pp. 67, 71; intro. and annotations
to his ed. of Peter Abelard, *Ethics*, pp. xvii–xviii, xxv, xxxiii, p. 14 n. 1, pp. 46–47
n. 1.

gians who take exception to this view, and to Augustine's categorical ban on lying for any reason whatever, make use of the counter-vailing analysis of pious fraud found in Gregory the Great. The issue, for Gregory, arises specifically in connection with the be-havior of the nurses of the enslaved Israelites in Egypt at the time of Moses's birth, who denied the existence of their charges in order to protect them from the Pharaoh's decree of death. Anselm of Laon and his followers, including the author of the *Summa sententiarum*, take the position that the nurses' intention of saving the infants' lives excuses their lie, buttressing their argument with Gregory.[5] On the other hand, Robert Pullen agrees with Augustine that this instance of lying, as with all acts of lying, was wrong. But, he argues, a good deed can wipe away a bad one. Thus, the nurses of Exodus 1:20 were given a dispensation by God concerning their lie because of their virtuous intentions.[6]

Another debate related to ethical intentionality was the one surrounding the virtue or vice with which people in different walks of life exercise their callings. Although all involved are proponents of intentionalism, not all the masters who take up this question deploy that principle consistently in practice. Anselm of Laon withholds his favor from merchants, who, he thinks, are motivated only by greed and fraud; Honorius Augustodunensis extends his criticism to knights, craftsmen, jongleurs, and even to public peni-tents, who, he thinks, are guilty of self-advertisement. He can find virtuous intentionality only in the profession of farming.[7] On the other hand, disciples of Anselm of Laon reverse his negative judg-ment on merchants, arguing that they perform a useful public service, and that they are just as capable of doing so for good as for selfish reasons. They find it possible as well to accept the idea that the songs of the jongleurs may inspire their audience to emulate the valiant deeds of great men and to serve the common weal, and that they do not always draw their hearers into immorality, in a striking reversal of the bad press generally given to members of this profes-sion by twelfth-century theologians.[8] Robert Pullen provides the

---

[5] *Sentences of Anselm of Laon*, no. 88; *Sentences of the School of Laon*, no. 47–72, 5: 76–77, 310; *Summa sent.* 4.5, *PL* 176: 122D–124B.

[6] Robert Pullen, *Sent.* 5.35, *PL* 186: 859B–C.

[7] *Sentences of Anselm of Laon*, no. 14, 5: 24; Honorius, *Eluc.* 2.54–59, 2.61, pp. 427–28, 429.

[8] *Sentences of the School of Laon*, no. 441–43, 5: 300–01. For the general attitude of theologians in this period toward jongleurs, see Charles Homer Haskins, *The Renaissance of the Twelfth Century* (New York: Meridian Books, 1957), p. 56.

most elaborate, and generous, analysis of professions as callings in the church which, while they do have their particular temptations, are all licit and capable of being conducted with virtue, thereby contributing to the salvation of their practitioners and the service of their fellow Christians. He ranges across the clergy and the laity, the *regnum* and the *sacerdotium*, the contemplative and the active lives, the celibate and the married, the rulers and the ruled, and the professions of magistrate, soldier, farmer, merchant, and miller, accenting the point that, in all cases, these callings can be seen as occasions for the practice of virtue if conducted with the proper intentionality.[9]

Still another debate concerned how the ethical intentionality defining moral states was itself to be understood and whether it conditions virtue and vice globally or not. Those contemporary theologians who give ethical intentionality a name describe it as a habit of mind (*habitus mentis*) focused on good, or evil, as the case may be. Despite the universality of the use of the term *habitus* by those who offer this definition, however, they do not always understand the term in the same way. Anselm of Laon, defining virtue as "a habit of mind well constituted" and vice as "a habit of mind badly constituted" (*virtus est habitus mentis bene constitute, et vicium habitus est mentis male constitute*), raises the question of whether a person can have virtues and vices at the same time. His understanding of the problem clearly goes back to the Stoic principle of intentionality as a fixed mental disposition which admits of no contrasting modalities at the same time. This notion, in Stoicism, had led to ethical claims regarded as paradoxes, such as the idea that he who possesses one virtue possesses them all, and the idea that all virtues and all vices are equal, since they all express equally a virtuous or a vicious intentionality. Augustine had considered these claims repeatedly. While he had agreed with the Stoics on the interconnection of the virtues, recasting all the virtues and vices as equal expressions of charity, or its absence, he had disagreed with the premise that all sins are equal or that an individual who is basically virtuous cannot experience backsliding in certain respects while retaining his paramount moral orientation. Anselm of Laon agrees with Augustine here. He sees the *habitus* of virtue as a mental disposition, but one that is not so total that its existence would be annulled by a minor peccadillo. He also agrees with Augustine that the reverse is the case, unsymmetrically, with a moral agent con-

---

[9] Robert Pullen, *Sent.* 7.7–9, 7.19–27, *PL* 186: 879C–922A, 931A–943B.

firmed in vice. Nothing that such a person does can be virtuous, since the absence of charity is his prevailing moral orientation. The same view of *habitus* and of the equality of the virtues as rooted in charity is found in Hermannus. The author of the *Sententiae divinitatis*, while he ignores the pendant to this question, likewise views the *habitus mentis* involved in ethical decisions purely from the perspective of the consent of the intellect to *suggestio* and *delectatio*.[10]

On the other hand, Peter Abelard understands *habitus* in a more Aristotelian sense. For him, a virtuous *habitus mentis* is to be defined not just as the willingness to obey God but also as a commitment that is confirmed in its exercise. It involves practice and improvement, and perdurance in virtue; and it is connected with the perseverance of the saints. While this attitude undergirds all modes of virtue and vice, Abelard agrees with Augustine that sins are not all equally important. He cites the standard distinction between mortal and venial sins, which he distinguishes in terms of the state of mind which the sinner displays in them. Venial sins spring from forgetfulness, carelessness, and triviality, while serious sins stem from deliberation and planning (*studio et deliberatione*). It is the degree of intentionality, and not the aspect of the human constitution from which sins derive or the amount of damage that they do, that counts.[11] Without the same elaboration on the difference be-

---

[10] *Sentences of Anselm of Laon*, no. 68, 5: 59; Hermannus, *Sent.*, pp. 141–48; *Sent. div.* 2.2.3, pp. 28*–29*.

[11] Peter Abelard, *Ethics*, pp. 68–70, 128–30. The quotation is on p. 70. Scholars who have noted the Aristotelian sense which Abelard gives to *habitus* here and the existence of an objective standard in his ethics include Bertola, "La dottrina morale," pp. 53–71; Robert Blomme, "A propos de la définition du péché chez Pierre Abélard," *ETL* 33 (1957): 319–47; *La doctrine du péché*, pp. 103–294; Davis, "The Unity of the Virtues," pp. 71–82; Frank De Siano, "Of God and Man: Consequences of Abelard's Ethics," *Thomist* 35 (1971): 631–60; Maurice de Gandillac, "Intention et loi dans l'éthique d'Abélard," in *Pierre Abélard, Pierre le Vénérable: Les courants philosophiques, littéraires et artistiques au milieu du XIIᵉ siècle* (Paris: CNRS, 1975), pp. 585–97; Angela Giuliano de Padova, "Alcuni relievi sull'etica abelardiana," *Atti dell'Accademia delle scienze di Torino*, classe di scienze morali, storiche e filologiche 102 (1967–68): 437–60; B. Landry, "Les idées morales du XIIᵉ siècle: Les écrivains en Latin," *Revue des cours et conférences* 40 (1938–39): 387–89; Luscombe, "The *Ethics* of Abelard," pp. 71, 80–84; Roger J. Van den Berge, "La qualification morale de l'acte humain: Ébauche d'une réinterpretation de la pensée abélardienne," *Studia moralia* 13 (1975): 143–73. These studies effectively refute the view of Abelard as a pure subjectivist in ethics put forth by G. de Giuli, "Abelardo e la morale," *Giornale critico della filosofia italiana* 12 (1931): 33–44 and Jean Rohmer, *La finalité morale chez les théologiens de Saint Augustin à Duns Scot* (Paris: J. Vrin, 1939), pp. 31–40; or the view of Abelard as an "ethical nominalist" as claimed by Richard J. Thompson, "The Role of Dialectical Reason in the Ethics of Abelard," *Proceedings of the American Catholic Philosophical Association* 12 (1936): 141–48.

tween mortal and venial sin, the author of the *Ysagoge in theologiam* agrees with Abelard's Aristotelian definition of virtue as a *habitus mentis* oriented to the highest good and developed by exercise, and adds to it another Aristotelian note, virtue as the mean between the extremes of excess and defect.[12] The author of *Sententiae Parisiensis* I agrees with the notion of *habitus* as a quality of soul that develops through exercise, as well as a mental disposition toward good or evil, and connects the point with the grading of the virtues.[13]

There are some theologians of the day who reflect on the question of the equality or gradation of vices and virtues and their mutual interdependence or lack of it without taking a stand on the nature of *habitus*. The followers of Anselm of Laon agree with him, and with Augustine, that all vices and virtues are interrelated, respectively, because of their common source in the absence or presence of charity. They agree with Abelard in distinguishing between venial and mortal sins on the basis of their accidental or deliberate character. To this they add that the severity of a sin depends on the particular vice inspiring it and on the status of the perpetrator. At the same time, they drop the Augustinian idea that a vicious person must, perforce, be vicious in all he does, unlike the virtuous person.[14] Robert Pullen also supports the critique of the Stoic principle that he who has one virtue, or vice, has them all. He offers no arguments or authorities in defense of this position, presenting the mix of vices and virtues in individual human beings as a phenomenon widely encountered and as a conclusion based on experience and common sense. It is one he finds compatible with the fact that people can, and do, change in their moral habits; this situation, for him, argues against anyone's moral state as a fixed intentionality.[15] Robert also grades the sins. With Abelard, Hugh of St. Victor, and others, he regards the degree of deliberation involved as an index of their seriousness. Also, with Abelard, he lists ignorance and unintentional error as factors mitigating or removing guilt, citing one of Abelard's examples, that of a man who inadvertently sleeps with another woman, believing that she is his wife. He adds another example of a case which he thinks ignorance excuses, and one usually reserved for the discussion of the condi-

---

[12] *Ysagoge in theologiam*, p. 76.

[13] *Sentences of the School of Laon*, no. 424–25, 458, 460, 462, 5: 293, 306, 307.

[14] *Sententiae Parisiensis* I, ed. Artur Michael Landgraf in *Écrits théologiques de l'école d'Abélard* (Louvain: Spicilegium Sacrum Lovaniense, 1934), pp. 50–52, 55–59.

[15] Robert Pullen, *Sent.* 5.31, 5.34–36, *PL* 186: 853D–854B, 856B–860B; cf. Hugh of St. Victor, *De sac.* 2.13.1, *PL* 176: 526B–C.

tions nullifying a marriage, that of a young man separated from his family as a child who returns to his native land and unknowingly contracts an incestuous marriage.[16] A more independent approach to the question of whether a person who has one vice or virtue has them all is taken by Roland of Bologna. He distinguishes between interior and exterior virtue (*in affecto interiori et in effectu exteriori*). With respect to their inner affects, he agrees that all the virtues are one and the same since they derive from an identical good intention. But, he adds, they manifest their outward effects in different ways. The same analysis holds for the vices. Here, Roland seeks to emphasize equally the primacy of intentionality and the idea that different people have their paramount virtues and vices, or that they may express these moral states in a variety of ways.[17]

The matter of ignorance, on which Robert Pullen touches, also evoked a range of opinions. As will be recalled, Hugh of St. Victor regards ignorance as a punishment for original sin, a view in which he is followed by the author of the *Summa sententiarum*. Ignorance is thus one of the conditions, along with concupiscence, that inclines fallen man to sin, in general, and it is not viewed by these masters as a circumstance that conditions or relieves the guilt of particular actions that would otherwise be regarded as actual sins. On the other hand, amplifying on the school of Laon here, Abelard reflects a more analytical approach to the problem of ignorance, and one displaying an awareness of the ways in which the canonists treat this issue.[18] Gratian, for example, gives a thorough analysis of the modes of ignorance and the ways in which they may or may not affect moral culpability. There is ignorance stemming from mental incapacity, which mitigates responsibility. There is ignorance of matters on which a person is humanly incapable of informing himself, which has a similar effect. On the other hand, there is ignorance of matters a person needs to know in order to conduct himself with propriety, matters of which he fails to inform himself through negligence. This type of ignorance, in Gratian's view, does not excuse a person from things he may say or do while acting under the resultant ignorance or misapprehension.[19] Abelard poses the question of ignorance in relation to intentionality in its most

---

[16] Robert Pullen, *Sent.* 5.35, 5.40, 6.2–11, *PL* 186: 854D–856A, 862A, 865C–871A.
[17] Roland of Bologna, *Sent.*, pp. 257–59.
[18] Lottin, *Psych. et morale*, 3: 12–13, 18–19, 56–57; *Sentences of the School of Laon*, no. 420, 5: 291.
[19] Gratian, *Decretum* pars 2. c. 22. q. 4. c. 23, dictum, col. 881–82.

extreme form, and in a manner calculated to raise the hackles of his contemporaries. He agrees with the consensus position that vice and virtue lie in inner intentionalities, whether or not they are expressed outwardly. A virtuous intention is the intention to obey God; a vicious intention is consent to an attitude or an act that stands in contempt of God. In order to make the intellectual judgment on which this consent rests, the moral agent has to know what God requires. His knowledge or belief in this respect is as critical as what the will of God actually may be, since different people in different dispensations or different states of faith may be given a differential access to that information. Abelard also includes ignorance, willy-nilly, of facts that are relevant to particular ethical decisions as excusing a person from culpability. In illustrating this point, he presents several highly charged examples. There is the example of the husband who mistakes another woman for his wife, also cited by Robert Pullen, and one that inspires a certain skepticism. Worst yet, in the eyes of contemporaries, there is the example of the people who put Christ to death. According to Abelard, they acted in good conscience since, in their view, He was a criminal and a blasphemer.[20] But, despite his vaunted reputation as a logician, Abelard is far from consistent in applying this principle. Another example he gives is that of a mother too poor to afford bedding for her infant, who takes him into her own bed to keep him warm, and accidentally smothers him while asleep. Despite Abelard's stand on the seriousness of sins as conditioned by deliberation, and not by the damage they may do, in this case he argues that the injury and scandal involved in the example given require that the woman be considered guilty of infanticide and punished, as an object lesson, notwithstanding the accidental nature of the event and the protective maternal intention informing her action.[21]

THE LOMBARD AS AN INTENTIONALIST

Peter Lombard subscribes to the consensus view that sees intentionality as the essence of the moral act and as a description of the moral status of the moral agent even in the absence of the act. At the same time, he places this question on a broader canvas than is the case with any of his contemporaries. He considers several definitions of the nature of sin, the initial context in which he

---

[20] Peter Abelard, *Ethics*, pp. 4–14, 16–20, 26–36, 53–56.
[21] Ibid., pp. 38–48, 68–70.

considers the psychogenesis of ethical acts, exploring their merits and demerits before presenting his own solution. He begins with two definitions drawn from Augustine, the *Contra Faustum* view that sin is any thought, word, or deed that contravenes the law of God, and the *De duabus animabus* view that sin is the will to retain and follow what justice forbids. In both of these definitions, Peter notes, Augustine accents the volitional character of sin, while conceding that sin may also be manifested externally. Next, he offers a definition drawn from Ambrose's *De paradiso*, where sin is treated as the disobedience through which a divine law is broken. Here, the malice of the perpetrator is central, but the presence of an objective external law that requires or forbids certain actions is given more prominence.[22] To this range of opinions, which he sums up as sin defined as bad will as such, irrespective of external action and as sin defined as both the bad will and the bad deed, he adds another view. This third position is found in Augustine as well and had been reprised recently by Anselm of Canterbury and Honorius. It argues that sin is non-being, in the sense of the privative theory of evil. Having observed that all three positions find support from Augustine, Peter opts for the first mentioned view. Sin, he states, is evil-doing in thought, word, and deed, with the accent falling most heavily on volition: "Sin consists principally in the will, from which evil deeds proceed as bad fruit from a bad tree" (*Praecipue tamen in voluntate peccatum consistit, ex qua tanquam ex arbore mala procedunt opera mala tanquam fructus mali*).[23]

Having displayed his colors early in this analysis, it now remains for Peter to disqualify the definitions of sin he rejects. His handling of the privative theory of evil is deft and knowledgeable. He begins by contextualizing it, accurately, as a cosmological, not as an ethical, doctrine, developed by Augustine in the first instance to refute the Manichees. From a metaphysical standpoint, he notes, if we equate being and goodness, then anything that exists is good, insofar as it exists, including evil thoughts and deeds. This position is clearly problematic in the field of ethics. At the same time, according to the privative theory of evil, evil is not a being but the corruption or absence of being. Sin is not a substance which, so far as it exists, is good. Rather, it is a rejection of the good, a departure

---

[22] Peter Lombard, *Sententiae in IV libris distinctae* 2. d. 35. c. 1, 3rd ed. rev., ed. Ignatius C. Brady, 2 vols. (Grottaferrata: Collegii S. Bonaventurae ad Claras Aquas, 1971–81), 1: 529–30.

[23] Ibid., c. 2.1–3, 1: 530–31. The quotation is at c. 2.3, p. 531. See also d. 44, 1: 577–80. For Honorius on evil as non-being, see *Eluc.* 2.2, p. 405.

from being, whose existence can be grasped only by applying to it
the epistemology of the *via negativa*. A far better way of understanding the condition of sin, in Peter's view, is to substitute for a
content-free absence of good a willed turning from the good. His
proposal is to invoke the theme of the *regio dissimilitudinis*, the region
of unlikeness, in which sinful man has placed himself by his own
voluntary action, thereby abandoning the image of God in himself.
As Peter explores this idea, he shows how far it had developed, by
the twelfth century, away from a cosmic Plotinian "fall of the soul"
over which the soul has no control, and away from a purely
monastic understanding of human existence apart from conversion
and adherence to the contemplative life. Now it has come to mean,
simply, the sinful state in which men find themselves thanks to
their own moral choices.[24] In effect, Peter disposes of the privative
theory of evil by substituting for it a notion of moral deprivation
rooted in man's will. The one point of agreement with the privative
theory that he feels he can maintain is the principle that sins, and
other evils, are not substances or natures. This idea is essential, he
concedes, in order to show that, although the punishment God
metes out to sinners is earned, God does not create evil. He is not
responsible for man's sins; they spring exclusively from man's bad
use of his free will, a use of free will which man is not constrained to
make.[25]

As to the argument that sin can be reduced entirely to subjective
intentionality, Peter turns the question around by observing that
the end of the good is charity. This is the goal toward which a good
will is oriented. To be sure, we can distinguish intentions from the

---

[24] Peter Lombard, *Sent.* 2. d. 35. c. 2.4–c. 6, 1: 531–36. Peter adverts frequently
to the theme of the *regio dissimilitudinis* in the same generic sense elsewhere in his
writings. See his *Sermo* 12, 13, 21, 23, 55, 99, 111, 112, *PL* 171: 397A, 404D,
435D–436A, 445C, 610C, 798B, 850D, 857B; *Sermo de adventu Domini* ed. Damien
Van den Eynde, "Deux sermons inédits de Pierre Lombard," in *Misc. Lomb.*, p. 78;
In Epistolam Pauli ad Galatas 2:23, *PL* 192: 128C–129A. Good studies of the changes
in interpretation undergone by this theme up through the twelfth century include
J. C. Didier, "Pour la fiche *Regio dissimilitudinis*," *Mélanges de science religieuse* 8 (1951):
205–10; Étienne Gilson, "*Regio dissimilitudinis* de Platon à Saint Bernard de Clair-
vaux," *MS* 9 (1947): 108–30; and, especially, Margot Schmidt, "*Regio dissimilitudinis*:
Ein Grundbegriff mittelhochdeutscher Prosa im Lichte seiner lateinischen Bedeutungsgeschichte," *Freiburger Zeitschrift für Philosophie und Theologie* 15 (1968): 63–83.
On the other hand, Pierre Courcelle, "L'Âme en cage," in *Parusia: Studien zur
Philosophie Platons und zur Problemgeschichte des Platonismus, Festgabe für Johannes Hirschberger*, ed. Kurt Flasch (Frankfurt: Minerva GMBH, 1965), pp. 103–16 treats the theme
by way of decontextualized *topos* research that offers no sense of how the meaning of
the theme changed over time.
[25] Peter Lombard, *Sent.* 2. d. 36–d. 37, 1: 536–47.

ends they serve. But, intentions are directionalities. They always have destinations in view, by definition; for the ends in question are what the moral subject wills when he wills. Now, when the will is disordered, that is, ordered to the wrong end, we sin. The will, in making a disordered choice, may misjudge what the good is, especially if it lacks the help of grace. The misguided choice is sinful, and so is the act that connects it with its inaccurately understood end. Peter is perfectly willing to grant that acts are not good or evil *per se*, but that they are good or evil in the light of the ethical intentionalities that inform them. At the same time, and here he argues against the Abelardian position concerning the people who put Christ to death, the acts themselves are not matters of indifference. Some acts, indeed, are objectively evil. In this connection he cites Augustine's rule in the *Contra mendacium* that lies stating an objective untruth are sinful even if spoken with a good intention, thereby distancing himself from contemporaries who accepted Gregory's justification of pious fraud. Like the lie which Augustine castigates, an evil act can be intrinsically evil and also evil in that it manifests an evil intention. Also, a person may have a good, or excusable, intention and at the same time he may express it in deeds that are not good or suitable. Where Peter draws the line is at the point where an intention, of whatever quality, is expressed in an act that is objectively wrong: "All human actions are judged good or bad according to their intention and cause, except those which are intrinsically evil, that is, those which are unconditionally prohibited" (*Omnia igitur hominis opera secundum intentionem et causam iudicantur bona vel mala, exceptis his quae per se mala sunt, id est quae sine praevaricatione fieri nequeunt*).[26]

Thus, for Peter, one can accept intentionality as the basic definition of the essence of the moral act, with two stipulations. First, one must acknowledge the normal continuity between the intention and its expression in appropriate action, in relation to the end with which it is connected. Second, one must acknowledge that an act cannot express a good intention if it stands in manifest opposition to one's own moral duties. The contemporary theologian to whom he comes the closest in articulating these conclusions is the author of the *Summa sententiarum*. Peter has sharpened the focus of his teaching. His position also takes account of Abelard's claim, and seeks to make it as palatable as possible, although he is not entirely responsive to Abelard's point that the executioners of Christ

---

[26] Ibid., d. 38–d. 40, 1: 547–61. The quotation is at d. 40. c. 12, pp. 560–61.

thought they were doing something right and appropriate. The Lombard does not expressly take up here the issue of ignorance. He does, however, include the issue of grace, in discussing the human will's judgment of the good, which Abelard omits. The Lombard's analysis here suggests that, had he included it, he would have felt comfortable with Gratian's treatment of ignorance, particularly the responsibility of an individual to inform himself of what he needs to know in order to carry out his duties virtuously, and his culpability if he fails to do so. As to the absence of grace in the will's erroneous judgments, it is on the same trajectory, for Peter, as the absence, or subtraction, of grace from those persons whom God does not pre-destine to salvation. As he sees it, such persons are none the less fully responsible for the consequences of the bad use which they make of their free will.

Before leaving this part of his analysis, Peter raises the related question of whether good intentions and good deeds require good faith. Here, he draws a distinction. An affirmative answer can be given if good faith means lack of hypocrisy. On the other hand, if we mean by faith the theological virtue of faith or the set of theological propositions to which faith constitutes assent, then we can answer in the negative. For, one does not have to be a Christian to possess good faith in the first sense, and hence to be capable of good intentions and good deeds. In support of this conclusion, Peter observes that the Jew or the non-believer is perfectly capable of good faith, good intentions, and good deeds, which he manifests in his own virtues and in ministering to the needs of his neighbors, "drawn by natural piety" (*naturali pietate ductus*).[27] While, in con-sidering man's capacity for virtue under the heading of human nature as such, before the fall, Peter, like Hugh of St. Victor, closes off the concept of natural virtue by arguing that ethical acts, to have merit, must be assisted by grace, here he opens up the concept of natural virtue and the possible existence of the virtuous pagan or non-Christian.

Vice and Sin

Another related question which Peter next takes up is whether all sins are reducible to a single, central, sinful intentionality and whether sins can be graded. His handling of these issues is some-what different from what we have found in other current theolo-

---

[27] Ibid., d. 41, 1: 561–66. The quotation is at d. 41. c. 2, p. 564.

gians. Peter is not always interested in the same aspects of this constellation of ideas as intrigue many of his compeers. He agrees with the principle that all sins stem from a central evil attitude or orientation, just as a bad will and a bad deed reflect the same bad intention. He uses the term *habitus* here but he does not pursue the question of whether the intention at issue is a mental disposition only, or an Aristotelian *habitus*, or both. Peter also agrees with those masters who think that sins can, none the less, be graded. The criterion for doing so, however, is not the degree of deliberation that informs particular sins, but rather the particular vice that inspires them. This rule obtains, for Peter, whether the sins are committed against God, oneself, or one's neighbor; whether they occur in thought, word, or deed, or all three; whether they are crimes as well as sins; and whether they involve the active perpetration of evil or the failure to do good. Peter also distinguishes between mortal and venial sins, and is inclined to invoke considerations of how much harm or outrage is done, and not the kind of intentionality involved, in making discriminations here.[28] Although he does not call upon the language used by Roland of Bologna at this juncture, he reflects Roland's idea that the same evil intention can be manifested by different people or even by the same person in different ways. In addition, and this is in line with his view that some sins are more serious than others because of the intrinsic evil they represent or because of their moral consequences, he brings to bear on this point the doctrine of the seven deadly sins given in Gregory the Great's *Moralia*. This was a standard topic in Peter's day, although theologians used it to illustrate a variety of points. Thus, Hugh of St. Victor introduces Gregory's scheme of the sins to underscore the idea that all sins spring from the mind, not the body.[29] The author of the *Summa sententiarum* uses it to illustrate the point that different passions give rise to different kinds of sin.[30] The author of the *Ysagoge in theologiam* treats the seven vices horizontally, as equal manifestations of man's bad use of free will.[31] William of

---

[28] Ibid., d. 42. c. 1–c. 5, 1: 566–70. Artur Michael Landgraf, "Some Unknown Writings of the Early Scholastic Period," *New Scholasticism* 4 (1930): 17 has noted that a *quaestio* found in an unpublished manuscript on the British Museum, dating to the mid-twelfth century, states that the Lombard distinguished between virtue *in habitu* and virtue *in usu*, in a manner approximating Roland of Bologna, although this language does not appear in the *Sentences*. Peter's reasons for distinguishing between mortal and venial sin are not noted by Landgraf, *Dogmengeschichte*, 4 part 2: 10–11, 110–16, 144–45.

[29] Hugh of St. Victor, *De sac.* 2.13.1, *PL* 176: 525A–526B.

[30] *Summa sent.* 3.16, *PL* 176: 113D–114C.

[31] *Ysagoge in theologiam*, p. 100.

Champeaux provides a detailed analysis of pride and envy, which later theologians drew upon, but stops there.[32]

The contemporary theologian closest to Peter in this area is one of the Porretan sentence collectors who, like him, is interested in viewing these vices vertically, hierarchically, and developmentally.[33] Pride, in the estimation of both this author and Peter, is the deadliest of the sins, not only because it involves the most exhaustive capitulation of the self to sin but also because it leads to the other sins, each engendered in turn by the one in back of it. As both masters see it, pride has four manifestations. It attributes the good things one has to oneself and not to God; it regards the good things one has from God as His response to one's own merits; it claims to have good things which one lacks; and it lords it over others on account of the good things one has. Envy springs from pride, in the estimation of the Porretan master, following William of Champeaux. For, unless one loved one's own excellence, one would not be jealous of another's good or resentful of another's pleasure. This jealousy and resentment in turn breed wrath, out of one's inability to attain equality with one's superiors or to deprive others of the desirable things they have. The frustrations emerging from this state in turn engender *accidia* or spiritual sloth, the deprivation of internal joy in the spirit. In that state, the sinner mistakenly turns to external pleasures, in the effort to derive joy from them, leading to avarice, gluttony, and lust.

Peter follows the same analysis, with equal fidelity to Gregory. His only gloss on this text is to include cupidity in the list of vices, as a species of pride, in the effort to harmonize Gregory's account with the biblical idea that love of money is the root of all evil.[34] The same sense that some sins are intrinsically more destructive and disabling informs Peter's conclusion that the single worst sin that can be committed is the sin against the Holy Spirit. This is not simply because God is the supreme being and sins against Him are weightier than sins against created beings. Rather, it is because this sin—the sin of despair, which makes a person obdurate in evil, impenitent, unwilling to accept the help of fellow Christians, and, worst of all, lacking in confidence in God's mercy and love—locks him in a state in which he rates his own self-importance more highly than God's grace. Reprising here his own analysis of the

---

[32] *Sentences of William of Champeaux*, no. 279, 5: 222–23.
[33] *Sent. mag. Gisleberti* I 10.19–26, pp. 158–59.
[34] Peter Lombard, *Sent.* 2. d. 42. c. 6–c. 8, 1: 570–72.

irremissibility of the sin against the Holy Spirit in his Romans commentary, Peter draws the same conclusion. This sin, he concludes, is irremissible not in the sense that God cannot or will not forgive it but in the sense that the sinner has so convinced himself of the hopelessness of his state that he rarely responds to God's call to repent.[35] The purpose of this discussion of the sin against the Holy Spirit in this particular context, however, is less to compare the three Augustinian reasons for why this sin is irremissible and to show why the solution chosen makes the best sense of both Augustine and St. Paul than it is to reinforce the principle that some sins are more serious than others, both objectively and subjectively, notwithstanding the principle that all sin stems from the same evil intentionality.

There are two striking features of the Lombard's handling of the subject of sin overall. In the first place, while he certainly participates in the consensus view that sees inner intentionality as paramount in defining the ethical status of moral agents and moral acts, he is concerned with defending the idea that ethics has an objective as well as a subjective dimension. He insists that both aspects of ethical reality need to be taken into consideration. While he acknowledges the fact that Abelard had included conscious and deliberate contempt of God in his own definition of sin, Peter is aware of the fact that Abelard's intellectualizing of that state of mind could lead to the reduction of God's express commands to those commands as misperceived and misinterpreted by fallible minds who would then use their own limited knowledge and understanding as an excuse for wrongdoing. The result, in Peter's estimation, would be an erosion of the very concept that man, in his fallen state, remains capable of grasping what God requires and capable of resisting temptations, including the temptation to self-delusion, that would incline him to flout those requirements. Secondly, Peter is eager to make man fully responsible for his own sins, even to the point of ignoring in this context the problem of diminished responsibility owing to invincible ignorance or defective mental states and circumstances, which other theologians and canonists bring to bear on the point, and helpfully so. The only place where Peter raises the

---

[35] Ibid., d. 43, 1: 572–77. René Wasselynck, "La présence des *Moralia* de Saint Grégoire le Grand dans les ouvrages de morale du XIIe siècle," *RTAM* 35 (1968): 236–38 has noted Peter's dependence of Gregory here, although he ignores the Porretan parallels to Peter's handling of this topic and sees the *Summa sententiarum* as his closest neighbor. For the comparison with the *Collectanea* on the sin against the Holy Spirit, see above, chapter 4, p. 209.

issue of ignorance is in connection with the fall of Adam and Eve, and, as we saw in chapter 6 above, he raises it there only to dismiss it categorically as a mitigating factor in original sin. While Peter rejects the privative view of evil, associated in western Christian theology primarily with Augustine's polemic against the Manichees, he shares fully with the anti-Manichean Augustine the desire to place the burden of sin squarely on man's shoulders in order to reinforce the point that God is in no sense the author of evil or sin. In this connection, Peter's treatment of the moral relations between man and God is consistent with his treatment of the metaphysical and physical relations between God and the creation more generally. Just as God creates a world containing beings capable of acting as secondary causes in their own spheres of activity, so, in His ethical relations with rational beings, He creates a universe in which they have the *posse peccare et non peccare*, the capacity to damage their own natures and to reject the moral law given for their own well-being. They are likewise free, in the realm of sin, to blemish their own similitude to God and to live at a lower level of existence than their natures make possible. And, this they can do on their own initiative and volition, whether prompted by internal or external temptation.

Virtue: Free Will and Grace in Its Attainment

In moving from sin to its correlative, virtue, we move to an area in which there is also a high degree of consensus in early twelfth-century theology, in this case regarding the relations between man's free will and God's grace in the development of virtue. Within this consensus position one can also detect some lesser points of disagreement, or differences in emphasis among the theologians of Peter Lombard's time. They may offer alternative definitions of virtue in general, of particular virtues and their interrelations, and of their applications in practice. They may also manifest a greater or lesser interest in this subject altogether. Their principal point of agreement is one deriving from their understanding of human nature. Some, like Hugh of St. Victor and his followers and like the Lombard himself, regard that nature, in its prelapsarian state, no less than after the fall, as requiring the assistance of grace in the acquisition of virtue that bears merit. In the case of postlapsarian man, they agree that he needs operating grace to gain the state of justification, on which man's subsequent moral growth is based with the help of cooperating grace. There is also general agreement on the freedom of the will, however much it may be damaged by original sin. The will, they hold, remains capable of resisting both of these types of grace. A middle-Augustinian position on this subject, in which the notion of irresistible grace is pointedly ignored, finds a wide hearing in the first half of the twelfth century, as we noted above in chapter 6.[36] The same understanding of grace and free will occurs in monastic writers in this period, such as Bernard of Clairvaux, as we find in the scholastic theologians, laying the foundation for the consideration of virtue on the part of Christian thinkers of the time in general. It has been claimed that the Abelardians taught an ethics of natural *eudaimonia*, in which the yearning for the good is seen as deriving from a psychic impulse arising in man himself and not from a moral capacity energized by God's grace.[37] This claim is not borne out by the evidence.[38] The Abelardians, like other theologians at this time, including the Lombard, see no difficulty in reconciling *eudaimonia* with a collaborative relationship between man and God. On this broad foundational issue, the Lombard's basic contribution is to explain clearly how divine grace can take the initiative and can do its work in man without thereby divinizing man or functioning as an immanental participation of the deity in man, and also how man's virtues and merits, although requiring the operation and cooperation of grace, can truly be his own possessions and can justly make of him the moral being on which his future reward depends.

Like his compeers, Peter grounds his analysis of virtue on the analysis of free will and grace. He first articulates his position on

---

[36] See above, pp. 289, 383–85. For the period in general, see Landgraf, *Dogmengeschichte*, 1 part 1: 44–48. For more on Hugh of St. Victor, in this connection, see A. Mignon, *Les origines de la scolastique et Hugues de Saint-Victor*, 2 vols. (Paris: P. Lethielleux, 1895), 1: 258–59; Roger Baron, "L'Idée de liberté chez S. Anselme et Hugues de Saint-Victor," *RTAM* 32 (1965): 117–21. The author of the *Sententiae divinitatis* is a salient example of the crossover between monastic and scholastic writers on this theme, citing verbatim Bernard of Clairvaux's "Tolle enim gratiam, et non erit unde salvetur; tolle liberum arbitrium, et non erit, in quo fiat salus vel cui fiat." *Sent. div.* 2.2.2, p. 20*. Bernard is also reprised by the *Summa sent.* 3.7–9, *PL* 176: 98D–105A, as noted by Mignon, *Les origines*, 2: 13. Robert Pullen preserves the general contemporary balance between grace and free will, although he grants more importance to angelic help in man's development of virtue than is typical in this period. Robert Pullen, *Sent.* 5.7–9, 6.22–50, *PL* 186: 834D–838A, 879C–896A.

[37] Philippe Delhaye, "L'Enseignement morale des *Sententiae Parisiensis*," in *Études de civilisation médiévale (IX–XIIᵉ siècles): Mélanges offerts à Edmond-René Labonde* (Poitiers: Centre d'Études Superieures de Civilisation Médiévale, 1974), pp. 197–207.

[38] *Sent. Parisiensis* I, pp. 58–59. See also *Ysagoge in theologiam*, pp. 91–99.

that subject in his Romans commentary and then develops it in
treating Adam's virtue before the fall in Book 2 of the *Sentences*,
expanding it to include the cardinal and theological virtues in Book
3, under the heading of the human Christ and His moral aptitudes.
He discusses the gifts of the Holy Spirit in both of these two latter
contexts. Having defined virtue as a good quality of mind, which
lives rightly and does not use anything badly, and having illustrated this point with justice and faith as works of God in man,
Peter raises the question of whether the grace that activates the will
is a virtue, and, if so, whether this means that virtue does not derive
from free will and that virtue is not a motion of the mind. He
concludes that virtue is not itself a motion or affect of the mind but
a good quality informing the mind, which free will activates to
develop good intentions and actions. Free will is thus an operative
condition of virtue, and virtue is a disposition to be motivated to
the good by means of it. In this sense, both free will and virtue are
sources of the good motion and good affection in the soul of a
virtuous person. Grace, for its part, is an enabling condition in this
process as well. But grace, Peter insists, cannot be defined as a
virtue, whether we understand virtue as a quality possessed by the
human soul or as the outcome of its disposition and action. We can
only regard grace as a virtue in the lexical sense of a *virtus*, a power
or force that activates something else.[39]

In explaining how this relationship works, Peter is heavily dependent on the account given in the *Summa sententiarum* of the
relationship between virtues and the gifts of the Holy Spirit, a topic
to which he himself turns after his discussion of grace and virtue.
The author of the *Summa sententiarum* invokes the analogy of agriculture in presenting his analysis. The gifts of the Holy Spirit, he says,
are "the first motions in the heart, as it were, like seeds of virtue"
(*primi motus in corde, quasi quaedam semina virtutum*). They are sown in
human hearts by God, Who, as He does so, operates without man's
collaboration. The virtues, for their part, are "effects of the disposition of the gifts" (*effectus donorum habitus*) in man, like the crops
growing from the seeds God has sown, which draw as well on the
fertility of the soil in which they are sown and on their active
cultivation by the husbandman; here God and man work
together.[40] As Peter expands on this analogy with respect to grace

---

[39] Peter Lombard, *Sent.* 2. d. 27. c. 1.1–3, 1: 480–81.
[40] *Summa sent.* 3.17, *PL* 176: 114D–115A. The quotation is at 114D. On this
passage and its influence, see Lottin, *Psych. et morale*, 3: 330–32.

and virtue, he adds another integer to the equation and reassigns the role of the seed. In agriculture, he notes, we have rain, the earth, the seed, and the fruit. The rain is analogous to divine grace; the earth is analogous to human free will; the seed is like virtue as a mental disposition or an inclination to the good; and the fruit resembles that inclination translated into virtuous intentions and actions. None of these four elements is identical with the others or can be substituted for them. The germination process that enables the seed to flower and the process enabling the flower to mature and to bear fruit are both assisted by grace, operating and cooperating, in Peter's terms. But in neither stage is the activation supplied by grace the same thing as the virtue it helps to produce.[41] What is striking about Peter's handling of this topic in comparison with the author of the *Summa sententiarum* and with Augustine, whom he cites profusely in support of his position, is that he sees the interaction of grace and free will in the engendering of virtue as a simultaneous division of labor, more than as a succession of cause and effect. This understanding endows his treatment of the theme with a theandric, synergistic view of the interaction of grace and free will that is in some ways more akin to the Greek patristic tradition than it is to Augustinianism. To be sure, Peter sees grace as the principal cause of the merit man gains in developing virtue, since it excites, heals, and aids the free will so that it can become a good will. At the same time, grace begins a process that in no sense constrains or excludes free will; and, for him, "there is no merit in man except by free will" (*nullum meritum est in homine quod non sit per liberum arbitrium*).[42]

As Peter sees it, man's reception and use of the gifts of the Holy Spirit is on the same trajectory as his reception and use of grace. These gifts are given by God and they are activated by man through his free will. Man plays an active role here in the use to which he puts the gifts. The virtues and merits he develops thereby are rewarded by God. Here, too, the gifts are not the same thing as the consequent virtues or merits and neither is man's free will. Rather, the gifts energize the will and the will is the agency through which virtue and merit arise, in the will's good exercise.[43] Throughout this entire analysis, Peter repeatedly cites the anti-Pelagian Augustine and reads his position as one that needs to be put into

---

[41] Peter Lombard, *Sent.* 2. d. 27. c. 1–c. 2.3, 1: 480–82.
[42] Ibid., c. 3.2, 1: 482–83.
[43] Ibid., c. 4–d. 28. c. 4, 1: 483–91. On this topic, see Johann Schupp, *Die Gnadenlehre des Petrus Lombardus* (Freiburg im Breisgau: Herder, 1932), pp. 243–55.

perspective, and judged, by the rhetorical needs of his polemic. He also, repeatedly, cites the anti-Manichean Augustine, along with other authorities, to defend a position on grace and free will and on the gifts of the Holy Spirit and virtue that is far less extreme than that of the late Augustine. At the same time, he distinguishes clearly between the divine *virtus*, as an enabling condition, and the human virtues which can develop with its help. Human virtues, for Peter, depend as well on the human contribution of will and effort; and, when they are attained, they are attributes of the human beings who possess them and who manifest them in their own particular ways. In rewarding such virtuous persons, God rewards those persons, and not the Holy Spirit. It is clear that neither Peter nor any of his contemporaries had yet emerged with the concepts of infused or created grace. But it is equally clear that his account of grace, free will, and the gifts of the Holy Spirit provides a terrain in which later scholastics could plant that doctrine, and that Peter has provided an environment congenial to that later development.

Peter's handling of the theological virtues, the cardinal virtues, and the gifts of the Holy Spirit in specific rather than in generic terms is placed in the third book of the *Sentences*, as a pendant to the human nature of Christ, along with the theme of Christ's human knowledge. As our discussion of that subject above in chapter 7 has shown, he is scarcely a maximalist in comparison with such thinkers as Hugh of St. Victor, although he certainly concedes that the human Christ knew more than any other human being and that He did not have to undergo a learning process of the type that ordinary mortals experience. Likewise, while seeking to preserve a human *posse peccare et non peccare* for the human Christ, a man spared from original sin, Who maintained throughout His life a perfect conformity between His human will and the will of God, Peter offers a human Christ Who, similarly, possesses a moral personality with a psychology that is different from that of other men. While Peter maintains that Christ truly could be tempted, he also thinks that, in resisting temptation, Christ experienced *propassio* and *consensus*, but not *passio*.[44] This being the case, the Lombard, along with Roland of Bologna and other masters who treat virtue in the context of Christ's human nature, faces something of problem. For Christ is, morally, *sui generis*. In what sense, then, can the virtues, as He may be held to have possessed them, function as norms or descriptions of virtues as they may be possessed by humankind?

---

[44] See above, pp. 442–43, 444, 447–48.

The Theological Virtues

It cannot be said that Peter resolves this problem entirely, given his chosen mode of organizing his treatment of virtue. He does make an approach to addressing it, however, by first asking what the virtues are, in themselves, and the capacity in which they are possible in ordinary mortals before considering whether and how the human Christ possessed them. This, however, is only one part of his agenda. For, in handling both the theological and the cardinal virtues, Peter also wants to take a stand on the issue of their definition and interrelation, a topic on which there was a wide range of contemporary opinions. He begins with the theological virtues, starting with faith. All theologians at this time agreed that faith is an epistemic state as well as a virtue. But attention had been distracted to the first of these considerations by Abelard and his followers, both with respect to the status of faith vis-à-vis other modes of knowledge and with respect to its content, in relation to what can be known by natural reason.[45] Abelard initially accents faith as an epistemic state and as a body of information by the schema he proposes in his *theologiae*, where he divides the material into faith, charity, and sacraments. According to this subdivision, "faith" covers the fundamental doctrines of the church which need to be held if a person is to be saved, while the other two subdivisions of theology deal with the Christian's practice of his faith. On faith itself, Abelard offers two main ideas, both of which proved to be controversial. The first is that Christ's incarnation and resurrection constitute the only Christian dogmas for which revelation and grace are required. As we have seen in our consideration of Trinitarian theology in this period in chapters 5 and 6 above, Abelard claimed that the doctrine of the Trinity was accessible to reason alone and that the pagan philosophers, especially the Platonists, had grasped its basic character, a claim that made his Trinitarian theology a cause célèbre for decades, even in the somewhat moderated form in which he eventually presents this teaching in his *Theologia "scholarium"*.[46] The claims Abelard made regarding the Trinity proved to be intellectually indigestible on the part of his contemporaries. But his second contribution to the discussion of

---

[45] For an overview on this issue in the period, see Georg Engelhardt, *Die Entwicklung der dogmatischen Glaubenspsychologie in der mittelalterlichen Scholastik*, Beiträge, 30:4–6 (Münster: Aschendorff, 1933), pp. 18–42.
[46] See above, pp. 51, 212–13, 239, 245, 254–59.

faith, while it evoked dismay from his monastic critics, proved to be more durable and acceptable among the scholastics.

This was his definition of faith, presented in its most influential form in his *Theologia "scholarium"*, as "the conviction of things not seen, that is, things not available to the corporeal senses" (*Fides est . . . existimatio rerum non apparentium, hoc est sensibus corporeis non subiacentium*).[47] The key word in this definition is *existimatio*. Now, *existimare* is a verb used in the Vulgate translation of the New Testament to describe epistemic states generically, regardless of their content. It can be rendered in English in most of these contexts as "to consider," "to deem," "to esteem," "to expect," "to suppose," or "to regard." *Existimare* is also used more specifically in St. Paul's Epistle to the Romans to refer to beliefs and hopes held firmly by Christians about the future, on the basis of which they comport themselves in accordance with Christ's teachings in the here and now, as at Romans 6:11, 8:18, and 14:14. But, despite its Pauline credentials, the word *existimatio* in Abelard's definition evoked a storm of protest. Bernard of Clairvaux and his associates thought that it stood for "opinion," which they, in turn, understood as knowledge that is uncertain. The disciples of Abelard sought both to clarify what he meant and to show that his language was Pauline, and that it had patristic support. Several of them point out that Paul's *argumentum non apparentium* in Hebrews 11:1 is basically the same cognitive state as the one to which the apostle refers in Romans with the use of *existimare*, and that this is what Abelard means by that term as well.[48] The authors of the two *Sententiae Parisiensis* seek, further, to explain how this *existimatio* is related to other forms of knowledge. One of them points out that conviction of this sort differs from knowledge (*cognitio*) in that its objects of knowledge are invisible. As he observes, once something has been seen, it is known and is no longer believed. The key to Abelard's definition of faith, then, is not its alleged lack of certitude but rather the certitude it possesses in the absence of empirical evidence. We may believe that the king of France is not in Paris, he notes, because we have not seen him in the city, as contrasted with knowing that he is in Paris because we have seen him there.[49] While

---

[47] Peter Abelard, *Theologia "scholarium"* 1.2, 1.11–15, ed. Constant J. Mews, CCCM 13: 318, 322–25.

[48] Hermannus, *Sent.*, pp. 25–30; Friedrich Stegmüller, ed., "*Sententiae Varsaviensis*: Ein neugefundenes Sentenzenwerk unter dem Einfluss des Anselm von Laon und des Peter Abelard," *Divus Thomas* 45 (1942): 318; *Ysagoge in theologiam*, pp. 79–84.

[49] *Sent. Parisiensis* I, p. 3; Johannes Trimborn, ed., *Die Sententie "Quoniam missio"*

this example enables us to localize this text, it ignores the fact that, unlike the data of faith, kings are not intrinsically invisible in this life.

The backdrop against which this Abelardian scenario was played out was the tradition, maintained by the school of Laon, of confining the understanding of faith to the substance of things hoped for, the argument of things not seen of Hebrews, while ignoring Paul's use of *existimare* elsewhere. Members of that school go on to note that faith can be understood as a substance in that it subsists in the heart of the believer. It is an argument in that it rests on heresay, concerning matters invisible to us, both with respect to events in the past and those in the hereafter which we in the present are unable to witness. It is also an argument in the sense of being a demonstration, in that it manifests its claims by its effects in the lives of believers.[50]

This language was deemed to be too imprecise by a number of theologians later in the century. The chief figure to succeed in moderating Abelard's account, or to succeed in explaining its acceptability in Pauline terms as well as its compatibility with the teaching of the Laon masters, was Hugh of St. Victor. He has an even keener interest than Abelard in considering the status of faith as a mode of knowledge, in relation to other kinds of knowledge. He agrees with Abelard that this is an issue requiring clarification, and supports the orthodoxy of *existimatio* against Abelard's critics. As a mode of knowledge, faith, according to Hugh, is a sacrament, in the broad sense in which he uses this term, and one that needs to be placed on a wide epistemological canvas that includes all forms of the knowledge of God man may have, direct and indirect, internal and external, up to and including contemplative vision. Hugh sees no tension between what later would be called the natural and supernatural modes of knowledge.[51] With this in mind, he agrees with the school of Laon's analysis of faith as the substance of things hoped for, in that it subsists in the believer's heart although he does not yet possess the things to which it refers. Likewise, he agrees, faith is the *argumentum non apparentium*, involving matters seen through a glass darkly, because it is a likeness of invisible realities although it is not corporeal itself. To this Hugh adds his own

---

aus der Abelardschule (Cologne: Photostelle der Universität zu Köln, 1962), pp. 152–58. The latter will be cited below as *Sententiae Parisiensis* II.

[50] *Sent. Anselmi* 2, p. 80.

[51] An excellent general orientation on Hugh's view of faith is provided by Roger Baron, "Le 'sacrement de la foi' selon Hugues de Saint-Victor," *RSPT* 42 (1958): 50–78.

refinement concerning the epistemic status of faith, which absorbs Abelard's view and makes it more precise. "Faith," he states, "is certitude concerning things that are absent; it is above opinion and below knowledge" (*Fides est certitudo rerum absentium supra opinionem et infra scientiam constituta*). As with the knowledge involved in opinion, the knowledge involved in faith is indirect. At the same time, unlike opinion, which is a more free floating cognitive state, faith constitutes knowledge that is certain. But, in comparison with *scientia*, faith also constitutes knowledge that is limited. Now, we know only in part. And, agreeing here with Abelard and his disciples, Hugh adds that when that fuller *scientia* becomes available, in the next life, the knowledge that it conveys will no longer be faith. Faith will have passed into sight. Hugh also imports another dimension into his discussion of faith. Despite his concern with the epistemological analysis of faith, a topic of deep importance to him, he reflects an appreciation of the fact that the debate surrounding Abelard on this subject had pushed to the side the idea of faith as a virtue and as an affective state. Here, he draws a distinction. The matter of faith, he states, is its cognitive content. The mode of faith, as he has described it above, is the limited yet certain knowledge of things not empirically available, above opinion and below science. But the substance of faith, that is, the act of faith and the spiritual attitude represented by faith, is grounded in affection. And, Hugh concludes, one can grow in faith, both as a cognitive and as an affective state.[52]

Hugh's treatment of faith exerted an influence on two mid-century theologians who, in turn, influenced Peter Lombard. Roland of Bologna agrees that Hugh's understanding of faith as the *substantia sperandum rerum, argumentum non apparentium, infra scientium et supra opinionum* is a large improvement over Abelard's *certa existimatio rerum absentium*. Aside from taking Hugh's analysis to heart here, another reason he advances for setting aside Abelard's definition is one derived itself from Abelard's own philosophy. *Existimatio*, in Abelard's sense, can include knowledge of many things that have nothing to do with religious faith. A conviction concerning something not present to the senses, in Abelard's logic, would also describe a concept standing for a sensible thing, which is capable of being thought about and used in propositions independent of the continued existence or present availability of its referent. Likewise,

---

[52] Hugh of St. Victor, *De sac.* 1.10.1–4, *PL* 176: 327D–333D. The quotation is at 1.10.2, 330C.

the certitude with which religious beliefs are held does not necessarily distinguish them from beliefs in other areas which may be
held with equal certitude. In Roland's estimation, a better reason
for elevating faith above opinion is that, although it is based on
heresay, it derives from authoritative sources, even though, since it
is indirect knowledge, it cannot be proved.[53]

The author of the *Summa sententiarum* also expands on Hugh.
Reprising the definition of faith as below science and above opinion
and as partial but certain, held in the absence of full evidence and
as not susceptible of proof in the sense of empirical demonstration,
he adds the point that faith cannot be held without the reception of
revelation, whether through internal inspiration or through external instruction by the words and deeds of other believers. In this
respect, faith differs from the knowledge of God that may be had
through natural theology. In particular, the key content of faith,
which differentiates it from the rational knowledge of God available
in philosophy, is the doctrine of God's unity and trinity as well as
the incarnation.[54] While he expatiates on the content of faith,
against Abelard, this author confines himself to faith as a body of
knowledge and as a cognitive state, and the special epistemic
conditions making it possible, and ignores Hugh's move to push
faith as a virtue and as an affective state back into the picture.

Although he does not use Victorine language, Peter Lombard's
definition and description of faith come down squarely in support
of the Victorine position, especially as articulated by the *Summa
sententiarum* and by Roland. He accepts their resolution of the
controversy inspired by Abelard. He combines this position with a
number of other ideas on which consensus reigned in the period,
with the effect of offering a fuller and more balanced account of
faith both as a virtue and as a mode of knowledge than any other
theologian of his time. Peter begins by defining faith as a virtue, one
which enables us to believe what we cannot see, insofar as the
knowledge at issue pertains to religion.[55] He uses the *argumentum non
apparentium* language of Hebrews and glosses "argument" by
adding the term *convictio*, derived from Augustine, in order to
emphasize the certitude of knowledge possessed by faith. He is also
concerned with locating faith among the diverse modes of knowledge. Its objects of knowledge, he notes, are not sensible. Thus,

---

[53] Roland of Bologna, *Sent.*, pp. 10–12.
[54] *Summa sent.* 1.1–3, *PL* 176: 43A–47C.
[55] Peter Lombard, *Sent.* 3. d. 23. c. 2.1, c. 7.1–c. 8.1, 2: 141, 145–47. The
quotation is at c. 7.3, p. 146.

what is known by faith is known "not corporally, not by imagination, but intellectually" (*non corporaliter, non imaginarie, sed intellectualiter*). Combining these definitions with a three-fold distinction concerning faith, articulated by the school of Laon and held widely in this period by many theologians, including the Peter of the Romans gloss, he notes that faith is a content of propositions to be believed, among them the doctrines of the Trinity and the incarnation, and confidence in the trustworthiness of the person who proposes those propositions. The third, and definitive aspect of faith, the faith that separates the justified believer from the believing reprobate or even from the devil, is the adhesion to God with love and confidence which inspires the faith working in love that is salvific.[56] As a virtue, Peter continues, here reprising as well a doctrine that states the consensus position, faith is the foundation of hope and charity. It covers the past, present, and future, and things both good and bad. It provides hope with the confidence it has in the goods to which it looks in the future; and it is the basis and the motivation for the charity that perfects faith and enables it to work in love.[57] Returning to faith as a mode of knowledge, Peter confirms the Victorine view that it refers to knowledge that is incomplete; it can, he adds, be supplemented by *intellectus* or intellectual clarification of the content of the faith, which can be added on by subsequent study and reflection.[58] Having tipped his hat here to Augustine and to Anselm of Canterbury, he then distinguishes between the faith possessed by mankind prior to the revelation of Christ and the faith possessed by simple Christians who do not understand all the points of faith which they profess. While the people of God before the time of Christ possessed all the revelation currently available and while they may have believed it fully, that faith, since it knew nothing of Christ, was not sufficient to save

---

[56] Ibid., c. 3–c. 6, c. 8, d. 25. c. 3–c. 4, 2: 143–45, 146–47, 155–58. On this trifold view of faith, see also *Sentences of the School of Laon*, no. 313, 415–16, 5: 247, 290; *Sent. Anselmi* 2, pp. 80–82, 86–90; Peter Abelard, *In Ep. ad Romanos* 4:57, CCCM 11: 24; *Sent. Varsaviensis*, p. 318; *Ysagoge in theologiam*, pp. 79–84.

[57] Peter Lombard, *Sent.* 3. d. 23. c. 9, d. 25. c. 5, 2: 147–48, 158–59. See also *Sent. Anselmi* 2, pp. 80–82; Hermannus, *Sent.*, p. 25; *Sent. Parisiensis* I, p. 3; *Ysagoge in theologiam*, pp. 79–84; *Summa sent.* 1.2, *PL* 176: 43C–45C. The author of the *Sent. Parisiensis* II, pp. 148–50, disagrees with the grounding of hope and charity in faith and treats each of these virtues as equally dependent on the others. On the relation of hope to faith in this period and in Peter's teaching, see Jacques-Guy Bougerol, *La théologie de l'espérance aux XIIe et XIIIe siècles*, 2 vols. (Paris: Études Augustiniennes, 1985), 1: 21–101; Servais Pinckaers, "Les origines de la définition de l'espérance dans les Sentences de Pierre Lombard," *RTAM* 22 (1955): 306–12.

[58] Peter Lombard, *Sent.* 3. d. 24. c. 3.3–5, 2: 151–52.

them. On the other hand, the simple Christian believer, whose faith is proportioned to his intelligence and education, and which may thus be anything but profound, does believe in Christ as the mediator and does assent to the other propositions of the creed. This faith, provided that it is manifested in works of love, is sufficient, for him.[59] With this last point, Peter signals the fact that he is going to make a significant departure from the Victorine position on the efficacy of the "sacraments" of the Old Law and on the redemption of persons lacking a specifically Christian faith.

Peter maintains a thoroughly consensus position on hope, as the virtue through which Christians look with confidence toward the spiritual and eternal goods to come in their future beatitude. He agrees that this virtue is based on faith and that the rewards it envisions derive from God's grace and the merits of the individual believer. Like faith, he notes, hope deals with things unseen. But, unlike faith, these things are all good things and they are to occur only in the future. He cites his own Romans gloss as his major source, although these views are the common coin of the period.[60] One line of analysis on hope which he ignores, although it was influential in other quarters in the twelfth century, is the Augustinian distinction among hope of pardon, hope of grace, and hope of glory (*spes venie, spes gratiae, spes gloriae*), popularized in this period by the school of Laon.[61] Instead, he moves on to the question of whether the human Christ possessed the virtues of faith and hope, and hits a major snag. On the negative side of the question, it would appear that, since Christ possessed a fullness of knowledge as well as a fullness of grace, like the beatified saints, He would have had no need of these virtues. However, Peter wants to argue that Christ, having decided to live the life of a man *in via* prior to His resurrection, did possess these virtues, as the saints do in this life, although to a much higher degree. For the saints, the knowledge attaching to faith and the confidence attaching to hope are partial. These limits, in Peter's estimation, were not present in the faith and hope possessed by the human Christ.[62] What remains unclear here, and understandably so, given the definitions of these virtues put forth by Peter above, is how, indeed, faith and hope can remain faith and hope when they lack the incompleteness that is an intrin-

---

[59] Ibid., d. 25. c. 1–c. 2, 2: 153–55.
[60] Ibid., d. 26. c. 1–c. 3, 2: 159–60.
[61] *Sentences of the School of Laon*, no. 313, 5: 247. On this theme, see Bougerol, *La théologie de l'espérance*, 1: 21–23, 65–76.
[62] Peter Lombard, *Sent.* 3. d. 26 c. 4, 2: 160–61.

sic feature of their nature, by definition. It has to be said that Peter
does not resolve this problem and that he does not succeed in
explaining comprehensibly how the human Christ, given the
psychology with which he endows Him, can truly be said to have
had faith and hope.

Peter does at least acknowledge that the human Christ, in the
light of His fullness of knowledge and grace, did not have faith and
hope in the same way that other human beings can possess these
virtues. But he insists firmly that Christ possessed the greatest
possible degree of human charity, both in heart and deed. This
virtue, he reminds the reader, is an essential condition of Christ's
accomplishment of His saving work, in displaying His love to man,
inspiring man's conversion, and instructing man in the love of God
and neighbor. The fact that there might be a problem regarding
Christ's charity, parallel to the problem regarding His faith and
hope, is simply not countenanced by Peter. He proceeds immediately to an analysis of charity. There were only two notable
areas in which there was any debate on this virtue in Peter's day.
One was the definition of charity and the other was the question of
whether, and how, it could be graded and manifested. In the first
case, the Abelardians and the author of the *Summa sententiarum* offer
a definition of charity as the love of the good (*amor honestus*) which
directs one's affections to their proper ends, and which loves other
people with respect to those ends. This definition, in its expanded
form, certainly views God himself and eternal life as the highest
ends in question and as the criterion of intermediate ends. At the
same time, Abelard's definition tends to emphasize the generic and
volitional aspect of the transaction.[63] The Laon masters and Hugh
of St. Victor, on the other hand, adhere to a more strictly conventional and Augustinian definition of charity as the love of God
for His own sake and the love of self and neighbor for God's sake.
Peter Lombard follows in this latter tradition,[64] drawing on some of

---

[63] Peter Abelard, *Theologia "scholarium"* 1.3–5, CCCM 13: 319–20; Hermannus,
Sent., p. 25; *Sent. Parisiensis* I, pp. 5, 48; *Ysagoge in theologiam*, pp. 85–91; Roland of
Bologna, *Sent.*, pp. 3, 5; *Summa sent.* 4.8, *PL* 176: 128A. On this point, see Robert
Wielocks, "La discussion scolastique sur l'amour d'Anselme de Laon à Pierre
Lombard d'aprés les imprimés et les inédits," Katholieke Universiteit Leuven,
Hoger Instituut vor Wijsbegeerte Ph.D. diss., 1981, pp. 277–96.
[64] *Sentences of Anselm of Laon*, no. 71–72, 5: 61–64; *Sent. Anselmi* 2, pp. 80–82;
Hugh of St. Victor, *De sac.* 2.13.6–12, *PL* 176: 528D–550C; Peter Lombard, *Sent.* 3.
d. 27, 2: 162–68. On this definition, see Ruggero Balducci, *Il concetto teologico di
carità attraverso le maggiori interpretazioni patristiche e medievali di I ad Cor. III* (Washington: Catholic University of America Press, 1951), pp. 148–53; Wielocks, "La
discussion scolastique," pp. 175–97, 297–99, 300–02, 306, 342–45.

the refinements added to Augustine by both the Laon masters and Hugh.

With the school of Laon, Peter holds that charity has several stages, although he expands the school's three levels of sweet and inchoate charity, wise and strengthening charity, and robust and perfecting charity into four stages. He retains the Laon masters' first three, which he labels *incipiens*, *proficiens*, and *perfecta*, and adds a final most perfect (*perfectissima*) phase denoting the charity enjoyed by the perfected saints.[65] The school of Laon's definition of charity as the Holy Spirit, "that is, the love between the Father and the Son" (*id est amor patris et filii*) is also one that influenced Peter. The Laon masters are straightforward in stating that those who dwell in charity are engrafted into the inner life of the Trinity. For his part, Peter is more guarded. He seeks to avoid a participatory or immanent view of the mission of the Holy Spirit. As Peter sees it, in communicating charisms, the Holy Spirit conveys the grace of the whole Trinity. He does not convey the divine nature to man.[66] While Peter draws on the school of Laon, at least in part, in these respects, he completely disregards the Laon masters' five-fold subdivision of charity as analogous to the five senses.[67]

Peter joins Hugh in drawing on Augustine's analysis of the goods to which charity should direct our attention, although each master imparts his own accent to this topic. Hugh distinguishes what is good in and of itself, namely God as the supreme and normative good; intermediate goods which are substantially good but good only in part, although they may also be good in relation to something or someone else; and purely derivative goods, which are not good in and of themselves but which may lead to good. Under this last heading he thinks some evils may be placed.[68] In his analysis, the first two goods, which are either wholly or partly good, will therefore be good for something or someone else as well. The

---

[65] *Sentences of the School of Laon*, no. 313, 5: 247; Peter Lombard, *Sent.* 3. d. 29. c. 3.1, 2: 177.

[66] *Sent. Anselmi* 2, pp. 80–82; the quotation is on p. 80; Peter Lombard, *Sent.* 1. d. 14. c. 1–c. 2, 1: 126–28. For Peter on the Holy Spirit as *caritas*, see above, chapter 5, pp. 260–62. The distinctions drawn by him on this subject, in relation to the school of Laon, are not given their due weight by Ignaz Siepl, "Die Lehre von der göttliche Tugend der Liebe in des Petrus Lombardus Büchern der Sentenzen und in der *Summa theologica* des hl. Thomas von Aquin," *Der Katholik*, 3:34 (1906): 37–49, 196–201; Franz Zigon, "Der Begriff der Caritas beim Lombarden, und der hl. Thomas," *Divus Thomas* 4 (1926): 404–11. Both of these authors draw too much of a contrast between Peter and Thomas.

[67] *Sentences of the School of Laon*, no. 431, 5: 296–97.

[68] Hugh of St. Victor, *De sac.* 1.4.15–20, *PL* 176: 240B–242D.

evident purpose of Hugh's distinction is to rationalize the existence
of evils as having a potential to serve the good, willy-nilly, as much
as it is to distinguish between the supreme good and lower goods as
objects of charity. On the other hand, Peter's focus on the levels of
goodness is specifically designed as an index of how men should
direct their loves. We should, he states, love God, Who is above us,
the most; and our souls and those of our neighbors, including the
angels, with a lesser degree of love and one that keeps their eternal
destiny in view. Human bodies, our own and others', are intimately
linked with the soul and are also destined for salvation; and so they
should also be loved, in the sense of promoting what is conducive to
their health and self-preservation. Finally, we should love what is
below us, insofar as it is conducive to the wellbeing of the body.[69]
Aside from his concern with the gradation of man's display of love,
and its rationale, Peter's treatment of this point emphasizes man's
hylemorphic constitution, a theme which he gives much more
prominence than Hugh does in his understanding of human nature
more generally.

Aside from the definition of charity itself, the other major topic
under this heading on which the theologians and their authorities
disagreed was the question of what criterion should be invoked in
extending charity to one's fellow man, given the finitude of the
means at one's disposal. The three criteria considered by theologians who wrestle with this point are virtue, need, and relationship
to the donor. Not all of them are able to make a decision here. The
author of the *Summa sententiarum* considers all three positions, and
their pros and cons, and draws no conclusions of his own.[70] The
author of the *Sententie Anselmi* opts for virtue, being particularly
concerned that we not grant charity or alms to notorious evildoers,
lest we thereby appear to condone their behavior.[71] Most of the
masters of the school of Laon think that need should be the primary
determinant, but that if need is not a factor, relationship should be
the guide, with charity dispensed first to parents, then to other
relatives, then to friends, members of one's household, neighbors,
and compatriots.[72] Roland of Bologna defends the principle of need
above all. He also imports into the discussion the same distinction
between interior *affectus* and exterior *effectus* which he draws in

---

[69] Peter Lombard, *Sent.* 3. d. 28. c. 1–c. 4, 2: 168–71.
[70] *Summa sent.* 4.7, *PL* 176: 125A–126A.
[71] *Sent. Anselmi* 2, p. 84; *Sentences of Anselm of Laon*, no. 79, 5: 67–68.
[72] *Sentences of Anselm of Laon*, no. 71–72; *Sentences of the School of Laon*, no. 432–33,
436, 5: 61–64, 297, 298–99.

considering virtue more generally. The needs that should determine our charitable responses will vary according to the nature and circumstances of the needy people we assist, he notes. Thus, the specifics of the *effectus* of charity will differ accordingly. But they will all be inspired equally by the same inner charitable *affectus*.[73]

Peter Lombard borrows this *affectus-effectus* distinction but uses it to support a view of the distribution of charity according to relationships, while going beyond the standard analysis to include enemies as well as relatives and friends. He agrees with Roland that all people are to be loved with the same charity, seen as a qualitative intentionality. With this idea in mind, it is possible to invoke the sliding scale of relationship, understanding that a different *effectus* will be appropriate to the different kinds of relatives and associates we have. Peter includes enemies not only in response to the biblical injunction to love one's enemies, but also as a means of reinforcing the point that the sliding scale of relationships speaks to charity as a virtue. We should love the people in question for the sake of God and their eternal life, not out of a merely natural affection. The rule of love of neighbor, moreover, is a general one. While it is harder to love those less closely bound to us than it is to love our nearest and dearest, and while, *a fortiori*, it is harder to love our enemies than our friends, it is also true that the virtue of charity is more perfect when it is exercised in the more difficult cases. Peter leaves open the question of whether we should aid relatives even if they are morally inferior to persons not related to us.[74] The Lombard also has two points to make on the perdurance of charity, in this case following Gratian.[75] When the apostle says that charity endures, he does not mean that individual people cannot grow stronger or weaker in this virtue. Rather, he is referring to the merits of charity *per se*, as a virtue. At the same time, while faith and hope will no longer be needed in the next life, having been superseded by sight and by the possession of what we hope for, charity will not be superseded but will rather be strengthened in Heaven, with all the limits and imperfections that may mar it in this life removed.[76] Peter concludes this treatise on the theological virtues on the same ambiguous Christological note as he had begun it. Having already stated that the human Christ had the most perfect charity possible for a human being *in via*, he now observes that,

---

[73] Roland of Bologna, *Sent.*, pp. 318–20.
[74] Peter Lombard, *Sent.* 3. d. 29. c. 2–c. 12, d. 30, 2: 172–76, 177–80.
[75] Landgraf, *Dogmengeschichte*, 1 part 2: 136–203.
[76] Peter Lombard, *Sent.* 3. d. 31. c. 1–c. 2, 2: 180–84.

while He was still alive, the human Christ possessed the even more perfect charity of the *patria*.[77] He thereby reinforces the problematic character of his treatment of Christ's humanity while at the same time raising questions, which he does not answer, about the very appropriateness of the consideration of the virtues under this heading in the first place.

The Cardinal Virtues

The same holds true for Peter's treatment of the cardinal virtues, which he considers in a primarily Christological context as well. Most of the theologians of the day did not place themselves under the constraints that follow from this decision. Many of them, including Anselm of Laon, William of Champeaux, the Porretans, and the authors of the *Sententiae divinitatis* and *Summa sententiarum*, display no interest in this topic at all. Those who do had available to them not only the classical definitions of these virtues, whether Platonic, Aristotelian, or Stoic, by means of both pagan and patristic intermediaries. They also had, as resources, the reformulations of the cardinal virtues in association with the theological virtues put forth by Ambrose and Gregory and the redefinition of them as modes of charity found in Augustine. Ambrose's treatment of the theological virtues as imparting the power to practice the cardinal virtues had no takers in this period. The Gregorian redefinition of the cardinal virtues had one supporter, the author of the *Sententie Anselmi*. Following Gregory, he presents these virtues as expressions of the Christian virtues of penance, obedience, poverty in spirit, and humility; all of them are fruits of the fear of the Lord. Also, with Gregory, he analogizes them to the figures in Ezechiel's vision, the man, ox, lion, and eagle standing for discretion, self-mortification, fortitude, and exaltation. The master adds that, along with memory, intellect, and will, contempt of the world, hope of eternal reward, and patience, these virtues will build the "house of God" within the human soul.[78]

A more Aristotelian approach to the cardinal virtues found favor with some theologians. Without placing them in an Aristotelian hierarchy, other members of the school of Laon join the Peripatetics in viewing the virtues as a mean between extremes. Prudence mediates between flightiness and sluggishness, temperance be-

---

[77] Ibid., c. 3, 1: 184.
[78] *Sent. Anselmi* 4, pp. 110–11.

tween luxury and insensibility, fortitude between rashness and timidity, and justice between the greater and the lesser good.[79] The Abelardians also tend to put an Aristotelian construction on the cardinal virtues. Abelard himself does not provide a discussion of the cardinal virtues as such, but singles out prudence or discernment as the mother of the virtues, a point associated with the Stoics.[80] His disciples reject that idea. According to the author of *Sententiae Parisiensis* I, prudence is not a virtue at all, since it involves knowledge of evil as well as good. As for the other three virtues, he follows Aristotle in making justice, defined as rendering to each his own and serving the common weal, the paramount virtue. Temperance and fortitude he sees as ordered to justice, aiding its exercise, with temperance strengthening the soul against the infrarational temptations that might deflect it from justice and fortitude arming the soul to repel whatever is opposed to justice.[81] Hermannus includes prudence as one of the cardinal virtues, but, like the author of *Sententiae Parisiensis* I, he places justice at the head of the list and gives all four of the virtues Aristotelian definitions. He adds that they can be possessed by virtuous pagans.[82] Hugh of St. Victor comes up with a list of virtues which also places justice at the head but whose relationship to Aristotle, or to any of Hugh's potential patristic sources, is difficult to see, as is its internal coherence. He begins with justice, followed by clemency, remorse, love of justice, mercy, purity of heart, and inner peace of mind. He does not explain the difference, if any, between justice and love of justice or between clemency and mercy. He neither redefines the cardinal virtues in Christian terms nor explores whether or how these virtues are antidotes to the seven deadly sins. This collection of virtues, to which he annexes the beatitudes and the gifts of the Holy Spirit, appears to be *sui generis* with Hugh.[83]

In relation to these contemporary and recent discussions, and to the patristic possibilities, the Lombard takes a line of his own on the cardinal virtues. In an early sermon, he echoes the language of the author of the *Sententie Anselmi*, although without his Gregorian overtones, in describing the four cardinal virtues as the four walls of the house of God, along with its four gates as the four evangelists,

[79] *Sentences of the School of Laon*, no. 424–25, 5: 293.
[80] Peter Abelard, *Ethics*, p. 128.
[81] *Sent. Parisiensis* I, pp. 52–54. On the Abelardian definition of justice, see Lottin, *Psych. et morale*, 3: 284–85.
[82] Hermannus, *Sent.*, pp. 145, 149.
[83] Hugh of St. Victor, *De sac.* 2.13.2, *PL* 176: 526C–527B.

its twelve towers as the apostles, and its roof as the gifts of the Holy Spirit. He does not provide definitions of the virtues here.[84]

In a still earlier sermon, he describes the cardinal virtues as antidotes of the vices of lust, vainglory, gluttony, and anger. In the same sermon, however, he proposes a non-Gregorian schedule of vices, including negligence, curiosity about things that are none of one's business, fleshly concupiscence, consent to sin, habituation to sin, contempt of the good, and delight in sin, proposing the gifts of the Holy Spirit as their remedies.[85] In the *Sentences*, Peter first brings up the cardinal virtues as virtues possessed by man before the fall. Like all meritorious action open to prelapsarian man, these virtues, he states, required the active collaboration of grace with free will.[86] In his treatise on Christology, Peter essays his only definition of these virtues. Although elsewhere he agrees with the Augustinian principle that charity is the ground of the virtues just as lack of charity is the ground of the vices, even though the internal *habitus* may be manifested outwardly in different ways in either case,[87] Peter does not follow Augustine's redefinition of the cardinal virtues as modes of charity. He does appeal to Augustine's authority here, but it is the Augustine of *De trinitate* 14.9.12, an Augustine in a less adaptive mood. In line with the definitions found in *De trinitate*, Peter states that justice is relief of those in misery, prudence is the outwitting or forestalling of attacks on virtue, fortitude is the calm bearing of suffering, and temperance is the restraining of evil pleasures. He adds that the human Christ, to Whom he accords both the perfect charity of the *via* and the still more perfect charity of the *patria*, possessed these virtues, which have their uses both in the *via* and in the *patria*.[88]

In examining the cardinal virtues more specifically, Peter begins with justice, but in no sense because he wants to put an Aristotelian construction on this virtue. The assuaging of need which marks this virtue *in via* will give way, in the *patria*, to the contemplation of the divine nature for which human nature was made, and than which nothing could be better, more amiable, or more appropriate, and hence, more just.[89] As for the other virtues, they too will remain in

---

[84] Peter Lombard, *Sermo* 32, *PL* 171: 497A.

[85] Peter Lombard, *Sermo* 4, *PL* 171: 354B–357B.

[86] Peter Lombard, *Sent.* 2. d. 29. c. 1–c. 2, 1: 492–93. Delhaye, *Pierre Lombard*, pp. 75–80, ignores this consideration of the cardinal virtues in Peter, and, in general, gives this subject shorter shrift than it deserves.

[87] Peter Lombard, *Sent.* 3. d. 36, 2: 202–06.

[88] Ibid., d. 33, c. 1–c. 2, 2: 188.

[89] Ibid., c. 3.2, 2: 189. Charles Lefebre, "La notion d'équité chez Pierre Lom-

the next life and their accent will likewise shift from the negative or disciplinary to the positive, since there will be, in the *patria*, no danger of error, no suffering, and no evil desires to be overcome. Instead, wisdom will propose God as the good; fortitude will adhere to Him; and temperance will enjoy Him with no impediments.[90] These remarks concerning the function of the cardinal virtues in the next life are also drawn from Augustine's *De trinitate*. This concludes Peter's extremely abbreviated treatment of the cardinal virtues. He does not redefine them as expressions of charity. He neither confirms nor denies in Book 3 the point made in Book 2 of the *Sentences* that they require the collaboration of grace and free will. He says nothing about how these virtues may be related or engendered. The virtuous pagan, who makes a brief potential appearance earlier in Peter's analysis of virtue, is neither claimed nor dismissed here. Peter offers no suggestions as to how, or whether, the cardinal virtues are related to the theological virtues or to the gifts of the Holy Spirit, although he places them in between his account of those two topics. This is clearly an area that called for further reflection, both in the mid-twelfth-century in general and in Lombardian theology more specifically.

The Gifts of the Holy Spirit

After considering the cardinal virtues, Peter next turns to the gifts of the Holy Spirit, which, in Book 3 of the *Sentences*, he treats as virtues, although in Book 2 he had distinguished quite sharply the gifts from the virtues which they enable man to develop, in collaboration with free will. That same distinction, as we recall, he had repeated at the beginning of his discussion of virtue in general, and the interaction of God and man therein. In any event, the first of these gifts which he takes up is the fear of the Lord. This provides him with the occasion to rehearse a topic that had received considerable attention in this period. Although there was some slight

---

bard," *Ephemerides Juris Canonici* 9 (1953): 291–304 gives a good overview of the meanings of justice in Peter Lombard, from the one given in this passage, to justice as justification, to justice as linked to or contrasted with mercy in the last judgment. The latter of these points in Peter is discussed by Landgraf, "Some Unknown Writings," p. 14. On the other hand, Hermenegildus Lio, *Estne obligatio iustitiae subvenire miseris? Quaestionis positio et evolutio a Petro Lombardo ad S. Thomam ex tribus S. Augustini textibus* (Rome: Desclée & Socii, 1957), pp. 1–4, 15–29, considers justice only from the narrow perspective of poor relief, more properly treated in conjunction with charity in Peter, and poses the question anachronistically in the light of the economic ethics of Aquinas.

[90] Peter Lombard, *Sent.* 3. d. 33. c. 3.3–4, 2: 189.

difference in the terminology used, there was a rather general agreement on the substance of the doctrine. Fear was divided, usually, into four categories, servile fear, mundane or worldly fear, initial fear, and chaste or filial fear. The first was seen as motivating action so as to avoid worldly punishment, the second as prompting action so as to avoid the loss of worldly good, the third as inspired by fear of eternal punishment, and the fourth as triggering virtuous action out of the love of God alone. Filial fear was generally held to be the only perfectly acceptable ethical motivation; but it was accepted that initial fear could serve as the beginning of wisdom in prompting the conversion of heart that would lead to filial fear.[91] This doctrine is found in Anselm of Laon and his followers and in Hugh of St. Victor, under the heading of ethics.[92] Robert Pullen agrees with the substance of the consensus position, but brings it up in considering the conditions making for acceptable contrition in the sacrament of penance.[93] William of Champeaux and the author of the *Summa sententiarum* discuss this topic in the context of the virtues possessed by the human Christ, agreeing that He had a perfect filial fear.[94] The Lombard follows these two latter theologians, but adds his own perspective to their common teaching.

The key to Peter's handling of the theme of fear as a moral motivation is his desire to apply to the gifts of the Holy Spirit as possessed by the human Christ a treatment parallel to the treatment he gives to the theological and cardinal virtues. There, he had been concerned to show that these virtues are needed in *via*, and that, with the exception of faith and hope, they will be retained in the *patria*, although in an altered and perfected form. He likewise wants to show that the human Christ possessed those virtues that will endure into the next life both according to the *via* and to the *patria* during His life on earth. In arraying his authorities on fear of the Lord, Peter's major concern is to tackle figures such as Bede and Augustine, who say that fear will cease in Heaven. Peter agrees that initial fear, in this life, can be a useful first step toward the filial fear which, again, in this life, is the sufficient and perfect motivation

---

[91] On this doctrine in the first half of the twelfth century, see Schupp, *Die Gnadenlehre*, pp. 164–66; Damien Van den Eynde, "Autour des 'Enarrationes in Evangelium S. Matthei' attribués à Geoffroi Babion," *RTAM* 26 (1959): 71–73.

[92] *Sentences of Anselm of Laon*, no. 31, 75; *Sentences of the School of Laon*, no. 420, 429, 5: 33, 65–66, 291, 294–95; *Sent. Anselmi* 3, pp. 105–06; Hugh of St. Victor, *De sac.* 2.13.5, *PL* 176: 528A–D.

[93] Robert Pullen, *Sent.* 5.30–31, *PL* 186: 851D–853C.

[94] *Sentences of William of Champeaux*, no. 276, 5: 220–21; *Summa sent.* 3.17, *PL* 176: 115A–116A.

for virtue. He resolves the problem provoked by Bede and Augustine by drawing a distinction. Initial fear, along with its even less worthy companions, servile and mundane fear, will, to be sure, cease in Heaven. On the other hand, filial fear will endure. But, like charity and the cardinal virtues, it will be perfected and manifested only in its most positive aspects. In Heaven, the filial fear that inspires the virtuous to avoid offending God and to desire never to be separated from God will be transformed into the desire to revere God always, now that they can remain with Him forever, in a reverence mixed with love.[95] As for the definitions of the modes of fear themselves, Peter is a bit more generous than are most of his contemporaries. He regards initial fear as a form of inchoate love of God, and not just as a fear of eternal punishment, and he sees the lower servile fear, while clearly outside of the state of wisdom to which initial fear can lead, as at least possessing the capacity to prepare the way to it in some sense. He affirms that the human Christ possessed a perfect filial fear, both of the *via* and of the *patria*, throughout His life and that, while as a human being He could experience the fear of death, such fear was not servile or mundane fear in His case.[96]

Peter's handling of the other gifts of the Holy Spirit is quite abbreviated. Aside from fear, the only other gifts he takes up are wisdom (*sapientia*) and knowledge (*scientia*). The chief framework of patristic authority in which he positions his analysis is Augustinian. Better, it can be read as a good case of Peter's use of Augustine against Augustine, in aid of his own desired conclusions. The first definition of wisdom he cites is the philosophical one given by Augustine in his *Contra academicos*, the knowledge of things divine and human. Against this idea Peter offers what he finds a better definition, one easier to gear to the notion of these mental states not as natural aptitudes and achievements but as gifts of the Holy Spirit. This is the definition of *sapientia* and *scientia* found in Augustine's *De trinitate*, where wisdom is seen as the knowledge of things divine, and science is seen as the knowledge of things human, omitting, that is, information that is vain, frivolous, or superfluous, and focusing on knowledge that nurtures, helps, and defends the faith and that therefore promotes beatitude.[97] According to Peter, wisdom can also be distinguished from understanding (*intellectum, intelligentia*). To be sure, understanding, like wisdom, applies to the

---

[95] Peter Lombard, *Sent.* 3. d. 34. c. 3.1–4, 2: 191–92.
[96] Ibid., c. 6.3–c. 9, 2: 196–98.
[97] Ibid., d. 35. c. 1.2–3, 2: 198–99.

knowledge of invisible, spiritual realities. But wisdom is eternal, while understanding operates temporally. In addition, wisdom has God alone as its object, and understanding is oriented both to God and to creatures. Further, through understanding we grasp what we know; through wisdom we delight in what we know. Both wisdom and understanding can thus be differentiated from *scientia*. *Scientia* applies to our right ordering and administration of temporal things and to the turning from evil to good things. *Intelligentia* applies to our speculation on the creator and the invisible creation in time. *Sapientia* applies to our contemplation and delectation of eternal truth. Following the model developed above for holy fear, Peter concludes that, at the end of time, it is *sapientia* that will endure.[98] In elaborating on this point, he once more reminds the reader that he is not talking about natural modes of knowledge here—a category to which he certainly assigns a place in Book 2 of the *Sentences*—but about gifts of the Holy Spirit that are given for the specific purpose of theological reflection, analysis, and enlightenment. The grace so imparted assists the human mind in turning its natural functions to subjects that lead to virtue and salvation.[99] Despite his dependence on Augustine here, Peter does not use the Augustinian language of divine illumination in discussing man's direct or indirect theological knowledge. At the same time, he marks a departure from the modes of knowledge outlined by Hugh of St. Victor, who places natural knowledge and knowledge for which divine assistance is required on more of a continuum than Peter does.

The Moral Law of the Old Testament

This willingness to depart from the Victorine tradition is also visible in the final area Peter addresses in connection with ethics in Book 3 of the *Sentences*, the Ten Commandments and other features of the Old Testament moral law, and the degree to which they continue to bind Christians. Following the consensus view, which goes back to Augustine, he observes that the first three of the Ten Commandments apply to the love of God and are more important than the next seven, which apply to the love of neighbor.[100] He also agrees with the consensus, shared by the canonists as well as the

---

[98] Ibid., c. 2, 2: 200.
[99] Ibid., c. 3.1–2, 2: 201.
[100] Ibid., d. 37. c. 1.1, 2: 206. Cf., for example, *Sentences of Anselm of Laon*, no. 12, 5: 23; *Summa sent.* 4.3, *PL* 176: 120D–125A.

theologians, that the moral rules of the Old Testament continue to bind, but that the ritual and ceremonial rites, which are subject to change and which in any case apply to religious practices that have been superseded for Christians, do not.[101] The master to whom Peter comes the closest in this area is the author of the *Summa sententiarum*. With him, the Lombard firmly rejects the placement of the Old Law on a broad "sacramental" trajectory, of the sort found in Hugh of St. Victor. The rites of the Old Law having been replaced, definitively, with those of the New, their salvific character even in their own day receives short shrift. Anticipating what he will say about the sacraments in Book 4 of the *Sentences*, Peter views these Old Testament ceremonies as significant, but not as a means for the transmission of divine grace. He also joins the author of the *Summa sententiarum* in asserting that the ethics of the New Testament likewise perfects and goes farther than the moral rules of the Old Testament, even in the case of those earlier rules that are retained. The reason for this is that Christ's teaching pays attention to intentionality and not just to action. Sexual ethics is an example cited by both authors to defend this claim. The author of the *Summa sententiarum* adds the example of homicide, which likewise can be committed "in deed, word, and intention" (*manu, lingua, consensu*). Thus, character assassination and compassing a person's death, in the Christian dispensation, count as murder.[102] Similarly, both Peter and the author of the *Summa sententiarum* take up, and condemn, usury under the heading of theft, a topic far less standard among theologians in the mid-twelfth century than it was later to become.[103]

On the other hand, Peter parts company with the *Summa sententiarum* and with the majority of his contemporaries in his treatment of the sin of lying, to which he gives extended attention. Two notes emerge in his discussion of this subject. First, reprising and expanding on what he had said in Book 2 of the *Sentences*, where he rejects the view of the school of Laon, the *Summa sententiarum*, and Robert Pullen on the admissibility of pious fraud in the lie of the Hebrew nurses of Exodus, he gives the most thorough analysis of the Augustinian position on lying of anyone of his time. And,

---

[101] Peter Lombard, *Sent.* 3. d. 40, 2: 228–29. Cf., for example, *Sentences of Anselm of Laon*, no. 51, 53, 5: 48–49, 50; Ivo of Chartres, *Decretum* prologus 2–6, *PL* 161: 50A–60A; Gratian, *Decretum* pars 1. d. 6. c. 3. dictum, col. 11.

[102] Peter Lombard, *Sent.* 3. d. 40, 2: 228–29. Cf. *Summa sent.* 4.3–6, *PL* 176: 120D–125A. The quotation is at 4.4 122B.

[103] Peter Lombard, *Sent.* 3. d. 37. c. 5.3, 2: 211; *Summa sent.* 4.4, *PL* 176: 122C–D.

second, he includes within his consideration of lying the discussion of perjury provided by Gratian, a topic not discussed in the work of his theological compeers. Peter brings four Augustinian texts to bear on his treatment of lying. He is aware of the fact that Augustine changed his mind on this subject, and that, in the *De mendacio*, he located the lie in the intention to deceive alone, while in the *Contra mendacium*, he included the objective untruth of the speaker's statement as well as his deceptive intention. Peter is also aware of the fact that, both in the *Contra mendacium* and in the *Enchiridion*, Augustine adds subjective certitude as a factor in the equation. According to his argument in these two works, then, a statement may be objectively false. But, if the speaker believes it to be true and speaks without a deceptive intention, he commits an error but does not tell a lie. Likewise, Peter is familiar with the three-fold distinction, found in Augustine's commentary on Psalm 5 as well as in the *De mendacio*, among a tall tale or jocose lie, told to entertain and understood as such, which therefore deceives no one, a lie told to protect someone else from harm—the case of the Hebrew nurses—and a lie told out of malice or duplicity. The Lombard, finally, is conversant with the example given by Augustine in the *Contra mendacium*, which illustrates the point that existing personal relationships and susceptibilities condition the way a hearer interprets a statement. In this example, a man gives misdirections to an acquaintance planning to take a trip, an acquaintance who, he knows, mistrusts him and will do the opposite of what he counsels, in the effort to prevent him from taking the dangerous route that he would otherwise take.

With this array of Augustinian materials on the subject before him, Peter composes a position on lying which combines insights from the *De mendacio* and *Contra mendacium* while squarely affirming the conclusions of the late Augustine against the countervailing opinion of Gregory the Great. All lies, he asserts, are sinful. They may be graded, as Augustine grades them, as more or less serious on the basis of their provocation. But, he agrees, no provocation, however acute, excuses a lie. This judgment excludes jocose lies, which deceive no one, and honest errors, or falsehoods told in good faith, or beliefs mistakenly but sincerely held, which report what the speaker really thinks is true. It does not excuse pious fraud, which is sinful, if perhaps venially so. For Peter, as for the late Augustine, a lie combines an objective untruth, except for the conditions noted above, with the speaker's knowledge that it is untrue and with the intention to deceive. The only example he will admit of a lie that is excusable is one also accepted by Augustine, the case of Jacob masquerading as Esau in order to obtain his father's blessing. Peter follows Augustine in saying that this is not a lie but a mystery, and that Jacob, in any event, is to be given a dispensation because he was obeying his mother's instructions under the guidance of the Holy Spirit.[104] The main issue on which he does not agree with Augustine is on the evaluation of the pious fraud as a venial, and not as a serious, sin. This analysis, both fuller and better informed than that of any contemporary, presents the strongest case against lying made by any theologian of the day, and one that is entirely consistent with Peter's desire to give wider scope to the objective dimension of sin side by side with ethical intentionality, in his ethical teaching more generally.

To this Peter adds an analysis of perjury, drawn from Gratian, and defined as a lie sealed by an oath. In line with this position, the Lombard notes that some say one can swear falsely, but unknowingly, thereby not lying or foreswearing oneself. In response, he draws a three-fold distinction. Perjury, first, is the voluntary taking of an oath while knowingly swearing what is false, for the sake of deception. A person can also swear that what he thinks is true is true, when it is false, and he can swear that what he thinks is false is false, when it is true. The two latter cases may involve honest mistakes. But, unlike the first case, or perjury proper, they do not involve a deceptive intention. In the first case, the speaker knows perfectly well that he is not telling the truth. In the second and third cases, the speaker may actually be in error, but his statement accurately reports what he thinks to be the case, in good faith. The latter two cases can be assimilated to the statements involving objective error but subjective conviction in the absence of deceptive intention in the foregoing analysis of lying. On the basis of the same reasoning, persons who swear to what is not objectively the case may not be guilty of perjury. Perjury, as such, requires both the deliberate distortion of the truth and the intention to mislead, as is the case with lying.[105] This account is quite faithful to Gratian, so far as it goes, although Peter is more interested in integrating the subject of perjury into the Augustinian theory of lying than Gratian is. He also omits a consideration which Gratian presents as essential in his own analysis of oaths, the question of ignorance, especially culpable ignorance, as a factor bearing not only on the accuracy of the statements to which one swears but also on the culpability of

---

[104] Peter Lombard, *Sent.* 3. d. 38. c. 1–c. 6, 2: 213–18.
[105] Ibid., d. 39. c. 1–c. 3, 2: 218–21.

the person taking the oath. Here as elsewhere in his ethical doctrine, Peter chooses not to take account of the issue of ignorance.

Peter also follows Gratian, while theologizing him, in dealing with
the related question of when it is appropriate to swear oaths and
when it is permissible to break them. He agrees that oaths should
not be sworn falsely, unnecessarily, or frivolously. But oaths are
acceptable in order to prove innocence, to confirm a peace treaty,
or to convince one's hearers of facts that are useful to them. These
conditions mitigate the Scriptural injunctions against swearing
oaths. But, no one should be forced to swear to something he knows
to be false, however good the end served by this action may be.
Peter adds that it is important to swear only on God, and not on
false gods or creatures. As to the breach of vows, he admits this in
cases where they were made foolishly or against faith or charity. It
is better, he thinks, to break one's oath in such a case than to
remain in a state of dishonor or bad faith.

Conclusion

It will be noted that the theme of the Old Law and its abrogation
or continuing applicability, which serves as the context for these
reflections on such subjects as lying, perjury, usury, and adultery,
has little or nothing to do with the subject of Christ's human
nature, His human knowledge, His human moral capacities, and
the gifts of the Holy Spirit, to which it has been annexed. This fact
underscores an observation made earlier and one which this chapter has explored more fully: ethics is the single most disorganized
subject in Peter Lombard's theology. There are, to be sure, a
number of powerful and consistent ideas that serve as overriding
themes, tying together what Peter has to say on ethics wherever the
material is presented in his *Sentences*. Of particular note is the desire
to moderate Abelard's teaching and to incorporate more of an
objectivist strain into the prevailing intentionalist consensus, a
consensus position which he supports. Also important is Peter's
desire to emphasize the need for the collaboration of grace and free
will in the development of human virtue and merit. He makes that
point very clearly, while preserving a crisp distinction between the
deity, or the Holy Spirit as such, and God's graces and gifts as His
effects, working in man, graces and gifts which man remains free to
reject and which, if voluntarily accepted and acted upon, enable
him to develop virtues and merits that are truly his own. This
process is understood by Peter as man's return from the *regio
dissimilitudinis* to which he has exiled himself by sin, and the recov-

ery of man's inborn similitude to God. Peter emphasizes that the working of grace in man does not divinize man; rather it helps him to restore his true humanity.

In other areas of his moral doctrine, Peter is less conclusive and consistent. While he teaches that the collaboration of grace and free will, in one form or another, is a necessary enabling condition in man's moral life, he also thinks that non-believers, who presumably lack knowledge of and access to that grace, are capable of the good faith, good intentions, and good deeds that express their natural *pietas*. Yet, Peter does not come to grips expressly with the problem of the virtuous pagan. It has to be said that his *Sentences* offer support for the acceptance of the virtuous pagan, as the Abelardians do, and for his exclusion, along with Hugh of St. Victor. Peter does not seem to be aware of his own ambiguity on this point. Another area in which the reader seeks clarification that he does not find is the relationship between natural reason, of the sort that makes possible proofs for God's existence and the grasp of the *invisibilia dei* by the rational inspection of the creation, on the one hand, with the *scientia* directed to created and temporal things with an eye to their ethical and theological significance, as a gift of the Holy Spirit, on the other.

Unquestionably the most problematic feature of the Lombard's ethics is his decision to deal with sin and with ethical intentionality and the psychogenesis of ethical decision-making in general as a pendant to his account of human nature and the fall, and with virtue in conjunction with Christ's human nature. Had Peter's Christ been a man like us in all but sin, this choice might not have made for any real difficulties. But, although he is not as extreme on this point as are many contemporaries, he endows the human Christ with a nature that does not have a fully human psychology. While Peter tries to circumvent the dilemmas flowing from this schematic decision, and from the Christology he professes, by analyzing the virtues as such before exploring their mode of possession by the human Christ, the fact remains that, with the human Christ as his paradigm, understood as Peter understands Him, a gap between mankind and the Son of man has been opened in which questions may legitimately be raised about Christ's role as a moral example for man. This arrangement of the material creates a pronounced asymmetry and disparity between the analysis of vice and sin, on the one hand, and of virtue, on the other, and one that transcends the differing operative factors conditioning the exercise of vice and virtue by man before and after the fall. The decision to treat virtue under the heading of Christology also leads, as we have seen, to the inclusion of the moral law of the Old Testament at the end of Book 3 of the *Sentences*, even though it has no immediately visible relationship to the moral capacities of the human Christ. As a schematic device, the one and only merit of Peter's placement of this material where he does is that it serves as a point of transition to the sacraments, to which he devotes most of Book 4, and on which, despite the deep and critical influence of Hugh of St. Victor which he reveals at many points, he plans to distance himself decisively from the broad and generic Victorine understanding of sacrament.

THE SACRAMENTS

In the first half of the twelfth century, there was a felt need, for the first time in the history of the western Christian tradition, for an organized, systematic, general theology of the sacraments. On one level, this fact is an expression of the emergence of systematic theology and systematic canon law as professional academic disciplines. Within each of these disciplines, practitioners felt the urge to present an organized treatise on the sacraments, conceptualized in such a way that it would cohere intellectually with the other subjects that a systematic account of their field of study would need to include. At the same time, and despite the difference in their guild mentalities and their division of labor, the canonists and theologians overlap and borrow from each other on the sacraments. It was the theologians who took the lead in organizing the authorities, defining the range of issues to be discussed, asserting their independence from earlier theory and practice, and considering the role of the sacraments in the Christian life and not just the juridical circumstances that would guarantee the validity of their administration. At the same time, the theologians drew on the canonists' dossiers of sources and cited them, sometimes to agree and sometimes to disagree with their reasoning and conclusions.[106] But,

---

[106] On the relations between theologians and canonists in the field of sacramental theology, the influence and greater independence of the theologians is accented by Paul Fournier and Gabriel Le Bras, *Histoire des collections canoniques en occident depuis les fausses décrétales jusqu'au Décret de Gratien* (Paris: Sirey, 1932), 2: 314–52; Nikolaus M. Häring, "The Interaction between Canon Law and Sacramental Theology in the Twelfth Century," in *Proceedings of the Fourth International Congress of Medieval Canon Law*, ed. Stephan Kuttner (Vatican City: Biblioteca Apostolica Vaticana, 1976), pp. 483–93; Artur Michael Landgraf, "Diritto canonico e teologia nel secolo XII," *Studia Gratiana* 1 (1953): 371–413. On the other hand, the dependence of theologians on canonists in this area is accented by Alfonso M. Stickler, "Teologia e diritto canonico nella storia," *Salesianum* 47 (1985): 695.

much more was at stake than the reinvigorating, institutionalizing, and crossfertilizing of pedagogy and reflection within and between these sister disciplines. Two other circumstances also fed into the explosion of interest in speculating on the sacraments in this period. One was the Gregorian reform movement. Focusing on the improvement of clerical morality and leading to partisan clashes within the church that left some clerics in the status of schismatics or excommunicates if they found themselves supporting an anti-pope or a bishop or ruler who was under papal censure, the reform movement, in raising for the first time since the days of the early church the question of the validity of sacraments administered by immoral, simoniac, or excommunicated priests also alerted Christians in the late eleventh and early twelfth centuries to the fact that they lacked a general theory of the sacraments in terms of which they could adjudicate such matters. Aside from the question of what validates a sacrament, arising from these struggles within the church, the emergence of anti-sacramental heresies on a wide scale demanded a justification and defense of the church's rites. And, as the controversy surrounding the Eucharistic heresy of Berengar of Tours revealed, a clearer definition of sacrament as such was required. For, in formulating his own grounds for rejecting the real presence doctrine, Berengar had collected a host of patristic citations that enabled him to give precise expression to his own position. In order to refute him, orthodox thinkers recognized, it was necessary to be equally precise, not only on the Eucharist but also on the nature of sacraments in general.[107]

The Idea of Sacrament in General

There was, initially, some uncertainty in this period as to where a treatise on the sacraments belonged in a more general work, how

---

[107] On these internal and external influences, see Nikolaus M. Häring, "Berengar's Definitions of *Sacramentum* and Their Influence on Mediaeval Sacramentology," *MS* 10 (1948): 109–46; "Character, Signum, und Signaculum: Der Weg von Petrus Damiani bis zur eigentlichen Aufnahme in der Sakramentslehre im 12. Jahrhundert," *Scholastik* 31 (1956): 41–69; "Character, Signum, und Signaculum: Die Einführung in die Sakramententheologie des 12. Jahrhunderts," *Scholastik* 31 (1956): 182–212; "The Augustinian Axiom: *Nulli Sacramento Injuria Facienda Est*," *MS* 16 (1954): 87–114; Gary Macy, "Berengar's Legacy as a Heresiarch," in *Auctoritas und Ratio: Studien zu Berengar von Tours*, ed. Peter Ganz et al. (Wiesbaden: Otto Harrassowitz, 1990), pp. 49–67; *The Banquet's Wisdom: A Short History of the Theologies of the Lord's Supper* (New York, Paulist Press, 1992), pp. 76–81; John Van Engen, *Rupert of Deutz* (Berkeley: University of California Press, 1983), pp. 118–21.

it should be introduced, and what it should cover. As will be recalled from our consideration of the schemata of the systematic theologians in chapter 2 above, only three of them, Honorius Augustodunensis, Hugh of St. Victor, and the author of the *Sententiae divinitatis*, here working under heavy Victorine influence, situate the sacraments in the context of an ecclesiology in which the sacramental ministry of the church is seen as an extension of Christ's saving work in time. Honorius follows this point with a discussion of the Eucharist, as the most important of the sacraments, after which he treats the priesthood, as needed to consecrate it. He interperses various ethical points in between the priesthood, baptism, and marriage, the only sacraments he considers, and never gives a general definition of sacrament. For Hugh, the church mediates the sacraments of the New Law, and he presents the clergy immediately after introducing the church, as their ministers.[108] But, as we have seen, and will observe again in more detail below, his extremely loose, broad-gauged, and sometimes contradictory understanding of "sacrament" blurs the focus of that idea in his work. The author of the *Sententiae divinitatis* picks up on the ecclesiological siting of the sacraments, describing the church as a nest where the mother bird protects and nourishes her young and, in even more Hugonian language, as Noah's ark, navigating believers through the flood, as the sacraments serve Christians *in via*, voyaging between birth, rebirth, and final arrival. The author does not, however, subscribe to Hugh's organization of the sacraments themselves, as we will see below.[109]

The principal definition of sacrament inherited by Christian thinkers in this period was the Augustinian visible sign of invisible grace, sometimes recast as a visible sign of a sacred thing or a visible form of an invisible grace or thing. There are some contemporary theologians and canonists who do not offer a general definition of sacrament at all. But many who do are satisfied with the Augustinian formula and repeat it.[110] On the other hand, some

---

[108] On the connection between Hugh's ecclesiology and his sacramental theology, see Jean Châtillon, "Une ecclésiologie médiévale: L'idée de l'église dans la théologie de l'école de Saint-Victor au XIIᵉ siècle," *Irénikon* 22 (1949): 115–38, 395–411; Marie-Dominique Chenu, *La théologie au douzième siècle* (Paris: J. Vrin, 1957), pp. 176–77.

[109] *Sent. div.* 5, proemium, pp. 105*–06*.

[110] Ivo of Chartres, *Decretum* 2. c. 8, *PL* 161: 148C; Peter Abelard, *Theologia "scholarium"* 1.9, CCCM 13: 321; *Sent. Parisiensis* II, p. 150; *Sent. mag. Gisleberti* I 4.2, pp. 132–33; Heinrich Weisweiler, ed. *Maître Simon et son groupe De sacramentis* (Louvain: Spicilegium Sacrum Lovaniense, 1937), pp. 1–2. On Abelard's purely

thinkers recognize the fact that this definition could be used to support the purely symbolic view of the Eucharist put forth by Berengar, that it was not responsive to his thesis, and that it was necessary to claim for at least some sacraments, such as the Eucharist,[111] baptism,[112] or baptism and the Eucharist,[113] that the sacred sign not only signifies but also conveys what it signifies. The authors in question, however, do not expand this definition beyond those horizons. Not all masters in this period manifest a sure-footed certitude about which sacraments to treat and where to do so. Even when they possess a definition of sacrament in general, they do not necessarily conduct a systematic inquiry into rites that might be thought of under that heading, testing them and ruling them in or out on the basis of their conformity to the definition, and organizing them according to some discernible plan. Abelard, for instance, has no systematic treatise on the sacraments, probably because of the incomplete nature of his theological works. He only treats three of the sacraments, baptism, marriage, and penance, and each is discussed in a different one of his works and in a different context. Marriage comes up in his *Hexaemeron*, in connection with the creation of Eve; baptism is addressed in his Romans commentary in conjunction with original sin; and penance is treated in his *Ethics* as a corollary of his analysis of the nature of ethical acts. Abelard inherits from Anselm of Laon the tendency to call Old Testament rites sacraments, although he confines this usage to circumcision, without explaining why it is apposite there but is not applied to other Judaic rites.[114] Gratian discusses the sacraments in two separate places, his *De consecratione*, where baptism and the Eucharist come up as an example of ceremonies performed in consecrated houses of worship, and the *De penitentia*, in which, despite its title, the other sacraments except unction are considered. Put together, these separate treatises offer a relatively full account of the sacraments, but the organization of the material has raised questions as to whether their author is the same as the

---

sign-oriented theory, see Richard E. Weingart, "Peter Abailard's Contribution to Medieval Sacramentology," *RTAM* 34 (1967): 164–66.

[111] Roland of Bologna, *Sent.*, pp. 154–56.

[112] *Sent. Parisiensis* I, pp. 4–5, 36.

[113] Hermannus, *Sent.*, pp. 26, 132–33. On Hermannus, see Wendelin Knoch, *Die Einsetzung der Sakramente durch Christus: Eine Untersuchung zur Sakramententheologie der Frühscholastik von Anselm von Laon bis zu Wilhelm von Auxerre* (Münster: Aschendorff, 1983), p. 150.

[114] *Sentences of Anselm of Laon*, no. 51, 5: 48–49; Peter Abelard, *In Ep. Pauli ad Romanos* 2:25; *Theologia christiana* 1.9, CCCM 11: 94, 12: 321.

author of Gratian's *Decretum*.[115]

There is also notable uncertainty as to how to classify the sacraments and on the order in which to discuss them. As we have seen, Honorius treats the Eucharist first, because he thinks that it is the most important sacrament, and holy orders next because priests are needed to administer it. Baptism is a sacrament that no one omits; and marriage would be the state of life to which most of the lay people who are the ultimate audience of the *Elucidarium* are drawn. But Honorius offers no insights into why he omits penance, a subject quite controversial at this time, or confirmation and unction, on which few debates raged, although they would be an ordinary part of the Christian life as well. The Porretans come up with a four-fold scheme of organization. There are sacraments of initiation, sacraments that fortify, sacraments that restore, and sacraments that perfect. The logic of this subdivision suggests that baptism should be the first sacrament treated. But the Porretan masters begin with the Eucharist, even though they have defined it as a sacrament of perfection. They give as examples of initiation, fortification, and restoration the sacraments of baptism, confirmation, and penance.[116] They do not indicate in which category marriage and unction, the other two sacraments they include, belong. The author of the *Ysagoge in theologiam* presents the sacraments in a sequence all his own—baptism, confirmation, marriage, unction, the Eucharist, and penance—and offers no rationale for it.

One of the most prevalent ways of distinguishing one type of sacrament from another and of prioritizing them was suggested early in the century by the canonist Alger of Liège. He separates sacraments of necessity from sacraments of dignity, a distinction that has two dimensions. Sacraments of necessity are necessary for salvation; sacraments of dignity are not. Furthermore, and here Alger reflects the canonists' concern with who can properly administer a sacrament and how the minister's moral or juridical state affects the validity of his sacramental ministry, sacraments of necessity are valid and efficacious (*vera et sancta*) so long as the minister has been validly ordained and so long as he uses the

---

[115] The most recent review of this debate, with a guide to the literature, is provided by John Van Engen, "Observations on the 'De consecratione'," in *Proceedings of the Sixth International Congress of Medieval Canon Law*, ed. Stephan Kuttner and Kenneth Pennington (Vatican City: Biblioteca Apostolica Vaticana, 1985), pp. 309–20. Van Engen supports the idea of Gratian's authorship.

[116] *Sent. mag. Gisleberti* I 4.61, p. 144; Nikolaus M. Häring, ed. "Die *Sententie magistri Gisleberti Pictavensis episcopi* II: Die Version der florentiner Handschrift" 4. 61, *AHDLMA* 46 (1979): 67.

correct verbal formula. On the other hand, in the case of sacraments of dignity, if immoral, excommunicated, heretical, or schismatic priests administer them, even if they use the correct form, the sacraments are true but not efficacious.[117] This distinction, in essence, is designed both to address the clerical fall-out of the Gregorian reforms and to exempt baptism, the only sacrament that Alger regards as a sacrament of necessity, from the strictures he places on the sacramental ministry of bad or unlawful priests in other respects. It is true that he holds that the moral status of the recipient affects his ability to internalize spiritually what he has received. But Alger's accent is on the minister's side of the transaction. Gratian absorbs the distinction between sacraments of necessity and other sacraments but defines these categories differently and disagrees with Alger on some of the specifics of the exercise of the sacramental ministry. For Gratian, the sacraments of necessity are those that cannot be repeated, and hence include baptism, confirmation, holy orders, and also penance. While he removes clerical immorality from the list of disqualifications, he agrees that, with sacraments of necessity, priests in poor standing juridically can administer them validly and efficaciously. With respect to the sacraments of dignity, that is, the Eucharist, unction, and marriage, validity and efficacy are present if they are administered "to the worthy, worthily, and by the worthy" (*digni, digne, a dignis*).[118] Gratian likewise sees an objective character in the sacraments and is less concerned with the verbal formula than Alger and more concerned with the standing and attitude of the minister and the recipient. But his handling of this topic reflects the same basic canonical priorities.

Some theologians pick up the distinction between sacraments of necessity and of dignity without always classifying the sacraments which they place under these rubrics in either Alger's or Gratian's way. The author of the *Sententiae Parisiensis* I classifies baptism,

---

[117] Alger of Liège, *De misericordia* 1.48, 1.55–50, 1.69, 1.72, 3.2–4, 3.16, 3.19–20, 3.55, 3.83, pp. 224, 231–34, 239, 242, 315–18, 325–27, 328–29, 333–34, 365, 379. An excellent account is Nikolaus M. Häring, "A Study of the Sacramentology of Alger of Liège," *MS* 20 (1958): 41–78. Kretzschmar, *Alger*, pp. 27–30 and Gabriel Le Bras, "Le *Liber de misericordia et justicia* d'Alger de Liège," *Nouvelle Revue historique de droit française et étranger* 45 (1921): 96–98 date the work, most probably, to 1105–06 and as not later than 1121.

[118] Gratian, *Decretum* pars 2. c. 1. q. 1. c. 39. dictum, col. 374. For this rule on baptism in particular, see ibid., c. 1. q. 1. c. 47. dictum, col. 377, 379, 380, and Gratian's summary and reprise at c. 54. dictum, c. 57. dictum, c. 97, dictum, col. 397.

confirmation, and the Eucharist as the sacraments of necessity.[119]
More of the theologians who invoke this distinction combine it with
some other prevalent way of organizing their material. Hugh of St.
Victor notes that we can subdivide the sacraments three ways.
There are those necessary for salvation, and here he includes
baptism and the Eucharist; those helpful for man's sanctification
but not necessary for man's salvation, and here he gives as examples such things as the ashes used on Ash Wednesday and holy
water; and those instituted so that the sacraments of necessity can
be administered, that is, holy orders. Yet another way of framing
this subdivision, he says, is to distinguish among sacraments of
sanctification, exercise, and preparation.[120] This classification has
its confusing elements, in that Hugh does not explain where confirmation, penance, unction, and marriage fit in, although, and
presumably by default, they would be placed in the second category. But if they were so placed, they would inhabit that category
side by side with rites that Hugh later rules out as sacraments
in any case, relegating them to the subordinate rank of
sacramentals.[121] He muddies the waters still more by adding that,
from the beginning, there were three sacraments necessary for
salvation, faith, the sacraments of the faith, and good works. He
makes this point in order to emphasize the idea that sacramental
ritual and reception are meaningless unless they are undergirded
by faith and manifested in good works.[122] But it is clear how
unhelpful his polyvalent use of the term "sacrament" is in this
connection. Another combination is made by Master Simon, a
theologian likely to have been writing in the lower Rhine area or
Flanders around 1145. He holds, like Alger, that baptism is the
only sacrament of necessity, and calls the other sacraments voluntary. To this he yokes an even more widespread distinction, between sacraments common to all Christians, and sacraments
received only by some Christians, such as marriage and holy
orders. As for the five common sacraments on Simon's list, they
cleanse, as with baptism; arm the cleansed, as with confirmation;
relieve the armed, as with penance; incorporate the relieved, as
with the Eucharist; and make present the vision of God, as with
unction.[123] The author of the *Sententiae divinitatis*, reflecting the

---

[119] *Sent. Parisiensis* I, p. 36.
[120] Hugh of St. Victor, *De sac.* 1.9.7, *PL* 327A–B.
[121] Ibid., 2.9.10, *PL* 176: 471D–478B.
[122] Ibid., 1.9.8, *PL* 176: 328A–B.
[123] Master Simon, *De sac.*, p. 2. For the dating and location of this work, see
Weisweiler's intro., pp. xlvi–lxii, lxxv, lxxx, xcvi, ccxii–ccxiv.

influence of both Hugh and Simon here, repeats the distinction between necessary and voluntary sacraments, placing baptism alone in the first category, and unites this idea with two other principles, the distinction between sacraments common to all Christians and orders and marriage, and, within the common sacraments, the treatment of the sacraments in the order in which they are received. Hence, his lists reads baptism, confirmation, the Eucharist, penance, and unction. This is how he states his case in principle.[124] In practice, he discusses only five sacraments. He mentions unction, but does not say anything about it. And, alone among the canonists and theologians of the time, he omits marriage. Roland of Bologna confines what he has to say about the relative necessity of individual sacraments to his commentary on each of them in course, and presents the common sacraments, in the order in which they are received, followed by marriage and an extremely abbreviated treatment of holy orders, confined to the power of the keys.

The theologian who did more to set the agenda on the nature of the sacraments in general to which the Lombard responded, both positively and negatively, was Hugh of St. Victor.[125] Hugh makes a major contribution to the development of doctrine in this field of theology by systematically expanding the Augustinian definition of sacrament well beyond the scatter-gun tactics of other thinkers in this period. For him, a sacrament is a sign of a sacred thing, whose external form resembles the internal thing (*res*) or divine power (*virtus*) contained within the sacrament. By its institution, moreover, the sacrament contains the grace it signifies and conveys it, through its material medium, to the recipient, for the purpose of sanctifying him. The exterior medium is visible and material; the interior *res sacramenti* is invisible and spiritual. The physical medium is a container of invisible and spiritual grace and, when the recipient comes to it properly disposed, it is efficacious in

---

[124] *Sent. div.* 5, proemium 2, pp. 108*–09*.

[125] The best account of Hugh's sacramental theology is Heinrich Weisweiler, *Die Wirksamkeit der Sakramente nach Hugo von St. Viktor* (Freiburg im Breisgau: Herder, 1932), pp. 5–154; see also his "Sakrament als Symbol und Teilhabe: Der Einfluss des Ps.-Dionysius auf die allgemeine Sakramentenlehre Hugos von St. Viktor," *Scholastik* 27 (1952): 321–43; "*Sacramentum fidei*: Augustinische und ps.-dionysische Gedanken in der Glaubensauffassung Hugos von St. Viktor," in *Theologie in Geschichte und Gegenwart: Michael Schmaus zum sechzigsten Geburtstag dargebracht von seinen Freunden und Schülern*, ed. Johann Auer and Hermann Volk (Munich: Karl Zink, 1957), p. 434; Knoch, *Die Einsetzung*, pp. 85–92; Paulo M. Pession, "L'ordine sacro e i suoi gradi nel pensiero di Ugo di S. Vittore," *La Scuola Cattolica* 64 (1936): 130–31.

conferring that spiritual grace upon him. The two new generic
keynotes of the sacraments that are important for Hugh are thus
the fact that they do not merely signify; they effect what they
signify. Also, they do so not merely because the physical medium
bears a resemblance to its inner *significatum* but because of the
express biblical institution of the sacraments.[126] This is, no doubt,
Hugh's single most significant contribution to sacramental theology; but there is more. The matter of the sacrament, that is, its
physical form as contrasted with its inner reality or *virtus*, has three
notes, for Hugh, "things, deeds, and words" (*rebus, factis, dictis*).
The first of these is the appropriate physical medium, such as water
in baptism and bread and wine in the Eucharist. The second,
deeds, speaks to the liturgical rite and the gestures used in the
administration of the sacrament, such as the ablution of the baptizand and the fraction of the host during the mass. The third is the
verbal formula, such as the invocation of the Trinity in baptism or
the words of consecration in the Eucharist.[127] Hugh also adds a
characteristic explanation of why the sacraments were instituted.
As he has already observed, they are there for the sanctification of
Christians. The way they carry out this function is by working in
the recipient's soul, for his "humbling, enlightenment, and exercise" (*humiliatio, eruditio, exercitatio hominis*). For God, they are a
dispensation, since He can save without them; for man, they are a
necessity.[128] What Hugh has accomplished here in a few brief
chapters is to redefine the sacraments as efficacious channels of
grace and to emphasize the importance of the sanctification they
impart in the inner lives of Christians. Just as the canonists stress
the external aspects of the sacraments and the juridical conditions
that validate them, principally from the standpoint of the minister,
so Hugh turns the subject around by considering sacraments as
valid because they effect what they signify and communicate an
ongoing growth in grace in the soul of the recipient. This shift in
emphasis and this expansion of the definition of sacrament in
general by Hugh proved to be an achievement of critical importance in the sequel.

---

[126] Hugh of St. Victor, *De sac.* 1.9.2, *PL* 176: 317C–318D.

[127] Ibid., 1.9.6, *PL* 176: 326B–327A. On the combination of these three elements in the thought of this period, see Damien Van den Eynde, "The Theory of
the Composition of the Sacraments in Early Scholasticism, 1125–1240," *FS* 11
(1951): 1–20.

[128] Hugh of St. Victor, *De sac.* 1.9.3–5, *PL* 176: 322A–326B. The quotation is at
1.9.3–4, 322A.

At the same time, this decided doctrinal advance travels in the company of Hugh's imprecise and often confusing handling of the idea of sacrament more widely, as anything manifesting God to man and anything helpful in man's restoration. From this perspective, sacraments have been available to man since the beginning of time, well before Christ's arrival, reflecting God's intention all along to save mankind and to provide an alternative to the sacraments of the devil.[129] Given his more specific definition of sacraments as rites of the church, just noted, or even his wider view of sacraments as manifesting God and restoring man, it is truly difficult to envision what these *sacramenta diaboli* may be, in Hugh's estimation. Black masses? Special rituals engaged in by fallen man? Unlike sacraments in any other of Hugh's conceivable senses of the term, these sacraments of the devil cannot be envisioned as stemming from God's institution or as playing a role in man's restitution. Without making any effort to explain this anomalous term, Hugh proceeds to extend the concept of sacrament to the moral precepts of the natural law, perceptible by reason, and to the Old Testament covenant. On the latter, he is far from consistent on whether the precepts and rites involved were salvific, in the same sense as Christian sacraments. On the one hand, he observes, the ritual prescriptions of the Old Law were morally neutral and not unchangeable. On the other hand, the rite of circumcision was salvific, although females could be saved without it, through faith and works. Yet again, these rites signified salvation only; they did not impart saving grace.[130] This inconsistency aside, there is also Hugh's conflation of sacramentals with sacraments in the Christian dispensation. Hugh retains the sacramentals within his general definition of sacrament, as we have seen above, even though he also takes pains to disqualify them because they signify only, and effect nothing.[131] Coupled with his disorganized and redundant discussion of the Christian sacraments in practice, these teachings prevent Hugh from offering a fully coherent sacramental theology.

Now, there was some carryover of Hugh's broad understanding of sacrament in the theology of the mid-twelfth century, as can be seen in Roland of Bologna.[132] But the key figures who serve as

---

[129] Ibid., 1.8.11, *PL* 176: 312B.
[130] Ibid., 1.12.1–2, 1.12.5–10, *PL* 176: 347D–351B, 352A–364A. On these inconsistencies, see Heinrich Weisweiler , "Hugos von St. Victor *Dialogus de sacramentis legis naturalis et scriptae* als frühscholastisches Quellenwerk," in *Miscellanea Giovanni Mercati* (Vatican City: Biblioteca Apostolica Vaticana, 1946), 2: 179–219.
[131] Hugh of St. Victor, *De sac.* 2.9.10, *PL* 176: 471D–478B.
[132] Roland of Bologna, *Sent.*, p. 194.

points of transition between Hugh and the Lombard are, rather, eager to repress this dimension of the Victorine legacy and to retain, or press further, what they perceive to be Hugh's more positive contributions. His influence extended into the Abelardian circle, as we may note in the *Ysagoge in theologiam*, whose author agrees that the sacraments are educational, bringing humility, insight, and exercise, and who repeats Hugh's point that sacraments are visible forms of invisible grace that are distinct from mere signs in that they confer grace as well as signifying it.[133] More detailed are the authors of the *Sententiae divinitatis* and the *Summa sententiarum*. The former master likewise distinguishes between a sign and a sacrament in that the sign "does not confer on us the thing it signifies" (*signum non confert nobis rem significantam*) while the sacraments "effect what they signify" (*efficiunt quod figurant*).[134] The author agrees that the sacraments were instituted *propter eruditionem, humilitatem, exercitationem*, although he accents enlightenment and behavior modification more than sanctification.[135] He also distinguishes between the *sacramentum* or physical medium and the *res sacramenti* or invisible grace it contains, and agrees that the recipient does not receive and internalize this grace fruitfully if he lacks the proper faith, intention, and attitude.[136] The main area in which he amplifies Hugh's teaching is in connection with the things, deeds, and words that constitute the matter of the sacraments. He follows Hugh's definitions of what these aspects are but adds that they reflect the remedial character of the sacraments, since Adam sinned *in rebus* in bringing damnation on the human race, *in factis* by taking the forbidden fruit, and *in dictis* by seeking to exculpate himself.[137]

The author of the *Summa sententiarum* also displays his fidelity to most of Hugh's formulae, although he annexes holy orders to the power of the keys as exercised in penance and emphasizes the salvific function of the sacraments as well as their educational and disciplinary functions.[138] Like the author of the *Sententiae divinitatis*, he incorporates a remedial view of the sacraments into their role as media of grace and as stimuli of moral action, in his handling of

---

[133] *Ysagoge in theologiam*, pp. 179–80.
[134] *Sent. div.* 5, proemium 1, 5.1, pp. 106*, 123*.
[135] Ibid., 5, proemium 2, p. 107*.
[136] Ibid., 5.1, pp. 113*–15*.
[137] Ibid., 5, proemium 2, p. 108*.
[138] On the *Summa sententiarum* in relation to Hugh of St. Victor, on the sacraments, see Knoch, *Die Einsetzung*, pp. 114–18, 120.

their work of *eruditio, humiliatio,* and *exercitatio* and their correction in *rebus, factis,* and *dictis.*[139] He agrees that all sacraments contain a *sacramentum* or physical medium and a *res sacramenti* or interior grace, which the exterior medium conveys.[140] He emphasizes very strongly the efficacy of sacraments, as contrasted with mere signs. In part, this is a function of his effort—and it is a successful one—to restrict sacraments to the rites of the church, eliminating both sacramentals on the one side and all ceremonies of the Old Law on the other. It is also a function of his desire to reinforce Hugh's point that the sacraments are efficacious not because their outward form resembles their inner spiritual content, but because of the power of divine institution. This is what enables sacraments, unlike signs, to serve as efficacious channels of grace. In placing sacraments, so understood, over against pre-Christian rites and practices, however, this master does not go the full distance in his criticism of Hugh, although his ethical doctrine, discussed above, gives him the tools to do so. He retains the use of the term "sacrament" in referring to the practices of men under the natural moral law, and the written or Mosaic law, as well as the Gospel. Sacraments have developed over time, he notes, and have improved until they have reached their current state of Christian perfection. While he does soft-pedal the salvific capacities of the earlier rites, and while he cuts the amount of space he allocates to this topic, in comparison with Hugh, he does not relegate them to the status of mere prefigurations of rites that alone can be called true sacraments according to his own definition of them.[141] Robert of Melun, on the other hand, is willing to offer what he regards as a correction of Hugh on this point,[142] and in this sense is bolder than the *Summa sententiarum,* which is somewhat inconsistent here, and than the *Sententiae divinitatis,* which does not raise the matter.

It is generally, and rightly, agreed that Peter Lombard's major contribution to the understanding of sacraments in general is both programmatic and substantive. He closes Book 3 of the *Sentences* and opens Book 4 with a crisp and unambiguous definition of sacraments in general, laying the foundation for the treatment he

---

[139] *Summa sent.* 4.1, *PL* 176: 118B–C.
[140] Ibid., 4.1, *PL* 176: 117B–C.
[141] Ibid., 4.1–2, *PL* 176: 118C–120D.
[142] Ulrich Horst, *Gesetz und Evangelium: Das Alte Testament in der Theologie des Robert von Melun* (Munich: Ferdinand Schöningh, 1971), pp. 3–5, 35–53. Horst is working from the unpublished manuscripts of that part of the incomplete section of Robert's *Sentences* where he takes up this question. We have not inspected the manuscripts ourselves.

gives to each of them in turn, a treatment which also reflects how
controversial or problematic each of them happened to be at this
time, Substantively, he relies on the Victorine and post-Victorine
masters just discussed. While underscoring his points of agreement
with them, particularly the idea that sacraments effect what they
signify, he also rigorously excludes the rites of the Old Law from
this designation.[143] Peter also integrates his definition of sacrament
with the Augustinian theory of signs and things, use and enjoyment, which he makes the overall theme of the *Sentences*.[144] In
addition, he takes his own position on the issue of remedy and
sanctification as functions of the sacraments. He distinguishes
clearly between the validity imparted by proper administration to
their material elements, on the one hand, and the sanctification or
remedy which they impart to the recipient, on the other, and
considers the conditions affecting both processes fully. In that same
connection, he devotes more attention than his theological predecessors to the role of the minister as an instrument in the transmission of grace through the sacraments.[145] As well, he provides a clear
and coherent basis for the definition of seven sacraments, omitting
none of the Christian rites ventilated by contemporaries in this
connection.[146] In all these respects, his handling of sacraments in
general seizes upon and redirects an emerging consensus and puts
it on a more articulate and at the same time a personal foundation.

Peter launches his discussion of sacraments in general with a
forthright statement on their relation to the rites of the Old Testa-

---

[143] For good accounts of Peter's relationship with his predecessors here, on
which there is a good deal of consensus, see Adriano Caprioli, "Alle origini della
'definizione' di sacramento da Berengario a Pier Lombardo," *La Scuola Cattolica*
102 (1974): 718–43; Chenu, *La théologie au douzième siècle*, pp. 309–10; Joseph de
Ghellinck, "Un chapitre dans l'histoire de la définition des sacrements au XIIᵉ
siècle," in *Mélanges Mandonnet; Études d'histoire littéraire et doctrinale du moyen âge*
(Paris: J. Vrin, 1930), 2: 79–96; Häring, "Berengar's Definitions," pp. 109–16,
128–32; Knoch, *Die Einsetzung*, pp. 227–29; Macy, *The Banquet's Wisdom*, pp. 89–91;
Mignon, *Les origines*, 2: 116–18, 121–22; Damien Van den Eynde, *Les définitions des
sacrements pendant la première période de la scolastique (1050–1240)* (Rome: Antonianum,
1950), pp. 31, 40, 42–46. These authors effectively refute the claim, made by
Elizabeth Frances Rogers, *Peter Lombard and the Sacramental System* (New York,
1917), p. 76, that Peter made no contribution to this subject.
[144] Seamus P Heaney, *The Development of the Sacramentality of Marriage from
Anselm of Laon to Thomas Aquinas* (Washington: Catholic University of America
Press, 1963), pp. 26–28.
[145] Häring, "The Augustinian Axiom," pp. 87–117; Landgraf, *Dogmengeschichte*,
3 part 1; 173–76.
[146] For Peter's relationship to his predecessors here, see Caprioli, "Alle origini,"
pp. 735–40; Édouard Dhanis, "Quelques anciennes formules septénaires des
sacrements," *RHE* 26 (1930): 574–608, 916–50; 27 (1931): 5–26.

ment. In contrast with the promises of earthly good embodied in those practices, he states, sacraments promise heavenly goods: "The sacraments are different," he asserts, "since the former [the rites of the Old Law] only signified, but they [the sacraments] confer grace" (*Diversa etiam sacramenta, quia illa tantum significabant, haec conferunt gratiam*).[147] The promise of future heavenly good that is made in each sacrament thus begins to work and is progressively activated by the grace transmitted to the recipient through the sacraments in this life. In addition to being promises, and the means by which Christians are made capable of attaining them, the sacraments are remedies repairing the damage caused by original and actual sin. As Peter points out in these introductory remarks, he plans to consider, in each individual case, what the sacrament is, why this particular one was instituted, in what it consists, and how it differs from the Old Testament rites that may parallel or prefigure it.[148] Before doing so, he cites the Augustinian definition of a sacrament as a sign of a sacred thing and notes its inadequacies, bringing the sign theory of the *De doctrina christiana* to bear on the point. As Augustine observes, signs are either natural or conventional. In the first case, they indicate natural processes or involuntary reactions, as smoke indicates fire and a grimace indicates pain. Conventional signs are signs whose significance is not automatic; it is, rather, imposed on the signs by the users of the verbal or non-verbal language in question, by common agreement. In neither case, however, is a sign identical with its *significatum* or productive of it. In relation to a sign, Peter observes, a sacrament does far more than to stand for its *significatum* or to bring it to mind. He agrees with Hugh of St. Victor and the *Summa sententiarum* that the material medium resembles the sacrament's inner spiritual content, or, in his terms, its interior grace, promise, and remedy. In that sense, sacraments may be compared with natural signs. But, here agreeing with these masters again while rephrasing the point in Augustine's semantic terms, the power of the sacrament is given, not an automatic consequence of that resemblance. Its given power, in this case, is not a function of the conventional understanding imparted to it by its users but is a consequence of its divine institution. It is the divine institution that empowers a sacrament to effect what it signifies. This is the basis on which it is different from a sign, which merely signifies but does not sanctify. And so, he

---

[147] Peter Lombard, *Sent.* 3. d. 40. c. 3.1, 2: 229.
[148] Peter Lombard, *Sent.* 4. d. 1. c. 1.1–2, 2: 231.

concludes, a sacrament properly speaking is more than the sign or
form of the invisible grace of God. It is also the cause of the
recovery of his image in man: "For it was not just to signify grace,
therefore, that sacraments were instituted, but also to sanctify"
(*Non igitur significandi tantum gratiam sacramenta instituta sunt, sed et
sanctificandi*).[149] Aside from the clarification imported into the Victorine position thanks to the Augustinian analysis of signs with
which Peter associates it, and which enables him to offer a crystal-
line rationale for departing from Augustine's definition of sacrament and for distinguishing the sacraments from both sacramentals
and from pre-Christian rites, Peter has expanded the understanding of sacraments by proposing that they have both a remedial
character and a sanctifying character, features that enable their
users to grow in grace so as to be worthy of the promise of salvation
which the sacraments also contain.

With this definition in place, Peter offers, as a concrete example
of the difference between sacraments, properly understood, and the
signs represented by Old Testament rites, a comparison between
circumcision and baptism. This example is not chosen at random.
For, even among contemporary theologians who may have been
inclined to dismiss other rites of the Old Law as *figurae* only, there
was a substantial inclination to regard circumcision as efficacious,
or as salvific, in its own time and place prior to the Christian era,
even if they did not go to the lengths of Hugh of St. Victor in this
connection.[150] Peter's opening salvo is a semantic one. When we use
the term "sacrament" to refer to these Old Testament rites, he
states, the word should not be understood literally. It is a courtesy
title only, since they only promised but did not give salvation. Peter
has no scruples about attacking and rejecting authorities such as
Augustine and Bede, who could be and had been used to support
the claim that circumcision was efficacious against original and
actual sin. In so doing, he raises the question of what happened to
the men, not to mention the women, who lived upright lives prior to
the institution of circumcision. Calling on Gregory the Great and
his own gloss on Romans, and the doctrine of justification found
there, he states that these people were saved by their faith and good
works. In this respect, circumcision, while its symbolism is useful
as a moral reminder of the need to cut off sin and to guard against

---

[149] Ibid., c. 2–c. 4.4, 2: 232–34. The quotation is at c. 4.2, p. 233.
[150] Ibid., c. 6–c. 10, 2: 235–39. For current treatments of circumcision and its
efficacy, see above and below, pp. 49, 52, 198, 199, 519, 525, 530–31, 533, 578 and
p. 533 n. 154.

concupiscence, is superfluous and was superfluous even in the pre-Christian dispensation. Unlike baptism, which is available to persons of both sexes and which not only forgives sin but communicates the grace that assists recipients in doing good and developing virtue, circumcision did not and does not justify. In this analysis, Peter brings the notion of justification by the faith that works in love to bear on the problem of pre-Christian rites as a cogent rationale for rejecting them as sacraments. The same principle will also afford a useful basis for his understanding of the salvation of the Old Testament worthies at the end of time. He departs quite pointedly from the Victorine position here. On the other hand, he endorses, essentially verbatim, the Victorine rationale for the institution of the sacraments *propter humiliationem, eruditionem, exercitationem,* as occasions for enlightenment, moral education, and self-discipline, and agrees that, as liturgical events, their celebration involves action, physical media, and the apposite verbal formulae.[151]

As for the sacraments of the New Law, Peter spells out seven, joining Master Simon, Roland of Bologna, and others who do the same. His own scheme for organizing them comes closest to that of Roland, but he presents another perspective on this issue. Sacraments, he notes, can be divided into three types. There are those that are remedies for sin and that also bring with them assisting grace (*gratia adiutrix*), such as baptism. There are those that bring a remedy, such as marriage. He hastens to add that marriage was ordained in the original creation as a sacrament, a good thing, and an office. It remains a sacrament after the fall but now is also a remedy. The third type of sacrament strengthens recipients in grace and virtue; the Eucharist and holy orders are given as examples. Of whichever type, he concludes, all sacraments are efficacious.[152] This typology of the sacraments, however, is not the order Peter uses in the discussion of the sacraments in particular which follows. In the sequel, to which we now turn, he joins Roland in reserving the remarks he wants to make about their necessity for salvation to each sacrament in turn, and presents the sacraments common to all Christians, in the order in which they are received, before turning to holy orders and marriage, as sacraments received only by some Christians. This fact, coupled with his comment on marriage in these stage-setting observations, raises a question concerning the status of that sacrament, in his mind. His actual mode

---

[151] Peter Lombard, *Sent.* 4. d. 1. c. 5.1–6, 2: 234–35.
[152] Ibid., d. 2. c. 1, 2: 239–40.

of organizing sacramental theology would suggest that marriage is a parallel of holy orders, a sacrament administered in order to convey to those receiving it a particular office in the church, which they alone are legitimately empowered to exercise and whose grace strengthens them in the conduct of that calling. On the other hand, Peter's remarks here suggest that marriage as a sacrament does not convey grace and is remedial only, in that it affords to the married a divinely sanctioned way of avoiding fornication. This apparent disjunction has provoked debate as to whether Peter truly extends his definition of sacrament in general to marriage, or whether his treatment of marriage is asymmetrical with his treatment of the other sacraments as means of grace.[153] It alerts us to the fact that we will need to be attentive to that question in considering his discussion of marriage below.

Baptism

As a theologian of baptism, the first sacrament received by all Christians, Peter registers the fact that there was considerable consensus among canonists and theologians on many aspects of this subject and that, at the same time, there were features of baptism that were debated, both because the practices of the early church were being called into question as inappropriate, because traditional authorities were coming under fire or being manipulated to support contrasting conclusions, and because some contemporaries were posing difficulties that demanded a response. Although there are a few topics aired in connection with baptism at this time that he does not address, such as conditional baptism, and the proper time of baptism, the latter of which was controverted, Peter reflects the consensus position in the areas that were not controversial in his time. In the areas attracting debate, he sometimes takes a conservative line while at other times he is far more flexible and critical of the established tradition. In these debates, it is occasionally the case that Peter is strongly influenced by one or another of the thinkers in his period, in terms of how he poses the question, or answers it, or both. At the same time, he often supplies his own rationale for the solutions he proposes, or imports his own emphasis into the subject.

---

[153] On this point, Heaney, *The Development*, pp. 26–28, asserts that marriage is a full sacrament for Peter, while Joseph de Ghellinck, "Pierre Lombard," in *DTC* (Paris: Letouzey et Ané, 1935), 12 part 2: 1999–2002, argues that Peter failed to extend his understanding of sacraments as a means of grace to marriage.

As might be expected from his remarks on circumcision as an example of a rite that was never a sacrament, properly speaking, Peter firmly distances himself from those theologians who place baptism on a sacramental trajectory that includes circumcision, and also the baptism of John, as efficacious in the remission of sin. He sides with those who draw a clear distinction between Christian baptism and its prefigurations, taking a stronger line here than his compeers.[154] For Peter, the baptism of John can similarly be called a sacrament only as a courtesy title. This being the case, the reason Christ accepted it although He did not need it was to signify His humility. The function of John's baptism, according to Peter, was to call mankind to repentance, as a preparation for the true baptism that would remit sin, and also to serve as the first occasion when the Holy Spirit disclosed the divinity of Christ.[155]

There were several other controversies surrounding baptism in the first half of the twelfth century. As we have already noted, a number of canonists and theologians described it as a sacrament of necessity. In supporting this position they could and did draw on the views of the late Augustine, who stressed, along with the unrepeatability of baptism, that it was mandatory for salvation and that persons neglecting to receive it, infants included, would be irrevocably damned. There are a number of thinkers in the early twelfth century who reflect the opinion that this teaching is too harsh. They take two lines of attack against the Augustinian view, one from the perspective of the damnation of unbaptised infants and the other from the perspective of the doctrine of baptism by desire and baptism by blood.[156] Early in the century, Anselm of

---

[154] Peter Lombard, *Sent.* 4. d. 2. c. 2–c. 6, 2: 241–43. Theologians admitting the sacramentality of circumcision include Hugh of St. Victor, *De sac.* 2.6.4, *PL* 176: 449D; *Sent. mag. Gisleberti* I 5.1–13, pp. 144–46; *Sent. div.* 5.1, pp. 110*–11*; Roland of Bologna, *Sent.*, pp. 194–96. Theologians who provide the background for Peter's position include Anselm of Laon, *Sententie divine pagine*, ed. Franz P. Bliemetzrieder in *Anselms von Laon systematische Sentenzen*, Beiträge, 18:2–3, (Münster: Aschendorff, 1919), pp. 42–43; the Laon master who wrote *Augustinus: Semel immolatus est Christus*, ed. Heinrich Weisweiler in *Das Schrifttum der Schule Anselms von Laon und Wilhelms von Champeaux in deutschen Bibliotheken*, Beiträge, 33:1–2 (Münster: Aschendorff, 1936), pp. 281–91; Hermannus, *Sent.*, p. 120; *Sent. Parisiensis* I, p. 37; *Ysagoge in theologiam*, p. 187; *Summa sent.* 5.2, *PL* 176: 128C. The author closest to Peter is Master Simon, *De sac.*, pp. 12–13, 15. See also Landgraf, *Dogmengeschichte*, 3 part 1: 61–108.

[155] Peter Lombard, *Sent.* 4. d. 2. c. 2–6, 2: 240–43. The *Sent. mag. Gisleberti* I 6.1–3, p. 146 supports this position on the baptism of John received by Christ as an act of humility.

[156] For an overview of this theme, see Landgraf, *Dogmengeschichte*, 3 part 1: 216–53.

Laon airs his own discomfort with the Augustinian hard line on baptism, indicating what he finds problematic with it. Noting that baptism is necessary for salvation, he observes that adult baptizands must bring faith to their reception of the sacrament if it is to be efficacious, while for infants, the sacrament is sufficient. There are exceptions, however. Catechumens and other people who desire baptism but who die before they can receive it, except in cases of negligence, are also saved. Anselm cites the case of Cornelius, to whom Christ gave the *res sacramenti*, the remission of sins, without the baptismal rite. The same is the case for infants who die unbaptized. In their case, the negligence involved will be charged to the account of their parents, who will be punished for it; but Anselm can see no reason why the infants themselves should be deemed responsible, or why they should be taxed with the sins of others.[157] In another connection, a different concern of his surfaces, which also informs his disquiet with the traditional teaching. The Holy Innocents, he notes, are venerated as saints, and there is a feast day in the liturgy in their honor. They are indubitably believed to have been received into Heaven and are rightly revered.[158] William of Champeaux does not cite the Holy Innocents or other biblical exceptions, but summarizes Augustine's opinion on the damnation of unbaptized infants and states that it is not at all clear that Augustine is correct.[159] Other followers of Anselm of Laon express other misgivings. Acknowledging that the correct faith is needed for the efficacious reception of baptism on the part of adults, they see infant baptism as efficacious on the basis of the sacrament alone, even if the faith of the parents is heterodox. Still, perfect charity is salvific, without baptism, and the martyrs' baptism by blood is another exception.[160]

Another anti-Augustinian perspective is presented by Abelard. His rejection of the need for infant baptism altogether, as a function of his rejection of the principle that infants are guilty of original sin, since all sin springs from intentionality,[161] was certainly the most extreme reason for opposing the traditional view. It did not catch

---

[157] Anselm of Laon, *Sent. divine pagine*, pp. 42–46; *Sentences of Anselm of Laon*, no. 57–59, 5: 53–54.

[158] *Sentences of Anselm of Laon*, no. 94–97, 5: 79–81.

[159] *Sentences of William of Champeaux*, no. 269, 5: 216.

[160] *Sent. Anselmi* 2, p. 84; *Sentences of the School of Laon*, no. 364–67, 5: 273–74. For the school of Laon on baptism, see Knoch, *Die Einsetzung*, pp. 27–44.

[161] Peter Abelard, *In Ep. Pauli ad Romanos* 5:9, CCCM 11: 164, 166, 170–72; Weingart, "Abailard's Contribution," pp. 166–69.

on, even among Abelard's disciples. The author of the *Ysagoge in theologiam* is only willing to go as far as stressing the priority of faith over the objective efficacy of the rite in the case of adults who receive baptism by blood and by desire. In the case of infants, who lack faith, this condition does not obtain, in his view. It is less the faith of the elders or the efficacy of the rite itself that counts than God's decision to accept them, which can occur if they die unbaptized or are raised by non-believers.[162]

Hugh of St. Victor launches another line of reflection on this subject, one based on source criticism. In treating the question of baptism by blood and by desire, he notes that authorities who support these ideas include Augustine but that Augustine hardened his position in the *Retractationes*. Faced with this conflict of Augustine against Augustine, the farthest Hugh is willing to go is to frame the problem in hypothetical terms. If a person could have perfect faith and charity without baptism, in a situation where it is impossible for him to receive it, it is not likely, in Hugh's opinion, that he would be condemned.[163] Hugh responds to the controversy on infant baptism by omitting that topic. Robert Pullen follows Hugh here, although only in part. He combines a reassertion of the Augustinian hard line on infant baptism and the need for adult baptizands to have faith with the exceptions of baptism by blood and by desire, citing not only Cornelius but the good thief on the cross received by Christ.[164] An equal effort to balance the unconditional necessity of infant baptism, yoking it to the objective efficacy of the sacrament in their case, with a willingness to make exceptions, in this case for baptism by desire, is found in Master Simon. But he is rather more repressive on the latter point than Robert or Hugh. Like the author of the *Ysagoge in theologiam*, he presents this exception as lying under the control of divine omnipotence but also as a privilege extended to biblical personages which is not the basis of a common rule.[165]

Much bolder in pulling together the misgivings of theologians in this area, whether those aired by Abelard or those articulated by the school of Laon, are the Porretans and the author of the *Summa sententiarum*. The *Summa sententiarum* reprises the notion that, when baptism is correctly administered, infants receive both the sacrament and the matter of the sacrament without faith, although

---

[162] *Ysagoge in theologiam*, pp. 187–88.
[163] Hugh of St. Victor, *De sac.* 2.6.7, *PL* 176: 452A–454C.
[164] Robert Pullen, *Sent.* 1.14, 5.17, *PL* 186: 702B–C, 843D–844B.
[165] Master Simon, *De sac.*, pp. 3–5, 9–10.

adults require faith; otherwise they receive the external sacrament only. Martyrs and those seeking baptism but prevented from receiving it receive the *res sacramenti* without the exterior rite. The author expressly rejects Augustine's exclusion of baptism by desire in his late work and thinks, regarding his own position, that it is proved by reason (*quod ratio probat*). He feels the same way concerning Augustine on infant baptism. Augustine's position, he argues, is not solidly grounded. "On this matter," he asserts, reprising William of Champeaux, "we have nothing definite" (*De quo nihil definitum habemus*). He cites the case of the Holy Innocents, who are believed to be saints, as an argument against the opposition. But he pulls back from asserting the contrary in a positive sense.[166]

The Porretans, taking a cue from the Abelardians, go even farther. Their method is both to cite other, countervailing, authorities against the Augustinian hard line on infant baptism, and also to introduce another tactic, the citation of Augustine on predestination, against Augustine on the damnation of unbaptized infants, possibly as suggested by one of the *quaestiones* in Abelard's *Sic et non*. They agree that faith is necessary, in the case of adults, and that the faith of their elders meets this condition in the case of infants. Baptism by blood and by desire are fully acceptable, provided that no contempt of the sacrament is involved, in the case of those who love God. Cyprian and Ambrose are the chief alternative authorities here. The Porretan master who expounds this position most fully goes on to note that faith and martyrdom, which can suffice for adults, do not suffice for children, who are incapable of bearing witness. Unless, that is, pagans overrun a Christian city and infants are put to death before they can be baptized. Such infants, the master asserts, are saved "although this opinion has not been expressly given by the learned" (*licet non sit hoc a doctoribus expositum*). None the less, it is a valid opinion that these infants should be regarded as martyrs, baptized by blood, "as we believe of the Holy Innocents" (*sicut de innocentibus credimus*). The clinching argument, however, is the one derived from Augustine on predestination. God has chosen His elect, from all eternity, the master observes; and His decree of predestination does not change. God will, therefore, save His elect, whether baptized or not.[167]

---

[166] *Summa sent.* 5.5–7, *PL* 176: 130B–C, 131B–133A. The quotations are at 5.5, 132B and 5.6, 133A, respectively.

[167] *Ysagoge in theologiam*, pp. 187–88; *Sent. mag. Gisleberti* I 7.6–7.7, 7.9–11, 7.19–20, 7.25, 7.28, pp. 148, 148–49, 150, 151, 152. The quotations are at 7.20, p. 150. Cf. Peter Abelard, *Sic et non* q. 106, ed. Blanche B. Boyer and Richard McKeon (Chicago: University of Chicago Press, 1976), pp. 343–46.

The independence of this line of thinking reflected by the theologians expressing discomfort with the Augustinian tradition on baptism can be better appreciated when we recognize the sternness of their contemporary opponents, who refused to budge one inch away from that tradition. This obduracy is found in canonists and theologians alike. The unconditional necessity of infant baptism, and the tendency to gloss over or omit exceptions, is found in Honorius Augustodunensis, Ivo of Chartres, and Gratian;[168] Roland of Bologna sums up this position by stating categorically that an unbaptized infant "is damned, without any doubt" (*procul dubio dampnatur*).[169] The toughest defense of this principle in our period, and one that also takes into account the claims made by opponents for baptism by blood and by desire and for the irrelevance of the sacrament for the elect, is indubitably the author of the *Sententiae divinitatis*. No one, of whatever age, he asserts, can escape damnation without baptism. While he is willing to admit that baptism by blood and by desire may have saved some people, his tactic for undercutting this claim as an ongoing possibility is to historicize it or to treat it as a unique personal exemption. The martyrs, he points out, lived at the time of the *ecclesia primitiva*, an age when Christians were a persecuted minority group. Circumstances then differed markedly from the situation today. And so, he concludes, while baptism by blood may have been efficacious in the past, it is now irrelevant. As for the good thief on the cross, the salvation extended to him by Christ can be viewed as a unique case. The thief's situation makes him *sui generis*. Picking up on a point made by Master Simon, the author insists that the thief, like the martyrs, does not constitute a category of persons who can serve as models or as precedents for contemporary twelfth-century theory or practice. The author pointedly ignores adult catechumens as well, although his technique of historical relativization could have been used to deal with them as well. As for those who say that baptism cleanses only the elect, who, in any case, will be saved, the author argues that, even for the elect, their salvation depends on their own behavior.[170]

Faced with this array of opinions, Peter Lombard aligns himself with the Victorine position, as articulated by the author of the

---

[168] Honorius, *Eluc.* 2.42–45, pp. 423–24; Ivo of Chartres, *Decretum* 1. c. 35, *PL* 161: 75D; Gratian, *Decretum* pars 3. c. 30. d. 4. c. 3–c. 7, c. 129, c. 132–c. 146, col. 1362–64, 1402–04, 1405–09.

[169] Roland of Bologna, *Sent.*, p. 209.

[170] *Sent. div.* 5.1, pp. 115*–17*, 122*–24*.

Summa sententiarum, while including some of the dimensions of the argument introduced by the *Ysagoge in theologiam* and the Porretans. He brings this constellation of ideas to bear on baptism by blood and by desire, which he defends strongly on the grounds of authority, reason, and theological appropriateness. On the other hand, he ignores the disquiet expressed by thinkers concerned with the Holy Innocents as a rationale for providing exceptions to the rule of infant baptism, while arriving at a defense of his own for the necessary and universal requirement of that practice. Peter begins with the distinction between the *sacramentum*, or external rite alone, the *res sacramenti*, or matter and effect of the sacrament alone, and the combination of the two, in the language common at this time, which had been articulated the most crisply to date in the *Summa sententiarum*. Infants, he continues, receive both the *sacramentum* and the *res*. All recipients are freed from original sin, although only those who are elect will be saved as well. Peter cites the late Augustine on this point, not for the purpose of confining salvation to the elect so much as to underscore the universality of the remission of original sin in baptism. Faith is not critical for infants, in Peter's view. For, infants who are not baptized cannot be saved even if the faith of the whole church supports them. In the case of infants, the efficacy of the sacrament is objective.[171]

In the case of adults, those who receive baptism without faith receive the *sacramentum* without the *res*. More than faith is required, he argues, if adults are to receive baptism efficaciously and fruitfully. They must come to the font with the sincere intention of abandoning a sinful way of life and any unfraternal or uncharitable attitudes they may harbor, in addition to assenting to the propositions in the creed. They must conform themselves to Christ in order to put on Christ in baptism. Those adults who receive the *res* without the *sacramentum* include the martyrs and those possessing faith and contrition whom necessity prevents from coming to the rite, although without contempt for it. On this point, Peter expressly acknowledges Augustine's change of opinion in the *Retractationes* and the objection to his later teaching raised by some contemporaries. He agrees with that objection. As for Augustine, Peter regards his retraction of the example of the good thief as an error on his part; according to the Lombard, the basic argument Augustine had made earlier concerning baptism by blood, which he had extended to baptism by desire, was a perfectly cogent one that

---

[171] Peter Lombard, *Sent.* 4. d. 4. c. 1, c. 4.12, 2: 251–52, 259.

embraces both cases. So, his position in the *Retractationes* has to be read as a lapse, not as a correction. Not only does the earlier Augustine make sense on this point, so do other authorities; and "reason also supports it" (*ratio etiam id suadet*). For, as Peter sees it, if baptism alone suffices for infants, who are incapable of belief, how much the more does faith suffice for an adult who desires baptism when it is not available? We should, therefore, accept that baptism is necessary for salvation, but with this stipulation. For, to insist that baptism is required in all cases would be to constrain God's power. Anticipating here what was later to be developed into a more elaborate distinction between God's absolute and ordained power in the order of salvation, Peter concludes that, while God instituted baptism as the path to be followed by mankind in ordinary cases, He Himself is not bound by the order of salvation that He lays down for man; "His own power is not constrained by the sacraments" (*suam potentiam sacramentis non alligavit*).[172]

Returning to infants and the importance of universal infant baptism, Peter adds a point that is an original opinion in defense of that practice. It is not only the objective efficacy of baptism in cleansing the infants of original sin that is critical, he observes, but also the grant of operating and cooperating grace which they receive at the same time. This grace will enable the infants, like adults, to gain access to a positive source of sanctification that will make it possible for them to develop virtue and merit when they reach the age of discretion. Peter harks back here to his definition of baptism as a sacrament with a double effect, that of imparting sanctifying grace as well as remitting sin. In the case of infants, to be sure, the grace remains latent in them until they are old enough to be able to accept it voluntarily and collaborate with it; until that time, it remains in them in a potential, not an active state (*in munere, non in usu*).[173]

The whole question of the effects of baptism on the recipient was another debated issue, although not one as widely controverted as the matters just discussed. In this area, there were three contemporary opinions.[174] The school of Laon holds that baptism destroys

---

[172] Ibid., c. 2–c. 4.10, 2: 252–58. The two quotations are at c. 4.8, p. 257 and c. 4.10, p. 258, respectively. For the positioning of Peter on these issues, see Landgraf, *Dogmengeschichte*, 3 part 2: 53–56, 130–34, although Landgraf accents too exclusively his Victorine sources and his desire to refute Abelard.

[173] Peter Lombard, *Sent.* 4. d. 4. c. 7.5, 2: 262–63.

[174] Lottin, *Psych. et morale*, 4 part 1: 288–97, for the school of Laon, the Victorines, Abelard, and Peter Lombard. See also above, chapter 6, pp. 381–85 for contemporary views on the effects of original sin.

the guilt of original sin, although the effects of original sin, that is, mortality, concupiscence, and the inclination to sin, remain. The Porretans agree with this view, adding that baptism also removes the eternal punishment due for original sin.[175] Hugh of St. Victor agrees that the guilt of sin and eternal punishment are removed and that the suffering imposed by sin remains; he includes in the subsisting inclination to sin both ignorance and concupiscence. His disciples follow suit. Since he does not think infants are guilty of original sin and that they are not yet capable of actual sin, Abelard argues that there is no need for baptism to wash away a culpability that does not, in his opinion, exist. At the same time, he admits that unbaptized persons share the consequences of original sin, in the form of mortality and the inclination to sin. To be sure, his handling of original sin itself makes it difficult for him to explain why this should be the case. In any event, he holds that baptism removes the punishment for sin. Roland of Bologna agrees with Abelard.[176] On this subject, Peter Lombard takes a modified Victorine line. Baptism, he holds, cleanses us of original sin and, in the case of adults, actual sin as well, removing the guilt and eternal punishment they bring upon fallen man. He agrees that baptized persons retain the inclination to sin and that this inclination involves concupiscence and ignorance. At the same time, and here he departs from Hugh and his followers, the inclination to sin is weakened in people who have received baptism. The operating and cooperating grace which they receive at the same time strengthens them and makes them better able to resist temptation, so that the inclination to sin is now no longer as automatic or as compelling as it would have been otherwise. As well, the grace of baptism, in the case of recipients whose actual and original sins are removed thereby, may relax the temporal punishment due for such sins.[177] Compared with his contemporaries, Peter widens the scope of the healing and empowering effects of baptism.

There were several other controversies surrounding baptism in this period which were less acutely felt and which did not receive attention from every master. Two of them had to do with the

---

[175] *Sent. mag. Gisleberti* I 7.1–4, pp. 146–47.

[176] Peter Abelard, *In Ep. Pauli ad Romanos* 5:9, CCCM 11: 164, 166, 170–72; Roland of Bologna, *Sent.*, p. 203.

[177] Peter Lombard, *Sent.* 4. d. 4. c. 4–c. 6, 2: 255–61. This position is also found in Peter's sermons. See Jean Longère, *Oeuvres oratoires des maîtres parisiens au XII*e *siècle: Étude historique et doctrinale*, 2 vols. (Paris: Études Augustiniennes, 1975), 1: 234.

administration of baptism and not with its basic theology; they are of interest as indices of how the participating masters used authority, or reason, or pastoral relevance, or liturgical symbolism, as a rationale for defending either their own desired departures from the tradition of the early church or their support for its practices. The subject of one of these controversies, single versus triple immersion, went back, as a debated question, to the patristic period. Augustine and Pope Leo I had required triple immersion, although the custom was not universal in the western church. In the sixth century, Leander, bishop of Seville, had signaled that fact by writing to Gregory the Great as pope and requesting a ruling on the practice. Gregory had recognized both the diversity of customs within the church and also the fact that single and triple immersion both have an edifying symbolic significance; the former signifies the unity of the deity and the latter signifies both the Trinity and the three days Christ lay in the tomb between His death and His resurrection, prefiguring the death to sin and the spiritual rebirth of the newly baptized Christian. In responding to Leander, Gregory does not require or rule out either practice, emphasizing that the unity of faith in the church is not obstructed by the diversity of baptismal custom. A fair number of the theologians who discuss this topic in the first half of the twelfth century advert to this Gregorian analysis, although they do not always put it to the same uses.

One can, to be sure, find supporters of triple immersion, such as the Laon masters, Hugh of St. Victor, the author of the *Sententiae divinitatis*, Master Simon, and Robert Pullen, who simply state that this is a required practice without referring to the contemporary debate, indicating support for the *triduum* symbolism where they can find it and saying nothing about, or to, the other side of the question.[178] Ivo of Chartres lists the pros and cons of both modes of administration while leaving the matter open, along Gregorian lines.[179] The author of the *Summa sententiarum* also invokes, and quotes, Gregory. He personally prefers triple immersion because he finds the *triduum* symbolism appealing. But his prime consideration is the principle that local custom ought to be followed.[180] On the other side of the debate, Roland of Bologna defends single immersion; he argues that, if triple immersion is used, it is on the first

---

[178] *Sent. Anselmi* 6, pp. 113–14; Hugh of St. Victor, *De sac.* 2.6.1–2, *PL* 176: 441D–447D; *Sent. div.* 5.1, pp. 118*–19*; Robert Pullen, *Sent.* 5.10–12, 5.24, *PL* 186: 838B–840C, 847D–848A; Master Simon, *De sac.*, p. 5.
[179] Ivo of Chartres, *Decretum* 1. c. 130, *PL* 161: 914A–B.
[180] *Summa sent.* 5.4, *PL* 176: 130A–B.

immersion that the baptizand's sins are remitted. But he offers no
reasons or authorities for that opinion.[181] A much fuller rationale
for single immersion is provided by the Porretans. Concerned with
the susceptibility to chills of infants, who now constitute the majority of baptizands in the church, their overriding reason for abandoning Leo's rule is pastoral utility. But they do not let the matter
rest just on that point. Their own patristic research indicates that
the first ancient authority to rule on the matter was Cyprian. He
imposed single immersion. How, then, did the church fathers and
early popes justify a departure from that practice? The Porretan
masters note that Augustine had cited Cyprian, and that, in so
doing, he had garbled Cyprian's text, thus substituting triple for
single immersion. And then, instead of cross-checking his sources,
Leo had simply repeated Augustine's corruption of Cyprian in
making his own ruling. In their own argument, the utility of citing
Gregory the Great is that he provides both a history of baptismal
practice in the primitive church and a way around both the triple
immersion tradition and the local custom theory advanced by
contemporary opponents. The Porretans' own quotation of Gregory, in their view, validates the sweeping away of the Leonine and
Augustinian departures from "true" tradition so that it can be
invoked as the rationale for universalizing single immersion.[182] This
daring exercise in source criticism finds, as a happy outcome, that
the earliest authority, Cyprian, supports the conclusions which the
masters want to reach, in any case. But, in the logic of their
argument, it is less Cyprian's antiquity than his correctness that
matters, from the Porretan standpoint, coupled with the fact that
Cyprian and Gregory together can be used to show that the more
widely held Augustinian and Leonine rulings are both based on
faulty patristic research. As for the Lombard, he gives this debate,
and the authorities used to support both sides of it, a full review.
Along with many others, he cites Gregory's maxim about the
diversity of custom and its lack of interference in the unity of faith.
His position is closest to that of the *Summa sententiarum*. While he
approves warmly of the *triduum* symbolism, and sees the more
general shift in the church to the practice of triple immersion as
hence desirable, he agrees that respecting local custom is the most
important consideration, and the reason for maintaining both

---

[181] Roland of Bologna, *Sent.*, p. 210.
[182] *Sent. mag. Gisleberti* I 7.14, p. 149.

forms of baptismal initiation; other necessary conditions obtaining, the sacrament is valid either way.[183]

There was another debate concerning the administration of baptism on which the Lombard does not feel inspired to take a stand, the question of when the sacrament should be administered. Ancient custom, as crystallized by Leo I and other early popes, required candidates for baptism to be received into the church on Easter or Pentecost Sunday, unless they were in danger of death. This ruling, and its congruity with the events in the life of Christ recalled by the Christian community on the great feasts of the resurrection liturgy, were duly noted and reinforced by a large number of masters in the first half of the twelfth century.[184] The chief opposition to this largely consensus view came from the school of Laon. Reflecting the same kind of pastoral concern which we have seen animating the Porretan defense of single immersion above, and which will also inform the Laon masters' view of the administration of the Eucharist below, their objection to the Easter-Pentecost rule is made with the needs of infants in mind. To be sure, the authorities were willing to waive this rule if the candidate were in danger of death. But, notes the Laon master who speaks to this point, the health of infants is very fragile, and they are unable to advertise the fact if they are in danger of death. Further, the church has a responsibility to minister as well to the anxieties of parents, who have a legitimate worry if their babies have to weather the hazards of their first winter without benefit of baptism. He accents the differences between the *ecclesia primitiva* and the present day here. Then, the majority of baptizands were adult converts. Their collective reception into the church on the great feasts of the Easter season was a source of group reinforcement for the struggling early Christian community and a powerful witness to the pagan society surrounding it. But now, he concludes, these conditions no longer obtain. For the sake of the current baptizands and their families, baptism should be administered whenever it is needed.[185] This argument is an authentic index of the pastoral considerations that often urged changes in sacramental practice in this period, as well as reflecting an authentic concern of

---

[183] Peter Lombard, *Sent.* 4. d. 4. c. 7, 2: 249.

[184] Ivo of Chartres, *Decretum* 1. c. 45–c. 58, *PL* 161: 79A–82B; Gratian, *Decretum* pars 3. c. 30. d. 4. c. 11–c. 18, col. 1364–67; *Sent. div.* 5.1, pp. 118*–19*; Master Simon, *De sac.*, pp. 9, 13–14.

[185] *Sentences of the School of Laon*, no. 371, 5: 275–76. See above, chapter 2, pp. 46–47.

current sacramental theology, the desire to remove impediments to the accessibility of sacramental grace, which twelfth-century masters often felt had been imposed too strictly in the early church. In this case, however, the Laon master finds himself swimming against the current. In the sequel, neither he nor the proponents of the majority view could look to Peter Lombard for support, for he does not take up this question.

The one remaining debate that he does enter on baptism is one that has neither a real theological nor a real pastoral significance. It was joined, by those who entered into it, more as a matter of biblical history. It was agreed that the sacrament of baptism was instituted personally by Christ. But when, in His career, did He do so?[186] Some masters, such as Anselm of Laon and Hermannus, ask this question only to review the options while making no personal determination.[187] Master Simon thinks that Christ instituted baptism when He told Nicodemus that rebirth through water and the Holy Spirit was required for salvation.[188] But Simon does not advert to the other positions taken on this subject, which received more support. Hugh of St. Victor and Roland of Bologna teach that the institution of baptism took place when Christ commissioned His apostles to baptize and to preach the Gospel in His name at Pentecost.[189] The majority view, and the one espoused by the Lombard, was the opinion that Christ instituted baptism at the time of His own baptism; here, he follows the *Ysagoge in theologiam*, the *Sententiae divinitatis*, and the *Summa sententiarum*. Peter thinks that Christ's speech to Nicodemus has something to be said for it as the moment of institution, but rules out the position taken by Hugh and Roland because he holds that baptism must have been instituted by Christ during His lifetime, and not after His resurrection. The preferability of Christ's own baptism to His response to Nicodemus as the key moment, in his view, lies in the fact that the name of the whole Trinity, a basic requirement of the verbal formula used in baptism since then, was first invoked at that time.[190]

These constituted the issues controverted regarding baptism,

---

[186] For an introduction to the range of opinions on this point, see Weisweiler, intro. to his ed. of Master Simon, *De sac.*, pp. lxxx–lxxxix.

[187] Anselm of Laon, *Sent. divine pagine*, p. 42; Hermannus, *Sent.*, pp. 120–24. On this point, see Knoch, *Die Einsetzung*, p. 150.

[188] Master Simon, *De sac.*, p. 3.

[189] Knoch, *Die Einsetzung*, pp. 92–94.

[190] Peter Lombard, *Sent.* 4. d. 4. c. 5, 2: 247.

and, as can be seen, they ranged from those directed to the essence of that sacrament, to those addressed to administration and liturgical practice, and to those that are relatively marginal. There were also a number of features of baptism on which all Christian thinkers agreed in the first half of the twelfth century and on which Peter joined his voice to the chorus without altering the consensus view. Under this heading we have the unrepeatability of baptism; baptism as a liturgical event composed of water as the sacramental medium, so chosen because of its general availability and cheapness and its symbolic resemblance to the *res sacramenti*, or the spiritual ablution it conveys, coupled with the correct invocation of the Trinity; the proper disposition and faith of the recipient with the stipulations regarding infants noted above; and the intention to baptize as the church intends, on the part of the minister. When these conditions are present, anyone can validly administer baptism, including a heretic, schismatic, non-believer, or lay person.[191] The necessity of a proper baptismal intention in the minister rules out, for Peter as for everyone else the validity of baptisms that are fictive or done in jest. Peter acknowledges that a baptism will be valid, assuming a proper intention, if the minister garbles the verbal formula as a consequence of poor grammar or a slip of the tongue, so long as this misadventure does not bespeak a heretical intention or malice on his part. Here, he departs from the stricter rulings of some of the canonists. His model is the *Summa sententiarum*.[192] In handling these standard points, Peter is fully aware of how the canonists treat them, especially Gratian. While he frequently finds himself in agreement with Gratian's conclusions, it is still to be noted that these two thinkers tend to pose the questions differently. Thus, while they agree that the virtue of the sacrament comes from Christ, and from the intentions of the minister and the recipient, Gratian accents the problem of whether a bad priest can validly confer the sacrament, while Peter approaches the instrumentality of the minister from the perspective of the idea that the gift of grace comes from God, not from man, and God's love and power cannot be obstructed by the shortcomings of the human ministers through whom He ordained its transmission. Finally,

---

[191] Ibid., d. 3. c. 1–c. 4, c. 6, d. 5–d. 6. c. 2, c. 5, 2: 243–47, 248–49, 263–69, 272–74. Ludwig Ott, *Untersuchung zur theologischen Briefliteratur der Frühscholastik*, Beiträge, 34 (Münster: Aschendorff, 1937), p. 160, draws some comparisons between Peter and other theologians but ignores the canonists.

[192] Peter Lombard, *Sent.* 4. d. 6. c. 4, 2: 272; cf. *Summa sent.* 5.9, *PL* 176: 135C–136A.

other consensus topics which Peter addresses are the point that the
ceremonies preceding and accompanying baptism, the appoint-
ment of godparents, the exorcisms, and the requests of the parents,
while decorous and appropriate, are not of the essence in baptism,
as well as the point that an infant cannot be baptized in the womb,
following, as everyone else does, Augustine's opinion that, in order
to be reborn in baptism, one must first be born. In both cases, he
follows most closely the language as well as the conclusions of the
Summa sententiarum.[193]

There are, finally, a few issues which other thinkers mention but
which, like the time of baptism, Peter ignores. Some are raised by
only one master. Thus, the author of one of the Porretan sentence
collections forbids the alarming possibility that people might baptize a baby by throwing him in a well, lest he be hurt or killed.[194]
The author of the *Sententiae divinitatis* raises and rejects the possibility that a person can baptize himself.[195] He also notes that, in the
ecclesia primitiva, thirty to forty days of penance were required of
adult converts prior to their baptism, and queries this practice,
given the fact that baptism washes away all sin. He concludes that,
while unnecessary, the custom was useful in helping to promote the
intention of the conversion needed for a fruitful reception of the
sacrament by an adult. The *Summa sententiarum* reviews the same
argument and comes down on the other side of it, agreeing with
Augustine that this penance should not be required.[196] The matter
of conditional baptism is also aired by a few thinkers. The Porretan
master thinks that, if there is any doubt at all as to whether a
person has been baptized, one should go ahead and baptize him;
the necessity of baptism for salvation, in his view, is more important than the canonical non-repeatability of the sacrament. On the
other hand, Master Simon points ahead to later usage, by suggesting that a conditional baptism be performed in such a case, and by
offering a formula for that purpose.[197] An item that is taken up more
widely, and by Peter as well, but more typically under the heading
of conditions that nullify or impede a marriage, is the question of
the continuing validity of the marriage of a couple who baptize

---

[193] Peter Lombard, *Sent.* 4. d. 6. c. 3, c. 6–c. 7, 2: 270–72, 274–76; cf. *Summa sent.*
5.4, 5.12, *PL* 176: 129C–D, 136D–138A.
[194] *Sent. mag. Gisleberti* I 7.24, p. 151.
[195] *Sent. div.* 5.1, p. 121*. Weisweiler, ibid., n. 1, notes that he is the only
theologian of the time to raise this question.
[196] Ibid., pp. 113*–15*; *Summa sent.* 5.5, *PL* 176: 130D.
[197] *Sent. mag. Gisleberti* I 7.21, p. 150; Master Simon, *De sac.*, pp. 15–16.

their infant in a circumstance of necessity, thus standing as godparents as well as parents to the child and contracting a condition of spiritual affinity. Both Master Simon and the author of the *Summa sententiarum* agree that such a situation does not automatically nullify the marriage. The latter author observes that there are decretals on both sides of this matter and indicates that he finds the more lenient position to be the more acceptable one.[198]

The Lombard is more concerned with engaging in reflection and debate on issues that he finds more central to the theology of baptism. He is not interested in the details of the ministry of the sacrament from the standpoint of canonical rules and regulations and their administrative corollaries. He is interested in what makes the sacrament valid, but largely from the perspective of the capacity of the valid sacrament to serve as an efficacious channel of God's grace to the recipient and as a condition of his fruitful reception of it. Both in his affirmation of the points on which consensus reigned and in the choices and contributions he makes in debated areas, he seeks to strike a balance between the principle of intentionality and the principle of the objective efficacy of baptism. He is incisive in distinguishing definitively between the precursors of Christian baptism and the baptism instituted by Christ, with only the latter justifying its recipient and putting him on the path to salvation. For Peter, the grace imparted by baptism is more than the spiritual ablution that washes away sin and remits the punishment that mankind would otherwise bear for it. Baptism, as well, conveys the operating and cooperating grace and the mitigation of the inclination to sin which still afflicts the human race. With this grace, and the weakening of the grip of ignorance and concupiscence on him, man can now make a new beginning. Baptism, for Peter, is hence a true rebirth, a renewal of the mind (*innovatio mentis*),[199] which cleanses, heals, and strengthens the recipient and arms him with the grace with which, latently in infants and immediately in adults, he can work voluntarily as he moves ahead into the Christian life. Altogether, Peter is far less interested in the social and ecclesiological dimensions of baptism than he is in its function as the hinge on which the capacity to grow in virtue and sanctification turns in the inner life of the individual Christian. The more corporative

---

[198] Master Simon, *De sac.*, pp. 8–9; *Summa sent.* 5.10, *PL* 176: 136B. Weisweiler, intro. to his ed. of Master Simon, pp. xci–xcii, is therefore incorrect in claiming that Simon is the only author to air this question at the time.

[199] Peter Lombard, *Sent.* 4. d. 3. c. 9, 2: 251.

aspects of the sacramental life he reserves for his discussion of some of the other sacraments. But baptism, for him, is a rather more strictly personal event.

Confirmation

Much the same can be said for Peter's understanding of confirmation. This sacrament evoked little attention in the first half of the twelfth century and inspired few controversies. Those that did arise give the appearance of having attracted only a half-hearted interest. There are several points on which all the masters agree. The sacrament of confirmation, they concur, was instituted to strengthen the recipient in the battle against sin; it must be administered by a bishop; and it is not repeatable. There are also a few areas in which they disagree, or where they give the subject a different emphasis.[200] The question of when and by whom the sacrament was instituted does not elicit wide interest. The masters who raise it, Simon, Roland of Bologna, and the author of the *Sententiae divinitatis*, assert that confirmation was instituted by Christ, Roland adding that He did so when He imparted the Holy Spirit to His apostles at Pentecost.[201] The Laon masters dissent from the view that confirmation remits sin, describing its effects, rather, as the communication of grace as a gift of the Holy Spirit; the Abelardian *Sententiae Parisiensis* I, Hugh of St. Victor, and the *Summa sententiarum* agree that the sacrament is a gift of the Holy Spirit.[202] Roland, the Porretans, and Master Simon see its effects as a combination of the gift of the Holy Spirit and the remission of venial sin.[203] It is agreed that confirmation should be administered after baptism, but how much later was disputed. Some authors,

---

[200] Heinrich Weisweiler, "Das Sakrament der Firmung in den systematischen Werken der ersten Frühscholastik," *Scholastik* 8 (1933): 481–523 provides the only existing overview. He considers only the debates over the age at which confirmation should be administered and by whom it was instituted. On the latter point, p. 483, he is in error in stating that Roland of Bologna held that confirmation was instituted by the apostles. For the patristic background on confirmation, see Franz X. J. Dölger, *Das Sakrament der Firmung, historisch-dogmatisch dargestellt* (Vienna: Mayer & Co., 1906), pp. 1–156.

[201] Master Simon, *De sac.*, p. 18; *Sent. div.* 5.2, p. 126*; Roland of Bologna, *Sent.*, p. 212.

[202] *Sentences of the School of Laon*, no. 372, 374, 5: 276–77; *Sent. Parisiensis* I, p. 40; Hugh of St. Victor, *De sac.* 2.7.6, *PL* 176: 462C; *Summa sent.* 6.1, *PL* 176: 137C–139A. For the school of Laon on confirmation, see Knoch, *Die Einsetzung*, pp. 44–47.

[203] Roland of Bologna, *Sent.*, p. 213; *Sent. mag. Gisleberti* I 8.1–3, p. 153; Master Simon, *De sac.*, p. 21.

such as Gratian and Simon, are not specific on the point.[204] Some, like Roland and the author of the *Sententiae Parisiensis* I, reflecting the Abelardian stress on intentionality, emphasize that the recipient should be an adult, or at least that he should have reached the age of discretion.[205] Robert Pullen contradicts himself on this point, saying that confirmation should be given "to children in their childhood" (*parvuli in parvitati*) and then supporting the view that candidates must have attained the age of discretion.[206]

Aside from the recipient's age, few masters display an interest in any of the other of the conditions or dispositions that he should bring to the reception of confirmation. The school of Laon teaches that he should approach it without sins on his conscience;[207] but for Master Simon, Gratian, the Porretans, and the author of the *Sententiae divinitatis*, the only consideration mentioned is that he should come to the sacrament fasting.[208] Most of the same masters are concerned with the condition of the ministering bishop, and agree that he, too, should be fasting, a view in which they are joined by Hugh of St. Victor and the *Ysagoge in theologiam*. Predictably, the author who devotes most of his attention to the technical aspects of administration is Gratian.[209] There is a fair degree of vagueness as to which aspect of the sacrament constitutes its physical medium. Most authors ignore this issue. Among those who do not, the author of the *Summa sententiarum* states that the *sacramentum* is the bishop's laying on of hands; but Hugh of St. Victor thinks that it is the unction used in the rite while the Porretans locate the *sacramentum* in both the unction and the laying on of hands.[210] There is wide support for the view that confirmation is not a sacrament of necessity, although it should not be neglected on that account. But the school of Laon and the *Sententiae divinitatis* depart from that consensus, the latter qualifying the point by conceding that confirmation is not required in the case of a baptized infant.[211] There is

---

[204] Gratian, *Decretum* pars 3. d. 5. c. 1–c. 2, col. 1413; Master Simon, *De sac.*, pp. 18–20.

[205] Roland of Bologna, *Sent.*, p. 214; *Sent. Parisiensis* I, p. 40.

[206] Robert Pullen, *Sent.* 5.23, *PL* 186: 847A–B.

[207] *Sentences of the School of Laon*, no. 374, 5: 276–77.

[208] Master Simon, *De sac.*, p. 21; Gratian, *Decretum* pars 3. d. 5. c. 3–c. 12, col. 1413–15; *Sent. mag. Gislebert* I 8.4, p. 153; *Sent. div.* 5.2. p. 128*.

[209] Master Simon, *De sac.*, p. 21; *Sent. div.* 5.2, p. 128*; Hugh of St. Victor, *De sac.* 2.7.1–6, *PL* 176: 459C–462C; Gratian, *Decretum* pars 3. d. 5. c. 3–c. 12, col. 1413–15. For Hugh on this sacrament, see Knoch, *Die Einsetzung*, pp. 94–96.

[210] *Summa sent.* 6.1, *PL* 176: 137C; Hugh of St. Victor, *De sac.* 2.7.1–6, *PL* 176: 459C–462C; *Sent. mag. Gisleberti* I 8.1–3, p. 153.

[211] *Sentences of the School of Laon*, no. 372, 374, 5: 276–77; *Sent. div.* 5.2, p. 127*.

also some dissent from the more generally held view that confirmation is less important than baptism. Both the author of the *Sententiae
Parisiensis* I, the Porretans, and Robert Pullen think that confirmation is greater in dignity because of the higher rank of the administering clergyman. Robert adds that its greater dignity lies as well
in its effects, using as an analogy the point that the regime for
training an athlete is better than one that merely cures an illness.[212]
Two other themes surface, of a more idiosyncratic nature. Predictably, Hugh of St. Victor devotes much attention to Old Testament
parallels of confirmation, getting rather confused in comparing it
with assorted forms of unction that are also used in other Christian
rites, and adding that the confirmand should not wash off the oil
until seven days have passed, in honor of the seven gifts of the Holy
Spirit.[213] And Roland of Bologna uses the agreed-on point concerning episcopal administration to expatiate on the need to revamp
ancient practices on the basis of the differing historical circumstances in the present. In the *ecclesia primitiva*, he notes, citing the
pertinent decretals, it was acceptable to waive the requirement of
episcopal administration and to concede it to priests, because, in a
missionary church with widely scattered Christian communities, a
bishop might not be easily available. But, since nowadays this
problem no longer exists (*quae hodie locum non habent*), the earlier
dispensation should be rejected.[214]

Peter Lombard does not address all the issues aired by contemporaries in connection with confirmation. He is not interested,
for instance, in the age of the recipient, the time and agency of
the sacrament's institution, or the condition of the ministering
clergyman.[215] Although other masters of the time serve as his
source for the idea that the *sacramentum* in each case involves words,
deeds, and a material medium, Peter is more consistent than his
contemporaries in adhering to this rule for confirmation. For him,
the external medium combines the words of the bishop, the chrism
he applies to the confirmand's forehead, and the sign of the cross
with which he signs him. Peter joins Roland of Bologna, Master
Simon, and the Porretans in seeing the effect of the sacrament as
both the remission of sins and the gift of the Holy Spirit. He is more
flexible than Roland in conceding that a priest may administer

---

[212] *Sent. Parisiensis* I, p. 40; *Sent. mag. Gisleberti* I 8.2, p. 153; Robert Pullen, 5.23, *PL* 186: 847B.

[213] Hugh of St. Victor, *De sac.* 2.1.6, *PL* 176: 462C.

[214] Roland of Bologna, *Sent.*, p. 214.

[215] Peter Lombard, *Sent.* 4. d. 7, 2: 276–80 for the entire treatise on confirmation.

confirmation if a bishop is lacking, and sees the ancient dispensations as retaining a continuing utility. He agrees with the standard consensus view concerning the ordinary episcopal ministry, the non-repeatability of confirmation, and its strengthening function, and joins the majority in disallowing the claim that it is more dignified than baptism, arguing that those who make this argument have confused the rank of the minister, whose role is purely instrumental in any case, with the effects of the sacrament and its relative necessity for salvation. All told, the strongest impression Peter's handling of this sacrament makes is his desire to avoid strictures that might impede its availability, his desire to make his account of confirmation conform to the guidelines he erects for the consideration of sacraments in general, and his affirmation of the broad view of its effects, as encompassing a remedial as well as a sanctifying and strengthening component.

The Eucharist

If confirmation received comparatively little attention in this period and if the debates it inspired seem to have been less than earthshaking in the eyes of the participants, the same cannot be said of the Eucharist. The Eucharist attracted considerable attention in the first half of the twelfth century, and with excellent reason. All orthodox Christian thinkers at the time warmly endorsed the words of the author of the *Sententiae divinitatis*, who elevated the Eucharist above all other sacraments as worthy of reverence "because, while in the other sacraments grace alone is given, in this one not only is grace given but also the giver of graces" (*quia cum in aliis sacramentis sola gratia detur, in isto non solum gratia, sed etiam dator gratiarum*).[216] The theological principle affirmed here was matched, in this period, by a surge of Eucharistic devotion in popular piety and mystical experience, one that would continue to flourish in the following centuries.[217] This fascination with the Eucharist is a genuine case of how the convergence between religious devotion and theological speculation helped to direct the

---

[216] *Sent. div.* 5.3, p. 128*; the same sentiment is expressed on p. 129*. The language of the *Summa sent.* 6.2, *PL* 176: 139B comes very close to this: "In hoc enim sacramento non solum gratia, sed ille a quo est omnis gratia sumitur."

[217] The best treatment of this subject, which integrates the history of theology with that of popular Eucharistic piety, is Gary Macy, *The Theologies of the Eucharist in the Early Scholastic Period: A Study of the Salvific Function of the Sacrament according to the Theologians c. 1080–c. 1220* (Oxford: Clarendon Press, 1984).

course of twelfth-century Christian thought. Aside from its appeal
both to the learned and the unlearned, the Eucharist demanded
attention because of the sharply felt need to defend it against
anti-sacramental heretics and against those who denied the real
presence doctrine. The terms of this debate had been shaped in the
late eleventh century by Berengar of Tours and antagonists of
Berengar such as Lanfranc of Canterbury. Whether or not they
traced their genealogy back to Berengar in the full doctrinal sense,
more recent heretics of a similar persuasion found his formulation
of the issues and the dossier of authorities he had assembled to
support his case to be of continuing utility. So, perforce, did their
orthodox opponents.[218] Given their concerted interest in defending
and promoting the importance of the Eucharist in the Christian
life, both canonists and theologians, in the backwash of the contemporary Gregorian reform movement, also sought to clarify the
conditions required for a valid administration of the sacrament, on
the part of priests who might be unworthy, heretical, schismatic, or
excommunicated, as well as the differential efficacy of the sacrament upon recipients who might bring heterodox and not orthodox
understandings of the Eucharist to their reception of it. Likewise,
the Berengarian controversy reimported into the arena topics that
had tended to remain in abeyance since the Carolingian period,
such as what happens if a consecrated host is accidentally dropped
on the ground, vomited by a recipient who is ill, or eaten by an
animal.[219] These, like virtually all the debates about the Eucharist
raised by the masters of the first half of the twelfth century, derive
from the conviction of the truth of the real presence doctrine. It is
either the desire to expound that doctrine more persuasively to
those who rejected it or the felt need to address questions that arise
within the orthodox consensus given the belief in the real presence
that set the contemporary agenda on the Eucharist.

The belief that the physical elements of bread and wine become
the body and blood of Christ when the celebrant utters the words of
consecration, echoing the personal institution of the Eucharist by
Christ at the Last Supper, coupled with the principle of concomitance, or the full presence of both the body and the blood of Christ

---

[218] For Berengar's continuing influence, see Häring, "Berengar's Definitions,"
pp. 109–46; Macy, "Berengar's Legacy," pp. 49–67, "Of Mice and Manna: *Quid
mus sumit* as a Pastoral Question," *RTAM* 58 (1991): 157–66; *The Banquet's Wisdom*,
pp. 76–84.
[219] Macy, "Berengar's Legacy," pp. 55–67; "Of Mice and Manna," pp. 157–
66. See also Landgraf, *Dogmengeshichte*, 3 part 2: 207–22.

in either of the two consecrated species, serves as the consensus position on which the theologians and canonists ground their differences of opinion and differences of emphasis in other areas of Eucharistic theology and practice.[220] It is the real presence of Christ that the Eucharist transmits, they agree. But, how best to respond to Berengar's efforts to reduce this claim to absurdity by posing objections such as the notion that Christ's body, as a finite physical entity, would be affected by repeated Eucharistic celebrations, damaged by the fraction of the host during the mass, or by the chewing and swallowing and digestion of the elements by the recipient, or physically added to, if repeated consecrations repeatedly convert more bread and wine into more of Christ's body and blood? Orthodox thinkers are unanimous in rejecting all these assertions; yet, they differ on the best way to go about refuting them.

One idea, inherited from Lanfranc's side of the debate, acknowledges that these problems would be insuperable if it were, indeed, Christ's historical body that was communicated in the Eucharist.[221] Orthodox thinkers could and did respond that this is not the body of Christ now given in communion, but rather the resurrected body of Christ, incorruptible and not subject to physical containment, growth, or diminution. Still, which body did Christ give to His disciples at the Last Supper? Was it His mortal or His immortal body? Some masters, such as Anselm of Laon, William of Champeaux, Ivo of Chartres in his *Panormia*, Hugh of St. Victor, and Master Simon, seize on the advantages offered by the doctrine that communion conveys Christ's resurrected body and argue that He gave this same resurrected body, which Christians now receive in the Eucharist, to His disciples at the Last Supper.[222] William

---

[220] Macy, *Theologies*, passim and esp. pp. 1–17 for a fine review of the previous literature on this subject; Walter Dürig, "Die Scholastiker und die Communio sub una specie," in *Kyriakon: Festschrift Johannes Quasten*, ed. Patrick Granfield and Josef A. Jungmann (Münster: Aschendorff, 1970), 2: 864–75; James J. Megivern, *Concomitance and Communion: A Study in Eucharistic Doctrine and Practice* (Fribourg: The University Press, 1963), pp. 36–47. Collectively, the work of these scholars corrects and supersedes all earlier accounts, such as Joseph de Ghellinck, "Eucharistie au XIIe siècle en occident," in *DTC* (Paris: Letouzey et Ané, 1913), 5: 1233–1302; Josef Geiselmann, *Die Eucharistielehre der Vorscholastik* (Paderborn: Ferdinand Schöningh, 1926); Josef A. Jungmann, *The Mass of the Roman Rite*, trans. Francis A. Brunner (New York: Benziger Brothers, Inc., 1955), 2: 385–86.

[221] Mariateresa Beonio-Brocchieri [Fumagalli] and Massimo Parodi, *Storia della filosofia medievale da Boezio a Wyclif* (Bari: Laterza, 1989), pp. 136–42.

[222] *Sentences of Anselm of Laon*, no. 26, 62; *Sentences of William of Champeaux*, no. 274, 5: 27, 55–56, 219; Ivo of Chartres, *Panormia* 1.134, *PL* 161: 1075B; Hugh of St.

responds to an objection that can be raised against this position, about which Hugh also worries: How can Christ's resurrected body be available before He received it, after suffering and dying on the cross? William's answer is that this was quite possible, in the same way that Christ could manifest His future glorified body in His transfiguration, while He was still alive. But Roland of Bologna uses this same point about the transfiguration as an argument for the countervailing view that Christ, by means of a miracle, gave His mortal body to His disciples, although without dismembering or destroying it, just as the transfiguration did not prevent Christ from continuing to possess the mortal body in which He completed the rest of His life and met His death. Robert Pullen agrees with this conclusion but manifests no awareness of the physical difficulties which it entails. He emphasizes the point that, whichever body Christ gave to His disciples, it was a miracle either way.[223] Ivo of Chartres, in his *Decretum*, appears to be groping toward an answer of this sort, in the statement that the body Christ gave His disciples was the one He currently possessed, although this has to be understood in a spiritual sense.[224] On the other hand, one of the Porretan sentence collectors seeks to split the difference between these two positions. Acknowledging that the theory that Christ gave to His disciples the body He possessed at the time of the Last Supper has the support of Augustine, he argues against it by making a distinction. The body of Christ had two physical modes, he asserts. It was immortal by nature and mortal by will. This natural immortality is something for which he offers no explanation. In any event, the master concludes that what Christ gave his disciples was the immortal body.[225] The Abelardians tend to hold themselves aloof from this problem. Hermannus and the author of *Sententiae Parisiensis* I raise the question and refrain from answering it.[226]

Even more taxing and fraught with metaphysical problems which theologians before the reception of Aristotle were ill equipped to handle was the vital issue of explaining how the change of

---

Victor, *De sac.* 2.8.3, *PL* 176: 462D–464C; Master Simon, *De sac.*, pp. 31, 38–40. Anselm's position is reported incorrectly by Ludwig Hödl, "Sacramentum und res-Zeichen und Bezeichnetes: Eine begriffsgeschichtliche Arbeit zum frühscholastischen Eucharistietraktat," *Scholastik* 38 (1963): 161–70.

[223] Roland of Bologna, *Sent.*, pp. 218–21; Robert Pullen, *Sent.* 8.4, *PL* 186: 964C–965C.

[224] Ivo of Chartres, *Decretum* 2. c. 5, *PL* 161: 140C–142C.

[225] *Sent. mag. Gisleberti* I 4.59, p. 143.

[226] Hermannus, *Sent.*, pp. 123–31; *Sent. Parisiensis* I, p. 43. On Hermannus's treatment of the Eucharist, see Knoch, *Die Einsetzung*, pp. 50–51.

the elements into the body and blood of Christ takes place. In some respects this topic offers a parallel with the contemporary problem of theological language. But, in Eucharistic theology the problem is more a question of the period's lack of a philosophical and scientific vocabulary precise enough and generally accepted enough with which to clarify the nature of the change and the metaphysical anomaly which it entails. While some of the thinkers who take a stand on this vexed question use terms such as *substantia*, which have a specific sense in Aristotelian philosophy, others do not. Even when the masters use Aristotelian-sounding language, they do not always give to *substantia* the technical meaning that it has in Peripatetic terms. And, while the term "transsubstantiation" does occur in this period, it does not have the denotation which it had acquired by the time of the fourth Lateran council in the usage of the master who employs it.[227]

Easily the most nebulous of the theologians who tackle the change in the elements is Anselm of Laon. He states, merely, that the species remain, although the substance changes into the body and blood of Christ. He neither defines the terms he uses nor displays an interest in explaining how this change occurs. The same laconic type of statement is made by William of Champeaux, and Roland of Bologna follows his lead.[228] Another member of the school of Laon claims that the *res sacramenti*, that is, the body and blood of Christ, cannot be separated from the *sacramentum*, or physical medium. This rather unclear statement is as far as he tries to go; he remarks, simply, that the change is a miracle which defies explanation.[229] Alger of Liège likewise says that the substance changes while the species remain, a process that transcends reason.[230] Gratian is also convinced of the reality of the change but

---

[227] A good sense of the overall terminological issues is provided by Ludwig Hödl, "Der Transsubstantiationsbegriff in der scholastischen Theologie des 12. Jahrhundert," *RTAM* 31 (1964): 230–59. Both Hödl and Hans Jorissen, *Die Entfaltung der Transsubstantiationslehre bis zum Beginn der Hochscholastik* (Münster: Aschendorff, 1965), pp. 4–7 state that the term *transsubstantio* was not used until the late twelfth century. In this claim they are, lexically, incorrect; although they are correct in noting that the use of this term in the same sense as it was given when written into orthodox theology by Lateran IV does not appear in the first half of that century.

[228] *Sentences of Anselm of Laon*, no. 25, 62; *Sentences of William of Champeaux*, no. 272–73, 5: 28–29, 62, 518; Roland of Bologna, *Sent.*, pp. 221–29. For a useful survey of discussions of the change in the Eucharistic elements in this period, see Damien Van den Eynde, "William of Saint-Thierry and the Author of the *Summa Sententiarum*," *FS* 10 (1950): 252–56.

[229] *Sentences of the School of Laon*, no. 375, 5: 277–78.

[230] Alger of Liège, *De misericordia* 1.48, 1.16–62, pp. 224, 235–36.

is vague on how to account for it. His principal concern here, and the one point which he feels he is able to determine with precision, is when the changes occurs, at the time of the consecration.[231] The Abelardian authors of the *Sentententiae Parisiensis* I and *Ysagoge in theologiam* agree that the change occurs and are more interested in considering why this is the case than how. Their answer is that the body and blood of Christ retain the physical attributes of bread and wine so that the sensibilities of recipients will not be offended.[232] Master Simon describes the change as a change in substance (*commutatio substantie*) which leaves the accidents intact, and presents this position as if it were non-problematic.[233]

On the other hand, Hugh of St. Victor, the Porretans, the *Sententiae divinitatis*, the *Summa sententiarum*, and Robert Pullen reflect a more circumspect effort to come to grips with the change in the elements, wrestling manfully with the difficulties which, they acknowledge, the orthodox teaching presents. Of these five masters, Hugh, Robert, and the Porretans are particularly bedevilled by the imprecision and inconstancy of their chosen lexicons.[234] Hugh notes that the Eucharist is made up of its visible appearance (*species*), on the one hand, and, on the other, of the real body and blood of Christ and the spiritual grace which its reception imparts to communicants. This sacramental *substantia* replaces the substance of bread and wine when the elements are consecrated. Hugh agrees that the species of bread and wine remain intact. He recognizes that it is difficult to see what these species now inhere in, and describes the change of substance very loosely as a transition (*mutatio*). His chief concern is to make the point that, although the grace conveyed by the sacrament makes use of a transitory physical medium which is swiftly assimilated into the recipient's digestive tract, its spiritual effects endure beyond the moment of his physical intake of the elements.[235]

The Porretans are also concerned with the idea that the physical elements are assimilated according to a different timetable than their spiritual content. One master holds that the body and blood of Christ remain united to the consecrated bread and wine so long

---

[231] Gratian, *Decretum* pars 3. d. 2. c. 35–c. 42, col. 1324–29.

[232] *Sent. Parisiensis* 1, p. 43; *Ysagoge in theologiam*, pp. 200–07.

[233] Master Simon, *De sac.*, p. 30.

[234] This point has been noted, à propos of Hugh, by Mignon, *Les origines*, 2: 171–79; Heinz Robert Schlette, "Die Eucharistielehre Hugos von St. Viktor," *ZkT* 81 (1949): 170–76.

[235] Hugh of St. Victor, *De sac.* 2.8.7–9, 2.8.13, *PL* 176: 466C–468C, 470B–471C.

as these elements retain the distinguishable species of bread and wine. Once they lose those traits in the recipient's digestive process, he assimilates the species like other food while he retains the union with Christ spiritually. The master's analysis of how the change in the elements comes about deploys a vocabulary that is unique to him. He distinguishes between essence and substance in the sacrament. He uses the term *substantia* in a very un-Aristotelian way. The *substantia* of the elements, he states, does not change; it is, rather, their essence that changes. Substance, for him, means the perceptible, physical aspects of the bread and wine. There is no *transsubstantio*, he argues, because these visible, tangible features of the consecrated species remain in them, unchanged. Equating substance with species in the Eucharist, he concludes that it is the essence which changes, not the substance (*mutantur secundum proprietatem essentie tantum et non secundum substantiam subiectam*). His reason for equating substance with species in the consecrated elements is that there can be no accidents unless they have a substance in which to inhere, a position which simultaneously distinguishes substance from accidents and identifies them with each other. The master's chosen formula also fails to explain how a substance subtending accidents is different from an essence, in his usage.[236]

Unclear and inconsistent language also haunts Robert Pullen's handling of this subject. On the one hand, he states that the *substantia* of the elements changes, although the form (*forma*) of bread and wine remains the same. Alternatively, he states that the *substantia* changes, although the properties (*proprietates*) of the bread and wine do not. Yet again, he says that the *substantia* changes, although the natural qualities (*qualitates naturae*) of the bread and wine are unaltered. Without offering definitions of any of these terms, Robert appears to think that these three statements are equivalent or synonymous; he does not acknowledge the diverse metaphysical significance which they may have.[237]

A much more energetic effort to pinpoint the issue is found in the *Sententiae divinitatis* and *Summa sententiarum*. The author of the first of these works indicates a clear-eyed awareness of the problem involved in the Eucharistic change, which he describes as a change in substance without a change in accidents. He understands these terms in an Aristotelian sense. He begins by distinguishing this

---

[236] *Sent. mag. Gisleberti* I 4.19–21, 4.23–24, 4.46, pp. 135–36, 136, 141. The quotations are at 4.19, p. 135.
[237] Robert Pullen, *Sent.* 8.9, *PL* 186: 966D–977A.

kind of change from a change in accidents only, which does not
bring with it a change in substance. Examples he cites to illustrate
the latter case are the change of Lot's wife into a pillar of salt and
the change of water into ice crystals. He is fully conscious of the
difficulty in explaining how the accidents of bread and wine can
remain when the substance in which they formerly inhered has
been changed into a different substance. He poses the question
lucidly and admits that he can find no philosophical answer to it,
falling back on the idea that the Eucharist involves a supernatural
miracle parallel with the miraculous mode of Christ's birth.
Beyond this, and the affirmation that the change does take place, he
feels he can say no more (*non amplius potest dici*); he agrees with the
Abelardians that the reason for the change is so that the reception
of the Eucharist will not be offensive, while adding that it is a test of
faith which brings merit to those who perceive the true body and
blood of Christ in the visible species of bread and wine.[238] The
Summa sententiarum makes essentially the same points, although
without the analysis of change from one accidental mode to
another. The author agrees that the *substantia* of the bread and wine
changes into Christ's resurrected body and blood and that this
event parallels the miraculous conception of His historical body.
Manifesting the same interest in why the elements retain the sensible appearance of bread and wine after the consecration, and giving
the same answer as the Abelardians and the author of the *Sententiae
divinitatis* to that question, he poses clearly the metaphysical difficulty which this doctrine entails. The accidents of bread and wine
remain, he concludes, although they no longer have the substance
of bread and wine in which to inhere (*et ut praeter substantiam*). He,
too, is able to pose the problem crisply, a problem which he
understands in Aristotelian terms, and to admit that he lacks an
explanation of the change, in those same terms.[239]

To the extent that progress is made on the matter of the Eucharistic change in the period just prior to Peter Lombard, the most
that can be said is that the thinkers who discuss it move from the
position that this article of faith should be restated but that it
cannot be explained to the position that it must be posed in
Aristotelian language and that the resources of philosophy currently available do not make possible an account of the change which

---

[238] *Sent. div.* 5.3, pp. 131*–33*. The quotation is on pp. 131*–32*.
[239] *Summa sent.* 6.4, *PL* 176: 141A–D. The quotation is at 141A. On this point,
see Van den Eynde, "William of Saint-Thierry," pp. 241–56.

the theologians see as required, and imperatively so. On these major issues surrounding the real presence doctrine, the Lombard comes the closest to the views of the *Sententiae divinitatis* and *Summa sententiarum*, particularly in his adherence to an Aristotelian vocabulary. On the other hand, in the debate over which body Christ gave to His disciples at the Last Supper, his closest immediate forerunner is Roland of Bologna. Peter's own account of the change of the Eucharistic elements uses language that reproves the terminology of Robert Pullen and the Porretans. The change in the Eucharist, he affirms, is a change in substance. The change cannot be a formal change, he notes, because the species of bread and wine are retained in those elements after the consecration. As for the claim that a change in substance is not the same thing as a change in essence, Peter expressly takes it up and rejects it. He also denies that support of this notion entails acceptance of the idea that all the Eucharists celebrated over time add new substance to Christ's historical body, since the body of Christ with which Christians have dealings in the Eucharist is His immortal, impassible, resurrected body, which can neither be enlarged, subdivided, or broken by the celebration and reception of the sacrament. As to the mode of existence of the accidents of bread and wine which remain after the change, Peter considers a range of opinions. Some say that these accidents continue to exist, even though they no longer possess a material substratum (*preiacentem materiam*) in which to inhere. They exist, anyway, inhering in nothing. Others thinks that the change in the elements is not total, and that enough of the bread and wine remains to provide a metaphysical foundation for the accidents of bread and wine. This latter view, he points out, is refuted by the authorities who say that the change is full and complete. Having ruled out the second opinion on these grounds, Peter is left with the first position cited.[240] He is not entirely happy with it, but he has clearly benefited from the way in which the *Sententiae divinitatis* and *Summa sententiarum* have posed the problem. He agrees that, normally, accidents cannot exist unless they inhere in a subject. At the same time, these particular accidents cannot inhere in the body and blood of the resurrected Christ. Peter thus comes to the conclusion that "these accidents remain, subsisting by themselves" (*Remanent ergo illa accidentia per se subsistentia*), attached

---

[240] Peter Lombard, *Sent.* 4. d. 8. c. 4, d. 10, d. 11. c. 1–c. 2, d. 12. c. 2–c. 3, 2: 282, 290, 296–97, 304–05.

to no substance.[241] Peter acknowledges the fact that this position is a metaphysical anomaly. The most that can be said about his handling of the topic of the Eucharistic change is that he articulates the problem and presents its difficulties more sharply than does anyone else in this period. And, like the masters who serve as his immediate models, he reflects the increasing tendency of mid-twelfth-century theology to conceptualize this question in Aristotelian terms, with Aristotelian meanings attached to the vocabulary used in this context. If Peter recognizes the metaphysical problem attached to the position he takes on the Eucharistic change, however, the same cannot be said of his espousal of the relatively unpopular view that it was His mortal and passible body that Christ gave to His disciples at the Last Supper.[242] The main point he wants to make here is that this mode of Eucharistic communion was no more or less efficacious, for the apostles, than the Eucharistic reception of Christ's resurrected body is for later Christians. But, uncharacteristically, Peter makes no attempt to acknowledge the difficulties, difficulties already in circulation since the time of Berengar of Tours, which this doctrine bears in its train; nor does he attempt to refute the opposing view.

The two debates concerning the real presence just discussed constitute the weightiest speculative controversies raised in connection with the Eucharist in this period. They both remained unresolved in the immediate sequel, pending the arrival of the richer philosophical resources on which the orthodox formulations later to develop could be grounded. There were also other aspects of the sacrament of the Eucharist which provoked disagreement, even though they were less philosophically intractable in mid-twelfth-century terms. It was agreed by all that, for the sacrament to be fruitfully received, the communicant had to approach it with the right intention and with a belief in the real presence. Yet, not all contemporary masters agreed on the kind of efficacy the sacrament had for different kinds of human recipients, and, indeed, subhuman ones as well. Debate also centered on the mode of administration of the Eucharist and the conditions empowering the minister to consecrate it validly. Also, the masters do not always define the *res sacramenti* received by the communicant in the same way.

The responses which the masters give to these questions are

---

[241] Ibid., d. 11. c. 2.5–10, d. 12. c. 1, 2: 298–99, 304. The quotation is at d. 12. c. 1, p. 304.

[242] Ibid., d. 11. c. 6.1, 2: 303.

usually related to the way they understand the nature of the *res sacramenti* transmitted efficaciously through the *sacramentum* of the Eucharist; in most cases, the position they take on that issue lays the foundation for their treatment of the effects of communion on the recipient. The distinction between the external physical medium of a sacrament, its spiritual content, and the capacity of an individual to receive either without the other had been drawn early in the twelfth century à propos of baptism, in which connection it had evoked considerable interest and support. Alger of Liège appears to have been the earliest thinker in this century to apply this idea to the Eucharist as well. For him, the *sacramentum* is the species of bread and wine, the *res sacramenti* is the body and blood of Christ, and the *effectum sacramenti*, the grace which reception conveys to the communicant, depends on his disposition, bringing him eternal life or damnation, depending on whether he believes in the real presence or not.[243] The same idea is found in masters writing closer to the middle of the century, who expand on Alger's theme. A good case in point is the author of the *Sententiae divinitatis*. As he sees it, the *sacramentum tantum*, or physical medium by itself, is the physical species, which, he notes, following Hugh of St. Victor on this point, resembles what it signifies, in that the individual grains and grapes that make up the bread and wine stand for the individual Christians united with each other and with Christ in the church. Likewise, the water added to the wine in the chalice recalls the blood and water issuing from the side of Christ on the cross, and symbolizes the combination of divine and human elements in the church. Along with the elements, he continues, the *sacramentum* includes the verbal formula of consecration and the rest of the Eucharistic rite, the mixing of water with wine in the chalice, the elevation, deposition, and fraction of the host, and the distribution of communion. For this master, the *res sacramenti* has two aspects, the body and blood of Christ, which the sacrament signifies and contains, and the union of Christians in the church, which it signifies but does not contain. To receive the *sacramentum tantum* is,

---

[243] Alger of Liège, *De misericordia* 1.48, 1.61–62, pp. 224, 235–36. On Alger, see Häring," A Study of the Sacramentology of Alger," pp. 41–78. Alger is left out of the account in the survey of the use of this distinction in our period by Hödl, "Sacramentum und res," pp. 161–82. He is also ignored by Macy, *Theologies of the Eucharist*, pp. 85, 96–98 and Van den Eynde, "William of Saint-Thierry," pp. 241–56, who both see William of St. Thierry as the first thinker to transfer the definition from baptism to the Eucharist and the *Summa sententiarum* as its only channel of entry into scholastic discourse.

like Judas, to receive the physical species only, but not what they signify and effect. According to this master, one can also receive spiritually the *res tantum*, the sacred matter of the Eucharist alone, if one is properly disposed and prevented from receiving the physical elements by some emergency. Such a spiritual communion, while clearly possible for the author of the *Sententiae divinitatis*, is not standard. A worthy, and normal, communion involves a reception of both the *sacramentum* and the *res sacramenti*.[244]

The essentials of this position, which offers the fullest account of the issue prior to Peter Lombard, are found in other thinkers in this period, although in a more abbreviated form. The author of the *Summa sententiarum* omits the sacramental ritual in defining the *sacramentum tantum*, although he adds that it signifies the spiritual nourishment of Christians as well as the body and blood of Christ and the union of Christians in the church. He, too, agrees that, for the *res sacramenti* to be internalized efficaciously by the communicant he must have the proper belief and disposition; failing those conditions, communion works to his damnation, not his salvation.[245] While he uses a different, and older, vocabulary, calling the physical medium the sign of a sacred thing (*sacre rei signum*) and the union of Christ and the church the visible sign of invisible grace (*visibile signum invisibile gratium*), and while he sees the body and blood of Christ as the hidden holy thing (*sacrum secretum*) conveyed by the sign, his pre-Victorine language describes, for Roland of Bologna, a *res sacramenti* that combines the bonding of Christians in the church with the salvific consequences of Christ's sacrifice in the remission of the recipient's sin and his sanctification through the gifts of the Holy Spirit. Roland, too, distinguishes between the mere physical reception of the consecrated elements, which, in the case of unbelieving or unworthy recipients leads to their damnation, as was the case with Judas, and the fruitful reception of both the sacrament and its sacred content by the properly disposed communicant. The former, he states, do receive the body and blood of Christ; but they are unable to assimilate and profit from its effects spiritually.[246] In omitting the idea of spiritual communion, Roland offers a less well developed version of this doctrine than the author of the *Sententiae divinitatis*; but he agrees with most of the main points presented in that master's teaching.

---

[244] *Sent. div.* 5.3, pp. 130*–31*, 135*–36*.
[245] *Summa sent.* 6.3, 6.5, *PL* 176: 140A–D, 142B.
[246] Roland of Bologna, *Sent.*, pp. 157, 216, 229–30. On Roland here, see Macy, *Theologies of the Eucharist*, p. 117.

One can find a similar kind of understanding of the differential effects of Eucharistic reception even in authors who do not refer overtly to Alger's distinction and its development by more recent masters. The Porretans offer their own scheme here, distinguishing among spiritual, sacramental, and neutral reception. Infants, martyrs, and people who cannot consume the physical elements but who unite themselves to Christ in spirit, faith, and good works communicate spiritually. The conditions which the Porretan master attaches to spiritual communion make it difficult to see why he includes infants on his list here. Sacramental communion, which involves the reception of the body and blood of Christ by means of the consecrated elements, he divides into two categories, fruitful and unfruitful. The first applies to people who keep the faith and it works toward their sanctification. The second applies to people who, like Judas, betray the faith, and it works toward their damnation. Neutral reception, in the eyes of this master, occurs when a non-believer receives communion. The master is regrettably vague on whether such a person receives more than just the physical elements. What he is sure of is that this kind of recipient is not saved by this kind of reception.[247]

One corollary of this issue that receives attention, in the wake of the Berengarian controversy, and which may or may not benefit from a master's possession of a well developed distinction among *sacramentum tantum*, *res tantum*, and *et sacramentum et res sacramenti*, is the problem of what happens if the consecrated species are inadvertently dropped on the ground or, worse yet, consumed by an animal. Berengar himself had raised these questions for their shock value in the effort to embarrass proponents of the real presence doctrine, well before Alger's distinction provided a way of disposing of it.[248] Master Simon offers the opinion that, in such occurrences, God withdraws the body and blood of Christ from the elements, keeping them invisibly suspended in the air, so that they will not suffer contact with the ground or be processed by the digestive system of a mouse, the animal typically singled out for attention since Berengar's time. The Porretans second this

---

[247] *Sent. mag. Gisleberti* I 4.11–15, 4.51–56, pp. 133–34, 142–43. To some extent this author here parallels Master Simon, *De sac.*, pp. 25, 28, 33–36, 41–42. Another parallel, although it is less marked, is Honorius, *Eluc.* 1.180–84, pp. 394–95. See Macy, *Theologies of the Eucharist*, pp. 106–11.

[248] Landgraf, *Dogmengeschichte*, 3, part 2: 207–22; Macy, "Of Mice and Manna," pp. 157–66; "Berengar's Legacy," pp. 49–67.

interpretation.[249] A less circumstantial account is given by the author of *Sententiae Parisiensis* I. He agrees that the mouse receives the species only, and not the body and blood of Christ, but declines to speculate on what happens to the body and blood in that event.[250] Oddly enough, Roland of Bologna, presenting pros and cons, leaves the matter undecided, even though the principle concerning the communion of Judas which he has articulated could have supplied him with a means of resolving it. The most he is willing to say is that he does not think that the mouse receives the *res sacramenti*; but he does not feel confident as to how this position can be defended.[251] It is perhaps noteworthy that the masters best qualified to deal definitively with the mouse, the authors of the *Sententiae divinitatis* and the *Summa sententiarum*, do not take up this question, and that Roland, who also has what he needs to do so, does not use his own armory effectively. The other contemporary masters interested in this topic are canonists such as Ivo of Chartres, who is more concerned with the culpability of persons who vomit the Eucharist, who allow it to fall on the ground, or who fail to guard it against animals, and the penance appropriate to them, than he is with the theological issues involved.[252]

Interest was much more widespread, and diverse, on another aspect of the distinction between the sacrament and its effects launched by Alger of Liège, the question of what these effects actually are. Although we have to wait until Hugh of St. Victor and his followers to find the full shift away from the Augustinian definition of sacrament in general as a visible sign of an invisible grace to its definition as a sign that contains and effects what it signifies, thinkers in this period, even if they write before or outside of this decisive Victorine development, none the less concur in the view that the Eucharist can be understood as efficacious as well as significant. Where they disagree is on the point of what the properly disposed recipient actually receives by means of the sacrament. Gary Macy has offered a distinction here, between what he calls the mystical and the ecclesiological understanding of the way the Eucharist was thought to be internalized in the twelfth century. Thinkers in the first group, according to Macy, accent the impact of communion on the inner life and religious experience of the recipient, whether or not it triggers mystic transports in the strict

---

[249] Master Simon, *De sac.*, pp. 40–41; *Sent. mag. Gisleberti* I 4.16–18, pp. 134–35.
[250] *Sent. Parisiensis* I, pp. 43–44.
[251] Roland of Bologna, *Sent.*, pp. 234–35.
[252] Ivo of Chartres, *Decretum* 2. c. 55–c. 61, *PL* 161: 172C–173D.

sense of the term. Thinkers in the second group see the primary if not exclusive effect of the Eucharist as the incorporation of the communicant into the church, seen as Christ's mystical body and as a historical institution.[253] Another way of putting the same point is to contrast thinkers who emphasize the subjective side of the sacramental transaction with those who emphasize its objective side. Macy's view in general can certainly be supported. One can, to be sure, find authors in our period who can be used to document these extremes in his interpretation. But a great many masters in the first half of the twelfth century present a much more eclectic or nuanced position on this question, and this irrespective of whether they are monks, scholastics, or canonists.

Perhaps the most extreme case of an author who views the reception of communion from a largely subjective standpoint is the Laon master who lists seven states of soul as needed for a proper reception and seven spiritual benefits which reception brings. In addition to the standard prerequisite of faith, the consensus position, he thinks that a communicant receiving worthily needs frequent thoughts about Christ, understanding, memory, and love of Christ, and adhesion to Christ, each state growing out of the one anterior to it. In turn, communion brings the communication of the effects of Christ's passion to the faithful, in their own measure. This, to be sure, is an objective gift. But, as noted, it is differential in the way it is appropriated by different communicants. This gift engenders six other benefits that enrich the inner life of the recipient: the thirst for God, the drink that quenches it, the inebriation of the spirit, tranquillity, and eternal life. The objective component that is undeniably present in this analysis is regarded from the perspective of how the soul of the communicant internalizes it.[254]

At the other end of the spectrum we may place Honorius Augustodunensis and Hugh of St. Victor. Each of these theologians, it will be remembered, is unusual in that he prefaces his account of the sacraments with an abbreviated ecclesiology, it being more typical, in this period, for theologians to leave ecclesiology to the canonists and publicists in their division of labor. Both Honorius and Hugh present the church as the mystical body of Christ. Honorius makes the connection even more organic than Hugh does, in that he takes

---

[253] Macy, *Theologies of the Eucharist*, passim.

[254] *Sentences of the School of Laon*, no. 381, 5: 280. For the school of Laon on communion, see Knoch, *Die Einsetzung*, pp. 47–55, although Knoch does not touch on all aspects of their teachings.

up the Eucharist as the first sacrament he discusses, rather than marriage, as the first sacrament instituted. Honorius describes the effects of communion as the engrafting of Christians into the ecclesial body of Christ and, through it, as obtaining the spiritual nourishment that begins in this life and that is perfected, for the community of the elect, in Heaven. The bread and wine, with their many grains and grapes, signify this union of Christians with Christ and with each other.[255] Hugh agrees that the Eucharist, since it contains the body and blood of Christ, is the sacrament of sacraments and the source of all sanctification. This sanctification, for him, is also a function of the incorporation of the recipient into the ecclesial body of Christ. The particularly Hugonian twist he imparts to this doctrine is to present it in terms of participation in the divine light, an idea which he derives from the *Celestial Hierarchy* of the Pseudo-Dionysius, a text on which he commented. This notion gives a rather Neoplatonic cast to the engrafting of Christians into the church through the Eucharist, in Hugh's account.[256]

Most masters in the first half of the twelfth century cannot be fitted so neatly into a framework bounded by personal religious experience on the one side and ecclesiology on the other. Not all the thinkers who accent the objective effects of communion conceive of this issue in ecclesiological terms. Ivo of Chartres, for instance, sees the effects of the Eucharist as a combination of the union of Christians in the church and the gift of eternal life; and he is seconded by the *Summa sententiarum*. But his fellow canonists, Alger of Liège and Gratian, who take an equally objective line, leave out the ecclesial dimension and describe the effects of communion as eternal life, salvation, and union with Christ.[257] The disciples of Abelard do not always distinguish what is a condition of fruitful reception from what is a consequence of it. Hermannus states that the effect of the sacrament is to remind us of Christ's love, while the author of *Sententiae Parisiensis* I asserts that the Eucharist helps us to recall Christ's crucifixion and that we should bring this recollection to

---

[255] Honorius, *Eluc.* 1.177–84, pp. 393–95.

[256] Hugh of St. Victor, *De sac.* 2.8.1, *PL* 176: 461D. This Dionysian slant has been noted by Erich Kleineidam, "Literaturgeschichtliche Bemerkungen zur Eucharistielehre Hugos von St. Viktor," *Scholastik* 20–24 (1949): 564–66; Knoch, *Die Einsetzung*, pp. 96–98; Schlette, "Die Eucharistielehre," pp. 193–99, 204–10; Weisweiler, "Sakrament als Symbol und Teilhabe," pp. 321–43. Macy, *Theologies of the Eucharist*, pp. 83–84, reads this point less Neoplatonically.

[257] Ivo of Chartres, *Decretum* 2. c. 4, *PL* 161: 138B; *Summa sent.* 6.3, *PL* 176: 139C–D; Alger of Liège, *De misericordia* 1.48, 1.61–62, pp. 224, 235–36; Gratian, *Decretum* pars 3. d. 2. c. 44–c. 53, col. 1130–33.

communion when receiving it. In addition, he thinks that the recipient is rendered immune from vice (*immunem facit ab omni vitio*) by the Eucharist.[258] Still, the accent of the Abelardians is on the subjective side, another unacknowledged legacy of Abelard's from the school of Laon. The master who accents this point most heavily is the Cambridge Commentator. If we do not respond to Eucharistic reception with love, he states, then Christ's saving work, itself understood as the conversion of man's heart, is frustrated in us and we cannot appropriate it in the Eucharist.[259] Other masters who may or may not have absorbed Abelardian influence on this point include Master Simon and the Porretans, who give as the effects of reception conversion, perfection, and the remission of venial sin;[260] Robert Pullen, who proposes spiritual nourishment;[261] and the author of the *Summa sententiatum*, who says that reception of the Eucharist remakes the communicant spiritually and liberates him from evil.[262] The one author who goes the farthest in balancing these diverse modes of understanding the effects of Eucharistic reception is Roland of Bologna. For him, the effects are threefold: the engrafting of Christians into the church, the remission of sin, and the sanctifying gifts of the Holy Spirit.[263]

In dealing with the fact that there are two material elements in the Eucharist, bread and wine, although the doctrine of concomitance stresses that they equally contain the body and blood of Christ, the theologians in this period tend not to defend the point simply on the grounds that this was the way Christ instituted the sacrament, but rather view the two species from the standpoint of man's needs and how the sacramental media are responsive to them, both as signs and as signs that effect what they signify. Here, is it not surprising that authors who see the prime effect, or one of the effects, of Eucharistic reception as the engrafting of Christians into the church should advert to the symbolism of the individual grains of wheat and grapes united in the Eucharistic bread and wine. This is the case with Roland and Honorius.[264] The instructive

---

[258] Hermannus, *Sent.*, p. 125; *Sent. Parisiensis* I, p. 43.

[259] *Comm. in Epistolam ad Hebraeos* 9 in *Commentarius Cantabridgensis*, 4: 782. Macy, *Theologies of the Eucharist*, pp. 114–16, 118, states that the Abelardians waver between an individual and a corporate view of the effects of communion. We have not found much to support the alleged corporative ingredient in their teaching.

[260] *Sent. mag. Gisleberti* I 4.60, p. 143. The author cites Simon by name as his source.

[261] Robert Pullen, *Sent.* 8.2, *PL* 186: 961C–963B.

[262] *Summa sent.* 6.2, *PL* 176: 139B.

[263] Roland of Bologna, *Sent.*, pp. 157, 216.

[264] Ibid., pp. 157, 216; Honorius, *Eluc.* 1.180–84, pp. 394–95.

power of this symbolism is so appealing that it also attracts masters who take a less ecclesial view of the effects of Eucharistic communion, such as the Laon masters, Master Simon, Robert Pullen, and the author of the *Ysagoge in theologiam*.[265] Some authors combine man's need for signs that enlighten him as to how the sacrament works in his soul with his need for redemption tout court. Although agreeing that both the body and blood of Christ are fully contained in each of the consecrated elements, they observe that the wine none the less stands for and nourishes man's soul while the bread stands for and nourishes man's body. Christ, they argue, took on both a human body and a human soul in order to redeem mankind both in body and soul; and, in the Eucharistic elements, He provided species that signify and effect this redemption of the whole human person. This Christological and soteriological argument is joined to the symbolism of the grains and grapes by the Porretans, Master Simon, and the authors of the *Summa sententiarum* and *Sententiae divinitatis*.[266]

There were two other issues related to concomitance that evoked a certain amount of discussion, as this doctrine affected the mode by which the Eucharist was administered to the laity. In this connection it is worth keeping in mind that the laity had been receiving the Eucharist under both species, separately, since the days of the early church. While communion in both kinds was the rule, there is evidence to suggest that some pastors were practicing intinction, or the dipping of the host into the chalice before giving it to the communicant. Pope Paschal II (1099–1118) had reproved this practice, citing the standard argument that intinction was unscriptural. The only one of the disciples to whom Christ gave communion in this way was Judas, another clear reason for prohibiting it. Paschal reinforced the traditional insistence on reception in both kinds, sequentially. He also granted a traditional dispensation, by conceding that aged, infirm, and moribund persons who are unable to consume solid food are allowed to receive

---

[265] *Sentences of the School of Laon*, no. 275, 5: 277–78; Robert Pullen, *Sent.* 8.2, *PL* 186: 961C–963B; *Ysagoge in theologiam*, pp. 200–07.

[266] *Sent. mag. Gisleberti* I 4.6–10, pp. 133–34; *Sent. div.* 5.3, pp. 129*–30*, 138*; Master Simon, *De sac.*, pp. 26–29; *Summa sent.* 6.5–6, *PL* 176: 142B–143B. Macy, *Theologies of the Eucharist*, pp. 68–69, 172 argues that the first person to develop this body-soul argument was Hervaeus of Bourg-Dieu in his Pauline commentary of ca. 1150; Philippe Delhaye, "Un dossier Eucharistique d'Anselme de Laon à l'abbaye de Fécamp," in *L'Abbaye bénédictine de Fécamp: Ouvrage scientifique du XIIIe centenaire, 658–1958* (Fécamp: L. Durand et Fils, 1960), 2: 156, rightly sees it as arising earlier than that. The notion was more widespread than either of these scholars thinks.

the chalice alone. This dispensation was a standard one, but it omitted, in Paschal's case, another category of communicant, infants in danger of death, who had been included in the dispensation in earlier decretals. Concomitance certainly supplied a rationale for Paschal's exception, but he made it less in defense of concomitance itself, or of pastoral need, than in conjunction with his ban on intinction.[267]

Whether they cite Paschal or rely on the authorities to whom he himself refers, the vast majority of masters in the first half of the twelfth century defend utraquism, oppose intinction, and connect this teaching with the doctrine of concomitance. Exceptions to this consensus are few; and they are interesting in that they reflect a desire to depart from established tradition on the basis of pastoral utility. The availablitiy of the Eucharist to the people who need it, and in the form in which they are able to receive it, is the operative norm here, a norm reflecting the more general desire to remove obstacles that might separate Christians from the grace available through the sacraments that is quite characteristic of this period. Considering, especially, the common wish to emphasize the sacred dignity of the Eucharist and its necessity for salvation, this criterion impelled several theologians to swim against the current of contemporary opinion on its behalf. Their views are thus more interesting for the concerns that animate them than for their ability to overturn the consensus position or to offer what could be regarded as another viable option within it. Roland of Bologna stands out as the one and only master to present a defense of intinction in the face of universal opposition to it on the part of the papacy, the canonists, and the theologians alike. He is fully aware of the objection based on Holy Scripture. In a remarkable if totally uninfluential turnabout of that objection, he argues that the fact that Christ gave the Eucharist to Judas in this form validates intinction, even though, as he has argued elsewhere, the bad faith which Judas brought to communion meant that it worked to his damnation. The reason why intinction should be permitted, according to Roland, is that it is an easier way to administer communion than by the host and chalice separately. The fear of dropping the host, or of accidentally spilling the contents of the chalice, he notes, may make some communicants anxious. This anxiety may undercut the proper state of devotion and receptivity which they need to bring to the

---

[267] See the references cited above, n. 220.

sacrament. Their worry, indeed, may keep them away from communion altogether. And so, for practical pastoral reasons (*curis
secularibus*) intinction should be allowed.[268]

As the twelfth century moved along, the clearer articulation of
the doctrine of concomitance, coupled with the increasing inci-
dence of "bleeding host" miracles, was to bring about a major
change in the administration of communion to the laity. By the end
of the century, the western church had abandoned the age-old
practice of utraquism for the laity and had made the reception of
the host alone the new standard. But, members of the school of
Laon, along with the Porretans, resisted this change. To be sure,
they could appreciate the rationale supporting communion in one
kind in the light of the doctrine of concomitance. What they sought
to retain, however, was the older custom of administering the
chalice alone, not only to the aged and infirm and to those in
danger of death, but also to infants, who are likewise unable to
consume solid food. Pope Paschal's recent ruling, they noted, while
it retained the dispensation permitting the chalice alone to the
aged, infirm, and moribund, had ignored the infants. The desire of
these masters to rush to the defense of the pastoral needs of infants
is exactly parallel with the desire of these same theologians to relax
the rule confining baptism to Easter and Pentecost, although their
stance in the face of ecclesiastical tradition differed in these two
areas of sacramental theology. In the case of baptism, as we have
seen above, they wanted to depart from a historically conditioned
rule which no longer spoke to the needs of the cohort of people now
largely receiving the sacrament. In the case of the Eucharist, on the
other hand, the masters defend the retention of an ancient practice
which, in their eyes, has as much pastoral relevance in the here and
now as it had ever had. Granting that, if no neccessity arises, the
first communion of infants can safely be deferred, Anselm of Laon
insists that, if the infant is in any danger, he should be given
communion at the next celebration of the Eucharist following his
baptism, by means of the chalice alone, because he cannot take
solid food. Anselm urges that this practice is essential since the
child's salvation will otherwise be placed in jeopardy. He adds that
the priest who fails to administer the chalice to the child has failed
miserably in his pastoral duty; Anselm compares him with a
shepherd who abandons his flock.[269] William of Champeaux force-

---

[268] Roland of Bologna, *Sent.*, p. 230.
[269] *Sentences of Anselm of Laon from the Liber Pancrisis*, no. 61–62, 5: 55–56.

fully seconds this opinion and connects it more specifically with the doctrines of the real presence and concomitance.[270] Another Laon master repeats Anselm's argument almost verbatim and adds a point which we see cropping up elsewhere in twelfth century sacramental theology, the idea that, should the priest be negligent, his failure to give the chalice to the infant will be charged to his own moral account by God, Who will not condemn the infant because of someone else's irresponsible behavior.[271] This observation also parallels exactly the reason why some members of the school of Laon reject the automatic damnation of the unbaptized children of negligent parents. Both the disciples of Gilbert of Poitiers and Gilbert himself strongly support the position of the school of Laon here, although they are fully conscious of the fact that it is a minority view, not given an extensive hearing in the schools (*Hec quaestio quamvis a doctoribus non sit ventilata*).[272]

There were two other issues related to the recipients of the Eucharist that provoked a mild flurry of interest, one illustrating a logical application of the agreed-upon conditions making for valid and fruitful reception held by all at this time and the other illustrating the desire to loosen older strictures. Anselm of Laon insists that communion should not be given to heretics and excommunicates, not even as a *viaticum*. His reasons are perfectly straightforward. Heretics lack the correct faith needed for fruitful reception, and severance from communion is precisely what excommunication is all about as well as being the penalty it imposes on the malefactor whose behavior has warranted such drastic requital.[273] The desire to make communion available to persons known or suspected of being evildoers or persons of bad character informs opinions on criminals, and on actors and magicians, at the hands of the Porretans and canonists, respectively. A priest should not deny communion to someone he knows to be a criminal, states the Porretan master, on the model of Christ's giving of the Eucharist to Judas, who, He knew, would betray Him. The only exception that the master admits is the case of a criminal who has also been publicly

---

[270] *Sentences of William of Champeaux*, no. 270, 5: 216–17.
[271] *Sentences of the School of Laon*, no. 372, 5: 276.
[272] *Sent. mag. Gisleberti* I 4.42, p. 140. As the editor notes, p. 140 n. 48, a gloss on this passage in a copy of the work preserved in MS. Paris BN lat. 14423, f. 97ᵛ states that this is Gilbert's teaching as well: "Parvuli debet dari, tamen in liquida forma . . . sicut magister Gillibertus instituit." This point has also been noted by Landgraf, *Dogmengeschichte*, 3 part 2: 192.
[273] *Sentences of Anselm of Laon*, no. 63, 5: 56.

excommunicated.[274] And, Ivo of Chartres and Gratian, although well aware of earlier canonical hostility to actors and magicians (*histrioni, magi*) as persons likely to have evil habits, noxious beliefs, or both, argue that they should be admitted to communion. Ivo cites the supporting authority of Cyprian; Gratian is not quite so generous, stipulating that the actors and magicians must first repent of their putative bad behavior and that they should not be given communion side by side with other, presumably Godfearing, Christians, but separately.[275]

This largely concludes the list of questions raised, by a greater or smaller range of masters, concerning the recipient of communion, the conditions affecting its efficacy in him, what it actually transmits to him, and how it ought to be administered. These debates have moved us from matters of pressing general concern to those that interest only a handful of authors, and from those directly connected with the essential definition of the sacrament itself to those embracing ecclesiastical policies and administrative matters regarded as subject to change. Looking at the Eucharist from the other side of the rite, the side of the minister and not that of the recipient, we encounter another debate, extremely widespread in this period, and one on which there was a decided range of views.[276] This aspect of the Eucharist, understandably, received detailed attention from the canonists, along with the rules and regulations for the liturgical celebration of the mass, provision of the reserved sacrament for sick calls, and other concerns of the clergy in this connection. Motivated by the reformist urge to deny priestly faculties to schismatics, excommunicates, or heretical clergymen, the canonists, by the mid-century, had arrived at a consensus among themselves that is aptly summed up by Roland of Bologna. For the Eucharist to be truly consecrated, he states, the minister must be a priest validly ordained, regardless of his moral qualities. Roland, however, withholds this capacity from priests who have been interdicted, deposed, or unfrocked, or who are heretics, schismatics, or excommunicates. The first set of disqualifications respects the fact that they are no longer in good standing canonically. Heresy obviates the correct faith and correct intention required for a valid consecration. Schismatics and excommunicates are ruled out by

---

[274] *Sent. mag. Gisleberti* I 4.49, p. 141.

[275] Ivo of Chartres, *Panormia* 1.152, *PL* 161: 1080C; Gratian, *Decretum* pars 3. d. 2. c. 95–c. 96, col. 1352.

[276] On this point, see Landgraf, *Dogmengeschichte*, 3 part 1: 119–45, 3 part 2: 223–34, 240–43.

definition; the Eucharist is the sacrament of unity, and it cannot be administered by a cleric who is not in union with the church.[277]

Many of the theologians of the day found this canonical position, for all its clarity and cogency, to be too restrictive. Another model was proposed by the Porretans, who argue that there are three conditions needed to validate the consecration of the Eucharist: *ordo*, *actio*, and *intentio*, or a validly ordained priest, the use of the proper canonical formula of consecration during the mass, and the intention to do what the church understands by the the celebration of the Eucharist. With this principle in hand, the Porretan master objects to the automatic disqualification of excommunicated priests. To be sure, he agrees that non-believers cannot consecrate validly; but, presumably, this category could exclude priests who had lost the faith themselves but who might be willing to be of service to communities of believers who would otherwise lack access to the mass and the Eucharist. The inclusion or exclusion of the non-believing priest is thus not a blanket one, in the master's estimation. In the case of the priest who is excommunicated, the master argues that it is perfectly possible for him to consecrate validly, so long as the notes of *ordo*, *actio*, and *intentio* apply to him.[278] The author of the *Sententiae divinitatis* also uses the *ordo*, *actio*, *intentio* model and expands the range of acceptable ministers still farther. Both heretics and schismatics may consecrate validly, in his opinion, so long as they are validly ordained, use the appropriate rite, and intend to do what the church intends. He does not take up the excommunicates or raise the question of why a heretic would want to participate in the sacramental ministry of the church.[279] Master Simon agrees that *ordo* and *actio* are required. He omits *intentio*, but concedes legitimacy to the consecrations of priests who display the first two traits.[280] In praise of flexibility in this area, he cites Gregory the Great's maxim that diversity of customs does not impede unity of the faith in the church, without noticing that it was directed by Gregory to the number of immersions required or permitted in baptism and not to who is to be barred from the Eucharistic ministry. The author of the *Summa sententiarum* also uses the *ordo*, *actio*, *intentio* formula, although he takes a harder line than some of his compeers. Agreeing with the *Sententiae divinitatis* here, he admits that a properly ordained heretic may be able to consecrate

---

[277] Roland of Bologna, *Sent.*, pp. 216–18, 235–37.
[278] *Sent. mag. Gisleberti* I 4.28, 4.32, 4.43–44, pp. 136, 137, 140.
[279] *Sent. div.* 5.3, p. 141*.
[280] Master Simon, *De sac.*, p. 38.

validly for the people who receive communion at his hands, although, in his own view, such a hypocrite would bring moral obloquy upon his own head. He disallows schismatics and excommunicates, since their own alienation from the church would prevent them from connecting their congregations with its unity by means of the Eucharist.[281] Robert Pullen shifts his focus from the issue of heresy, schism, or severance from communion as impediments to valid consecration to the problem of morally unworthy priests. He agrees that their Eucharistic ministry is valid. But he is less concerned with what gives the formula of consecration its efficacy than he is with the blame and punishment attached to clerical misconduct in this area.[282]

Three other observations are needed to complete our survey of Eucharistic debates in the first half of the twelfth century before turning to the question of how Peter Lombard addresses the issues of reception, administration, and appropriation of the grace made available by the Eucharist, in comparison with his contemporaries. One area in which those canonists and theologians who take up the issue agree in softening the rigor of an earlier age is the matter of a nocturnal emission experienced by a priest scheduled to celebrate mass the following morning, and whether this accident places him in a state of ritual pollution which would bar him from celebrating. The consensus position in this period rejects the strict idea of ritual pollution and distinguishes among the reasons why the individual experiences the seminal emission in the first place. He is guilty of sin, it is agreed, if he has brought the event upon himself by overindulgence in food or drink or by deliberately entertaining lustful thoughts. For these offenses he must do penance and he may not approach the altar as a minister of the Eucharist until he has done so. On the other hand, if the seminal emission occurred willy nilly, out of the superabundance of the man's animal spirits, then no sin has been committed. Here, the principle of intentionality in ethics is clearly at work. In the latter case, the priest should cleanse his person, clothing, and bedclothes but he is not prohibited from celebrating the Eucharist. Among the theologians, not all of whom take up this topic, the canonico-theological consensus position is spelled out the most crisply by the Porretans.[283] Another matter addressed by both canonists and theologians, although far less

---

[281] *Summa sent.* 6.4, *PL* 176: 141A–D.
[282] Robert Pullen, *Sent.* 8.6, *PL* 186: 968A–D.
[283] *Sent. mag. Gisleberti* I 4.47–48, p. 141.

often, is the frequency of communion for the laity. Robert Pullen is the best guide to the state of play on this subject. Even though he does not name the authorities he cites, he gives an accurate report of the tradition reprised by the canonists. This tradition states that lay people should receive communion three times yearly, at Christmas, Easter, and Pentecost. Robert offers no recommendation of his own on the timetable, but stresses, rather, that what is most important is receiving worthily, however frequently or infrequently reception occurs.[284] Finally, and the point is worth mentioning mainly to illustrate a shift of major dimensions in the agenda of writers on the Eucharist at this time, there is the evaporation of the polemic against the Greek church, which had been given sustained attention as recently as the final years of the eleventh century. Only one scholastic in our period, Roland of Bologna, attacks the Greeks for using leavened bread in the Eucharist; and he is the exception who proves the rule.[285]

While in the field of Eucharistic theology, as in theology more generally, one can find Peter Lombard characterized as the good, gray mediator, striking a compromise or middle-of-the-road position in relation to his contemporaries,[286] a consideration of the opinions he gives, or declines to give, on the range of Eucharistic questions just discussed shows him taking sides, more often than not, in areas where there was a range of views among the orthodox. As we have seen, in addressing the critical debates stemming from the defense of the real presence, he takes the relatively unpopular line of Roland of Bologna on the matter of Christ's giving His mortal body to His disciples at the Last Supper. And, he takes, and sharpens considerably, the most recent and most Aristotelian way of formulating the question of the Eucharistic change presented by the authors of the *Sententiae divinitatis* and *Summa sententiarum*, rather than trying to coordinate it with other modes of framing the issue. It is likewise from the latter two masters that Peter derives his clearly stated distinction among the *sacramentum*, the *res sacramenti*, and the existence of either without the other in the Eucharist. He is closest of all to the *Summa sententiarum* here; for, as with its author, he confines the physical medium to the species of bread and wine, omitting the liturgical rite which the *Sententiae divinitatis* includes in

---

[284] Robert Pullen, *Sent.* 8.7, *PL* 176: 968D–969A. Cf. Ivo of Chartres, *Decretum* 2. c. 27–c. 30, c. 33–c. 51, *PL* 161: 167A–168A, 168B–171A.
[285] Roland of Bologna, *Sent.*, p. 231.
[286] See, for instance, Domenico Bertello, 'La problematica eucaristica in Pier Lombardo," in *Misc. Lomb.*, pp. 149–61.

his definition of the *sacramentum*. As with both of these authors and
with Roland, he sees the *res sacramenti* as having two components,
using the language of the *Sententiae divinitatis* here. This *res* includes
the body and blood of the resurrected Christ, which it signifies and
contains, and the union of Christians in the church. He adds,
qualifying the latter point, that the *societas ecclesiastica* involved is
both the mystical body of Christ and its institutional manifestation,
and that this Christian community includes all those who are
predestined, called, justified, and glorified.[287] This double *res sacramenti*, he adds, is one of the reasons why there are two species in
the physical *sacramentum*. He agrees with the Victorine idea that there
is a similitude between the elements and their sacred *significata*.
The new twist he imparts to this theme is that both the bread and
the wine signify both aspects of the *res sacramenti*. The Eucharistic bread and wine, in Peter's handling of this point, do not stand
for the ministry of the sacrament to different components of the
human constitution. Both severally and together, the two species
nourish the human body, and, in so doing, both species stand for
and transmit Christ's nourishment and support of the human soul.
At the same time, Peter agrees with the widely held idea that the
many grains and grapes that make up the elements stand for the
union of Christians in the society of the church. Another reason, in
his estimation, for the double physical medium, and here Peter
concurs as well with the *Sententiae divinitatis* in particular, is their
Christological symbolism and soteriological effects. Notwithstanding the fact that Christ's body and blood are both fully present
under each species, He provides this mode of sacramental ministry
in the Eucharist in order to show that He assumed both a human
body and a human soul so as to redeem mankind in both body and
soul. In this connection, Peter accepts the idea that the bread
signifies and ministers to the salvation of the body and the wine
signifies and ministers to the salvation of the soul. He agrees with
the Abelardians, and those influenced by them, that the body and
blood of Christ are made available under the species of bread and
wine both as a test of faith and in the light of human sensibilities. In
his teaching here, Peter firmly links concomitance with his ecclesial, soteriological, and Christological agendas alike, as do the
Porretans, Master Simon, the *Sententiae divinitatis*, and the *Summa
sententiarum*, while at the same time connecting the point organically
with the notion of a double *res sacramenti*. Just as this does not make

---

[287] Peter Lombard, *Sent.* 4. d. 8. c. 7, 2: 284–86.

the Eucharist two sacraments in its institution, so concomitance does not mean, for Peter, that the reception of both elements, sequentially, constitutes more than one act of communion.[288]

Peter omits the topic of spiritual communion through the reception of the *res tantum*, concentrating on people who receive, in the normal course of events, the *res sacramenti* by means of the *sacramentum*. But he is fully appreciative of the point that the idea of the *sacramentum tantum* provides a basis for analyzing the differential effects of communion on people who bring different beliefs and intention to the Eucharist. He also extends the notion of the double *res sacramenti* into a broader understanding of what the worthy communicant appropriates. Peter states firmly that the beliefs and intentions of communicants do not alter the objective content of the Eucharist, and criticizes thinkers who, in his estimation, have failed to grasp and to support this principle. Human failings and limitations cannot override what God has decided will happen when the elements are consecrated. What they can do, and here Peter agrees with the *Sententiae divinitatis* and *Summa sententiarum* in their formulation of the issue, is to interfere with the capacity of the recipient to make a spiritual appropriation of that objective content.[289] The recipient must bring to communion both belief in general and belief in the real presence in particular. Also, he must be morally and intentionally in concord with Christ. Peter gives full weight to these subjective considerations as controlling what the recipient derives spiritually from the Eucharist. But he gives more weight to the objectivity of the body and blood of Christ which even the unworthy communicant receives. For Peter, the same *res sacramenti* is received by whoever communicates, but not to the same effect. He is not presenting a view of the objective efficacy of the Eucharist so sweeping that it is internalized the same way by all communicants irrespective of persons. The unworthy, he agrees, receive to their condemnation. As to what the worthy communicant receives, Peter sides with those masters who see both a subjective and an objective, an individual and a corporative, dimension to this question.[290] The masters to whom he comes the closest are Roland of Bologna and the author of the *Summa sententiarum*, but he goes beyond both of

---

[288] Ibid., d. 8. c. 7, d. 10. c. 2.8, d. 11. c. 3–c. 4, c. 6.2, 2: 285–86, 296, 299–300, 303. On the basis of Peter's recognition of the ontological as well as the redemptive and ecclesial significance of the two species, Megivern, *Concomitance and Communion*, pp. 134–38, has rightly stated that, in his hands, the doctrine of concomitance comes of age.

[289] Peter Lombard, *Sent.* 4. d. 12. c. 4.3, 2: 308.

[290] Knoch, *Die Einsetzung*, pp. 233–35. Macy, *Theologies of the Eucharist*, pp.

them. Roland had seen three effects of communion, the engrafting of the recipient into the church, the remission of sin, and the sanctifying gifts of the Holy Spirit. The author of the *Summa sententiarum* had seen the effects of communion as fourfold, the engrafting of the Christian into the church, spiritual renewal, spiritual nourishment, and eternal life. For his part, Peter combines the personal union of the communicant with Christ and with Christ's redemptive ministry with the union of the communicant with his fellow Christians in the church, as a function of the fact that these are the two aspects of the double *res sacramenti* which he receives. As he appropriates these graces in his own inner life, they provide both a spiritual remedy and a means of spiritual growth. The Eucharist, Peter observes, was ordained both to remedy our daily infirmities and to increase our virtue. As a pendant to baptism, the Eucharist remakes us spiritually; it nourishes and redeems us in body and soul; it perfects us in the good. It is not only an augmentation of virtue and grace, but "it is the source and origin of all grace" (*est fons et origo totius gratiae*).[291] Peter's language has as a strongly Victorine coloration here. But, while he certainly underscores the ecclesial dimensions of the effects of communion, he inclines more to the consequences of communion in the recipient's inner life than the *Summa sententiarum* does, and more than Roland does, although, with the latter, he sees these effects as both remedial and perfective.

Another area in which he follows the Hugonian line of argument to a conclusion reflecting Victorine influence which is, none the less, post-Victorine, is the relation of the Eucharist to its pre-Christian parallels. Hugh himself is inclined to grant salvific power more to circumcision than to the Old Testament precursors of other Christian sacraments. When it comes to the paschal lamb, the forerunner of the Eucharist, he is vague on whether it saved the Israelites in more than a political sense.[292] In the next generation, the authors of the *Sententiae divinitatis* and *Summa sententiarum* are more insistent on the point that Old Testament analogies, such as the manna in the desert and the sacrifice of Melchisidech, are *figurae*, which merely foreshadow the Eucharist and do no more.[293] Peter refers to all these types as only pointing ahead to Christ and

---

122–23; and *The Banquet's Wisdom*, p. 90 takes too preclusively ecclesial a line on this point, in our estimation.

[291] Peter Lombard, *Sent.* 4. d. 8. c. 1, c. 7, d. 12. c. 6.1, 2: 280, 284–86, 310. The quotation is at d. 8. c. 1, p. 280.

[292] Hugh of St. Victor, *De sac.* 2.8.5, *PL* 176: 465A.

[293] *Sent. div.* 5.3, p. 120*; *Summa sent.* 6.3, *PL* 176: 139C–D.

to His sacrifice on the cross, which endows the Eucharist with a unique salvific efficacy. He draws here with particular sharpness the distinction between mere sign and efficacious sign which he draws in his definition of sacraments in general. In order to accentuate the supersession of all of these Old Testament prefigurations, he calls the reader's attention to the fact that, while communion is now received fasting, at the Last Supper Christ gave it to His disciples at the end of the Passover meal. This unique circumstance, he notes, is designed to point up both the continuity and the discontinuity between past and present; the recollection of a past, physical, and collective deliverance merges with and is radically transformed into a rite that is not only corporative and commemorative but is also a transfusion of grace that sanctifies and glorifies the soul of the individual communicant in the here and now.[294]

When Peter turns to the conditions validating the consecration of the Eucharist by its minister, he displays considerable independence from the theologians, largely of Victorine provenance, on whom he draws in other areas of Eucharistic doctrine, whether to edit, streamline, refine, or embroider upon their views. In this case Peter sides wholeheartedly with the canonists, repudiating the efforts of most mid-century theologians to admit priests with certain kinds of canonical disqualifications to the Eucharistic ministry. Peter stands foursquare with masters such as Gratian and Roland of Bologna in barring heretics, schismatics, and excommunicates. Heresy of any kind, and not just the failure to believe in the real presence, is an obstacle to valid consecration on the part of the minister just as much as it is to the salvific appropriation of communion on the part of a recipient with the same liability. A heretic, Peter agrees, cannot have the same understanding of the Eucharist as an orthodox priest does, and cannot bring to it the same intention as the church brings. Peter also sees the full cogency of excluding schismatics and excommunicates. Men who are separated from the Christian community cannot act for it. Nor can they draw their congregations into a deeper unity with a church from which they themselves are detached. Here, he affirms both the canonists' conclusions and the rationale behind them. Peter also assents to the principle that the moral failings of a duly ordained

---

[294] Peter Lombard, *Sent.* 4. d. 8. c. 2–c. 3, c. 5, 2: 280–81, 283–84. Here, Peter also reflects the canonical consensus on the reception of the Eucharist fasting; cf. Ivo of Chartres, *Panormia* 1.152, *PL* 161: 1080C; Gratian, *Decretum* pars 3. d. 2. c. 54, col. 1133–34.

priest in good standing canonically are not an impediment, although he gives a somewhat different reason than the canonists do. It is not so much the dignity and authority of holy orders that is the key, for him, as the idea that the efficacy of the sacrament lies in God's power. The human minister plays an essentially in-strumental role; and God will not allow His grace to be impeded by the unworthiness of its intermediaries. Aside from this important shift in emphasis, the other personal nuance Peter gives to this essentially canonical reading of the topic is to distinguish between moral weaknesses that do not affect the priest's capacity to conse-crate the Eucharist validly and sins so heinous that they have resulted in drastic disciplinary action, such as his unfrocking or ejection from the church.[295]

Although, as we have just seen, Peter reflects a generous use of the canonists, especially Gratian, at some points in his Eucharistic theology, there are also some points which concern the canonists, and, to a lesser extent, other theologians of the day, in which he displays no interest. The nocturnal emission of a priest scheduled to celebrate mass the following day is not on his agenda. Nor is the dispensation concerning communion in one kind, by means of the chalice, for the aged, infirm, or moribund as given in the ancient canons and more recently by Paschal II in connection with his renewal of the ban on intinction. Peter certainly supports the contemporary consensus on utraquism and against intinction, but without mentioning these exceptions.[296] Nor does he refer in any way to the argument of the Laon masters and Porretans concerning the communion of infants. Another consensus position he reflects is a disinterest in arguing with Greek Eucharistic practices. Noting that water is added to the chalice to signify the Christian people who are redeemed by Christ's blood, he adds that the Greeks do not do this, but judges that the omission, if it stems from ignorance, does not invalidate the celebration of the Eucharist.[297]

There are two points taken up concerning the Eucharist by some masters in this period on which Peter is less conclusive, or outright dismissive, even though the general orientation he takes toward this sacrament might have suggested another course of action. Along with Robert Pullen and the canonists, he considers the matter of the frequency of communion for the laity. He provides a fuller array of authorities than anyone else does here. In addition to

---

[295] Peter Lombard, *Sent.* 4. d. 13. c. 1–c. 7, 2: 311–14.
[296] Ibid., d. 11. c. 6.2, 2: 303.
[297] Ibid., c. 5, 2: 301–03.

citing the standard rule that Christians should communicate on Christmas, Easter, and Pentecost, to which he adds, on his own account, at the very least, he brings in the position, ascribed to Augustine although it is actually the view of Gennadius, recommending communion every Sunday. Like Robert Pullen, he declines to take an overt stand of his own on this issue, and emphasizes that the essential point is to receive worthily.[298] Still, the logic of his handling of the topic is to suggest the desirability of frequent communion, a conclusion which, had he articulated it more decisively, would certainly have been in harmony with his general inclination to encourage Christians to avail themselves of the benefits of sacramental grace as much as they can, or as much as they need. Perhaps even more surprising, given Peter's keen interest in the speculative issues surrounding the defense of the real presence doctrine and his own clear statement that the body and blood of Christ do not depart from the consecrated species when they are received by a communicant whose unworthiness prevents him from appropriating the grace of the sacrament in a fruitful and salvific way, is his handling of the question *quid sumit mus*. Peter can evidently compass the idea that the objective content of the Eucharist may be appropriated, or not, depending on the status of the human recipient. But he regards the extension of this state of affairs to a mouse as an entirely frivolous question. His response to it is: "What does the mouse receive? What does it eat? God knows!" (*Quid ergo sumit mus? quid manducat? Deus novit*).[299] This effort to dismiss the problem, even though, in principle, like Roland and the authors of the *Sententiae divinitatis* and *Summa sententiarum*, he has the means at hand to resolve it, did not prove determinative, either in the middle of the twelfth century or in the sequel, when a fresh supply of philosophical and scientific analysis would be brought to bear upon it.

The unwillingness or inability of Peter and some of the masters best equipped to do so to engage themselves with the last-mentioned question is a reminder of the fact that the more speculative aspects of Eucharistic theology were less amenable to principled resolution in the 1150s than was the case with other problem areas in which this sacrament provoked debate. Even the most philosophically minded of the theologians recognized that the conceptual resources available to them were adequate to do no more

---

[298] Ibid., d. 12. c. 6.2, 2: 310–11.
[299] Ibid., d. 13. c. 1.8, 2: 314. See Macy, "Of Mice and Manna," p. 160.

than to pose the questions connected with the real presence doctrine
clearly, but that they were not adequate to provide a resolution
of those questions or a comprehensible rationale for the mys-
teries they embody. Peter's contribution in bringing this idea to
consciousness is most notable in connection with the account of the
change in the elements. Neither he nor anyone else in this period
was able to articulate, with a similar degree of lucidity, the physical
and metaphysical difficulties embedded in the questions of which
body Christ gave to His disciples at the Last Supper and *quid sumit
mus*. In other areas of Eucharistic theology, Peter takes a stance
that is highly selective. He agrees with the consensus, or majority,
positions on the institution of the Eucharist, the real presence,
concomitance, communion in both kinds sequentially, and the idea
that the unbelieving or unworthy recipient receives to his damnation. When it comes to the conditions that validate the consecration
of the Eucharist, he sides unhesitatingly with the canonists in
rejecting the efforts of other theologians to make the rules more
flexible. He finds it perfectly reasonable to rule out heretic,
schismatic, and excommunicate priests, although, in admitting the
validity of the Eucharistic ministry of immoral priests, he accents
the instrumentality, and not the authority, of the priest in this
context. Concerning the reception of the Eucharist, what makes for
its efficacious appropriation, and what, indeed, is appropriated
when the communicant receives worthily, Peter concurs with the
idea of the double *res sacramenti* found in Roland of Bologna, the
Sententiae divinitatis, and the *Summa sententiarum*, which he understands as the personal and the ecclesiological dimensions of the
sacrament. The personal appropriations are the ones that he
emphasizes the most heavily. In so doing, he combines an appreciation of the subjective dispositions which the communicant needs
to bring to the sacrament if it is to do its work of healing and
sanctifying in him with a heightened sense of the objectivity of the
content of the sacrament, which remains present in the physical
elements received by the unworthy communicant as well, although
he does not appropriate them. Peter's conviction that man lacks the
power to thwart God in blocking access to the sacramental grace
which God institutes and administers through the Eucharist is thus
coupled with his equally clear conviction that man can and must
dispose himself, in belief and attitude, so that he can make spiritual
use of this grace in his own inner life. Above all, Peter accentuates
the positive. He is far more interested in how the effect and the
affect of this sacrament of sacraments can be realized in the bonding of members of the Christian community and, even more so, in

the sanctification and perfection of individual Christians, than he is in discussing impediments or conditions that would deactivate or delegitimize it.

Penance

Penance was a sacrament that also attracted considerable attention in the early twelfth century. Both the administration and the theological understanding of this sacrament had undergone substantial change since the days of the early church.[300] Penance had originally been viewed as a single, solemn, public event, one that was unrepeatable during the penitent's lifetime, and one that required heavy and protracted satisfaction before he could be restored to communion. In the spread of Christianity to the Germanic and Celtic peoples during the early Middle Ages, private confession was introduced and penances remained lengthy and heavy. Up until the late eleventh century, the fact that those performing satisfaction were visibly distinct within the community led to a tendency to regard the completion of satisfaction as the point at which the penitent's sins were remitted. The early twelfth century witnessed a shift in the way in which penance was understood and practiced. Penances became much lighter; public, solemn confession became the exception not the rule; and attention shifted to the intention of the penitent and the role of the sacrament in his spiritual growth and development. With this, the idea that penance was an unrepeatable sacrament came under sharp attack and was demolished. Prior to this time, writers on penance had approached it from a polemical perspective, or from the standpoint of the practical guidelines for its administration and the appropriate satisfactions to be required for particular sins. In the formulation of a theology of penance, to all intents and purposes for the first time in the history of the western church, the masters before and during Peter Lombard's generation were not only expressing the need to systematize this subject and to coordinate it with what they had to say on the sacraments in general. They also wrote in order to

---

[300] Good general overviews are provided by Paul Anciaux, *La théologie du sacrement de pénitence au XIIe siècle* (Louvain: É. Nauwelaerts, 1949), pp. 164–231, 329–35; Polycarp Schmoll, *Die Busslehre der Frühscholastik: Eine dogmengeschichtliche Untersuchung* (Munich: J. J. Lentnerschen Buchhandlung, 1909), pp. 3–14, 18–74; Amédée Teetaert, *La confession aux laïques dans l'église latine depuis le VIIIe jusqu'au XIVe siècle: Étude de théologie positive* (Wetteren: J. De Meester et Fils, 1926), pp. 1–101. This last-mentioned work covers much more than what is indicated by its title.

rationalize the changes from the ancient and more recent practice which penance was actually undergoing in their own century. While there existed a good deal of consensus on the idea that this was the contemporary agenda on penance, there were still two broad areas of disagreement. One was on the best kind of argument to be made for the repeatability of penance and for the principle that, if a sin were repeated, it could be remitted again, as needed, by this sacrament. The other debate focused on when, in the three-part process of contrition, confession, and satisfaction inherited from Augustine and Gregory the Great, the penitent's sin was remitted. In both of these areas, canonists and theologians sometimes came to the same conclusions, and relied on each other's work. Yet, even on occasions when this was the case, their ways of conceptualizing the common problems they faced were often quite different. In addition, the study of penance in this period reveals a geographical differentiation between the practices of the Roman and the Gallican churches. The latter church was swifter in setting aside ancient practices. The question of where a master taught in this period and which theory and practice of penance he was most familiar with is thus, on occasion, a factor that he may bring to bear on the finding of his own solutions to the debated questions on penance.

The fact that canonists and theologians, even when they agreed on the need to rationalize the changes that penitential practice was undergoing in their own day, tended to do so in ways reflecting their respective guild mentalities is well illustrated in the first debate, on the repeatability of penance, and the associated question of the reviviscence of sins.[301] Like the theologians, the canonists are advocates of change here, and seek to make the remedy provided in the sacrament of penance more generally available to Christians.[302] They are well aware of the ancient strictures banning the repetition of penance and confining it to a single, solemn penance. They are equally familiar with the ancient argument that, if a person commits the same kind of sin for which he did penance earlier, this proves that his earlier penance was hypocritical and he cannot be forgiven again. Gratian does not shrink from listing the authorities

---

[301] For a survey of contemporary views on the reviviscence of sins and the repeatability of penance, see Landgraf, *Dogmengeschichte*, 4 part 1: 195–228; Joseph de Ghellinck, "La réviviscence des péchés pardonnés à l'époque de Pierre Lombard et Gandulphe de Bologne," *Nouvelle Revue Théologique* 41 (1909): 400–08, although the latter paper is not a reliable guide to Gratian's position.

[302] The best study of this motive in twelfth-century sacramental theology is

who support these ancient policies. He thinks they are wrong. In his view, penance should be available as often as it is needed, since human vices do not get eradicated all at once. If the same kind of sin recurs, he maintains, it should be confessed and forgiven. Gratian's tactic in defending this position against the authorities on the other side of the issue is a twofold one. In the first place, he uses countercitation. Penance is not a subject on which he thinks he can find a middle ground or on which he tries to harmonize irreconcilable opinions. He cites the anti-Donatist Augustine as his main weapon against the opposition. In attacking this sect, Gratian notes, Augustine had defined penance as the method of handling post-baptismal sin, in order to refute the Donatist idea that rebaptism could be used to deal with it. In this particular instance, then, Augustine had contrasted penance, as a repeatable sacrament, with baptism, as an unrepeatable one. Augustine thus comes in very useful as a means of undermining the ancient rules and their supporters, who include Augustine himself, writing in other contexts. In Gratian's hands, the rejection of the repeatability of penance becomes tantamount to a belief in Donatism, or in the idea that one cannot fall from grace once having received it. This line of argument, as we will see below, attracted theologians as well as canonists. Far more indicative of his canonical mentality is Gratian's conclusion that, although the ancient tradition is wrong, for the reasons he has given, the existing rules should still remain on the books. But they should not be enforced, on grounds of charity. This recourse to the principle of dispensation from the rules, rather than the outright abandoning of the rules and their replacement by new ones, is a hallmark of the canonists' caution with respect to past precedents.[303] Roland of Bologna shows an analogous kind of caution, in connection with local custom. Agreeing entirely with Gratian on the desirability of repeated penance, he notes that there is a difference between the Gallican church and "us," that is, the Roman church, on the repeatability of penance. The Italians adhere to the hard line on the practice of only a single, solemn, public penance. While his own reasoning would support the idea that the practice followed north of the Alps should be extended to the whole church, Roland shrinks from advocating an institutional revamping of the Roman practice.[304]

Häring, "The Augustinian Axiom," pp. 87–117.

[303] Gratian, *Decretum* pars 2. d. 2. c. 1–c. 20, d. 3. c. 1–d. 4. c. 24, col. 1189–97, 1211–38.

[304] Roland of Bologna, *Sent.*, pp. 237–43, 249–51.

For their part, the theologians display no such hesitations. They feel perfectly free to reject out of hand the ancient tradition as fundamentally incompatible with the purposes for which penance was instituted. Yet, there are a number of ways in which they defend this common conviction. The members of the school of Laon, convinced, with Gregory the Great, that the cure of souls is the art of arts (*ars artium est regimen animarum*) and that pastoral need requires the repeatability of penance, invoke the principle of historical criticism as a basis for overturning the traditional rules. Back in the time of the primitive church, they note, the idea of a single, solemn, public penance may have made good pastoral sense. In those days, only the truly committed risked membership in the church. The early Christians, moreover, were largely adult converts. The single, solemn, public penance was a useful device for putting the fear of the Lord (*propter incutiendem terrorum*) into new Christians who might think they could join the church without true moral conversion. But, nowadays, the situation is a different one. The church is no longer a community of zealots. The current needs of real, and fallible, Christians have to be taken into account, lest people fall into despair. The abandoning of the old practice is thus a real and relevant desideratum. It is now better to rule that penance should be received as often as people sin (*item salubriter provisam est ut quotiens peccarent totiens ad penitentiam recipirentur*). Each of the rules, the old rule to be set aside and the new rule to be observed in its place, is suitable to the conditions of its own time (*suo tempore congruum est*). The Laon masters also see that private penance can be invoked to circumvent the old rule. If a person has already done public penance for a serious sin, his subsequent penances for subsequent sins can be done in private.[305] This pressure to change the rules, in the estimation of the Laon masters, stems from the necessity of penance for salvation,[306] given the present membership of the church and its pastoral requirements.

Historical criticism is not the only tack that a theologian in accord with this conclusion may take. Hugh of St. Victor offers a different rationale for rejecting the unrepeatability of penance. He combines a cogent appeal to reason with an exegetically based attack on the opposition. Once a person does penance for a sin, he

---

[305] *Sentences of Plausible Authenticity*, no. 200; *Sentences of the School of Laon*, no. 383, 385–87, 5: 134, 280, 282–83. The first quotation is at no. 383, p. 280; the others are at no. 200, p. 134. See also *Sent. Anselmi* 8, pp. 122–23.
[306] *Sentences of the School of Laon*, no. 363, 5: 272.

observes, it is forgiven and God does not tax him with it again. But, a person can commit the same kind of sin again. This is not the same act of sin that he committed and repented of earlier, Hugh stresses, but a different, if analogous, event. Consequently, the penitent can repent and be pardoned again. When this happens, neither the sincerity of the penitent nor the mercy of God on the first occasion needs to be called into question. This being the case, how, Hugh asks, did the ancient fathers make the error in judgment that led them to the imposition of the rule declaring that penance was unrepeatable? Hugh's technique for exposing this error is the countercitation of authorities, all deriving from the Bible, in order to show that the opposition's view is founded on an incorrect understanding of Holy Scripture. While his basic motive is certainly the desire not to limit the occasions of divine mercy in the lives of Christians, his tactic is to put the debate on an exegetical foundation, and one that can be subsumed by the principle that the Bible cannot be read correctly if it is read so as to undercut God's goodness and His wish to redeem and to sanctify mankind.[307]

The author of the *Sententiae divinitatis* provides yet another kind of argument in support of the new twelfth-century consensus position, an argument by definition. He cites as his definition of penance one derived from Augustine and Gregory and one widely held at this time. Penance, he states, is sorrow for past sin and the sincere desire not to commit it again. This sincere desire is laudable; but human beings are fallible. Since people can and do sin again, they can and do repent again. Thus, by its very nature as defined, penance is repeatable. Its repetition does not obviate the sincerity of an earlier penance. Further, the master warns sternly, the opinion of those who reject this conclusion is impious and merciless (*impia et immisericors sententia ista*). As with the members of the school of Laon, he invokes private penance as a remedy for fresh outbreaks of repentance, although he draws a different distinction than they do between public and private penance. It is not the intrinsic seriousness of the sin that mandates public penance, in his view, but the fact that sin so remedied has social implications or has given public scandal. In contrast, private penance can be used, repeatedly, for sins that affect only the sinner himself, whether the sin is major or minor. The master does not have a recommendation, however, on how to deal with renewed occasions when sins having a public impact need to be repented, since he retains the

---

[307] Hugh of St. Victor, *De sac.* 2.14.4, 2.14.9, *PL* 176: 556C–559D, 570C–578A.

rule that public penance can be performed only once.[308]

The author of the *Summa sententiarum* takes still another line of attack, and one, perhaps, that is less persuasive than the aggressive appeals to pastoral need, history, exegetical accuracy, and the nature of penance as such made by the masters just mentioned. His approach is to try to relativize the force of the prohibition of the repeatability of penance by asserting that the authorities who advocate that position were referring only to public penance. He ignores the fact that they may have been writing before private penance had been developed as a substitute for public penance, or as a simultaneous option. In his estimation, this reading of the anti-repeatability authorities clears the field for the defense of repeated private penance, although the master offers no positive rationale for that practice.[309] Other masters simply reiterate the conclusions that can be drawn from all the above arguments for the repeatability of penance, without developing a rationale for it, as if the position were in no need of support.[310]

The second major debate concerning penance in our period, and it is one involving the substance of the doctrine and not just the tactics of argument adopted to defend a particular mode of administration, concerns the question of when, in the standard three-part event embracing contrition, confession, and satisfaction, the sins of the penitent are remitted. Here, the terrain was divided between the contritionists and the confessionists. The canonists were inclined to take the confessionist position and the theologians the contritionist one, but the battle lines were not drawn hard and fast and, as we will see, there were some masters on both sides who broke ranks.[311] There are, to be sure, masters who ignore this

---

[308] *Sent. div.* 5.4, pp. 142*–44*, 148*–51*. The quotation is on p. 143*. Other authors who give the same definition of penance include Ivo of Chartres, *Decretum*, 15. c. 1, *PL* 161: 857C; Peter Abelard, *Ethics*, p. 76; *Sent. mag. Gisleberti* II 10.65, pp. 85–86; Master Simon, *De sac.*, p. 22. Master Simon, ibid., pp. 22–24 agrees that public penance is not repeatable but that private penance is, although without taking up the reviviscence of sins.

[309] *Summa sent.* 6.12, *PL* 176: 149B–150C.

[310] Thus the *Ysagoge in theologiam*, p. 207; *Sent. mag. Gisleberti* II 10.63–64, p. 85; Robert Pullen, *Sent.* 5.41, 6.24, *PL* 186: 847C–D, 862D–863A. Knoch, *Die Einsetzung*, pp. 196–97 misinterprets Robert here.

[311] An extensive and excellent survey of this debate is provided by Anciaux, *La théologie du sacrement de la pénitence*, pp. 164–223. Briefer but still useful are Francesco Carpino, "Consensi e critiche ad una teoria sull'assoluzione sacramentale nel sec. XII," *La Scuola Cattolica* 67 (1939): 308–21; "Un tentativo al secolo XII per valorizzare l'assoluzione sacramentale," *La Scuola Cattolica* 66 (1938): 281–98; Jean Gaudemet, "Le débat sur la confession dans la Distinction 1 du "de penitentia" (Décret de Gratian, C. 33, q. 3)," *Zeitschrift der Savigny-Stiftung für Rechtsgeschichte*,

debate, noting merely that the sacrament has these three parts and venturing no opinion on which of them is of the essence in the remission of sin. In this category we can find Honorius Augustodunensis, and Ivo of Chartres.[312] As the century progressed, however, the only writer on the sacraments who manages to ignore this question is Master Simon. Gratian takes a commanding lead in the elaboration of the confessionist view. He is important here not only for the classic rendition of this position which he provides, but also for the elaborate dossier of authorities pro and con which he assembles, material on which other masters draw whether they agree with him or not. After his exhaustive review of the evidence, Gratian concludes that the authorities supporting contritionism have made a good case, but only up to a point. They are useful in rebutting a totally unqualified confessionist line that would ignore, or undervalue, the penitent's attitude, while placing the emphasis purely on the external acts of confession and the completion of satisfaction. This pure confessionism Gratian rejects as too mechanical. He asserts that true contrition is necessary if penance is going to be efficacious and fruitful. But, if it is a necessary step, contrition is only the first step. It is required but, for Gratian, it is not sufficient. In particular, it is in the confession stage of the sacrament that he locates the moment when the penitent's sins are remitted, at the point when the priest pronounces the words of absolution. As for the satisfaction, it may be public or private, depending on whether the sins confessed were confessed in public or in private. The distinction Gratian draws here combines the criteria given by the Laon masters and the author of the *Sententiae divinitatis*. Public penance is reserved for serious sins that affect others; while private penance is for lesser sins that affect only the penitent. Both types of sins, Gratian stresses, need to be confessed. Confession perfects the sacrament which contrition initiates. It is mandatory, otherwise the power of the keys vested in the priesthood would be frustrated. Further, refusal to confess is a sign of pride that compounds the penitent's existing moral problems and

---

kanonistische Abteilung 71 (1985): 54–56; Landgraf, *Dogmengeschichte*, 3 part 2: 244–45, 264–65, 273; 4 part 1: 275–99; Longère, *Oeuvres oratoires*, 1: 257–58; Jean Charles Payen, "La pénitence dans le contexte culturel des XIIe et XIIIe siècles: Des doctrines contritionistes aux pénitentiels vernaculaires," *RSPT* 61 (1977): 399–428; Joseph A. Spitzig, *Sacramental Penance in the Twelfth and Thirteenth Centuries* (Washington: Catholic University of America Press, 1947), pp. 38–67.

[312] Honorius, *Eluc.* 2.72, p. 432; Ivo of Chartres, *Decretum* 2. c. 71, *PL* 161: 857C–902A.

indicates that his contrition is insincere. Confession, Gratian concludes, is, to be sure, first offered to God in contrition. But it must
also be offered, orally, to a priest. Appreciative as Gratian is of the
need for a truly contrite disposition in the penitent, he holds that
penance, in order to be ratified and perfected, must be carried from
the internal forum of conscience to an external, judicial forum. The
penitent's placement of himself under the judgment of the priest is
necessary for him, if he wants his sins to be remitted. It is also
necessary for the church, in its guarantee of the proper exercise of
priestly authority, both in the priest's loosing of the penitent's sin with
the words of absolution and in his assigning of the satisfaction.[313]

This argument requires Gratian to make the claim that the
contritionist authorities are not talking about contrition as the
point when the forgiveness of sins occurs, although that is precisely
what they are in fact doing, but merely about contrition as the
sacrament's necessary but not sufficient first step, as he holds it to
be. This is the way in which he seeks to adjust their view to the
confessionist position that he, and the confessionist authorities as
moderated by his analysis, maintain. Gratian's technique here
involves the same sort of creative misreading of authorities as what
we have found in the *Sententiae divinitatis* on the repeatability of
penance. This manhandling of the sources forces them into alignment with the largely institutional view of penance which Gratian
presents.[314] It is the legitimate exercise of the priestly power of the
keys that is foremost in his defense of the necessity and centrality of
confession, not the moral education of the penitent. This emphasis
is reflected in a range of other topics which Gratian takes up à
propos of penance, which likewise view it from the standpoint of the
minister of the sacrament, not the recipient. He devotes a good deal
of attention in this connection to how priests should administer
penance, whether, if they are penitents themselves, they should
hear the confessions of others—a question which, in its very formulation, suggests that Gratian has not fully emancipated himself
from the idea that penance means the completion of satisfaction—
and how to deal with a penitent who the priest suspects of making a
hypocritical confession or who tries to buy absolution by bribing
the priest. Gratian also has urgent words of support for the princi-

[313] Gratian, *Decretum* pars 2. d. 1. c. 87–c. 89, col. 1181–89. Good accounts are
found in A. Debil, "La première distinction du De poenitentia de Gratien," *RHE*
15 (1914): 251–73, 442–55; Gaudemet, "Le débat," pp. 54–56.
[314] Gratian's handling, or mishandling, of the contritionist authorities is ana-
lyzed fully by Gaudemet, "Le débat," pp. 52–75.

ple that the seal of confession must be respected at all costs. The defense of this principle, in his estimation, requires the deposition of a priest whose ability to maintain confidentiality is compromised. Finally, penance, for Gratian, can and should be administered up to the point of death; and priests should not fail, in their ordained responsibility as the ministers of penitential absolution, to hear the confessions of the moribund.[315] In all these areas, as well as in his stress on confession as the point in the sacrament of penance when the penitent's moral state is determined, Gratian emphasizes the institutional, sacerdotal side of the transaction.

This point of view is quite typical of the canonists, both before and after Gratian. Alger of Liège also takes a strongly confessionist line, stressing that it is the priest who has the power to forgive sin, to loose and to bind, an authority he possesses *ex officio*, regardless of his personal merits.[316] Roland of Bologna summarizes Gratian's argument and refines it slightly. He devotes attention to the charity and lack of dissimulation that must inform the contrition which begins the process of penance. While the penitent's guilt (*culpa*) is remitted in contrition, in his view, Roland agrees that confession and satisfaction are sure signs (*certa signa*) of that state and that it is they that remit the temporal punishment due for sin. Contrition alone would suffice only in cases of necessity where confession and satisfaction are impossible. Otherwise, time permitting, both are required. When we sin, Roland observes, we sin against both God and the church. Thus, when we repent, we must satisfy both, God by our contrition and the church by our auricular confession and satisfaction. While Roland grants more attention to contrition than Gratian does, his outlook, if marginally less clericalist, is equally institutional.[317]

Not all of the masters in the first half of the twelfth century who concur with Gratian's confessionism are fellow canonists. Among the theologians, both Robert Pullen and the author of the *Summa sententiarum* offer strong support for this position. With Gratian, they argue that all three steps are required for penance to be real penance. Sincere contrition, in which none of the penitent's sins are held back, begins the process and is a critical factor in his capacity to make moral progress by means of this sacrament. But the decisive moment, at which his sins are forgiven, occurs when the

---

[315] Gratian, *Decretum* pars 1. d. 50, pars 2. d. 5–d. 7, col. 178–203, 1236–47.

[316] Alger of Liège, *De misericordia* 1.64–65, pp. 237–38.

[317] Roland of Bologna, *Sent.*, pp. 343–49; *Summa* c. 33. q. 3, pp. 193–94. Schmoll, *Die Busslehre*, pp. 249–51 depicts Roland as more of a contritionist than he is.

priest pronounces the words of absolution following the penitent's oral confession. Following Anselm of Laon here, Robert states that the worthy celebration of this rite demands absolution (*quoniam in ipsa digne celebrata peccatorum est absolutio*). Further, taking a firmly clericalist line, both masters insist on the right and duty of the priest to impose satisfaction. Robert acknowledges the fact that the confessor may be delinquent and fail to do so. The *Summa sententiarum* adds that the confessor may lack good judgment and may impose an unsuitable satisfaction, noting as well that the penitent may neglect to do or to complete the satisfaction that he does impose, whether it is appropriate or not. If so, additional time in Purgatory will be required of the penitent by God so that the deficiency can be remedied. The only exception to the need for confession and satisfaction, in Robert's eyes, is martyrdom, or the case of the good thief on the cross, on the analogy with baptism by desire and baptism by blood.[318]

Likewise, not all of the canonists are confessionists. Paucapalea, the earliest commentator on Gratian, whose work dates to the years between 1144 and 1150, takes the point about contrition being sufficient in emergencies and contrition being the moment when God removes the penitent's *culpa* also found in Roland of Bologna and develops it into a defense of contritionism that does not square with Gratian's position.[319] Without repeating the thoroughgoing analysis of the confessionist authorities on whom Gratian bases his own solution, he summarizes the contritionists' arguments and presents his own view as a logical inference from them. While he does not seem particularly comfortable with the conclusions he draws, he presents them as a position which he can find no way of refuting or relativizing, being unwilling, evidently, to make use of Gratian's own strategy of argument here.

Indeed, discomfort with the logical corollaries of contritionism can also be found in some of the most ardent defenders of that

---

[318] Robert Pullen, *Sent.* 5.30–31, 6.52–53, 6.59–61, 7.1–5, *PL* 186: 851D–853C, 902B–904D, 908C–912C, 911C–913A. The quotation is at 6.61, 912C. Schmoll, *Die Busslehre*, pp. 60–64 presents Robert as offering a more balanced view than he does. See also *Summa sent.* 6.10, 6.13–14. *PL* 176: 146D–147B, 152A–153A. Cf. *Sentences of Anselm of Laon*, no. 64, 5: 57, where it is stated that forgiveness of sins does not occur "nisi per ministros ecclesie solvitur." On Anselm, see Francesco Carpino, "Una difficoltà contro la confessione nella scolastica primitiva: Anselmo di Laon e la sua scuola," *Divus Thomas* ser. 3ª, 16 (1939): 94–103.

[319] Paucapalea, *Summa über das Decretum Gratiani*, ed. Johann Friedrich von Schulte (Aalen: Scientia Verlag, 1965 [repr. of Giessen, 1890 ed.]), p. 132. For the dating of this text, see Schulte's intro., pp. viii–x.

position. What troubles them is the fact that they are hesitant to dismiss the desirability of confession and satisfaction. But they face real difficulties in trying to explain why these steps in the sacrament should be retained, given their conviction that the contrition stage is when the penitent is forgiven by God. Proponents of contritionism deal with this problem more or less cogently. The members of the school of Laon are a good index of the unsuccessful effort to resolve this dilemma. In general, they find Anselm of Laon's position unacceptable. It is the intention of the penitent that they accent. What inspires God to remit his sin is his true sorrow for sin and for having offended God. If, after having been released from his sin on account of such true contrition, the penitent fails to proceed to confession and satisfaction, God does not withdraw the forgiveness He has already given; nor does God grant it conditionally.[320] But, side by side with this assertion that contrition is sufficient in the eyes of God, the Laon masters make other statements suggesting the opposite. Noting that, when we sin, we sin in thought, word, and deed, and so we must do penance in thought, word, and, deed, they also say that, while contrition provides the cleansing (*ablutio*), God does not actually remit the sin until the penitent is absolved by the priest.[321] Another member of the school makes the equally confusing observation that, while the confession made to God in the contrite penitent's soul purges sin, it remains for the priest to teach how this sin is to be purged.[322] At the same time, one can find points made by the Laon masters suggesting adherence to the opinion that penance can be defined as satisfaction, that it is the works done under this heading that rise to God as an evening sacrifice, and that a penitent has not truly repented and is not to be given communion until the yoke of satisfaction has been lifted from his shoulders.[323]

Hugh of St. Victor manifests some of the same kinds of inconsistency and self-contradiction as we have just seen in the school of Laon, a fact reflected in the inability of modern scholars to decide whether he is a contritionist or a confessionist, or something in between.[324] On the one hand, he presents the contritionists as

---

[320] *Sentences of the School of Laon*, no. 383, 5: 280–81.

[321] *Sent. Anselmi* 8, pp. 121–25; *Sentences of the School of Laon*, no. 64, 363, 389, 5: 56–57, 272–73, 280.

[322] *Sentences of the School of Laon*, no. 199, 5: 134.

[323] *Sentences of the School of Laon*, no. 384, 385–88, 5: 281, 281–82. Knoch, *Die Einsetzung*, pp. 58–61 does not appreciate these inconsistencies.

[324] Carpino, "Un tentativo," pp. 281–95 presents Hugh as a would-be confessionist; Knoch, Die *Einsetzung*, pp. 103–09 sees him as a full-fledged confessionist;

people seeking to avoid the biblical injunction to confess sins, one to another, and as thinkers who have abandoned patristic as well as apostolic authority. Yet, in his own treatment of penance, he distinguishes between interior and exterior penance. The first is the grief and sorrow for sin and the firm purpose of amendment. Interior penance, for Hugh, is penance proper. Exterior penance is its fruit, and works to correct the sin. Hugh sees exterior penance as satisfaction, omitting confession here, and states that the satisfaction is not penance proper. Having made that point, he next asks what happens to people who do not complete their penance in this life, thus equating penance with satisfaction. The scenario he has in mind is not that of a person whose completion of satisfaction is cut off by death but rather that of a person given an inadequate satisfaction by an imprudent confessor. Hugh's response is that God will not tax this penitent with the inadequacies of his priest. Anyway, leftover satisfaction can be dealt with in Purgatory.[325] After pausing to discuss other aspects of the sacrament, Hugh returns to this issue later in the same section of the *De sacramentis*. There, he asserts that what is efficacious in penance is repentance, not satisfaction. To be sure, a good will seeks to express itself in good deeds. But, should the good deeds be thwarted or incomplete, the good will suffices, and it is on this basis that God judges the penitent. In addressing the question of when, in the penitential process, the remission of sin occurs, he ventilates both sides of the debate and takes what he tries to present as a compromise view, which has the effect of muddying the waters. With the contritionists, he states that it is contrition which is efficacious. Also, he points out, it is God Who forgives, not the priest. But, as in all sacraments, so here as well God has chosen to use physical means as channels of His grace. In this case, God associates Himself with the ministry of the priest, and the forgiveness He grants is given through the words of absolution spoken by the priest. Further, satisfaction must be done, in Hugh's estimation, even though he has stated that it is not the sacrament proper. The necessity of satisfaction is offered to buttress the argument for the necessity of confession, as the point at which sin is forgiven officially. The exchange between the penitent and the confessor reflects the penitent's humility, good faith, and willingness to undertake satisfaction. It also provides the occasion for the priestly exercise of the

Schmoll, *Die Busslehre*, pp. 47–57 argues that he is a contritionist. None of these authors notes Hugh's inconsistencies.

[325] Hugh of St. Victor, *De sac.* 2.14.1–3, *PL* 176: 549D–556C.

power of the keys. The priest not only absolves, assigns satisfaction, and counsels the penitent; Hugh presents him also as interceding with God on the penitent's behalf, persuading God to forgive the sinner in addition to persuading the sinner to repent. Here, Hugh neglects to note that, at this point in the process, by his own account, the penitent no longer needs to be so persuaded. And, having ordained this mode of remedy for post-baptismal sin, neither does God.[326] This effort at finding a middle road between confessionism and contritionism thus emerges as a non-solution, rather than as a coherent and viable compromise between those two positions.

Judging from his overall stance on the role of intentionality in ethics, and in sacraments such as baptism, we are not surprised to find in Peter Abelard a staunch defender of contritionism. What is surprising in his handling of penance is his unwillingness, or inability, to press or even to follow the logic of his own position.[327] As with the author of the *Sententiae divinitatis*, he states that contrition is the very definition of this sacrament; penance is nothing other than the sorrow for sin in the penitent's mind. Furthermore, and here Abelard opposes the school of Laon, Robert Pullen, and the author of the *Summa sententiarum*, who allow that *timor initialis*, or fear of eternal punishment, can be an acceptable trigger to contrition, at least if it leads to love of God as the penitent's motive, Abelard asserts that, in order for contrition to be fruitful, contrition must stem from the love of God and the hatred of sin because it offends God, and not in any sense from the fear of punishment. If that state of contrition is present, for Abelard, God grants the remission of sin: "In the sigh of inner repentance inspired by charity we are instantly reconciled to God for our past sins" (*In hoc statim gemitu Dei reconciliamur et precedentis venium assequimur*).[328] Abelard follows up

---

[326] Ibid., 2.14.6–8, *PL* 176: 560C–570C.

[327] Abelard's inconsistencies on penance have been noted by Schmoll, *Die Busslehre*, pp. 28–35; Sikes, *Peter Abailard*, pp. 196–200; Weingart, "Abailard's Contribution," pp. 173–77; *The Logic of Divine Love*, pp. 197–200; Amédée de Zedelghem. "L'Attritionisme d'Abélard," *Estudis Franciscans* 35 (1925): 178–84, 333–45.

[328] Peter Abelard, *Ethics*, p. 76; the translation is Luscombe's, p. 77. On this point, see Amédée de Zedelghem, "Doctrine d'Abélard au sujet de la valeur morale de la crainte des peines," *Estudis Franciscans* 36 (1926): 108–25. For the countervailing position on fear in the masters he opposes, see *Sentences of the School of Laon*, no. 383, 5: 280–81; Robert Pullen, *Sent.* 5.30–31, *PL* 186: 851D–853C; *Summa sent.* 6.10, *PL* 176: 146C–D. In agreement with Abelard on this point we find not only disciples of his such as Hermannus, *Sent.*, pp. 156–57 but also Master Simon, *De sac.*, pp. 24–25.

this forthright assertion of contritionism with the point that, since contrition involves a complete inner reorientation toward the good, one cannot be forgiven if he retains any unacknowledged sins on his conscience, a consensus position. The forgiveness applies to the remission of the eternal punishment due for sin, but not to the temporal punishment. This claim establishes why satisfaction is needed and provides Abelard with the occasion to observe, as other masters do, that a person who dies before completing his satisfaction is detained in Purgatory on that account.[329]

It is not, however, the relations between contrition and satisfaction but the relations between contrition and confession where the real, and perceived, problems lie in Abelard's doctrine of penance. Despite the clarity and force of his contritionist claims, Abelard wants to argue that confession is still necessary, even though the penitent's sin has already been forgiven before he speaks to the priest. It must be said that, notwithstanding his reputation as a logician, Abelard is aware of the difficulties he imposes on himself in seeking to make confession mandatory, and he makes heavy weather of his argument here, jumping from one idea to another in a kind of scatter-gun effort to distract the reader from the logical insufficiency of any of the claims he makes. There is a pastoral argument for confession, he notes: the prayers of the confessor will assist the penitent. There is an argument for the moral education of the penitent: the knowledge that we have to confess our sins may serve as a deterrent to sin, for going to confession is difficult and embarrassing. In this sense, the act of confessing is part of the satisfaction. Moving to an ecclesiastical argument, Abelard notes that priests have the right and duty to impose satisfaction, and penitents have the duty to accept correction.[330]

This last-mentioned observation leads Abelard to a discussion of the power of the keys, where he gets even more deeply ensnared in contradicitions which he recognizes and shrinks from resolving. Having noted the penitent's duty to accept correction, Abelard asks what one should do if one cannot find a confessor who is religious, discreet, and trustworthy, and who is intelligent enough to impose a suitable satisfaction and to counsel the penitent effectively. This is by no means a frivolous question. Abelard's posing of it here reflects the fact that, the Gregorian reforms notwithstanding, the improvement in the quality of clergymen at which they aimed was

---

[329] Peter Abelard, *Ethics*, pp. 76–98.
[330] Ibid., pp. 98–100.

being outpaced by the rising expectations of the Christian people to whom these clerics ministered. Having aired this real and vexing question, Abelard says that, even if a good priest cannot be found, one should go to confession anyhow. Agreeing with Hugh here, he states that God will not charge the failings of His ministers to the penitent's account. Listing in some detail, and even with some relish, the assorted sacerdotal shortcomings which penitents may encounter in the practice of confession, he still insists that they are not excuses for refusing to confess to an unworthy priest, even though this conclusion is incompatible with the educational and pastoral benefits which the penitent is supposed to derive from the encounter.[331] With respect to the power of the keys on the priest's side of the transaction, Abelard argues that, in penance, the role of the priest is not to loose and bind, on the grounds that it is God Who does the loosing, and that He does it in the contrition stage of the sacrament. In his view, the priest exercises the power of the keys here only in connection with the imposition of satisfaction, which falls under the heading of the key of discretion, not the key of power. But, here Abelard notes that not all priests in fact possess the attribute of discretion. Some priests lack the intelligence and good judgment needed to exercise their faculties, in the administration of the sacrament of penance, in a seemly and circumspect manner. Now, Abelard continues, if individuals do not possess these attributes by nature, the reception of the sacrament of holy orders on their part does not in itself remove that regrettable defect. Abelard here tries to glide away from the dilemma in which he leaves penitents confronted by such inadequate priests by trying to turn the discussion toward the moral problems that unworthy priests create for themselves. But, as for the moral problems that they create for others, Abelard simply abandons the point. The final observation he has to make about the power of the keys creates another inconsistency, however. As we have seen, he has left the power to loose and to bind, understood as the power to excommunicate and to readmit to communion, out of the reckoning à propos of penance. There is good reason for this omission, since this dimension of the power of the keys is not really pertinent to penance. Still, Abelard brings it up at the close of his analysis of that sacrament. The power to excommunicate and readmit, he states, is canceled when it is exercised unjustly. This observation may or may not have been included as a reference to Abelard's own

---

[331] Ibid., pp. 106–10.

misadventures. In any event, he does not see that a parallel judgment might be made, for the sake of logical symmetry, in the case of
the unworthy or deficient exercise of the key of discretion, despite
the harm that it may do. Why the power of discretion should not be
subject to the same logical analysis as the power of excommunication and readmission is a matter that Abelard declines to discuss.[332]
He ends by leaving penitents in a double bind by insisting on the
necessity of confession, a requirement that does not follow from his
definition of penance itself, and which, in the event of a counterpro-
ductive spiritual encounter with an indiscreet confessor, he fails to
justify.

Precisely the same problems are found in Abelard's disciples,
mitigated only to the extent that their treatment of this topic is
much more abbreviated than his own, giving them fewer opportunities to get ensnared in their own reasoning. Still, the basic contradiction remains. They are contritionists; they see contrition as valid
only if it is inspired by the love of God; they seek to insist on the
necessity of confession; they recognize the fact that priests may not
possess the key of discretion in actuality; and they leave the penitent in the same impasse as Abelard does.[333] The same can be said
for the Porretans and for Gilbert of Poitiers himself, whom his
disciples cite as teaching that sins are forgiven in the contrition
stage of penance. They agree, but likewise require confession and
satisfaction and are not successful in explaining why, given their
recognition of the fact that discretion is no respecter of persons and
that holy orders are no guarantee that an individual will possess it.
One of the Porretan masters describes priests as having the official
function of discerning (officium discernandi); but he leaves the reader
in the dark as to how priests will be able to exercise this function if
they lack the mental and moral wherewithal required to do so.[334]

We can see little real effort to break the log-jam which the
mid-century defenders of contritionism create for themselves until
we get to the Sententiae divinitatis. The author of this work is an
unqualified contritionist. After reviewing with great thoroughness
the arguments on both sides, he invokes the definition of penance as
contrition noted above, and states firmly that sins "are remitted in
contrition of the heart" (dimissa sunt in cordis contritione). He adds
forthrightly that confession and satisfaction "have no effect on the

---

[332] Ibid., pp. 112–26.

[333] Hermannus, Sent., pp. 156–65; Ysagoge in theologiam, pp. 207–16.

[334] Sent. mag. Gisleberti II 10.57–62, 10.66–67, pp. 84–85, 86. The quotation is at
10.67, p. 86.

remission of sins" (*valet quidem non ad peccatorum remissionem*). One should go to confession, he recommends, not because it has any effect on the forgiveness of sin, but so as not to put the institutions of the church in despite.[335] In dealing with the problems surrounding priests handled so inconclusively by the Abelardians and Porretans, this master imports into the discussion an authority whom they do not cite, the *De vera et falsa poenitentia*. This work, written anonymously in the mid-eleventh century, was ascribed to Augustine. It validates a principle that had been part of the orthodox consensus for centuries, and one which was to remain there during and after the middle of the twelfth century if as a minor current of opinion, confession to a lay person. Says the master, citing the Pseudo-Augustine, if a priest is not available, confess to a deacon. If a deacon is not available, confess to a neighbor (*confiteatur proximo*). Such a confession will be valid and worthy so long as the proper contrition is present and the desire to confess to a priest is present, were one at hand.[336] Further, the master adds that if the penitent knows that a particular priest is excommunicated or is under a disciplinary ban, as a punishment for sin, he should avoid that priest and seek another confessor. But, he warns, one should not avoid a priest simply because one does not like him personally. Also, priests should not seek to rob their brother priests of their penitents, reaping a harvest where someone else has sown.[337] Displaying more interest in the priest's side of the transaction than is typical of the theologians, the master considers what priests ought to bear in mind when they judge the severity of the sins confessed to them and assign satisfaction. The conditions, in his view, should be the quantity, quality, place, time, and occasion of the sin and the person who has committed it. With respect to the person, the priest should consider the individual's office, age, sex, wealth, and circumstances. Also, he should consider whether the sin was committed in thought only or also in act, whether it implicated or affected others, and whether it was committed in public or in private.[338] These concerns give the master's treatise on penance as much the look of a penitential guidebook for confessors as the look of a

---

[335] *Sent. div.* 5.4, pp. 145*–48*. The quotations are on p. 148*.
[336] Ibid. 5.4, pp. 151*–52*. The quotation is on p. 152*. For the background on confession to lay people, see Teetaert, *La confession aux laïques*, pp. 1–142. For the *De vera et falsa poenitentia* and its influence, see in particular ibid., pp. 50–56, 102–42; on the *Sent. div.*, see pp. 134–37.
[337] *Sent. div.* 5.4, p. 152*.
[338] Ibid., 5.4, pp. 152*–55*.

sacramental theology. He does not raise the issue of the power of
the keys or the problem of priestly indiscretion in connection with
penance. Still, it has to be said that this master goes farther toward
assisting contritionism to a cogent resolution of its difficulties than
does any of his predecessors. His influence on Peter Lombard is
considerable.

The *Sententiae divinitatis* is not, however, the only recent source on
which the Lombard draws in elaborating his doctrine of penance.
Another author whom he uses extensively, both in a positive sense
and in order to turn his argument on its head, is Gratian.[339] Abelard
receives both criticism and homage and Hugh of St. Victor and the
Summa sententiarum are treated as helpful only intermittently. While
the Lombard has been characterized as doing no more, and no less,
than summarizing the aspects of the doctrine of penance on which
consensus reigned in his time,[340] in actual fact he does much more.
In areas where he agrees with the consensus position, he anchors
his points in his own way, and with a richer array of authorities
than is generally the case. In addition, he takes a forceful stand in
debated areas, a stand which is typically both more extreme and
more coherently defended than is usual among recent and contemporary masters.

One striking and unusual feature of Peter's handling of penance
is that he offers his fullest definition of the *sacramentum* and the *res
sacramenti* at the end of his treatise on the subject, rather than at the
beginning. While he has a clear understanding all along of how he
proposes to define these terms, and one that certainly controls his
exposition of the topic throughout, Peter adopts this strategy because he seeks to present the definitions with which he concludes as
following logically from the analysis and argumentation that pre-
cede them. At the start of his discussion, then, he confines himself
to observing that penance was given to help people reapproach
God after they had distanced themselves from Him by falling into
the *regio dissimilitudinis* of post-baptismal sin. Penance is both a
sacrament and a virtue of the mind. The exterior rite is the
sacrament.[341] The virtue of the mind is interior; and here Peter

---

[339] This point is noted, correctly, by Debil, "La première distinction," pp.
252–53, 255–56; Gaudemet, "Le débat," p. 66.
[340] Thus Landgraf, *Dogmengeschichte*, 3 part 2: 244–45, 264–65, 273.
[341] Peter Lombard, *Sent*. 4. d. 14. c. 1, d. 19. c. 1.3, 2: 315–16, 365–66. Alister E.
McGrath, *Iustitia dei: A History of the Christian Doctrine of Justification* (Cambridge:
Cambridge University Press, 1987), 1: 93 is thus incorrect in stating that Peter
Lombard's definition of penance excludes a physical element.

joins the *Sententiae divinitatis* and Abelard in reprising the Augustinian and Gregorian definition of contrition as sorrow for sin and a
sincere purpose of amendment. He thus agrees, at the outset, that
contrition is of the essence in penance, by definition; but the idea of
calling penance a virtue of the mind is not found in any current
canonist or scholastic theologian. It bears a closer affinity to the
treatment of this question by monastic authors such as Bernard of
Clairvaux, who is interested in the subjective disposition involved
in the state of compunction which he seeks to inflame in his
audience in his writings on this subject.[342]

This understanding of contrition sets the stage for Peter's treatment of the reviviscence of sins and the repeatability of penance.
He agrees with Hugh of St. Victor's clarification of the topic of
reviviscence. When the same type of sin is committed again, this is
not the identical sin which was committed on another occasion.
The fact that the earlier sin may have been remitted in penance
does not obviate the need, and the desirability, of returning to this
remedy, if circumstances should require it subsequently. One
should not, he warmly agrees, cut off access to the channels of grace
which God in His mercy has made available. Peter also concurs
with Hugh, and with everyone else, that for a repeated reception of
penance to be fruitful, or for any reception of penance to fruitful, for
that matter, a proper attitude is required, which includes the
willingness to admit and to repent of all one's sins, holding nothing
back, except for sins already remitted in penance, unless they have
been repeated. The only stipulation he adds to this common
teaching is that a penance will not be fruitful if the penitent,
knowing that he can have future recourse to the sacrament, fails to
bring to his reception of penance a truly sincere purpose of amendment. Peter also seconds wholeheartedly Gratian's argument on
the repeatability of penance, making use of his dossier of authorities. Noting that the pro-repeatability authorities can offer cogent
pastoral and moral reasons in defense of their position, while those
who would limit penance to the single, solemn, public penance can
offer no rationale at all for this restriction, he likewise caps his
conclusion by citing the anti-Donatist Augustine, observing that
the doctrine of nonrepeatability gives lefthanded support to a
Donatist, sectarian view of the church. His argument is an effective

---

[342] Peter Lombard, *Sent.* 4. d. 14. c. 1–c. 3.1, 2: 315–18; Jean Leclerq, "S.
Bernard et la confession des péchés," *Collectanea Cistercensia* 46 (1984): 122–30;
Schmoll, *Die Busslehre*, pp. 23–24.

synthesis of the pastoral considerations put forth by the school of
Laon, the moral analysis of Hugh, and the broad-gauged grasp of
tradition afforded by Gratian, not to mention Gratian's elegant use
of the anti-Donatist argument. He is, however, more interested in
invoking reason than historical criticism in rejecting ancient tradition and does not follow Gratian in urging that the old rules should
remain on the books but that Christians should be systematically
dispensed from observing them. Rather, he argues for the repeatability of penance tout court, and the abandonment of any restric-
tions on that principle. Peter rejects the efforts to hedge the idea of
the single, solemn penance by introducing the possibility of using
private penance repeatedly for certain kinds of sins, introduced by
less independent-minded masters. He boldly sweeps away their
distinctions. Since we should not spurn the grace provided in
penance for our spiritual healing and spiritual growth, Peter concludes, we can retain the single, solemn penance if we wish to. But,
in his hands, this rite has become fundamentally irrelevant. Repeated private penance replaces it as the norm. It is to be used as
often as it is needed, and for all kinds of sins.[343] This solution had the
decided effect of clearing the air, paving the way to the dropping of the
single, solemn, public penance altogether as a practice in the western
church, one that is optional, and one that is essentially marginal to
the way in which penance is normally administered and received.
Here, while certainly confirming the contemporary consensus position on the repeatability of penance, Peter pushes beyond the
boundaries set on this subject by his compeers. He succeeds in
placing the discussion of this aspect of the sacrament in a new state
of equilibrium. By anchoring his solution in the positive pastoral
and moral rationale that supports it, and by urging that the authorities who defend the ancient practice be rejected out of hand
because of their inability to adduce any coherent reasons for the
rule they advocate, Peter effectively raises the ante to the point
where his opponents are forced to leave the game.

On the matter of confessionism versus contritionism, as we have
seen, there was no consensus in this period, either on the particular
point in the penitential process when sins are remitted or, for the
contritionists, on the way to support the idea that confession and
satisfaction are desirable practices even though they are held to
take place after the remission is granted and therefore to have no
effect on it. In this area Peter emerges as a staunch contritionist,

---

[343] Peter Lombard, *Sent.* 4. d. 14. c. 3.2–d. 15. c. 7, d. 22. c. 1, 2: 318–36, 386–88.

and as the only supporter of that side of the debate in the mid-twelfth century who refuses to shrink from the logic of its claims, who goes on to develop a coherent and non-contradictory theory of the relations between contrition and the other two traditional elements in the penitential rite.[344] In taking his stand on this controversy, Peter adheres consistently to the principles he advocates, and does not hesitate to offer arguments that are relatively extreme in their defense. Peter's opening salvo is a quotation from John Chrysostom, actually the Pseudo-Chrysostom, cited as well by the Laon masters and by Peter himself in his treatment of sin, in general, under the heading of ethics, a point making it clear that he intends to consider the remission of sins in penance in a parallel manner. When we sin, says the authority, we sin in thought, word, and deed. And so, perfect penance involves compunction of heart, oral confession, and satisfaction. Both inner and outer penance must be sincere, an idea on which he amplifies by noting that we should not confess one sin to one priest and another to another.[345] Moving at once to the heart of the matter, he next introduces a trio of related questions. Can sins be remitted without confession and without satisfaction? Can one confess just to God, purely by one's contrition of heart, without a priest as accessory? Can one confess to a lay person?

Peter plans to answer each of these questions with a resounding "yes." He recognizes the fact that, in order to do so successfully, he needs to take account of the authorities and arguments on the other side of the debate and to de-fang them convincingly. In dealing with the first two of these questions, he borrows not only from Gratian's dossier but also takes a leaf from his book, methodologically speaking. Peter's own chosen solution is that the remission of sin is a gift of God that is given in the contrition stage of penance. The gift is given and received within the penitent's heart. If the penitent has time, he should also confess to a priest, although the sin has already been remitted. Peter presents this issue as if penitents are people with such busy schedules that, for perfectly legitimate reasons, they may be unable to go to confession. And, just as Gratian "adjusts" the contritionist authorities he cites to make

---

[344] Good accounts of Peter's stance in the confessionist-contritionist debate are provided by Anciaux, *La théologie du sacrement de la pénitence*, pp. 223–31, 329–35; Schmoll, *Die Busslehre*, pp. 67–74; and Spitzig, *Sacramental Penance*, pp. 67–85. Briefer but also useful accounts are Carpino, "Consensi e critiche," pp. 321–25; Gaudemet, "Le débat," pp. 56–57; Longère, *Oeuvres oratoires*, 1: 257–58.

[345] Peter Lombard, *Sent.* 4. d. 16. c. 1–c. 3, 2: 336–40.

them read as if they were supporting the idea of contrition as a necessary first step, but not as the point when the sin is remitted, so Peter likewise "adjusts" the confessionist authorities, interpreting them to mean that confession is not required but only recommended, as a desirable event taking place after the sin has been remitted in contrition, and also as taking place if time permits.[346] We may say, in surveying this line of attack, that if the fudging of authorities comes into play here, alongside of the exposure of their relevance or irrelevance or their possession or lack of a cogent rationale, this process occurs on both the contritionist and the confessionist side of the debate.

Moving to the question of confession to a lay person, Peter appropriates the argument of the *Sententiae divinitatis* derived from the *De vera et falsa poenitentia*, yokes it with the analysis of the power of the keys found in Abelard's *Ethics*, and goes both authors one better. To the point that a lay person may be a substitute for a priest if a priest is not available Peter adds the idea that this substitution may also be made if priests are thick on the ground but if none can be found who possess wisdom and discretion, that is to say, who possess sound judgment, and not just authority. In such a case, he recommends, one should confess to a friend who possesses the requisite mental and moral attributes (*Quaerendus est enim sacerdos sapiens et discretus, qui cum potestate simul habeat iudicium; qui si forte defuerit, confiteri debet socio*).[347] In any event, Peter emphasizes, while it is a good idea, confession is not necessary, "since the sin has already been forgiven in contrition" (*cum in contritione iam deletum sit peccatum*). Confession and satisfaction, that is to say, may be helpful in increasing caution and humility in the penitent's moral life, but they are not strictly necessary.[348] In explaining this point, Peter observes that we need to understand what role this non-requisite confession plays in penance. He begins by emphasizing here, as he does in the case of the other sacraments, that the confessor plays a purely instrumental role. It is God Who remits the sin; and He does so before the penitent goes to confession. If the confessor is a priest, then, in what sense does he exercise the power of the keys in the sacrament of penance? Since God has lifted the penitent's eternal punishment, in what sense does the priest loose and bind? In

---

[346] Ibid., d. 17. c. 1–c. 2.3, 2: 342–50.
[347] Ibid., c. 4, 2: 351–55. The quotation is at c. 4.6, p. 352. A good analysis of Peter's handling of this point is given by Teetaert, *La confession aux laïques*, pp. 137–42.
[348] Peter Lombard, *Sent.* 4. d. 17. c. 5, 2: 355.

Peter's estimation, and here he takes the point farther even than Abelard does, the key of loosing and binding is exercized by priests only in the acts of excommunication and readmission to communion. This authority is given to all priests *ex officio*, irrespective of their personal qualifications. The other key, the key of discretion, is given only to some priests. These individuals are men who already possess this quality. If they lack it naturally, holy orders, unfortunately, does not supply them with it. If that is the case, as Peter has already observed, they cannot display a soundness of judgment which they personally lack in the counsel they may give or in the satisfaction they may impose on a penitent. This is why a discreet and intelligent lay confessor should be substituted in that event. If a priest does possess discretion, Peter concedes, then he does indeed manifest it *ex officio* in the conduct of these pastoral functions. But, and this is the critical point, for Peter, in pronouncing the words of absolution, priests are not loosing or binding. They do not loose and bind in confession. What they do, and all that they do, is to announce the forgiveness that God has already granted, and to impose, for better or for worse, such satisfaction as they deem appropriate. Essentially, the role of the priest is declaratory only. For, not only does God alone forgive the sin; it is God alone Who purges the sinner, and it is God alone Who has the authority to waive satisfaction, partially or altogether, if, in His judgment, the situation and the penitent's state of mind warrant it.[349]

As a concrete example of a circumstance which might incline God to make this kind of judgment, Peter brings up penance when the sinner is in danger of death. That such a person could always repent, up to the end, and that penance should not be denied him, was a consensus view, as was the idea that his contrition would be acceptable to God even if he died before being able to complete his satisfaction. Hugh of St. Victor adds the qualification that this arrangement would not work with a person who hedged his bets, looking forward to a deathbed conversion, since that attitude is entirely incompatible with sincere contrition.[350] Peter, using the

---

[349] Ibid., d. 18–d. 19, 2: 355–71. For Peter on the power of the keys, see Ludwig Hödl, *Die Geschichte der scholastischen Literatur und der Theologie der Schlüsselgewalt*, Beiträge, 37:4 (Münster: Aschendorff, 1960), pp. 193–96; Knoch, *Die Einsetzung*, pp. 235–36; Longère, *Oeuvres oratoires*, 1: 260–61. These authors correct François Russo, "Pénitence et excommunication: Étude historique sur les rapports entre la théologie et la droit canonique dans le domaine pénitentiel du XIIe et XIIIe siècles," *Recherches de science religieuse* 33 (1946): 274–75, 441, who fails to observe the distinctions that Peter draws.
[350] Hugh of St. Victor, *De sac.* 2.14.5, *PL* 176: 559D–560C.

issue of penance *in articulo mortis* to illustrate his doctrine of penance more generally, agrees with the consensus position and expands on it in a manner rather different from Hugh. To begin with, and here he narrows the rule of admissible motivations, in comparison with his own handling of the four kinds of fear in the moral life more generally, repentance is acceptable only for penitents who seek it out of the love of God. Aligning himself with the Abelardians here, he redefines the nature of the evening sacrifice that rises gratefully to God in Psalm 140. In contrast with Hugh, he sees it not as the penitent's satisfaction but as his contrition. In Peter's view, perfect contrition, the contrition arising from the love of God alone, suffices to waive not only the penitent's eternal punishment but also his temporal punishment for sin. Granted, if his contrition is less than perfect, and if he dies before completing his satisfaction, the fires of Purgatory will make up the difference. But, if his contrition is perfect, no punishment at all will follow.[351] Likewise, the penitent will not be punished if his confessor has been indiscreet or foolish and has imposed an inappropriate satisfaction. For, in that event as well, the penitent's interior sorrow for sin will right the balance. No minister of the church, Peter emphasizes, can judge the quality of another man's contrition. The state of his soul can only be known to the God Who alone scrutinizes hearts. And God will not reject perfect contrition, even if the satisfaction performed under these conditions is insufficient.[352] In any event, since a person about to die will not be likely to be able to perform satisfaction himself, Peter urges that priests called to minister to the moribund should require prayers and almsgiving from the penitent's kinsmen and friends instead. But, most importantly, in times of necessity, penance and reconciliation are not to be withheld. Necessity cancels many requirements, Peter insists, including episcopal permission for the reconciliation of excommunicates and of certain other classes of penitents that would otherwise obtain. Throughout this passage in his treatise on penance, Peter uses the concept of necessity to relax the strictures of the authorities he cites who are speaking to non-emergency situations. Similarly, he insists that the intention to

---

[351] Peter Lombard, *Sent.* 4. d. 20. c. 1–c. 2, 2: 371–74. He gives a more extended comment on Purgatory, forecasting his remarks on that subject to be made under the heading of Last Things, at d. 21. c. 1–c. 6, 2: 379–83. On fear as a motive in penance in this period, see Landgraf, *Dogmengeschichte*, 4 part 1: 277–99 who, however, does not note Peter's departure from his more general ethical analysis in this context.

[352] Peter Lombard, *Sent.* 4. d. 20. c. 3, 2: 375–76.

confess will be taken as confession if a person is overtaken by death enroute to his confessor.[353] All of this is perfectly consistent with Peter's strong defense of contritionism and his emphasis on the importance of intention over outward acts in the moral life more generally.

In moving to the close of his discussion of penance, Peter takes up a few additional questions, which are of interest not only because of the answers he gives but also because, reflecting his use of Gratian, they are issues rarely addressed by contemporary theologians. What if someone makes a general confession and inadvertently omits a sin because he has honestly forgotten about it? Here, distinguishing between the event as described and the willful omission of a sin that one remembers perfectly well, Peter rules that the confession is valid, even if the sin forgotten is a mortal one. Another case he raises, admittedly more difficult to envision, is that of a person who accuses himself of a sin he has not committed. Without exploring whether the person holds himself guilty out of a genuine misapprehension or because he is in a delusional state, Peter agrees with his canonical source in accounting his confession a lie, and hence as a sin.[354] Finally, he agrees with Gratian that priests have a solemn obligation to respect the confidentiality of confession, and that they should be deposed if they fail in this responsibility.[355]

Having presented this thoroughly, and consistently, contritionist analysis of penance, which lays the foundation for the doctrine of repeatability, the stress on private penance as normal in all cases, the suspension of the necessity of confession and satisfaction, not only in times of emergency but also in the standard observance of the sacrament, reducing them to desirable and recommended practices whose importance is a function of how they help the penitent grow in virtue and not how they reinforce the authority of the clergy, Peter now turns, at the end of his treatise on penance, to the definition of the *sacramentum* and *res sacramenti*, definitions which have certainly functioned as governing principles in the foregoing analysis. Some say, he notes, that the exterior penance is the sacrament, signifying the interior penance, or the contrition in the penitent's heart. This Hugonian position he rejects, and on Victorine grounds. A sacrament of the New Law, he reminds the reader, "effects what it signifies" (*efficit quod figurat*). This is not the case,

---

[353] Ibid., c. 4–c. 7, 2: 376–79.
[354] Ibid., d. 21. c. 7–c. 8, 2: 384–86.
[355] Ibid., c. 9, 2: 385–86.

however, with exterior penance, since it is the contrition that is efficacious, not the external manifestation or declaration of the fact, which follows it. Others say, he continues, that both the interior and the exterior penance are the sacrament, the exterior acts being the *sacramentum tantum* while the interior contrition is both *sacramentum* and *res*. Peter agrees with this view, with a qualification of his own, and one in which he reminds the reader that penance is a virtue. The *res sacramenti* in penance, strictly speaking, is the grace of God that forgives sins. This forgiveness occurs in the contrition stage and it is a divine response to the virtue of contrition which the penitent offers to God. Like all virtues, the virtue of contrition can also be seen as the human response to the grace of God that enables the penitent to acknowledge his sins as sins, and to turn away from them and seek reconciliation. In this sense, Peter concludes, the contrition stage of penance is both the *res* and the *sacramentum*. Contrition is both the remission of sins and a sign of the remission of sins. For its part, thus, exterior penance is not an efficacious sign but a visible manifestation of the fact that the efficacious sign has been received and internalized by the penitent.[356]

Of all the masters on the contritionist side of the debate, the Lombard is the only one who is truly and wholly faithful to the logic of that position, to the point of being willing to regard confession and satisfaction as optional, to abridge dramatically the power of the keys in penance, and to exempt penitents, whose spiritual welfare comes first, for this is the reason why the sacrament was instituted, from having to subject themselves to the ministrations of indiscreet priests, encouraging them instead to seek the counsel they need wherever they may find it. While his views on the reviviscence of sins and the repeatability of penance help substantially in strengthening the argument for the consensus position that emerged in his century, Peter's systematic and consistent defense of contritionism, along with the corollaries of that stance, which he does not hesitate to draw, put Peter in a rather more exposed position. It was one that lay well within the orthodox consensus of his own day, to be sure, but it came close to locating itself on the radical fringe just inside the limits of that orthodox consensus. Peter Lombard is the only contemporary contritionist able to offer as strong, as well-reasoned, and as well-documented a case on behalf of its cause as Gratian was able to offer on behalf of confessionism. Neither side achieved a salient victory over the other in the

---

[356] Ibid., d. 22. c. 2.2–c. 5, 2: 389–90.

twelfth century. When a new balance was struck and a new consensus was formed in the thirteenth century, it was one that accepted many of the exceptions and exemptions promoted by Peter, under the heading of removing obstacles between the penitent Christian and the grace available in the sacrament of penance. But it was also a consensus that could appreciate the values for which Gratian's position had stood, in locating the moment when forgiveness is given in the moment when God acts through the words of priestly absolution. The motive for making that choice, in the sequel, combined a more Aristotelian way of framing the notion of sacramental causality with an ongoing and increasingly felt need to guard the dignity of the priestly office from the attacks of anti-clerical and anti-sacramental heretics. Peter Lombard's position on penance thus stands not so much as the occasion for the emergence of a new consensus on all features of penance as it stands as an index of his combative, principled, and systematic spirit.

Unction

In the case of penance, as we have seen, the debates and arguments of the canonists and theologians were, to a large extent, sparked by the desire to defend changes in the practice of penance which they were eager to promote and support. The existence of changing attitudes between the early church and the twelfth-century present, visible in liturgical rites, saints' lives, and canonical and theological texts alike, can also be documented in the case of unction. This fact, however, is not always registered faithfully in the sacramental theology of our period. While differences of opinion on unction certainly do occur, the masters do not pursue them with dedication and zeal. Nor do they give the impression that a great deal hangs on their resolution. Comparatively little effort is made to integrate unction coherently into whatever general theory of the sacraments a master may propose, and themes normally treated in the case of the other sacraments, such as the ordinary minister and the proper disposition of the recipient, are frequently omitted.

Unction had been a popular practice in the early church.[357] At that time, it was seen as a sacrament instituted for the healing of the sick and was widely administered, by lay people as well as by

---

[357] Excellent background is supplied by Antoine Chavasse, *Étude sur l'onction des infirmes dans l'église latine du IIIe au XIe siècle*, vol. 1 (Lyon, 1942); Placid Murray, "The Liturgical History of Extreme Unction," in *Studies in Pastoral Liturgy*, ed. Vincent Ryan (Dublin: Gill & Son, 1963), 2: 18–38.

the clergy. By the sixth century, the idea that unction also remits
sin had emerged, although the corporal effects it was believed to
convey received more attention. It was only in the Carolingian
period that unction started to be seen as a *viaticum*, or extreme
unction, the last opportunity of a moribund person to receive
sacramental grace, which often occurred in conjunction with deathbed penance. This development enhanced the tendency to view a
cleric as the only suitable minister. Despite this shift in practice,
which had become quite general in the western church by the end
of the eighth century, the theologians of the first half of the twelfth
century do not always take note of the change. While a number of
them, including Honorius Augustodunensis, the Abelardians, and
the author of the *Summa sententiarum* define unction as extreme
unction,[358] Anselm of Laon and the Porretans retain the older
definition of unction as the annointing of the sick.[359] Another tack is
taken, most influentially by Hugh of St. Victor, who is followed by
Master Simon and Roland of Bologna, in defining unction as
serving both as the annointing of the sick and as *viaticum*.[360]

While the masters therefore do not agree on what unction is, in
terms of the class of persons for whose needs it has been instituted,
there are a number of points on which a consensus, or a virtual
consensus on unction, does exist. All who raise the point agree that
unction is not a sacrament of necessity but that it should not be
neglected out of contempt for the institutions of the church. Gilbert
of Poitiers appears to be alone in rejecting the sacramentality of
unction, giving the opinion that it is no more a sacrament than the
washing of feet on Maundy Thursday; he gives no grounds for this
exclusion. Gilbert's own disciples criticize him for departing from
orthodoxy on this point;[361] and every other master at the time sees
unction as a sacrament, including Hermannus, even though he
states that it does not effect what it signifies.[362] There is also

---

[358] Honorius, *Eluc.* 2.94, p. 439; Hermannus, *Sent.*, pp. 132–33; *Sent. Parisiensis* I,
p. 47; *Ysagoge in theologiam*, p. 199; *Summa sent.* 6.15, *PL* 176: 153A. This definition
of unction at the time is ignored by Henry S. Kryger, *The Doctrine of the Effects of
Extreme Unction in Its Historical Development* (Washington: Catholic University of
America Press, 1949), pp. 1–11. On Hermannus, see Knoch, *Die Einsetzung*, pp.
151 52.
[359] *Sentences of Anselm of Laon*, no. 57, 5: 53; *Sent. mag. Gisleberti* I 9.1, p. 154. On
Anselm, see Knoch, *Die Einsetzung*, p. 62.
[360] Hugh of St. Victor, *De sac.* 2.15.2, *PL* 176: 577D–578B; Master Simon, *De
sac.*, pp. 42–43; Roland of Bologna, *Sent.*, pp. 261–62. On Hugh, see Knoch, *Die
Einsetzung*, pp. 107–09.
[361] *Sent. mag. Gisleberti* I 9.6, p. 155; *Sent. mag. Gisleberti* II 9.5, p. 75.
[362] Hermannus, *Sent.*, pp. 132–33.

widespread agreement on the point that unction was instituted by the apostles, on the authority of the Epistle of James.[363] Hardly anyone discusses the question of the ordinary minister, but of those who do, the Porretans say it should be a priest while Roland of Bologna states that it may a priest or a bishop.[364]

The two areas where the masters rise from their extremely lethargic and laconic treatment of unction and seek to coordinate it with the other sacraments they treat are the repeatability of unction and its effects on the recipient. In handling penance, as we have seen, there was a concerted effort on the part of theologians in this period to repudiate the early church rule that the sacrament could not be repeated. In the case of unction, on the other hand, the early church view of unction as a sacrament designed to heal the sick led to the principle, supported in theory as well as practice, that it is a repeatable sacrament. Even with the development of the shift in perception that led unction to be seen as a *viaticum*, there was no reason, in theory, to refuse to administer it more than once, if a person happened to find himself in danger of death more than once. The general interest in keeping open the channels of sacramental grace to Christians and in removing obstacles to their reception of it, so richly documentable elsewhere in the sacramental theology of this period, suggested to a number of mid-century masters that unction should be repeatable as well, on the analogy of the other repeatable sacraments. Hugh of St. Victor compares unction with penance here, while the Porretans draw a parallel with the Eucharist.[365] Hugh's warrant for his position is common sense and the lack of any countervailing authorities, or, at least, any that he chooses to acknowledge. For the Porretans and for the other masters who agree on repeatability, no arguments at all are given.[366] Yet, the alternative view is maintained by Hermannus and Master Simon. The former offers no reasons; but Simon's basis for his opinion is a garbled citation from Augustine, coupled with the idea

---

[363] *Sent. mag. Gisleberti* I 9.1, p. 154; Hugh of St. Victor, *De sac.* 2.15.2, *PL* 176: 577D; *Summa sent.* 6.15, *PL* 176: 153A; Master Simon, *De sac.*, p. 42; Roland of Bologna, *Sent.*, pp. 161–62.

[364] *Sent. mag. Gisleberti* I 9.2, p. 154; Roland of Bologna, *Sent.*, p. 163.

[365] Hugh of St. Victor, *De sac.* 2.15.3, *PL* 176: 578B–580B; *Sent. mag. Gisleberti* I 9.4–5, pp. 154–55.

[366] *Sent. Parisiensis* I, p. 48; *Ysagoge in theologiam*, p. 200; Roland of Bologna, *Sent.*, p. 164; *Summa sent.* 6.15, *PL* 176: 154C. On this debate, see Heinrich Weisweiler, "Das Sakrament der Letzten Ölung in den systematischen Werken der ersten Frühscholastik," *Scholastik* 7 (1932): 321–53, 524–60, although he is not entirely reliable on all the members of the Abelardian school, the *Summa sententiarum*, or Roland of Bologna.

that a married person should abstain from sexual relations after
receiving unction, which would suggest a once-and-for-all approach to this sacrament, confining it to the extremely elderly or
to persons whose recovery from serious illness is given a highly
negative prognosis.[367]

To a large extent, the decision as to whether to regard unction as
repeatable or not is tied to the master's understanding of what it
accomplishes, at least in the case of authors capable of following the
logic of their own arguments. Hermannus, for instance, thinks that
unction remits sin, although, as noted, he does not regard it as
efficacious, a manifest self-contradiction. If unction does remit sin
despite the latter claim, it is also difficult to see why he thinks it
should not be repeated; it has to be said that his exposition does
nothing to clarify why he thinks this is the case. Simon also thinks
that unction remits sin, as an exit sacrament parallel with baptism;[368] but it is the marital conditions he imposes on recipients
that account for its non-repeatability in his eyes, not the baptismal
analogy. On the other hand, those masters who accept the repeatability of unction connect this point with the remission of sin,
whether or not, like Hugh of St. Victor, they compare unction with
penance. Typically, they expand the effects of unction beyond the
remission of sin to include the restoration of health, if God wills it,
and to the strengthening of the recipient's soul if God wills that he
should now pass into the next life. They may also add the purgation
of vice as an effect of unction.[369] Anselm of Laon, who has no
position on the repeatability of unction, stands alone in confining
its effects to the stimulation of devotion.[370]

In his own extremely terse discussion of unction, Peter Lombard
is clearly influenced by Hugh of St. Victor, and, to a lesser extent,
by the author of the *Summa sententiarum*.[371] From the latter master he
takes the idea that the *sacramentum* is the oil used in unction and that
the *res sacramenti* is the remission of sins.[372] But he yokes this point to

---

[367] Hermannus, *Sent.*, p. 134; Master Simon, *De sac.*, pp. 43–44.

[368] Hermannus, *Sent.*, pp. 132–33; Master Simon, *De sac.*, pp. 42–43.

[369] Hugh of St. Victor, *De sac.* 2.15.2, *PL* 176: 577D–578B; Roland of Bologna,
Sent., pp. 262–63; *Sent. Parisiensis* I, pp. 47–48 join the remission of sin to the gifts of
the Holy Spirit in all their plenitude. *Sent. mag. Gisleberti* I 9.2, p. 154 adds the
purgation of vice. On the other hand, *Ysagoge in theologiam*, p. 200 and the *Summa
sent.* 6.15, *PL* 176: 153A–B confine themselves to the remission of sin.

[370] *Sentences of Anselm of Laon*, no. 57, 5: 53.

[371] This point is developed well by Knoch, *Die Einsetzung*, p. 237; Weisweiler,
"Das Sakrament der Letzten Ölung," pp. 324, 329, 341–42, 525–31, 555.

[372] *Summa sent.* 6.15, *PL* 176: 153A–B; Peter Lombard, *Sent.* 4. d. 22. c. 3.3, 2:
391.

the wider, Hugonian understanding of the effects of the sacrament as curing the sick, if God wills it, and as increasing virtue in the recipient. For him, the spiritual benefit extends both to the unction of the sick and to the moribund in need of *viaticum*, while the corporal benefit extends only to the sick person who does, indeed, recover. It was for all these purposes that the apostles instituted the sacrament.[373] Peter also agreed with Hugh about the repeatability of unction and sees Simon as the main thinker he needs to refute. He does so by going back to the Augustinian text that Simon had garbled, the *Contra epistolam Parmeniani*, and by showing that what Augustine was really placing under the heading of unrepeatable sacraments were baptism and holy orders, not unction. Further, he notes, we should not confuse the reconsecration of the oil used in unction, which is to be avoided, with the repetition of unction itself, which he supports, in order to make the grace of the sacrament available whenever it is needed.[374] Peter takes a harder line than most of his compeers in saying that it is damnable to omit unction out of neglect or contempt; and he certainly stands alone in insisting that this sacrament must be administered by a bishop.[375] But, in most respects, his teaching on unction is a reprise at Hugh's, with the amplifications noted. He retains the balance between unction as the sacrament of the sick and unction as *viaticum* despite the historical shift in practice to the latter understanding, in his time. He retains a combination of physical and spiritual benefits in the sacrament, although he views the latter as constant and the former as contingent. He insists on the repeatability of unction, as part of his consistently applied general rule on the availability of sacramental grace. There is, however, one respect in which Peter fails to integrate his theology of unction into his sacramental theology as such. Despite his firm insistence on intentionality and the proper disposition as conditioning the recipient's appropriation of sacramental grace in his account of other sacraments, Peter remains as silent on the question of the disposition of the recipient of unction as does every other contemporary master. The one, and the only, idiosyncratic note in his treatment of unction is his requirement of episcopal administration.

---

[373] Peter Lombard, *Sent.* 4. d. 22. c. 1–c. 3.1–3, 2: 390–91.
[374] Ibid., c. 4, 2: 391–93.
[375] Ibid., c. 1, c. 3.3, 2: 390, 391.

Holy Orders

The one sacrament that is taken for granted, to such an extent that it is frequently passed over in silence or given a very scanty treatment even by masters seeking to promote its dignity and its necessity elsewhere in their sacramental theology, is holy orders. This tendency can be found in canonists and theologians alike. Alger of Liège displays only one preoccupation in treating this topic, the problem of unworthy priests and the validity of the sacraments they may administer. The intentions of such unworthy ministers are of interest to him in relation to the efficacy of the sacrament of holy orders in itself as guaranteed by the proper formula and ritual in the administration of holy orders. He never goes into the matter of what makes holy orders a sacrament in the first place and how it operates in the ministry and in the inner life of priests whose status and behavior are not problematic.[376] Honorius Augustodunensis is also preoccupied with the problem of bad priests; but, consistent with the interests of the ultimate audience for which he writes the *Elucidarium*, he is more concerned with how lay people should respond to them and whether the laity should accept their directives. Other than that, he confines his analysis of their ministry to the consecration of the Eucharist. He joins those who argue that excommunication, but not moral weakness, invalidates this priestly function.[377] Roland of Bologna confines himself to the priestly power of the keys in his treatise on holy orders, even though he clearly thinks that priests play a wider role than merely excommunicating and readmitting to communion, hearing confessions, and imposing satisfaction. On the one point he raises, he follows the standard canonical line in viewing the power to loose and bind as embracing the forgiveness of sins in penance as well as the excluding and readmitting of persons to communion with the church. As for the key of discretion, he admits that people who are not priests sometimes have this quality and that not all priests display it. Still, he maintains, discretion is granted to priests *ex officio* thanks to their ordination; they have the capacity to use it whether they do so or not.[378]

---

[376] Kretzschmar, intro. to his ed. of *De misericordia*, pp. 31–57; Le Bras, "Le *Liber de misericordia et justicia*," pp. 92–94, 115; Friedrich Merzbacher, "Alger von Lüttich und das kanonische Recht," *Zeitschrift der Savigny-Stiftung für Rechtsgeschichte*, kanonistische Abteilung 66 (1980): 233–34, 246–50.

[377] Honorius, *Eluc.* 2.185–92, 2.198–202, pp. 395–403.

[378] Roland of Bologna, *Sent.*, pp. 265–68.

Roland does not manifest any interest in the technical or administrative side of holy orders that is the typical preserve of the canonists and that is, indeed, often the only aspect of the subject that concerns them. In this respect, Gratian is prototypical. He is concerned, and concerned only, with the rights and duties of priests, the correctness of their ordination, the age limits, qualifications, and other norms to be enforced in admitting men to this or that grade of orders, and the impediments and disqualifications that should prevent ordination or give rise to disciplinary action, suspension, or deposition. Insofar as he distinguishes the functions of one grade of ordination from another, he presents them as a job description, not as a mode of sacramental grace, which will enable the individual's superior to ascertain whether or not he is performing appropriately. The only mild debate into which Gratian enters, and it is an echo of a controversy to which Honorius had alluded earlier in the century, is whether there is any difference between a secular priest and one living under a monastic rule. Given his emphasis on the juridical aspects of the question, Gratian's solution, predictably, is that all priests, whether they are monks or not, have the same rights and duties.[379]

Some theologians adopt this canonical perspective as well. Robert Pullen shows a similar concern for the qualifications, rights, and duties of clerics, accenting in particular their right to receive tithes and their duty to avoid simony or the acceptance of payment for their services. While he ignores the question of what makes holy orders a sacrament, he deals primarily with the priesthood as a calling in the church, and one that has certain ethical requirements attached to it. His chief effort is to outline the moral responsibilities of priests, such as celibacy, detachment from military, political, and commercial affairs, hospitality, generosity to the poor, studiousness, honesty, purity of faith, mercy, soundness of judgment, and freedom from the abuse of the authority entrusted to them by their office.[380] Aside from listing the ways in which clerics are expected to give good moral example, he has one and only one point to make about holy orders as a sacrament. Ordination, he notes, imparts a permanent character to a priest. And so, if a priest is suspended for disciplinary reasons and then restored to his

---

[379] Gratian, *Decretum* pars 2. c. 16. q. 1. c. 40. dictum, c. 69. dictum, col. 773, 781.
[380] Robert Pullen, *Sent.* 7.6, 7.10–11, 7.13, 7.16–17, *PL* 186: 913A–914B, 922B–924A, 927A–B, 928B–930C.

sacerdotal duties, he is not to be reordained.[381]

The two quarters from which we first see the effort truly to develop a sacramental theology of holy orders, and a theology in which the way sacramental grace is seen to operate is differentiated according to the clerical rank involved, are Ivo of Chartres and the school of Laon.[382] Ivo spells out seven grades of holy orders. More than merely being a division of labor, these grades, as he sees them, are designed to signify the church and the various forms of grace that its ministers are given in order to empower them to perform the different ecclesiastical functions of their offices. The ranks of the ministry signify, as well, the moral qualities that these ministers should possess. In treating minor orders, Ivo accents the ecclesiological dimension or significance of each rank, while in discussing subdeacons, deacons, and priests, he focuses on the personal moral qualities required in ministers at these ranks. For Ivo, the porter signifies the church's role in distinguishing good from evil. The lector performs the church's function of announcing the prophesies of the Old Testament and the good news of the New. In the office of exorcist the church casts out evil spirits, both in catechumens and in its people more generally, for which the exorcist needs to have purity of spirit. In the office of acolyte, the church sheds light into the darkness and conveys Christ as the light of the world. The subdeacon's role is to carry the liturgical vessels in which the Eucharist is contained, and the aquafer used in the priest's ablution in that rite. This function both signifies and requires the virtue of continence and imparts the grace that helps the subdeacon to preserve it. Noting that seven deacons were ordained by each of the apostles, Ivo explores the symbolism of that number, signifying the gifts of the Holy Spirit, the seven-branched candelabrum of which the Bible speaks, and other septiform allegories. In ordination to this rank, the deacon receives the charge, and the grace, to evangelize and to dispense the sacraments, to elevate the host and carry the chalice in the celebration of the Eucharist. For this, he must be chaste in mind and body and free from greed and lust. Priests, finally, are the successors of the original apostles. Ivo points out that the word *presbyter*, in Greek, refers to the elders, which suggests the ethical and behavioral maturity that must be brought to this grade of holy orders. The role of the priest is fourfold, for Ivo. He

---

[381] Ibid., 7.15, *PL* 186: 927C–D.
[382] Cf. Knoch, *Die Einsetzung*, p. 237, who claims that the Lombard was the first to give a sacramental definition of holy orders.

mediates between man and God; he forgives sins; he prays for his people; and he offers the Eucharist. Ivo observes in passing that some of the other functions exercised by priests in the early church were later transferred to bishops. But the chief point he wants to make about the priesthood is that, in all four respects, priests provide an extension in time of Christ's saving work. The grace they are given enables them to serve as channels of God's power, to that end. The moral corollary of this fact is that the entire life of priests should be an imitation of Christ.[383]

This theme of the imitation of Christ is given a much more sustained development in the school of Laon.[384] As the Laon masters see it, the life of Christ is a model for each and every grade in holy orders. This, in turn, is the inner spiritual meaning of the sacrament for the men who receive it. As with the porter, Christ served as a gatekeeper when He ejected the money-changers from the temple. Christ functioned as a lector when He interpreted the prophesy of Isaiah. He was an exorcist when He cast out demons. He was an acolyte when He described Himself as the light of the world and when He illuminated the minds of those who accepted Him in faith. Christ acted as a subdeacon when He turned water into wine at the marriage of Cana. He was a deacon when He washed the feet of His disciples at the Last Supper and when He preached the coming of the kingdom of God. Christ, also, was a priest when He celebrated the Eucharist at the Last Supper. The Laon masters add to this list of seven grades of orders the rank of bishop. This office Christ exercised as well, when He ordained and commissioned His disciples to preach the gospel and to baptize in His name, and to loose and to bind, and when He raised people from the dead.[385] It is true that the members of this school go on to discuss, in some detail, the canonical regulations validating or invalidating ordination or the exercise of priestly functions, taking a rather more generous line here than most masters do on the capacities of excommunicate and heretic priests, unless they have been unfrocked by their bishops, but also urging that, if a priest has been unfrocked for a grave crime, such as murder or adultery, he

---

[383] Ivo of Chartres, *Sermo 2, PL* 162: 514B–519D.

[384] This point is ignored by Knoch, *Die Einsetzung,* pp. 54–57, in his account of the Laon masters on holy orders.

[385] *Sentences of the School of Laon,* no. 359, 5: 271. This interest in discussing the sacramental functions of bishops is comparatively unusual in the first half of the twelfth century. See Landgraf, *Dogmengeschichte,* 3 part 2: 277–96.

should not be readmitted to the ministry.[386] Still, they clearly understand holy orders as a sacrament, in which the *res sacramenti*, the grace that imparts discretion, power, and knowledge (*discretio et potentia et scientia*) is transmitted by the rite of ordination, if the ordinand is moved by the appropriate intention in receiving it. If he is not suitably motivated, he receives the *sacramentum tantum* and not the *res*.[387] And, as we have seen above, the grace which the clergyman receives not only imparts authority, enabling him to perform his public sacerdotal functions. It also is a grace that strengthens him inwardly and assists him in developing the virtues needed for the *imitatio Christi* which is the meaning of ordination in his own spiritual life.

The school of Laon plays a critical role in the development of the sacramental understanding of the priesthood in the twelfth century. Subsequent masters who contributed to that development, within our period, are heavily influenced by the position of the Laon masters although they expand on it, introducing additional considerations. Hugh of St. Victor strengthens the point that the grace imparted to the clergy in holy orders has the double role of empowering them to serve as the sacramental channels of grace to other members of the Christian community in the ecclesiastical dispensation and of enriching their own spiritual lives. To the imitation of Christ in the grades of holy orders from porter to priest as given by the Laon masters he adds both Old Testament parallels and insights drawn from the *Ecclesiastical Hierarchy* of the Pseudo-Dionysius, thus imparting a somewhat more participatory and Neoplatonic cast to the notion that clerics are associated with Christ's own ministry in performing their own and in achieving personal sanctification thereby.[388] Hugh goes on to explore the parallels, in the lay and clerical estates, between groups arranged in hierarchical order with a single ruler at the top, the king and pope respectively, adding that the clerical order precedes the secular power in honor and dignity and that it has the right to judge its

---

[386] For the rules and regulations in general, *Sentences of the School of Laon*, no. 393–97, 400, 5: 283–84, 285–86; for the points about unfrocked priests and their ineligibility for reinstitution, no. 376, 380, 390–92, 399, 479, 5: 279, 280, 283, 285, 313.

[387] *Sentences of the School of Laon*, no. 391, 5: 283.

[388] Hugh of St. Victor, *De sac.* 2.2.1–2, 2.3.6–19, *PL* 176: 415B–417D, 423A–431D. This point is brought out well by Paolo M. Pession, "L'ordine sacro e i suoi gradi nel pensiero di Ugo di S. Vittore," *La Scuola Cattolica* 64 (1936): 133–49, although he sees the influence of Ivo of Chartres here and not that of the school of Laon. See also Knoch, *Die Einsetzung*, pp. 98–103; Mignon, *Les origines*, 2: 221–33.

exercise, a mild pass at church-state relations atypical in theological *summae* of this period.[389] Also, in considering the seven clerical
grades, Hugh observes that some of them, such as deacon and
priest, are distinguished from each other in that they have different
faculties, while others, such as deacon and archdeacon, are distinguished from each other as having the same faculties but a different
range of powers. Still other grades, such as priest and bishop, have
both different faculties and a different range of powers.[390] Like the
Laon masters, Hugh includes the rules and regulations governing
ordinands, material which he derives from the canonists and which
he explores in rather more detail than is typical of theologians at
this time.[391] Unlike the school of Laon, he appends a discussion of
liturgical vessels and vestments as used by the clergy, how to
deploy them, and their symbolism.[392] He also picks up a point
made by Gratian while responding to it differently. Monks, he
agrees, can validly exercise the priestly ministry; and, of course, it
is appropriate for them to do so within their own monastic communities. Beyond that, however, this faculty should be seen as an
indulgence, not as an intrinsic part of their calling, which, for
Hugh, is prayer, penitence, and contemplation.[393] But, while
adding to the Laon masters in these respects, he preserves faithfully
their sense of the double effect of the grace of holy orders on
clergymen, both authorizing them to serve the church and sanctifying them in their inner lives, and he retains their understanding
of how clergymen participate in and manifest the life of Christ at all
levels of the ministry.

Master Simon is another theologian strongly influenced by the
school of Laon on holy orders, whether directly or by way of Hugh,
although he amplifies the Laon analysis in a different way. Simon is
less interested than either Hugh or the Laon masters in the juridical dimensions of this subject. He does discuss the power of the keys,
which he takes up here rather than in his treatise on penance. He
agrees with the view that this power includes loosing and binding
in confession as well as in excommunication and readmission to
communion. He acknowledges the fact that not all priests have
discretion and fails to deal with the problem. Aside from making the
standard observation that bishops are responsible for performing

---

[389] Hugh of St. Victor, *De sac.* 2.2.4, *PL* 176: 417D–418D.
[390] Ibid., 2.2.5, *PL* 176: 418D–419B.
[391] Ibid., 2.3.20–24, *PL* 176: 431D–434A.
[392] Ibid., 2.4.1–7, 2.5.1–3, *PL* 176: 433C–438D, 439A–442C.
[393] Ibid., 2.3.4, *PL* 176: 422D–423A.

ordinations,[394] he leaves rules, regulations, and jurisdictional matters to the side and concentrates his attention on the sacramental quality of holy orders, giving much more attention than his sources to the effects of sacramental grace on the recipient. Simon agrees with Robert Pullen that ordination imparts an indelible character. For him, this means that even an excommunicated priest can validly consecrate the Eucharist as well as validly baptize, a permission which, as we have seen, was not so freely granted by all contemporary masters.[395] Even more important than the permanent faculty to minister in the sacramental lives of others which a priest acquires through the grace of holy orders, for Simon, is the effect which this grace has in the cleric's spiritual life. Simon gives more sustained attention to this aspect of the sacrament than do the Laon masters and Hugh of St. Victor. He agrees firmly that each grade of holy orders manifests the life and ministry of Christ: "Each of these, in itself, shows forth our Lord and savior" (*Hos ipse Dominus et Salvator noster in se ostendit*).[396] But, what Simon does in developing this theme is to use some of Ivo of Chartres' definitions of the grades of orders, and some of his own, as descriptions of aspects of Christ's ministry, side by side with other definitions inherited from the Laon masters and Hugh. He also expands this topic by exploring how the grace of ordination is manifested in the gifts of the Holy Spirit as associated with the grades of ministry.

Thus, for Simon, the porter suggests Christ's ejection of the money-changers from the temple; the lector represents Christ's teaching under the inspiration of the Holy Spirit; the exorcist reflects Christ's casting out of demons. The acolyte, as Simon presents him, shows forth Christ's healing miracles that opened the eyes of the blind, a note not found either in Ivo or in the Laon tradition. The subdeacon, Simon agrees, imitates Christ in washing the feet of the disciples, the deacon in administering the Eucharist, and the priest in consecrating the bread and wine. As with the Laon masters, he sees the ministry of these last two orders in a rather more narrowly Eucharistic light than is the case with Ivo. With the former, he also adds the episcopate as a grade of holy orders. Bishops imitate Christ by instructing and consecrating others. And, whether bishops, archbishops, or popes, they are successors of the apostles as well as participants in and conveyors of the ministry of Christ.[397]

---

[394] Master Simon, *De sac.*, pp. 66–67, 70–81.
[395] Ibid., p. 70.
[396] Ibid., p. 65.
[397] Ibid., pp. 65–66.

To this account Simon attaches an analysis of how the grades of holy orders are informed by the gifts of the Holy Spirit. The porter manifests fear of the Lord, the beginning of wisdom. Here, Simon reprises the four modes of fear and concludes that it is filial fear which is involved in the porter's case, not initial fear. The lector manifests piety. His desire to read expresses his desire to teach others. The exorcist is informed by knowledge, the discretion or discernment of spirits that enables him to help others come to grips with and to purge themselves of the moral problems that may be troubling them—a notable interiorization of the idea of exorcism, we may observe. The acolyte, for Simon, manifests fortitude, in that he holds up the candelabra that light liturgical ceremonies. The subdeacon reflects counsel. He reads the Epistle during the mass; he mixes water and wine in the chalice; and he thereby enlightens his hearers and inspires the love of God in them. The deacon is granted the gift of intelligence, to be used in his preaching and in his distribution of the Eucharist. The priest, finally, shows forth the gift of wisdom. His truest office, according to Simon, is the consecration of the Eucharist. Other sacerdotal functions which priests may exercise he lumps together under the vague phrase *et cetera*. The gifts of the Holy Spirit, he concludes, enrich the inner lives of clerics and assist them in developing the virtues needed for these different grades of ministry. Having himself occupied each step along this clerical *cursus honorum*, the priest will have acquired all of these virtues as he completes what, for Simon, is better understood as a *cursus gratiarum et virtutum*.[398]

In placing Peter Lombard's theology of holy orders in the context of the treatments of this topic current in his day, it can be said that he stands in the tradition of the school of Laon both in emphasizing, and in defining clearly, the sacramentality of holy orders. In outlining the grades of holy orders he draws on Hugh and Simon, as well as Ivo of Chartres, while adding some ideas of his own. In one important respect he departs from the Laon masters, Hugh, and Simon alike. He removes bishops and other prelates from the grades of holy orders and considers them, instead, as occupying different ranks within the priesthood but not as different orders. Another notable difference between Peter and the other masters, whether canonists or theologians, is that he eliminates a number of topics which they discuss under this heading. He does not concern himself with what qualifies a man to enter the

---

[398] Ibid., pp. 67–69.

priesthood or what disqualifies him. Nor is he interested in the circumstances under which a priest may be deposed, disciplined, or restored to service. The regulations governing the supervision of clerics, once ordained, by their superiors are not, in his view, to the point here. The only juridical considerations that he imports into his theology from the canonists have to do with the conditions validating or invalidating the administration and reception of the sacrament of holy orders itself.[399]

Peter begins by seconding Hugh, in placing the doctrine of holy orders within the context of a brief ecclesiology, in which Christ is the head and church members are the parts of His mystical body. He agrees that the seven grades of holy orders all exemplify aspects of Christ's own ministry, participating in it when the incumbents accede to ecclesiastical office with a worthy intention. Leaving aside Hugh's mini-treatise on hierarchy and on the two-swords theory, he agrees with Simon that the seven grades of holy orders manifest the gifts of the Holy Spirit as well and that ordination imparts not only an office in the church, with the power and authority needed for its exercise, but also provides a means through which clerics can unite themselves with Christ in both their inner and their public lives. Peter places more emphasis than either of these masters on the importance of quality control, citing Pope Clement to the effect that it is better to have fewer priests who are truly worthy of the dignity to which they are called than to have many useless ones not capable of rising to the demands of their office or of internalizing its graces.[400] While Peter refers to the gifts of the Holy Spirit in these opening remarks, he does not schematize them, as Simon does, in conjunction with the different grades of orders. In handling that topic, Hugh is his model, especially for the Old Testament parallels and for his frank interest in the symbolism of the roles of Christian clerics. At the same time, he often borrows Ivo's definitions and substitutes them for those of Hugh and the Laon masters, sometimes but not always in the way that Simon

---

[399] Cf. Joseph de Ghellinck, "Le traité de Pierre Lombard sur les sept ordres ecclésiastiques: Ses sources, ses copistes," *RHE* 10 (1909): 290–302, 720–28; 11 (1910): 29–46, who presents the doctrine as one of mere sterile and servile imitation. Knoch, *Die Einsetzung*, pp. 237–39, while he credits Peter with more originality than he in fact displays, gives an accurate description of many if not all features of his teaching on holy orders.

[400] Peter Lombard, *Sent.* 4. d. 24. c. 1–c. 3.1, 2: 393–94. The particular Clement is not indicated. As Brady notes, *ad loc.*, p. 394, Peter's citation of Clement is derived from Gratian.

does; and he appends to the definitions he chooses some further reflections of his own.

All clerics receive the tonsure. With Hugh, Peter takes up its symbolism. Like a king's crown, he observes, the tonsure is a mark of office. It bares the head because the head is where the mind, man's highest faculty, is located. Baring the head signifies the opening of the mind to revelation. The tonsure is cut in a small round shape because this, according to Peter and Hugh, signifies the removal of obstructions from the senses, which have to do their part in informing the cleric. Completing this introduction to the grades of orders with tonsorial types and parallels of clerical commitment from the Old Testament, Peter commences his itinerary through the seven grades of orders, noting both the Old Testament analogies, the ways in which the grades of orders participate in Christ's ministry, and the ways in which they manifest a moral imitation of Christ. Christ accepted the office of porter, he agrees, when He drove the money-changers out of the temple. He Himself is the gate, the way, as well as controlling access to it. The janitors guarding the entrance to the temple of Jerusalem are the forerunners. And, porters must possess the judgment that Christ displayed, in carrying out their functions. The lector reads and preaches. For these duties, Peter adds, he must be literate and have a clear and carrying voice, and eloquence. Christ manifested these qualities when He debated the book of Isaiah among the elders in the temple. The Old Testament prophets are the forerunners of the lectors. Exorcists, for Peter, have the traditional role of casting evil spirits out of catechumens, as Old Testament exorcists did more generally and as Christ did in the New Testament. Peter does not pick up on Master Simon's more psychological reading of this function. Exorcists must have purity of spirit. The acolyte holds up the candelabra that shed light when the Gospel is read and the Eucharist is offered and he helps prepare the Eucharistic elements on the altar. Candelabra were also used in the Old Testament temple services and their keepers are the earlier analogies of Christian acolytes. The acolyte needs a specific acquaintance with his duties, as Christ did, in being the light of the world.[401]

Moving to the three higher grades of orders, Peter offers an expanded description of their roles, in comparison with his sources. The subdeacon receives the offerings of the people, arranges the materials used in liturgical rites on the altar, such as the paten,

---

[401] Peter Lombard, *Sent.* 4. d. 24. c. 5–c. 8, 2: 396–99.

chalice, and other vessels used in celebrating the Eucharist. The sacrifices that took place in the temple service in Old Testament times, and the ministers who coordinated them, are the types here. Christ manifested this mode of ministry when He washed the feet of the disciples at the Last Supper. Peter assigns this role to the subdeacon, not to the deacon, as the Laon masters do. Continence is the virtue required of subdeacons. The deacon is analogous to the Old Testament Levites. These functionaries carried the ark and tabernacle, and, like the Christian deacons whom they prefigure, they must have reached a mature age. Peter here shifts the note of maturity from the office of priest, where Ivo had located it, to the office of deacon. Deacons minister by distributing communion and by assisting in baptism and in other sacramental rites. Deacons also preach and carry the cross in processions. In comparison with his sources, Peter widens the scope of the deacon's activities. He also observes that they wear a stole as a sign of office. To fulfill that office they must have the capacity to announce and to warn. Christ performed the ministry of the deacon both when He distributed the Eucharist at the Last Supper and when He enjoined His disciples to watch and to pray on the night before His passion. While Peter enlarges the office of the deacon well beyond the Eucharistic ministry, or that ministry combined with preaching, he narrows the office of priest to an essentially Eucharistic one, unlike Simon and Ivo. The priest, for Peter and for the Loan masters, consecrates the Eucharist. His role is paralleled by that of Aaron and other Old Testament priests who offered sacrifices. Priests, like deacons, need maturity. They also require the virtue of prudence. Here, Peter combines the gift of wisdom prescribed by Simon with the lexical understanding of *presbyter* offered by Ivo. Christ fills this particular clerical office, and to perfection, by offering Himself as a sacrifice on the cross, according to Peter; he replaces Christ's institution and first celebration of the Eucharist with the act that gives it its ongoing sacramental efficacy.[402] Throughout this discussion of the seven grades of holy orders, then, Peter preserves the overall schema of the Laon masters and Hugh, while at the same time he feels perfectly free to incorporate ideas from Simon and from Ivo, to rearrange the material when he feels moved to do so, and to add his own insights and perspectives.

Peter asserts much more independence in dealing with bishops and prelates of a still higher level of authority. As we have seen,

---

[402] Ibid., c. 9–c. 11, 2: 400–05.

both the Laon masters, Hugh, and Simon treat the episcopacy as a grade of holy orders. Peter does not. He draws a sharp distinction between ranks within the clergy that are dignities, and ranks that are orders. Bishops and those above them fall clearly into the first category. The bishop, be he a bishop alone or a metropolitan, archbishop, or patriarch as well, has a specific office, along with a specific dignity. The dignity refers to the scope of his jurisdiction and whether it embraces a diocese or a province, or some larger unit of church governance. The office refers to those sacramental functions which are reserved to bishops. These include confirmation and ordination, and, in Peter's eyes at least, unction as well. The Lombard also accords two brief lines to the papacy. He remarks, rather laconically, that the pope is the supreme priest in the church and that he disposes all other ecclesiastical orders. Peter shows no interest in explaining how the pope exercises these functions or in his juridical relationship with other church leaders or with the secular power.[403] His lack of interest in these subjects is quite typical of systematic theologians in the middle of the twelfth century; Hugh of St. Victor and Robert Pullen, who do take up jurisdictional matters and the relation between *regnum* and *sacerdotium*, are the exceptions who prove the rule. Still, by making mention of the papacy at this juncture, however vague and abbreviated his remarks may be, Peter offers a location in the *Sentences* where later theologians, if inclined to discuss these matters at greater length in this kind of setting, could find a natural home for the subject. To round out his consideration of dignities in the church that convey rank, but not a new degree of orders, and in some cases do not involve, necessarily, any degree of orders at all, Peter mentions seers (*vates*), who may be priests, prophets, or poets.[404] His inclusion of poets under this heading, as holding rank within the church, is a remarkable expression of belief in the inspirational power of art when it is turned to the service of edification and the glorification of God. Literary art is not the only kind of art of which Peter takes cognizance, for he includes, as a final example of a rank within the church that is not necessarily associated with ordination, the office of cantor. The cantor may be the *praecentor*, the singer who leads the choir, or the *succentor*, his deputy.[405] Either way, the art of the musician gives him an office in the church since he embellishes

---

[403] Ibid., c. 14–c. 16, 2: 405–07.
[404] Ibid., c. 18, 2: 407.
[405] Ibid., c. 19.1, 2: 407.

divine worship and uplifts the spirit of the Christian people. Peter appears to have been unique among scholastic theologians in this period for the official rank in the church which he accords to literary and musical artists, in recognition of the services they perform for the faithful.

These addenda or exceptions to the seven grades of holy orders having been duly noted, Peter concentrates his attention in the rest of his treatise on holy orders on defining what it is, as a sacrament, and on outlining the conditions required for its valid administration and reception. Here, he applies his standard distinction between the *sacramentum* and the *res sacramenti*. The ceremony of ordination, and, specifically, the laying on of hands by the ministering bishop, constitute the sacrament. By means of it, the ordinand receives a permanent spiritual character. With it he also receives the grace empowering him to perform those actions which only the clergy can perform with efficacy and the grace enabling him to develop the virtues he needs in order to show forth the ministry and the sanctity of Christ in his own ministry. As with the school of Laon, Hugh, and Simon, and especially the latter two masters, Peter sees a double effect of sacramental grace in holy orders. On the one hand, this grace assists in the recipient's personal and internal sanctification, and, on the other, it also enables him to function as a channel of grace for others in his public sacramental ministry.[406] Peter agrees with Simon and with Robert Pullen on the imparting of an indelible and permanent sacramental character to the priest in his reception of ordination, a fact which entrenches this doctrine firmly in the understanding of the priesthood after his time.

Yet, more is required to convey this *res sacramenti* to the ordinand than the correct celebration of the ceremony of ordination. The intentions of both the minister and the recipient also play a critical role. This is the heading under which Peter takes up the question of whether bishops in a state of heresy or schism can validly ordain. He gives a thorough review of the opinions offered on this subject by the canonists and by his fellow theologians and he takes a hard line, and one that is perfectly consistent with the position that he takes on the valid consecration of the Eucharist in his treatise on that sacrament. Heresy and schism alike, in Peter's eyes, deprive a bishop of the capacity to ordain validly. A heretic will not have the requisite faith and intention, and a minister not himself in com-

---

[406] Ibid., c. 13, c. 19.2, 2: 405, 407.

munion with the church cannot induct other men into its sacerdotal ministry.[407] The situation is a bit more complicated, in his estimation, in the case of ordination by simoniacs. This is the only aspect of clerical morality which Peter raises in connection with ordination. Simony may be brought to the rite by would-be ordinands as well as by bishops who have themselves obtained preferment in this vicious manner. Here, Peter argues that the state of knowledge of the parties involved is a relevant factor in the equation. If the ordinand is not himself trying to purchase ordination, and if he is honestly unaware of the fact that his bishop is a simoniac, his ordination should be accepted as valid. On the other hand, if the ordinand knowingly seeks ordination from a simoniac bishop, his ordination should be rejected. In general, if ignorance is not a facter, Peter thinks that three circumstances should be taken into account in making a ruling. If both bishop and ordinand are simoniacs, both should be deprived of office. If a simoniac is ordained by a non-simoniac, the simoniac should be deprived of office. Finally, if a non-simoniac is ordained by a simoniac, he should be allowed to remain in office on the condition that the loss of his services would be a serious deprivation to the faithful, a proviso Peter derives from Pope Nicholas II along with the above-mentioned condition that the ordinand is unaware of his bishop's simoniac state. Another dispensation which Peter accepts is the validity of an ordination in which the candidate has been forced by violence to receive ordination at the hands of a schismatic or heretic.[408] In all these cases, it is clear that proper intentionality, and free will, on both sides of the transaction, are vital determinants of sacramental efficacy. And, while in the case of other sacraments, where the moral unworthiness of the minister is not seen as capable of impeding the workings of grace through the sacramental medium, the deep horror of simony, and the recognition that it remains a serious and ongoing problem in the middle of the twelfth century, inform the massive exception to that rule that Peter makes in the case of holy orders. Also, while he does pay brief and passing attention to the rules and regulations attached to ordination, as with the age requirements for advancing to different grades of orders,[409] it is also clear that this matter of the status, and morality, of both minister and recipient is the only major aspect of

---

[407] Ibid., d. 25. c. 1, 2: 408–13.
[408] Ibid., c. 2–c. 6, 2: 413–15.
[409] Ibid., c. 7, 2: 415–16.

the canonical approach to ordination that Peter is truly concerned with, and it is a concern which he reformulates so as to align it with intentionality as it applies both to the objective efficacy of the sacramental ministry and to the efficacy of the recipient's appropriation of sacramental grace subjectively.

Marriage

The sacrament that received the fullest discussion on the part of canonists and theologians alike in the first half of the twelfth century, and the one that has inspired the most research on the part of modern scholars is, indubitably, marriage.[410] In contrast with the situation that affected sacraments such as the Eucharist, this chorus of concern does not mirror a change in the practice of marriage on the part of twelfth-century Christians at large, a change which the masters of the day might seek to oppose or to rationalize. On the other hand, in line with other branches of sacramental theology at this time, marriage was strongly affected by the felt need of orthodox thinkers to defend it against the attacks of heretics, such as the Cathars, who rejected it. The central fact that most differentiates marriage as a sacrament from other sacraments in the writings of canonists and theologians in the first half of the twelfth century is that marriage existed as a social and legal institution, and always had, regardless of what Christian thinkers might say about it. It had a life of its own, apart from Christianity, a circumstance which was not the case with the other Christian rites treated under the heading of sacramental theology. The mas-

---

[410] For helpful overall surveys, see James A. Brundage, *Law, Sex, and Christian Society in Medieval Europe* (Chicago: University of Chicago Press, 1987), pp. 182–245; Jean Dauvillier, *Le mariage dans le droit classique de l'église depuis de Décret de Gratien (1140) jusqu'au la mort de Clément V (1314)* (Paris: Sirey, 1933), pp. 5–32, 183–94, 279–92, 310–18, 473–79; Gérard Fransen, "La formation du lien matrimonial au moyen âge," *Revue de droit canonique* 21 (1971): 106–26; Heaney, *The Development of the Sacramentality of Marriage*, pp. 7–14, 75–79, 82–83; T. P. McLaughlin, "The Formation of the Marriage Bond according to the *Summa Parisiensis*," *MS* 15 (1953): 208–12; Hans Zeimentz, *Ehe nach der Lehre der Frühscholastik: Eine moralgeschichtliche Untersuchung zur Anthropologie und Theologie der Ehe in der Schule Anselms von Laon und Wilhelms von Champeaux, bei Hugo von St. Viktor, Walter von Mortagne und Petrus Lombardus* (Düsseldorf: Patmos-Verlag, 1973). Briefer overviews are provided by Longère, *Oeuvres oratoires*, 1: 251; Michael M. Sheehan, "Choice of Marriage Partner in the Middle Ages," *Studies in Medieval and Renaissance History*, n.s. 1 (1978): 1–33; Rudolf Weigand, "Kanonistische Ehetraktate aus dem 12. Jahrhundert," in *Proceedings of the Third International Congress of Medieval Canon Law*, ed. Stephan Kuttner (Vatican City: Biblioteca Apostolica Vaticana, 1971), pp. 59–67.

ters writing on this subject in our period are not always very successful in coming to grips with this basic fact. Their debates on marriage, for this reason, often have a curiously airless quality about them; they read as if the masters were talking only to each other in some empyrean realm, without acknowledging the practical realities attached either to marriage itself, as it operated in real life, or even to the workability of the rules, principles, and procedures which they themselves advocate. There are, to be sure, major aspects of marriage on which a solid contemporary theological consensus existed. All masters at this time, for instance, agree with the Augustinian view that marriage was instituted in Eden before the fall, as an index of the creator's ordinance that sexual intercourse was to be the means for the propagation of the human race; after the fall, they agree, as well, marriage was designed to serve as a remedy for sin.[411] This consensus position was expounded both to refute Origen's views on human nature and the Catharist position on human sexuality. On another level, under the heading of the status of a marriage once made, all the masters hold that, once a valid marriage has come into being, it is indissoluble. Indissolubility, indeed, is part of what the agreement to marry involves, in their view, and it is seen as one of its goods, remaining in effect even if the couple are physically separated or if one puts aside the other on account of infidelity.[412] Another consensus position relates to impediments to marriage, or grounds for the nullification of a marriage. All agree that prior vows, especially those involved in entry into the monastic life or the priesthood, spiritual affinity, such as that created between a godparent and a godchild, or ignorance as to the identity or status of the other contracting party, constitute such impediments. There are many other areas where a principle at stake, such as consanguinity as an impediment, may receive general approval, but where the masters disagree as to the precise. understanding of the principle in practice. There are also aspects of marriage on which the debates reveal sharp differences of opinion on questions of fundamental substance, as well as divergences of opinion on procedure as well as substance that reflect regional rules and not merely personal preferences. But the single debate on marriage that generated the most discussion was the question of

---

[411] Michael Müller, *Die Lehre des hl. Augustinus von der Paradiesesehe und ihre Auswirking in der Sexualethik des 12. und 13. Jahrhunderts bis Thomas von Aquin* (Regensburg: Friedrich Pustet, 1954), pp. 19–103.

[412] Heaney, *The Development of the Sacramentality of Marriage*, pp. 154–56.

what makes the association of two people a marriage that can be regarded as a sacrament of the New Law.

In the field of marriage formation, the battle lines were drawn between those who argued that consummation makes the union a marriage and those who argued that it was consent that makes the marriage. This dispute was a bitter one, not only because of the serried ranks of authorities who could be, and were, marshalled in support of both of these positions but also because of the need to counter objections, both practical and theoretical, that could be leveled against each of them. On the consummationist side, for instance, it was hard to explain the difference between marriage and concubinage, recognizing that the latter institution, legitimate in Roman law and most forms of medieval secular law in the twelfth century, remained in existence, however much Christian moralists might deplore the fact. There was also the difficulty of proving non-consummation of a marriage, for the purpose of ad-judicating it as a cause of nullification, without violating personal and conjugal privacy and without admitting the evidence of witness-es who were likely to be partisan. Most serious of all, in the light of twelfth-century religious sensibilities, if a valid marriage required consummation to bring it into existence, then the consummationist position made it difficult to see how the marriage of the Virgin Mary and St. Joseph could have been a valid, sacramental marriage, given the fact that it was recognized to have been a celibate union.

For its part, the consent theory presented difficulties of its own. If consent to a common life, without the necessity of sexual commu-nity, were sufficient to make a marriage, how is marriage different from arrangements in which two relatives share a common house-hold? If consent alone is sufficient, can the exchange of vows on the part of two persons legally capable of marriage and lacking in impediments constitute a valid marriage in the absence of wit-nesses, a priestly blessing, the permission of the parents, and the standard provision of a dowry? If clandestine marriage is admitted, is this permission not a disservice to the legitimate interests of the state, the family, the church, and even the principals themselves? If consent makes a marriage, can consent unmake it, as was the case in Roman law, a logical and symmetrical conclusion even though it flies in the face of the Christian principle of indissolubility? All these questions and difficulties, and more, proved to be extremely intractable. Defenders of both the consummationist and the con-sent positions found their ingenuity taxed to the utmost in finding responses to the opposition while supporting their own positive solutions in the authorities and dealing with the authorities who supported the other side of the debate. We find both canonists and theologians in the consummationist camp, or Italian school, with Gratian emerging as its leading champion. The consensus, or French, school is also populated with both canonists and theologians, Hugh of St. Victor providing it with its most powerful insights and arguments and Peter Lombard articulating this position in its fullest and most sharply honed form. He also goes farther than anyone else in the debate in taking seriously the argument on the other side of it, borrowing from its perspectives, while at the same time staunchly refusing to compromise the principles he defends.

Although the members of the school of Laon are, generally, supporters of consent, one Laon master, the author of *Decretum dei fuit*, gives an early inkling of the position to be articulated much more powerfully by Gratian later in the century. The master sees the centrality of consummation, in marriage formation, as a corollary of the institution of marriage in Eden for the purpose of procreation and its later reinstitution as a remedy for fornication after the fall. Therefore, what marriage is all about, in his view, is sexual relations. Marriage is, simply, the carnal union of the spouses. This is the sacrament, the external physical sign. What it signifies is the union of Christ and the church. This author writes before, or outside of, Hugh of St. Victor's important expansion of the definition of a sacrament as a sign that effects what it signifies, as well as bearing a physical resemblance to it, and so he does not take up the question of whether, or how, the *sacramentum* conveys or effects this *res sacramenti*. He regards the intentions which the spouses bring to their marriage as important, and defines them, purely, as the hope of offspring. He does not raise the question of whether the validity and sacramentality of their marriage would be jeopardized were they to bring other intentions to it, or if they omit this one. The one item he adds to the point that consummation makes the marriage is that marriage also requires public celebration before witnesses. He does not specify whether one of those witnesses must be a priest. The master makes no direct mention of consent, whether of the spouses themselves or their parents, as in any way required. To the extent that consent, in an implicit sense, can be read into their intention, or wish, to have children, it would be a consent to carnal relations only. The master makes no reference to the problem of Mary and Joseph or to the difference between marriage and concubinage.[413]

---

[413] *Decretum dei fuit*, ed. Heinrich Weisweiler in *Das Schrifttum der Schule Anselms*

In turning from this Laon master to Gratian, we can clearly see that, while the latter has profited from the reflections of the theologians, he is determined to place the topic of marriage formation on a far wider canvas and to handle it in a much more circumspect way. Gratian's treatment of marriage has typically been studied in isolation, as a subject in its own right, by historians of canon law.[414] Much can be gained, however, by comparing his analysis of this subject with his discussion of penance. Marriage and penance are given parallel treatment by Gratian in two respects. In both cases, he agrees that an initial stage is necessary in which the correct intention is manifested by the recipient of the sacrament, but that the sacrament itself cannot be held to have been received in fact unless and until a second stage occurs that is public and institutional and presided over by a priest. It is in this second stage that the alteration in the recipient's status imparted by the sacrament takes place. The second clear parallel is that, in the case of both sacraments, Gratian collects and discusses thoroughly a large dossier of authorities who say that the first, or consensual, stage is the point at which that change of status occurs. Several of these authorities are as weighty as they are unequivocal. They include Pope Nicholas II, who locates marriage formation in consent not coitus, John Chrysostom, who says that consent, and not the marriage ceremony, the formal handing over of the bride to the groom, or their sexual union makes the marriage, and Ambrose, who states crisply that it is not the defloration of the virgin but the conjugal pact that makes the marriage. To be sure, Gratian is concerned with showing that consent is necessary and that it cannot be omitted. He is also willing to recognize that, while the public celebration of weddings is required and appropriate, it is not the ceremony itself but the consummation of the marriage following it that is the critical determinant of the status of the spouses. As with his handling of the

---

von Laon und Wilhelms von Champeaux in deutschen Bibliotheken, Beiträge, 33:1–2 (Münster: Aschendorff, 1936), pp. 371–73. Heinrich J. F. Reinhardt, *Die Ehelehre der Schule des Anselms von Laon: Ein theologie- und kirchenrechtsgeschichtliche Untersuchung zu den Ehetexte der frühen Pariser Schule des 12. Jahrhundert*, Bieträge, n.F. 14 (Münster: Aschendorff, 1974) is unaware of this text and its departure from the support of consent by other Laon masters. His study is otherwise the best guide to their position. Knoch, *Die Einsetzung*, pp. 62–73, omits marriage formation in his account of the school of Laon on marriage.

[414] See, in particular, Brundage, *Law, Sex, and Christian Society*, pp. 235–45; Raymond G. Decker, "Institutional Authority versus Personal Responsibility in the Marriage Section of Gratian's *A Concordance of Discordant Canons*," *The Jurist* 32 (1972): 51–65; Fransen, "La formation," pp. 119–26; Fournier and Le Bras, *Histoire*, 2: 314–52; John T. Noonan, "Power to Choose," *Viator* 4 (1973): 419–34.

authorities supporting confessionism, whom he reads as deeming the critical act of confession and absolution as having been inspired by a rightly motivated spirit of contrition, whether or not this is what they actually argue, so he reads the consummationist authorities as saying that the consent of the spouses is also required, whether the authorities in fact make this point or not. As for the pro-consent authorities, whatever the literal sense of their opinions may be, he reads them as speaking only to a consent that is necessary but not sufficient, in a manner directly parallel with his handling of the contritionist authorities in his treatment of penance. In Gratian's own solution, he presents marriage, like penance, as a two-part process. In the case of marriage, a truly sacramental, and hence indissoluble, bond is not forged until the second part has been completed. Marriage begins, as he sees it, at the time of the betrothal of the couple, when consent to the marriage is given. But it does not become truly binding until it is consummated. As he puts the point: "It must be known that marriage is begun by betrothal and completed by [sexual] mixing. Hence between the betrothed there is a marriage, but only a beginning; between the couple there is a ratified marriage" (*Sed sciendum est, quod coniugum desponsatione initiatur, con mixtione perficitur: Unde inter sponsum et sponsam coniugum est, sed initiatum; inter copulatos est coniugum ratum*).[415]

Consistent with this clear distinction between *matrimonium initiatum* and *matrimonium ratum* which he draws, Gratian states, at one point, that, since the marriage does not become indissoluble until it is consummated, engaged persons may break their engagements if they prefer different marital partners or in order to undertake religious vows, although elsewhere he gives the opposite view.[416] Where does this leave the marriage of Mary and Joseph? Gratian's first sally is to argue that their union includes the three Augustinian goods of marriage, faith, offspring, and sacrament. It manifests faith in their fidelity to each other. It manifests sacramentality in the permanence of their union. And, it manifests offspring in their rearing and education of Jesus. Still, when push come to shove, Gratian is an honest man. He recognizes the fact that the goods of marriage are not the same thing as marriage itself. Marriages can

---

[415] Gratian, *Decretum* pars 2. c. 27. q. 34, col. 1073. The translation is that of John T. Noonan, *Marriage Canons from the Decretum* (Berkeley: School of Law, 1967), p. 12. For the argument in this paragraph more generally, see *Decretum* pars 2. c. 27. q. 34–c. 30. q. 5, col. 1073–1108.

[416] Gratian, *Decretum* pars 2. c. 27. q. 50–q. 51, col. 1077–78.

and do exist which lack these goods. And, given the fact that there was no *matrimonium ratum* in the case of Mary and Joseph, their marriage was not truly sacramental, and could have been dissolved.[417] A marriage that is *ratum*, for Gratian, requires consummation, even if this is the one and only time that the spouses come together in the flesh.[418] If the condition is met, the marriage is indissoluble.

As noted, notwithstanding his firm consummationism, Gratian thinks that consent, involving an appropriate intention, is also a required if not a *per se* constitutive part of marriage. In comparison with the author of the *Decretum dei fuit*, he widens appreciably his understanding of what marital consent includes. More is at issue here, for Gratian, than merely the consent to sexual relations. For, that would not make it possible to distinguish between marriage and concubinage. In his terms, consent that is specifically marital consent requires marital affection.[419] This idea, which goes back to Roman law, means, neither for the civilians nor for Gratian himself, romantic or erotic love. Indeed, the civilians contrast the two attitudinal states. Rather, marital affection involves according to one's spouse the respect, the honor, the moral standing and regard, and the acknowledgement consistent with one's recognition of the spouse as one's partner in an upright, lawful union. This is not the kind of attitude one would display toward a partner whom one would not or could not marry, toward whom one felt no enduring commitment, and whose offspring would not be part of one's legitimate lineage. Gratian's incorporation of the idea of marital affection guarantees the continuing availability of this principle in both canonical and theological treatments of marriage in the sequel. Important as it is, he none the less makes it plain that, while the couple's inner intention, in the form of marital affection, is necessary, the consent reflecting it is *matrimonium initiatum* only, not *matrimonium ratum*.

Gratian's earliest commentators tend to confirm his position, although they do not always use his exact language and while they may subtract from, add to, or amplify on his teaching. Paucapalea

---

[417] Ibid., pars 2. c. 27, col. 1062–78.

[418] Ibid., pars 2. c. 27. q. 29, col. 1071.

[419] Ibid., pars 2. c. 28. q. 1. c. 17, col. 1089. On marital affection, see John T. Noonan, "Marital Affection in the Canonists," *Studia Gratiana* 12 (1967): 479–509; "Power to Choose," pp. 419–34; Rudolf Weigand, "Liebe und Ehe bei Dekretisten des 12. Jahrhunderts," in *Love and Marriage in the Twelfth Century*, ed. Willy Van Hoeke and Andries Welkenhuysen (Leuven: Leuven University Press, 1981), pp. 41–58.

agrees that, while consent is necessary, it is consummation that makes the marriage. He thinks that the consent involved must include that of the parents as well as the principals, and makes a point of insisting on the spouses' taking of their vows in person, ruling out the acceptability of proxies. He disallows clandestine marriage although, inconsistently, he says that it is licit and indissoluble.[420] Roland of Bologna who, like his canonical associates, is far more interested in impediments, grounds for nullification or separation, and other actionable matters than he is in the sacramental character of marriage, takes a somewhat different line in his *Summa* and in his *Sentences*. In the former work, which is more a commentary on Gratian, he reprises that master's view that consent, expressed at the time of the betrothal, supplies only *matrimonium initiatum*, while it is consummation that makes the union an indissoluble *matrimonium ratum*. He presents marriage as having three aspects, or parts: consent, the conjugal pact or engagement, and the absence of obstacles to a legal union. This analysis associates the consent with the engagement. But Roland contradicts himself by introducing a distinction which he finds in contemporary theologians on the opposing side of the debate, the distinction between present and future consent. The engagement embodies future consent. It is the present consent voiced at the wedding itself that conveys the consent needed for the *matrimonium initiatum* phase of the event. While the husband and wife may be called spouses from the time of their engagement, they are not actually married until the union is consummated sexually. Roland follows Gratian's first line of the defense of the marriage of Mary and Joseph as a true marriage by stating that the raising of Jesus enabled them to fulfill the marital good of children. But he does not acknowledge the logic of Gratian's conclusion that their marriage was, technically, no marriage at all according to the consummationist theory.[421] In his *Sentences*, Roland omits the distinction between future and present consent and does not consider whether the consent required is given at the betrothal or at the wedding. He cites the pro-consent authorities in discussing this point, without using Gratian's creative reinterpretation of their views so as to make them compatible with a consummationist position which they plainly reject. This gives a rather inconclusive tone to Roland's defense of that position. One thing he does that is not found in Gratian is to discuss the

---

[420] Paucapalea, *Summa* c. 27, c. 28. q. 5, pp. 110–11, 112, 115, 123.
[421] Roland of Bologna, *Summa* c. 20. q. 3, c. 27 prologus, c. 27. q. 2. pp. 72–73, 113–14, 126–30.

sacramental character of marriage, in line with his treatment of the other sacraments. The *sacramentum* in any such rite must be the physical, perceptible sign. In the case of marriage, this is the sexual union of the spouses. Roland adds this theological rationale to Gratian's argument in favor of consummationism. The sexual union of the spouses signifies the union of Christ and the church, which is the *res sacramenti*. Roland does not discuss whether this *sacramentum* serves as a channel of grace as well.[422] But his emphasis on the sexual union as the *sacramentum* is associated with a view of marriage that limits it to its sexual purposes only and that omits Gratian's idea of marital affection.

Canonists no less than theologians are to be found supporting the consent position as well. Indeed, one of the earliest of twelfth-century canonists to devote attention to this topic, Ivo of Chartres, gives a strong statement of the position that marriage is made by consent. Unlike other canonists writing on this subject in the period, and unlike the theologians, Ivo was a bishop. As an ecclesiastical statesman, he needed not only to rule on delicts occurring within his own sphere of jurisdiction; he was also called upon by other bishops to give advice concerning cases on which they had to render judgment. Many of these marriage cases, starting with the flagrant and protracted affair between King Philip I and Bertrada de Montfort, countess of Anjou, both of whose spouses were still alive when they decided to live together openly, involved mighty personages who regarded themselves as the makers of manners and whose behavior demanded correction, not only on general principles but also because of their high social profile and rich capacity to give scandal. While Ivo, in his letters no less than in his more systematic decretals, was a man of principle, fully capable of maintaining strict and rigorous opinions, the political necessities surrounding particular cases sometimes lead him to accept a compromise position for the sake of resolving practical problems. For the same reasons, he is willing to take seriously the practices which the civil law condemns or permits, whether he approves of them or not, and his emphasis often has more to say about the frequency and urgency of the problems that he confronts as a sitting bishop than it does about their importance to him in the abstract. In this

---

[422] Roland of Bologna, *Sent.*, pp. 116, 157, 270–72. On Roland here, see Gietl, intro. to his ed., pp. lxii–lxvii; Brundage, *Law, Sex, and Christian Society* p. 263; Jean Gaudemet, "Sur Trois 'Dicta Gratiani' relatifs au 'matrimonium ratum'," in *Études de droit et d'histoire: Mélanges Mgr. H. Wagnon* (Louvain: Faculté Internationale de Droit Canonique, 1976), pp. 550–54.

respect, Ivo's position on marriage formation can be read as much as a reflection of the ways in which northern French aristocrats understood marriage in actuality as it is an effort on his part, however successful or unsuccessful, to impose Christian values on this group and to persuade them to regard marriage as a sacrament and not merely as a matter of political and dynastic policy or of personal convenience.[423]

Ivo launches his discussion of marriage formation with a forthright assertion that consent, not consummation, makes the marriage, citing Ambrose, Chrysostom, and Nicholas, the standard authorities who support this view. He does not seek to disarm the authorities on the other side of the debate, but simply anchors his own position with the pro-consent authorities and goes on to elaborate on its implications.[424] This position undergirds his own ruling that physical separation, of the sort that might occur thanks to pilgrimage, crusading, or long-distance trading, does not terminate a marriage, since the physical union of the spouses is not what created the marriage in the first place.[425] In addition to being a logical application of the consent principle, these examples are also a sign of the times; it is difficult to envision any writer on the subject before Ivo who would refer so casually to these indices of early twelfth-century behavior. Ivo's stress on the consent principle also informs his insistence on the point that underage children, too young to give informed consent, cannot be married off by their parents; nor should they be betrothed by their parents before the age of seven. The attention that Ivo gives to this issue reflects three things: the fact that the consent of the principals was frequently ignored in actuality, the need for the principals themselves to consent knowingly and of their own free will, and the idea that the principle of consent extends in some sense to the parents as well as to the spouses.[426] The same point of view can be seen in Ivo's judgment concerning rape as the basis for establishing a marital

---

[423] Good assessments of Ivo which take his circumstances into account include Brigitte Basdevant-Gaudemet, "Le mariage d'après la correspondance d'Yves de Chartres," *Revue historique de droit française et étranger* 61 (1983): 195–215; A. Foucault, *Essai sur Ives de Chartres d'après sa correspondance* (Chartres: Petrot-Garnier, 1883), pp. 140–77; Paul Fournier, *Yves de Chartres et le droit canonique* (Paris: Bureau de la Revue, 1898), pp. 1–10, 36, 39–47, 57–62.

[424] Ivo of Chartres, *Decretum* 8. c. 2–c. 3, c. 16–c. 17, c. 20, c. 35, *PL* 161: 583D–584D, 587B–588A, 588B, 591C; *Epistolae* 99, 134, 168, 243, 246, *PL* 162: 118D–119A, 143C–144C, 153B–154D, 251A, 253B–C.

[425] Ivo of Chartres, *Decretum* 8. c. 9, c. 12–c. 14, c. 189–c. 193, c. 244–c. 245, *PL* 161: 586A–D, 623D–624D, 637D–638C.

[426] Ibid., 8. c. 21–c. 22, c. 169, *PL* 161: 588C–D, 620A.

claim on an unmarried woman. As we will see below, this topic
tends to surface frequently in the list of impediments to marriage at
this time, and the masters reflect a general inclination to reject this
claim, in contrast to their Carolingian predecessors. In handling
this point, Ivo states that the rapist can be refused but sees this
decision as requiring the consent of both the victim and her
parents.[427]

These efforts to accommodate the principle of consent to the
social realities of the day can be seen in other areas of Ivo's
treatment of marriage formation. He draws no distinction between
the consent given at the time of the betrothal and the consent given
at the time of the wedding, and does not consider the question of
which of these moments is the time when the union becomes
indissoluble. Given his admission of the age of seven as an acceptable age at which a child may be betrothed, he does not, in
practice, offer much protection to the consensual rights of young
spouses, although he seeks to defend them. Similarly, he adds other
conditions which propose that more than consent is required to
initiate a marriage. A marriage is valid, Ivo says, if the vows are
sworn in church (*in oratorio*) in a public ceremony, even if there is no
written document attesting the event and no dowry; although he
contradicts himself concerning the dowry and elsewhere says that
there can be no wedding without one.[428] Ivo clearly opposes clandestine marriage, but declines to rule on its validity.[429] As for the
intentions that spouses ought to bring to marital consent, he takes
the same broad-gauged line later followed by Gratian. He does not
confine himself to the consent to sexual relations alone, but invokes
the principle of marital affection, and defines it in the same way as
Gratian does later in the century, as the dignity, courtesy, and
standing as an honorably wedded spouse which it accords. In
making this point, however, Ivo is not interested in reflecting on
what makes Christian marriage a sacrament, a question which,
indeed, he never raises. Rather it comes up in the context of his
effort to distinguish marriage from concubinage, not in defense of
consummationism but as a critique of the relationship between
Philip and Bertrada. Despite the fact that Philip had browbeaten
several French prelates into witnessing a fictitious wedding cere-

---

[427] Ibid., 8. c. 23, c. 40–c. 41, c. 170–c. 177, *PL* 161: 588D–589A, 593A–B,
620A–621C.
[428] Ibid., 8. c. 44, *PL* 161: 594A. For his retraction of this position on the dowry,
see 8. c. 144, *PL* 161: 616C.
[429] Ibid., 8. c. 141, *PL* 161: 616B.

mony between himself and Bertrada, an event loudly deplored and denounced by Ivo, the lovers were not, he insists, married. Rather, they were living in a state of adulterous concubinage, which Ivo certainly disapproves of although he is constrained to recognize that it is a licit relationship, according to the secular law. So, he does what he can to explain why concubinage is not marriage.[430]

The theologians on the pro-consent side of the debate feel, on the whole, less constrained than Ivo to take the realities of life as it was lived in their time into account, however much they may have agreed with him. The influence of Ivo can be marked in the treatment of marriage typical in the school of Laon, whose members also amplify considerably on his position.[431] As one Laon master forthrightly states, "where there is no mutual consent, there is no marriage" (*ubi non est consensus utriusque non est coniugum*).[432] And, two other Laon masters, evidently the earliest source for this critical distinction, specify that the consent required to make a marriage is the present consent given at the wedding, not the future consent given at the betrothal.[433] The author of the *Sententie Anselmi* goes on to indicate three aspects of this present consent. It must involve the manifest, not tacit, consent of persons who are present—no proxies are allowed—who have the legal capacity to marry, and who lack impediments to marriage. The spouses must also bring to their marriage vows two intentions, the desire for children and the commitment to welcome their arrival whether it is convenient or not, and the commitment of mutual fidelity until death.[434] Another author in this group treats the production of offspring, and the sexual relations required for it, and the consummationist authorities who stress this aspect of marriage, as speaking merely of what happens in a typical marriage after it has come into being, although this sequel is not of the essence in making the union a marriage. Others agree that the three Augustinian goods of marriage do not constitute the marriage, since marriages continue to remain in force in their absence.[435] Masters in this school are

---

[430] Ibid., 8. c. 32, c. 36, c. 60, c. 153, *PL* 161: 591A–B, 591C–D, 597A, 617C–D.

[431] For Ivo's influence on the Laon masters, see Reinhardt, *Die Ehelehre*, pp. 86–98, 132, 184. This book as a whole gives a good account of the pro-consent arguments of the school.

[432] *Sentences of Plausible Authenticity*, no. 206, 5: 135. See also no. 405, 5: 287.

[433] *Sentences of the School of Laon*, no. 527, 5: 365–66; *Sent. Anselmi* 5, pp. 146–47. Cf. Brundage, *Law, Sex, and Christian Society*, p. 237, who attributes this distinction, in the first instance, to Abelard.

[434] *Sent. Anselmi* 5, pp. 112–13, 139–40, 141, 149.

[435] *Deus de cuius principio et fine tacetur*, ed. Heinrich Weisweiler in "Le recueil des

sensitive to the problem of Mary and Joseph, and harness it to their cause. The author of *De coniugo* uses this point to hammer home his conclusion that sexual relations, although usually present, are not required to make a marriage. The content of consent which accomplishes the end of marriage formation is, rather, the spouses' commitment to a common life, their common will to live together under the laws of the church. He is willing to push the principle of consent, so defined, with nothing added, to its ultimate logical conclusions, by admitting that a clandestine marriage is valid, so long as consent is present and the parties are legally marriageable.[436]

Also on the pro-consent side of the controversy stands Robert Pullen, although he is less interested in the question of marriage formation than he is in marriage as a calling within the church, and one that has special ethical notes attached to it. While his basic concern in his treatise on marriage is sexual ethics within marriage, and not marriage as a sacrament, and while he omits many standard topics relating to this subject, he agrees that consent is of the essence. He does so without profiting from the Laon masters' distinction between present and future consent. Marital consent, in his eyes, should embody an appropriately religious intention. Only God's reasons for marrying, the procreation of offspring as given by His first institution of marriage in Eden and the avoidance of fornication attached to its reinstitution after the fall, are acceptable. Robert objects to worldly reasons, such as the enjoyment of the beauty, desirability, wealth, or social position of one's spouse, although he does not go so far as to say that such defective intentions invalidate a marriage. In any event, he holds that a marriage that is validated by consent remains in force irrespective of whether it leads to mutual fidelity, offspring, or permanence.[437]

It is striking that neither the Laon masters, nor Robert Pullen, nor Ivo of Chartres has much to say about the sacramentality of marriage. This is by no means invariably the case among the defenders of consent. Much more of an effort to see how, or if, marriage can be brought into accord with their general definitions of sacrament is found in other masters in this group. Peter Abelard

---

sentences 'Deus de cuius principio et fine tacetur' et son remaniement," *RTAM* 5 (1933): 270–72; *Sentences of the School of Laon*, no. 527, 5: 365; *Sent. Anselmi* 5, p. 112; *De coniugo*, ed. Franz Bliemetzrieder in "Theólogie et théologiens de l'école épiscopale de Paris avant Pierre Lombard," *RTAM* 3 (1931): 274–75.

[436] *De coniugo*, pp. 274, 283.

[437] Robert Pullen, *Sent.* 6.4, 7.35, 7.39, *PL* 186: 867B, 952A, 956D–960B.

and his followers wrestle with this problem rather inconclusively, and also inconsistently in some respects. To be sure, Abelard himself bring up marriage only indirectly, in discussing the creation of Eve in his *Hexaemeron* and as a gloss on Paul's remarks on the subject in his Romans commentary. Elsewhere, he treats marriage in a hortatory vein in addressing a monastic audience, Heloise especially, who must put aside thoughts about marriage. The circumstances and contexts in which marriage comes up in Abelard's writings help to account, in part, for the line he takes on it. In his view, marriage is purely a concession to the regrettable fact of human carnality. It exists as a remedy for sin, only, and it is burdened with worldly cares, sorrow, and luxury. The wise man, he argues, here invoking Jerome and the anti-matrimonial argument of his *Adversus Jovinianum*, will avoid marriage and spare himself its aggravations. At the same time, Abelard asserts that marriage is a sacrament and, presumably, as such, it ought to be viewed as something holy. Yet, he can find nothing in the relations between spouses that signifies a divine grace, his general definition of sacrament.[438]

The fullest exposition of marriage within the Abelardian school is provided by Hermannus, who faithfully perpetuates Abelard's negative appraisal of it and his logical inconsistency regarding its sacramentality. Hermannus is a firm proponent of consent as what makes the marriage and accepts the distinction between present and future consent. Indeed,this distinction is of use to him because he sees the content of marital consent as extending specifically and only to the agreement of spouses to exclusive sexual rights to each other, which rights come into being only at the wedding. "It is this pact that initiates the marriage" (*Et hoc federatio ad primum facit coniugum*), he asserts.[439] Marital vows make licit and blameless the sexual relations which are the sole point of marriage, and which exist purely as a concession to human weakness. The wise man, Hermannus agrees, citing Theophrastus as well as Jerome, does not marry. In other areas one can try before one buys. Not so with marriage. A wife is either chaste or unchaste. If chaste, she is

---

[438] Peter Abelard, *Hex.*, pp. 133–35; *In Ep. Pauli ad Romanos* 4:18–19, CCCM 11: 148. Good treatments of Abelard on marriage are provided by Weingart, "Abailard's Contribution," pp. 172–73; *The Logic of Divine Love*, pp. 195–96; Philippe Delhaye, "Le Dossier anti-matrimoniale de l'*Adversus Jovinianum* et son influence sur quelques écrits latins du XIIe siècle," *MS* 13 (1951): 65–86.

[439] Hermannus, *Sent.*, p. 135. For Hermannus on marriage, see Knoch, *Die Einsetzung*, pp. 152–53.

proud; if unchaste, she embroils her husband in a life of never-
ending suspicion and embarrassment. Marriage, in short, is a yoke,
an obstacle to a man's freedom.[440] At the same time, Hermannus
states that marriage is a sacrament. He gives the standard Augustinian definition of a sacrament as a visible sign of invisible grace or
as the sign of a holy thing. As for marriage, however, it conveys no
merit in the sanctification or salvation of those who enter it; it
stands for nothing sacred; and it confers no *donum*, no gift of
grace.[441]

Precisely the same position is taken by the author of *Sententiae
Parisiensis* I. Although sex is what marriage is all about, in his eyes,
he agrees that consent to it, and not its actual exercise, is what
makes the marriage. The concession of exclusive sexual rights to
each other is all that the spouses promise. Marriage itself is a
purely negative, remedial, concession. It is, he states, a sacrament,
although, illogically, "it conveys no gift of grace" (*non confert
donum*).[442] On the other hand, this master does think that marriage
signifies something sacred, the union of Christ and the church.[443]
But, given his treatment of marriage in general, it is understandably difficult for him to explain why and how this is the case. He
makes no effort to do so. The same can be said for the authors of
Sententiae Parisiensis II and the *Ysagoge in theologiam*.[444] The latter
master also makes the mistake of mentioning the marriage of Mary
and Joseph, although it does not help his argument. Since he has a
purely sexual understanding of the content of marital consent, he
has as much difficulty accounting for that marriage as the consummationists do.[445]

Most of the masters on the pro-consent side of the debate show
far more sensitivity to the usefulness of the Mary and Joseph case to
the defense of their position. This fact has already emerged in our
consideration of the school of Laon. But the contemporary master
who, more than any other, capitalizes on this theme, and uses it to
promote a generous and expanded understanding of marriage, both
in itself and as a sacrament, is Hugh of St. Victor.[446] Hugh first

---

[440] Hermannus, *Sent.*, pp. 137–38.
[441] Ibid., pp. 120, 135, 136.
[442] *Sent. Parisiensis* I, p. 44.
[443] Ibid., p. 46.
[444] *Sent. Parisiensis* II, p. 150; *Ysagoge in theologiam*, pp. 196, 199.
[445] *Ysagoge in theologiam*, pp. 196–99.
[446] The best treatment of Hugh's contribution to the understanding of marriage
is provided by Henri A. J. Allard, *Die eheliche Lebens- und Liebesgemeinschaft nach Hugo*

develops his position in his *Epistola de beatae Mariae virginitate*, not initially in the context of sacramental theology. He then reprises what he says in that work in his *De sacramentis*. This fact accounts for the way he approaches the nature of marriage in the first instance. The question he poses at the beginning of the *Epistola* is whether, as a woman already betrothed at the time of the annunciation, Mary changed the nature of her marital consent when she married Joseph so as to retain her virginity, and, if so, whether she was marrying him under false pretenses. This issue leads Hugh to a consideration of the essential content of marital consent, and whether it must include consent to sexual relations. Repeating the position of the ancient pro-consent authorities without expressly citing them by name, he insists that "marriage is not made by sexual union, but by consent" (*matrimonium non facit coitus, sed consensus*).[447] This consent, he continues, must be mutual. In it the spouses promise fidelity and permanence. The agreement to sexual relations is not required to make a marriage. But, when sexual relations are included in a vow that also contains the other and the essential ingredients, their exercise is a duty flowing from the vow, and not the bond itself (*officium et non vinculum*).[448] In Hugh's eyes, the bond itself is a bond of charity, not one forged by sexual intercourse. A true marriage is marked by its spiritual and affective character. In it, the spouses are one in heart (*duo in corde uno*). This union of hearts signifies the union of God and the individual human soul. The relationship of spouses that Hugh envisions is marked by constancy, sincerity, solicitude in all things, affection, piety, consolation, devotion, care, and compassion. They mutually support each others as companions and partners, bearing tribulation and suffering in undivided unity (*semper in omni sinceritate dilectionis, in omni cum sollicitudinis, in omni affectu pietatis, in omni studio compassionis,*

---

von St. Viktor (Rome: Analecta Dehoniana, 1963). See also Fransen, "La formation," pp. 114–17; Corrado Gneo, "La dottrina del matrimonio nel 'De B. Mariae virginitate' di Ugo di S. Vittore," *Divinitas* 17 (1973): 374–95; Penny S. Gold, "The Marriage of Mary and Joseph in the Twelfth-Century Ideology of Marriage," in *Sexual Practices and the Medieval Church*, ed. Vern L. Bullogh and James Brundage (Buffalo: Prometheus Books, 1982), pp. 102–17; W. E. Gössman, "Die Bedeutung der Liebe in der Eheauffassung Hugos von St. Viktor und Wolfram von Eschenbach," *Münchener theologische Zeitschrift* 5 (1954): 205–08, 213; Heaney, *The Development of the Sacramentology of Marriage*, pp. 14–16; Knoch, *Die Einsetzung*, pp. 110–13; Ott, *Untersuchung*, pp. 404–15; Christian Schütz, *Deus absconditus, Deus manifestus: Die Lehre Hugos von St. Viktor über die Offenbarung Gottes* (Rome: Herder, 1967), pp. 121–24; Zeimentz, *Ehe*, pp. 136–40.
[447] Hugh of St. Victor, *Epistola de beatae Mariae virginitate*, *PL* 176: 858A.
[448] Ibid., *PL* 176: 859D.

in omni virtute consolationis, et fide devotionis . . . in bonis et in malis omnibus, sicut consolationis socium ac participem, ita et tribulationis et sufferentiae indivisum exhibeat).[449] Hugh certainly agrees that God intended spouses to reproduce sexually from the very beginning. This activity, however, does not constitute the bond of love that makes the marriage. Also, it is a duty that not all couples are required to perform. When it is included in their marriage, it signifies the union of Christ and the church. This physical union is sacramental, for Hugh, just as the spiritual and affective union of spouses is sacramental. But, in his view, the union of hearts is the greater sacrament of the two, and it is *per se* constitutive of marriage and sufficient.[450] The marital union of hearts, he adds, here address-ing an objection raised by the consummationists, is not the same thing as a common household shared by relatives who may also be bound by affection. For, the former union signifies the union of the soul and God, which the latter does not. Pointing out that the consummationists, if they are honest, are forced to admit that the marriage of Mary and Joseph was not a real marriage, he returns to the question he had posed at the beginning of the *Epistola* and concludes that Mary and Joseph had already agreed on a celibate union before the annunciation, so that neither of them changed what they intended in their actual marriage vows.[451]

Hugh repeats the essentials of this doctrine in the *De sacramentis* and adds to it, drawing not only on ideas found in other contempo-rary thinkers but also on his own general theory of the sacraments. He reiterates the point about the double sacramentality of mar-riage, with the spouses' pure love of the mind (*pura mentis dilectione*) standing for the union of God and the soul and their sexual associa-tion, if any, standing for the union of Christ and the church. He agrees that it is the spiritual society that is of the essence, although he does not give the effusive description of it that he provides in the *Epistola*. To the double institution of marriage, before and after the fall, he adds that, in addition to being a remedy for sin in the latter case, marriage, like the other sacraments, is given for our instruc-tion and for our growth in virtue; he thus adds a positive moral dimension to this state of life.[452] Reaching out to include points made by other masters, whether pro-consent or not, and whether

---

[449] Ibid., *PL* 176: 860A–D.
[450] Ibid., *PL* 176: 864A–B.
[451] Ibid., *PL* 176: 858C, 865C–867D, 873B–876C.
[452] Hugh of St. Victor, *De sac.* 1.8.13, *PL* 176: 314C–318A. The quotation is at 316B.

canonists or theologians, he observes that, along with mutual consent, the spouses must both possess the legal right to marry. The
content of their consent, moreover, must include consent to marital
affection and honor, in the sense that Ivo and Gratian give to this
term, as well as being a compact of love and a spiritual society. It is
a commitment, as well, to mutual fidelity in spirit, and not just to
mutual fidelity and reciprocity in their sexual relations, when the
latter are included.[453] Hugh also concerns himself with the question
of when the marriage comes into being.[454] He agrees with the
distinction between present and future consent and sides with the
Laon masters and those influenced by them in asserting that it is
the present consent given at the wedding, not the future consent
given at the betrothal, and not the consummation, if any, that
follows the wedding that initiates the bond. He would like to see
this consent confirmed before witnesses; but, like the author of the
De coniugo, he recognizes that the logic of his position forces him to
recognize the validity of clandestine marriages, the other necessary
conditions being present. Hugh accepts the distinction drawn between the goods of marriage and marriage itself, and maintains
that the latter remains in force in the absence of the former.[455]

There is no question of the fact that Hugh offers the most solidly
grounded defense of the principle of consent in marriage formation
of any master up through his time. He also widens considerably the
range of issues pertinent to the understanding of marriage as a
sacrament. Consistent with the emphasis on consent, he provides a
detailed and broad analysis of the kind of intentionality that
spouses need to bring to the reception of this sacrament, including
the marital affection of the canonists and going beyond it to
embrace a spiritual, moral, and affective bonding, seen as symbolizing the intimate union of God and the soul. His description of
this state, especially in the *Epistola de beatae Mariae virginitate*, offers a
richer and more positive assessment and account of what marriage
means, or should mean, to those persons who commit themselves to
this state of life. Hugh also moves well beyond the remedial in his
consideration of the help which marriage can give to Christians in
becoming better, wiser, and more virtuous people. Yet, there are
two salient areas where he does not integrate marriage fully into the
general theory of sacrament that undergirds his innovations in

---

[453] Ibid., 2.11.4, *PL* 176: 483A–485D.
[454] Ibid., 2.11.5–6, *PL* 176: 485D–494A.
[455] Ibid., 2.11.7–9, *PL* 494A–496D.

these other respects. While in the case of other sacraments, he is
deeply concerned with the intention which the recipient brings to
the sacrament as conditioning his ability to profit from its reception, Hugh does not deal with the question of whether people who
marry for purely worldly reasons, and not for the exalted and idealistic
reasons which he imputes to spouses, are therefore not validly married
in the eyes of God and Christian society, whatever the civil law and
civil society may think. And, mindful of the fact that Hugh's definition
of sacrament in general is a sign that is a medium of grace, a sign that
effects what it signifies, it is odd to note that he never raises the
question of how the spiritual union of spouses can be thought of either
as a physical sign or as a sign that effects as well as symbolizes the
union of God and the soul, or how the sexual union of the spouses,
when present, although it certainly is a physical transaction, can be
thought of as effecting as well as symbolizing the union of Christ and
the church. Nor does he explain in what sense either of these *sacramenta*
functions as a container or medium of grace. None the less, the
contribution of Hugh of St. Victor proved to be quite important in the
sequel. His definition of marriage and his defense of present consent as
the point when it comes into being, informed as they are by his ardent
Mariology, provide the framework within which supporters of consent
in marriage formation came to view the subject during and after his
time.

A good index of Hugh's wide influence, coming as it does from a
perhaps unexpected quarter, is the treatment of marriage formation by the early Porretans. The goal of these masters is to try to
mediate between the consent and the consummation schools by
arguing that both consent and carnal union are required, without
specifying when in the course of events the spouses' change in
status occurs and when the union becomes an indissoluble one.
There is, to be sure, an inclination on their part to favor the consent
position, reflected in their acknowledgement of the point that future
consent is not binding. None the less, they bypass the issue of
whether it is the exchange of wedding vows or the subsequent
consummation of the marriage that is determinative. This unwillingness to take a stand on a matter that was quite clear cut for all
other masters at the time, including Hugh, does not prevent the
Porretans from viewing marriage as a double sacrament, just as he
does. Agreeing that marriage is both a union of a man and woman
for the purpose of leading a common life and a union, by consent, of
two persons legally capable of marrying, they view the consent as
the consent to establish a conjugal society in a spiritual sense,
which symbolizes the union of God and the soul, as well as a carnal

union, which symbolizes the union of Christ and the church. Consistent with this position, they do not condemn clandestine marriages outright, although they note their disadvantages.[456] On their own account, they add a point not found in Hugh, the idea that sexual relations were ordained both before and after the fall, apart from the other reasons God had in mind, in order to engender a human genealogy for Christ.[457] At the same time, they agree that lack of offspring, like lack of fidelity and permanence, does not invalidate a marriage.[458]

Another master who shows the ability to combine Hugonian insights with ideas on marriage that Hugh does not countenance is Master Simon. Although he introduces his remarks on marriage in a manner similar to that of Robert Pullen, by describing marriage as a calling, indeed, as the only calling for the laity in this sphere of personal life, Simon rapidly moves to the sacramentality of marriage and its formation. Given the reasons why marriage was instituted both before and after the fall, that is, the propagation of offspring and the remedy for incontinence, marriage must require sexual union, in his estimation. Although he agrees with all the other pro-consent masters that it is consent that makes the marriage, he agrees with the Abelardians that the consent itself is consent to sexual relations (*Nam et per consensum efficiter et propter carnalem copulam celebratur*).[459] Yet, at the same time, what is required and reflected in this consent is not just a commitment to the exclusivity of sexual rights between the spouses but a union of wills and mutual love (*voluntatis unionem, mutuam dilectionem*),[460] which, according to Simon, is manifested by the husband in his protection of his wife and by the wife in her submission to her husband. This combination of love, protection, and subjection signifies the spiritual union of Christ and the church, for Simon, just as the carnal union of the spouses signifies the union of Christ and the church viewed institutionally. With Hugh, Simon holds that it is in the spiritual rather than in the physical bond that the *sacramentum* is truly and essentially located. He brings in Mary and Joseph and the pro-consent authorities to buttress this conclusion, which is where he rests his case.[461] It has to be said that Simon emerges with

---

[456] *Sent. mag. Gisleberti* I 11.30–33, pp. 160–61; *Sent. mag. Gisleberti* II 11.5–6, 11.8–9, pp. 86–87, 89.
[457] *Sent. mag. Gisleberti* II 11.1–4, p. 86.
[458] Ibid., 11.8–9, p. 89.
[459] Master Simon, *De sac.*, p. 47.
[460] Ibid.
[461] Ibid., pp. 45–49.

a rather inconsistent position, because his insistence on the priority and efficacy of the spiritual union undercuts his point about sexual relations being required to fulfill the purposes for which marriage was instituted. Further, the model of protection and subjection as descriptions of the mutual love of the spouses is rather a travesty of Hugh's extended vision of true mutuality in their relations. Still, the appeal of Hugh's conception of marriage is so strong, for Simon, that he incorporates the Victorine understanding into his account despite the inconsistencies that result.

A much more faithful follower of Hugh on the consent side of the debate is the author of the *Summa sententiarum*, although he does not hesitate to disagree with Hugh at times or to amplify on points that Hugh ignores or to which Hugh, in the master's opinion, gives short shrift. With respect to the intentions informing the decision to marry, he asserts that the procreation of offspring and the avoidance of fornication are the only theologically acceptable reasons. Other possibilities advanced by some authorities, such as the reconciliation of enemies, he rejects as not found in Holy Scripture. The less upright, or worldly reasons, such as sexual pleasure, riches, and connections, he deplores; but he affirms that they do not invalidate a marriage so long as the spouses are bound by mutual consent. Consent is of the essence; and it provides the master with a way of addressing the all-too evident gap between marriage, as it exists in the real world, and marriage, as theologians would like it to be.[462] When it comes to marriage formation and the relation of marriage to the goods of marriage, he follows Hugh in observing that, when a valid marriage exists, the absence of the goods does not alter that fact. With Hugh, he holds that the requirements for a valid marriage are the absence of legal impediments and consent. While citing the standard pro-consent authorities, he is particularly concerned with enlarging the dossier used by Hugh to include those who condemn parents who interfere with or undermine their children's liberty of choice, especially in the case of their daughters. He emphasizes as well that spouses must be of age, so that they can render informed consent. For the same reason, he rejects future consent as determinative, given the fact that children can be betrothed at an early age. With Hugh, he brings the marriage of Mary and Joseph to bear on the defense of consent, and acknowledges that his position admits the validity of clandestine marriage. Although he does not stop to consider, and to refute, the authorities

---

[462] *Summa sent.* 7.1, *PL* 176: 153D–155B.

on the other side of the debate, he comes down firmly on the conclusion that consent is sufficient, even in the absence of a dowry, a solemn, public wedding ceremony, and a priestly blessing, and that this is the case whether or not the marriage is consummated.[463] The master adds to this analysis of marriage formation a paean of praise to marriage itself, not so much as a way by which man assists in the continuing work of creation, as Hugh would have it, but as a means of refuting heretics who impugn its goodness. For, as he says, marriage "is a good thing and in no way evil" (*rem esse bonam et nullo modo malam*), and this is so both because of its double divine institution and because of the honor with which Christ endowed it by performing His first miracle at the marriage of Cana, a point also made by the author of the *Sententie Anselmi*.[464] This is a sentiment which Hugh would certainly have endorsed although he himself does not put such an expressly antiheretical construction on the point. But there is also an area in which the author moves away from Hugh. He does not speak about the inner quality of mutual love that describes a sacramental marriage, and he does not see the friendship of the spouses that proceeds from their spiritual conjugal society as essential. He puts this condition in the same category as the goods of marriage, which may flow from marital consent, but which do not obviate it if they are absent. Likewise, the union of minds and hearts may be absent, both as an intentionality flowing into consent or out of the spouses' common life. Consistent with his initial point, it is the consent to a permanent common life that counts, with or without these desiderata.[465] In this respect, the author shows himself to be less interested in the quality of the commitment made by the spouses and the ways in which marriage may help them to grow as persons than he is in the unimpeded, conscious, and deliberate character of the consent which initiates the marriage.

In positioning Peter Lombard's view of marriage as a sacrament and marriage formation in the contemporary context, three main features of his account stand out: his solid support for the principle of consent, coupled with an appreciation of the values and realities to which his consummationist opponents speak, rare for a defender of consent; a generous use of the work of his predecessors, with the guiding spirits being Gratian, Hugh of St. Victor, and the *Summa sententiarum*; and his ability, notwithstanding his appeal to these

---

[463] Ibid., 7.4, 7.6–7, *PL* 176: 157B–C, 158C–160C.
[464] Ibid., 7.2, *PL* 176: 155C; *Sent. Anselmi* 5, pp. 129–30.
[465] *Summa sent.* 7.4, *PL* 176: 176B–C.

masters and to many well-worn themes and opinions, to impart to these topics a quality that is Lombardian in its own right, and that moves reflection on marriage forward.[466] Peter begins with the double institution of marriage before and after the fall, for the purpose of procreation and the avoidance of fornication. He immediately tips his hand on how he plans to present sex in marriage by remarking that the postlapsarian institution was for the protection of nature, and not merely for the repression of vice. In explaining this point, he adds that, while marriage was a precept in Eden, and again after the flood when the repopulation of the world was required, it is now an indulgence. An indulgence can be regarded as a concession, or for remission, or as a permission. Marriage, he states, is conceded. What this means is that it is granted for a good purpose, and not just merely allowed as a dispensation from a rule that would otherwise be binding or as a mere permission. The goodness of marriage after the fall is a notion which Peter, like the author of the *Summa sententiarum*, wants to stress specifically against the heretics who condemn marriage. No names are named but the Cathars are clearly in the dock. The fact that marriage is a good thing (*res bona*), he agrees, is shown not only by its divine institution in Eden, but also by the fact that Christ chose to perform His first miracle at the marriage of Cana. For, he concludes, were marriage not good, it would not be a sacrament. As the sign of a sacred thing, a sacrament must resemble what it signifies, he reminds the reader; and Christ, in turning water into wine at the marriage of Cana, indicates how, through the blessing He thus imparts to marriage, it can be transformed from a purely human institution into one drawing spouses to the holy thing it signifies.[467]

This holy thing, the *res sacramenti* of which marriage is a sign is, for Peter, who here departs from Hugh and follows Master Simon, the union of Christ and the church. There is a single *res sacramenti*,

---

[466] Helpful treatments include Gold, "The Marriage of Mary and Joseph," pp. 102–17; Orio Giacchi, "Voluntà e unione coniugale nella dottrina matrimoniale di Pier Lombardo," in *Misc. Lomb.*, pp. 341–43; Heaney, *The Development of the Sacramentality of Marriage*, pp. 28–31; Knoch, *Die Einsetzung*, pp. 239–41; Zeimentz, *Ehe*, pp. 118–23, 136–40. Mignon, *Les origines*, 2: 241–42, 248–49 makes the unsupported claim that Peter rejects Hugh in favor of Abelard, while Ludwig Ott, "Walter von Mortagne und Petrus Lombardus in ihrem Verhältnis zueinander," in *Mélanges Joseph de Ghellinck S.J.*, 2 vols. (Gembloux: J. Duculot, 1951), 2: 656, 666 n. 35, 669 claims that Walter of Mortagne was his source for ideas found in all the defenders of the principle of consent.

[467] Peter Lombard, *Sent.* 4. d. 26. c. 1–c. 5, 2: 417–19. The quotation is at c. 5.2, p. 419. Peter makes the same point about the marriage of Cana in *Sermo* 13, *PL* 171: 402B.

he holds, but marriage signifies it in two ways, since Christ is united to the church in two ways. Christ associates Himself to the church both in will and in nature (*voluntate et natura*). His intention and desire to make His love and His salvation available to the believers who make up His mystical body is made efficacious through the church as a visible institution. Its existence as an institution is a manifestation and expression of the loving intentionality of Christ which is its inspiration and source. So, as Peter sees it, marriage is a bond "according to the consent of souls and according to the union of bodies" (*secundum consensum animorum et secundum permixtione corporum*). Consent signifies the bond of charity joining Christ and the church by will, while the sexual union of the spouses signifies Christ's union with the church by nature, in that He Himself took on the nature of man and continues to make Himself available to man in modes that can be appropriated physically in the ecclesiastical dispensation. And, just as the visible church expresses the invisible bond of love which created it and which informs it, so the physical union of the spouses expresses and reinforces the union of souls which animates it.[468]

It is clear from his posing of the definition of marriage in this way that Peter is planning to adhere forcefully to the principle that a marriage comes into being when the spouses give their consent, while at the same time acknowledging that their life together in the flesh is not an irrelevancy or a mere option in the vast majority of cases. Rather, he wants to present the sexual relations of spouses as something that can, and should, be joined meaningfully to their union of souls, in such a way as to express and to strengthen that spiritual bonding. This being the case, he has a clear idea of how to handle the authorities on both the consent and the consummation side of the controversy. He borrows Gratian's dossier here and also his tactic of relativizing the judgments of those authors whose statements are made without the qualifications that he himself wants to impose on them. Peter also has a way of dealing effectively with the marriage of Mary and Joseph, without having to urge or even to imply that a mariage blanc is normative or desirable for most couples. He begins by citing the authorities who say that the consummation is the point at which a true and indissoluble marriage comes into being. This position is flatly in error, he asserts. A marriage can be perfect, valid, sacramental, and indissoluble without sexual union. Such was the case with Mary and Joseph. Since

---

[468] Peter Lombard, *Sent.* 4. d. 26. c. 6, 2: 419–21.

the union of souls signifies a sacred thing, the bond of charity between Christ and the church, it is a sacrament, although it is not a visible one. A standard marriage, on the other hand, is sacramental in a twofold sense, since both the union of souls and the union of bodies stand for a *res sacramenti*. Further, and this is the way the consummationist authorities should be understood, he argues, while in a standard marriage the sexual union is just as sacramental as the union of souls, the former is a manifestation of the latter. The spiritual communion of love comes first and is the ground; "for marriage is the sign of spiritual bonding and of the love uniting souls, and, on this account spouses ought to come together in the flesh" (*Est etiam coniugum signum spiritualis coniunctionis et dilectionis animorum, qua inter se coniuges uniri debent*).[469]

In one stroke, by means of this argument, Peter has managed to accomplish three things at once, which move forward the understanding of marriage in his time. He has retained the notion of deliberate and loving consent as the essential basis of marriage and of marriage formation as put forth by Hugh of St. Victor, but without Hugh's asceticism. He has acknowledged, with the consummationists, that life in the body is natural and commensurate with the purposes for which marriage was instituted. But, rather than seeing the sexual union as what perfects a consensual union that serves only as the incomplete beginning of a marriage, he regards the sexual union as sacramental in that it expresses the union of minds and hearts that is constitutive of the marriage. This perspective dignifies the sexual relations of spouses, in seeing them as more than merely remedial, and provides the foundation for Peter's treatment of sexual ethics in marriage later in his treatise on this subject.

But before he gets to that point, and to the other topics pertinent to marriage that he intends to treat, he offers a more specific and more institutionally framed definition of marriage which includes a consideration of when it begins, which he discusses under the heading of the efficient cause of marriage; of the intentions which the spouses bring to it in rendering their consent, which he does not label a cause but which might well be called the formal cause; and of the ends of marriage, understood as its final cause. His handling of these themes reflects his familiarity with Gratian's terminology and concerns, even if his own conclusions are not always substantively the same as Gratian's. Peter agrees with the canonical notion

---

[469] Ibid. The quotation is at c. 6.5, p. 421.

that marriage is a union of a man and woman who are legitimate persons (*legitimas personas*), that is, legally able to contract a marriage, who come together to live a common life under a common custom (*individuam vitae consuetudinem retinens*). This means that the spouses recognize that they have a common, and, Peter stresses, a mutual, set of rights and obligations. Aside from the standard point about the rendering of the marriage debt and the requirement that spouses may not withdraw into continence without their spouses' consent, he adds their common agreement to a permanent union and a union in which there is no double standard; each spouse commits himself or herself to the same conjugal chastity and fidelity that he or she requires of his or her partner.[470]

As to the efficient cause of this union, it is clearly, in Peter's eyes, the consent of the spouses verbally and freely given, a present not a future consent (*Efficiens autem causa matrimonii est consensus, non quilibet, sed per verba expressus; nec de futuro, sed de praesenti*). If the principals are unable to speak, they may substitute some other perceptible sign indicating that they are aware of the commitment that they are undertaking and that they bring to it the requisite intentions. This stress on the articulate word or sensible sign in the taking of marriage vows reflects Peter's desire to make the marriage ceremony symmetrical with the rites in which the other sacraments are administered, which involve a visible or sensible sacramental medium, with the possible exception of penance, in his case. For the same reason, he rules here as well that vows taken fraudulently or under coercion are invalid.[471] Having disposed of the consummationist authorities as he does above, he does not debate with them here, but concentrates on presenting the main pro-consent citations, with which he plainly agrees. Also, having already laid to rest, to his own satisfaction, the claim that the marriage is not valid until it is consummated, he focuses his attention rather on the claim that the marriage begins at the time of the betrothal. The way to read those authorities who support the latter position, he argues, is with a lexicographical clarification. A couple can be called spouses (*sponsus, sponsa*), as a courtesy title, from the time of their engagement (*desponsatio*), just as they can properly address their in-laws-to-be with the titles of relatives. But they are not actually husband and wife (*coniuges*) until they render their present consent at their wedding. This distinction, Peter shows, can be reinforced by the

---

[470] Ibid., d. 27. c. 2, 2: 422.
[471] Ibid., c. 3.1, 2: 422–23. The quotation is on p. 422.

fact that an engaged person may choose a monastic vocation uni-
laterally, while *coniuges* cannot withdraw into monastic life except
with the express consent of their husbands or wives. It is only at the
point of the exchange of marriage vows that the union becomes
indissoluble. There is no hesitation in Peter's mind as to whether
an engagement can be broken. Engagements manifestly can be
broken, since they are merely promises to do something in the
future and not the doing of the thing itself. He points not only to the
rule regarding entrance into monastic life, and other canonical
rules pertaining to engaged persons to buttress this position, but
also to the civil law. If a woman's fiancé should die prior to the
marriage, he points out, she does not gain the legal status of a
widow vis-à-vis his estate. Likewise, if it is the fiancée who dies, the
man in question is not held to have been married, insofar as that
might be a bar to his ordination.[472] Through arguments of this type,
Peter seeks to show that those authorities who collapse present
consent into future consent or who ignore present consent
altogether are both erroneous and self-contradictory, just as he has
sought to show that those who argue for consummationism, or who
require a dowry, confuse the marriage itself with events that come
later and which are consequences of the marriage and not its point
of inception.

In turn, this argument leads Peter to assert that we must distinguish what is necessary to initiate a marriage from what is decorous
in conjunction with it. As in the case of other sacraments, he notes,
there are ceremonies surrounding marriage which are and should
be observed. But the marriage remains a valid marriage if they are
omitted. It is under this heading that he places parental consent,
along with the formal handing over of the bride to the groom, and
priestly blessing. Peter is as frank as Hugh of St. Victor, the author
of the *Summa sententiarum,* and the school of Laon in recognizing that
the logic of this position means the acceptance of clandestine marriage. Peter does not shrink from drawing this conclusion. He
admits the validity of such marriages, the other necessary conditions obtaining, although he does not seek to encourage them. Like
the Porretans, his tactic for handling this admittedly uncomfortable
corollary of the pro-consent view is to discourage people contem-
plating a clandestine marriage by pointing out that it is not to their
enlightened self-interest to enter into such a union. If problems
should arise later on and the principals should need to have to

---

[472] Ibid., c. 3-d. 28. c. 1, 2: 422–32.

prove that they are really married, the ability to produce witnesses will be to their advantage. Still, when push comes to shove, Peter's desire to defend the principle of consent is unyielding, and he rules that such couples must be received as truly married on their own testimony.[473]

Peter also discusses the intentions brought to a marriage under the heading of the content of the present consent of the spouses. Here, he addresses a number of debated points by the way he defines his terms. This consent, he notes, is more than the commitment to share a common life. For, if this were all that were required, brothers and sisters and other relatives sharing a common household would be considered married, and they are not. Nor is the sole content of marital consent the consent to sexual relations, he states, herewith rejecting the position of the Abelardians. If this were the case, the marriage of Mary and Joseph would be no marriage, a weapon that can be used against this group of pro-consent theologians as handily as it can be deployed against the consummationists. While marriage, for Peter, typically does include both consent to a common life and consent to sexual relations, it is exhausted by neither of these ingredients nor by both of them together. What is of the essence, for Peter, is the agreement to form an association that is, specifically, a conjugal one (*consensus coniugalis societatis*), an association constituted and guided by marital affection (*coniugali affectu*).[474] In his discussion of these conditions, which inform both the intentions of spouses as they render present consent and which serve as the final causes of their union, Peter reveals his familiarity with the canonists' understanding of the term *maritalis affectio*, although he does not use their precise language. He also reveals his familiarity with the substitution of this canonical notion by the author of the *Summa sententiarum* for the more effusive and idealistic view of marital intentionality proposed by Hugh of St. Victor. Peter accepts the canonists' idea that marital affection means the honor, dignity, and respect which people recognize that they owe to their spouses as such, and that the concept does not refer to erotic or romantic love, although he does not manifest their interest in endorsing this principle as a means of distinguishing marriage from concubinage. He joins the *Summa sententiarum* in advancing marital affection as a more workable and reasonable norm than the counsels of perfection advocated by Hugh; few

---

[473] Ibid., d. 28. c. 2, 2: 433–34.
[474] Ibid., c. 3.2, d. 31. c. 2.5, 2: 435, 444.

validly married couples can be expected to approximate the exalted example of Mary and Joseph, who, in any case, were granted special charisms because of their unique role in the Christian story. The aspect of marital affection and conjugal society that Peter emphasizes is found neither in the canonists, Hugh, nor the *Summa sententiarum*. Here, he reintroduces the observation he had made about the creation of Eve in Book 2 of the *Sentences*, an idea which he shares with Hugh and with many other masters of the time, as a means of reinforcing his point. Eve was taken from Adam's side, he reminds the reader, and not from his head or his feet, to indicate that the wife is neither the ruler nor the servant of her husband but rather his equal associate in a common life. This equality and mutuality extend to the moral relationship of spouses and not only to their sexual relationship. In making this point, what Peter omits is as striking as what he says. While he is certainly willing to put forth the idea in his Pauline glosses, he does not refer here to the subjection of wives to husbands as a punishment for sin or to the principle of hierarchy within the family as a foregone conclusion both socially and theologically. Unlike Master Simon, the union of souls he has in mind is not based on the model of protection and subjection but on the model of spiritual and sexual equality.[475]

While putting this egalitarian construction on the principle of marital affection, Peter joins the author of the *Summa sententiarum* in applying it to what he calls the final causes of marriage, from a sexual point of view. Recognizing that there are spiritual values that marriage confirms and promotes, he agrees fully with the idea that there are two proper and honest sexual causes at work in marriage, the propagation of offspring and the avoidance of fornication. He acknowledges that people in fact often marry for less unselfish reasons. Unlike the author of the *Summa sententiarum*, he reimports the sealing of peace and the reconciliation of enemies into the question, under the heading of lesser but still worthy reasons for marrying. These motives may not have Scriptural foundations but he finds them eminently reasonable none the less. Motives still less worthy, and, in this case, not honest either, include marriage for the sake of wealth, social position, or the gratification of erotic desire. Confronted with the problem of whether marriages undertaken for essentially worldly and selfish reasons are truly sacramental unions, Peter recognizes fully that the intentions which

---

[475] Ibid., d. 28. c. 4, 2: 435. This point has been emphasized correctly by Zeimentz, *Ehe*, pp. 220–21.

spouses bring to such unions are defective. In the case of other sacraments, as we have seen, defective intentionality on the part of either the recipient or the administrator is enough to rule out the validity of the sacrament and its fruitful appropriation by the recipient, for Peter. On this point, apparently recognizing the limited force which sacramental theology can have with respect to legal and social institutions such as marriage, fully capable of existing independent of the sacramental understanding which theologians may seek to impose on them, he bows to the perceived need to depart from his otherwise symmetrical treatment of sacramental intentionality in the case of marriage. He agrees, with the *Summa sententiarum*, that if a couple give their mutual and unforced present consent, they are validly married, even if the marriage serves ends which he holds to be dishonest and inappropriate, from a Christian perspective. The goodness of the sacrament, he reluctantly concludes, is not contaminated by the less than good ends that it serves in such marriages.[476] Agreeing as well with the host of contemporaries who distinguish the Augustinian goods of marriage from marriage itself, the only category of spousal intentionality which he thinks pollutes the sacrament to such an extent that it warrants the withdrawal of the title of married from those who engage in the practices it informs has to do with contraception and abortion. Those spouses who procure poisons seeking to prevent conception or induce abortion are in a class with simoniac clergymen, in his estimation. But, in stating that they should no longer be considered married, Peter acknowledges tacitly that he is making a hortatory and rhetorical point only, for there is no way of stripping such people of their marital status on this account analogous to the canonical procedures for unfrocking a simoniac priest or invalidating his ordination.[477]

In practice, then, as well as in theory, Peter adheres to the principle of consent in marriage formation, whether the intentions spouses bring to present consent are truly in keeping with the sacramental character of marriage or not. Without falling into inconsistency, what he manages to do, better than any of the other defenders of consent, and, indeed, better than any of the defenders of consummation, is to find a way of integrating, positively, the importance of sexual relations between spouses into the position that marital consent, not consummation, is of the essence in mar-

---

[476] Peter Lombard, *Sent.* 4. d. 30. c. 3, 2: 440–41.
[477] Ibid., d. 31. c. 1–c. 4, 2: 442–46.

riage formation. In the immediate sequel, his doctrine of marriage
formation proved to be decisive for both theologians and canonists.
It was adopted officially in the decretals of Pope Alexander III in
the next generation.[478] This is not to say that the victory of the
consent position, with the particular emphasis Peter gives to it, was
able to come to grips with the many ways in which it fails to square
with marriage as practiced in medieval societies and as regulated
by medieval codes of secular law in and after Peter's time. Parents
continued to force children into unwanted marriages; dowries remained essential requirements for marriage; breach of promise
remained a cause of action; the notary, rather than the priest,
continued to be the official personage of choice in nuptial agree-
ments; the high and the mighty continued to ignore or to manipu-
late the principle of marital indissolubility when it suited their
convenience; and the dependent, the poor, and the semi-free found
that their status and circumstances stood in the way of making
their own free choice of marriage partners. In all these respects,
while Peter's definition of marriage and of marriage formation
proved determinative for the masters in the schools of theology and
canon law, and for the leaders of the church, it neither responded to
the perceived needs of married Christians nor informed their
understanding of marriage in practice.

   The definition of marriage and of marriage formation was the
single biggest debated question raised with respect to this sacrament in the first half of the twelfth century. There were, however,
other controversies into which some if not all of the contemporary
masters entered. The two remaining topics, sexual relations in
marriage and impediments to marriage, are subjects which a considerable numbers of masters felt a need to address and on which
they expressed a range of opinions. In the case of the first of these
topics, the terms of the debate were set by the position articulated

---

[478] For Peter's influence, see Brundage, *Law, Sex, and Christian Society*, pp.
268–70. Brundage writes as if there were an automatic trickle-down process and as
if the views of the theologians and canonists actually informed the attitudes of high
medieval Christians concerning marriage. The same kind of over-simplification,
but one which treats ecclesiastical authorities and theologians as having a monolithic position, is found in Georges Duby, *Medieval Marriage: Two Models from
Twelfth-Century France*, trans. Elborg Forster (Baltimore: Johns Hopkins University
Press, 1978); and *The Knight, the Lady, and the Priest: The Making of Modern Marriage
in Medieval France*, trans. Barbara Bray (New York: Pantheon Books, 1983). A
more realistic appraisal is given by Jean Gaudemet, *Le mariage en occident: Les moeurs
et le droit* (Paris: Éditions du Cerf, 1987) and Michael M. Sheehan, "Theory and
Practice: Marriage of the Unfree and the Poor in Medieval Society," *MS* 50
(1988): 457–87.

by Augustine. As a pendant to his view that the sexual relations of Adam and Eve in Eden, had they not fallen, could have taken place entirely under the direction of reason and will, exclusively for the procreation of offspring, and devoid of sexual desire or sexual pleasure, he argued that, in man's fallen state, they could not be engaged in, even in pursuit of the legitimate goods of marriage, without lust, and hence without at least venial sin. This position continued to receive support from some twelfth-century masters, such as the author of the *Sententie Anselmi*.[479] But, wherever they stood regarding consummation versus consent in marriage formation, and regardless of whether they saw the content of marital consent as sexual only or as broader than that, a number of masters expressly reject the Augustinian position. Indeed, within the same school of Laon in which the *Sententie Anselmi* was produced, the majority opinion is that sex in marriage is a good thing, or at least that it is excused when applied to the ends of marriage.[480] Hugh of St. Victor agrees that the sexual relations of spouses can take place without sin,[481] and so does Master Simon, who, however, adds a distinction taken from Gregory the Great: if the spouses are acting with a procreative intention, they act "for a conjugal good, . . . so that sin in no way attaches to them" (*per bonum coniugale, . . . ut nullo modo peccatum reputetur*). But, if the couple are acting in order to avoid fornication, venial sin does attach to their behavior, while serious sin is imputed to them if they unite merely for the sake of pleasure.[482] Both the author of the *Summa sententiarum* and Robert Pullen take a much more generous line, distancing themselves still more sharply from Augustine. For the author of the *Summa sententiarum*, sex in marriage is exempted from all vice when it is intended to minister to the physical needs of the couple as well as to their wish to produce offspring (*absque omni vitio et sola intentione guerandi*). It only becomes venially sinful if neither of these intentions is present and if the couple come together for erotic pleasure alone. But, even in that event, he holds the fault to be quite mild. His accent is on the fact that sexual relations are required for the bearing of offspring and for the rendering of the marriage debt, and that this situation is approved by God. The pleasure necessarily attending the use of sex for the ends of marriage, he adds, is no

---

[479] *Sent. Anselmi* 5, pp. 131–34.
[480] *De coniugo*, p. 386; *Decretum dei fuit*, p. 364; *Sentences of the School of Laon*, no. 401, 403, 527, 5: 286, 365; *Deus de cuius principio et fine tacetur*, p. 270.
[481] Hugh of St. Victor, *De sac.* 2.11.4, *PL* 176: 481B–482D.
[482] Master Simon, *De sac.* pp. 53–54. The quotation is on p. 53.

more evil *per se* than the pleasure attending eating, so long as moderation is observed.[483] Robert Pullen is equally interested in accentuating the positive. At the very worst, he holds, any sins found in marital sex will be slight (*levia peccata*). But, in those who are baptized and married sacramentally, this sin, if any, is excused in virtue of the sacrament. Since spouses commit no sin in the married use of sex, sin should not be imputed to them. Robert agrees with the *Summa sententiarum* in observing that sexual relations, like eating and sleeping, are natural acts that have nothing intrinsically evil in them, although, like these other functions, our use of them may be virtuous or depraved. He adds that there are also some virtuous acts that are inspired by, or are concomitant with, certain emotions, to which they are appropriate. Righteous indignation is a case in point. The same is true of sexual pleasure in marital relations. No blame attaches to it when sex in marriage is used for the sake of offspring, to render the marriage debt, and to avoid fornication.[484]

While the effort to moderate, or to reject, the rigors of Augustinianism on sex in marriage attracts support from a large number of masters in the mid-twelfth century, we can also find evidence of a more ascetic approach to this issue. Consistent with their narrow, negative, and purely concessive treatment of marriage itself, the Abelardians elevate celibacy above marriage and see nothing positive in married sex.[485] The only thing that marriage does in this connection, in their view, is to make legitimate a form of activity which the wise man should rise above, and which is not licit except for married persons. Given the fact that all the masters just discussed, whether Abelardians or not, are proponents of consent in marriage formation, it is hard to agree with the claim of James A. Brundage that defenders of consent took that position in order to elevate the spirit above the flesh, out of ascetic inclinations.[486] That view would seem to describe the Abelardians primarily, and not most of their scholastic compeers.

In the context of contemporary opinions on sexual ethics in marriage, the Lombard comes closest to the *Summa sententiarum* and Robert Pullen, similarly repudiating Augustine, and dignifying sex

---

[483] *Summa sent.* 7.3, *PL* 176: 156A–157A. The quotation is at 156A.

[484] Robert Pullen, *Sent.* 6.4, 7.28, 7.30, *PL* 186: 867B, 945C–D, 948C–949C. The quotation is at 6.4, 867B.

[485] Hermannus, *Sent.*, pp. 120, 137–38; *Sent. Parisiensis* I, pp. 44, 46; *Ysagoge in theologiam*, p. 196.

[486] Brundage, *Law, Sex, and Christian Society*, pp. 237, 268.

in marriage still farther. Because it is required in order to attain the goods of marriage, Peter agrees, the sexual union of spouses is freed from blame (*excusetur coitus carnalis*). Having noted that some people marry for purely worldly reasons and that they are considered to have a valid sacramental marriage none the less, he extends that same reasoning to the good of offspring as one of the three Augustinian goods of marriage. To be sure, Augustine was referring to the bearing and rearing of children in the faith, as good citizens of the church. Peter observes that many couples pursue this good not for religious reasons and not because they see the family as a cellular unit within the church, but for the sake of maintaining and expanding the importance of their own lineage, for the sake of self-perpetuation through children, or for other selfish reasons. Nevertheless, a procreative intention that is defective, from a theological or moral standpoint, does not remove the freedom from sin attaching to the sexual relations of such couples. The only point at which Peter draws the line is the case of sexual relations engaged in by spouses purely out of the desire for pleasure. This activity he sees as no better than fornication. But, in developing a sliding scale that places the rightly motivated desire for children at the top and the pleasure principle at the bottom of the hierarchy of ethical motivations and ethical evaluations of sex in marriage, what is striking is the way he describes the term in between. While all his contemporaries see the avoidance of fornication as one of the reasons for the institution of marriage, and while most of them see sexual relations undertaken for this purpose either as totally blameless, as with the *Summa sententiarum* and Robert Pullen, or as blameworthy but only to a slight degree, as with Master Simon, they still put the matter negatively. Peter sides here with Simon on the venial character of sin attached to this type of sexual activity, but he puts the point positively. The reason for the acceptability of this motive for sexual relations is that it serves the fidelity of the spouses. It is a positive motive, not a negative one springing from the view that it obviates the need for the spouses to seek satisfaction with other partners, in illicit relations. Peter presents this type of sex in marriage not as a means of preventing sin but as a means of strengthening the couple's mutual commitment. In concluding that sexual behavior that exceeds the norms he outlines, behavior that ends in incontinence that is selfish and immoderate is hence blameworthy, the point that Peter wants to stress is not that marital sex is restricted in its virtuous use but that sexual pleasure in marriage is no more evil than the satisfactions accompanying other natural functions and activities, such as rest and recreation after work and eating when one is hungry. As for the more ascetic and concessive authorities, Peter holds that they should be read in the light of the principle that human sexuality is a good when exercised in the service of the ends of marriage. Also, while in certain legal contexts the husband is the head of the wife, in their sexual relations they have equal rights and obligations. Peter acknowledges the idea that there are certain time in the church year when the canonists think spouses should abstain from sexual relations. But he is far more permissive than they are. He asserts that the payment of the marriage debt for the sake of preserving marital fidelity must always be seen as a higher priority. This willingness to recognize that sexual relations play a positive role in the lives of married couples, joined, as it is in Peter's eyes, to the mutuality of the spouses' rights and duties, is a teaching that Peter presents in the light of his understanding of sexual relations in marriage as expressing and as reinforcing the union of minds and hearts in mutual consent, on which the sacrament is based and which is its fundamental definition.[487] And, while agreeing with Hugh of St. Victor and with other proponents of consent that Mary and Joseph were joined in a holy and sacramental marriage, entered into without false pretenses concerning its celibate nature, and reflective of the good of offspring in their rearing of Jesus as well as in the goods of fidelity and permanence, he reminds his reader that this marriage is not the norm of Christian marriage in that it lacks the full sacramental significance of the union of Christ and the church that the standard marriage possesses in its combination of the union of souls with the union of bodies.[488]

A final set of issues confronting theologians and canonists who wrote on marriage in the first half of the twelfth century has to do with impediments to marriage, the conditions that nullify a marriage, and grounds for separation, coupled with the question of when and if either or both parties have the right to take another spouse in the event that their marriage has been dissolved. There are certain points on which there is general agreement here. All concede that the only grounds for separation is infidelity and that, if a spouse is dismissed on that account, the marriage remains in effect and neither party can remarry. Those masters who take up the question also agree that physical separation, as might be

---

[487] Peter Lombard, *Sent.* 4. d. 27. c. 1, d. 31. c. 1–c. 2.4, c. 5–d. 32. c. 4, 2: 421–22, 442–45, 446–56. Zeimentz, *Ehe*, pp. 226–28, 237–45 gives a sensitive appreciation of these points.
[488] Peter Lombard, *Sent.* 4. d. 30. c. 2, 2: 439–41.

brought about by pilgrimage, crusade, long-distance trade, or capture by an enemy, does not dissolve a marriage either; and, if a new union has been made by either or both parties, it is not valid, and the original partners must return to each other if the absent spouse reappears. It is also a consensus position that consanguinity to the sixth or seventh degree, depending on whether one counts the parent-child relationship or not, and spiritual affinity, of the type created by godparenting or serving as a sponsor at a person's confirmation, are a bar to marriage. Likewise, holy orders at the rank of subdeacon or above, vows of celibacy whether public or private, in association with a monastic profession or not, are generally accepted as impediments to marriage or as grounds for nullification if they were not known at the time of the marriage and are subsequently discovered. These views are shared by canonists and theologians alike, although, faithful to their own guild mentality, the canonists revel in the discussion of consanguinity, giving it protracted and enthusiastic attention; and in considering impediments and decrees of nullity they are deeply interested in the identification and prosecution of delicts and the procedures to be followed in these kinds of cases, themes that do not appeal very much to the theologians.

There are also a number of topics in this same general category where a range of opinions can be detected, both in areas where masters take opposing views on the same questions and areas where they agree on the substance of the issue but disagree on the rationale supporting their common conclusions. A good example of the latter is the observation that the rules and regulations affecting marriage have changed over time, to a greater extent than those affecting other sacraments. In Old Testament times, polygamy and concubinage were acceptable; the rules on consanguinity were drastically different from those obtaining later on; and divorce and remarriage were permitted. Some masters merely register these changes without much comment, or content themselves with the observation that these are disciplinary regulations, which are changeable by nature, as opposed to the sacramental character and purposes of marriage, which are not.[489] One Laon master, however, dissents, arguing that polygamy was and always is wrong, but that God tolerated it among the Old Testament patriarchs on a lesser of

---

[489] Honorius, *Eluc.* 2.51, p. 426; *Sent. Anselmi* 5, p. 112; *Sentences of the School of Laon*, no. 402, 404, 5: 286–87; *Deus de cuius principio et fine tacetur*, pp. 272–73; Gratian, *Decretum* pars 2. c. 32. q. 3, col. 1127–30; *Sent. Parisiensis* I, pp. 44–55; *Ysagoge in theologiam*, p. 196; Master Simon, *De sac.*, p. 54.

the two evils basis.[490] Robert Pullen sees the change in marriage customs as an index of the moral weakness of mankind in earlier times and the hardness of heart and selfishness of pre-Christian family life.[491] On the other hand, Hugh of St. Victor, Hermannus, and the author of the *Summa sententiarum* explain the change in customs on historical grounds. In the earliest chapters of Old Testament history, they observe, as well as after the flood, polygamy and concubinage were permitted in order to populate or repopulate the world; and the small number of people available for that purpose made it necessary to marry relatives who would now be ruled out as too closely connected. Hugh is anxious to make the point, following Augustine, that the patriarchs took multiple wives out of piety and public spirit, not lust. The author of the *Summa sententiarum* adds that these necessities and constraints have now been superseded, and Christian marriage can operate according to rules that are better (*honestior*).[492]

Concerning impediments to marriage and grounds for nullification, the topics on which we see substantive disagreement do not agitate all masters to the same extent. Sometimes their positions are related to their theory of marriage formation and sometimes not. Thus, while all agree that being underage is an impediment, Gratian sets the age limit at seven, reflecting his position that the *matrimonium initiatum* begins with the betrothal. Although Roland of Bologna supports Gratian on the point that the union is not a *matrimonium ratum* until it is consummated, he insists on the age requirement of twelve, for a girl, and thirteen, for a boy, or adequate physical maturity, both because this is necessary for consummation and because he thinks that persons below these ages are not likely to know their own minds or to be capable of rendering the informed consent required before the consummation. For his part, the author of the *Summa sententiarum*, as a defender of consent, sees the latter ages, which he gives as twelve and fourteen, as needed from the sole perspective of the capacity of spouses to consent intelligently.[493] Although members of the school of Laon are generally on the side of consent, one Laon master discusses the status of a marriage in which one partner is above the age of consent and the other is below it. He rules, unhelpfully, that the marriage is valid

---

[490] *Sentences of the School of Laon*, no. 527, 5: 366.

[491] Robert Pullen, *Sent.* 7.28–29, *PL* 186: 946A–947D.

[492] Hugh of St. Victor, *De sac.* 2.11.10, *PL* 176: 496D–497C; Hermannus, *Sent.*, p. 136; *Summa sent.* 7.5, *PL* 176: 157C–158C.

[493] Gratian, *Decretum* pars 2. c. 30. q. 2, col. 1099–1100; Roland of Bologna, *Sent.*, pp. 279–80; *Summa sent.* 7.15, *PL* 176: 166C.

for the first party but not for the second.[494] Another impediment which is usually, although not always, related to the master's theory of marriage formation is insanity. While it is generally agreed that insanity, as with any other malady that may strike a married person after he is married, has to be seen, like sterility, as a misfortune that does not alter the valid status of his marriage and that gives his spouse no grounds for dismissing him, insanity is seen as an impediment to the creation of a marriage by Gratian, the Porretans, and the *Summa sententiarum*.[495] Gratian's argument is linked to the requirement of informed consent in the first phase of marriage formation, the betrothal that initiates but does not perfect the marriage, while the other masters connect it to their view that consent alone suffices to make the marriage. Despite their strong support for the principle of consent, however, Hugh of St. Victor and Master Simon omit this question altogether, notwithstanding its pertinence, and Ivo of Chartres, although a defender of consent as well, oddly enough treats insanity as not being an impediment to marriage.[496] All involved, wherever they come down on insanity as a bar to informed consent, and not always consistently with the position they take on that matter, agree that insanity does not prevent people from carrying out the duties of marriage, even if they see marriage as involving a union of souls, and one that requires a self-discipline in the use of sex that is difficult to envision in a relationship in which one or both partners are deranged or not fully responsible for their actions. The principal argument the masters make in support of their position is that spouses who are insane should not be required to separate lest the benefits of marriage be lost to them.

Another debated topic under the heading of impediments to marriage and grounds for nullification, which also may or may not be related to a master's views on marriage formation, has to do with the religious beliefs of the spouses. On this topic, as well, conflicting legal and Scriptural injunctions and concessions collide. Noticing the fact that, unlike the other sacraments, marriage was not invented in the dispensation of Christ, Hermannus and the author of the *Sententiae Parisiensis* I see no reason to object to the

---

[494] *Sentences of the School of Laon*, no, 528, 5: 368.
[495] Gratian, *Decretum* pars 2. c. 32. q. 26, col. 1147; *Sent. mag. Gisleberti.* II 11.20, p. 90; *Summa sent.* 7.15, *PL* 176: 166C.
[496] Ivo of Chartres, *Decretum* 8. c. 168, *PL* 161: 619D. Ivo's *Panormia* 6–7, *PL* 161: 1244D–1304A gives a summary of his position on impediments both on this and on other points.

validity of marriages between infidels. Master Simon agrees, pointing out that these marriages conform to the Roman law definition
of marriage, which he cites by way of Isidore of Seville, the union of
a man and woman possessing the right to marry, for the purpose of
living a common life.⁴⁹⁷ On the other hand, the members of the
school of Laon raise a plausible objection, to which none of the
abovementioned masters responds. The marriages of infidels cannot be valid, the Laon masters assert, because the union of spouses
signifies the union of Christ and the church, which simply cannot
apply in the case of infidels. Also, marital consent includes the
consent to live together under the laws of the church, which similarly is not the case with infidels.⁴⁹⁸ Gratian attempts to mediate in
this dispute by ruling that marriages between infidels are valid in
civil law, but not in canon law, while Hugh of St. Victor seeks to
bring the topic into line with his sacramental theology in general by
observing that such marriages are legally valid but that they are
not sacramental. He agrees with Gratian that they could be dissolved, according to the civil law, and that, were this to occur, the
former partners could remarry. But, unlike Gratian, he mentions
this point only to dispose of it as irrelevant to the positive exposition of the doctrine of sacramental marriage that is his subject.⁴⁹⁹

In a related area, the question of disparity of faith as an impediment and as a basis for dissolving a marriage receives lively attention in this period. The treatment which the masters give to this
topic reflects, on the one hand, an emerging consensus that seeks to
restrict the biblical and patristic permission of mixed marriages
while, on the other, it manifests disagreement as to the best arguments to offer in support of that departure from the practice of the
early church. There are, to be sure, some sturdy defenders of the
Pauline principle that such marriages should be allowed, in that
the believing spouse sanctifies the unbelieving one, and can assist
him or her in moving from unbelief to faith. Hermannus and the
author of *Sententiae Parisiensis* I give an affirmative ruling, citing this
biblical reason.⁵⁰⁰ Both Hugh of St. Victor and Master Simon
expand on the point, urging that the Christian spouse take an
active role in working for the conversion of his or her spouse, seeing

---

⁴⁹⁷ Hermannus, *Sent.*, p. 139; *Sent. Parisiensis* I, p. 44; Master Simon, *De sac.*, p.
59.
⁴⁹⁸ *Sentences of the School of Laon*, no. 406, 5: 287; *Sent. Anselmi* 5, p. 137; *Deus de
cuius principio et fine tacetur*, pp. 272–73.
⁴⁹⁹ Gratian, *Decretum* pars 2. c. 28. q. 1, col. 1078–89; Hugh of St. Victor, *De sac.*
2.11.7–9, *PL* 176: 494A–496D.

in such marriages a missionary opportunity. Since it is apposite to his case, Simon adds that this practice is supported by the earliest authorities, starting with St. Paul, and that it follows the guidelines laid down by the *ecclesia primitiva*. He also adds that Christian spouses should not invoke the Pauline privilege on the other side of this issue, by dismissing unbelieving partners merely on that account; he suggests that some spouses who do so invoke it for frivolous or self-serving reasons.[501] Ivo of Chartres looks at both sides of the question. He agrees that mixed marriages are licit, and also that the unbelieving spouse may be dismissed if he or she is interfering in the Christian spouse's practice of the faith. His main goal is to try to iron out marital dissension in such cases and to help spouses make their marriages work.[502] One member of the school of Laon agrees with this view, although he omits Ivo's concern with marriage counseling and is more forthright in extending permission to the Christian spouse to dismiss the unbelieving partner.[503] Another member of the school offers the unworkable ruling that the marriage is valid for the believing spouse but not for the unbelieving one.[504] The most exhaustive defender of the legitimacy, and even of the desirability, of mixed marriages, the master who rules out disparity of cult as an impediment to marriage most vigorously, is Paucapalea. This is, perhaps, surprisingly so. As a commentator on Gratian, he refers to the very full dossier of citations, pro and con, that Gratian brings forward, from St. Paul on up, and he overturns the conclusions of his master.[505]

It is the same Gratian who occupies a pivotal role in turning the twelfth-century consensus away from the idea that mixed marriages are acceptable. Gratian offers the most solidly based arguments in favor of disparity of cult as an impediment to marriage and as a basis for nullifying a marriage of anyone in this period. In so doing, he also manifests a distinctly canonical approach to the question. Gratian is well aware of the fact that Paul both permits mixed marriages and that he permits the dismissal of the non-believing spouse. He is also aware of the fact that the church fathers and early decretals emphasize the first of these permissions. His

---

[500] Hermannus, *Sent.*, p. 139; *Sent. Parisiensis* I, p. 47.

[501] Hugh of St. Victor, *De sac.* 2.11.9, *PL* 176: 504D–510C, Master Simon, *De sac.*, p. 59.

[502] Ivo of Chartres, *Decretum* 8. c. 147, c. 195–c. 197, c. 246–c. 253, *PL* 161: 617A, 625B–C, 638C–639C.

[503] *Decretum dei fuit*, pp. 368–70.

[504] *Deus de cuius principio et fine tacetur*, p. 272.

[505] Paucapalea, *Summa* c. 28, p. 117.

reason for rejecting that tradition is not, ultimately, based either on a "creative" reading of the authorities he rejects or on the historical criticism that might have been used to relativize early church practice in the light of the missionary posture of the church at that time. Rather, Gratian's argument comes down upon a lawyer's point. The notion of two spouses living within the same household being governed by two different legal systems with respect to marriage is intellectually indigestible. It is also an administrative nightmare, in the event that it should prove necessary to adjudicate a marital dispute. And so, he rules that disparity of cult is an impediment.[506]

Support for Gratian's position was not slow in coming. Roland of Bologna follows his analysis, although he confines himself to citing the authorities who favor this conclusion, departing from his master by ignoring those who permit mixed marriages.[507] There are also other masters who agree with Gratian's solution, but who offer quite different, and less legalistic, reasons for defending it. Some members of the school of Laon see disparity of cult as an impediment because they think it is very likely that the Christian spouse will be obstructed in the practice of his or her religion.[508] The Porretans and Robert Pullen agree with that idea but put the question more under the heading of the grounds for the dissolution of a marriage. The situation they envisage is not one in which a Christian and a non-Christian seek to marry but one in which both spouses start out as pagans and one converts to Christianity or one in which two Christians marry and one of the spouses subsequently falls into heresy or embraces another religion. They thus yoke this issue to the principle that a spouse may be dismissed for fornication. Since they see the union of spouses as a spiritual as well as a physical one, they view the commission of spiritual fornication that is involved in renouncing the Christian faith as an extension of this same principle. But, because these masters have linked disparity of cult with fornication, they see the separation to which it should lead as just that, a separation and not a nullification of the marriage that would allow either or both partners to remarry.[509] For his part, the author of the *Summa sententiarum* agrees with this notion of spiritual fornication and links it to a defense of disparity of cult as an

[506] Gratian, *Decretum* pars 2. c. 28. q. 1–q. 2, col. 1078–90.
[507] Roland of Bologna, *Sent.*, p. 275.
[508] *Sent. Anselmi* 5, pp. 137–38; *De coniugo*, p. 282.
[509] *Sent. mag. Gisleberti* II 11.15, 11.22, 11.34–35, pp. 89, 158, 161; Robert Pullen, *Sent.* 7.33, 7.35, *PL* 186: 950B–952A.

impediment that is as religiously motivated as it is ungallant. Dismissing cavalierly the Pauline concession, he argues that disparity of cult is an impediment to marriage because Christian marriages must be chaste. In his opinion, the marital attitudes and practices of non-Christians are, *ipso facto,* unchaste. A Christian would thus be put into an impossible situation morally if he or she were united to a partner whose sexual rights over him or her would force the Christian to traduce Christian values.[510]

Certain kinds of sexual relations, or the lack of them, give rise to another set of disputed questions concerning impediments to marriage. One topic that is of interest, on which the masters invoke earlier principles derived from Roman law over more recent Carolingian rulings that reflect Germanic attitudes and practices now seen as unacceptable, has to do with rape as an impediment. For the Roman lawyers and the church fathers whom they influenced, the heinous crime of rape, far from giving the perpetrator any status as a claimant for the hand of his victim, made him liable to prosecution for a crime seen as a capital offense. In Germanic custom, on the other hand, cultural norms made it acceptable for men to raid other tribes of their women and to marry them by forcibly reducing them to their own power. Canonists such as Ivo of Chartres, Gratian, and Roland of Bologna seek to resurrect the older Roman principle in the case of the rape of an unmarried girl. In so doing, they also take note of the fact that a Roman girl was married by the consent of her *paterfamilias,* not by her own consent. They are not always clear on whose consent is required in this particular connection. Gratian views rape as an impediment, although he allows that it is one that can be waived if the principals consent to marriage. But, who are the principals? On the question of whether it is the woman's consent, or her father's, that binds her, he contradicts himself, although he asserts that compulsion itself is an impediment to marriage.[511] Ivo of Chartres agrees that rape establishes no claim on an unmarried girl and sees it necessary for both the girl and her parents to assert her right to view rape as an impediment.[512] Like Gratian, Roland is more forthright in treating rape as an impediment tout court and not as a possible way of initiating a marriage unless it is specifically rejected as such. He

---

[510] *Summa sent.* 7.8 *PL* 176: 160C–161B.

[511] Gratian, *Decretum* pars 2. c. 31. q. 2. c. 2.13–c. 16, c. 36. q. 2. c. 7–c. 11, col. 1112–14, 1124–25, 1291–92.

[512] Ivo of Chartres, *Decretum* 8. c. 23, c. 40–c. 41, c. 170–c. 177, *PL* 161: 588D–589A, 593A–B, 620A–621B.

concedes that, as an impediment to marriage, rape may not be automatic or intrinsic. He also observes that the girl and her parents may not agree on this point. If that is the case, he rules that it is the consent of the victim that is determinative, although he is not entirely clear on whether he means the consent to the illicit sexual activity represented by the rape itself or to the subsequent marriage, if any.[513] On the other hand, the author of the *Decretum dei fuit* shows both an inclination to adhere to the Carolingian authorities and a disinclination to consider the opinion of the victim that ill accords with the school of Laon's general support for the principle of consent. He flatly asserts that rape is not an impediment to marriage.[514]

Another form of sexual misbehavior discussed as a bar to marriage is a prior adulterous affair between the principals, their having lived together in concubinage, the wife-to-be having been a prostitute with her intended husband as one of her former clients, or the more general issue of prior unchastity. The handling of this range of topics is conditioned by the context in which a given master places it and also by the fact that there was a standard pair of opposing authorities on this issue, Pope Leo I and Augustine, whose reasoning the master might or might not bring to bear on his solution. Leo had ruled that a prior adulterous affair was an impediment to marriage. The situation he envisages is one in which a married woman commits adultery and she and her lover conspire to murder her husband, in order to clear the way for their own marriage. This type of behavior, of course, he seeks to discourage; and so he bans their subsequent union. Augustine has in mind a different kind of situation, in which adulterers or two people living together illicitly come to see the error of their ways and seek to regularize their relationship when events make this possible. He applauds such a conversion of heart and and the intention of reparation, and permits the marriage for the spiritual healing of the couple.

This question is the only one on marriage raised by Anselm of Laon. Reviewing the arguments on both sides and the rationales of Augustine as well as Leo, he comes down squarely in support of Leo. In his estimation, Leo's point of view is entirely cogent. Murder should not be encouraged or countenanced. Criminals should not be allowed to profit from their crimes, and thereby to imply that the church sanctions, or turns a blind eye to, their

---

[513] Roland of Bologna, *Sent.*, pp. 308–10.
[514] *Decretum dei fuit*, p. 377.

scandalous behavior. On his own account, he adds that inheritance rights may become confused in the event that the lovers are allowed to marry. The disciples of Anselm follow his lead.[515] Roland of Bologna seeks to split the difference. If the lovers have committed murder, he agrees that Leo's ruling should be applied. But, if their only crime is adultery, they should be permitted to marry, following Augustine, assuming that they have first done penance for that sin.[516] The author of the *Summa sententiarum* is also supportive of Leo's position and seeks to vaporize the authority of Augustine in the alembic of historical criticism. As he argues the case, Augustine was referring to an earlier time, the age of David and Bathsheba, when such unions were allowed, not excluding the *de facto* elimination of Bathsheba's husband by David's ordering him to the front lines of the army, where he was dispatched by the enemy. On the other hand, according to this master, Leo was addressing a later age, in which such unions were forbidden. In his view, we are still living in the age to which Leo spoke and for which he was legislating. Leo's ruling thus still holds, and, pending any more recent dispensations, it should be followed.[517] In this reading of the question, the reasons why Leo and Augustine take the positions they take are set aside and the matter is treated simply in the light of one set of customs succeeding another, with the idea that it is fitting to observe the conventions in place. The master sees Leo not so much as legislating new rulings for his own age as he is making a declaratory statement about current norms. It is quite possible that the master takes this tack because he cannot produce a satisfying refutation of Augustine's position. For his part, one of the Porretan masters carefully reviews the position of both Leo and Augustine and the concerns that animate them. We are, unfortunately left in suspense concerning his solution, because there is a lacuna in his sentence collection and the text breaks off just at the point where he would have rendered his verdict.[518]

Ivo of Chartres' whole focus on sexual misconduct as a bar to marriage is informed by his desire to come to grips with the affair between Philip I and Bertrada de Montfort. There actually was a point during this affair when the adulterers could have married, the spouses of both parties having died. In his effort to terminate the

---

[515] *Sentences of Anselm of Laon.* no. 66–67; *Sentences of the School of Laon*, no. 409; 5: 57–58, 288; *De coniugo*, p. 283; *Sent. Anselmi* 5, pp. 146, 148–49. See above, chapter 2, pp. 47, 87.
[516] Roland of Bologna, *Summa* c. 31. q. 1, pp. 154–56.
[517] *Summa sent.* 7.13, *PL* 176: 165A–B.
[518] *Sent, mag. Gisleberti* I 11.39, pp. 161–62.

scandal, which had also brought a decree of excommunication upon the head of the king, a situation impeding the resolution of the investiture controversy in France, Ivo sees much to be said in favor of Augustine's position. He rules that it is acceptable for a man to marry a woman who has been his concubine, providing that no impediments of any other kind exist.[519] Ivo writes, clearly, before Bertrada herself had resolved the problem by acquiring a monastic calling and retiring to a nunnery. Since the Philip-Bertrada affair is the only context in which Ivo takes up this matter, it is difficult to know how much the felt need to lay the scandal to rest influenced his thinking. For his part, Gratian associates prior adultery with a range of other illicit or problematic forms of sexual behavior. He recognizes the general difficulty that Leo wants to address, but thinks that his prohibition is far too sweeping. The couple, in his estimation, ought to be allowed to marry provided that they do penance first, so long as they have not committed murder. On the other hand, he rules out as acceptable a marriage between a rapist of a matron and his victim if she is later widowed, a position consistent with his view of rape as an impediment. In Gratian's opinion, Augustine is not entirely to the point here, because he was talking about marriage to one's concubine or to a mistress who had been repudiated by her husband because of her infidelity. Marriage to the latter sort of woman might have been permitted under the divorce laws of the Old Testament, he notes, but in the New Testament such a woman would not be considered marriageable. Gratian thus criticizes both Augustine and Leo, although he turns Leo's prohibition into a legitimate if qualified opportunity. A propos of marriage to one's concubine, he yokes this problem to the larger question of marriage to a woman who has been unchaste or who was a prostitute whom her intended husband had patronized. Gratian feels distinctly uncomfortable at the thought of permitting such marriages. In his view, the moral horizon of such women, and of the men who resort to them, is so low that they will be inclined to import the sexual ethics governing their past lives into their nuptial relations as Christian spouses, thereby debasing Christian marriage. They will engage in sexual relations immoderately, and for pleasure only, and not in accordance with the ends of marriage. They will be much more likely to succumb to the temptation of aborting unwanted offspring than will other people. Gratian views

---

[519] Ivo of Chartres, *Decretum* 8. c. 32, c. 34, c. 38, *PL* 161: 591A–B. 591B, 592A; *Epistola* 16, ed., and trans. Jean Leclercq in Ivo of Chartres, *Correspondence* (Paris: Les Belles Lettres, 1949), 1: 64–71.

with the deepest misgivings the capacity of sexual sinners genuinely to abandon their past lives and to enter into Christian marriage with a firm purpose of amendment. Yet, much as he dislikes the idea, he agrees that such unions are licit.[520] Paucapalea puts the subject in the same context as Gratian and rules as well that the wife's status as a former concubine or prostitute is not an impediment to marriage. But he is far less grudging than Gratian and far less worried about the sexual temptations likely to be present in such marriages.[521]

Leo I also looms as a standard authority in an even stickier debate concerning another impediment and basis for dissolving a marriage, sexual dysfunction. During the first half of the twelfth century, this problem went by the name of *frigiditas*; and it was, almost universally, held to be an affliction of the male sex only. Another contemporary assumption, also almost universal, was that *frigiditas* comes in two forms. There is natural impotence, as a congenital disability, whether structural or functional in character, or as a disability brought about by accident, illness, or injury. And, there is impotence that is a consequence of witchcraft (*maleficium*).[522] This distinction in turn reflects a more basic assumption, the idea that any two members of the opposite sex will, automatically, desire and be able to have sexual relations with each other under any circumstances. This belief that the sex drive is no respecter of persons, times, and conditions and that it is always translatable into coitus unless malevolent supernatural forces intervene is what informs the view that temporary sexual dysfunction or impotence with a particular partner whom one finds sexually unattractive or with whom one is a bad physical match must be caused by *maleficium* These beliefs are brought to the discussion of *frigiditas* as an impediment and as grounds for nullification of a

---

[520] Gratian, *Decretum* pars 2. c. 31. q. 1, c. 32. q. 1–q. 2, col. 1106–12, 1115–22.

[521] Paucapalea, *Summa* c. 32. q. 1, p. 125.

[522] Good overviews are provided by James A. Brundage, "Impotence, Frigidity, and Marital Nullity in the Decretists and Early Decretalists," in *Proceedings of the Seventh International Congress of Medieval Canon Law*, ed. Peter Linehan (Vatican City: Biblioteca Apostolica Vaticana, 1988), pp. 407–23 and Josef Löffler, *Die Störungen des geschlechtlichen Vermögens in der Literatur der autoritativen Theologie des Mittelalters: Ein Beitrag zur Geschichte der Impotenz und des medizinischen Sachverständigensbeweises im kanonischen Impotenzprocess*, Akademie der Wissenschaften und der Literatur in Mainz, Abhandlungen der geistes- und sozialwissenschaftlichen Klasse, 6 (Wiesbaden: Franz Steiner Verlag GMBH, 1958), pp. 9–10, 14–15, 17, 63–91. As Löffler, himself a historian of medicine, shows, the progressive refinements on these concepts in later medieval theology and canon law can be read as an index of the reception of Greco-Arabic medical science and its accessibility to thinkers outside of medical circles.

marriage by all contemporary masters and cause them to labor
under the same liabilities in the effort to resolve this question. And,
despite what one might be inclined to think, the pressure to address
frigiditas, the inclination to regard it as an impediment or as a cause
for nullification, and the recognition that this view requires a
means of verifying the claims of the aggrieved spouse were not
confined to those masters who judged that consummation makes
the marriage or even to those who deemed that sexual relations are
all that marriage involves.

A good index of that lack of symmetry, and even of logical
inconsistency, can be found in the treatment of *frigiditas* among the
Abelardians. Since they agree that marriage was conceded only as
a remedy for human concupiscence and they argue that the consent
to exclusive sexual relations is the sole content of marital consent,
one would expect them to rule that marriages are null in which
sexual relations are impossible. But, instead of following this, the
Leonine ruling, such is their ascetic distaste for the sexual relations
whose legitimization is the only rationale for marriage that they
agree with the authority who undergirds the other side of the
debate, Gregory the Great. They join him in ruling that, in cases
where a marriage cannot be consummated, the spouses cannot file
for an annulment but should live together as brother and sister.
The fact that such an arrangement would defeat the primary, and
indeed, the only, purpose of marriage as they see it give them no
qualms at all.[523] Roland of Bologna, in his *Summa*, also agrees that
frigiditas affords no grounds for dissolving a marriage.[524]

The Laon master who wrote the *De coniugo* suggests that the
preference for the Gregorian over the Leonine position may be
regionally, if not rationally, induced, and that it is also a function of
whether one distinguishes between natural *frigiditas* and *frigiditas*
caused by witchcraft. Like other members of the school and like the
majority of theologians and canonists in this period, he sides with
Leo. In the case of natural *frigiditas*, which he thinks must be
proved by the testimony of seven witnesses (*septima manu*), the
marriage can be nullified and the wife may remarry. If the husband
loses his disability later, the wife must set her new husband aside
and return to her original husband. If witchcraft is involved, the
master prescribes a regime of fasting, prayer, and almsgiving for a
period of five years. After that time, the Gallican church permits

---

[523] Hermannus, *Sent.*, p. 136; *Sent. Parisiensis* I, pp. 45–46; *Ysagoge in theologiam*,
pp. 197–99.
[524] Roland of Bologna, *Summa* c. 33. q. 1, pp. 188–89.

the dissolution of the marriage and the marriage of the wife to another partner, but not the remarriage of the husband. The Roman church, he notes, withholds that permission and requires the dysfunctional marriage to remain in force. This master does not discuss how the witnesses in the first case come by their evidence and whether the testimony of interested parties, such as relatives of the wife, will be admitted. He offers no advice on how natural *frigiditas* which later disappears can be distinguished from temporary dysfunction brought about by *maleficium*.[525] Another member of the school tries to address the intractable problem of proving the non-consummation of a marriage, in an area where, admittedly, empirical verification of the facts is impossible to obtain without violating personal modesty and connubial privacy. In order to avoid selfish or frivolous claims against husbands, he says, the evidence must be given under oath. This still leaves to the side the question of how the evidence is to be obtained in the first place. Leaving that problem unresolved, he rules that, if a man whose marriage has been annulled on account of his *frigiditas* finds himself capable of having sexual relations with another woman, he must return to his wife. The possibility that the wife may have been the problem in the first place is never considered. Regarding *maleficium*, he prescribes the same five-year regime as the author of the *De coniugo* and, siding with the Gallicans, admits not only the remarriage of the aggrieved spouse but also, if the spell passes, of the formerly dysfunctional one as well. He does not require the original partners to reunite, a view not widely shared in this period. Other members of the school are in basic agreement, except for that last point, although they display even less interest in how allegations in this area can be proved.[526]

The distinction between natural impotence and impotence caused by witchcraft is not always so clearly marked in the teaching of other masters, even though many of them who join the members of the school of Laon in viewing *frigiditas* as grounds for nullification and for the prohibition of a marriage also join them in regarding consent, not consummation, as the essence of the marriage. In strict logic, their doctrine of marriage formation would seem to make it a moot point whether or not a marriage had been consummated. The attention they give to this point and their support of

---

[525] *De coniugo*, pp. 279–80.

[526] *Decretum dei fuit*, pp. 371–73. See also *Sentences of the School of Laon*, no. 528, 5: 367, where the regime for *maleficium* is reduced to two years; *Deus de cuius principio et fine tacetur*, p. 273.

Leo suggest that their awareness of what most people expect in a marriage takes pride of place over their view of what makes a marriage valid and sacramental, even in the case of masters who have a broader understanding of marriage than do the Abelardians. The Porretans treat *frigiditas* as grounds for annulment, but only if it is a permanent, congenital disability. They are unique, up to their time, in observing that this disability may afflict women as well as men. That consideration aside, the author of the *Summa sententiarum* agrees with the Porretans' narrow definition of the problem and thinks that the permanence of the dysfunction can be assumed after a trial period of two years. He notes that the couple are not required to separate but that, if they do, the dowry is to be returned by the husband. He offers no recommendation of his own.[527] Master Simon and Robert Pullen also see *frigiditas* as grounds for annulment and make no distinction as to its type. Simon offers some vague remarks about oaths and witnesses but provides no real understanding as to how a claim of non-consummmation can be proved.[528]

This murkiness on how to test allegations of impotence in the authors just noted is not just a function of the fact that they are theologians a bit out of their depth in handling forensic matters. For it is found, to an equally bemusing degree, among the canonists as well. Ivo of Chartres demands that proof must be obtained, whether one is dealing with *maleficium* or with natural *frigiditas*. He is not at all clear on how one gathers it. If one has the proof, he states that a wife can repudiate an impotent husband after two years, and, her marriage having been nullified, she may remarry. But, if the wife lays a charge and the husband denies it, the husband's word is to be taken, even if they both give their word under oath, for the husband is the head of the wife in legal matters. This ruling gives the wife no legal remedy for the non-payment of the conjugal debt which Ivo elsewhere agrees is just as much the wife's right as the husband's. Ivo does not appear to recognize that his opinion here is inconsistent and unfair. However, consistent with his emphasis on consent, he states that if a man who, knowing that he is impotent, marries, he has committed perjury, which invalidates his marital consent. Ivo grants that, when witchcraft is at work, and if the prayers, tears, and almsgiving prove ineffective,

---

[527] *Sent. mag. Gisleberti* II 11.15, p. 89; *Summa sent.* 7.15–17, 7.20, *PL* 176: 165B–166B, 170C–D.
[528] Master Simon, *De sac.*, pp. 50–51, 54–58; Robert Pullen, *Sent.* 7.36, *PL* 186: 956A–D.

the marriage may be dissolved and the aggrieved partner may remarry. If the remedy is effective, the spouses should remain with each other. One finds in Ivo's imprecision about evidence and in his dismissive treatment of the testimony of wives almost a wish, unspoken, that spouses in unconsummated marriages should not air their problems in public but rather should suffer in silence.[529]

Gratian does no better in providing a real remedy for the wife when her husband contradicts her, a fact which also stands at odds with his guarantee of the equality of spouses in rendering the marriage debt and his firmly evenhanded treatment of the right to dismiss a spouse on grounds of fornication.[530] He agrees that *frigiditas* is a cause for nullification. He also agrees that the husband is to be believed if the spouses are not in agreement on the facts. He offers no suggestions on how the authorities who sit in judgment can or should substantiate the allegations or disclaimers of the spouses. As for the impotence caused by *maleficium*. Gratian joins other masters of the day in offering no insight on how to prove that witchcraft is, indeed, afoot, and no remedy for the new husband of a woman freed from a marriage on this account, if her first husband recovers.[531] Nor do Gratian's earliest commentators offer much further help. Paucapalea ignores natural impotence altogether, as well as how one would go about proving it. He confines himself to *maleficium* and agrees with Gratian on that subject.[532] Roland of Bologna, taking a totally different position in his *Sentences* from the one he offers in his *Summa*, states that natural *frigiditas* both impedes and dissolves a marriage, so long as it is not pretended or falsely and maliciously charged. In treating *maleficium* as a cause of impotence, he is the one and only master in this period to recognize the fact that a man may be sexually functional with one partner and not with another. Without pausing to notice that this conceptual breakthrough places the whole idea of *maleficium* on a very shaky foundation indeed, and without indicating what the regime for exorcism should be, he takes the unpopular line, along with the author of *Decretum dei fuit* that, if a man dysfunctional because of

---

[529] Ivo of Chartres, *Decretum* 8. c. 79–c. 80, c. 178–c. 180, c. 182, c. 194, *PL* 161: 600C–D, 621C–622A, 622B–C, 624D–625A.

[530] Gratian, *Decretum* pars 2. c. 32. q. 6–q. 7, q. 25, col. 1136–44, 1146–47. See James A. Brundage, "Sexual Equality in Medieval Canon Law," in *Medieval Women and the Sources of Medieval History*, ed. Joel T. Rosenthal (Athens, GA: University of Georgia Press, 1990), pp. 68–78. I am indebted to Professor Brundage for the latter reference.

[531] Gratian, *Decretum* pars 2. c. 33. q. 1, col. 1148–50.

[532] Paucapalea, *Summa* c. 33, pp. 130–31.

witchcraft should recover, he should be allowed to take a new wife, in contrast with the naturally impotent man, who is not permitted to do so after his first marriage is annulled. On the vexed question of proving non-consummation, or proving which kind of impotence is at issue, Roland waffles. He dislikes the idea of witnesses, thinking that anyone close enough to a married couple to be able to claim certitude about their intimate relations is likely to be prejudiced. He prefers adverting to the oaths of the plaintiff and defendant, but offers no advice on what to do if they disagree.[533]

There is one other major debate over an impediment to marriage, this one focusing on status and not on sexual conduct or its absence. The problem in part derives from the ambiguous meaning of the term *servus* in medieval Latin. It can have the same sense of the word as classical Latin gives it and refer to a slave, who, by definition, in Roman law, is a thing and not a person and who lacks *connubium*, or the legal right to marry. But *servus* can also mean serf, a person of semi-free legal status and one who did have assorted private and public rights in law and custom, rights that could be quite diverse depending on the part of Europe in which he lived and on his relative degree of semi-freedom and semi-servitude. Slavery, to be sure, was far less in evidence in the twelfth century than it had been in the Roman world, but it was still to be found, although to a different extent in different parts of Europe. Now, the ancient authorities who had ruled on the question of whether servile status was an impediment to marriage had done so in the late Roman period, when the institution of slavery was normal, for Christians and non-Christians alike. It is true that, in the later centuries of Roman history, the crystal-clear distinction between slavery and free status found in Roman jurisprudence grew blurred, as a sizable group of upgraded slaves and downgraded freemen replaced, as the labor force, the slaves who had now become an insupportable drain on the capital resources of their masters. But the *servi*, or partially free former slaves in this category, while they bore the same name as the Roman slave and as the later medieval serf, had fewer legal rights than the serf did, rights which, in the latter case, were difficult to generalize about in the twelfth century given the profusion of local variations of law and custom.

Faced with these institutional and regional discrepancies and

---

[533] Roland of Bologna, *Sent.*, pp. 280–82.
[534] Ivo of Chartres, *Decretum* 8. c. 51–c. 55, c. 139, c. 156–c. 157, c. 164–c. 165, c. 167, *PL* 161: 594–D–595D, 615C, 618B–C, 619B–C, 619C–D.

terminological imprecisions, it is perhaps no surprise that theologians and canonists in the first half of the twelfth century reached no consensus on the question of whether servile status, however defined, was an impediment to marriage. The confusion is registered by Ivo of Chartres, who flounders about inconclusively on the question of whether marriage partners need to be of equal legal status and whether persons of servile status can marry.[534] Most other masters take a more definite stand. The Porretans and the Abelardian authors of the *Ysagoge in theologiam* and the *Sententiae Parisiensis* I assert that servile status is an impediment.[535] Gratian and Roland of Bologna take the opposing position and draw some distinctions. Disparity of status, or unfree status, they agree, are not impediments or grounds for nullifying a marriage. Error as to the identity of the person one is marrying or as to his legal status would, they think, impede or nullify a marriage, in contrast with inaccurate information as to his wealth and condition, the latter term embracing his moral character as well as his health.[536] The theme of error, or misinformation, or even disinformation, is picked up by Hugh of St. Victor, Hermannus, and Master Simon, who concur that servile status is not an impediment or a cause of nullification, so long as the *servus* has not tried to pass himself off as a *liber*, or free man, in order to marry a free woman; Simon adds the stipulation that a *servus* must obtain his master's consent.[537] The author of the *Summa sententiarum* agrees with that proviso and offers a historical and geographical gloss on this point. He notes that in some local churches, in places where Roman law is followed, persons of servile status are denied the right to marry. This is not the case in the Gallican church, where people of unequal status do have the right to marry, each person retaining his or her original status thereby. He supports this latter rule because he is a member of the Gallican church and because he advocates the following of local custom, and not necessarily because he thinks that it is the correct and fair position. The observance of the rules in force where one lives is a sufficient justification, in his eyes, for this conclusion. Thus, he makes no effort to plead for an extension to other parts of the church of the Gallican practice; within the Gallican jurisdiction, at any rate, it is fitting for a *servus* to marry another *servus* or

---

[535] *Sent. mag. Gisleberti* II 11.10, p. 88; *Ysagoge in theologiam*, p. 196; *Sent. Parisiensis* I, p. 45.

[536] Gratian, *Decretum* pars 2. c. 19, col. 1091–95; Roland of Bologna, *Sent.*, p. 275.

[537] Hugh of St. Victor, *De sac.* 2.11–19, *PL* 176: 497D–520C; Hermannus, *Sent.*, p. 136; Master Simon, *De sac.*, pp. 60–61.

for a *servus* to marry a *liber*, so long as the consent of the master of any *servus* involved is obtained.[538]

The debates just discussed, whether they involve substantive disagreements among the masters or areas where they draw the same, or similar, conclusions but for different reasons, constitute the principle controversies concerning impediments to marriage or grounds for dissolution on which contemporaries of Peter Lombard took a stand. Before positioning his own handling of this aspect of marriage doctrine in relation to the ideas of other masters, we might mention three other issues, topics much more restricted in the interest they elicited. Under this heading, several masters place monstrous crime as an impediment to marriage. Roland of Bologna gives this opinion without indicating what sort of crimes he has in mind.[539] Gratian specifies uxoricide. He displays no concern with women who may murder their husbands, but appears to think that a man who has murdered one wife is likely to be a serial killer whose right to remarry should be withdrawn.[540] The author of the *Summa sententiarum* also thinks that punitive action should be taken against serious criminals in the matrimonial forum but is more interested in the status of the marriage of such a person once his crime is discovered In this master's view, the criminal should be separated from his spouse. This would mean that neither of them would have the right to remarry, and it would thereby punish the innocent wife as well as the guilty husband—for this master, along with Gratian, envisions the criminal as being the husband—but it would at least mean that she was not forced to live with a horrible felon.[541]

The other two mini-debates are triggered by the departure of the Porretans from views standard at this time. Under the heading of the point that misfortunes or vicissitudes in the areas of health, wealth, or the discovery of sterility in a spouse do not provide grounds for an annulment or separation, the defenders of the consensus position, citing Augustine as their authority, urge that not even leprosy, should it supervene, offers an exception from this rule. Leprosy is singled out, among misfortunes, both for its loathsome manifestations and for its alleged contagiousness, in the eyes of Augustine and his followers. One of the Porretan masters objects specifically to this Augustinian notion. In his view, leprosy does

---

[538] *Summa sent.* 7.14, *PL* 176: 165B–166B.
[539] Roland of Bologna, *Sent.*, p. 280.
[540] Gratian, *Decretum* pars 2. c. 33. q. 2. c. 9. dictum, col. 1154.
[541] *Summa sent.* 7.20, *PL* 176: 170B.

offer grounds for dismissing a spouse.[542] Another area in which the same master finds himself swimming against the current has to do with the horror of incest that informs the elaborate consanguinity rules of this period In order to dramatize how seriously this principle has to be taken, the Laon master who wrote the *Deus de cuius principio et fine tacetur*, reflecting the contemporary consensus in so doing, poses a hypothetical case whose plot has all the trappings of a Hellenistic romance. Imagine that a brother and sister are separated in childhood, he suggests. The brother is stolen and taken to a faraway land, there to be raised in ignorance of his true homeland and identity. After he grows up, he finds his way back to his native land, and chances to meet his sister. The two young people fall in love and marry. But then, evidence of their close blood relationship comes to light. What to do? The master is quite unequivocal in his ruling. He states the standard opinion that the marriage must be annulled forthwith.[543] Now, the Porretan master tells the same gripping tale by way of example. He pointedly fails to agree with the consensus position. If, and only if, legitimate witnesses can be found, in sufficient number, to testify to the sibling status of the spouses, should the couple be parted. But if not, they should be allowed to stay together, for they married in perfectly good faith. And, in any event, he reminds the reader, in this unsuccessful sally against the serried ranks of ancient and contemporary opinion, the purpose of theologizing about impediments to marriage and grounds for nullification is not to obstruct people from seeking the solace of marriage, whenever possible, but to try to find as many ways as possible of keeping marriages together and of enabling spouses to work out their difficulties within its embrace.[544]

This last sentiment, if not the Porretan master's position on incest, is one warmly shared by Peter Lombard. It certainly colors the way he addresses the whole subject of marital impediments. Irrespective of the alignment of his position, or not, with this or that contemporary master on particular impediments, he does something that no other scholastic theologian of the time does, in his generous incorporation into his account of material drawn from the canonists and in his effort to rationalize the treatment of the entire subject. When one reads the discussion of matrimonial impediments provided by other theologians and canonists in this period, one is struck by the randomness of their attack on the

---

[542] *Sent. mag. Gisleberti* I 11.29, p. 160.
[543] *Deus de cuius principio et fine tacetur*, pp. 273–74.
[544] *Sent. mag. Gisleberti* I 11.37, p. 161.

subject. There seems to be no individually or generally understood reason for the sequence in which impediments are presented; and the ordering of this material differs considerably from one author to another. From the very outset, the Lombard gives his own treatment of impediments a look that sets it apart from the marriage treatises of his compeers. He offers a clear and cogent principle of organization. He first presents conditions that may interfere with the consent that is constitutive of the marriage. Next, he considers who has a legitimate right to marry. His way of posing this question is of interest. Instead of presenting impediments in negative terms, as obviating legitimate marriages, he accents the positive qualities possessed by marriageable persons as rights that they have, insofar as they have not ceded them by their own free will or as a result of forces beyond their control. In handling other impediments, Peter organizes them in two categories, those that are intrinsic, natural, and unchangeable and those that are accidental, existing because of human choices or contingencies that are not graven in stone, or because of disciplinary rulings that can and do change. This mode of organization gives the whole subject of impediments a much more coherent and comprehensible shape in Peter's *Sentences* than it finds anywhere else in this period.[545]

Under the heading of circumstances that impede the consent which is of the essence in marriage formation, Peter lists coercion, fraud, and error. He is in full agreement with the consensus position, which invalidates marriages in which defective consent of these kinds is present. His own concern, notwithstanding his vigorous defense of the need for free and informed consent, is to ask whether there is any basis for accepting as valid marriages in which these defects are present. With respect to coercion, he cites an oft-mentioned case of a crusader baron who forced his daughter into a political marriage that was initially repugnant to her. But, as time went on, she grew to appreciate her husband or at least to make her peace with her situation. Peter concedes that such a marriage is, initially, invalid. But he thinks it can become valid if, in the sequel, the dissenting spouse changes her opinion to one of assent. Peter's position on this case can be understood two ways. It can be seen as a rare concession on his part to the realities of

---

[545] Peter outlines this organizational scheme at *Sent.* 4. d. 27. c. 1, 2: 421–22. None of these points are noted by the only general study of Peter Lombard on marital impediments to date, Leon M. Smiśniewicz, *Die Lehre von den Ehehindernissen bei Petrus Lombardus und bei seinen Kommentaren* (Posen: Druckarnia Katolicka, 1917), which is very sketchy and not to be recommended. The author treats the subject as a mere curtain-raiser for Peter's thirteenth-century commentators.

marriage as it was actually practiced in the twelfth-century world. It can also be read in another light. Peter is as interested in the possibility that the experience of conjugal life can engender, over time, the true consent needed to make the marriage sacramental as he is interested in objecting to coercion. In this instance, his view of marriage as a means of moral education emerges strongly. On the other hand, on the question of fraud, error, or *bona fide* ignorance as impediments, he follows Gratian very closely. Not all error, he agrees, vitiates consent. If there is error, deliberate or otherwise, as to a person's identity or legal status, this error is an impediment. But error, and even disinformation, as to a person's fortune, condition, and moral qualities, or as to his past history, is not an impediment. Along with Gratian, Peter argues this case on both rational and legal grounds. Error as to person and status is deception, and is hence wrong. It may also infringe on the legal rights of the spouse who marries such an individual and thereby suffers disparagement. Deception may also be present in the case of error as to fortune and condition. This, he concedes, is also immoral. But, no infringement on the spouse's legal rights results. And so, error as to fortune and condition is not an impediment or grounds for the dissolution of a marriage.[546] To this common doctrine which he shares with Gratian Peter adds a theological problem not of such concern to the canonists, the question of whether the father of Leah, who passed her off as Rachel in marrying her to Jacob, committed a sin or refuted the principle that error as to person is an impediment to a valid marriage. His opinion is that this event was designed to state a mystery and not to lay down a legal or theological precedent.[547]

Peter opens his discussion of who is legally entitled to marry by remarking on the point that some of the rules relative to this question, and to other regulations governing marriage, have changed over time. Agreeing that the deity has altered these rules in accordance with His estimate of human needs and capacities in various times and places, he adds to the stand taken on this matter by Hugh of St. Victor, the author of the *Summa sententiarum*, and Hermannus by noting that, aside from population statistics as a controlling consideration, the deity, in His successive dispensations

---

[546] Peter Lombard, *Sent.* 4. c. 29, 2: 436–37. Teodoro Ruiz Josué, "Los efectos juridicos de la ignorancia en la doctrina matrimonial de Hugo de San Victor y Roberto Pulleyn," *Revista española de derecho canónico* 8 (1948): 63, 65, 68–105 sees Hugh, whether directly or indirectly by way of Robert Pullen, as Peter's chief source for the doctrine of error, ignoring Gratian.

[547] Peter Lombard, *Sent.* 4. d. 30. c. 1, 2: 437–38.

on this subject, moved from a covenant in which religion was held to be passed on by hereditary succession to a covenant potentially embracing all mankind, by faith. God also moved from a sexual ethic in which marriage alone was valued to one in which celibacy as well was esteemed. Peter places the differences between the Old Testament and New Testament rules on marriage on a trajectory that includes the rules changed by men in the ecclesiastical dispensation, including the enforcement of clerical celibacy, suggesting the understanding that some of the impediments to marriage to be discussed later on are of man-made invention and that others are not.[548] Thus, with respect to who a legitimate person is, one has to take account not only of the changes in marriage before the law, under the law, and in the time of grace but also the changes between the rules obtaining in the *ecclesia primitiva* and those obtaining in the present day, an observation designed to suggest that historical criticism may need to be invoked in disallowing earlier rules which Peter means to reject. In addition, even regarding those regulations that are currently in force, some are fully legitimate, others are fully illegitimate, and still others, in an intermediate group, are neither fully legitimate nor fully illegitimate. In the first category Peter places unions that do not violate vows of continence, holy orders, cognation, legal status, disparity of cult, or natural *frigiditas*. In the second category he places unions that include persons with prior vows, ordination, cognation, and disparity of cult. In the intermediate category are unions made problematic by impotence or by the legal status of one or both spouses. The principle underlying this distinction is whether the marriage is indissoluble, as it is in fully legitimate unions, whether marriage must be prevented or annulled, as in the case of the fully illegitimate unions, or whether the marriage presents a range of options in this connection, as in the case of the intermediate type of union, especially if the marriage has been contracted in ignorance.[549]

These distinctions having been clearly laid down, Peter now proceeds to group impediments under the headings of natural and permanent impediments and impediments conditioned by will, circumstance, or changeable disciplinary rulings. The first of the natural impediments are *frigiditas* and insanity, because these defects speak to the natural capacities needed to express the two aspects of marital sacramentality that Peter sees in a valid union. Peter sides firmly with the majority of contemporary masters who

---

[548] Ibid., d. 33. c. 1–c. 4, 2: 456–62.
[549] Ibid., d. 34. c. 1, 2: 462–63.

follow Leo in supporting the dissolution of marriages that cannot be consummated on the basis of natural *frigiditas*. In line with his egalitarian treatment of the sexual rights of spouses, he departs from the contemporary consensus and agrees with the Porretans that this rule applies to husbands and wives alike. He considers the problem of obtaining proof and mentions both the swearing of oaths, on relics, by the contending parties, and the use of witnesses. Peter is not particularly interested in these procedural issues, but appears to think that the inclusion of relics will deter litigants from bringing frivolous or malicious charges or from lying about the facts under oath. Peter rejects the idea, found in Ivo of Chartres and Gratian, that the wife's testimony is to be disallowed if it conflicts with her husband's. Peter recognizes the contemporary distinction between natural *frigiditas* and *frigiditas* caused by witchcraft. He includes the latter in his discussion here because, although it is not congenital, it is a result of forces beyond the control of the couple in question. He agrees with the generally held notion that a regime of prayer, fasting, and alsmgiving should be undertaken and that, if exorcism fails, the marriage should be dissolved. Just as in the case of natural *frigiditas* the functional partner may remarry. In the case of a person whose marriage has been annulled because of his own dysfunction and whose former spouse has remarried, who subsequently finds himself able to have sexual relations with another partner, Peter attacks the consensus position as being too harsh and too lacking in equity. He joins Roland of Bologna and the author of the *De coniugo* in ruling that the new marriage or marriages should not be broken up and the original spouses should not be forced to reunite. As he points out, it was by the judgment of the church that the original marriage was annulled, because it could not be consummated. But now, both of the original partners find themselves in new, and functional, marriages. They both originally entered the state of marriage in recognition that they were called to this state and that they need its consolations. Thus, the forced reconciliation of the original spouses, in despite of the rights of their new spouses, should not be automatic and rigidly enforced. Rather, the range of personal circumstances involved and the demands of fairness should be taken into account, a perspective which, in Peter's eyes, is likely to favor the new, and functional union or unions over the original, and dysfunctional, one.[550]

Just as sexual relations in a marriage are a sacrament, in that

---

[550] Ibid., c. 3, 2: 465.

they signify the physical and institutional union of Christ and the church, and their impossibility renders the sacrament null, so, *a fortiori*, insanity must be viewed as a natural impediment to marriage in that it makes impossible the consent and the union of minds and hearts that signify the bond of love between Christ and the church. It is this aspect of the sacrament, as we have seen, that, for Peter, initiates a marriage and that animates, or should animate, its external expression in sexual relations. The reason why Peter considers insanity under the heading of natural impediments and not under the heading of error, ignorance, fraud, or compulsion is that these latter obstacles are products of the exercise of human free will. On the other hand, insanity is a congenital defect. People who are mentally ill (*furiosi*) or who are mentally incapacitated (*in amentia*), should not be allowed to marry, in Peter's view, because they are persons of diminished responsibility who are not capable of giving informed consent. If it is not entirely self-consistent, Peter's position on this point, along with his view that insane persons already married should be allowed to stay together and that, when insanity, like physical illness or deformity, supervenes, it is not grounds for dismissing a spouse, is consistent with the consensus on that subject.[551] As with his contemporaries, his treatment of insanity is not symmetrical, either with itself or with his treatment of *frigiditas*, even though in both cases he draws a distinction between a disability that is inborn and a disability that is acquired later. For, although he sees the union of minds and hearts involved in marital consent as essential, he does not permit the annulment of marriages in which the mental condition of one or both spouses makes that union of minds and hearts problematic, or even impossible, after the marriage has come into being, even though he sees the impossibilities involved as an obstacle to the creation of a marriage in the first place. It is not entirely clear why he admits this discrepancy. He offers no grounds for his ruling, except the idea that marriage requires a commitment, for better or for worse.

All the other conditions to be considered as impediments to marriage, and grounds for dissolution, or not, fall under Peter's second heading, since they are subject to human will, circumstance, or changeable convention. The first item on his agenda here is sexual misconduct. He agrees with the consensus position that fornication is a basis for separation but that it does not dissolve a marriage and permit the remarriage of either the guilty or the

---

[551] Ibid., c. 4–c. 6, 2: 465–67.

innocent party. The particular accent which the Lombard gives to this standard opinion is derived, in part, from Gratian, and, in part, from his own pastoral outlook on marriage. With Gratian, he argues that a spouse who himself or herself has been unfaithful has no business seeking to dismiss his or her spouse for the same offense; a single standard of marital chastity must apply to both husbands and wives. And, since, even if a spouse is legitimately dismissed for this reason, neither party can remarry, it is a better idea to aim at forgiveness and reconciliation than to activate the permission to separate.[552] The second kind of sexual misconduct to which Peter adverts is the prior adulterous affair as a bar to marriage in the first place, on which there was no contemporary agreement. Here, Peter comes the closest to the position taken by Gratian and Roland of Bologna, although, again, with an emphasis on how the church can best minister to the spiritual needs of the parties involved. In comparing the analyses of Leo and Augustine, Peter prefers Augustine's concern with penance, reparation, and the regularization of the couple's relationship when events make this possible over Leo's more legalistic and punitive approach. He also agrees with Gratian and Roland that, if the couple have indeed succumbed to the temptation to murder the obstructive spouse, they should not be allowed to profit from their crime. In that event, he thinks that Augustine would join Leo in forbidding the marriage, as he would himself. But, if this condition does not obtain, the spiritual healing of the couple takes priority, and is the reason why Augustine should be supported.[553] This is as far as Peter takes the subject of sexual misconduct, before or outside of marriage, as an impediment to marriage. By his omission of the range of worries on this score ventilated by Gratian and Paucapalea, he suggests, at least by implication, that marriage creates a new status, morally and sacramentally. Sincere commitment to its values is what counts, rather than the past history of the partners before they accepted its rights and duties.

Like the decision to commit fornication or adultery, the decision to take vows of celibacy, to enter into holy orders, and to commit a serious crime are matters deriving from the exercise of free will, which Peter logically includes under the heading of impediments to marriage that are not part of the natural givens of a person's life. He agrees entirely with the consensus position on ordination at the rank of subdeacon or above as an impediment to marriage. With

---

[552] Ibid., d. 35. c. 1–c. 3, 2: 467–71.
[553] Ibid., c. 4, 2: 471–72.

Gratian, he withdraws from uxoricides the right to remarry. Peter also adds his own insights to these topics. In handling holy orders, he is less concerned than are the canonists in showing that authorities in the early church support clerical celibacy. With respect to the murder of a spouse, he shares the assumption that this form of felony is to be conceived of as a crime on the husband's side, not the wife's. The evenhanded treatment of wives and husbands more typical of Peter's theology of marriage deserts him on this subject. The chief point that he wants to make in this connection is that, even if the provocation of a husband's uxoricide was his wife's adultery, a motive that might be excused in the civil courts, he should be punished by the spiritual penalties of the church.[554] On the subject of vows, Peter is somewhat more lenient than is typical in this period. He is also deft in turning a legalistic point against a ruling of the canonists. While he agrees with the canonists, and with everyone else, that vows of celibacy are an impediment to marriage and a cause of nullification if they are discovered later on, whether the vows involve a monastic commitment or a calling to virginity, celibacy, or widowhood in a non-monastic context, he draws a distinction between vows taken in public and vows taken in private, one not found in contemporary masters. According to Peter, if a person takes a private vow of celibacy and later marries, the marriage should not be dissolved. While Peter acknowledges that such conduct is morally wrong, especially if the individual passes himself off as someone who has not taken such a vow, he notes that, in the absence of witnesses, there is no way of proving that the vow was ever taken.[555]

There are other impediments that Peter addresses under this same heading. While they may not be volitional, they reflect conditions that are conventional, accidental, and subject to change. One such circumstance is servile status. Peter places it here because he regards it as accidental and not as built into the nature of things. On this subject, while his dossier of sources is derived from Gratian, his solution has more in common with that of Hugh of St. Victor, Hermannus, and Master Simon. With them, he agrees that servile status is not an impediment to marriage and it is not a cause of nullification unless a person of servile status has defrauded his spouse by pretending to be free. If there is disparity of legal status in a marriage, and if both partners have entered into the marriage

---

[554] Ibid., d. 37. c. 1–c. 2, 2: 475–77.
[555] Ibid., d. 38. c. 1–c. 2.7, 2: 478–80.

with their eyes wide open, the union is not to be dissolved. Peter further agrees that the permission of the lord is required in the marriage of a person of servile status, whether to another *servus* or to a person of higher status. Peter does add a legalistic touch, found in the canonists and not in the theologians on whom he draws. As he observes, a free man who is already married to a wife of free status cannot accept a servile status for himself that would also disparage his wife, without the wife's consent. He should neither dismiss her on this account nor force her to accept servile status. Peter's recommendation, in situations of this kind, is that the husband should gain his wife's consent, or else he should not accept servile status for himself.[556] One thing curiously absent from this analysis, deriving as it does from patristic authorities familiar with the downgrading of the Roman free farmer into a semi-free *colonus* during their own time, is the fact that neither Peter nor the canonical sources from whom he derives this question ask whether it has any real pertinence to mid-twelfth-century society.

Unfree status may be an accident of birth, or a condition accepted voluntarily, but it is a condition that can be changed. A circumstance that is totally accidental is captivity, the extreme form of a range of conditions that impose a physical separation between spouses. Without considering the other cases that can be grouped together with captivity, such as pilgrimage, crusading, and long-distance trade, Peter agrees wholeheartedly with Ivo of Chartres and Gratian that this circumstance does not terminate a marriage and that it does not allow either of the spouses to take a new partner. He is, however, somewhat more lenient than the canonists in addressing this topic. If the captive or absent spouse is honestly believed to be dead and his partner remarries, in all ignorance of his continued existence, the partner commits no sin, Peter allows. And, if the absent spouse should return, he thinks, the spouse left behind should return to him and renounce a new marriage that may have been made, but only if this can be accomplished without bad will. These conditions soften the rigor of the canonical position notably.[557]

There are four other impediments which Peter considers as serious obstacles to marriage but which he sees as impediments deriving from convention and from the disciplinary and legal rules which, although currently in force, have not always been in force,

---

[556] Ibid., d. 36. c. 1–c. 3, 2: 473–75.
[557] Ibid., d. 38. c. 3, 2: 482–83.

and which, in principle, are subject to change. Under this heading
he places disparity of cult, age, cognation, and affinity, impediments which other contemporary masters are more inclined to view
as natural or voluntary. To be sure, a person's age and his blood
relationships can be viewed as natural and his religion is a matter
of choice. But Peter treats these four impediments as conventional
because he wants to focus on the point that the rules governing
them, or the rules that he thinks should govern them, are man-
made and have not always been the same. Peter joins Gratian's
sturdy defense of the growing contemporary sense that mixed marriages should not be allowed. He holds as well that disparity of cult
is a basis for dismissing a spouse. Rather than presenting religious
commitment as a matter of choice, Peter treats this whole topic of
the two Pauline concessions, and which should be followed, from a
historical standpoint. He takes this tack so as to undermine the
permission to marry a non-Christian given by Paul and supported
by the early church. But, rather than seeking to relativize the
practice of the *ecclesia primitiva* directly, as irrelevant to the historical conditions of the twelfth-century church, he makes use of a more
roundabout historical argument, which appeals at the same time to
the perceived contradictions of the authorities who permit mixed
marriages, starting with Paul himself. Here, the Lombard cites the
Pauline permission to dismiss the unbelieving spouse in 2 Corinthians 5:14 as proof that Paul was in error in allowing mixed
marriages in 1 Corinthians 7:12–13. He admits that the Christian
partner is not required to dismiss the unbelieving spouse and that
Paul was correct in stating that the Christian spouse may win over
the unbelieving spouse. But, still, on what grounds can it be argued
that the Paul of 2 Corinthians is more to be believed than the Paul
of 1 Corinthians? Peter's main argument rests on the claim that
Paul's permission of mixed marriages, which was seconded by the
early church, was a mistaken departure from a still earlier rule
which continued then, and continues now, to remain in effect. This
is the Old Testament prohibition of mixed marriages This earlier
historical precedent, according to Peter, remained in effect in the
new Christian dispensation. It was not one of the Mosaic laws that
was abrogated or superseded by the New Law. To be sure, this
argument from historical priority is offered not because Peter thinks
that antiquity, in and of itself, is normative, but rather because, in
this instance, the Old Testament rule conforms to the rule he wants
to advocate. At the same time, his handling of this topic is a good
index of the fact that Peter does not hesitate to criticize St. Paul, in
this case for having made what he holds to have been an erroneous

and unwarranted departure from a law still binding, an error then compounded by the church fathers which Peter intends to reject. While his conclusion is certainly in line with that of many masters of his day, who join him in viewing disparity of cult as a marital impediment, his argument here is all his own. Peter shares with Hugh of St. Victor and thinkers influenced by him the idea that disparity of cult, in the case when a Christian spouse falls into heresy, non-belief, or another religion, is an index of spiritual fornication that permits dismissal of the apostate. In line with that theological appraisal of the problem, his most telling reason for banning mixed marriages is one that stands at antipodes from Gratian's, notwithstanding their strong and substantive agreement on that policy. For Gratian, as we have seen, it is both intellectually unthinkable and administratively prohibitive for two spouses in a single household to live under two different legal systems pertaining to marriage. For Peter, disparity of cult is to be disallowed because the union of minds and hearts essential to marital consent cannot, in his estimation, exist if the two spouses have different religious beliefs and values concerning marriage.[558]

Peter also confronts the question of whether, having dismissed an unbelieving spouse, the Christian partner can marry again. Here, he contrasts the position of Ambrose, who allows remarriage, with that of Augustine, who does not. Peter basically sides with Augustine, not in the interests of harshness, but in the hope that, since such a remarriage is forbidden, the Christian spouse will be motivated to work for the conversion of the unbelieving spouse whom he has dismissed, with an eye to achieving a marital reconciliation and reunion. His strategy here is to try to show that Ambrose contradicts himself, just as St. Paul does. But the argument is in line with Peter's more general interest in keeping couples together, or reuniting them if they have been separated, and encouraging them to be reconciled and to work out their differences.[559] This kind of proposal he sees as reflecting the educational value of marriage as a sacrament. With respect to the marriages between infidels, he joins Hugh of St. Victor in ruling that they are legitimate, but not sacramental, and that they are important to mention only to show that they are irrelevant to sacramental theology.[560]

Peter's handling of the other three impediments, age, consanguinity,

---

[558] Ibid., d. 39. c. 1–c. 4, 2: 483–88.
[559] Ibid., c. 5, 2: 488–90.
[560] Ibid., c. 6–c. 7, 2: 490–91.

and affinity, is of a piece in that he does not treat these conditions as natural but as conventional. In accepting the ages of
twelve, for girls, and fourteen, for boys, for present consent, norms
derived from Roman law, and the age of seven, for engagement, he
observes that these regulations are in force and that they make
sense although he is able to see that different age limits have
applied and do apply in other legal systems.[561] His source is the
Digest of Justinian which, he knows, is not the law of the land
everywhere. The affinities set up by spiritual relationships are, to
be sure, created by regulations imposed by the church for the
administration of the sacraments, regulations that can, and do,
change. While Peter agrees entirely with the consensus view on
affinity, here, following Gratian in all details, including the point
that parents who baptize their own child in a case of neccessity, and
who therefore become the child's godparents as well as his parents,
are exempt from the rule that affinity annuls a marriage, he presents this impediment as based on disciplinary regulations that are
essentially mutable.[562] What is perhaps more surprising is that
Peter treats consanguinity in exactly the same way, although blood
relationships would appear to be natural givens. Consanguinity is a
matter which he dispatches with signal brevity and with a good
deal of impatience. He agrees that consanguinity to the sixth or
seventh degree is an impediment, and a cause for nullification, and
that one arrives at the seventh or the sixth degree depending on
whether one begins with the parent-child or the brother-sister
relationship. On the problem of a consanguineous relationship, if
subsequently discovered in spouses innocent of the knowledge
when they married, he sides with the mainstream view by briskly
stating that the couple cannot be allowed to stay together since no
legitimate marriage between them ever existed. The only point he
finds debatable is whether the witnesses in such a case should be
relatives or informed neighbors, which he leaves open. But, Peter's
whole attitude to the issue of blood relationships, and, *a fortiori*, to
relationships with in-laws, as an impediment to marriage is that the
rules are conventional. They have changed over time, just as the
rules governing polygamy and monogamy. They are not rules for
the ages. And, in practice, and in the last analysis, people are so
frequently dispensed from them that it is a waste of time to belabor
the point.[563]

---

[561] Ibid., d. 36. c. 4, 2: 475.
[562] Ibid., d. 42. c. 1–c. 6, 2: 501–08.
[563] Ibid., d. 40–d. 41. c. 4, d. 42. c. 3, 2: 491–99, 505.

There is one sexual delicit, rape, that is treated by many other masters as an impediment to marriage, or not, which Peter handles in a different way. Instead, he discusses it under the heading of crimes or sins against marriage, so defined because they involve the illicit use of sex when sex is legitimate only for the married. Here, he distinguishes five types of illicit sexual behavior. There is fornication, which can refer to illegal sexual activity in general, but which also refers specifically to this activity in persons who are not married, such as widows, concubines, and prostitutes. There is dishonor (*stuprum*), which is the illicit defloration of a virgin. There is adultery, or sexual relation with someone's else's spouse. There is incest, or the sexual relations between relatives. And there is rape. Peter offers a definition of rape that blends Roman law with later Germanic practice. He sees it as the stealing of a girl by violence from her father's house in order to take her as a wife corruptly. His response to this behavior is exactly the same as Gratian's and that of the other canonists. Rape establishes no marital claim whatever, in his eyes, but rather makes the rapist liable to criminal indictment, which bears the penalty of death if he is convicted. Peter offers one qualification on this judgment. It is not one relating to the victim's consent to marriage with her rapist, a possibility which he finds hard to countenance, since she has been taken violently and against her will. Nor does this act, *ipso facto*, reflect or augur well for the union of minds and hearts needed for the consent that makes a marriage. The one exception to the dire and richly deserved punishment that awaits the rapist if he is apprehended and convicted is, rather, the immunity that he can gain if he seeks and finds sanctuary in a church or consecrated place.[564]

This disquisition on crimes against marriage aside, the point of these remarks is to emphasize that no one should be forced into marriage, or into sexual relations, and that freely rendered consent is of the essence. Marriage should not be denied to people, except in the cases where real obstacles exist, whether natural, circumstantial, freely willed, or conventional. Even in these cases, Peter is rather more generous in allowing exceptions, with regard to remarriage, than are most of his contemporaries, in the interest of not condemning people, especially innocent, people, to a celibate life to which they are not called and for which they have not received the necessary charisms, whether as single people or as spouses in a

---

[564] Ibid., d. 41. c. 5–c. 9, 2: 500.

dysfunctional marriage. By the same token, drawing on his own commentary on 2 Corinthians, he dismisses the authorities who restrict second and third marriages, or even more. Since marriage itself is good, and since it is a school for virtue in a positive and not merely a remedial sense, the remarriage of widowed persons called to this state of life and needing its consolations is desirable, "for the virtue of the sacrament" (*pro sacramenti virtute*).[565]

If the sacrament helps spouses to grow in virtue and contributes to their salvation thereby, there are still major respects in which the Lombard's theology of marriage falls short of being fully symmetrical with the rest of his sacramental theology. Two aspects of his treatment of marriage stand out here, which can be highlighted by a comparison of the Lombard on holy orders and penance with the Lombard on marriage. The insistence on an upright intention and on a blameless motive for receiving the sacrament, which informs his analysis of the valid and fruitful reception of the sacrament in the case of these other rites, is not found in Peter's theology of marriage. In this case, and in agreement with the *Summa sententiarum*, he holds that free, unfeigned, and unforced consent is all that is required, even if the couple bring essentially worldly or selfish reasons into play in their decision to marry and to seek the goods of marriage, rather than the union of souls, the wish to help each other to grow in virtue, a commitment to fidelity, and the wish to bear and to rear children for the love of God and the Christian community and not out of dynastic self-interest and the egotistical desire for self-perpetuation. The criticism he extends to priests who abuse their office can be paralleled by his objection to the immoderate or selfish use of sex in marriage and to worldly philoprogenitiveness; but a defective intention of this sort brought to marriage does not in itself disqualify the recipients as it does in the case of holy orders, or as inadequate and less than sincere and exhaustive sorrow for sin does in the case of penance.

The lack of symmetry noted above may derive from an inclination, on Peter's part, to accommodate marriage as he would like it to be to marriage as it exists in the real world, in an unequal contest in which realism achieves one of its rare victories over theological principle in his handling of marriage. The second major discrepancy between Peter's sacramental theology in general and his theology of marriage is one he shares with Hugh of St. Victor, who is far less willing to make concessions to real life on the matter of marital

---

[565] Ibid., d. 42. c. 7, 2: 508–09. The quotation is at c. 7.4, p. 509.

intentionality. Although Peter joins Hugh in advancing the understanding of sacrament in general as involving more than the visible sign of invisible grace, moving, with Hugh, beyond the Augustinian definition of sacrament to the notion that the sacramental sign is a medium of grace which effects what it signifies, he also joins Hugh in failing to extend this understanding of sacramentality to marriage.[566] It would not have been difficult for Peter to have done so, treating marriage on the analogy of holy orders or on the analogy of penance. On the analogy with holy orders, the vows articulated at the wedding could have been viewed as the sensible sign of the consent that constitutes the spiritual union of the couple, the point at which they are given the grace to model their union on the bond of love joining Christ and the church. As with penance, their physical union could likewise have been envisioned as the external expression of the grace already received through their union of minds and hearts as mediated through their articulation of their vows. As with holy orders, their physical union could have been seen as an occasion of grace that enables the couple to model their common life on the physical and institutional union of Christ and the church, an occasion of grace that empowers them fitly to exercise their unique office in the church, in the proper use of human sexuality, and that gives them the strength to do so without selfishness and for the sake of the Christian community. All these pieces are in place. The Lombard could have extended his theology of marriage in these directions, advancing the concept of its sacramentality farther than he does and bringing marriage into full accord with his treatment of the other sacraments. But this he does not do. As a sacrament, marriage, for him, remains a mere Augustinian sign, not a sign that effects what it signifies, or a spiritual or physical medium of grace. The inconsistency between Peter's theology of marriage and his sacramental theology as a whole can also be charged to Hugh of St. Victor's account. Still, for the Lombard, it is a missed opportunity. Dependent as he is on Hugh, he does not hesitate to move the Victorine project forward in other respects. It has to be said, therefore, that, significant as his contribution to the theology of marriage may have been in his day, Peter's conception of marriage as a sacrament remains, in the end, sub-sacramental in comparison with his understanding of the other sacraments and of sacraments as such.

---

[566] Both Heaney, *The Development of the Sacramentality of Marriage*, pp. 26–28 and Knoch, *Die Einsetzung*, pp. 239–41 overinterpret Peter on this score. Ghellinck, "Pierre Lombard," col. 1999–2002 is correct in noting his inconsistency here.

At the same time, Peter does make some notable contributions to the development of the doctrine of marriage. While maintaining an unwavering commitment to the principle of consent in marriage formation, his understanding of marriage as having a double sacramentality gives strong support to the goodness and naturalness of the sexual relations of spouses. His approach to this aspect of marriage has none of the praise of asceticism and none of the grudging and concessive distaste for human sexuality, and the pleasure it bears with it, found in much of the previous Christian tradition and in some of the masters of his own day. To be sure, he thinks, as they do, that sexual relations in marriage have been authorized, and blessed, so that they can be used for the ends of marriage. He does not regard them as ends in themselves. But he makes a generous and positive appraisal of what those ends are, viewing them as more than merely procreative and as more than merely making a preemptive strike against the illicit satisfaction of sexual needs outside of the bonds of marriage. He sees the rendering of the marriage debt not in negative, remedial terms, but as a way in which spouses can strengthen their bond of fidelity while at the same time growing in virtue by replacing egotism with unselfishness, mutuality, and egalitarianism. Peter's stress on the equality of spouses in their sexual relations is enriched by his use of Gratian on that point, but he goes farther than the canonists, both by extending the single standard to the equality of the wife in marriage litigation, where her sworn testimony is to be taken just as seriously as her husband's, and also by recasting this theme, not as a statement about legal rights alone but as an index of how Christian marriage can be not merely a school for virtue but a sign of contradiction in a society where patriarchy is the rule. In contrast with his handling of intentionality, and how it informs marital consent, while he feels constrained to admit that one cannot withhold the sacrament from spouses who bring sub-Christian intentions to it, in this area Peter does not hesitate to preach counsels of perfection and to rule that they are normative.

In treating the impediments to marriage and the grounds for nullification or separation, Peter states the consensus position of his day to a large extent, enlarging the theological outlook on it thanks to his borrowings from Gratian. There are points on which he modifies and softens rulings that he thinks are too harsh or inequitable, as with the remarriage of a person whose spouse has been absent for a long time and who is honestly presumed to be dead Another notable area in which he takes a minority view in relaxing the rigor of a rule is the case of a man whose first marriage he was unable to consummate, leading to its dissolution, but who finds himself able to function with a new partner. Peter does not require him and his first wife to return to a dysfunctional union but allows them to remain with their new spouses. Thus, while Peter generally supports the consensus position, he is certainly willing to nuance it and also to challenge it, in the interests of fairness and charity as opposed to the rigid and mechanical enforcement of norms. In this area he also takes a stand on disputed matters where there was no contemporary consensus, such as the prior adulterous affair as an impediment to marriage. In such cases, his solutions consistently reflect the appreciation of the principle that spiritual growth, repentence, reconciliation, forgiveness, and associated values are what the church should be promoting, in making marriage as accessible as possible and by concentrating more on the quality of life it affords for spouses and less on the occasions, especially the man-made ones, that prevent a union, that require its nullification, or that afford opportunities for separation or litigation.

Another major achievement of the Lombard's theology of marriage lies in his handling of impediments to marriage, which imposes a clear and logical order on this topic for the first time. According to his scheme, impediments to free, honest, and unforced consent come first, since such consent is of the essence in making a marriage in the first place. This category is swiftly followed by impediments built into the nature of things, regardless of human will or convention, such as mental and physical incapacity. The two parts of the theme of incapacity which he takes up here reflect not only the fact that both of these kinds of incapacity exist, but also his own notion of the double sacramentality of marriage. There is both the union of minds and hearts, for which sufficient mental health is needed, and the union of bodies, in the vast majority of marriages, which expresses that union of souls and which requires the capacity to consummate the marriage. While his treatment of mental and physical incapacity as impediments to marriage is perfectly symmetrical, Peter shares an inconsistency found as well in the contemporary consensus by failing to treat them in a parallel way as a cause for nullification. In any event, all other impediments he relegates to the category of those affected by choice, circumstance, and human legislation, and, hence, as subject to change. While, as noted above, Peter does not see insanity as a basis for ending a marriage, however incapable its victims may be of carrying out their marital responsibilities, he supports the emerging consensus view on disparity of cult as an impediment to marriage and as authorizing the dismissal of the non-Christian spouse, seeing as critical the inability of the unbelieving partner to play his or her necessary role in the union of minds and hearts that is of the essence in the sacrament of marriage. Peter places this solution to the problem of disparity of cult on a thoroughly theological and psychological foundation, not on a legal or administrative one. He does not seize upon the opportunity to promote the Pauline permission to dismiss an unbelieving spouse over the Pauline permission to take a non-Christian spouse as an example to be supported on the historical grounds that it speaks more realistically to the situation of the present church, one no longer in the missionary position of the early church. Had he done so, Peter could have integrated the topic of disparity of cult more smoothly into his exposition of the other impediments to marriage which he addresses in his third and final subdivision of this subject, since he treats age limits and the definitions of cognation and affinity as man-made conventions that have changed over time, along with other rules attached to marriage which can change and which have changed over time.

In adopting the doctrine of consent in marriage formation, as taught by Peter, in his marriage decretals later in the century, Pope Alexander III gave recognition to one of the principal areas in which the Lombard's theology of marriage could be seen as superior to that of his contemporaries. Advances there indubitably were, however much this theory managed to impress itself on the consciousness and practice of medieval Christians. Yet, as this conclusion to Peter's doctrine of marriage and to his sacramental theology more generally suggests, he left soft spots and inconsistencies for his followers to puzzle over in the sequel. And, irrespective of his concessions to the world in which he lived at some points, there remains an air of unreality about his theology of marriage, an air of trying to turn the hortatory into the normative, that is just as apparent in Peter's work as it is in the treatments of marriage offered by his compeers.

LAST THINGS

The subject of Last Things is a field in which we can detect a real difference between authors who write in the light of popular belief and the exegesis of the Book of Revelation, on the one hand, and the systematic theologians, on the other. The period during which the Lombard lived and worked was marked, on the part of the former group, by a rash of apocalyptic thinking, mostly in the ranks of the monastic authors. Their works are marked by a highly speculative reading of Revelation, which anxiously seeks to answer questions arising from the worries of people concerned with what is going to happen to their own souls, and the souls of others, at every step of the way during the coming last days. It also reflects a tendency to politicize the idea of Antichrist, in the context of the current papal-imperial feud, sometimes connecting this theme with the tradition of Nero as Antichrist. At times, Last Things is a subject linked by these monastic authors with liturgical reflection, or is treated as an agency for, or an expression of, visionary experience. At the very least, it affords an opportunity for meditation, and exhortation, in helping individuals in the writer's audience to contemplate their own moral state in preparation for their own impending deaths.[567] On the other hand, the scholastics take a different tack on Last Things altogether. They have no hortatory or visionary concerns and they take a dim view of apocalyptic speculation. They distance themselves from the effort to attach the doctrine of Antichrist to any particular political events or personalities, or to an allegorical view of human history. As a group, they seek to base what they have to say on the authorities who, they hold, are the most reliable. They draw heavily on Gregory the Great's *Moralia* and, even more so, on the final chapters of Augustine's *City of God*. Above all, since they are systematic theologians, they seek to show the connection between their doctrine of Last Things and the main themes that animate their *summae* and sentence collections, at least in the case of those scholastic theologians who address the subject at all. Since the mainstream effort draws essentially on the same sources, from the school of Laon through Hugh of St. Victor, Robert Pullen, and Robert of Melun, there is a high degree of consensus on the main outlines of the end-of-time scenario among scholastics in the first half of the twelfth century. Disagreements tend to be on matters of detail. Peter Lombard reflects the attitude of his fellow scholastics. He helps to crystallize the consensus treatment of Last Things on the part of scholastic theology, while at the same time imparting his own highly individual coloration to a number of the standard topics which his contemporaries treat. As well, both in his manner of handling those themes relevant to Last Things which he takes up,

---

[567] Good general background is supplied by Richard Kenneth Emmerson, *Antichrist in the Middle Ages: A Study of Medieval Apocalypticism in Art and Literature* (Seattle: University of Washington Press, 1981), pp. 78, 11–33, 37–57, 63–67, 74–107, 158, 166–72; Bernard McGinn, *Visions of the End: Apocalyptic Traditions in the Middle Ages* (New York: Columbia University Press, 1979), pp. 94–121; Horst Dieter Rauh, *Das Bild des Antichrist im Mittelalter: Von Tyconius zum deutschen Symbolismus*, Beiträge, n.F. 9 (Münster: Aschendorff, 1973), pp. 1–18, 165–365, 416–540.

in addition to those he pointedly ignores, he conveys his own opinion as to what is knowable, suitable and proper to discuss, and important in this area of theology, suggesting the desire to take a stand on the broader range of treatments of this topic found outside the schools as well as within them.

The Non-Scholastic Challenge

That the non-scholastic theology of Last Things presented a de-cided challenge to the more sober leanings of Peter and his colleagues can be appreciated by a consideration of the way Honorius Augusto-dunensis handles this assignment. Honorius straddles the divide that can be seen between the monastic and scholastic authors here. He is a systematic theologian, who makes a clear connection between the doctrine of Last Things and the rest of his exposition, presenting it as the conclusion of the ecclesiastical dispensation in which Christians will be rewarded or punished eternally according to their practice of the ethical and sacramental life as members of the church. This highly coherent integration of the subject into the fabric of his theological system is combined, however, with a wild-eyed fascination with the last days and the state of souls in the life to come that reflects both Honorius's own interests and those of the lay people for whose ultimate consumption his *Elucidarium* was written. His exposition of Last Things is extremely lengthy. Freighted with much detail, it reflects his eagerness to describe the events he relates in vivid and concrete terms, an eagerness so great that it inspires him to go beyond the standard patristic authorities and to appeal to other sources less reputable and more inventive. The most important of these is the *Prognosticon futuri saeculi* of Julian of Toledo (d. 690). Indeed, much of the flamboyant and circumstantial material in Honorius's account, material for which there is no Scriptural war-rant whatever, is drawn from Julian.

From its very outset, Honorius's treatment of Last Things speaks to the questions that worry ordinary people, starting with death. Death, he somberly notes, comes in many forms, including the premature death of children, the cruel death of people in the prime of life, and the natural death of the aged. Yet, even God's elect need to die. He offers the consoling thought that however they die, their death is precious in the sight of God, whether or not they can be interred in consecrated ground.[568] Honorius is keenly interested in

---

[568] Honorius, *Eluc.* 2. 96–97, 2.101–04, pp. 440, 441–42.

how the souls of the departed occupy themselves between their death and the end of time. Before the last judgment, he avers, the souls of the damned know both the souls of other people who are damned, as well as those of the saved, and suffer on that account. The souls of the saved know other just souls, as well as what is happening on earth. They take an interest in earthly affairs, praying for their friends and relatives as well as for each other and for the souls undergoing purgation. The latter, who, he thinks, sometimes begin their purgation while they are still alive, suffer, but they are assisted by the prayers of the saints even as they are helped by the prayers, masses, and good works of their fellow Christians on earth. Those souls who will be damned in the last judgment are housed in an upper part of Hell, envisioned by Honorius, following Gregory, as a kind of holding tank where they are not yet punished except by their separation from God.[569]

Next comes the reign of Antichrist, which Honorius describes in extremely elaborate detail. According to him, Antichrist is the offspring of the devil and a prostitute from the tribe of Dan. He will govern the world with terror and cruelty, deluding even clerics and monks by his eloquence and false miracles. Readers, he implies, should take this as a warning, although he allows that those who succumb to the deceptions and threats of Antichrist will be granted forty years in which to repent. On the authority of Julian, who, apparently, invented the idea, Honorius claims that the human body during the time of Antichrist will be smaller than it is now. The only mitigating feature of his reign will be that it will witness the conversion of the Jews to Christianity, a point which, however, Honorius ignores later in the scenario.[570]

The general resurrection, Honorius affirms, will occur instantaneously. It will be a double resurrection of the body and the soul, paralleling the double death of the body and the soul. The instant in which the resurrection occurs will be the same time of day as Christ's resurrection. Following Augustine, Honorius explains that everyone will be resurrected with a perfect body, at the perfect age of thirty, the age when Christ died, whatever his physical condition at the time of his own death. Those with deformities or disabilities will lack them, in the next life. Infants who died in the womb, if ensouled at the time, will be resurrected as adults; if not, they will be raised as part of their mothers' bodies. In the case of fetuses

---

[569] Ibid., 3.1–11, 3.19–32, pp. 443–46, 449–52.
[570] Ibid., 3.33–37, pp. 452–54.

miscarried or aborted, the cells belonging to their father and their
mother will be restored to each parent, to be raised as part of him
or her. As to the troubling issue of people who were eaten by wild
animals, Honorius counsels his readers not to worry. The God Who
created the universe *ex nihilo* will see to it that they are resurrected,
none the less.[571]

The last judgment, too, will occur in the twinkling of an eye,
according to Honorius, following Augustine. In the second coming,
Christ will appear in the glorified body which He manifested to His
disciples in His transfiguration. Ushered in by an elaborate angelic
procession, as the book of Revelation foretells, He will judge mankind seated in the midst of His twelve apostles. Following Gregory,
Honorius states that the angels will go among the people and sort
them out into four groups, those who are perfect and who do not
need to be judged, but who judge along with Christ; the just who
are both judged and saved; the impious who are judged and condemned; and the damned who have already been judged and condemned. Unlike Gregory, his source for this distinction, he extends
the system of classification to people in certain callings or states of
life, irrespective of how they conducted themselves therein. In the
first category he places the apostles, martyrs, monks, and virgins.
In the second he places married people, those who have done good
works, and who have done penance for their sins. In the third
group are non-Christians who, whether they were there at the time
or not, are held to have consented to the death of Christ because of
their non-belief in Him. In the category of the damned, Honorius
places not only those Christians who have sinned, unrepentant,
under the new dispensation but also the Jews who sinned, before
Christ's coming, according to their own law. The books that are
opened during the last judgment, according to Honorius, are to be
understood allegorically as the books of the Bible and the examples
of the saints, held up as a model to which the judged are compared,
for the purpose of assigning them to one or another of these four
groups.[572]

After the judgment, the damned will be dragged to Hell by the

---

[571] Ibid., 3.38–49, pp. 454–57. This Augustinian account of the resurrection
shapes the contemporary consensus position, as is noted by Richard Heinzmann,
*Die Unsterblichkeit der Seele und die Auferstehung des Leibes: Eine problemgeschictliche
Untersuchung der frühscholastischen Sentenzen- und Summenliteratur von Anselm von Laon bis
Wilhelm von Auxerre*, Beiträge, 40:3 (Münster: Aschendorff, 1956), pp. 148–67;
Colleen McDannell and Berhard Lang, *Heaven: A History* (New Haven: Yale
University Press, 1988), pp. 54–66.
[572] Honorius, *Eluc.* 3.50–78, pp. 457–63.

devil and his minions, the saved ushered to Heaven by their guardian angels, and those undergoing purgation returned to the place of purgation, which Honorius envisions as a less obnoxious zone of Hell, in which suffering is temporal and marked by both heat and cold. The damned will be consigned to a Hell with two general subdivisions, one involving physical torments and the other, more loathesome, involving torment specifically by fire, a distinction he derives from Gregory. From Julian he reprises a more specific distinction of the grades of punishment in Hell, designed to parallel the nine orders of angels.

In vivid, and lurid, sensory detail, he describes these punishments as fire, cold, serpents and dragons, disgusting stench, the blows of demons, palpable darkness, hatred, the fearsome sight of demons and dragons, and the cacophonous cries of the victims and their torturers alike. This infernal arrangement is also an antithesis of the varieties of bliss enjoyed by the saints in Heaven, which will include beauty, joy, health, swiftness, freedom, concord, comfort, power, and honor. Honorius is deeply interested in what the resurrected bodies of the damned and the saved will look like. He allays his own curiosity, and that of his intended audience, with an appeal to Julian. On this rather dubious foundation, he affirms that the new body will be not only incorruptible but also translucent as glass. Moreover, it will be color-coded. The resurrected bodies of the damned will be of somber hue. But the glorified bodies of the saints will come in an assortment of bright colors—blue, green, red, and the like, each assigned to a particular type of saint. Thus, their fellow-citizens in Heaven will be able to see, at a glance, whether they are united in happy concord with a virgin, a martyr, or whatever.[573] Once the souls, truly visible saints or visible reprobates, have taken their places, the world will be destroyed. Honorius offers an elaborate description of the celestial fireworks accompanying that event. Time will cease, and the heavenly bodies will stop moving, as the alternation of night and day is replaced by eternal light. Then, he concludes, the world will be recreated, as a *locus amoenus* just like the original paradise, without suffering and pain.[574] Having brought his story to an end, symmetrical with the creation of the universe at the beginning of time, Honorius thankfully lays down his pen.

---

[573] Ibid., 3.1–18, 3.79–121, pp. 443–49, 463–77.

[574] Ibid., 3.78, p. 463. This elaborate description of Heaven, Hell, and the new earth follows the monastic approach to Last Things, as noted by McDannell and Lang, *Heaven*, pp. 72–73, 78–79, 107–10.

The Scholastic Response

Faced by the competition represented by this extremely circumstantial, not to say fanciful, account of Last Things, the systematic
theologians of a scholastic persuasion responded in a number of
ways. Some, like the Abelardians and the authors of the *Summa
sententiarum* and *Sententiae divinitatis*, simply react to Honorius and
his ilk by omitting the topic of Last Things altogether. Other
masters view the tactic of strategic omission as irresponsible. The
Porretans grasp the nettle, and indicate by their extremely abbreviated and repressive treatment of the subject that it needs to be
reduced, radically, to what can be established by reference to
Scripture and the more reliable authorities, especially Gregory. In
the leanest discussion of Last Things found among the scholastics
in the first half of the twelfth century, an account which they place
not at the end of their sentence collections but as a pendant to the
devil's temptation of Adam and Eve, they raise the question of
where Hell is located, and what it is like. This question is introduced, in the first instance, to permit the masters to disclaim our
ability to know very much about Hell. They note that Gregory says
that Hell has two sections. In the superior part are the souls of
those awaiting judgment; in the inferior part are the souls of the
damned. On the other hand, others say that Hell does not have two
compartments, but that it is a single zone in which the damned and
the just undergoing purgation by fire are mingled, led there, respectively, by demons and angels. Offering no comment on Heaven,
they observe that it is the destination of souls who have completed
their penance. But, as to where the purgatorial fire is located, they
remark, in such a way as to dismiss the whole question of Last
Things, "we say that we do not know" (*dicimus quod nescimus*).[575]

In the eyes of most other scholastic theologians, and Ivo of
Chartres as well, a better plan was to state what could be known
more fully and to acknowledge that the Bible and the reliable
authorities permitted a rather larger number of positive statements
to be made than the Porretans allow. Ivo, for example, relies
heavily on Gregory here. In effect, he gives a swift reprise of the
Moralia on Last Things, adverting to the *City of God* only for

---

[575] *Sent. mag. Gisleberti* I 13.75–76, p. 174. The quotation is at 13.76. Even in this
most repressive account of Purgatory in the period, it is clear that the doctrine of
Purgatory exists; the claim of Jacques Le Goff, *The Birth of Purgatory*, trans. Arthur
Goldhammer (Chicago: University of Chicago Press, 1984), p. 135: "Purgatory
did not exist before 1170 at the earliest," cannot be sustained.

Augustine's descriptions of Heaven and Hell. Ivo clearly sees the next life as divided into Heaven and Hell, representing permanent states of being, and Purgatory, as a transitional state in which souls are purged by the refining fire and aided by the prayers and masses offered by the living on their behalf. He declines to speculate on where Purgatory may be located, just as he indicates that we have no clear information on where the souls of the departed are to be found before the general resurrection. He thinks that the damned and the saved will be aware of each other's condition in the next life and will suffer and rejoice the more, accordingly. Souls in both Heaven and Hell will dwell in different mansions. It is unavailing for the saints to pray for the souls of the damned, and the saints recognize that this is the case, because their status is unalterable. This last observation is one that Ivo adds in acknowledgment of the contemporary felt need to refute Origen's doctrine of the permanent capacity of souls to reform, or to fall, in the next life, up to and including the salvation of Satan. The saved must endure death, Ivo agrees, because it is a consequence of original sin affecting everyone, even God's elect. The joy of the blessed will be an intellectual joy, the vision of God and a knowledge greater than any that can be had on earth. For their part, the damned will suffer physical as well as mental pain, the former in the torments afflicting their bodies and the latter in the sorrow of mind which includes the knowledge that they will never experience consolation, light, or joy.[576] Having outlined this Gregorian description of the next life, Ivo concludes with an account of what will happen before souls arrive there. After a trimmed-down description of the reign of Antichrist taken from Gregory, he ends with Augustine's views on the general resurrection, the last judgment, and a reprise of his earlier remarks on Heaven and Hell.[577]

Ivo, to be sure, does not present this doctrine as the finale of a systematic theology. He includes it merely because of its general interest, a choice in which he is not seconded by the other canonists in this period. The members of the school of Laon, likewise, do not propose their views on Last Things in the context of a systematic sentence collection. While they advert to Gregory at some points, they mainly follow the *City of God*, while bringing in some other issues and authorities. These masters appear to be more interested in the state of the blessed in Heaven than in any other aspect of

---

[576] Ivo of Chartres, *Decretum* 17. c. 67–c. 103, *PL* 161: 993A–1009A.
[577] Ibid., 17. c. 104–c. 120, *PL* 161: 1009A–1015B.

Last Things. Anselm of Laon agrees with Gregory that the souls
and bodies of the saved are not beatified in the same way. Only the
souls receive complete brightness, incorruptibility, and glory (*cla-
ritas, incorruptio, glorificatio*).[578] But other members of the school dwell
on the resurrected body and its qualities. It will have no physical
needs—although there is some inconclusiveness here about eating
—and it will be subtler and lighter than the earthly body, and not
dependent on the senses for knowledge.[579] One Laon master, citing
Gregory Nazianzus by way of Eriugena, argues that, in the next
life, the senses will be converted into reason, reason into intellect,
and intellect into God. The resurrected saints, he holds, will enjoy
the direct apperception of non-sensible objects of knowledge. This
perfect, intuitive knowledge will constitute the joy of the saints; the
exclusion from it of the damned constitutes their punishment.[580]
Anselm worries about how the souls of the departed will recognize
the bodies to which they were attached in this life, given the
changed nature of these bodies in the resurrection. He proposes
that a nexus of some sort will remain between the soul and the body
after death enabling the soul to claim the correct body in the
resurrection.[581] Mostly, the members of the school are interested in
following up on Augustine's account of the resurrection. They
agree that all will be raised at the age of thirty in a perfect physical
state, lacking in any defects which they may have had in life.
Miscarried fetuses are included in this rule. The only exception to it
is the scars of the martyrs, which they will retain in Heaven and
wear as badges of honor. With respect to the foodstuffs men have
eaten in this life, the masters agree, they are not a problem in the
resurrection because they were assimilated and have become part
of the human bodies of the people who ate them. As for fingernail
clippings and hair that has been cut off in this life, they suggest,
with Augustine, that we should not worry about what becomes of
them. They support his view that people will be resurrected in the
male and female sexes, although there is no marriage in Heaven,
and affirm that hermaphrodites will receive the physical attributes
of whichever of the two sexes was preponderant in their earthly
constitution.[582] The saints, the Laon masters agree, will all enjoy
beatitude but in different degrees, just as the damned will suffer

---

[578] *Sentences of Anselm of Laon*, no. 93, 5: 79.
[579] *Sentences of the School of Laon*, no. 500, 530, 5: 322, 395.
[580] *Sent. Anselmi* 11, pp. 152–53.
[581] *Sentences of Anselm of Laon*, no. 91, 5: 78.
[582] *Sentences of the School of Laon*, no. 498–500, 530, 5: 320–22, 396–97.

different degrees and modes of punishment. They will hear the prayers of the living, and of those in purgatory who need their assistance, and, if God has decided to save them, these suppliants will be aided by the prayers of the saints.[583] The Laon masters also refer to the identification of Antichrist with Nero in 2 Thessalonians, seeking but failing to explain it.[584] They think that Purgatory is a fiery place located in the air.[585] But their treatment of the end of time is less a treatise on Last Things in general than a discussion of the resurrection and the beatitude of the saints.

The first scholastic theologian to attempt a more systematic treatment of Last Things, and one that he seeks to correlate with the overarching themes of his theology in general, is Hugh of St. Victor. He follows in the Laon tradition, in that his account is largely a reprise and abridgement of the last three chapters of the *City of God*. But he presents a more connected story as well as raising a wider variety of questions than do the Laon masters. The fact that he raises questions, however, is not always an index of his ability or desire to answer them. In some instances, like the Porretans, his queries are introduced as a means of pinpointing issues on which he thinks speculation should be discouraged. The latter is the case with the question with which he opens his treatise on Last Things, the whereabouts of the souls of the departed in between their separation from their bodies in death and the general resurrection. Hugh thinks, with some pertinence, that this is a question mal posée. Pointing out that the soul is spiritual, he concludes that souls do not need, and indeed, they cannot have, a local habitation once detached from their bodies. In any event, he warns, this is a subject on which there is little secure information. Of greater interest to him, and an area in which he is not disinclined to speculate, is the question of whether such souls can return to earth as ghosts in visible form, a possibility which he by no means rules out.[586]

Since Hugh follows a generally historical model in his *De sacramentis*, this is the way he approaches Last Things as well. Reprising Augustine throughout, he states that we cannot know the day or the hour when the Antichrist will arrive and trigger the rest of the end-of-time scenario, an observation perhaps also aimed at the too-enthusiastic monastic exegetes of Revelation in this period.

---

[583] *Sentences of the School of Laon*, no. 501–02, 504–05, 5: 322–23.
[584] *Sentences of the School of Laon*, no. 530, 5: 397.
[585] Ibid., p. 394.
[586] Hugh of St. Victor, *De sac.* 2.16.2, *PL* 176: 580C–584C.

After the Antichrist has completed his reign of three years and six months, the general resurrection and last judgment will occur, each in the twinkling of an eye.[587] Hugh reports Augustine's views on the perfection of the resurrected body faithfully, except for the fact that he disclaims knowledge of when, in the gestation process, the fetus becomes a person and will be resurrected as himself and not as part of his mother's body. He admits that the resurrected body will have physical needs and desires, but not those that can aggravate the soul.[588] In treating the punishments of the damned, Hugh agrees that they will be afflicted by corporeal fire and finds this doctrine problematic, since it is a punishment they start to receive as soon as they die and before their resurrected bodies have been joined to their souls. Hugh can find no explanation either in authority or in reason for the claim that a soul not attached to a body can suffer physical punishment. He states that this teaching should be held by faith alone. The punishment by fire, which he takes from Gregory as well as Augustine, can also be understood, metaphorically, as spiritual torment. Hugh does not think that the damned can see the blessings of the saved. He does think that the punishments of the damned in Hell are graduated. He holds that Hell is located in the nether regions, somewhere in the bowels of the earth; but, in his view, its exact location cannot be ascertained.[589]

Hugh also takes exception to those authors who think they can give a precise location for Purgatory. He reviews the principal opinions on this issue. Some say that people begin their purgatorial punishment on earth while they are still alive, in the same places where their sins were committed. Others say that Purgatory is in or near Hell. The most likely opinion, in Hugh's estimation, is that of Gregory, who locates it underground in an upper, and less loathesome, part of Hell. Still, the best course of action, Hugh advises, is to acknowledge that we do not know for certain where Purgatory is. What is more important, in Hugh's eyes, is what happens in Purgatory It is a zone, he agrees, where people predestined to salvation, who died still possessing faults on their consciences which they need to eliminate, undergo purgation temporarily. He adds that these souls are aided by the prayers, masses, and almsgiving offered on their behalf by the living.[590]

As for the saved in Heaven, Hugh confirms Augustine's view

[587] Ibid., 2.17.5–8, *PL* 176: 598B–600C.
[588] Ibid., 2.17.13–20, *PL* 176: 601C–606A.
[589] Ibid., 2.16.3–5, 2.18.1–2, 2.18.5–6, *PL* 176: 584C–593C, 609B–C, 610B–C.
[590] Ibid., 2.16.4–10, *PL* 176: 586C–596A.

that part of their edification consists of their ability to witness the torments of the damned. They do not pity the damned or pray for them, since they know that the fate of the damned is sealed and that it is just.[591] For Hugh, the bliss of Heaven can be defined primarily and essentially as the vision of God. As with the Laon masters, he treats beatitude as a cognitive state, in which perfect knowledge and perfect sight replace the partial knowledge available to man by faith in this life. At the same time as he seconds this Augustinian theme, he puts his own Victorine construction on it. At the opening of the *De sacramentis*, he had outlined the modes of human knowledge and had placed systematic theological investigation on a trajectory starting from the knowledge of God one gains through reason, the knowledge of God one gains through revelation, and the knowledge of God one gains through contemplation. This quest for knowledge, in Hugh's understanding of Heaven, is consummated in the vision of God enjoyed by the saints. While they possess other kinds of beatitude as well, including immortality, love without offense, the forgetting of all past sufferings and the memory and reexperiencing of all past joys, it is ultimately the perfection of knowledge, and not only the knowledge of lesser things without error, but first and foremost, the knowledge of the creator and redeemer Himself, that brings Hugh of St. Victor's envisioned work of institution and restitution to its close.[592]

This Victorine focus on knowledge aside, Hugh sets the agenda for succeeding accounts of Last Things on the part of the systematic theologians in this period. This fact is visible in the slender gleanings that have been found of Robert of Melun's teaching on this subject.[593] It is also the case with Robert Pullen. Like Hugh, Robert Pullen draws heavily on Augustine and Gregory and emphasizes the events that will take place between the official end of this world and the final assignment of souls to their ultimate places of punishment and reward. The coming of Antichrist, his reign, the general resurrection of all into perfect bodily form, and the last judgment claim Robert's primary attention. He discusses all these processes in considerable detail.[594] He acknowledges that some of the saints will be brighter than others, as there are many mansions in Heaven. But he is far less interested than Hugh or, for that matter, Augustine, in what the existence of the blessed and the damned will

---

[591] Ibid., 2.18.5–6, 2.18.13, 2.18.15, *PL* 176: 610B–C, 612A, 612C.
[592] Ibid., 2.18.16–19, 2.18.21–22, *PL* 176: 613A–616D, 617B–618B.
[593] Raymond-M. Martin, ed., "Un texte intéressant de Robert de Melun (Sententiae, libr. II, part 2, cap. cxcvii–ccxiii)," *RHE* 28 (1932): 322–26, 328–39.
[594] Robert Pullen, *Sent.* 8.15–17, 8.26–32, *PL* 186: 982D–988B, 1003A–1010B.

be like in Heaven and Hell. All he has to offer on that subject is the observation that the mental and moral attitudes (*habitus mentis*) which they had at the time of their death will be intensified, and that Hell involves extremes of cold as well as heat.[595] Robert largely omits Purgatory from Last Things. He takes it up primarily as a pendant to his discussion of penance. He follows Gregory's teaching on that subject, locating Purgatory somewhere underground, and in the upper portion of Hell, where repentant souls complete any satisfaction still owing, the length of their stay depending on the needs of the individual. He omits the idea that the prayers and masses of the living may speed up their purgation, but concentrates on the sufferings they undergo, which, he says, will be worse than the sufferings they endured in this life but far lighter than the punishments of the damned. Robert also thinks that this purgatorial upper zone of Hell was where the Old Testament worthies awaited Christ's harrowing of Hell,[596] another context in which he brings up the subject. But, aside from the elaboration of the stages through which souls will pass before attaining these habitations, Robert's chief concern is to combat Origen's teaching on the possibility that souls in the next life may undergo repeated backsliding, or conversion, *ad infinitum* and even that the devil may be saved.[597] The finality of God's judgment is the principal reality he wants to stress.

Peter Lombard on Last Things

In placing Peter Lombard's doctrine of Last Things in the context of contemporary accounts, modern scholars, while noticing the range of his sources, including the same Julian of Toledo used by Honorius to such cinematic effect, see his contribution largely as the amplification of Hugh of St. Victor.[598] There is certainly strong evidence indicating that Peter has drawn on Hugh, and on Augustine, Hugh's own major source. Yet, in comparison with both of

---

[595] Ibid., 4.14–24, 8.32, *PL* 186: 823B–828A, 1008B–1010B.
[596] Ibid., 1.14, 4.17–18, 8.21, *PL* 186: 705A, 823B–824D, 994A–D.
[597] Ibid., 8.25, *PL* 186: 999C–D.
[598] Ghellinck, "Pierre Lombard," col. 2002; Coloman Viola, "Jugements de Dieu et jugement dernier: Saint Augustine et la scolastique naissante (fin XIᵉ-milieu XIIIᵉ siècles)," in *The Use and Abuse of Eschatology in the Middle Ages*, ed. Werner Verbeke, Daniel Verhelst, and Andries Welkenhuysen (Leuven: Leuven University Press, 1988), pp. 242–98; Nikolaus Wicki, "Das 'Prognosticon futuri saeculi' Julians von Toledo als Quellenwerk der Sentenzen des Petrus Lombardus," *Divus Thomas* 31 (1953): 349–60; *Die Lehre von der himmlischen Seligkeit in der mittelalterlichen Scholastik von Petrus Lombardus bis Thomas von Aquin* (Freiburg in der Schweiz: Universitätsverlag, 1954), pp. 4–17, 62–63, 175–76, 186, 239–40, 280, 319.

these authors, and, indeed, with most other early twelfth-century treatments of Last Things, what is striking in the Lombard's account is his sobriety and his accent on positions that can be documented in Holy Scripture. At the same time, and by the same token, he ruthlessly suppresses anything smacking of fanciful or wild-eyed speculation. His principal tactic for enforcing his views concerning what can be known about Last Things with certitude and what cannot is his appeal to St. Paul and to the strategy of selective omission, which he uses not only against Hugh and Augustine but against Paul himself. Another major feature of Peter's treatment of Last Things is that he, like Hugh, is interested in harnessing this subject to the overall themes animating his systematic theology as a whole; but the themes, in his case, are different ones.

Peter largely follows the scenario laid out by Paul in 1 Thessalonians in describing the events leading to the permanent assignment of souls to the two cities of Augustine, although he reverses the emphasis in such authors as Robert Pullen by giving this part of his assignment a rather streamlined treatment, reserving more space for the actual state of being of the damned and the saved. He draws as well on his own biblical exegesis here. The story begins with the descent of Christ from Heaven in the voice of the archangel and in the trumpet's blast, the sound of the trumpet being the cause that triggers the general resurrection (*causa . . . resurrectionis*) in the sense of being the efficient cause of what happens next. The second coming of Christ will occur at an unexpected moment, he stresses. Peter is just as unsympathetic as Hugh toward efforts to spell out the day and the hour; the middle of the night to which the apostle refers points to no specific time, he observes. The books that will be opened are the consciences of the individuals now to be judged.[599] Peter declines to speculate on some of the matters of interest to other theologians, including his patristic and post-patristic sources, in connection with the resurrection. He thinks it likely that the elect will remember the troubles they endured, and overcame, in this life, but not in such a way as to interfere with their present happiness. There is no forgetting of all past suffering, as in Hugh's account. But he points out that there is no evidence in Scripture as to whether people who are not members of the elect will remember their past sins. The most he is willing to concede is that facts that occurred openly will be known openly in the next life. Peter dismisses the question of whether people still alive when the trumpet

---

[599] Peter Lombard, *Sent.* 4. d. 43. c. 2–c. 4, 2: 511–12. The quotation is at c. 2.1, p. 511.

blows will be taken immediately into immortality, their bodies swiftly changed from living, earthly ones to resurrected ones, or whether they will have to die before they can be resurrected, like everyone else. We have no basis for answering this question, he observes. Likewise, the idea that Christ judges the living and the dead may be taken literally, in the sense that those people still alive at the time of the second coming will be judged, along with the departed. It may also be understood figuratively, in the sense that the living stand for the saved and the dead stand for the damned. No precise or preclusive determination can be given here, in Peter's view. Furthermore, none is required. Likewise, while Peter follows the standard Augustinian account of the perfection of the bodies of the resurrected saints, pointedly declining to appeal to the technicolor version of this theme provided by Julian of Toledo and Honorius, he argues that we have less evidence about the nature of the resurrected bodies of the damned. The most we can say is that their bodies will be able to burn without being consumed and that their souls will be able to suffer along with their bodies.[600]

Peter moves immediately to the last judgment, and, in so doing, he draws on the doctrine of Gregory the Great, which he had also developed in his Psalms commentary, and to which Honorius refers as well. The saints, he affirms, will participate in the last judgment along with Christ, starting with the twelve apostles in whose midst He conducts the proceedings. Four categories of souls will emerge in this judgment. There are those who are not judged and who are condemned to perdition. It is not necessary to judge them in the hereafter, because they have openly condemned themselves to damnation as unrepentant sinners in this life. Then, there are those who will be judged and condemned. These are people who professed the faith but did not manifest it in good deeds. There are, thirdly, those who are judged and who will rule. These are the souls who died with unexpiated but repented sins on their consciences. They will be admitted to glory, but only after their purgation. Finally, there are those who are not judged and who rule. These souls, like those in the first category, do not need to be judged. For them, this is the case because they have already shown their true character in this life, having manifested their perfect virtue through works of supererogation. They are the saints who will assist Christ and His apostles in the last judgment.[601] This description of the

---

[600] Ibid., c. 5–d. 44, 2: 513–22.
[601] Ibid., d. 47. c. 2–c. 3, 2: 537–40. See above, chapter 4, pp. 176–77.

four categories of souls departs from Honorius's account of them, as referring to different callings, belief systems, or states of life, and restores to them the authentic Gregorian note of moral choice and moral action.

In the judgment itself, Christ, with His angelic and saintly assistants, will gather the saved from the four corners of the earth, leaving the damned behind to be dragged to their punishment by demons. Peter gives passing attention to the issue of where the last judgment will take place, and agrees with the authorities who say that it will occur in the firmament somewhere, and not on earth. He dismisses as irrelevant and as unknowable the matter of why the heavenly bodies will remain in existence after time stops and is replaced by perpetual day. The points he really wants to accent about the last judgment are two other ones. First, the form in which Christ will preside over the last judgment is the form of His resurrected body. This, says Peter, is eminently fitting, since Christ's resurrection is the earnest of our own. Further, since this is the form in which He communicates Himself to believers sacramentally in the Eucharist, Christ's resurrection is also the cause of our own salvation.[602] The other major teaching Peter wants to emphasize concerning the last judgment, before going on to the condition of souls in their posthumous states, is, in effect, the *Leitmotiv* of his entire account of Last Things. The judgment of Christ is just. And, the judgment of Christ is merciful. True, for those who are condemned, this judgment means eternal and unchanging punishment. This point, developed by Robert Pullen as an argument against Origen, is focused on a different objective by Peter. The punishment of the damned is not in conflict with God's mercy, he observes, because God punishes them less than they actually deserve. In any event, he reminds the reader, the justice and mercy of God are one and the same. Therefore, nothing in the judgment of God is lacking in mercy, since these attributes are identical in, and with. the divine essence itself. Here. Peter refers his readers to the extended account of the radical unity of the divine essence and of how divine attributes are to be understood in connection with it that he had provided in the first book of the *Sentences*.[603]

In surveying the steps that lead to the manifestation of this justice and mercy of God in the states of souls in the next life, on

---

[602] Peter Lombard, *Sent.* 4. d. 47. c. 4–d. 48. c. 5, 2: 540–47.

[603] Ibid., d. 46. c. 1–c. 5, 2: 529–37. On this point, see Landgraf, *Dogmengeschichte*, 4 part 2: 268–70.

which he plans to lavish much attention, we may say that Peter has
been pointedly concerned with pruning the florid display of fantasy
found in many of his sources and with dismissing as inappropriate
or as unanswerable many of the questions that they are willing to
consider. His tactic of strategic omission can be seen most strik-
ingly in the fact that he begins his own end-of-time scenario with
the second coming of Christ and the general resurrection, not with
the reign of Antichrist. Indeed, the single most original feature of
Peter's treatment of Last Things is that, unlike all of his predecessors, ancient and modern, he ignores the Antichrist altogether.
This decision is fully conscious. As we have seen above, in his
exegesis of 2 Thessalonians, he develops a thoroughgoing and a
quite innovative interpretation of the meaning of Antichrist, one
that unshackles it completely not only from the Emperor Nero, the
initial problem in that epistle, which he sets out to correct, but
also from any kind of institutional manifestation or historical
phenomenon.[604] Peter relies on St. Paul for much of his account of
Last Things, but it is noteworthy that the Paul he relies on is only
the Paul of 1 Thessalonians, and his own gloss on that epistle, and
not the Paul of 2 Thessalonians, and his gloss on the latter text. A
more sharply pointed rejection of the tendency of some contemporaries to speculate on the apocalypse and to cater to the fears,
worries, and yearnings for certitude to which the chiliastic imagination gave free rein would be difficult to envision. While Peter is
ready and willing to offer his own interpretation of Antichrist, as an
exegete, in order to bring the Paul of 2 Thessalonians into line with
the Paul of 1 Thessalonians and with Pauline theology more generally, when it comes to the systematic theology of Last Things, his
goal is to excise this topic from the syllabus altogether. It is not a
subject on which responsible theological research can be done, in
his estimation. It is not a field in which certitude is available. Thus,
it should not be allowed to obstruct the logical and theological
passage of the student from the ethical and sacramental lives of
Christians on earth to their posthumous outcomes.

This point having been made by the radical surgery he performs
on the theme of Antichrist, in the *Sentences*, Peter turns to those
posthumous conditions, presented as expressions of divine justice
and mercy. With respect to Purgatory, he declines to raise the
question of whether it can be localized and, if so, where it is. But he
has a perfectly clear understanding of its nature. For Peter, this

---

[604] See above, chapters 4 and 6, pp. 196, 204, 205–07, 350.

state is one that souls requiring purgation enter immediately after their deaths, although their condition therein is altered following the general resurrection. The third category of person who is judged in the last judgment, and who will attain to glory, is the population found in Purgatory. The inhabitants of this state of being are assisted, according to Peter, by the prayers of the saints. They are also helped by the prayers, masses, and almsgiving which the living offer on their behalf, before the end of time. What is striking about Peter's handling of Purgatory under the heading of Last Things, a point also visible when he discusses it as a corollary of the sacrament of penance, is that he is not interested in expatiating on the nature of purgatorial punishments. Rather, what he wants to emphasize, along with Gregory, is the doctrine of the communion of the saints and the connections uniting all Christians, living and dead, in the bond of love that is the church. He has an ecclesiological point to make here, as well as a piece of earnest advice to his contemporaries. The aids that living Christians can offer to the souls in Purgatory are efficacious, he observes, and it is much more important to spend one's time and money on them than on elaborate and expensive funerals or funerary monuments.[605] Equally basic, he agrees with Gregory, is the justice and mercy God expresses in providing this transitory realm for people who died in a contrite state of mind, so that the continuing grace of forgiveness of sins acknowledged and repented can be made available to them in the hereafter.

Turning to the souls permanently damned and saved, Peter appeals largely to Augustine, and to his own personal appropriation of Augustine in his orchestration of the idea of use and enjoyment as the main theme of his *Sentences*. There are two conditions which the saints and sinners will share, he agrees, outside of the eternalization of the prevailing state of their love in the city of God or the city of man, respectively. They will be disposed in differing degrees of punishment and bliss in Hell and Heaven, all equal in the sense that the damned will all have what they deserve and the blessed will all have what they want. Just as the blessed will enjoy the incapacity to sin (*non posse peccare*), so the damned will be confirmed in their possession of a bad will. Even though they will not be able to engage in all their earlier earthly modes of sin, they will still be incapable of not sinning by intention. Hence, Peter observes, they will continue to merit their punishments, to all

---

[605] Peter Lombard, *Sent.* 4. d. 45. c. 1–c. 6, 2: 523–29.

eternity, since they will continue to add to their own viciousness and demerit. Therefore, their eternal punishment is just. The outer darkness into which the damned are cast is their separation from God, which they earn thanks to the inner darkness of soul that led them into sin. Their inability to see, and to see God, is a terminal case, for Peter, of the dissimilitude to God and to their true selves which they have created for themselves; Hell, as he sees it, is the ultimate, and permanent, *regio dissimilitudinis*. So greatly does citizenship in this anti-city blind its inhabitants that they cannot recognize God or even remember Him. The only tiny glimmer of humanity that Peter, following Augustine, is willing to grant to the damned is the capacity to feel sorrow or empathy with other people's punishments. On the model of the *dives et Lazarus* story, it would seem that they do care about the fates of their living relatives. Other than that, bad will and total moral blindness characterize their condition.[606] Unlike Augustine, Peter focuses on the spiritual horrors of Hell, and ignores the idea of physical punishment.

The blindness of the damned, according to Peter, will make it impossible for them to see the bliss of the saints. This condition, too, is an act of divine mercy and justice; for the damned are spared a vision of joy that is totally closed to them. For the blessed, on the other hand, faith will be replaced by sight. They not only see God face to face, and all things in Him, but, confirmed in their rectitude, they understand His justice. They grasp the fact that the punishment of the damned is just, and unalterable, and their capacity to observe it does not diminish their own beatitude. The question of their praying for the damned does not arise. For Peter, the beatitude of the saints will consist largely of knowledge and joy. Peter acknowledges his debt to Hugh of St. Victor here and goes beyond him. Despite the different mansions they inhabit, the saints will all see God, although in different ways. Each will possess all the knowledge and joy of which he is capable; each will attain everything for which he has hoped and yearned. This gift, for each of the saints, is the consummation of God's power, mercy, and justice as it is displayed to man. In the grand finale Peter orchestrates, before laying down his pen, the bliss of heaven consists in the confirmation of the saints' recovery of the image of God in themselves. Indeed, it consists in their acquisition of a condition better than the one in which man was created. For they have now moved beyond signs to the possession of the things signified. They have moved beyond use

---

[606] Ibid., d. 49–d. 50. c. 1–c. 4, 2: 547–57.

to the enjoyment of God, the supreme good Who can now be loved, fully, and without impediment, for Himself alone.[607] And, even more than that, they have now transcended the mutabilities of their condition as creatures, the limits of their earthly modes of interaction with the God Who manifests Himself to man within the temporal and physical boundaries of the order of creation and redemption. They now share in an eternal communion with the deity Who transcends time. Peter, thus, unites his treatment of Last Things, with which he concludes his *Sentences*, with his own reworking of the Augustinian motifs which he recasts as the framework, and the agenda, of his own systematic theology, as an enterprise uniting intellect and will in the final attainment, through God's mercy, of that God Himself, the deity Who transcends His own manifestation of Himself to man in time, as the highest object of knowledge and love, and the highest good.

---

[607] Ibid., d. 49, d. 50. c. 4–c. 7, 2: 547–53, 557–61.

CONCLUSION

In the foregoing pages, care has been taken to present the contemporary state of play in western theology, among Peter Lombard's scholastic compeers, when he entered the field, in order to locate his own teachings in the environment in which he worked. As we have seen, his relationship to his coevals is not a simple one. Sometimes, the Lombard's role is essentially that of strengthening, restating, or confirming the current consensus position. Sometimes he draws together, in his own eclectic mix, ideas derived from other masters, canonists and theologians alike. Sometimes his concern is to criticize and to demolish the teachings of some one master, or group of masters. Sometimes his contribution is to find a fresh way of conceptualizing issues that other thinkers had raised and had failed to resolve. Sometimes he takes a decidedly polemical approach in areas keenly debated at the time, areas in which there was no consensus. In so doing, he often contributes a clear articulation of one side of a controversy that was not settled in the mid-twelfth century. In other areas, his reasoning, as a partisan, plays a decisive role in defeating the opposition and in contributing to the emergence of a new consensus. In addition to positioning the Lombard's theology in these several ways, we have also, in the body of this book, sought to explore Peter's sources, and his use of them. His address to the inheritance of the Christian tradition, whether ancient or more recent, is, as we have seen, both thoroughgoing and independent. The same can be said for his attitude toward the *artes* and to the philosophy available in the schools of his day. In the conclusion which now follows, we plan to set aside these questions of context and comparison in order to draw together the strands of the Lombard's teaching in their own right, in order to set forth the main outlines of Lombardian theology as such.

We begin, as Peter himself does, with the single most important subject with which he thought theologians should be concerned, and the subdivision of theology in which he thought western Christian thought in his own day most needed a massive overhaul, the doctrine of God. The supremacy, and centrality, of the deity as a subject of attention is one that Peter signals not only by the notable amount of space he devotes to this topic, but also by the place he assigns it in the reformulation of the Augustinian idea of signs and things, use and enjoyment, which is the guiding theme he announces at the beginning of his *Sentences*, and which is to govern his doctrinal priorities throughout. God alone is to be enjoyed in and for Himself. He is the supreme being and the supreme good, to which everything else points and in relation to which everything else, and not least, systematic theology itself, is to be used. Peter states a positive doctrine of man's knowledge of God that displays no interest whatever in the claims of negative theology. He is quite confident in man's ability to prove God's existence by the use of natural reason, and launches his doctrine of God by doing so.

This foundation laid, he proceeds to tackle the two most important aspects of the doctrine of God which he regards as needing clarification and rigorous enforcement. The first is the doctrine of the Trinity. In Peter's eyes, it is mandatory to make a clear and intelligible distinction between the divine nature and the divine persons in the Trinity, one that neither collapses the personal determinations of the Trinity into the common essence which the Trinitarian persons share, nor confuses each person with a particular divine attribute or a particular divine mission *ad extra*, in such a way as to produce tritheism or subordinationism in the Trinity. This first task was, initially, complicated for Peter by the absence in his day of a common, a speculatively adequate, and a generally understood vocabulary of the terms needed to discuss the distinction between nature and person in the Trinity. Not the least of the Lombard's contributions here, and a prior condition on which it depends, is his circumspect treatment of the problem of theological language as it applies to the Trinity. Peter's theological agenda, with respect to the Trinity, is of a piece with his agenda for the second major concern he addresses in treating the doctrine of God, the stress on God's transcendence. With respect to the Trinity, he emphasizes this principle by insisting that the determinations distinguishing the Trinitarian persons from each other are, and only can be, the relationships They bear to each other *in se*, in the eternal and unmanifested Trinity, and not in anything They do *ad extra*. When he turns to the divine nature as such, shared by the persons of the Trinity quite apart from any outward manifestation of it that They may make, Peter strongly emphasizes the idea that God is absolute being, utterly one and simple, infinite and unbounded in all His attributes, immutable and incommutable despite the differing ways in which He can be understood or be seen to act in relation to His creation. For Peter this principle has two critical and irrefragable corollaries. God acts not by emanation or by immanence in the world. His workings in man and nature are His effects and are not participations in the divine being. Above all, they are not responses to any internal necessities of His own nature. Secondly, and consequently, the divine being is always greater than any expression of it that God may make in the creation. God is never limited, exhausted, or circumscribed by anything He does *ad extra*. He acts, to be sure, to create, to sustain, to govern, and to empower man and nature; but His role as a God of agency in these respects does not override or subsume His transcendent reality as a God of essence.

With the reinforcement of this doctrine of God in mind, over against a purely or primarily economic understanding of the deity, Peter launches forthwith into his proofs of God's existence, on the basis of natural reason. His lead-in is the *invisibilia dei* passage from St. Paul's Epistle to the Romans. But, although he certainly starts with evidence that can be found in the visible creation, whose causes inductive reason can infer, Peter also imparts a metaphysical look to this topic as well. In this area he is confident and unhesitating about the powers of reason and about the corroboration of the proofs he bases on it in pagan philosophy. He offers four proofs. The first is an *a posteriori* proof from effects to causes and from causes to a first cause, and from design and order in the creation to the notion that this first cause is also an intelligent supreme orderer. The second is an *a posteriori* proof from motion to a ground of being that is itself immutable. Here we see the beginning of Peter's shift from physical to metaphysical analysis. It is not how the deity acts, as a cause, that is the crux of this proof, but what He is. Peter seeks to show how a structure of being in creatures that involves change is metaphysically grounded in a being that has a different kind of nature. The analysis of being offered in the second proof undergirds the third and fourth proofs. In the third proof, Peter notes that the universe yields evidence of hierarchy, a favorite theme of his. There are degrees of being and degrees of excellence. A supreme being is required as a cause of this phenomenon. And, it cannot be one that is merely the highest term in the hierarchy. It must be a being that transcends the hierarchy. In the fourth proof, Peter observes that the universe contains beings marked by compositeness as well as by changeability. Thus, the supreme ground of the being of such creatures must be simple as well as unchanging.

Four general observations may be made about these proofs. First, in each case, the cause of the phenomena induced by the proofs is not merely a cause that is like those phenomena, but one that is merely greater than they are. Rather, for Peter, it is a cause that utterly transcends them. Secondly, and therefore, what the *ea quae facta sunt* show forth is not how the creation resembles the creator, but, rather, how the creator differs from the creation. The ontological dependence of the world upon God as its ground of being reflects both the world's connection with God and His radical independence from the world. Thirdly, the prime attribute of God accented in the demonstration of God's otherness is God's immutability, which attribute plays a key role in two out of the four proofs. It is adverted to more frequently than the divine notes of primacy, intelligence, unity, and simplicity. Finally, while these are *a posteriori* proofs, Peter is concerned not merely with what causes the phenomena and events that occur in time. He understands priority and posteriority primarily in the order of being, not in the order of time. The proofs, in short, offer grist for the mills of the metaphysicians as well as for those of the natural theologians.

For Peter, natural reason is an epistemic reality that can certainly prove the existence of God and elicit some extremely basic aspects of His nature; but it cannot prove that God is three and one. With respect to the Trinity, the most reason can do is to offer similitudes and analogies, with the clear-eyed recognition of the fact that, as analogies, they always fall short of what they resemble. This is a form of the knowledge of God that requires revelation and faith, in Peter's eyes. Any apparent parallels to the doctrine of the Trinity found in pagan philosophers are the shadow, not the reality. They stop short well before they can attain to the doctrine of the Trinity held by Christians. Peter's consideration of man's natural knowledge of the Trinity is also a concerted effort to banish the idea that this knowledge is found in economic descriptions or similitudes of the Trinitarian persons, especially when they refer to attributes shared equally by those persons. The Trinity of which man can have knowledge by analogy is, for Peter, first, last, and always the unmanifested Trinity. The analogies must speak to the interactions of the Father, Son, and Holy Spirit among Themselves.

This being the case, Peter focuses on two such analogies, bequeathed by Augustine, that are found in human psychology. The fact of threeness in oneness in the human soul can be seen in its simultaneous possession of memory, intellect, and will and in the simultaneous presence of the mind, its knowledge of itself and its love of itself. Critical to either of these analogies, and to Peter's stress on the intratrinitarian interaction of the divine persons as the only basis for the denomination of those persons, is his handling of the concept of relation, an idea he also borrows from Augustine and nuances. Relation, he stresses, must, in this context, be purged of its Aristotelian acceptation as an accident, one of the predicables that may, or may not, be attributed to a substance susceptible of modification by accidents. Rather, relation here should be understood in the light of relative nouns, such as right and left or light and dark. So understood, a relative, comprehensible in connection with its correlative, provides a means of describing the association and the distinction among the Trinitarian persons, whose determinations as unique individuals vis-à-vis each other, the determinations of unbegottenness, filiation, and procession, have always been structured into the eternal Trinitarian family. In comparing the two Augustinian analogies that he cites, Peter sees the analogy of *memoria-intellectus-voluntas* as having more limitations than that of *mens-notitia-amor*, although Augustine places them in the reverse order of priority. Also, Peter is less interested in the light these analogies may shed on human psychology than in the structure of being that they display. In any case, and this is another advantage of these analogies in Peter's eyes, they make relatedness in the deity, and not splendid isolation, the supreme reality.

With this discussion of what can be known and proved about the deity as such and about the Trinity in place, Peter proceeds logically to explore the distinction between person and nature in the Trinity. In his own vocabulary, substance can be used in this connection, as indeed it must be used, for it is in the creed. Deliberately refraining from associating this term with any particular philosophical definition of it in this context, he treats substance as the intrinsic qualities that make a being itself, whatever kind of being it happens to be. With this understanding of substance in mind, Peter consistently yokes substance to nature, as denoting the divine essence shared equally and in the same way by the Trinitarian persons. One can, properly, attribute the terms substance and nature to the Trinitarian persons only when one is referring to the divine essence which They share. In sharing it, They do not do so numerically, as parts that make up a whole, or as species within the same genus. The Godhead is not a level of being metaphysically prior to the Trinitarian persons. Rather, the divine nature is wholly possessed by each of Them; there is not "more God" present when two or three of the persons are considered together than when one person is considered by Himself. These are the respects in which the persons of the unmanifested Trinity are one in nature and being. The respects in which they are three, and distinct, are the respects in which they are both bonded to and distinguishable from each other, also in that unmanifested state, as unbegotten, begotten, and proceeding. In these particular relations, and only there, is

each Trinitarian person a specific individual whose personal properties are unique to Him. The same simply cannot be said of any of
the other denominations that the Trinitarian persons may be given.
For, in their role *ad extra*, what They manifest and exercise is the
divine nature, not Their divine personhood. The divine persons are
fully coactive in anything They do *ad extra*, including missions
which may be delegated to one or another Trinitarian person in
particular.

Thus, for Peter, it is the Godhead Who interacts with the world
and man, and not some one of the Trinitarian persons, in an array
of cosmological and charismatic activities limited to any one of
those persons. And, while God is engaged in His various modes of
activity *ad extra*, He remains utterly immutable, incommutable,
incomparable, simple and transcendent over His creation, never
identical with or consumed by His effects in the orders of nature
and grace. Given the infinite store of being that God possesses, or,
better put, is, Peter stresses very heavily the point that God always
has, or is, more than He does or chooses in actuality. In general
terms, in handling the issues that arise under the heading of the
divine nature in this connection, Peter resolutely emphasizes the
metaphysics of that subject. He dislikes, and criticizes, the tendency found in some quarters, ancient and modern, to collapse
metaphysical questions concerning the deity into logical questions,
especially if the logic used is a propositional logic which, on its own
accounting, disclaims the ability of logic to verify conclusions that
lie outside its own formal bailiwick. This basic outlook informs
Peter's handling of the three most important issues he raises in
discussing the divine nature in relation to the universe, God's
ubiquity; the compatibility of God's providence, predestination,
and foreknowledge with contingency and free will; and the vexed
question of whether God can do different, and better, than He does.

In treating God's ubiquity, Peter rejects a substantialist or im-
manentalist understanding of God's presence in the universe, for
such a mode of presence would blur the difference between divine
and created being. The only created being in which God is present
substantially is the man Jesus. But, He is the exception Who proves
the rule. In every other case, God is present in creatures ontologi-
cally, as their ground of being, not as their essence or as their form,
but as the source that creates and sustains them and that gives
them the capacity to carry out their natural functions. Likewise, in
the order of grace, a theme Peter plans to develop more fully in his
ethics and sacramental theology, what God communicates, except
in the case of the Eucharist, is not Himself but a *virtus* or power that

leaves intact the creaturely status of the human beings to whom He grants it. They must, and can, cooperate with it, in developing their own virtues and merits, and they can reject it. In this sense, God is less ubiquitous in the charismatic order than He is in the order of nature, in that not all people receive and act on His grace, and not all of those who do receive and act on it do so to the same degree or in the same way. Nevertheless, in both cases, God's presence in the world and man is a presence by way of ontological grounding and by way of enabling power, not by way of participation.

In comparison with thinkers who viewed God's relation to the world in terms of the logical or physical relations between necessity, possibility, and contingency, Peter recasts the question into a metaphysical investigation into God's foreknowledge, providence, and predestination in relation to contingency and free will. In so doing he seeks to make two basic points. In the first place, the function of this inquiry is to shed light on the divine nature, not on the creation or on human logic. Secondly, and in particular, the aspect of the divine nature which is at issue here is God's omniscience. God's exercise of this attribute is the focus. And, like God's exercise of any of His attributes *ad extra*, it is not exhausted by the ways in which He actually chooses to exercise it. Although we can think of God's knowledge in relation to the world in terms of foreknowledge, disposition, predestination, and wisdom, God's knowledge is, intrinsically, as one and as simple as it is eternal and complete. As Peter defines these terms, foreknowledge is God's knowledge of everything that will happen from all eternity, irrespective of who or what the causes of those events will be. Disposition is God's governance of the universe, including His foreknowledge of the natural laws He will create, before He puts them in place. Predestination is the grace of preparation, which God grants to His elect, His salvation of them in the next life, and His knowledge from all eternity of who they will be, before they have a chance to acquire merit. Wisdom is God's knowledge of all things, past, present, and future. The dimension of time included by Peter in this definition of wisdom refers not to God's knowledge as such, but to that knowledge as applied, in a relative sense, to a universe that exists in time. This application in no sense diminishes or conditions the intrinsic eternity and infinity of divine omniscience, for God's knowledge is of His essence.

On the other hand, the things that are in God's knowledge are not God Himself. This is true of His predestination, which is causative, but which does not mean that the elect share the divine nature or that they do not have to cooperate with the grace of predestination in order to profit from it. For its part, divine fore-knowledge is not *per se* causative. Some of the things God foreknows He also causes. But He also foreknows things that will occur contingently. The fact that God does not cause events that stem from contingency or from free will in the case of rational creatures is not an imperfection or a limitation on God's knowledge or on God's role as a cause, for He freely chose to create beings capable of acting as secondary causes and as agents possessing free will. The fact that God knows contingent events, and events that have not yet occurred, does not mean, moreover, that He knows them better when they do eventuate. For, His knowledge has always been exhaustive. The events in question are conditioned by time; God is not. Also, God's knowledge cannot increase because it is, and always has been, total. This same principle also means that God does not alter His immutable decree as to the people He predes-tines. His omniscience in this regard is immutable although the grace of predestination is not irresistible. Peter, therefore, creates a clear zone for the existence of contingency and free will, one just as well garrisoned as those provided by his confrères from the side of natural philosophy or formal logic. He shows the compatibility of these possibilities both with divine foreknowledge and disposition, and with the existence of direct divine causation in some areas. Yet, the whole topic, in his hands, is firmly guided back to his own metaphysical point of departure, the principle that the omniscience of the immutable and transcendent God is not limited by or defin-able as the way His cosmological and charismatic order works its way out in time.

In addressing the question of whether God can do different, and better, than He does, Peter develops an argument parallel to the one just noted, this time placing the issue under the heading of God's omnipotence. His analysis here is likewise designed to re-place a purely logical argument or an argument from theodicy with one whose first concern is to illustrate this particular divine attrib-ute. Similarly, he seeks to show that God's actual arrangements in the temporal world do not exhaust His power and that God acts freely and not in response to any internal necessity of His own being. Peter grounds his argument on the distinction between God's power and God's will. God's omnipotence, he notes, is not God's power to do everything. For "everything" includes the doing of evil, and the doing of things that require a body, things which, in God's case, would be imperfections and antithetical to His nature. Rather, God's omnipotence is God's power to do whatever He wills. Peter agrees that what God does do is just and good. But,

God is not constrained by His justice and goodness in the exercise
of His power; and, the choices that He in fact does make in this
connection do not limit what He might have done otherwise. God's
omniscience, further, includes His knowledge of the range of options out of which He selects the ones He chooses to perform. Not
only can God do whatever He wills; He always remains, in principle, capable of doing more than He actually decides to do.

What Peter is really stating here, and it is a principle that
animates his discussion of the divine nature more generally, is the
distinction between God's absolute and ordained power, although
he does not use this express terminology. Beyond that, Peter rejects
the idea that the world we have is the best possible world that God
could have created because the world is not perfect. Only God is
perfect. Created beings are capable of improvement. The life they
lead, under the natural law He created, could have been an easier
one, had God chosen to dispose things differently, just as He could
have ordained a different mode of human redemption than He did
ordain. Peter presses this argument to the point of saying that, just
because Christ was born, crucified, and resurrected once for all,
this does not mean that God lacks the power to do all these things
again, should He choose to do so. This example is Peter's most
extreme and rigorous application of the principle that God's power
always transcends His actual use of it. To man, God, manifests His
will in His precept, prohibition, permission, operation, and counsel. These manifestations, Peter points out, are all signs of the
divine will, signs of the way an unchanging will is shown forth *ad
extra*. Signs are not to be confused or equated with their *significata*,
Peter notes, adverting to the Augustinian analysis of signs and
things with which he begins the *Sentences*. Likewise, the unchanging
and simple will of God cannot be collapsed into the ways He
chooses to signify it to man. By the same token, man's exercise of
his God-given free will in contravention of God's precepts or pro-
hibitions does not circumscribe God's power. Here, in a manner
analogous to his handling of divine foreknowledge and related
matters in connection with contingency and free will, Peter guarantees a zone of independence for creatures, even as he underscores
the inexhaustibility of God's transcendent omnipotence.

This analysis of the divine nature and its manifestations *ad extra*,
in addition to accomplishing Peter's objectives for the doctrine of
God, thus sets the stage for his intended treatment of the creation,
angels, man, and the fall. While these topics are all related to the
doctrine of God, Peter conveys much less of a sense, in the second
book of the *Sentences*, that these individual subjects are themselves

tied together as organically as are those in Book 1. Also, in treating the questions he takes up in Book 2, especially on the creation, Peter departs from his usual practice of citing authorities by name and title, quoting or paraphrasing them *in extenso*, and evaluating their reasoning as well as the conclusions to which it leads before rendering his own opinion. He thus appears, uncharacteristically, to have relied on *catenae* or other intermediary sources, which report merely the conclusions of the authorities, for this part of his work. This fact may either be a cause or an effect of Peter's comparative lack of interest in cosmological speculation in its own right as a suitable focus for theologians.

With respect to creation, this perspective is notable in Peter's deep lack of sympathy with the project of considering how or whether the account of cosmogenesis in Plato's *Timaeus* squares with the Book of Genesis. Peter marshals both philosophical and theological weapons against both the plausibility of that enterprise and the particular conclusions reached by some of its partisans. His own solutions on creation are grounded in the exegetical and patristic traditions. He is, typically, less interested in the specula- tive side of the subject than are many thinkers in that heritage. Peter's own contribution to the doctrine of creation is a threefold one. He discovers a cogent way of including the creation of the angels within a primarily hexaemeral account of creation. He also finds a way of combining the six-day account in Genesis with a modified doctrine of creation *simul*. And, he also finds a way of acknowledging the pertinence of presenting creatures in an order reflecting their relative metaphysical status, even while retaining the standard six-day model which does not order creation in that manner.

According to Peter, God and God alone is the cause of creation *ex nihilo*. He rejects the idea of exemplary causes, however understood, along with preexistent matter. Further, he sees God as such as doing the whole work of creation, and not as delegating different aspects of it to this or that Trinitarian person, a notion consistent with his conception of the unity of God's actions *ad extra*. Likewise compatible with his doctrine of God are the principle that God cannot be equated with the forces of nature He creates and the principle that He does not create in response to any necessity of His own nature, but freely. In all these respects, God transcends the world He creates. Since, as Peter sees it, God clearly did not need to create the universe, why did He do so? In response to that question, Peter asserts that He creates rational creatures, such as angels and men, out of His benevolence, so that they can come to a knowledge

and love of God and hence possess beatitude. Following the principle of use and enjoyment, everything else in the creation was
brought into being for the utility of rational creatures in attaining
that end. With respect to human beings, this also means that Peter
has a positive reason for their creation that allows him to dismiss
the claim that they were created to make up the numbers of the
fallen angels. It also means that man's possession of a body can be
given a solid and generous foundation. God gave human bodies to
human souls, according to Peter, so that man could serve as a
microcosm of creation. Thus, in loving and serving God in body
and soul and in attaining beatitude both in body and soul, man
brings the whole of creation back to God; and it is metaphorically
redeemed and glorified in him. Peter does not expressly use the
term "microcosm;" but is it is clearly what he intends here. This
notion also lays the foundation for the doctrine of human nature
which he develops later in Book 2 of the *Sentences*. He firmly rejects a
Platonizing anthropology in which man is equated with his soul, a
soul merely using or even trapped in a body seen as the source of
his problems. He favors a more Aristotelian view of man as a
hylemorphic unit, both aspects of which are integrally human.
From this perspective, God created man with a body and a soul in
order to redeem and glorify man in both body and soul, a process in
which body and soul are interdependent.

Having explained why God created what He created in metaphysical order, Peter turns to the timetable of the creation. In the
scenario he presents, angels and primordial matter are created
simul and before anything else. Then, the other creatures are produced according to the biblical six-day plan. Peter rounds out the
Genesis account by including God's creation of seminal reasons
during the hexaemeron to account for developments that occur
later. Peter thinks that it is possible to grasp the idea of unformed
matter conceptually by analogy with our use of negative or privative language that refers not to species but to the absence of species.
In his view, God creates directly and immediately the specific
forms which He unites with unformed matter in making actual
creatures. Both unformed matter and the forms are created *ex nihilo*.
When He creates individual creatures, God inserts seminal reasons
into them, which will enable them to carry out their natural functions as well as accounting for any new beings that may arise. Peter
presents a literal, straightforward, and streamlined treatment of
creation. He shows no interest in extrapolating moral and allegorical meanings from the Genesis account of creation, and no concern
for the scientific anomalies it contains. Here, as in his handling of

cosmogenesis itself, he shows no desire to wear the hat of the natural philosopher.

While Peter disagrees with some theologians as to when the angels were created, he states the consensus view on their nature, disposition, and attributes and on why they constitute a subject important for theologians to consider in the first place. For Peter, angels are spiritual beings who possess intelligence and free will. They are sempiternal once created; and they are arranged in nine hierarchical ranks, headed by the seraphim, as Gregory the Great and the Pseudo-Dionysius propose. They function as divine messengers and guardians of men in this life, as well as having certain ceremonial roles to play in the last judgment. All of this is standard. So is Peter's chief concern in the field of angelology, the fall of the angels. This interest in how the fall occurred, the moral states and capacities of the good angels confirmed in their goodness and of the fallen angels confirmed in their fall, is an agenda framed largely by the felt need to refute Origen's teaching on the eternal capacity of souls, including those of angels, to backslide or to be converted, not excluding the possibility of the salvation of Satan. Peter keeps this agenda firmly before his own and the reader's eyes. He omits question that have nothing to do with it, or which he thinks are frivolous or unanswerable, such as the metaphysical status of the bodies that angels may take on in performing their missions to men, or the status of *incubi* and the offspring they allegedly may engender in union with human partners. Peter's discussion of the angelic attribute of free will, defined as the capacity to choose good or evil without violence or constraint, affords him the first opportunity to consider free will. The definition of it he gives here is one he extends to free will in prelapsarian man as well. He is less interested in how angels know what they know. With respect to the angelic hierarchy, Peter expands on it to embrace not only gradations of function but also gradations in the angelic nature itself. While he holds that all angels are equal in possessing personhood, immortality, and a simple and immaterial nature, he thinks that they also possess different grades of tenuousness and different degrees of wisdom and will.

In exercising the latter faculties in their decision to fall or not to fall, the angels, for Peter, are dependent on divine grace. The good angels remain loyal to God thanks to their cooperation with the grace God gives them. The fallen angels fall, not only because they choose to be malicious and disobedient, but also because God subtracts or withdraws His grace from them. This subtraction of grace from the fallen angels then becomes a permanent and

unalterable consequence of their fall. Lacking grace, their only option
is to continue to make vicious choices, and thus to continue to merit
their expulsion from Heaven. They are incapable of repenting or
improving. On the other hand, the good angels are confirmed in
goodness, and continue to receive grace. They do not have the *non
posse peccare* as possessed by God. But they continue to choose to
cooperate with grace and to grow in virtue. The fact that these two
sets of angels now consistently will only evil and good, respectively,
does not mean, for Peter, that their free will has been abrogated.
Rather, it has been intensified. The angels of either sort now
experience no conflicting desires. Thus, they will entirely what they
want, without violence or constraint. Other than that, there is a
basic lack of symmetry between them. The fallen angels cannot
improve. The good angels do grow in virtue. Also, since they live in
time, they continue to grow in knowledge as well, knowledge of the
events that unfold in time. Peter draws a distinction here, with
respect to the good angels. Their orientation toward the good,
being confirmed in them, does not change. Likewise, in their contemplation of God, their knowledge does not change. The quality of
of their merit does not change. But the quantity of their cognition of
temporal affairs, and the number of opportunities they have to
express their virtue, do increase over the course of time. By means
of this distinction Peter accomplishes two objectives at the same
time. His distinction between the quality and quantity of virtue in
the good angels sets up the terms in which he is going to discuss the
human Christ as a moral agent in Book 3 of the *Sentences*. And, his
argument that the angels continue to grow in virtue and knowledge, despite their confirmation in the good and their possession of
a pure and simple spiritual nature, enables him to distinguish
between these exponents of the highest and best of the spiritual
creation and the creator, a God Who is eternally omniscient, good,
and immutable. Despite their nature and their excellence, angels,
as creatures, lack these divine attributes. Thus, in addition to his
fidelity to the concerns agitating contemporaries on this subject,
Peter's angelology is connected organically to his doctrine of God,
just as it has links to his Christology and to his understanding of
free will and grace and their ultimate outcomes in Last Things, in
the case of men.

The theological agenda concerning man before the fall was a less
clear one, in Peter's day. His own handling of this subject offers a
striking reorientation of it, dominated by his desire to de-Platonize
anthropology and to consider human nature as such, as an important topic in its own right. This interest leads Peter to reflect at

length on human nature before the fall, in a manner that is often quite speculative, given the leanness of the biblical data and the fact that fallen man is now the only kind of man available for empirical study.

Most of the theologians of Peter's time give pride of place to the soul of prelapsarian man, its faculties and attributes. They have far less to say about the human body before the fall. In this connection, they focus primarily on human sexuality. In treating human nature they typically distinguish between male and female nature, regarding Eve as inferior to Adam in mind, in body, or in both. Peter's own handling of this subject reflects a distaste for these extremes of subordinationism, both of woman to man and of the body to the soul. He holds that creation in God's image and likeness applies to all human beings regardless of their sex. All human souls resemble God in their possession of reason, will, immortality, and indivisibility; in their natural capacity for virtue; and in their possession of the Trinitarian analogy of memory, intellect, and will. He sees the similarities between the human soul and God as operational as well as structural. The differing modes by which Adam and Eve were created do not imply or entail an intrinsic hierarchy between man and woman. Rather, these differences speak to their consubstantiality and equality in the bond of marital love that unites them. It is primarily the physical and metaphysical implications of Eve's creation, rather than the moral or matrimonial, that interest Peter.

Dismissing the claim that the investigation of human nature before the fall is a matter of vain curiosity, he concurs with the idea that human sexuality is the chief topic to be considered under the heading of man's physical nature. Agreeing that prelapsarian man had the capacity to die or not to die, and the ordinary functions of life in the body, such as the need to eat and drink, he places human sexuality in the same naturalistic perspective. He agrees with the consensus position framed against Origen by Augustine which states that the sexual procreation of offspring was part of God's original plan and that, before the fall, its exercise would have been free from lust and fully under the rational and volitional control of Adam and Eve. Peter annexes the procreation, gestation, birth, and growth of offspring to man's other natural processes, as goods that are part of the creation, not punishments for sin. Likewise, growth in knowledge and virtue are natural human aptitudes which would have continued in Eden. In Peter's view, while man before the fall had the rational capacity to distinguish good from evil, the capacity to choose freely between them, a knowledge of the other creatures and why they had been created, self-knowledge, and an awareness of God's presence, these prelapsarian aptitudes were just that, aptitudes. They were not perfections, but capacities through which Adam and Eve could have been translated to a higher state of wisdom and virtue. Peter describes two faculties in the human soul. There is the sensual soul, an inferior power of the soul which man shares with the animals, and which he uses to regulate the body and to dispose of temporal matters. The rational soul is the superior power of the soul, the intelligence which enables man to grasp higher things, whether scientific or contemplative. Although Peter divides reason, in its exercise, into the functions of knowledge and wisdom, his bipartite faculty psychology is an unusual one, for his time. As for man's will, Peter gives it the same treatment as he accords to the angelic will. Prelapsarian man had the natural capacity to choose good or evil without violence or constraint. A twofold process is involved here, which basically parallels Peter's analysis of grace and free will in the life of postlapsarian man. In each case, an initial grace is given by God, although, in the case of Adam, it is the grace of creation while in the case of fallen man it is the operating grace needed to help him turn away from sin. This distinction aside, acceptance of the initial grace, in each case, enables man, whether before or after the fall, to go on to collaborate with God's cooperating grace in the development of virtue and merit. To be sure, Adam also lacked a burden borne by fallen man, the inclination to sin. None the less, the choice of evil, for Adam as well, was the only moral choice he could make with complete autonomy, purely on the basis of his natural endowment of free will.

This evil choice, Peter agrees, is the one that in fact was made by the primal parents. The Lombard has a very definite view of the motivations leading to that choice, the faculties through which it was activated in Adam and Eve, the consequences they suffered as a result, and the mode by which original sin is passed on to the rest of mankind. His account of the fall leads Peter to propound two inconsistencies concerning the two primal sinners. Although, as noted above, he insists on the metaphysical, moral, and intellectual equality of Adam and Eve, he argues that the devil tempted Eve first because she was less rational than Adam. This external tempter makes an appeal, in Eve's case, to the internal temptations of vainglory, gluttony, and avarice and, in particular, to her immoderate and presumptuous desire for knowledge. Peter situates this analysis of Eve's fall in the more general context of his psychogenesis of moral choice. It is not the temptation to sin itself, be it external or internal, or the contemplation of the temptation, but the rational consent to sin that counts. Notwithstanding his claim of

Eve's rational inferiority, Peter does not think that her responsibility for capitulating to sin is any less than Adam's. Indeed, he finds her the more culpable of the two, even thought he thinks that original sin can be imputed to Adam more seriously. Eve may not have been as intelligent as Adam, but she cannot be excused on grounds of ignorance. She was intelligent enough to understand what God required. Her state, like that of Adam, displayed neither invincible nor vincible ignorance, a topic that Peter includes here only for the purpose of disqualifying ignorance of any kind as a mitigating factor in the fall. Both Adam and Eve sinned consciously. But each exercised a different aspect of the rational faculty in so doing. Eve's sin was a function of consent made through knowledge. She sought to enjoy knowledge as an end in itself. This sin is serious; but it is not so serious as the sin of Adam, which was a function of consent to sin made through wisdom. Now, wisdom, the highest exercise of the rational faculty, involves more than knowledge. It involves the capacity to place knowledge in the context of man's ultimate destiny. It must hence rule over knowledge. Adam's sin was thus more serious, even if Eve's motivation was more reprehensible, and even though she was just as responsible for her sin as Adam was for his. For, he failed to take the wider perspective into account and he failed to govern Eve, thus bringing mortality on both of them and on the entire human race. While Eve can be reckoned the greater sinner because of her greater presumption, Adam bears the greater guilt because he sinned more profoundly, with a more comprehensive faculty of the mind, and with disastrous results that are universal.

In considering the consequences of original sin, while Peter notes that it brought with it physical suffering and death, the removal of man's capacity to exercise his sexual functions without lust, concupiscence understood more generally, and ignorance, the particular effect that he emphasizes above all others is the depression of the will. Man's free will, for Peter, is partially lost in the fall; and, what remains is weakened. While the Lombard staunchly holds that man still possesses a conscience that inclines him to seek the good and avoid evil and while man still remains free to reject grace, he argues that fallen man no longer is free from necessity. The freedom to choose good or evil without violence or constraint has gone by the boards. Man now has an inclination to sin which undercuts his freedom. Man continues to need grace in order to will the good. In postlapsarian man, grace is not a substitute for free will. What it does, in conjunction with free will, is enable the free will to be a good will. But the choice of the good that it enables man to make is not just a choice of the good; it is a choice of the good in the face of a tidal pull drawing him toward evil, with which prelapsarian man did not have to contend. Aside from freedom from necessity and freedom from an existing state of sin, man before the fall had freedom from misery. This latter freedom has been lost to all men by the fall, since no one now can avoid suffering and death. In sum, for Peter, the will after the fall, like the will before the fall, is completely free and completely autonomous only in willing evil. But, it has now lost the freedom not to incline toward evil which man possessed before the fall. Peter stops well short of taking the late Augustinian line that man must, necessarily, will evil unless prevented by God, and that God's prevenient grace is irresistible. Inclination, for Peter, is not the same thing as necessity; and man can resist grace. Fallen man is less free in willing the good than in willing evil, and is less free in willing the good with God's assistance than he was before the fall. Man now needs operating or prevenient grace, which helps him to turn away from sin and prepares him for virtue, and cooperating grace, which works with his free will thereafter. Free will is as essential a condition as grace in both stages if this process. Peter holds that there can be no merit where there is no liberty of will. But the human will now operates under different, and more difficult, conditions of labor. The major continuity between Peter's understanding of the relations between grace and free will before and after the fall is that, in both situations, both grace and free will are required. And, in both situations, man cannot acquire virtue and merit without both grace and free will, virtue and merit that then become characteristics inhering in the moral personality of the human agent. In both situations, as well, Peter views the interaction of grace and free will synergistically. Each provides the operative conditions for its collaborator. Grace comes first, to be sure, empowering the will to do the good. But what it excites and heals is a natural human faculty which then becomes the agency through which the moral subject acquires human virtue and merit.

Peter firmly believes that when that happy outcome occurs, those elected to respond to grace will enjoy a glory far greater than the happiness of Adam and Eve before the fall. But the fall, and its consequences, as they are conveyed to the rest of the human race by the primal sinners, constitute the rocky road that the Christian must traverse while he is still *in via*. How that regrettable condition is passed on from parent to child, especially given the fact that Peter sees the depression of the will as its main consequence, is a highly problematic question. Peter is staunchly anti-traducianist.

The parents, he holds, transmit only the body to their offspring. It is God Who directly creates each person's soul. The soul is good as a result of its divine creation. It contains the rational faculties, free will included. How, then, can the parents transmit the guilt, the punishment for sin, and the inclination to sin that spring from or are consequences of the consent of the will to a soul that they do not create themselves in their children?

Like everyone else in his period, Peter finds himself forced to address this intractable problem with the weapons forged by Augustine's theory of the transmission of original sin through the sexual mode of generation ordained by God for the procreation of offspring. After the fall, it was agreed by Augustine and his followers, however reluctantly, spouses would no longer be able to engender offspring without the desire and pleasure accompanying sexual relations. This condition might be seen as a moral problem for the spouses themselves. But the fetus so engendered is not capable of experiencing these sexual feelings at the point when it is engendered. Peter deals with this objection by answering that what the parents necessarily convey to their offspring is not the sexual feelings that they personally may experience in the act of conception. Rather, what they pass on is a flesh that has been corrupted as a consequence of the fall, along the lines of the inheritance of acquired characteristics. This must occur, perforce, because their own bodies have been weakened as a result of the fall; and, genetically, their own vitiated physical endowment is the only one they have to pass on to their children. This vitiated body bears with it the inclination to sin. In due course, it will make the sexuality of their children incapable of functioning without lust. Moreover, thanks to the intimate union between the human body and the human soul, the vitiated body inherited from the parents will fuse with the innocent God-given soul in the womb and corrupt that soul as well.

For Peter, the fact that the parents are baptized Christians themselves who have been cleansed of original sin, and spouses united in holy matrimony who come together for the goods of marriage and whose sexual feelings are therefore free from any imputation of sin, does mitigate the concupiscence of the parents. This exemption, in his estimation, is a real one. Yet, enough concupiscence remains to inspire them to the sexual union that, unavoidably, transmits a corrupted body to their child which, in turn, corrupts his soul. Whether Peter has completely resolved the problems stemming from the Augustinian account of the transmission of original sin or not, and the question remains moot, he is forthright in his acceptance of that account and circumspect in recognizing the kinds of objections that can be, and had been, raised against it. He can see no other way to explain the transmission of original sin, and, with it, the universal necessity of baptism for salvation. Nor can he see much reason for essaying an alternative analysis. The account that he himself offers, in his own eyes, has, at least, the signal merit of reinforcing the major point he makes about the nature of man. Man is an integral unit of body and soul. It was as a unit of body and soul that man was created. It was as a unit of body and soul that he fell. It was, also, as a unit of body and soul that he was afflicted with the consequences of original sin. While the fall depresses the will more than any other faculty, it also vitiates the body. The negative side of the intimate union of body and soul in man is that this vitiated body then afflicts the soul to which it is joined and corrupts it as well. At the same time, it is as an integral unit of body and soul that man will be redeemed and glorified. This fundamental reality controls, for Peter, God's chosen mode of redemption for man in the incarnation of Christ. It also controls God's ordinance for the extension of Christ's saving work in the ethical and sacramental life of the church.

There are three main areas in the field of Christology on which the Lombard takes a clear stand, areas that are logically and theologically interrelated in his thought, although the nature of his contribution to western theology differs in each of the cases. The first of these is the hypostatic union. In this area there were three prevailing opinions at the time, the *assumptus homo* theory, the subsistence theory, and the *habitus* theory, all inherited from the patristic period and all finding contemporary adherants. Peter acknowledges that they all have support in the Christian tradition. He also finds something to criticize in all of them. His contribution in this field of Christology is to lay out clearly how these opinions are to be understood and, from his own perspective, why they are all problematic. He refuses to choose among them, concluding that the most prudent course of action is to leave the matter open, pending further investigation. In the second subdivision of Christology, Christ's human nature, and, in particular, His psychology, His human knowledge, and His moral aptitudes, Peter maintains a definite positive position. Against the tendency of some theologians to divinize the human Christ, in effect, he seeks to stress the full consubstantiality of the human Christ with the rest of the human race. At the same time, and this constitutes the single most massive inconsistency in Peter's theology as a whole, he endows the human Christ with a psychology that is quasi-superhuman. In the third area of Christology, the doctrine of Christ's saving work, Peter reflects a powerful contemporary tendency, visible in his ethics as well, to accent the internalizing of the Christian message in the lives of believers. This orientation leads him to join thinkers of the time who reject both the "rights of the devil" understanding of the redemption as well as any effort to view it from a political, military, or forensic perspective. He emerges with a personal theology of the redemption which, while it retains an objective dimension in its view of what Christ accomplishes and what man receives, accents the subjective side of the transaction, both in Christ's inner disposition and in the appropriation of His saving work in man that it makes possible.

Peter's handling of the first of these problems, the hypostatic union, is throughly informed by the clarification, with respect to theological language, that he had brought to bear on the doctrine of God and on human nature. His distinction, in the Trinity, of personhood as the relations of the Father, Son, and Holy Spirit vis-à-vis each other, in contrast to the divine essence, substance, and nature which They all commonly share, enables him to specify what the divine contribution to the hypostatic union is, while his view of human nature as involving the integral substantial union of body and soul helps him to explain the human contribution to it as well. These same lexical clarifications assist him not only in describing the hypostatic union looked at from a constitutional point of view, but also serve him in dealing with the incarnate Christ's behavior during His earthly life.

Reminding his readers that the work of any one person of the Trinity *ad extra* is the work of the divine nature that inheres equally in all of its members, even though the assignment may be delegated to a particular Trinitarian person, he observes that the Word joins the divine nature to human nature in the person of the Son, just as the divine task of accomplishing the incarnation in the Virgin Mary is delegated to the Holy Spirit. In explaining what the Word took on, Peter stresses three points. In the first place, and seeking to avoid Adoptionism, he emphasizes the point that the human Christ was not a man already in existence prior to His union with the Word, a man possessing a human person. For, this would make the incarnate Christ an individual with two persons, an idea which, for Peter, is a contradiction in terms. Equally unacceptable would be the formation of a composite, semi-divine and semi-human person out of the union of the two natures. This, too, would be impossible because the person of the Word, being divine, is, by definition, simple and immutable. Thus, rather than taking on a preexisting human nature or human person, the Word took on a human body and a human soul, infrasubstantial ingredients that go to make up a human nature, which were not yet in existence and which had not yet been joined together until they were simultaneously created and united with each other and with the person of the Son. In this union, the Word took on the human body through the mediation of the human soul. Peter takes sharp exception to the idea that the substance of the human Christ, that is, the union of a human body and a human soul in Him, can be conflated with the idea that He had a human person. It is the proponents of that conflation, he points out, who make themselves vulnerable to the charge of Christological nihilianism in rejecting the notion that Christ had a human person.

Secondly, Peter stresses the point that the man Jesus was a specific, historic, human being. In taking on a human nature, the Word did not unite Himself with an abstraction. This principle is firmly linked to Peter's soteriology. Only a God-man Who was a specific individual could perform Christ's saving work. Thirdly, and of equal importance to Peter for equally strong soteriological reasons, the human nature of the individual man Jesus is the same as that of the rest of mankind. Otherwise, the ability of this God-man to extend the benefits of His redemption to the whole human race would be severely compromised. Thus, Peter holds that the Word was joined to human nature both in the sense of being joined to a concrete human being and in the sense of being joined to humanity in general. Both aspects of this union are critical. The exception to Christ's identity with the rest of the human race as it currently exists lies in His exemption from original sin. Given Peter's understanding of the transmission of original sin, which, as he sees it, involves the passing on of corrupted genetic materials as well as the presence of lust in the engendering of offspring, this exemption must also be extended to the Virgin Mary as well, and at some unspecified time prior to the moment when she conceived Christ. This dogmatic imperative provides an opening for pushing back the moment when the Virgin's exemption took place. The Lombard's theology of the hypostatic union thus has implications for the development of western Mariology.

Peter's positive doctrine of the incarnation informs the way that he understands the three prevailing opinions on the hypostatic union, and explains why he finds all of them defective. As he sees it, the *assumptus homo* theory, in emphasizing the intimate union between the divinity and humanity of Christ, in effect absorbs the human nature into the divine nature in such a way as to blur the distinction between the two natures which proponents of this theory claim to be defending. The chief problem with the subsistence theory is similar, although it arises out of a different estimate of what occurs in the hypostatic union. Proponents of that theory maintain that this union produces a composite person, and, in some quarters as well, a composite of three substances, divinity, a human body, and a human soul. Given his own understanding of human nature, Peter objects to the idea that the body and soul, the infrasubstantial components that combine to make up a human nature, can each be described as a substance. More problematic still is the idea of a mixed or duplex person. This would entail the alteration, and dilution, of the simple and immutable divine personhood of Christ. Also, were He a composite person, the incarnate Word would introduce a fourth member into the Trinity, side by side with, but not equal in divinity with, the Word as unmanifested. In any case, no person, by definition, can be understood as made up of parts. *A fortiori*, this is true of the Word, Who has been and Who remains a "whole" person from all eternity and Who does not require the incarnation for His completion. As Peter presents the *habitus* theory, according to which the Word took on human nature like a habit, or garment, which conforms to the shape of the person wearing it, he sees it as overemphasizing the divinity of Christ at the expense of His humanity. As with the *assumptus homo* theory, the humanity is conformed to the divinity and the human Christ is thereby divinized. But, where the *assumptus homo* theory views that process as a substantial one, the *habitus* theory regards is as a purely spatial and adventitious one. From Peter's standpoint, this conclusion is equally alarming, for it suggests that Christ's humanity is not integrally united with His divinity once it is taken on, and that it remains accidental and partible. Indeed, proponents of the *habitus* theory did teach that the incarnate Christ laid aside His human nature, in between His death and His resurrection, a claim that Peter vigorously opposes.

Difficulties therefore exist, for him, in all three opinions, although it can be said that he finds the subsistence theory the thorniest of the three. While some readers in the twelfth century, and even today, have failed to take seriously Peter's advice that the matter not be foreclosed prematurely, this counsel was, to a large extent, accepted in his own century. Further research and reflection did, in the event, take place, permitting a consensus on the hypostatic union to emerge in the thirteenth century in a field where no consensus existed in the Lombard's day. This topic is the crispest index imaginable of Peter's espousal of the generally held twelfth-century view that Christian orthodoxy does not have to be monolithic, even on very basic issues. As Peter's handling of the hypostatic union indicates, *diversi, sed non adversi* is a real and operational guideline for him, delineating the working conditions under which he thinks theologians of good will should labor.

While, as a theologian of the hypostatic union, Peter is consistent, and insistent, on the point that the divinity and humanity of Christ were integrally united, that the union was not partible, and not accidental, and that neither the divinity nor the humanity was altered thereby, is has to be said that he does not push the latter conviction to its ultimate logical conclusion in treating the nature of the human Christ. On the one hand, Peter stresses that Christ's body and soul were fully human, consubstantial with those of His mother and those of all other human beings. While His conception was miraculous, He underwent gestation, birth, physical growth and development from infancy to adulthood, just as all other human beings do. He lived at a particular time and place in history; He was capable, as a man, of being predestined; and He was endowed with a sexual nature, in this case a masculine one, although Peter sees this choice on God's part not as necessary but as useful in the light of the morés of the community into which He was born. In all these ways, Peter asserts the full humanity of Christ, over against theologians who argued that His humanity was divinized accidentally or substantially by its union with the Word.

At the same time, Peter's treatment of Christ's human knowledge and His moral aptitudes endows Him with a psychology that is more than human. To be sure, these endowments are gifts of grace, not Christ's natural human inheritance, as he sees it; but they exempt Christ from the intellectual and volitional processes which other human beings undergo in acquiring knowledge and in making ethical decisions. While he is scarcely as extreme here as are other masters of the day, Peter assents to the proposition that Christ, as a man, enjoyed a fullness of grace and wisdom from the moment of His conception. His wisdom is created wisdom, and not the uncreated wisdom possessed by the Word. But, not only did the human Christ know everything that God knows, He never had to undergo a learning process. The most that Peter will concede here is that, although the quantity of knowledge possessed by the human Christ was the same as God's, He knew what He knew less exhaustively than God knows what He knows. Also, unlike God, the human Christ could not translate everything He knew into fact. This is certainly a knowledge far transcending the knowledge possessed, at least potentially, by Adam before the fall.

The same must be said of Peter's estimate of the moral condition and aptitudes of the human Christ. Christ was exempted from original sin, although He voluntarily took on some of its consequences, such as mortality, and the ability to feel hunger, thirst, exhaustion, pain, affection, and fear. These consequences of sin Christ took on because they were expedient for Him. They were essential to His mission and did not derogate from His dignity. On the other hand, He did not take on the major consequences of original sin, ignorance, concupiscence, and the depression of free will. In these respects, the human Christ as Peter presents Him was not like the rest of mankind in all but sin. To be sure, it could be argued that prelapsarian man was capable of making moral decisions unhampered by the ignorance, concupiscence, and the constraints on free will under which fallen man must labor. But Peter gives the human Christ a psychology of ethical decision-making different from Adam's. Adam, like all men, underwent a three-step process, involving temptation, the contemplation of temptation, and the conscious consent that is the essence of the moral act. According to Peter, however, Christ experienced only the contemplation of the temptation and the consent stages. At the same time, and inconsistently so, Peter maintains that Christ really experienced the temptations set before Him by the devil, as well as the temptation to despair during His passion, experiences which the Lombard regards as critical in enabling Christ to know and to empathize with the human weaknesses that He came to heal. Peter's human Christ lacks the defective knowledge that leads to sin. He does not experience temptation in the psychogenesis of His moral decisions. His flesh does not lust against His spirit. Hence, in the exercise of His fully free will, Christ at all times chose to bring His human will into perfect conformity with the will of God. Hence, He always possessed perfect virtue, marked especially by the notes of obedience and humility. The impulse to grant that the human Christ be given worship, and not just veneration, while it reflects Peter's awareness that, even here, a distinction must be observed between the creature and the creator, also reflects the fact that the human Christ he envisions is actually more than human.

If Peter's treatment of the human Christ accents His functional differences from other men more than His constitutional similarities with them, his doctrine of the atonement, one very much his own, draws on both of these ideas. Peter takes a firm stand in opposition to the externalist and politically or militarily envisioned doctrine that Christ's saving work was to free mankind from the power of the devil, whether that power is seen as just or unjust. He also opposes, just as vigorously, the critique of the "rights of the devil" position offered by Anselm of Canterbury, holding it to be just as externalist as the "rights of the devil" account in that Anselm sees Christ's saving work as the changing of God's mind about man thanks to the imputation of His own merits to man, enabling man to rectify his account with God and to repay a debt justly owed, but without man's inner life being changed thereby. Instead, Peter warmly embraces the countervailing tendency to ignore the category of justice and to see Christ's redemption as effecting a change in man himself, and adds his own personal coloration to this teaching.

As he sees it, the atonement has both an objective and a subjective dimension. On the objective side of the account, the key point he makes is that Christ possessed all the virtues perfectly, especially obedience and humility. Christ's ethical merit is total. At all times in His earthly life, His will was in accord with that of the Father, so that nothing He did, up to and including His crucifixion, could have improved His virtue in the Father's sight. Here the distinction between the quality of virtue and the quantity of virtue that Peter draws in discussing the good angels also comes into play. From this perspective, the crucifixion of Christ merely gave Him an opportunity to display the perfect obedience and humility that He had always had. Startling as is this claim, Peter makes it in order to explain why God chose this particular mode of redemption, although, as he had noted under the heading of his doctrine of God, He was in no sense constrained to do so. While the passion and crucifixion did not enhance the quality of Christ's merit in the eyes of God, the drama and pathos of His heart-rending sacrifice is critical from the standpoint of man. Christ, in offering this electrifying expression of His love for man, provides an affective catalyst that is essential for man's appropriation of the redemption subjectively. Christ's saving work revolutionizes man's heart and changes man's mind, enabling him to respond in love to God and to his fellow man. Christ's role is to change man's inner being, his inner moral orientation. This change empowers man to think, feel, and act with charity, to accept God's grace and to work with it voluntarily. This appropriation of Christ's death justifies man, for Peter, not by transferring unearned merits to man that clear his debt with God and not by changing God's mind about man, but by changing man's mind and by exciting charity in his soul.

Peter does not fail to address the "rights of the devil" debate, and drastically subjectivizes this whole idea. As he sees it, the devil is not an external power whom Christ defeats on the passive battleground of the human soul. The devil, rather, is nothing other than man's own internal slavery to sin, from which the new power to love inflamed in man's heart by Christ enables him to liberate himself. The devil, Peter observes, remains a psychological reality even after that liberation has taken place, in the form of the temptations that continue to afflict redeemed and justified mankind. Once again, it is the power to love unleashed in man's soul by Christ, in their continuing relationship, that enables the redeemed to resist temptation. For Peter, just as the fall leads to the depression of the will, so the redemption, when subjectively appropriated, restores a measure of the radical freedom to choose good or evil without constraint possessed by man before the fall. While some inclination to sin will still be present in the redeemed, the appropriation of Christ's saving work in man relaxes the pressure to choose evil under which man had labored as fallen and unredeemed. We may note that this relaxation of the *fomes peccati* is an objective consequence of Christ's saving work, and that it is efficacious only when that saving work is appropriated subjectively, a relationship that will reappear in Peter's sacramental theology. Although the inclination to sin is weakened in the redeemed, it is still present in their lives. In this sense, the devil is not completely vanquished by the cross, but his power is significantly reduced. What is equally important, the devil's power is dramatically reinterpreted by Peter as a function of man's own internal psychology of sin.

The merits which Christ possesses, and which He offers to man in lifting man's guilt and punishment for sin, are real and objective. At the same time, Christ makes this release efficacious within the human soul by empowering an equally real inner conversion, in which man's soul is active, and not a passive terrain on which contending armies clash or advocates offer briefs. Christ's virtue is exemplary for man; but it is also efficacious in inspiring the change of heart that will enable the redeemed to develop their own virtues and to acquire their own merits, in collaboration with divine grace. It is through His human mortality, which Christ's virtue led Him to offer up on the cross, that He accomplishes this aspect of man's redemption. It is through His divine immortality that He is able to grant eternal life and posthumous glory to man. In Peter's view, this is why the Father ordained man's redemption by means of a God-man, given the fact that He could have ordained it some other way. Yet, what gives the Lombard's soteriology its own distinctive cast is his ability to unite an objective understanding of the atonement, based on Christ's nature and action both as God and as man, with a subjective understanding of the atonement, based on a psychological and existential reading of the moral change that

Christ's human love and human virtue inspire in man. Peter's accent on Christ's humility, as His most paramount and efficacious virtue, is consistent with his view that humility is needed to supply the sufficient corrective to the pride that brought about the fall. So important is this point, for Peter, that he takes the unusual step of regarding the crucifixion as unnecessary, except for its unique capacity to provoke an emotional response from man. The enabling act which Christ performs within man's heart is also what allows Peter to marginalize and to internalize the "rights of the devil" theory and, in effect, to remove it from the agenda of scholastic theology. This accomplishment, and the rest of his account of Christ's saving work, are related organically to his stress on intentionality in his moral teaching and to his effort to balance the objective with the subjective in his sacramentology, as the continuing relationship between man and God specified by Christ's atonement works its way through the Christian life.

This point brings us next to ethics, although it has to be said that Peter's handling of that subject is not necessarily presented as a logical corollary of Christ's atonement. His ethical teaching is marked by a serious organizational disjunction, and one that requires a certain amount of repetition on his part, in that he treats the vices and the psychogenesis of sin under the heading of man's nature as created and man's fall, while he discusses the virtues primarily under the heading of the moral capacities and achievements of the human Christ. In that latter location he considers the theological virtues, the cardinal virtues, and the virtues understood as the gifts of the Holy Spirit. The question of ethical intentionality in its relation to sins and virtues appears as well in connection with his treatment of a number of the sacraments, while the relations between grace and free will in man's ethical life crop up in several contexts. Peter's decision to place virtue largely under the rubric of the moral aptitudes of the human Christ is not without its difficulties, given the fact that he endows the human Christ with a greater than human psychology. The Lombard is sensitive to this problem and seeks to correct for it by discussing the virtues as such before considering Christ's possession of them. This tactic, however, is not in the end fully responsive to the question of how Christ can be seen as a moral exemplar for man. That problem aside, and notwithstanding the repetition which his chosen mode of organizing his ethical doctrine entails, there is a good deal of consistency in what Peter has to say on this subject. If that consistency is notable, however, it is not total. There is one major point on which he gives with one hand and takes with the other, the question of whether natural virtue is possible. And, he leaves unexplained what connection there is between human reason as an endowment of nature and the knowledge and wisdom that are gifts of the Holy Spirit.

On the face of it, the bulk of the evidence would suggest a clear negative answer to the question concerning the virtuous pagan, for one of the earmarks of Lombardian ethics is the principle that all meritorious acts require the interaction between free will and grace. This principle extends backwards from man as redeemed, justified, and sanctified in the ecclesiastical dispensation to man before the fall and even to the angels. At the same time, the second central attribute of Peter's ethics is his stress on voluntary consent as the essence of the ethical act and on intentionality as the critical determinant of the moral agent's moral status. While he seeks to provide an objective ethical norm as well, holding that some acts are intrinsically immoral, and while he thinks that good intentions ordinarily need to be translated into good, and appropriate, actions, he also holds that inner intentionality remains of the essence, present or absent its external expression. He also holds that the capacity to possess a good will is a generic human possibility.

This latter point is reinforced by Peter's agreement with the three-part analysis of the psychogenesis of ethical decision-making standard in his time. Whether using the language of *passio, propassio,* and *consensus* or that of *suggestio, delectatio,* and *consensus,* he agrees that there is temptation, internal or external, the entertaining of the temptation, and the conscious and voluntary decision to reject it or to succumb to it. Inner intellectual consent is where sin and virtue lie, not in the outward manifestation of that consent. The active exercise of volition is critical, for Peter. When it comes to sin, this conviction leads him to dismiss the privative theory of evil and to invoke the theme of the willed fall into the *regio dissimilitudinis,* in which man deliberately rejects the image of God in himself. To be sinful, an act must manifest an evil intention. At the same time, intentions cannot be severed from the ends they serve. One cannot, therefore, serve an objectively good end by wrongdoing. Peter's strong intentionalism is thus qualified by the principle that a good intention cannot inform a bad end or an action that is unconditionally prohibited, or one that conflicts with the moral subject's acknowledged moral duties. As noted, Peter considers the question of ignorance, its modes, and the degree to which it mitigates or removes moral culpability under the heading of the fall, essentially as a means of ruling it out as an extenuating circumstance in the case of Adam and Eve. He does not reimport this theme into his analysis of ethical intentionality, of the way in which a person identifies ends as morally good or bad, or of the quality of his grasp of what is categorically prohibited or required in his own case. Peter's handling of these topics might have been enriched had he done so. But, before he leaves this point, he acknowledges that good deeds require good faith. Leaving aside faith here as a theological virtue, which would require consent to specifically Christian teachings, he agrees that good faith means the absence of hypocrisy as well as good intentions in a positive sense, and concedes that non-Christians are capable of expressing it, in their own virtues and in their service to their neighbors inspired by natural piety. The virtuous pagan rears his head here, however briefly.

While Peter agrees with other intentionalists, ancient and modern, that vice, and virtue, spring respectively from a vicious or a virtuous intention, he does not think that all sins or virtues are equal or that intentions or actions in either category can be collapsed into each other. He grades the sins as more or less serious. Seriousness is determined by the nature of the vice that inspires them; by whether they are sins committed against self, neighbor, or God; by whether they occur in thought, word, or deed, or all three; by whether they are crimes as well as sins; and by whether they involve the active perpetration of evil or the passive failure to do good. The intrinsic nature of the sin, and the extent of the harm it does, are the criteria, for Peter, rather than the degree of deliberation involved. This analysis yokes the standard seven deadly sins with the understanding of how they engender each other in the psyche of the sinner, which was a common inheritance of the time from Gregory the Great. In agreement with that tradition, Peter sees pride as the most serious sin and the sins of the flesh as less important than the sins of the intellect. Sins, of whatever type, are entirely accountable to the people who commit them. Both Peter's dismissal of the privative theory of evil and his disinterest in considering how ignorance may limit moral responsibility point to his desire to place the burden of sin squarely man's shoulders, and to emphasize the point that the creator, Who endowed man with the freedom to sin, is in no sense to be charged with man's evil use of that freedom.

As we have already seen, despite the common thread of intentionalism that binds vice to virtue in Peter's ethics, his treatment of virtue, as a pendant or alternative to vice, is not and cannot be symmetrical with his analysis of vice, in that men can and do sin purely on their own initiative, while virtuous choices and actions require collaboration between free will and grace, both operating and cooperating grace since the fall. Both forms of grace can be rejected by man. When he accepts grace and works with it, man can acquire virtue. Peter defines virtue as a good quality of the mind, inclining it to live rightly and not to use anything badly. In this stage of his analysis, virtue is seen not primarily as what the moral subject acquires by means of upright moral activity but rather as a disposition of the mind to such activity. Both grace and free will are needed to activate this disposition. In exploring their relations, Peter develops an agricultural analogy. Grace is like the rain; free will is like the earth; virtue as a disposition of the mind is like a seed. The fruit borne by the seed, the other necessary conditions obtaining, is virtue in the sense of the good intentions and actions that ornament the soul of the moral subject and that are accounted meritorious in him.

Peter treats grace and free will as enabling conditions that work simultaneously, and synergistically, upon man's natural moral inclinations, rather than from the standpoint of cause and effect. An important consequence of his doctrine of grace and free will, which provides the conceptual model that he also uses for the gifts of the Holy Spirit as virtues, is that it allows him to preserve and to develop, in his ethics, an idée maîtresse found throughout his theology, most notably in his doctrine of God: God's interaction with His creation, whether in the order of nature or in the order of grace, preserves the distinction between God as the transcendent supreme being and His effects in His mission *ad extra*. Neither God's grace, nor even the gifts of the Holy Spirit, afford man a participation in the divine nature. The virtues and merits which that grace or those gifts assist man in acquiring are, and remain, purely human attributes, spiritual characteristics of the moral subject in whom they inhere. In rewarding such a meritorious person, God rewards that person; He does not reward Himself. The human being so transformed by the acquisition of virtue is not divinized thereby. Rather, he reacquires his full humanity, the image of God in himself lost in his earlier state of sinful fall into the *regio dissimilitudinis*.

In handling the three categories of virtue that he treats specifically, Peter displays more interest in the theological virtues than in the cardinal virtues or in the gifts of the Holy Spirit as virtues. His handling of the cardinal virtues is quite abbreviated. It reflects no interest in considering them from the perspective of any of the available philosophical definitions of them, whether Platonic, Aristotelian, or Stoic. Nor does Peter show any interest in redefining them in Christian terms, on either an Ambrosian, an Augustinian, or a Gregorian basis. He does not treat them as natural virtues. For, he states that they were possessed by Adam before the fall, when all virtue required the collaboration of grace. The chief point that Peter wants to make about these virtues concerns their perdurance beyond the Christian's life *in via* into the *patria* in the next life. In all cases, their posthumous manifestations will shift from the negative or disciplinary to the positive. Wisdom will propose God as the good; fortitude will cling to Him; temperance will enjoy Him unopposed; and justice will engage in the contemplation of the divine nature. Peter has no insight to offer about the relationship of the cardinal virtues to the theological virtues, on the one side, or to the gifts of the Holy Spirit, on the other, even though he places them, in his table of organization, between those two topics. This fact, as well as the extreme leanness of his account of the cardinal virtues, in the light of what the philosophical and patristic traditions had to offer on this subject, suggests that this was an area of Lombardian ethics ripe for subsequent development.

The one point of connection that Peter draws between the cardinal virtues and the gifts of the Holy Spirit is the idea of perdurance into the next life, along with the carryover of the positive features of the virtues in that transition. This notion informs Peter's treatment of holy fear, knowledge, and wisdom, the only three of these charisms which he considers in any detail. The theme of holy fear in this context is where he orchestrates the oft-cited distinction among servile fear, worldly fear, initial fear, and chaste or filial fear, as ethical attitudes and motivations. Peter takes a generous line on this subject. He treats initial fear not as fear of eternal punishment but as an inchoate love of God, which he thus sees as being on more of a continuum with filial fear, or reverence for God for His own sake, than is typically the case. This initial fear, he agrees, will no longer be needed in Heaven, where it will have been superseded by the filial fear which, he also agrees, Christ possessed perfectly in the *via* as well as the *patria*. Peter offers a parallel account of knowledge and wisdom. Reprising, to some extent, the distinction he had drawn between the different functions of the intellectual faculty in assigning guilt to Adam and Eve in the fall, he defines knowledge as the right ordering and administering of temporal things, with beatitude as their end, and the turning from evil to good things. Wisdom can be distinguished from knowledge, and also from understanding. Like wisdom, understanding addresses itself to invisible, spiritual realities. But it is concerned with the grasp of these realities in this life; so it, too, along with knowledge, will be superseded in the next life. Wisdom alone endures. To be sure, in this life, wisdom is concerned with the knowledge of God, and of creatures in Him, through the temporal thought processes available to man *in via*. But, in the *patria*, wisdom will be able to contemplate these objects of knowledge without temporal constraints. Peter makes no effort to explain how, or if, these mental operations seen as gifts of the Holy Spirit are related to knowledge, understanding, and wisdom as natural functions of human reason *tout court*. The question of whether charismatic intervention is needed to activate man's mental faculties in some connections, but not in others, is a question that he does not take up, although this *locus* in Book 3 of the *Sentences* could provide a natural habitat for scholastics who might want to orchestrate that theme, in one way or another.

The major topic under the heading of the virtues that Peter is interested in addressing is the theological virtues. To be sure, one point of carryover we can see here between this sub-set of virtues and the other two is the notion that some virtues perdure, in more exalted form, while others are ordered to man's life *in via* and terminate once it is over. In this case, charity endures, while faith is replaced by sight and hope by the possession of the blessings hoped for in this life. It is not the urge to gloss the St. Paul of 1 Corinthians on this subject that animates Peter's extended discussion of the theological virtues, so much as the felt need to come to grips with the definition of faith, and, to a lesser extent, the desire to offer a policy statement on charity in action in this life. The definition of faith is certainly complicated by Peter's wish to ascribe this virtue to the human Christ, although, since He is deemed to have known everything that the Word knows, it is difficult to make a case for this claim. Also pressing is the need to locate faith as an epistemic state, inspired by the contemporary misunderstanding of Abelard's use of the term *existimatio* in this connection. Peter puts his stamp of approval on the Victorine resolution of this problem by agreeing that faith, the substance of things hoped for and the argument of things not seen, lies below knowledge that can be empirically proved and above opinion, owing to its certitude. He clarifies the point that the objects of knowledge addressed by faith as a theological virtue are religious ones, not available to the senses or the imagination. Another major issue that Peter wants to consider is the salvific character of faith. Here, he articulates the consensus view by distinguishing among faith, as intellectual assent to a body of theological propositions held to be true, faith as assent to what a person says because one has confidence in his trustworthiness, and the faith that saves. The latter involves adhesion to God in love and confidence and a faith that works in love. Peter acknowledges that the faith that saves may also be proportioned to the intellect and education of the believer. But, in its content, it needs to embrace the propositions in the creed, however imperfectly they may be understood. Overall, the chief quality that Peter imparts to faith is to give equal attention to its nature as an epistemic state and its nature as a virtue, both in itself and in its informing of hope and charity.

Peter's remarks on hope are brief, and largely uncontroversial. He agrees that, unlike faith, the things hope addresses are all good things, not good as well as bad, and that, like faith, hope points to the future, to things unseen and not yet in our grasp. Thus, by definition, like faith, hope is incomplete in this life. As well, and as with faith, Peter grapples with the difficulties involved in arguing that the human Christ possessed the virtue of hope, despite His omniscience and His fullness of grace. As with faith, his proposal for resolving this problem is to withdraw, in Christ's case, the condition of incompleteness from hope, although that is part of its very definition. This effort is not a particularly successful one. Peter has far less trouble arguing that the human Christ possessed the greatest possible charity, and one that was as perfect, for Him, in the *via* as it was in the *patria*. This claim is, of course, central to his account of Christ's saving work and its ability to evoke the loving response of man in man's appropriation of it.

The same definition of charity, love of God for His own sake and love of self and neighbor for God's sake, applies to the charity that human beings are enjoined to develop, despite their constitutional inability to possess this virtue to the degree to which the human Christ did. Manifesting his general propensity for hierarchy, Peter posits four grades of charity, incipient, proficient, perfect, and most perfect, the latter descriptive of the saints in Heaven. As a gift of grace, charity, for Peter, remains, like all other charisms, an effect of God in His mission *ad extra* and not a participation of the divine nature in man. He resists the tendency to view those dwelling in charity as becoming so bonded to the Holy Spirit, understood as the love uniting the Father and the Son, that they become engrafted into the inner life of the Trinity. The principle of hierarchy also informs Peter's gradation of goods under the heading of charity, as a guide to how men should order their loves. We should love God the most, as the supreme good. We should love the souls of rational creatures next, for they have an eternal destiny. We should love the human body next, for it is intimately linked to the soul and it is destined, as well, for future glory. Therefore, its health and self-preservation in this life are legitimate goods. Finally, we should love those things that are below us in the creation, insofar as they are conducive to the well-being of the body. This ladder of love recapitulates, from the standpoint of man's return to God, the metaphysical and moral hierarchy of the creation set forth by Peter at the beginning of Book 2 of the *Sentences*. Finally, there is the problem of charity understood as the practical assistance of other men, given the finitude of means at anyone's disposal. Departing from those who make the principle of need the only or the primary determinant, Peter adopts the criterion of relationship, starting with parents and moving to other relatives, members of one's household, neighbors, and compatriots, and ending with enemies. His inclusion of enemies is to be noted, stemming from his wish to support the biblical injunction to love one's enemies, and from his desire to emphasize that the sliding scale he proposes is grounded not merely in natural ties and natural responsibilities but in charity as a virtue expressing a commitment that transcends nature. It is charity in this wider sense that perdures, after our natural obligations in time are no more. While Peter is clearly willing to grade the outward expressions of charity, both by the closeness of blood ties and social relations and by the difficulty of its exercise in the case of enemies, and while he agrees that its *effectus* should be proportioned to the recipient, he holds that its inner, intentional *affectus* is the same in all cases, as controlled by the general definition of charity which he provides.

Peter concludes his consideration of ethics by exploring the moral precepts of the Old Law in relation to the New, treated as a general approach to the question of which Old Testament rules and practices merely prefigure Christian ones and which carry over into the new dispensation. This is also the context in which he develops an extended analysis of lying and of perjury, under the rubric of not bearing false witness. Peter's lengthy and extremely well documented treatment of lying emphasizes the point that a lie involves both objective untruth and a deceptive intention, and that lies are never justifiable, whatever the provocation or the good end one may be trying to serve in such a devious way. This single topic, in short, is designed to reinforce his more general position on the relations between ethical intentions and the ends they serve, and the relations between the objective dimension of ethics and subjective intentionality. Peter treats perjury as a pendant to his analysis of lying, in a parallel way, adding only the points that perjury is a lie sealed by an oath and that there are occasions when the lesser of the two evils is to break an oath. This topic, like that of the abrogation of the Old Law or its continuity in force, which ends his consideration of ethics, is placed at the end of Book 3 of the

Sentences, where his main subject is Christology. As has been noted, Peter's decision to treat virtues under the heading of the moral aptitudes of the human Christ leads to certain difficulties, in his effort to argue that Christ possessed virtues that seem inapposite in an individual who possessed a fullness of grace and wisdom at all times. Even more problematic is the inclusion of the material just referred to under the same Christological umbrella. The abrogation of the Old Law, or not, and the analysis of lying and perjury, have no manifest connection with the nature of Christ or the atonement as such. They point to the fact that Peter's schematic decisions, in the field of ethics, do not always make sense. The one, and the only, advantage of Peter's arrangement of his material at the end of Book 3 is that it permits him to introduce the rituals of the Old Testament as a transition to the sacraments, his subject in most of Book 4, and one on which he plans to take a distinct and vigorous stand in differentiating between these Old Testament rites and those of the New.

Peter's most important contribution to sacramental theology is his absorption and refinement of Hugh of St. Victor's redefinition of sacraments in general, not merely as visible signs of invisible grace, but as signs that resemble what they signify and, more important, as signs that contain and serve as physical media of divine grace and make it effective in the inner life of the recipient. It is on the basis of this Victorine definition of sacrament that Peter decisively rejects the Victorine claim that Old Testament rites, which the Lombard holds to be signs and signs only, are truly comparable with the efficacious, sanctifying, and salvific sacraments of the Christian church. In general, he holds that the sacraments were ordained as mediating an objective content of sanctifying grace, and as sanctifying the recipient by strengthening his soul, enhancing his moral education, and helping him to grow in virtue. According to Peter, sacraments contain and convey divine grace objectively thanks to their divinely ordained capacity to do so, assuming that the sacrament is administered in the appropriate way, by the appropriate minister, with the appropriate intention. The capacity of the recipient to receive and to make fruitful use of the grace mediated by the sacrament, in turn, is conditioned by the faith and intention that he brings to his reception of it. In addition to the particular form of remedy, or sanctification, or both, that particular sacraments impart, the sacraments promise a future heavenly good, and one that begins to be activated in the inner life of recipients in the here and now, by helping them to recover the image of God in themselves. Peter associates this understanding of sacraments in general with Augustine's sign theory, a comparison designed to show how sacraments partake of both natural and conventional signification, and go beyond both, thanks to their status as efficacious signs. For Peter, the Christian's journey back from the *regio dissimilitudinis* of sin is concretely moved along, and not just signposted, by the sacraments. As extensions of Christ's saving work in time, the sacraments partake of the combination of objectivity and subjectivity that the Lombard sees in the atonement. The divine healing, cleansing, and strengthening that they contain is objective; and it is made operational by the recipient's subjective disposition. Another way in which he makes this point is in noting that sacraments have two aspects. There is the *res sacramenti*, the divine grace contained in the sacrament. There is also the *sacramentum*, the physical medium. By divine ordination, the *sacramentum* is endowed with its *res sacramenti*, in the proper administration of the rite. A worthy recipient who brings the proper disposition to the *sacramentum* receives the *res sacramenti* by means of it. On the other hand, if a person approaches a sacrament without the proper intention, he receives the *sacramentum tantum*, the physical medium alone. Even in cases where Peter is unwilling to grant that the objective content of the sacrament goes by the boards, he insists that the unworthy recipient cannot profit from it in his own inner life.

Sacraments in general can be differentiated, for Peter, in terms of whether they supply sanctification, a remedy, or both. But his preferred scheme for presenting sacramental theology is to group the seven rites so considered in two subdivisions. The first contains the sacraments received by all Christians, in the order in which they are received—baptism, confirmation, the Eucharist, penance, and unction. The second contains the sacraments—holy orders and marriage—received only by some Christians. The relative necessity and importance of each sacrament is a question which he treats in considering each sacrament in turn. There are two salient features of the Lombard's handling of the sacraments as a whole that stand out clearly. In each case, while he is interested in the conditions that validate the administration of the sacraments, leaning more heavily here on the canonists, especially Gratian, than is typical of contemporary theologians, his chief concern, and it is one that differentiates him and other theologians from the canonists, is how the sacraments work to heal and sanctify in the inner lives of Christians. Secondly, and given that the purpose of the sacraments is precisely that, he is interested, as are most of his contemporaries, in removing obstacles to the reception of sacramental grace.

Whether this emphasis speaks to the rationalization of changes in the liturgical and devotional practice of the church that had already taken place, or to changes that he wants to promote, its effect is to widen the access he grants to the sacraments, to insist on the repeatability of all but baptism, confirmation, and holy orders, and to view the departures from the sacramental theory and practice of the early church which this policy entails as a rational, pastoral, and theological desideratum.

In the case of baptism, for instance, Peter agrees with the consensus on the universal necessity of baptism, arguing for its objective efficacy in the case of infants who are incapable of bringing to it the faith required of adult baptizands. He prefers this solution to the idea that the adults presenting the infant for baptism supply the requisite faith. He offers a strong defense of baptism by desire and baptism by blood; in cases where physical baptism is impossible, the sincere intentions of the persons at issue enable them to receive the *res tantum*, the grace of baptism, without the external *sacramentum*. This exception recognizes the point that, while God has ordained the rite of baptism as the normal way in which that grace is to be received, His mercy cannot be limited by emergency conditions. Nor can it be limited by the availability of a priest, the ordinary minister of the sacrament. Given the necessity of baptism for salvation, and given the mere instrumentality of any minister of the sacraments, Peter agrees that, in an emergency, anyone using the correct rite with the intention of the church to baptize can validly administer baptism. Peter offers a still wider exception, and one that underscores the organic connection between his sacramental theology and his doctrine of God, a doctrine that consistently stresses the point that God's power always transcends the particular ordinances He imposes by means of it. Even though baptism is normally mandatory, Peter asserts, to insist that it is mandatory in all cases would be to constrain God's power. For God Himself is not bound by the order of salvation that He lays down for man, by means of the sacraments. The specific effect of baptism, when received by a properly disposed baptizand, and when received by any infant, is a double one, for Peter, and in two senses. Baptism washes away all sin, and it imparts sanctifying grace. The eternal punishment owing for original sin is remitted. Also, the temporal punishment owing for actual sin may be relaxed as well. And, while inclination to sin remains in baptized Christians, along with ignorance and concupiscence, it is weakened. The grace that baptizands receive in the sacrament makes them better able to resist temptation, so that the inclination to sin is not as compelling, for them, as it otherwise would be. These effects are immediate, in the case of adult recipients. In the case of infants, the effects of baptism remain latent and potential until these baptizands are old enough to accept and to cooperate with baptismal grace.

These are the features of baptism that are of central interest to Peter. He relaxes rules that might prevent a baptism from being performed, such as the inadvertent garbling of the baptismal formula by the minister. He notes that the ceremonies surrounding baptism are decorous but not of the essence. He ignores issues such as the time of baptism, whether penance should be required before baptism in the case of adults, and whether a person can baptize himself, questions he dismisses as marginal or frivolous. The moral and liturgical symbolism of triple, as versus single, immersion in baptism appeals to him, although he does not devote major attention to it and does not seek to enforce his personal preference. His concern lies, rather, with what makes the sacrament valid, and largely from the perspective of the capacity of the valid sacrament, worthily received, to serve its ordained role in liberating mankind from original sin and in enabling recipients to make fruitful use of that gift of grace as they grow in sanctification. He sees the change effected in the baptizand on a personal and individual basis. The role of baptism in incorporating a new Christian into the Christian community is not his focus. The renewal of mind, the healing, strengthening, and cleansing function of the sacrament, and its role in empowering the individual Christian's first steps on the *via* that leads back to the *patria*, is his focus.

Peter likewise streamlines his treatment of confirmation, setting to the side such matters as the recipient's age, the time and agent of the sacrament's institution, and whether the ministering clergyman should be fasting or not. As with other sacraments, confirmation involves an external rite, which is composed of the verbal formula, the chrism placed on the confirmand's forehead, and the sign of the cross made by the bishop in so doing. The *res sacramenti* so imparted is the grace that strengthens the Christian against temptation and that arms him in the struggle against sin. It also remits sin and imparts the gifts of the Holy Spirit. Like baptism, confirmation cannot be repeated. But it is less critical for the Christian's salvation, although it should not be ignored out of disrespect for the rites of the church. This stripped down account of confirmation reflects both the general lack of controversy which this sacrament inspired in Peter's day and his systematic and successful effort to bring his discussion of it into conformity with his general theory of the sacraments.

The theology of the Eucharist was fraught with many problems in the middle of the twelfth century, some embedded in the need to defend it against heretics who rejected the real presence doctrine or the sacrament altogether, and others embedded in the difficulties faced by orthodox theologians in explaining coherently the Eucharistic doctrines on which they disagreed among themselves and even those position on which they stood in agreement. That the Eucharist is the greatest of sacraments, in that it conveys not only grace but the giver of all graces, they all heartily and devoutly supported. The real presence, concomitance, and the necessity of Eucharistic reception for salvation are also consensus positions. The chief line of subdivision that is visible in the Lombard's treatment of this sacrament can be traced between the questions flowing from the belief in the real presence, and the conceptual and terminological problems deriving from the difficulty in explaining this belief, given the speculative vocabulary available at the time, and the questions addressed to the administration and reception of the Eucharist. Peter is drawn above all to the first set of questions. The conditions of labor under which he works in tackling them share the same limits that affected other theologians writing before the reception of Aristotle. His solutions, to the extent that he reaches them, are thus, of necessity, provisional ones, from the standpoint of the history of scholastic theology. There are two main topics he addresses here. One is the question of which body Christ gave His disciples at the Last Supper, the resurrected body which Christians now receive in communion or the historical body which He then possessed. Peter supports the relatively unpopular view that it was the historical body Christ gave to His disciples. He neither lays out nor accounts for the physical and metaphysical understanding which this claim requires. The second is the problem of accounting for the change undergone by the elements of bread and wine when they are turned into the body and blood of Christ at the time of the consecration, and the retention by the elements of the physical attributes of bread and wine notwithstanding that change. Here, Peter's achievement is notable if partial. It consists of his rigorous effort to pose the problem in Aristotelian terms. The change undergone by the elements is thus a change of substance. The physical attributes of the elements are seen as accidents. The difficulty, as Peter spells it out, is that these accidents, after the consecration, no longer have a substance subtending them and serving as a material substratum in which they can inhere. Yet, they subsist anyway, inhering in no substance. Peter is no more successful than anyone else at the time in accounting for this anomaly. He does not solve the problem. But he does pose it very clearly indeed, in a philosophical vocabulary that provides a congenial setting for further essays on this subject, to be drafted in that same vocabulary in the sequel.

As with other orthodox theologians of the day, Peter agrees that the Eucharist is subject to differential effects in its reception, despite its objective divine content, depending on the belief and disposition that the recipient brings to it. The *res sacramenti* itself, as he sees it, is a double one. It includes the body and blood of Christ, which nourish and sanctify the communicant's soul by means of his body, and which signify and help to accomplish his redemption in both body and soul. It also includes the union of Christians in the church, and with Christ, the head of that body, as signified in the many grapes and grains of wheat that unite to make up the Eucharistic elements. This twofold significance of the sacrament is symmetrical with the rule that it should be received under both species, sequentially, although the body and blood are equally and concomitantly present in each of the species individually. Peter ignores the question of the communion of infants by means of the chalice alone sometimes attached to this last point, and the theme of spiritual communion, or the reception of the *res tantum* without the *sacramentum* in emergency cases, although the latter has a clear parallel with his handling of baptism by desire or by blood. He is concerned, rather, with how people appropriate the *res sacramenti* by means of the sacramental medium in the normal course of events. Nothing that recipients believe or intend, he argues, can change the objective content of the Eucharist, for this would allow mere mortals to frustrate God's merciful and gracious ordinance with respect to the sacrament. What the immoral or unbelieving recipient can do is to frustrate his own capacity to profit from communion. Indeed, such a person receives to his condemnation. Conversely, the upright and believing recipient appropriates a personal union with Christ that remakes him spiritually, remits his sin, and perfects him, as well as bonding him with other Christians in the church. As between the ecclesial and the subjective dimensions of this event in the inner life of the communicant, Peter emphasizes the personal. As between the remedial and the perfective consequences of communion, he emphasizes the perfective. The same principle which he uses to distinguish the effects of unworthy from worthy communion could have provided Peter with an answer to a vexed question of the day, concerning what happens if a mouse consumes the consecrated species. But, perhaps surprisingly, and in a response that was scarcely determinative, he dismisses this question as pointless and irrelevant.

While the recipient's side of the Eucharistic transaction is of greater interest to him, Peter also pays sustained attention to the Eucharistic ministry and the conditions that validate it. Here, parting company with most of his theological confrères and with his own general disinclination to circumscribe the availability of grace through the sacraments, he finds the strictures imposed on the sacramental ministry by the canonists eminently convincing, and supports them wholeheartedly. Thus, he agrees with Gratian, priests who are heretics, excommunicates, or schismatics, however validly ordained they may have been, are *ipso facto* barred from celebrating the Eucharist. These impediments are intrinsic, because they bespeak a defective faith and a state of dissociation from the community of faith which prevent such priests from intending what the church intends and from officiating in and for a congregation from which they are severed. Peter also agrees with the canonists' ruling that a priest's moral failings are not an impediment in his Eucharistic ministry, but he offers a different rationale for this conclusion. It is not the authority of the priesthood that he accents, but its instrumentality. Once again, he stresses the point that God will not allow His grace to be impeded by the personal failings of His human instruments. These themes constitute Peter's main concerns à propos of the Eucharist. Other questions, such as the problem of a celebrant's nocturnal emission as a possible bar to his officiating and the frequency of communion for the laity, he either ignores or gives only passing attention. This is not because they are philosophically intractable or incapable of principled solution. It is, rather, because the other aspects of the Eucharist are more central to him. Although he is less flexible in the rules he imposes on the minister's side of the sacrament than he is in other areas of his sacramental theology, Peter is consistent in placing more emphasis on the sanctification that individual Christians can attain by means of the Eucharist than on the conditions or impediments that would deactivate or delegitimize it.

The centrality of the recipient, and of the role of the sacrament in his inner life, come through even more forcefully in Peter's doctrine of penance. Here, he stands foursquare with his contemporaries in insisting on the repeatability of penance, in dismissing the single, solemn, public penance of the early church as now marginal and irrelevant, and in acknowledging that, if the same type of sin recurs in a penitent's life, penance itself can and should recur, so that the channels of divine forgiveness and reconciliation remain open. He takes a firm and consistent stand on the controversial issue of when, in the three-part process of contrition, confession, and satisfaction, the remission of the penitent's sin occurs, siding vigorously with the contritionist position. He does not shrink from pressing the logic of this position to its ultimate conclusions, even when this forces him to espouse views that place him close to the radical fringe within the orthodox consensus. Thus, he states that confession is optional. If confession is made to a priest, all that the priest does is to declare the fact that the penitent has already received divine forgiveness in the confession of the heart that he had already made to God in his contrition. Since Peter agrees with the definition of penance as sincere sorrow for sin and a firm purpose of amendment, as well as the willingness to acknowledge all of one's sins, penance is contrition, by definition. While confession may be desirable, it is desirable only to the extent that the counseling the penitent receives from the confessor is useful in his moral education. While priests are authorized to loose and to bind, in excommunication and in readmission to communion, they do not exercise this aspect of the power of the keys in confession, as Peter sees it. The other aspect of the power of the keys is discretion. This function can be served by priests, according to Peter, if they happen to be discerning and intelligent men, in advising those penitents who confess to them and in assigning appropriate satisfactions. But, Peter resolutely acknowledges the fact that not all priests indeed possess discretion. A penitent who chooses to seek guidance from a confessor is thus entitled to choose a lay person with discretion as his confessor, if a discreet priest is not available. In any event, Peter notes that the matter of performing satisfaction comes under the discretion of God. He may waive it entirely, if He judges the penitent's contrition to have been perfect, or if some emergency prevents him from fulfilling it, or if his confessor has assigned an inappropriate satisfaction. Peter does concern himself, if marginally, with the confessor's duties, when he is a priest, and takes a hard line in punishing any priest who fails to respect the confidentiality of confession. But his account places the question of the ordinary minister to the side, given his view that confession to a priest, indeed, confession at all, is optional and not required, and that, in any case, it is not the point in the sacrament when the moral status of the penitent is altered. Penance, as he sees it, is a transaction between the penitent and God. Insofar as there is a human minister of penance, it is the penitent's own conscience. In this respect, in assigning to the different aspects of penance the terms *sacramentum* and *res sacramenti*, Peter holds that both the *res sacramenti* and the *sacramentum* are to be found in contrition. The matter of the sacrament is God's forgiving grace. It is a divine response to the sorrow for sin presented by the penitent. This sorrow for sin, like all virtues, can be seen as a product of the collaboration of the penitent's free will with cooperating grace. It is by means of this virtue that God grants His forgiveness to the penitent and it is by means of contrition that he appropriates this grace. Confession, if any, is merely the outward indication that the matter of the sacrament has already been given and received through contrition.

As the foregoing analysis suggests, there is a lack of symmetry between penance and the other sacraments, in the Lombard's teaching, and in two respects. First, there is no human minister of the sacrament other than the penitent himself. Second, there is no physical medium that signifies and conveys grace. The penitent's confession of the heart may be made in silence and solitude. None the less, contrition, for Peter, is both the remission of sin and the efficacious sign of the fact that this remission of sin has been granted and internalized. As for exterior penance, it is neither a sign of the remission of sin, nor does it effect it. It merely indicates or gives formal recognition of the fact that the penitent has been reconciled to God. The just-noted absence of a physical medium aside, the logic and elegance of the Lombard's reasoning on penance has much to recommend it, both in itself and as a specific application of the principles that hold pride of place in his sacramental theology as a whole. The healing and sanctification of Christians through the sacrament are absolutely primary; and anything that interferes with this objective is to be dismissed or drastically marginalized. In the event, this logic did not prove powerful enough in Peter's day to eliminate the confessionists from the game. The matter remained unsettled. And, when a new consensus emerged in the next century, it was one that required sincere contrition but that made confession, and, specifically, the statement of the words of absolution by the priest, the moment when the penitent was reconciled. This step was taken in the name of an Aristotelian analysis of sacramental causality not available in the Lombard's day and in the effort to heighten the importance of the institutional side of penance. This latter consideration is one that Peter is perfectly prepared to undercut, in giving pride of place to the penitent's intentions and the penitent's growth in virtue. This is not to say that he ignores, or underrates, the objectivity of God's forgiveness. What it does say is that, in this sacrament at any rate, the communication of divine grace can be objective and efficacious without being physically manifested.

While, Peter can be regarded as being within the pale on penance, even if somewhat extreme in his admission of confession to a layman and in the radical surgery he is willing to perform on the priestly power of the keys, he strikes an idiosyncratic note in his treatment of unction as well. Unique among his compeers, he insists that a bishop should be the ordinary minister of this sacrament. Another unusual feature of his handling of unction, in relation to his own sacramental theology in general, is that he says nothing about the disposition which the recipient needs to bring to the sacrament in order to profit from it. In other respects, his theology of unction, laconic though it may be, brings together the range of opinions that existed in his day on what the sacrament had been instituted to accomplish; and in this sense, it is as synthetic as it is non-problematic. Peter holds the *sacramentum* to be the oil used in unction and the *res sacramenti* to be the remission of sins. In addition, it imparts physical healing, if God wills it, when it is the unction administered to the sick, and the spiritual strengthening of *viaticum*, when it is administered to the dying. Since a person may be seriously ill or in danger of death more than once, unction is repeatable. Like confirmation, it is not a sacrament of necessity. But Peter condemns more harshly people who neglect unction out of disrespect for the rites of the church. The very perfunctory discussion which he allots to unction reflects the fact that, like confirmation, it ranked very low on the list of sacraments that inspired controversy at this time. Oddly, that same characteristic fails to take note of the substantial changes in the understanding and practice of unction which this sacrament had undergone since the days of the early church, changes which neither Peter nor his contemporaries felt strongly motivated to justify, or even to mention.

In considering holy orders, Peter makes a decisive move away from the canonists' tendency to view clerics merely as functionaries with particular job descriptions, qualifications, and impediments, and presents, instead, a broad-gauged theological understanding of holy orders as a sacrament. Each of the seven grades of holy orders, for Peter, signifies and makes efficacious in the ministry of its recipient the various modes of service performed by Christ in His own personal ministry. As this *res sacramenti* is internalized by the properly disposed recipient, it empowers him to perform his own duties vis-à-vis his fellow Christians and it also grants him the grace that enables him to carry out this *imitatio Christi* in his own inner life. In this respect, the ordinand receives the gifts of the Holy Spirit, although Peter does not coordinate the particular gifts or virtues in question with the different grades of orders. Peter sees the culminating clerical office as the Eucharistic ministry of the priest.

He treats the ranks of bishop, archbishop, and pope not as grades of holy orders beyond the priesthood but as dignities or ranks within the priesthood, referring to the scope of their jurisdiction in church governance and to the forms of sacramental ministry which bishops alone can perform, such as confirmation, ordination, and, for Peter, unction. He is not interested in the juridical interrelationships of clerics in these various ranks, or with the relations of *regnum* and *sacerdotium*, which he leaves to the canonists and the publicists in his division of labor. Peter also considers other official functions within the church that, in his view, convey rank, although they are not new grades of holy orders and although they may be exercised, in some cases, by people who are not ordained at all. These include prophets, poets, and priests who have foresight. Musicians as well as poets hold a rank within the church, for the contribution which they make to the inspiration and edification of the Christian people and to the embellishment of the liturgy through the power of their art.

Peter devotes more attention here than elsewhere in his sacramental theology to the conveying of the *res sacramenti* in ordination. In his treatment of holy orders, there is more of a balance between this side of the sacrament and the recipient's appropriation of it than is typical, for Peter. His handling of this subject is symmetrical with the way he deals with the qualifications of the minister of the Eucharist. In this case, as well, he is equally supportive of the reasoning of the canonists. While he is unconcerned with such matters as age qualifications, he is supremely interested in the intentions, faith, and canonical status of the minister no less than that of the recipient of ordination. Heretics, schismatics, and excommunicates cannot validly ordain, in his view, for precisely the same reasons why they cannot validly consecrate the Eucharist. In the case of this one sacrament, Peter departs from one of his general rules by granting that there is also a form of immorality, namely simony, that is an impediment to valid ordination for both the minister and the recipient. In his eyes, simony is also grounds for depriving a cleric of office after the fact. Peter admits that ignorance as to the true state of the minister or the ordinand, on either side, may be a mitigating factor, even as pastoral need may be in the case of a non-simoniac ordained by a simoniac whose deposition would be a serious deprivation to the lay people he serves. So strong is Peter's horror of the sin of simony that, in this single case, he allows the immorality to stand as a barrier, obstructing God's grace from reaching the ordinand and from enabling him to perform the clerical functions that it would otherwise authorize him to undertake in his ministry. *A fortiori*, for Peter, such a state would prevent a cleric from making use of the grace of holy orders in his personal sanctification. But, lacking such impediments, this *res sacramenti* is conveyed by the bishop's laying on of hands as the physical *sacramentum*, and it imparts an indelible clerical character to the recipient.

The single sacrament that evoked the most controversy in the twelfth century and that warranted, for Peter, the lengthiest exposition, is marriage. In some ways his approach to marriage can best be appreciated by comparing it with penance and holy orders. As with penance, and symmetrical to a significant extent with his treatment of it, marriage, for Peter, involves more than one stage in the joining of the couple. In his view, it is the stage expressing their intentionality, and not a later, optional, and physical expression of that intentionality, that is determinative in creating a change of status. Thus, with respect to marriage formation, it is not the betrothal, which promises future consent, and not the sexual consummation that normally follows a marriage, but the present consent of marriageable parties, freely and consciously given at the time of the wedding, that makes the marriage. Just as Peter rejects the confessionists on penance, in arguing that confession, if any, is strictly *ex post facto*, so he defends the principle of consent in marriage formation against the argument of the consummationists who urge that, while consent is required, it is not sufficient, and that the marriage is ratified, perfect, and indissoluble only after it has been consummated. In both cases, Peter develops a parallel line of reasoning in support of consent, and contritionism; and, in both cases, it is the consummationism and confessionism of Gratian that is the chief challenge he wants to overcome and a major source of the material that he uses against this opponent.

Peter's insistence on the sufficiency of the intentional stage in marriage formation is so thoroughgoing that he acknowledges the validity of clandestine marriages lacking in any witnesses, parental consent, or priestly blessing, much as he would like couples pondering such a course of action not to follow it on grounds of enlightened self-interest. In contrast with his defense of contritionism in penance, however, Peter does require a sensible sign as the vehicle of the spouses' present consent. Typically, this is an exchange of vows expressed verbally. But, it may be a non-verbal means of signifying their consent, so long as it is a physically perceptible sign. Once such a marriage has been formed, it is sacramental, even if it is never consummated. Like the marriage of the Virgin Mary and St. Joseph, it is a union of minds and hearts, a spiritual

union in which the spouses pledge their fidelity and their commitment to a permanent common life. This sacrament signifies the
spiritual union of Christ and the church. If this already valid and
sacramental marriage should be consummated in the sequel, as is
usually the case, the physical union of the spouses is also a sacrament.
It manifests and reinforces the spouses' spiritual union and it signifies
the institutional union of Christ and the church. Unlike penance, in
this case the external manifestation of the intentional state that is of
the essence is regarded by Peter as a sacrament as well.

As with penance, there is no consideration in Peter's discussion
of marriage formation of who the ordinary minister of the sacrament is. In both cases, however, the implicit answer to this question is that the recipient, or recipients, perform this function for
themselves or for each other. As with penance, Peter seeks to
remove obstructions that would limit its availability to Christians,
so far as possible. He is generous on the matter of remarriage, both
for widowed persons and for a number of categories of persons
whose marriages have been dissolved or placed, in effect, in limbo,
by the extended absence and presumed death of a spouse or by the
spouse's sexual dysfunction. At the same time, there is a striking
and major discrepancy between Peter's treatment of marriage and
penance, more important than the need for a physical means of
indicating consent and the sacramentality of its sexual expression,
which must be noted side by side with the many ways in which his
treatment of these two sacraments is parallel. In penance, the *res
sacramenti* is the grace of God's forgiveness, communicated in the
penitent's contrition. He receives sanctifying grace, as well as the
opportunity to undergo moral education and improvement. On the
other hand, while Peter certainly thinks that marriage affords an
alternative to sin and while he regards it as a school for virtue, the
union of Christ and the church, the *res sacramenti* signified by
marriage, is a theological and ecclesial reality already in existence
whether or not any two people marry. Moreover, the marital
consent which constitutes and initiates their union is not seen by
Peter as a medium though which divine grace is transmitted to
them. Their marital consent, and their sexual expression of it in the
standard marriage, are seen as sacraments, but as sacramental
signs only. They each signify a divine reality but neither is an
efficacious channel of that reality in the common life of the spouses.
For the Lombard, therefore, marriage, alone among the sacraments, remains a still-Augustinian and pre-Victorine sacrament.
In the light of Peter's own doctrine of sacraments in general,
marriage is sub-sacramental.

A comparison between Peter's handling of marriage and his treatment of holy orders is also instructive in clarifying what he does, and does not do, with his doctrine of marriage. In both cases, these are sacraments received only by some but not by all Christians. The persons receiving these sacraments do so out of a calling to lead a particular kind of life, with the intention of receiving its authorizations, and embracing its responsibilities and commitments, as the church intends, for the service of the Christian community. Selfish, immoral, or manipulative abuses of the powers that these sacraments convey are equally to be deplored in the case of each of them. With respect to the clergy, what is granted is the capacity to function as an instrument of Christ's own ministry and to exercise it in their own communities. With respect to marriage, what is granted to the spouses is the right to engage in sexual relations, legitimately and without the imputation of sin, for the sake of the goods of marriage. In Peter's eyes, these goods include the propagation of offspring for the building up of the Christian community and the rendering of the marriage debt, which he views less as a purely remedial activity that prevents spouses from seeking illicit sexual satisfaction than as an opportunity for spouses to strengthen their bond of mutual fidelity and to grow in unselfishness and equality in their life together. Just as the right to exercise clerical faculties is unique to holders of clerical office, so the right to sexual relations pertains, legally and morally, only to married people.

So much for the parallels. The lack of symmetry between these two sacraments is also noteworthy. If a would-be ordinand fails to present a proper intention, Peter holds that he receives the *sacramentum tantum* in his ordination, and not the *res sacramenti* as well, just as an unworthy or unbelieving adult baptizand receives only physical ablution, and not the spiritual ablution of baptism. On the other hand, Peter is well aware of the fact that many people marry for mercenary, political, erotic, or other self-serving reasons, and that their marital relations, even when philoprogenitive, are often motivated by the same kinds of sub-theological considerations. Yet, he does not deny to such spouses a valid, sacramental marriage, despite the faulty intentionality which they may bring to marital consent. The spouses may be united in mind and heart, but for thoroughly worldly and unchristian reasons. Still, the marriage stands. The marital rights of the spouses are not withdrawn from them. Aside from a defective intention, Peter recognizes simony as an impediment to holy orders and as a basis for deposing a cleric who obtained his post in this way. Serious crime, notably uxoricide, is one of the impediments to marriage that he accepts, as preventing a widower made such by his own crime from marrying again. In other respects, a person's previous moral history, even if he supplies disinformation about it to a potential spouse, is not seen by Peter as an impediment to marriage or as grounds for nullification. Yet, while there are a range of disciplinary actions that can be taken to suspend or to disqualify a simoniac priest, or one abusing the confidentiality of confession, no analogous range of disciplinary actions exists for punishing irresponsible spouses or for terminating their marriage on grounds of immorality. Marriages continue to remain in force even if they lack the notes of fidelity and permanence understood to be present in the marriage vows. These imbalances reflect two discrepancies between holy orders and marriage, which the Lombard's treatment of marriage does not eliminate. One is the fact that simony, in his view, does interfere with the efficacy of ordination, as a means of authorization and as a channel of grace to the recipient. But, since he envisions no transmission of grace in marriage, the immorality of spouses or their abuse of their authority cannot be seen as obstructions, from a sacramental standpoint, however much such behavior may place them in jeopardy ethically speaking. Secondly, Peter is forced to recognize the fact that, alone among the sacraments, and apart from the church's sacramental view of it, marriage already exists as a legal and social institution. As such, it is thought of, governed, and practiced in ways that are not necessarily commensurate with the theological values that he wants to impart to it. This is a fact that he sometimes tries to accommodate, and sometimes not.

Consistent with his desire to focus on what marriage is all about, in a positive sense, Peter devotes more of his attention to the problem of marriage formation than to the impediments to marriage, grounds for nullification, and grounds for separation. He agrees that marriage was instituted in Eden before the fall and that sexual reproduction was part of God's original plan; after the fall, marriage was reinstituted for the purpose of avoiding fornication as well. Peter takes a fairly generous line on sexual relations in marriage by observing that the avoidance of fornication means the protection of nature and the service of marital fidelity; it is not just the repression of vice. His stress on the idea that the union of bodies typical of most marriages, although not required, is no less sacramental than the union of souls that it expresses, dignifies the sexual relations of spouses. A procreative intention, whether Christian or sub-Christian, removes all blame from the lust that unavoidably accompanies these relations. Rendering the marriage debt, a requirement that takes precedence over the counsels suggesting abstention during certain seasons, is, at worst, minimally sinful. Peter draws the line only at marital relations pursued for the sake of selfish erotic pleasure alone. His handling of the sexual rights of the spouses is uniformly egalitarian, whether it comes to rendering the marriage debt, conjugal chastity and fidelity, voluntary temporary withdrawal from marital relations, or the seriousness with which the sworn testimony of both spouses is to be taken in marriage litigation. Included in the present consent that makes the marriage is marital affection. This concept, as a marital intention, is one that Peter borrows from the canonists. He agrees with them in defining it as the commitment to accord to one's spouse the honor, dignity, and respect owed to a lawfully wedded spouse as such. With this notion he sets to one side both an excessively idealistic assessment of what most people can be expected to bring to their intention to marry, and a purely erotic understanding of married love, as well as the common lives that may be lived by like-minded relatives who are not thereby married. The same idea underlies his admission that unforced present consent creates a sacramental marriage even when the spouses use their marriage in the service of ends that he regards as inapropriate or even dishonest. The same holds true for marriages that may lack the goods of fidelity, permanence, and offspring.

In turning from marriage formation and the morality of sex in marriage to impediments, the single most notable feature of Peter's treatment of this range of questions is the coherent order he imposes on the material, coherent not only in and of itself but also in relation to the principle of consent as making the marriage. He begins by considering circumstances that would impede consent or lead to defective consent, such as coercion, fraud, and error. He next discusses the positive attributes possessed by marriageable persons, insofar as they have not ceded these rights freely or to forces beyond their control. Under the heading of involuntary or congenital impediments he takes up sexual dysfunction and insanity. The former may be temporary or permanent; the latter he sees as an unchangeable and incurable condition. All other impediments, such as servile status, vows, disparity of cult, age, cognation, and affinity, he places under the heading of impediments that exist not in the nature of things but as a consequence of choice, accident, or conventional regulations subject to change.

Peter is firm on the need for free consent, although he thinks there are cases in which a union based initially on coercion, which was therefore not sacramental when it came into being, may ripen into true sacramentality if the dissenting spouse undergoes a

change of heart within the course of married life. Fraud always
obviates a valid marriage. Error does so when it is error as to an
individual's personal identity and legal status, but not if it is error
as to his fortune and condition. Noting that the rules have changed
over time as to who is marriageable, Peter observes that there are
also basic natural incapacities that impede marriage. His handling
of *frigiditas*, or impotence, reflects the idea that, notwithstanding
the fact that it is consent, not consummation, that makes the
marriage, marriages normally are consummated; and, the inability
to do so constituties grounds for annulment, in that impotence
makes impossible both the procreative and the remedial reasons for
the institution of marriage. Peter also adheres to the contemporary
distinction between natural impotence and impotence caused by
witchcraft. He is quite as unhelpful as anyone else at the time in
explaining how reliable proof of non-consummation can be obtained,
although he also expresses a minority viewpoint both in acknowledging that sexual dysfunction can afflict females as well as males
and by granting wives as much credibility in court as husbands in
litigation on this point. He is also more generous than most in
allowing the dysfunctional partner, no less than the other spouse, to
remarry if the dysfunction vanishes after the original marriage has
been dissolved. For its part, insanity or mental incapacity renders
persons incapable of giving informed consent and of participating
in the union of minds and hearts that constitutes marriage. Yet,
and unsymmetrically with his treatment of *frigiditas*, Peter holds
that this condition prevents a marriage from being formed; but, if it
should supervene after a marriage has come into being, it provides
no grounds for nullification, any more than any other illness or
misfortune that may supervene, or the discovery that a spouse is
sterile.

Peter next turns to the second class of impediments, those conditioned by convention, circumstance, or free will. He takes up
illicit sexual behavior before or outside of marriage, and rules that,
while fornication provides grounds for a separation in which neither partner may remarry, sexual misconduct before marriage is not
an impediment to marriage in the first place. He does not view rape
either as an impediment to marriage or as grounds for making a
marital claim, but rather as a sexual sin which, like other kinds of
illicit sexual relations, is a sin against marriage and which, in this
case, is a crime as well. As with sexual sins, the taking of vows of
celibacy, the entry into holy orders, and the commission of the
serious crime of uxoricide are matters of choice. But unlike sexual
sins, they all impede marriage; and the first two are grounds for

nullification if subsequently discovered. For its part, servile status is an accident which may occur voluntarily or not. Peter does not regard it as an impediment to marriage, so long as a *servus* does not seek to dissimulate his real status in making a marriage with a free person whose status would be disparaged thereby, and so long as the masters of any *servi* involved give their consent. In Peter's view, a married person should obtain his spouse's consent if he seeks to accept servile status. But he cannot force that status upon his spouse willy nilly, nor dismiss the spouse on that account. Also circumstantial is captivity, which does not terminate a marriage *per se*. But Peter is more generous than most in leaving open to negotiation the status of the relict spouse who remarries, if and when the absent spouse returns.

The other obstacles to marriage, which include disparity of cult, age, cognation, and affinity, are all treated under the heading of impediments defined by convention and as subject to change, even though one might think of age and cognation as naturally determined and of religious commitment as a matter of choice. Still, Peter points out that the rules governing all these matters are not the same in all times and places, and have been altered in the course of church history. They are not graven in stone. With respect to disparity of cult, he thinks that St. Paul's dispensation from the rule barring mixed marriages in 2 Corinthians was unauthorized, and that Paul, and the patristic authorities who compounded this error, should be rejected in favor of the Old Testament rule, also stated by Paul in 1 Corinthians, in his permission to dismiss an unbelieving spouse. Peter presents this latter rule as one that was not abrogated in the Christian dispensation and as still in force. The policy he prefers also makes sense, in his estimation, since he thinks that spouses who have differing religious beliefs will lack the union of minds and hearts that defines marriage. If such a situation should arise in an otherwise valid marriage, Peter regards it as spiritual fornication. As with physical fornication, it would entitle the aggrieved spouse to dismiss the unbelieving one, but it is not grounds for an annulment. He hopes that, if such a circumstance should arise, this fact will encourage the believing spouse to work for the conversion of the unbelieving spouse, and for reconciliation with him or her. Peter follows the standard Roman law principles on age requirements, of twelve for girls and fourteen for boys, recognizing at the same time their conventional character and the fact that Justinian's code is not in force everywhere. His handling of consanguinity and spiritual affinity does not depart from consensus views on the substance of these impediments. But

Peter is notably impatient with these subjects, spending little time elaborating them. He observes, in so doing, that it is pointless to waste energy on these man-made rules, rules from which, in any case, people are dispensed so frequently.

Altogether, impediments and grounds for nullification and separation are less to the point, for Peter, than the positive qualities a sacramental marriage has or should have. He sees marriage as the state of life to which most people are called and whose consolations they need. These same consolations were ordained by God in His institution of marriage. As well as serving as a remedy for sin, they afford couples the opportunity to grow in virtue and in an unselfish mutual affection. This being the case, Peter generally seeks to relax the conditions enabling people to marry, rather than taking a harsh, legalistic, ascetic, or punitive approach. He is consistent in centering marriage on the free and unfeigned present consent of the spouses. The content of that consent always includes marital affection and the union of minds and hearts that is constitutive of the marriage. In the vast majority of cases, marital consent also includes consent to the expression and reinforcement of that spiritual union in the sexual union of the spouses. Peter sees both kinds of union as sacramental. The use of sex for the ends of marriage he frees, virtually completely, from any imputation of sin. By the same token, although the spiritual bond is of the essence for him, impotence can be accepted as a real and reasonable impediment to marriage. The major advance Peter makes in the theology of marriage is his persuasive defense of the principle of consent in marriage formation. He offers this teaching in the light of his stress on intentionality more generally and in the effort to defend the sacramentality of the marriage of Mary and Joseph. Yet, he presents the principle of consent in such a way as to address the values and concerns articulated by his opponents on the consummationist side of the debate. In his treatment of sex in marriage, he is typically more generous and more egalitarian than they are. Peter's second major contribution is to impose a coherent order on the subject of impediments. While it has to be said that, in relation to his sacramental theology as a whole, his doctrine of marriage falls short, in that he does not see either the spiritual or the physical union of spouses as a means of grace, he does see marriage as assisting spouses in the acquisition of virtue and merit.

Looking at Peter's sacramental theology over all, this point is one among several areas in which his handling of a particular sacrament fails to square with his theology of sacraments in general. He does not discuss the topic of the ordinary minister in the case of either marriage or penance. His understanding of penance as contrition means that a physical medium of grace is not required in this sacrament; any subsequent external manifestation of the penitent's reconciliation is a sign of the sacrament and is not a sacrament itself. In the case of unction, Peter omits the issue of the disposition or intention that the recipient needs to bring to the sacrament in order to receive it worthily and to appropriate its grace fruitfully. In the case of holy orders, and uniquely so, he allows a moral failing, simony, to obstruct the efficacy of grace in the valid administration and reception of the sacrament. This is the one and only instance in which Peter accepts the idea that the personal weaknesses of fallible men can block the workings of the sacraments despite their God-given power. It is a departure from his more general tendency to see the ministers of the sacraments merely as instruments in their transmission of divine grace. These anomalies aside, Peter's treatise on sacramental theology imparts a higher level of coherence and consistency to the topic, as a field of systematic theological inquiry, than it had yet received in western Christian theology. Peter's sacramentology makes frequent use of canonical insights and material, especially from Gratian, even though Peter finds himself on the opposing side of controversies, such as consent versus consummation and contritionism versus confessionism, as much if not more than he agrees with Gratian. Even when the two masters are in accord, Peter often offers a different rationale for his conclusions. The single most important feature of Peter's teaching on the sacraments is his acceptance and elaboration of the Victorine view of a sacrament as a sign that effects what it signifies. His adoption of this principle puts it at the center of scholastic sacramental theology in the high Middle Ages. The Lombard's treatment of the sacraments also puts sacramental theology on a continuum with his doctrine of God and God's relations with His creation, with his soteriology, and with his understanding of the relations between intention and action, and grace and free will, in the moral life. The healing, the sanctification, and the growth in personal virtue and merit for which the sacraments were instituted are likewise means by which God's power and mercy and man's effort combine to bring the Christian through the life *in via* to the *patria* at the end of time.

It is as the culmination of that journey that Peter views Last Things, the subdivision of systematic theology embracing the final set of questions included in his *Sentences*. In relation to that of his scholastic confrères, Peter's eschatology is notable for its resolute refusal to raise questions that he thinks are unanswerable and for his equally firm dismissal of anything that smacks of wild-eyed speculation. He makes no concessions whatever to the chiliastic imagination or to creative apocalypticism. This norm is one he applies to his appropriation of the work of his own contemporaries and also to his patristic authorities and to the New Testament itself. The single most striking index of Peter's outlook here is his total omission of the Antichrist from his end-of-time scenario, even though he had developed a cogent and independent position on that subject in his Pauline exegesis. He leads off, instead, with, the general resurrection and the second coming of Christ. On balance, he is far less interested in catering to curiosity about the sequence of events leading to the last judgment than he is in discussing its consequences in the assignment of souls to their posthumous habitations. He imports into the last judgment the Gregorian subdivision of four categories of souls, evaluated in terms of how they have lived their lives on earth and the moral state in which they died. Both the saints who have demonstrated their merit by their charity and their works of supererogation and the unregenerate and unrepentant sinners who have confirmed their damnation by their evil choices up to the end are already judged, and saved or damned accordingly. There are other sinners, less comprehensively evil, who will be judged and condemned, as well as repentant sinners who died penitent but without having fully expiated the sins on their consciences, who will be judged and saved, after a purificatory interim in Purgatory.

In dealing with the fates of the inhabitants of Heaven and Hell, Peter seeks to integrate this subject into the larger themes informing his systematic theology. One of these themes, orchestrated throughout the *Sentences*, is his reformulation of Augustine. Here, he sees the damned and the saved as expressing, eternally, the city of man and the city of God. He also coordinates Last Things with the idea of signs and things, use and enjoyment, applied to his view of the Christian life and his doctrine of God. Peter offers a strong defense of the principle that the judgment of God is just, and that it is merciful. Since they are attributes of a divine essence that is radically simple, God's justice and mercy are identical. Further, Peter maintains, the damned have fully earned their punishment. As with the wills of the fallen angels, moreover, their wills remain free in the next life. Deprived, for all time, of access to the grace that they have spurned in this life, they will continue to consent to evil, and to evil alone. Thus, they will continue to merit their punishment, eternally. None the less, God punishes them less than they deserve, and He mercifully spares them from the sight of the joys of the blessed, which would only increase their suffering. The blessed will experience God's justice and mercy with even greater intensity. Like the angels confirmed in the good, they too will be freed totally from any obstacle to their willing of the good. They will have everything they have hoped for, and more. Most of all, having completed their journey home from the *regio dissimilitudinis*, they will have recovered a full humanity, indeed, a greater humanity than that possessed by man before the fall. Having collaborated with grace in working out their salvation, through the good use of earthly things, including the sacramental signs that are efficacious means of grace as well as things, they will have moved, through and past the mutabilities of the world in time and the time-bound modes of human cognition and volition to the direct, unconditioned love and knowledge of the immutable God Himself, the supreme being and the supreme good Whom they can now enjoy eternally and without impediment.

This conclusion to Peter's *Sentences* thus connects the entire enterprise of systematic theology with the basic doctrine of God stated at the outset of that work and the basic principles and emphases that govern his exposition throughout it. Peter never forgets that the subject of subjects is the deity. Nor does he forget that this deity's ordinances, in the order of nature and the order of grace, have been laid down for the sake of man. They become meaningful, and functional, in man's instruction and redemption by providing the means, starting with Christ's saving work, by which man's latent desire for the good can be activated and energized. Notwithstanding the depression of the will in fallen man, man's will can and must collaborate with God's grace. This collaboration grows easier with the partial relaxation of the depression of the will when man is redeemed and justified. Together, God's grace and man's freedom continue to cooperate in the growth of virtue and merit in the ethical life and in the sacramental life. With the exception of the body and blood of Christ given in the Eucharist, the gifts of grace given by God are His effects, not God Himself. The moral progress made by man is his sanctification, not his divinization, the recovery of the image of God in himself, not a participation in the divine nature. God's transcendence over His creation, His concession of freedom and contingency to that creation, and His simultaneous refusal to let its limitations circumscribe His power or frustrate His mercy and love, are notes which Peter carries clearly and systematically throughout his presentation of Christian theology, from his discussion of the knowledge of God to his eschatology. The end-point, for the blessed, in which their mutability as creatures has been overcome in their eternal enjoyment of God, still preserves Peter's vivid sense that there are two distinct kinds of beings here who are now joined in loving communion.

The force and cohesion of this vision of systematic theology yet bears with it occasional inconsistencies, soft spots, and areas that could be seen as requiring further reflection or refinement, not merely in the light of some theology or other to come but in the context of Peter's own century. This point can be made with respect to Peter's address to philosophy, no less than to theology itself. Peter goes a long way toward the clarification of theological language and toward a constructive use of philosophy, and the other *artes*, as ways of posing and of settling questions. In some quarters he reflects a propensity toward Aristotelianism. His view of human nature as a substantial and integral unity of body and soul is central to his anthropology, his understanding of the incarnation of Christ, his ethics, and his sacramentology alike. This propensity makes these topics hospitable locations for the expansion of these themes by thinkers of a still more Aristotelian bent. It causes Peter to dismiss a Platonizing view of human nature that would likewise influence the treatment of those related subjects. It also inspires him to reject Boethius's definition of a person as the individual substance of a rational nature, a definition he finds as inapposite to human beings and to the human nature of Christ as it is to the Trinitarian persons. None the less, in using the term "substance" to refer to the divine nature, Peter resolutely and deliberately avoids any particular philosophical acceptation of that term. His use of it is specifically devoid of the Aristotelian sense of substance as denoting a composite being made up of matter and form that is susceptible to modification by accidents. In describing the change in the Eucharistic elements, Peter formulates the problem in clearly Aristotelian language. At the same time, he is unable to find an explanation, in that same vocabulary, for the anomaly involved when accidents have no substance in which to inhere, much as he thinks that this is the vocabulary that needs to be used in that connection.

In handling issues such as God's foreknowledge, providence, predestination and free will or contingency, Peter parries the Aristotelian tendency to conceive of the problem in terms of a logic framed in the first instance to describe events *in rerum natura*. He is also unsympathetic to the Boethian, and, more recently, the Abelardian, effort to impart a post-Aristotelian gloss to this question by reframing it in terms of formal logic. Here, as with the parallel issue of whether God could do different and better than He does, Peter insists on treating the question philosophically but as a problem in metaphysics, looked at from the standpoint of the supreme being and His attributes, not from the perspective of natural philosophy or the inferences that can be made from certain kinds of propositions. He dismisses the debate over universals as inapposite to theology, and, at the same time, makes constructive use of the nominalist analysis of the unitary signification of nouns and verbs in defending this metaphysical address to the themes of divine omniscience and omnipotence. In these contexts, he never forgets that what he is talking about is God, and not the created world or the workings of the human mind. His selective criticism of Aristotelianism can also be seen in his substitution of relation, understood in the sense of relative nouns, for relation, understood in the sense of an Aristotelian accident modifying created substances, in his delineation of the distinction between person and nature in the Trinity and in the service of his vigorous effort to restore to the understanding of the Trinitarian persons their individual determinations, as structured eternally into the connections among the members of the unmanifested Trinitarian family, while insisting on the notion that God's action *ad extra* is not an adequate index of the differences among those persons. If he offers a criticism of Aristotelianism in this treatment of Trinitarian relations, Peter's doctrine of God more generally can be seen as a thoroughgoing effort to de-Platonize that subject, whether from the standpoint of emanationism, participationism, exemplary causation, or the *via negativa*. In still another quarter, his analysis of marriage, Peter is largely comfortable with the Aristotelian view of causation, in labeling the consent that makes the marriage the efficient cause and the ends of marriage the final cause. He does not expressly describe the intentions of the spouses as the formal cause, although his handling of the topic would make it amenable to that denomination.

In these several ways, the Lombard shows that he is anything but uninterested in or hostile to philosophy. He draws on it freely; and, when he substitutes one version of it for another, he does so as a matter of circumspect and principled choice. As indicated, he seeks radically to de-Platonize western theology, with respect to the Trinity, with respect to a preclusively economic view of the deity, with respect to human nature, and with respect to the interaction of man and God in the charismatic order. Thinkers with a more Platonic or Neoplatonic perspective would feel the challenge of reclaiming the terrain from him on these points. As we have noted, there are areas in his *Sentences* that provide a natural habitat for Aristotelianism, areas where more of this philosophy could be added without stretching the fabric of Lombardian theology out of shape. There are also points at which his theology presents a challenge to the Aristotelians as well, and also to proponents of a post-Aristotelian logic. Indeed, it may be argued that the very fact of Peter's philosophical eclecticism, no less than his clear preferences in this field, was what made his *Sentences* a useful vehicle for budding philosophers in the later medieval centuries.

There are also inconsistencies and soft spots in Peter's theology that are less conditioned by his philosophical inclinations and tolerances. In our view, Christology must be put at the head of the list here. This is not because of his refusal to take what he thought would have been a premature stand on the three opinions concerning the hypostatic union. Much as the outsiders and obscurantists in the Lombard's time and in the following generation may have misunderstood him, charging him erroneously with Christological nihilianism or with the proposing of a quaternity in the Trinity, his own unwillingness to rush to judgment here, and his clear analysis of the three opinions, should be counted as an advantage of Lombardian theology, and not as a disadvantage. More important, and more problematic, is his treatment of Christ's human nature. While arguing that the exemptions and privileges received by the human Christ were gifts of grace, not endowments of nature, and while asserting that the human Christ was entirely consubstantial with other men, Peter gives to the human Christ a psychology that is more than human, an epistemology in which Christ is virtually omniscient and in which He never had to undergo a learning process, and a psychogenesis of ethical decision-making in which the temptations suffered and resisted by Christ are alleged to have been real temptations, although He is also held never to have experienced *passio*, but only *propassio* and *consensus*. In addition, Peter's decision to treat the virtues in connection with Christology, although he treats vice and sin in connection with human nature and the fall, is an impediment to his resolution of this discrepancy. Since Peter's human Christ is functionally superhuman, His role as a moral exemplar for man and His capacity to possess virtues such as faith and hope, which involve incompletion by definition, are put into question. Peter does not resolve the contradiction between the human Christ, full of grace and wisdom, as he understands Him, and the human Christ Who is like us in all but sin.

There are a few other theological inconsistencies in Peter's work, notable and annoying if perhaps less fundamental in doctrinal terms, which we have flagged above and here reprise. Peter's Eve is consubstantial with Adam and equally a bearer of God's image and likeness in her soul. Yet, according to Peter, she was less rational than Adam and her fall can be credited to her misuse of knowledge, the lower of the two functions of the higher intellectual faculty, as contrasted with Adam's misuse of wisdom. Along with the angelic nature, human nature at all times is regarded by Peter as requiring the assistance of grace in the development of virtue. Yet, he thinks that non-Christians, who can be presumed to lack that grace, are capable of possessing good faith and of developing virtue out of their natural *pietas*. Through his natural endowment of reason, man possesses, for Peter, the capacity to come to a positive natural knowledge of God and to prove God's existence. What relationship this faculty and aptitude bears to the knowledge, understanding, and wisdom that he sees as gifts of the Holy Spirit Peter leaves unexplained. Finally, notwithstanding the fact that he places on a firm foundation the new Victorine conception of sacraments as efficacious signs, severed from the Victorine idea that they are really on a continuum with pre-Christian rites, Peter does not extend his theory of the sacraments in general to all the sacraments, fully and completely. There are asymmetries with respect to intentionality in unction and with respect to the capacity of human immorality to impede the efficacy of the administration and reception of the sacrament in the case of holy orders. The question of the ordinary minister does not arise in the case of penance and marriage. Penance lack a physical medium, in his understanding of that sacrament. And marriage, while it signifies a *res sacramenti* and, indeed, does so in a double sense, is not viewed by Peter as an efficacious channel of grace to spouses, whether in their spiritual or their physical union.

Both the strengths of the Lombard's achievement, the questions that he deliberately leaves open, the areas in his theology in which he presents different philosophical options and challenges, and the topics on which he contradicts himself or fails to press the logic of his position to its ultimate conclusions, all provided a wealth of problems and opportunities for later theologians. So did the many *loci* in the *Sentences* that offered natural homes for the new materials and the new debates that lay on the immediate intellectual horizon of western Christendom. The tradition launched by the Lombard's *Sentences* was well served by the fact that it possessed a schema and a methodology that could accommodate these new materials, in whatever camp a commentator might choose to plant his standard. It must also be said that Peter was fortunate in his critics. They were, and they were perceived to be, men who were misinformed, poorly educated, and hostile to scholarly progress, men, in short, who could be dismissed as people who had nothing to contribute to the development of mainstream western theology. It must also be said that Peter was fortunate in his supporters, the scholastics who took on his mantle and who made Lombardian theology tantamount to mainstream Paris theology in the generation after his death. How they rose to the challenges and opportunities presented by his work is the subject of another investigation. The talents and insights and the new instruments which they brought to this task constitute their own endowment and their own contribution. The terrain which that they were able to cultivate thereby was the legacy of the Lombard.

BIBLIOGRAPHY

Primary Sources

Abelard, Peter. *Abaelardiana inedita*. Ed. Lorenzo Minio-Paluello. Rome: Edizioni di Storia e Letteratura, 1958.
———. "A Critical Edition of Peter Abelard's 'Expositio in Hexameron'." Ed. Mary Foster Romig. University of Southern California Ph.D. diss., 1981.
———. *A Dialogue of a Philosopher with a Jew and a Christian*. Trans. Pierre J. Payer. Toronto: Pontifical Institute of Mediaeval Studies, 1979.
———. *Dialectica*. 2nd ed. Ed. L. M. DeRijk. Assen: Van Gorcum & Comp. N.V., 1970.
———. *Dialogus inter Philosophum, Iudaeum et Christianum*. Ed. Rudolf Thomas. Stuttgart: Friedrich Frommann Verlag, 1970.
———. *Du bien suprême*. Trans. Jean Jolivet. Montreal: Bellarmin, 1978.
———. *Ethics*. Ed. and trans. David E. Luscombe. Oxford: Clarendon Press, 1971.
———. *Historia calamitatum*. Ed. J. Monfrin. Paris: J. Vrin, 1959.
———. *Hymnarius Paraclitensis*. Ed. Joseph Szövérffy. 2 vols. Albany: Classical Folia Editions, 1975.
———. *Opera*. Ed. Victor Cousin, with C. Jourdain and E. Despois. 2 vols. Hildesheim: Georg Olms Verlag, 1970 [repr. of Paris, 1849 ed.].
———. *Opera. Patrologia latina, cursus completus*. Ed. J. P. Migne. Vol. 178. Paris, 1885.
———. *Opera theologica*. Ed. Eligius M. Buytaert and Constant J. Mews. Corpus christianorum, continuatio medievalis, 11–13. Turnhout: Brepols, 1969–87.
———. *Philosophische Schriften*. Ed. Bernhard Geyer. Beiträge zur Geschichte der Philosophie und Theologie des Mittelalters, 21:1–4. Münster: Aschendorff, 1919–33.
———. *Scritti di logica*. 2nd ed. Ed. Mario Dal Pra. Pubblicazioni della facoltà di lettere e filosofia dell'Università di Milano, 34, sezione a cura dell'Istitito di storia della filosofia, 3. Florence: La Nuova Italia, 1969.
———. *Sermones. Patrologia latina, cursus completus*. Ed. J. P. Migne. Vol. 178. Paris, 1885.
———. *Sic et non*. Ed. Blanche P. Boyer and Richard McKeon. Chicago: University of Chicago Press, 1976.
———. *Theologia "summi boni"*. Ed. Heinrich Ostlender. Beiträge zur Geschichte der Philosophie und Theologie des Mittelalters, 25:2–3. Münster: Aschendorff, 1939.
———. *The Story of Abelard's Adversities*. Trans. J. T. Muckle. Toronto: Pontifical Institute of Mediaeval Studies, 1964.
Abelard, Peter and Heloise. *The Letters of Abelard and Heloise*. Trans. Betty Radice. Harmondsworth: Penguin Books, 1974.
Alberic of Trois Fontaines. *Chronaca. Monumenta Germaniae Historica, Scriptores rerum Germanicarum*. Vol. 23. Hannover, 1874.
Alger of Liège. *Alger von Lüttichs Traktat "De misericordia et iustitia": Ein kanonistischer Konkordanzversuch aus der Zeit des Investiturstreits*. Ed. Robert Kretzschmar. Sigmaringen: Jan Thorbecke Verlag, 1985.
Alulf of Tournai. *De expositio novi testamenti. Patrologia latina, cursus completus*. Ed. J. P. Migne. Vol. 79. Paris, 1903.
Anselm of Canterbury. *Opera omnia*. Ed. Franciscus Salesius Schmitt. 2 vols. Stuttgart: F. Frommann, 1968.
Augustine. *Eighty-Three Different Questions*. Trans. David L. Mosher. Washington:

Catholic University of America Press, 1982.
────. *De diversis quaestiones octoginta tribus.* Ed. Almut Mutzenbecher. Corpus christianorum, series latina, 44A. Turnhout: Brepols, 1975.
────. *Enarrationes in Psalmos.* Ed. D. Eligius Dekkers and Ioannes Fraipont. Corpus christianorum, series latina, 38–40. Turnhout: Brepols, 1956.
Baron, Roger, ed. "Hugonis de Sancto Victore *Epitome Dindimi in philosophiam.*" *Traditio* 11 (1955): 91–148.
────. ed. "Textes spirituels inédits de Hugues de Saint-Victor." *Mélanges de science religieuse* 13 (1956): 157–78.
────. ed. "*Tractatus de trinitate et de reparationis hominis* du MS. Douai 365." *Mélanges de science religieuse* 18 (1961): 111–23.
Bernard of Clairvaux, *On Grace and Free Choice.* Trans. Daniel O'Donovan. Intro. by Bernard McGinn. Kalamazoo: Cistercian Publications, 1977.
────. *On the Song of Songs.* Trans. Kilian Walsh and Irene Edmonds. 4 vols. Spencer, MA/Kalamazoo, MI: Cistercian Publications, 1971–80.
────. *Opera.* Ed. J. Leclercq, C. H. Talbot, and H. M. Rochais. Vols. 1–8. Rome: Éditiones Cistercienses, 1957–77.
Bernard Silvestris. *Cosmographia.* Ed. Peter Dronke. Leiden: E. J. Brill, 1978.
────. *The Cosmographia.* Trans. Winthrop Wetherbee. New York: Columbia University Press, 1973.
Biblia latina cum Glossa ordinaria. 4 vols. Editio princeps. Strassburg: Adolph Rusch, 1980/81. Anastatic reprint. 4 vols. Intro. by Karlfried Froelich and Margaret T. Gibson. Turnhout: Brepols, 1992.
Bliemetzrieder, Franz P., ed. *Anselms von Laon systematische Sentenzen.* Beiträge zur Geschichte der Philosophie des Mittelalters, 18:2–3. Münster: Aschendorff, 1919.
────, ed. "Théologie et théologiens de l'école épiscopale de Paris avant Pierre Lombard." *Recherches de théologie ancienne et médiévale* 3 (1931): 273–91.
Boethius. *The Theological Tractates.* Ed. and trans. H. F. Stewart, E. K. Rand, and S. J. Tester. Cambridge, MA: Harvard Universiy Press, 1973.
Bruno the Carthusian. *Expositio in Psalmos. Patrologia latina, cursus completus.* Ed. J. P. Migne. Vol. 152. Paris, 1879.
Burnett, Charles S. F., ed. "Peter Abelard, Confessio fidei 'Universis': A Critical Edition of Abelard's Reply to Accusations of Heresy." *Mediaeval Studies* 48 (1986): 111–38.
Chronica Pontificum et Imperatorum Mantuana. Monumenta Germaniae Historica, Scriptores rerum Germanicarum. Vol. 24. Hannover, 1879.
Chronique de Morigny (1095–1152). Ed. Léon Mirot. Paris: Alphonse Picard et Fils, 1909.
Cicero. *Tusculanae disputationes.* 5th ed. Ed. Otto Heines. Leipzig: B. G. Teubner, 1959.
Continuatio Beccensis. Ed. Robert Howlett. Rerum Britannicarum medii aevi scriptores, 82:4. London: H. M. Stationery Office, 1889.
Continuatio Sanblasiana. Monumenta Germaniae Historica, Scriptores rerum Germanicarum. Vol. 20. Hannover, 1868.
Dante Alighieri. *La Divina Commedia.* Ed. Fredi Chiapelli. Milan: Ugo Mursia, 1965.
Ebbesen, Sten, et al., ed. "Compendium logicae Porretanum ex codici Oxoniensi Collegii Corporis Christi 250: A Manual of Porretan Doctrine by a Pupil of Gilbert's." *Université de Copenhague, Cahiers de l'Institut du moyen-âge grec et latin* 46 (1983).
Eberhard of Bamberg. *Epistolae. Patrologia latina, cursus completus.* Ed. J. P. Migne. Vol. 193. Paris, 1854.
Flint, Valerie I. J., ed. "Honorius Augustodunensis: *Imago mundi.*" *Archives d'histoire doctrinale et littéraire du moyen âge* 49 (1982): 7–153.
Florus of Lyon. *Expositio in Epistolas beati Pauli ex operibus sancti Augustini collecta. Patrologia latina, cursus completus.* Ed. J. P. Migne. Vol. 119. Paris, 1880.

Fontana, Maria, ed. "Il commento ai Salmi di Gilberto della Porrée." *Logos* 13 (1930): 283–301.

Gallia Christiana, in provincias ecclesiasticas distributa. Opera et studio Monachorum Congregationis S. Mauri Ordinis S. Benedicti. Vol. 7. Paris: H. Welter, 1899 [repr. of Paris: Ex Typographia Regia, 1744 ed.].

Gerhoch of Reichersberg. *Epistolae. Patrologia latina, cursus completus.* Ed. J. P. Migne. Vol. 193. Paris, 1854.

————. *De gloria et honore Filii hominis. Patrologia latina, cursus completus.* Ed. J. P. Migne. Vol. 194. Paris, 1855.

————. *Letter to Pope Hadrian about the Novelties of the Day.* Ed. Nikolaus M. Häring. Toronto: Pontifical Institute of Mediaeval Studies, 1974.

————. *Opera inedita.* Ed. Damien and Odulph Van den Eynde and Angelinus Rijmersdael, with Peter Classen. 2 vols. in 3. Rome: Antonianum, 1955–56.

Geyer, Bernhard, ed. *Die Sententiae divinitatis: Ein Sentenzenbuch der Gilbertischen Schule.* Beiträge zur Geschichte der Philosophie des Mittelalters, 7:2–3. Münster: Aschendorff, 1909.

Gilbert of Poitiers. *The Commentaries on Boethius by Gilbert of Poitiers.* Ed. Nikolaus M. Häring. Toronto: Pontifical Institute of Mediaeval Studies, 1966.

Glossa ordinaria. Patrologia latina, cursus completus. Ed. J. P. Migne. Vols. 113–14. Paris, 1879.

Gratian. *Decretum.* Ed. Aemilius Friedberg. Corpus iuris canonici, 1. Leipzig: Tauchnitz, 1879.

————. *Marriage Canons from the Decretum.* Trans. John T. Noonan. Berkeley: School of Law, 1967.

Guérard, M., ed. *Cartulaire de l'église Notre-Dame de Paris.* 4 vols. Collection des cartulaires de France. Vols. 4–7. Paris: Crapelet, 1850.

Guibert of Nogent. *Self and Society in Medieval France: The Memoirs of Abbot Guibert of Nogent.* Ed. and trans. John F. Benton. New York: Harper & Row, 1970.

Häring, Nikolaus M., ed. "A Commentary on the Pseudo-Athanasian Creed by Gilbert of Poitiers." *Mediaeval Studies* 25 (1965): 23–53.

————, ed. "A Treatise on the Trinity by Gilbert of Poitiers." *Recherches de théologie ancienne et médiévale* 39 (1972): 14–50.

————, ed. "Die *Sententie magistri Gisleberti Pictavensis episcopi* I." *Archives d'histoire doctrinale et littéraire du moyen âge* 45 (1978): 83–180.

————, ed. "Die *Sententie magistri Gisleberti Pictavensis episcopi* II: Die Version der florentiner Handschrift." *Archives d'histoire doctrinale et littéraire du moyen âge* 46 (1979): 45–105.

————, ed. *Life and Works of Clarenbald of Arras, A Twelfth-Century Master of the School of Chartres.* Toronto: Pontifical Institute of Mediaeval Studies, 1965.

————, ed. "The *Eulogium ad Alexandrum Papam tertium* of John of Cornwall." *Mediaeval Studies* 13 (1951): 257–300.

————, ed. "The Treatise 'Invisibilia dei' in MS Arras, Bibl. mun. 981 (399)." *Recherches de théologie ancienne et médiévale* 40 (1973): 104–46.

Hermannus. *Sententie magistri Petri Abelardi (Sententie Hermanni).* Ed. Sandro Buzzetti. Pubblicazioni della facoltà di lettere e filosofia dell'Università di Milano, 101, sezione a cura di storia della filosofia, 31. Florence: La Nuova Italia, 1983.

Hervaeus of Bourg-Dieu. *Commentaria in Epistolas divi Pauli. Patrologia latina, cursus completus.* Ed. J. P. Migne. Vol. 181. Paris, 1854.

Hugh of St. Victor. *De sacramentis fidei christianae. Patrologia latina, cursus completus.* Ed. J. P. Migne. Vol. 176. Paris, 1880.

————. *Didascalicon: De studio legendi.* Ed. Charles Henry Buttimer. Washington: Catholic University of America, 1939.

————. *Didascalicon.* Trans. Jerome Taylor. New York: Columbia University Press, 1961.

————. *Epistola de beatae Mariae virginitate. Patrologia latina, cursus completus.* Ed. J. P. Migne. Vol. 176. Paris, 1880.

————. *On the Sacraments of the Christian Faith.* Trans. Roy J. Deferrari. Cambridge,

MA: Medieval Academy of America, 1951.

Huygens, R. B. C., ed. "Guillaume de Tyr étudiant: Un chapitre (XIX, 12) de son 'Histoire' retrouvé." *Latomus* 21 (1962): 811–29.

———, ed. "Metamorphosis Goliae." *Studi medievali* 3:2 (1962): 764–72.

Ivo of Chartres. *Correspondance*. Vol. 1. Ed. and trans. Jean Leclercq. Paris: Les Belles Lettres, 1949.

———. *Opera omnia. Patrologia latina, cursus completus*. Ed. J. P. Migne. Vols. 161–62. Paris, 1889.

Jacques de Vitry. *Chronicon Legenda aurea inserto. Monumenta Germaniae Historica, Scriptores rerum Germanicarum*. Vol. 24. Hannover, 1879.

Jerome. *Vita Pauli. Patrologia latina, cursus completus*. Ed. J. P. Migne. Vol. 23. Paris, 1883.

Joachim of Fiore (attributed). *Liber contra Lombardum*. Ed. Carmelo Ottaviano. Rome: Reale Accademia d'Italia, 1934.

John Damascene. *De fide orthodoxa: Versions of Burgundio and Cerbanus*. Ed. Eligius M. Buytaert. St. Bonaventure, NY: The Franciscan Institute, 1955.

———. *Writings*. Trans. Frederic H. Chase, Jr. New York: Fathers of the Church, Inc., 1958.

John of Salisbury. *Historia Pontificalis*. Ed. and trans. Marjorie Chibnall. Oxford: Clarendon Press, 1986.

———. *Memoirs of the Papal Court*. Ed. and trans. Marjorie Chibnall. London: Thomas Nelson and Sons Ltd., 1956.

———. *Metalogicon*. Ed. Clement C. J. Webb. Oxford: Clarendon Press, 1909.

———. *Metalogicon*. Trans. Daniel D. McGarry. Berkeley: University of California Press, 1955.

John Scottus Eriugena. *Commentaire sur l'Évangile de Jean*. Ed. and trans. Édouard Jeauneau. Sources chrétiennes, 180. Paris: Les Éditions du Cerf, 1972.

———. *Periphyseon*. Bk. 3. Ed. I. P. Sheldon-Williams and Ludwig Bieler. Scriptores latini hiberniae, 11. Dublin: Dublin Institute for Advanced Studies, 1981.

———. *Periphyseon*. Trans. Myra L. Uhlfelder. Comm. by Jean A. Potter. Indianapolis: Bobbs-Merrill Company, Inc., 1976.

Juvenal. *Saturae*. Ed. Ulrich Knoche. Munich: Max Hueber Verlag, 1950.

Landgraf, Artur Michael, ed. *Commentarius Cantabridgensis in Epistolas Pauli e schola Petri Abaelardi*. 4 vols. Notre Dame; University of Notre Dame Press, 1937–45.

———. ed. *Commentarius Porretanus in primam epistolam ad Corinthios*. Vatican City: Biblioteca Apostolica Vaticana, 1945.

———, ed. *Écrits théologiques de l'école d'Abélard*. Louvain: Spicilegium Sacrum Lovaniense, 1934.

Lanfranc of Canterbury. *In omnes Pauli epistolas commentarii cum glosula interjecta. Patrologia latina, cursus completus*. Ed. J. P. Migne. Vol. 150. Paris, 1880.

Lefèvre, Yves, ed. *L'Elucidarium et les lucidaires: Contribution, par l'histoire d'un texte, à l'histoire des croyances religieuses en France au moyen âge*. Paris: É. de Boccard, 1954.

Letbert of Lille. *In Psalmos LXXV commentarius. Patrologia latina, cursus completus*. Ed. J. P. Migne. Vol. 21. Paris, 1878.

Liber de sex principiis Gilberto Porretanae ascriptus. Ed. Albanus Heysse. Rev. ed. Damianus Van den Eynde. Münster: Aschendorff, 1953.

Lottin, Odon, ed. "Les 'Sententiae Atrebatenses'." *Recherches de théologie ancienne et médiévale* 10 (1938): 205–24, 344–57.

———, ed. *Psychologie et morale aux XII⁰ et XIII⁰ siècles*. Vols. 1–5. Louvain: Abbaye de Mont-César, 1940–59.

———, ed. "Quatre Sommes théologiques fragmentaires de l'école d'Anselme de Laon." In *Mélanges Auguste Pelzer: Études d'histoire littéraire et doctrinale de la scolastique médiévale offerts à Monseigneur Auguste Pelzer à l'occasion de son soixante-dixième anniversaire*. Louvain: Bibliothèque de la Université, 1947, pp. 81–108.

———, ed. "Questions inédits de Hugues de Saint-Victor." *Recherches de théologie ancienne et médiévale* 26 (1959): 177–213; 27 (1960): 42–66.

Luscombe, David E., ed. "Peter Abelard and His School." Vol 2. King's College

Cambridge Ph.D. diss., 1962 = *Sententiae Parisiensis* II.

Maccagnolo, Enzo, trans. *Il Divino e il megacosmo: Testi filosofici e scientifici della scuola di Chartres*. Milan: Rusconi, 1980.

Martin, Raymond-M., ed. "Un texte intéressant de Robert de Melun (Sententiae, libr. II, part. 2, cap. cxcvii–ccxiii)." *Revue d'histoire ecclésiastique* 28 (1932): 313–29.

Ordericus Vitalis. *The Ecclesiastical History*. Ed. and trans. Marjorie Chibnall. 6 vols. Oxford: Clarendon Press, 1969–80.

Ostlender, Henricus, ed. *Sententiae Florianensis*. Bonn: Petri Hanstein, 1929.

Otto of Freising. *Deeds of Frederick Barbarossa*. Trans. Christopher C. Mierow. New York: Columbia University Press, 1953.

Paucapalea. *Summa über das Decretum Gratiani*. Ed. Johann Friedrich von Schulte. Aalen: Scientia Verlag, 1965 [repr. of Giessen, 1890 ed.].

Peter Lombard. *Collectanea in omnes d. Pauli apostoli Epistolas*. Patrologia latina, cursus completus. Ed. J. P. Migne. Vols. 191–92. Paris, 1880.

———. *Commentaria in Psalmos*. Patrologia latina, cursus completus. Ed. J. P. Migne. Vol. 191. Paris, 1880.

———. *Sententiae in IV libris distinctae*. 3rd ed. rev. Ed. Ignatius C. Brady. 2 vols. Grottaferrata: Collegii S. Bonaventurae ad Claras Aquas, 1971–81.

———. *Sermones*. Patrologia latina, cursus completus. Ed. J. P. Migne. Vol. 171. Paris, 1893.

Peter of Poitiers. *Sententiae*. Patrologia latina, cursus completus. Ed. J. P. Migne. Vol. 211. Paris, 1855.

———. *Sententiae*. Bk. 1. Ed. Philip S. Moore and Marthe Dulong. Notre Dame: University of Notre Dame Press, 1961.

Piazzoni, Ambrogio M., ed. "Ugo di San Vittore 'auctor' delle 'Sententiae de divinitate'." *Studi medievali* 23:2 (1982): 861–955.

Pseudo-Bede. *De Psalmorum libro exegesis*. Patrologia latina, cursus completus. Ed. J. P. Migne. Vol. 93. Paris, 1862.

Pseudo-Bruno of Würzburg. *Expositio Psalmorum*. Patrologia latina, cursus completus. Ed. J. P. Migne. Vol. 142. Paris, 1880.

Quaestiones et decisiones in Epistolas d. Pauli. Patrologia latina, cursus completus. Ed. J. P. Migne. Vol. 175. Paris, 1879.

Ricobaldus of Ferrara. *Historia imperatorum Romano-Germanicorum a Carolo M. usque ad an. 1298 producta*. Ed. L. A. Muratori. Rerum Italicarum Scriptores. Vol. 9. Milan, 1726.

Robert of Melun. *Oeuvres*. Ed. Raymond-M. Martin. 4 vols. Louvain: Spicilegium Sacrum Lovaniense, 1932–52.

Robert of Torigni. *Chronica*. Ed. Richard Howlett. Rerum Brittanicarum medii aevi scriptores, 82:4. London: H. M. Stationery Office, 1889.

Robert Pullen, *Sententiarum libri octo*. Patrologia latina, cursus completus. Ed. J. P. Migne. Vol. 186. Paris, 1854.

Roland of Bologna. *Die Sentenzen Rolands*. Ed. Ambrosius M. Gietl. Amsterdam: Editions Rodopi, 1969 [repr. of Freiburg in Breisgau: Herder, 1891 ed.].

———. *Summa magistri Rolandi*. Ed. Friedrich Thaner. Aalen: Scientia Verlag, 1962 [repr. of Innsbruck, 1874 ed.].

Rupert of Deutz, *De sancta Trinitate et operibus eius*. 4 vols. Ed. Rabanus Haacke. Corpus christianorum, continuatio medievalis, 21–24. Turnhout: Brepols, 1971–72.

Sicard, Patrice, ed. *Hugues de Saint-Victor et son école*. Turnhout: Brepols, 1991.

Stegmüller, Friedrich, ed. "*Sententiae Berolinensis*: Eine neugefundene Sentenzensammlung aus der Schule des Anselms von Laon." *Recherches de théologie ancienne et médiévale* 11 (1939): 33–61.

———, ed. "*Sententiae Varsaviensis*: Ein neugefundenes Sentenzenwerk unter dem Einfluss des Anselms von Laon und des Peter Abaelard." *Divus Thomas* 45 (1942): 301–423.

Suger of St. Denis. *Vie de Louis VI le gros*. Ed. and trans. Henri Waquet. Paris:

Honoré Champion, 1929.
Thierry of Chartres. *Commentaries on Boethius by Thierry of Chartres and His School.* Ed.
Nikolaus M. Häring. Toronto: Pontifical Institute of Mediaeval Studies, 1971.
Trimborn, Johannes, ed. *Die Sententiae "Quoniam missio" aus der Abaelardschule.*
Inaugural-Dissertation, Köln. Cologne: Photostelle der Universität zu Köln,
1962 = *Sententiae Parisiensis* II.
Van den Eynde, Damien, ed. "Deux sermons inédits de Pierre Lombard." In
Miscellanea Lombardiana. Novara: Istituto Geografico de Agostini, 1957, pp.
75–87.
Victorinus, Marius. *Opera exegetica.* Ed. Franco Gori. Corpus scriptorum ecclesias-
ticorum latinorum, 83:2. Vienna: Hölder-Pichler-Tempsky, 1986.
———. *Opera theologica.* Ed. Paul Henry and Pierre Hadot. Corpus scriptorum
ecclesiasticorum latinorum, 83:1. Vienna: Hölder-Pichler-Tempsky, 1971.
Vincent of Beauvais. *Memoriale omnium temporum. Monumenta Germaniae Historica,
Scriptores rerum Germanicarum.* Vol. 24. Hannover, 1879.
Walter of Mortagne. *De trinitate. Patrologia latina, cursus completus.* Ed. J. P. Migne.
Vol. 209. Paris, 1855.
———. *Epistola ad Hugonem de S. Victore. Patrologia latina, cursus completus.* Ed. J. P.
Migne. Vol. 186. Paris, 1854.
Walter of St. Victor. "*Contra quatuor labyrinthos Franciae.*" Ed. P. Glorieux. *Archives
d'histoire doctrinale et littéraire du moyen âge* 19 (1952): 185–335.
Weisweiler, Heinrich, ed. *Das Schrifttum der Schule Anselms von Laon und Wilhelms von
Champeaux in deutschen Bibliotheken.* Beiträge zur Geschichte der Philosophie und
Theologie des Mittelalters, 33:1–2. Münster: Aschendorff, 1936.
———, ed. "Le recueil des sentences 'Deus de cuius principio et fine tacetur' et
son remaniement." *Recherches de théologie ancienne et médiévale* 5 (1933): 245–74.
———, ed. *Maître Simon et son groupe De sacramentis.* Louvain: Spicilegium Sacrum
Lovaniense, 1937.
Westra, Haijo Jan, ed. *The Commentary on Martianus Capella's De Nuptiis Philologiae et
Mercurii Attributed to Bernard Silvestris.* Toronto: Pontifical Institute of Mediaeval
Studies, 1986.
William Andrensus. *Chronica. Monumenta Germaniae Historica, Scriptores rerum Germa-
nicarum.* Vol. 24. Hannover, 1879.
William of Conches. *De philosophia mundi. Patrologia latina, cursus completus.* Ed. J. P.
Migne. Vol. 172. Paris, 1854.
———. *Elementorum philosophiae. Patrologia latina, cursus completus.* Ed. J. P. Migne.
Vol. 90. Paris, 1862.
———. *Glosae in Iuvenalem.* Ed. Bradford Wilson. Paris: J. Vrin, 1980.
———. *Glosae super Platonem.* Ed. Édouard Jeauneau. Paris: J. Vrin, 1965.
———. *Philosophia mundi.* Bk. 1. Ed. Gregor Maurach. Pretoria: University of
South Africa, 1974.
William of St. Thierry. *De erroribus Guillelmi de Conchis. Patrologia latina, cursus
completus.* Ed. J. P. Migne. Vol. 180. Paris, 1855.
———. *Expositio in Epistolam ad Romanos. Patrologia latina, cursus completus.* Ed. J. P.
Migne. Vol. 180. Paris, 1902.

Secondary Sources

Affeldt, Werner. *Die weltliche Gewalt in der Paulus-Exegese: Röm. 13, 1–7 in den
Römerbriefkommentaren der lateinischen Kirche bis zum Ende des 13. Jahrhunderts.* Göt-
tingen: Vandenhoeck & Ruprecht, 1969.
———. "Verzeichnis der Römerbriefkommentare der lateinischen Kirche bis zu
Nikolaus von Lyra." *Traditio* 15 (1957): 369–406.
Alesandro, John A. *Gratian's Notion of Marital Consummation.* Rome: Officium Libri
Catholici, 1971.
Allard, Henri A. J. *Die eheliche Lebens- und Liebesgemeinschaft nach Hugo von St. Viktor.*
Rome: Analecta Dehoniana, 1963.

Alszeghy, Z. *Nova creatura: La nozione della grazia nei commentari medievali di S. Paolo.* Rome: Universitas Gregoriana, 1956.

Anastos, Milton V. "Some Aspects of Byzantine Influence on Latin Thought." In *Twelfth-Century Europe and the Foundations of Modern Society.* Ed. Marshall Claggett, Gaines Post, and Robert Reynolds. Madison: University of Wisconsin Press, 1961, pp. 131–87.

Anciaux, Paul. *La théologie du sacrement de pénitence au XII* siècle.* Louvain: É. Nauwelaerts, 1949.

Anders, F. *Die Christologie des Robert von Melun.* Paderborn: Ferdinand Schöningh, 1927.

Annat, J. "Pierre Lombard et ses sources patristiques." *Bulletin de littérature ecclésiastique,* ser. 3:8 (1906): 84–95.

Arduini, Maria Lodovica. "Considerazioni sul Liber III del *De misericordia et iustitia* e del *De sacramentis* di Algero di Liegi: Ipotesi interpretativa." *Proceedings of the Seventh International Congress of Medieval Canon Law.* Ed. Peter Linehan. Vatican City: Biblioteca Apostolica Vaticana, 1988, pp. 171–95.

Balducelli, Ruggero. *Il concetto teologico di carità attraverso le maggiori interpretazioni patristiche e medievali di I ad Cor. XIII.* Washington: Catholic University of America Press, 1951.

Baldwin, John W. *Masters, Princes, and Merchants: The Social Views of Peter the Chanter and His Circle.* 2 vols. Princeton: Princeton University Press, 1970.

Baltus, Urbain. "Dieu d'après Hugues de St.-Victor." *Revue bénédictine* 15 (1898): 109–23, 200–14.

Baltzer, Otto. *Die Sentenzen des Petrus Lombardus: Ihre Quellen und ihre dogmengeschichtliche Bedeutung.* Leipzig: Dieterich'sche Verlags-Buchhandlung, 1902.

Bardy, G. "La littérature patristique des '*Quaestiones et responses*' sur l'Écriture sainte." *Revue biblique* 41 (1932): 210–36, 341–69, 515–37; 42 (1933): 14–30, 211–29, 328–52.

Barkholt, Erich. *Die Ontologie Hugos von St. Viktor.* Inaugural-Dissertation, Universität Bonn, 1930.

Baron, Roger. "Étude sur l'authenticité de l'oeuvre de Hugues de Saint-Victor d'après les MSS. Paris Maz. 717, BN 14506, et Douai 360–366." *Scriptorium* 10 (1956): 182–220.

———. "Hugues de Saint-Victor: Contribution à un nouvel examen de son oeuvre." *Traditio* 15 (1959): 223–97.

———. "La pensée mariale de Hugues de Saint-Victor." *Revue d'ascétique et de mystique* 31 (1955): 249–71.

———. "La situation de l'homme d'après Hugues de Saint-Victor." In *L'Homme et son destin d'après les penseurs du moyen âge.* Louvain: Éditions Nauwelaerts, 1960, pp. 431–36.

———. "Le 'sacrement de la foi' selon Hugues de Saint-Victor." *Revue des sciences philosophiques et théologiques* 42 (1958): 50–78.

———. "L'Idée de liberté chez S. Anselme et Hugues de Saint-Victor." *Recherches de théologie ancienne et médiévale* 32 (1965): 117–21.

———. "L'Idée de nature chez Hugues de Saint-Victor." In *La filosofia della natura nel medioevo.* Milan: Vita e Pensiero, 1966, pp. 260–63.

———. "L'Influence de Hugues de Saint-Victor." *Recherches de théologie ancienne et médiévale* 22 (1955): 56–71.

———. "Note sur la succession et la date des écrits de Hugues de Saint-Victor." *Revue d'histoire ecclésiastique* 57 (1962): 88–118.

———. "Note sur l'énigmatique 'Somme de Sentences'." *Recherches de théologie ancienne et médiévale* 25 (1958), 26–46.

———. *Science et sagesse chez Hugues de Saint-Victor.* Paris: P. Lethielleux, 1957.

Basdavant-Gaudemet, Brigitte. "Le marriage d'après la correspondance d'Yves de Chartres." *Revue historique de droit français et étranger* 61 (1983), 195–215.

Baumkirschner, Robert. "Bernhard von Clairvaux als Kirchenlehrer in dogmengeschichtlicher Schau." *Cistercienser Chronik* 86, n.F. 145 (1979): 85–102.

Bautier, Robert-Henri. "Paris au temps d'Abélard." In *Abélard en son temps*. Ed. Jean Jolivet. Paris: Les Belles Lettres, 1981, pp. 21–77.

Bavel, Tarsicius J. van. *Recherches sur la christologie de Saint Augustin: L'humain et le divin dans le Christ d'après Saint Augustin*. Fribourg, Suisse: Éditions Universitaires, 1954.

Bazán, Bernardo C. "La *quaestio disputata*," In *Les Genres littéraires dans les sources théologiques et philosophiques médiévales: Définition, critique et exploitation*. Louvain-la-Neuve: Institut d'Études Médiévales, 1982, pp. 31–49.

Bell, David N. "Esse, Vivere, Intelligere: The Noetic Triad and the Image of God." *Recherches de théologie ancienne et médiévale* 52 (1985): 5–43.

Benton, John F. "A Reconsideration of the Authenticity of the Correspondence of Abelard and Heloise." In *Petrus Abaelardus (1079–1142): Person, Werk und Wirkung*. Ed. Rudolf Thomas. Trier: Paulinus-Verlag, 1980, pp. 41–52.

———. "Consciousness of Self and Perception of Individuality." In *Renaissance and Renewal in the Twelfth Century*. Ed. Robert L. Benson and Giles Constable. Cambridge, MA: Harvard University Press, 1982, pp. 263–95.

Beonio-Brocchieri [Fumagalli], Mariateresa. "Concepts philosophiques dans l'Historia Calamitatum et dans autres oeuvres abélardiennes." In *Petrus Abaelardus (1079–1142): Person, Werk und Wirkung*. Ed. Rudolf Thomas. Trier: Paulinus-Verlag, 1980, pp. 121–24.

———. *Introduzione a Abelardo*. Rome: Laterza, 1974.

———. "La relation entre logique, physique et théologie chez Abélard," In *Peter Abelard*. Ed. Eligius M. Buytaert. Leuven: Leuven University Press, 1974, pp. 153–62.

———. *The Logic of Abelard*. Trans. Simon Pleasance. Dordrecht: D. Reidel, 1969.

Beonio-Brocchiere [Fumagalli], Mariateresa and Parodi, Massimo. *Storia della filosofia medievale da Boezio a Wyclif*. Bari: Laterza, 1989.

Bergeron, M. "La structure du concept latin de personne: Comment, chez les Latins, 'persona' en est venu à signifier 'relatio'." In *Études d'histoire littéraire et doctrinale du XIIIᵉ siècle*, 2nd ser. Paris: J. Vrin, 1932, pp. 121–61.

Bertola, Ermenegildo. "I commentari paolini di Pietro Lombardo e la loro duplice redazione." *Pier Lombardo* 3:2–3 (1959): 75–90.

———. "Il problema delle creature angeliche in Pier Lombardo." *Pier Lombardo* 1:2 (1957): 33–54.

———. "Il problema di Dio in Pier Lombardo." *Rivista di filosofia neo-scolastica* 48 (1956): 135–50.

———. "I precedenti storici del metodo del 'Sic et non' di Abelardo." *Rivista di filosofia neo-scolastica* 53 (1961): 255–80.

———. "La dottrina della creazione nel *Liber Sententiarum* di Pier Lombardo." *Pier Lombardo* 1:1 (1957): 27–44.

———. "La dottrina lombardiana dell'anima nella storia delle dottrine psicologiche del XII secolo." *Pier Lombardo* 3:1 (1959): 3–18.

———. "La dottrina morale di Pietro Abelardo." *Recherches de théologie ancienne et médiévale* 55 (1988): 53–71.

———. "La 'Glossa ordinaria' biblica ed i suoi problemi." *Recherches de théologie ancienne et médiévale* 45 (1978): 34–78.

———. "La scuola di Gilberto de la Porrée." In *Saggi e studi di filosofia medioevale*. Padua: CEDAM, 1951, pp. 19–34.

———. "Le critiche di Abelardo ad Anselmo di Laon ed a Guglielmo di Champeaux." *Rivista di filosofia neo-scolastica* 52 (1960): 495–522.

———. "Le 'Sententiae' e le 'Summae' tra il XII e il XIII secolo." *Pier Lombardo* 2:2 (1958): 25–41.

———. "Le 'Sententiae Florianenses' della scuola de Abelardo." In *Saggi e studi di filosofia medioevale*. Padua: CEDAM, 1951, pp. 5–18.

———. "Pietro Lombardo nella storiografia filosofica medioevale." *Pier Lombardo* 4 (1960): 95–113.

———. *San Bernardo e la teologia speculativa*. Padua: CEDAM, 1959.

Beumer, Johannes. "Der theoretische Beitrag der Frühscholastik zu dem Problem des Dogmenfortschrittes." *Zeitschrift für katholische Theologie* 74 (1952): 205–26.

———. "Zur Ekklesiologie der Frühscholastik." *Scholastik* 26 (1951): 364–89.

Bischoff, Bernhard. "Aus der Schule Hugos von St. Viktor." In *Aus der Geisteswelt der Mittelalter: Studien und Texte Martin Grabmann zur Vollendung des 60. Lebensjahres von Freunden und Schülern gewidmet.* Vol. 1. Ed. Albert Lang, Joseph Lechner, and Michael Schmaus. Beiträge zur Geschichte der Philosophie des Mittelalters, Supplementband, 3:1. Münster, Aschendorff, 1935, pp. 346–50.

———. "Das griechische Element in der abendländischen Bildung des Mittelalters." *Byzantinische Zeitschrift* 44 (1951): 27–35.

———. "Zur Kritik der Heerwagenschen Ausgabe von Bedas Werken (Basel, 1563)." In *Mittelalterliche Studien: Ausgewählte Aufsätze zur Schriftkunde und Literargeschichte.* Vol 1. Stuttgart: Anton Hiersemann, 1966, pp. 112–17.

Blic, J. de. "L'oeuvre exégètique de Walafrid Strabon et la *Glossa ordinaria*." *Recherches de théologie ancienne et médiévale* 16 (1949): 5–28.

Bliemetzrieder, Franz. "Autour de l'oeuvre théologique d'Anselme de Laon." *Recherches de théologie ancienne et médiévale* 1 (1929): 435–83.

———. "Gratian und die Schule Anselms von Laon." *Archiv für katholische Kirchenrecht* 112 (1932): 37–63.

———. "L'oeuvre d'Anselme de Laon et la littérature théologique contemporaine: I. Honorius d'Autun." *Recherches de théologie ancienne et médiévale* 5 (1933): 275–91.

———. "L'oeuvre d'Anselme de Laon et la littérature théologique contemporaine: II. Hugues de Rouen." *Recherches de théologie ancienne et médiévale* 6 (1934): 261–83; 7 (1935): 28–51.

———. "Note sur la 'Summa sententiarum'." *Recherches de théologie ancienne et médiévale* 6 (1934): 411–12.

———. "Robert von Melun und die Schule Anselms von Laon." *Zeitschrift für Kirchengeschichte* 53 (1934): 117–70.

———. "Trente-trois pièces inédits de l'oeuvre d'Anselme de Laon." *Recherches de théologie ancienne et médiévale* 2 (1930): 54–79.

———. *Zu den Schriften Ivos von Chartres (d. 1116): Ein literargeschichtlicher Beitrag.* Kaiserliche Akademie der Wissenschaften in Wien, philosophisch-historische Klasse, 186:6. Vienna, 1917.

Blomme, Robert. "A propos de la définition du péché chez Pierre Abélard." *Ephemerides Theologicae Lovanienses* 33 (1957): 319–47.

———. *La doctrine du péché dans les écoles théologiques de la première moitié du XIIe siècle.* Louvain: Publications Universitaires de Louvain, 1958.

Blumenthal, Uta-Renate. "Cardinal Albinus of Abano and the *Digesta pauperis scholaris Albini*, MS. Ottob. lat. 3057." *Archivum Historiae Pontificiae* 20 (1982): 7–49.

Boh, Ivan. "Divine Omnipotence in the Early *Sentences*." In *Divine Omniscience and Omnipotence in Medieval Philosophy: Islamic, Jewish and Christian Perspectives.* Ed. Tamar Rudavsky. Dordrecht: D. Reidel, 1985, pp. 185–211.

Borst, Arno. "Abälard und Bernhard." *Historische Zeitschrift* 186 (1958): 497–526.

Bougerol, Jacques-Guy. *La théologie de l'espérance aux XIIe et XIIIe siècles.* 2 vols. Paris: Études Augustiniennes, 1985.

Bournazel, Éric. *Le gouvernement capétien au XIIe siècle, 1108–1180: Structures sociales et mutations institutionnelles.* Paris: PUF, 1975.

Boussard, Jacques. *Nouvelle histoire de Paris: De la fin du siège de 885–886 à la mort de Philippe-Auguste.* Paris: Hachette, 1976.

Brady, Ignatius C. "Peter Lombard." In *New Catholic Encyclopedia.* Vol. 11. New York: McGraw-Hill Book Company, 1967, pp. 221–22.

———. "Peter Lombard: Canon of Notre-Dame." *Recherches de théologie ancienne et médiévale* 32 (1965): 277–95.

———. "Peter Manducator and the Oral Teachings of Peter Lombard." *Antonianum* 41 (1966): 454–90.

———. "The Distinctions of Lombard's Book of Sentences and Alexander of Hales." *Franciscan Studies* 25 (1965): 90–116.

———. "The Rubrics of Peter Lombard's Sentences." *Pier Lombardo* 6 (1962): 5–25.

———. "The Three Editions of the 'Liber Sententiarum' of Master Peter Lombard (1882–1977)." *Archivum Franciscanum Historicum* 70 (1977): 400–11.

Brancaforte, Antonio. "Contributo di Pietro Lombardo all'unità del pensiero medioevale." *Teoresi* 8 (1953): 230–45.

Bresch, Jean. *Essai sur les Sentences de Pierre Lombard considérées sous le point de vue historico-dogmatique.* Strasbourg: Imprimerie de la Veuve Berger-Levrault, 1857.

Brinckmann, Hennig. "Verhüllung ('integumentum') als literarische Darstellung im Mittelalter." In *Der Begriff der Repraesentatio im Mittelalter: Stellvertretung, Symbol, Zeichen, Bild.* Miscellanea mediaevalia, 8. Ed. Albert Zimmerman. Berlin: Walter de Gruyter, 1971, pp. 314–39.

Brooke, Christopher N. L. *Marriage in Christian History.* Cambridge: Cambridge University Press, 1978.

Browe, Peter. "Die Letzte Ölung in der abendländischen Kirche des Mittelalters." *Zeitschrift für katholische Theologie* 55 (1931): 515–61.

Brown, Stephen F. "Abelard and the Medieval Origins of the Distinction between God's Absolute and Ordained Power." In *Ad litteram: Authoritative Texts and Their Medieval Readers.* Ed. Mark D. Jordan and Kent Emery, Jr. Notre Dame: University of Notre Dame Press, 1992, pp. 199–215.

Bruder, Karl. *Die philosophischen Elemente in dem Opuscula sacra des Boethius: Ein Beitrag zur Quellengeschichte der Philosophie der Scholastik.* Leipzig: Felix Meiner, 1928.

Brundage, James A. "Impotence, Frigidity, and Marital Nullity in the Decretists and Early Decretalists." In *Proceedings of the Seventh International Congress of Medieval Canon Law.* Ed. Peter Linehan. Vatican City: Biblioteca Apostolica Vaticana, 1988, pp. 407–23.

———. *Law, Sex, and Christian Society in Medieval Europe.* Chicago: University of Chicago Press, 1987.

———. "Marriage and Sexuality in the Decretals of Pope Alexander III." In *Miscellanea Rolando Bandinelli papa Alessandro III.* Ed. Filippo Liotta. Siena: Accademia senese degli Intronati, 1986, pp. 59–83.

———. "Sexual Equality in Medieval Canon Law." In *Medieval Women and the Sources of Medieval History.* Ed. Joel T. Rosenthal. Athens, GA: University of Georgia Press, 1990, pp. 66–78.

Bünger, Fritz. "Darstellung und Würdigung der Lehre des Petrus Lombardus vom Werke Christi (Sentent. 1. III, dist. 18–20)." *Zeitschrift für wissenschaftlichen Theologie* 45 (1902): 92–126.

Burnett, Charles S. F. "A New Text for the 'School of Abelard' Dossier?" *Archives d'histoire doctrinale et littéraire du moyen âge* 55 (1988): 7–21.

Burns, J. Patout. "The Concept of Satisfaction in Medieval Redemption Theory." *Theological Studies* 36 (1975): 285–304.

Buytaert, Eligius M. "Abelard's *Collationes.*" *Antonianum* 44 (1969): 18–39.

———. "Abelard's 'Expositio in Hexaemeron'." *Antonianum* 43 (1968): 163–94.

———. "Abelard's Trinitarian Doctrine." In *Peter Abelard.* Ed. Eligius M. Buytaert. Leuven: Leuven University Press, 1974, pp. 127–54.

———. "An Earlier Redaction of the 'Theologia Christiana' of Abelard." *Antonianum* 38 (1961): 481–95.

———. "Critical Observations on the 'Theologia Christiana' of Abelard." *Antonianum* 38 (1963): 384–433.

———. "St. John Damascene, Peter Lombard, and Gerhoh of Reichersberg." *Franciscan Studies* 10 (1950): 323–43.

———. "The Anonymous Capitula Haeresum Petri Abaelardi and the Synod of Sens, 1140." *Antonianum* 43 (1968): 419–60.

———. "The Greek Fathers in Abelard's 'Theologies' and Commentary on St. Paul." *Antonianum* 39 (1964): 408–36.

———. "Thomas of Morigny and the 'Apologia' of Abelard." *Antonianum* 42 (1967): 25–54.

———. "Thomas of Morigny and the 'Theologia Scholarium' of Abelard." *Anto-*

nianum 40 (1965): 71–95.

Caprioli, Adriano. "Alle origini della 'definizione' di sacramento: Da Berengario a Pier Lombardo." *La Scuola Cattolica* 102 (1974): 718–43.

Carpino, Francesco. "Consensi e critiche ad una teoria sull'assoluzione sacramentale nel sec. XII." *La Scuola Cattolica* 67 (1939): 308–25.

———. "Una difficoltà contro la confessione nella scolastica primitiva: Anselmo di Laon e la sua scuola." *Divus Thomas* ser. 3ª, 16 (1939): 94–103.

———. "Un tentativo al secolo XII per valorizzare l'assoluzione sacramentale." *La Scuola Cattolica* 66 (1938): 281–98.

Carra de Vaux Saint-Cyr, M. B. "*Disputatio catholicorum Patrum adversus dogmata Petri Abaelardi.*" *Revue des sciences philosophiques et théologiques* 47 (1963): 205–20.

Cavallera, Ferdinand. "D'Anselme de Laon à Pierre Lombard." *Bulletin de littérature ecclésiastique* 41 (1940): 40–54, 103–14.

———. "Les *De sacramentis* de Hugues de Saint-Victor: Rapports du Dialogue et du Traité." *Bulletin de littérature ecclésiastique* 41 (1940): 207–10.

———. "Saint Augustin et le Livre des Sentences de Pierre Lombard." In *Études sur Saint Augustin* by Régis Jolivet et al. Paris: Gabriel Beauchesne, 1930, pp. 186–99.

Châtillon, Jean. "Abélard et les écoles." In *Abélard en son temps.* Ed. Jean Jolivet. Paris: Les Belles Lettres, 1981, pp. 133–60.

———. "Achard de Saint-Victor et les controverses christologiques du XIIᵉ siècle." In *Mélanges offerts au R.P. Ferdinand Cavallera.* Toulouse: Bibliothèque de l'Institut Catholique, 1948, pp. 117–37.

———. "De Guillaume de Champeaux à Thomas Gallus: Chronique d'histoire littéraire et doctrinale de l'école de Saint-Victor." *Revue du moyen âge latin* 8 (1952): 139–62, 245–72.

———. "La Bible dans les écoles du XIIᵉ siècle." In *Le moyen âge et la Bible.* Ed. Pierre Riché and Guy Lobrichon. Paris: Beauchesne, 1984, pp. 163–97.

———. "La culture de l'école de Saint-Victor au 12ᵉ siècle." In *Entretiens sur la renaissance du 12ᵉ siècle.* Ed. Maurice de Gandillac and Édouard Jeauneau. Paris: Mouton, 1968, pp. 147–60.

———. "Latran III et l'enseignement christologique de Pierre Lombard." In *Le troisième concile de Latran (1179): Sa place dans l'histoire.* Ed. Jean Longère. Paris: Études Augustiniennes, 1982, pp. 75–90.

———. "Les écoles de Chartres et de Saint-Victor." In *La scuola nell'occidente latino dell'alto medioevo.* Settimane di studi del Centro italiano di studi sull'alto medioevo, 19:2. Spoleto: Presso la Sede del Centro, 1972, pp. 795–839.

———. "L'Influence de S. Bernard sur la pensée scolastique au XIIᵉ et au XIIIᵉ siècle." In *D'Isidore de Seville à saint Thomas d'Aquin: Études d'histoire et de théologie.* London: Variorum, 1985, pp. 268–88.

———. "Quidquid convenit filio dei per naturam convenit filio hominis per gratiam: A propos de Jean de Ripa, *Determinationes*, I, 4, 4." *Divinitas* 11 (1967): 715–28.

———. "Une ecclésiologie médiévale: L'Idée de l'église dans le théologie de l'école de Saint-Victor au XIIᵉ siècle." *Irénikon* 22 (1949): 115–38, 395–411.

Chavasse, Antoine. *Étude sur l'onction des infirmes dans l'église latine du IIIᵉ au XIᵉ siècle.* Vol. 1. Lyon, 1942.

Chenu, Marie-Dominique. "Involucrum: Le mythe selon les théologiens médiévaux." *Archives d'histoire doctrinale et littéraire du moyen âge* 22 (1955): 75–79.

———. *La théologie au douzième siècle.* Paris: J. Vrin, 1957.

———. "Platon à Cîteaux." *Archives d'histoire doctrinale et littéraire du moyen âge* 29 (1954): 99–106.

———. "Une opinion inconnue de l'école de Gilbert de la Porrée." *Revue d'histoire ecclésiastique* 26 (1930): 347–52.

———. "Un essai de méthode théologique au XIIᵉ siècle." *Revue des sciences philosophiques et théologiques* 24 (1935): 258–67.

Chibnall, Marjorie. *The World of Ordericus Vitalis.* Oxford: Clarendon Press, 1984.

Chossat, Marcel. *La Somme des Sentences: Oeuvre de Hugues de Mortagne vers 1155.* Louvain: Spicilegium Sacrum Lovaniense, 1923.

Cioni, Laura. "Il concilio di Reims nelle fonti contemporanee." *Aevum* 53 (1979): 273–300.

Claeys-Boúúaert, P. "La Summa Sententiarum appartient-elle à Hugues de Saint-Victor?" *Revue d'histoire ecclésiastique* 10 (1909): 278–89, 710–19.

Clanchy, M. T. "Abelard's Mockery of St. Anselm." *Journal of Ecclesiastical History* 41 (1990): 1–23.

Clark, Elizabeth A. "Vitiated Seeds and Holy Vessels: Augustine's Manichean Past." In *Ascetic Piety and Women's Faith: Essays on Late Ancient Christianity.* Lewiston, NY: Edwin Mellen Press, 1986, pp. 291–349.

Classen, Peter. *Burgundio von Pisa: Richter, Gesandter, Übersetzer.* Sitzungsberichte der heidelberger Akademie der Wissenschaften, philosophisch-historische Klasse, 4. Heidelberg: Carl Winter, 1974.

———. *Gerhoch von Reichersberg: Eine Biographie.* Wiesbaden: Franz Steiner Verlag GMBH, 1960.

Clerck, D. E. de. "Droits du démon et nécessité de la rédemption: Les écoles d'Abélard et de Pierre Lombard." *Recherches de théologie ancienne et médiévale* 14 (1947): 32–64.

———. "Le dogme de la rédemption de Robert de Melun à Guillaume d'Auxerre." *Recherches de théologie ancienne et médiévale* 14 (1947): 253–86.

———. "Questions de sotériologie médiévale." *Recherches de théologie ancienne et médiévale* 13 (1946): 150–84.

Clerval, A. *Les Écoles de Chartres au moyen-âge du Vᵉ au XVIᵉ siècle.* Mémoires de la Société archéologique d'Eure-et-Loir, 11. Chartres: R. Selleret, 1895.

Cloes, Henri. "La systématisation théologique pendant la première moitié du XIIᵉ siècle." *Ephemerides Theologicae Lovanienses* 34 (1958): 277–329.

Colish, Marcia L. "Another Look at the School of Laon." *Archives d'histoire doctrinale et littéraire du moyen âge* 53 (1986): 7–22.

———. "Early Porretan Theology." *Recherches de théologie ancienne et médiévale* 56 (1989): 58–79.

———. "From *sacra pagina* to *theologia*: Peter Lombard as an Exegete of Romans." *Medieval Perspectives* 6 (1991): 1–19.

———. "Gilbert, the Early Porretans, and Peter Lombard: Semantics and Theology." In *Gilbert de Poitiers et ses contemporaines: Aux origines de la logica modernorum.* Ed. Jean Jolivet and Alain de Libera. Naples: Bibliopolis, 1987, pp. 229–50.

———. "Peter Lombard and Abelard: The *Opinio Nominalium* and Divine Transcendence." *Vivarium* 30 (1992): 139–56.

———. "Peter Lombard as an Exegete of St. Paul." In *Ad litteram: Authoritative Texts and Their Medieval Readers.* Ed. Mark D. Jordan and Kent Emery, Jr. Notre Dame: University of Notre Dame Press, 1992, pp. 71–92.

———. "*Psalterium Scholasticorum*: Peter Lombard and the Development of Scholastic Psalms Exegesis." *Speculum* 67 (1992): 531–48.

———. "*Quae hodie locum non habent*: Scholastic Theologians Reflect on Their Authorities." In *Proceedings of the PMR Conference*, 15. Ed. Phillip Pulsiano. Villanova: Augustinian Historical Institute, 1990, pp. 1–17.

———. "St. Anselm's Philosophy of Language Reconsidered." In *Anselm Studies*, 1. Ed. Gillian R. Evans. London: Kraus International, 1983, pp. 113–23.

———. "Systematic Theology and Theological Renewal in the Twelfth Century." *Journal of Medieval and Renaissance Studies* 18 (1988): 135–56.

Colker, Marvin L. "The Trial of Gilbert of Poitiers, 1148: A Previously Unknown Record." *Mediaeval Studies* 27 (1965): 152–83.

Cottiaux, Jean. "La conception de la théologie chez Abélard." *Revue d'histoire ecclésiastique* 28 (1932): 247–95, 533–51, 788–828.

Courcelle, Pierre. "Étude critique sur les commentaires de la Consolation de Boèce (IXᵉ-XVᵉ siècles)." *Archives d'histoire doctrinale et littéraire du moyen âge* 12 (1939): 5–140.

————. "L'Âme en cage." In *Parusia: Studien zur Philosophie Platons und zur Problemgeschichte des Platonismus. Festgabe für Johannes Hirschberger*. Ed. Kurt Flasch. Frankfurt: Minerva GMBH, 1965, pp. 103–16.

Courtenay, William J. *Capacity and Volition: A History of the Distinction of Absolute and Ordained Power*. Bergamo: Pierluigi Lubrina, 1990.

————. "Newly Identified 'Sentences' Commentaries in the Stuttgart Landesbibliothek." *Scriptorium* 41 (1987): 113–15.

————. "*Nominales* and Nominalism in the Twelfth Century." In *Lectionum varietates: Hommage à Paul Vignaux*. Ed. Jean Jolivet et al. Paris: J. Vrin, 1991, pp. 11–48.

————. "Sacrament, Symbol, and Causality in Bernard of Clairvaux." In *Bernard of Clairvaux: Studies Presented to Dom Jean Leclercq*. Washington: Cistercian Publications, 1973, pp. 111–22.

————. "Schools and Schools of Thought in the Twelfth Century." Unpublished.

Courtney, F. *Cardinal Robert Pullen: An English Theologian of the Twelfth Century*. Rome: Universitas Gregorianae, 1954.

Creussen, J. "'Tractatus magistri Symonis de sacramentis,' eine Vermutliche Quelle der 'Sententiae Divinitatis'." *Theologische Revue* 11 (1912): 125–26.

Crocco, Antonio. *Gioacchino da Fiore: La più singolare ed affascinante figura del medioevo cristiano*. Naples: Edizioni Empirico, 1960.

Crouse, Robert D. "Honorius Augustodunensis: Disciple of Anselm?" In *Analecta Anselmiana*, 4:2. Ed. Helmut Kohlenberger. Frankfurt: Minerva, 1975, pp. 131–39.

Croydon, F. E. "Abbot Laurance of Westminster and Hugh of St. Victor." *Mediaeval and Renaissance Studies*, 2 (1950): 169–71.

Dahmen, Reiner. *Darstellung der Abälardischen Ethik*. Münster: Robert Noske, 1906.

Daly, Saralyn R. "Peter Comestor: Master of Histories." *Speculum* 32 (1957): 62–73.

Dane, Joseph A. "*Integmentum* as Interpretation: Note on William of Conches's Commentary on Macrobius (I, 2, 10–11)." *Classical Folia* 32 (1978): 201–15.

Daniel, E. Randolph. "The Double Procession of the Holy Spirit in Joachim of Fiore's Understanding of History." *Speculum* 55 (1980): 469–83.

Dauvillier, Jean. *Le mariage dans le droit classique de l'église depuis le Décret de Gratien (1140) jusqu'à la mort de Clément V (1314)*. Paris: Sirey, 1933.

Davis, Scott. "The Unity of the Virtues in Abelard's *Dialogues*. In *Proceedings of the PMR Conference*, 11. Ed. Phillip Pulsiano. Villanova: Augustinian Historical Institute, 1986, pp. 71–82.

Debil, A. "La première distinction de De poenitentia de Gratien." *Revue d'histoire ecclésiastique* 15 (1914): 251–73, 442–55.

Déchanet, Jean-Marie. "La christologie de saint Bernard." In *Bernhard von Clairvaux: Mönch und Mystiker*. Ed. Joseph Lortz. Wiesbaden: Franz Steiner Verlag GMBH, 1955, pp. 63–75.

————. "La christologie de S. Bernard." In *Saint Bernard théologien*. Rome: Tipografia Pio X, 1953, pp. 78–91.

————. "L'Amitié d'Abélard et de Guillaume de Saint-Thierry." *Revue d'histoire ecclésiastique* 35 (1939): 761–73.

Decker, Raymond G. "Institutional Authority versus Personal Responsibility in the Marriage Canons of Gratian's *A Concordance of Discordant Canons*." *The Jurist* 32 (1972): 51–65.

Delhaye, Philippe. *Enseignement et morale au XIIᵉ siècle*. Fribourg, Suisse: Éditions Universitaires, 1988.

————. "La nature dans l'oeuvre de Hugues de Saint-Victor." In *La filosofia della natura nel medioevo*. Milan: Vita e Pensiero, 1966, pp. 272–78.

————. "Le Dossier anti-matrimoniale de l'*Adversus Jovinianum* et son influence sur quelques écrits latins du XIIᵉ siècle." *Mediaeval Studies* 13 (1951): 65–86.

————. "L'enseignement de philosophie morale au XIIᵉ siècle." *Mediaeval Studies* 11 (1949): 77–99.

————. "L'Enseignement morale des *Sententiae Parisienses*." In *Études de civilisation médiévale (IX–XIIᵉ siècles): Mélanges offerts à Edmond-René Labande.* Poitiers: Centre d'Études Supérieures de Civilisation Médiévale, 1974, pp. 197–207.

——. "L'organisation scolaire au XIIᵉ siècle." *Traditio* 5 (1947): 211–68.

——. *Pierre Lombard: Sa vie, ses oeuvres, sa morale.* Montreal: Institut d'Études Médiévales, 1961.

——. "Un dossier eucharistique d'Anselme de Laon à l'abbaye de Fécamp." In *L'Abbaye bénédictine de Fécamp: Ouvrage scientifique du XIIIᵉ centenaire, 658–1958.* Vol. 2. Fécamp: L. Durand et Fils, 1960, pp. 153–61.

DeLubac, Henri. "A propos de la formule: *diversi sed non adversi.*" In *Mélanges Jules Lebreton = Recherches de science religieuse* 40 (1952): 2: 27–40.

——. *Corpus Mysticum: L'Eucharistie et l'église au moyen âge.* 2nd ed. Paris: Aubier, 1949.

——. *Exégèse médiévale: Les quatre sens de l'écriture.* Vol 2:1–2. Paris: Aubier, 1961–64.

——. "La *res sacramenti* chez Gerhoh de Reichersberg." In *Études de critique et d'histoire religieuses.* Lyon: Facultés Catholiques, 1948, pp. 35–42.

Denifle, Heinrich. *Die abendländischen Schriftauslegung bis Luther über justitia Dei (Rom. 1, 17) und justificatio.* Mainz: Kirchheim & Co., 1905.

——. "Die Sentenzen Abaelards und die Bearbeitung seiner Theologia vor Mitte des 12. Jahrhunderts." *Archiv für Literatur- und Kirchengeschichte des Mittelalters,* 1 (1885): 402–69, 584–624.

——. "Quel livre servait de base à l'enseignement des maîtres en théologie?" *Revue thomiste* 2 (1894): 149–61.

DeRijk, L. M. "De quelques difficultés de nature linguistique dans le vocabulaire de Gilbert de la Porrée." In *Actes du Colloque Terminologie de la vie intellectuelle au moyen âge.* Ed. Olga Weijers. Turnhout: Brepols, 1988, pp. 19–25.

De Siano, Frank. "Of God and Man: Consequences of Abelard's Ethics." *Thomist* 35 (1971): 631–60.

Dhanis, Édouard. "Quelques anciennes formules septénaires des sacrements." *Revue d'histoire ecclésiastique* 26 (1930): 574–608, 916–50; 27 (1931): 5–26.

Didier, J. C. "Pour la fiche *Regio dissimilitudinis.*" *Mélanges de science religieuse* 8 (1951): 205–10.

——. "Un scruple identique de Saint Bernard à l'égard d'Abélard et de Gilbert de la Porrée." In *Mélanges Saint Bernard.* Dijon: Association bourgignonne des sociétés savantes, 1953, pp. 95–100.

Di Napoli, Giovanni. "Gioacchino da Fiore e Pietro Lombardo." *Rivista di filosofia neo-scolastica* 71 (1979): 621–85.

Dolch, Josef. "Lehrplanfragen in der Frühscholastik." *Philosophisches Jahrbuch* 62 (1955): 433–44.

Dölger, Franz X. J. *Das Sakrament der Firmung, historisch-dogmatisch dargestellt.* Vienna: Mayer & Co., 1906.

Dondaine, Antoine. *Écrits de la "petite école" porrétaine.* Montreal: Institut d'Études Médiévales, 1962.

Doucet, Victorinus. *Commentaires sur les Sentences: Supplément au Répertoire de M. F. Stegmüller.* Quaracchi: Collegii S. Bonaventurae ad Claras Aquas, 1954.

Dronke, Peter. *Fabula: Explorations into the Uses of Myth in Medieval Platonism.* Leiden: E. J. Brill, 1974.

——. "New Approaches to the School of Chartres." *Anuario de estudios medievales* 6 (1969): 117–40.

Dronke, Peter, ed. *A History of Twelfth-Century Western Philosophy.* Cambridge: Cambridge University Press, 1988.

Duby, Georges. *Medieval Marriage: Two Models from Twelfth-Century France.* Trans. Elborg Forster. Baltimore: Johns Hopkins University Press, 1978.

——. *The Knight, the Lady, and the Priest: The Making of Modern Marriage in Medieval France.* Trans. Barbara Bray. New York: Pantheon Books, 1983.

Dürig, Walter. "Die Scholastiker und die Communio sub una specie." In *Kyriakon: Festschrift Johannes Quasten.* Vol. 2. Ed. Patrick Granfield and Josef A.

Jungmann. Münster: Aschendorff, 1970, pp. 864–75.

Dutton, Paul Edward. "The Uncovering of the *Glosae super Platonem* of Bernard of Chartres." *Mediaeval Studies* 46 (1984): 192–221.

Elswijk, H. C. van. "Gilbert Porreta als glossator van het Psalterium." In *Jubileumbundel voor Prof. Mag. Dr. G. P. Kreiling, O. P.* Nijmegen: Dekker & Van de Vegt N.V., 1953, pp. 286–303.

———. *Gilbert Porreta: Sa vie, son oeuvre, sa pensée.* Louvain: Spicilegium Sacrum Lovaniense, 1966.

Emmerson, Richard Kenneth. *Antichrist in the Middle Ages: A Study of Medieval Apocalypticism, Art, and Literature.* Seattle: University of Washington Press, 1981.

Endres, Josef A. *Honorius Augustodunensis: Beitrag zur Geschichte des geistigen Lebens im 12. Jahrhundert.* Kempten: Jos. Kösel'schen Buchhandlung, 1906.

Engelhardt, Georg. *Die Enwicklung der dogmatischen Glaubenspsychologie in der mittelalterlichen Scholastik.* Beiträge zur Geschichte der Philosophie und Theologie des Mittelalters, 30:4–6. Münster: Aschendorff, 1933.

Engels, L. I. "Fons olei: Abélard, sermon 4 et hymne 34." In *Festoen: Opgedragen aan A. N. Zadoks-Josephus Jitta blj haar zeventigste verjaardag.* Groningen: H. D. Tjeenk Willink, 1976, pp. 235–47.

Esmein, Adhémar. *Le mariage en droit canonique.* 2 vols. 2nd ed. Ed. Robert Génestal and Jean Dauvillier. Paris, 1929–35.

Espenberger, Joh. Nep. *Die Philosophie des Petrus Lombardus und ihre Stellung im zwölften Jahrhundert.* Beiträge zur Geschichte der Philosophie des Mittelalters, 3:5. Münster, Aschendorff, 1901.

Evans, Gillian R. "*Alteritas*: Sources for the Notion of Otherness in Twelfth-Century Commentaries on Boethius' *Opuscula sacra*." *Bulletin Du Cange* 40 (1975–76): 103–13.

———. *Anselm and a New Generation.* Oxford: Clarendon Press, 1980.

———. *Anselm and Talking about God.* Oxford: Clarendon Press, 1978.

———. "*Cur Deus Homo*: St. Bernard's Theology of the Redemption: A Contribution to the Contemporary Debate." *Studia Theologica* 36 (1982): 27–36.

———. "Godescalc of St. Martin and the Trial of Gilbert of Poitiers." *Analecta Praemonstratensia* 57 (1981): 196–209.

———. "Hugh of St. Victor on History and the Meaning of Things." *Studia Monastica* 25 (1983): 223–34.

———. *Old Arts and New Theology: The Beginnings of Theology as an Academic Discipline.* Oxford: Clarendon Press, 1980.

———. "*Speculatio* and *Speculativus*: Boethius and the Speculative Theology of the Twelfth Century." *Classical Folia* 32 (1978): 69–78.

———. "The Academic Study of the Creeds in Twelfth-Century Schools." *Journal of Theological Studies* n.s. 30 (1979): 463–80.

———. "The Borrowed Meaning: Grammar, Logic, and the Problem of Theological Language in the Twelfth-Century Schools." *Downside Review* 96 (1978): 165–75.

———. *The Language and Logic of the Bible: The Earlier Middle Ages.* Cambridge: Cambridge University Press, 1984.

———. *The Language and Logic of the Bible: The Road to Reformation.* Cambridge: Cambridge University Press, 1985.

———. *The Mind of St. Bernard of Clairvaux.* Oxford: Clarendon Press, 1983.

Fabro, Cornelio. "Teologia dei nomi divini nel Lombardo e in S. Tommaso." *Pier Lombardo* 4 (1960): 77–93.

Faust, Ulrich. "Bernhards 'Liber de gratia et libero arbitrio': Bedeutung, Quellen und Einfluss." In *Analecta Monastica: Textes et études sur la vie des moines au moyen âge,* 6th ser. Rome: Herder, 1962, pp. 35–51.

Ferruolo, Stephen C. *The Origins of the University: The Schools of Paris and Their Critics, 1100–1215.* Stanford: Stanford University Press, 1985.

Flatten, Heinrich. "Die 'materia primordialis' in der Schule von Chartres." *Archiv für Geschichte der Philosophie* 40 (1931): 58–65.

———. *Die Philosophie des Wilhelm von Conches.* Koblenz: Görres-Druckerie, 1929.

Flint, Valerie I. J. "Heinricus of Augsburg and Honorius Augustodunensis: Are They the Same Person?" *Revue bénédictine* 92 (1982): 148–58.

———. "Some Notes on the Early Twelfth-Century Commentaries on the Psalms." *Recherches de théologie ancienne et médiévale* 38 (1971): 80–88.

———. "The Career of Honorius Augustodunensis: Some Fresh Evidence." *Revue bénédictine* 82 (1972): 63–86.

———. "The Chronology of the Works of Honorius Augustodunensis." *Revue bénédictine* 82 (1972): 215–42.

———. "The 'Elucidarius' of Honorius Augustodunensis." *Revue bénédictine* 85 (1975): 179–89.

———. "The Place and Purpose of the Works of Honorius Augustodunensis." *Revue bénédictine* 87 (1977): 97–127.

———. "The 'School of Laon': A Reconsideration." *Recherches de théologie ancienne et médiévale* 43 (1976): 89–110.

———. "The Sources of the 'Elucidarius' of Honorius Augustodunensis." *Revue bénédictine* 85 (1975): 190–98.

Forest, Aimé. "Gilbert de la Porrée et les écoles du XIIe siècle." *Revue des cours et conférences* 35:2 (1934): 410–20, 640–51.

———. "Le réalisme de Gilbert de la Porrée dans le commentaire du 'De Hebdomadibus'." *Revue néo-scolastique de philosophie* 36 (1934): 101–10.

Forest, Aimé, Van Steenberghen, Fernand, and Gandillac, Maurice de. *Le mouvement doctrinal du XIe au XIVe siècle.* Paris: Bloud & Gay, 1956.

Forster, William J. *The Beatific Knowledge of Christ in the Theology of the 12th and 13th Centuries.* Rome: Pontificium Athenaeum Internationale "Angelicum," 1958.

Fortman, Edmund J. *The Triune God: A Historical Study of the Doctrine of the Trinity.* Philadelphia: The Westminster Press, 1972.

Foucault, A. *Essai sur Ives de Chartres d'après sa correspondance.* Chartres: Petrot-Garnier, 1883.

Fournier, Paul. *Yves de Chartres et le droit canonique.* Paris: Bureau de la Revue, 1898.

Fournier, Paul and Le Bras, Gabriel. *Histoire des collections canoniques en occident depuis les fausses décrétales jusqu'au Décret de Gratien.* Vol. 2. Paris: Sirey, 1932.

Franks, Robert S. *The Work of Christ: A Historical Study of Christian Doctrine.* 2nd ed. London: Thomas Nelson and Sons Ltd, 1962.

Fransen, Gérard. "La formation du lien matrimonial au moyen âge." *Revue de droit canonique* 21 (1971): 106–26.

Fuehrer, M. L. "The Principle of Similitude in Hugh of Saint Victor's Theory of Divine Illumination." *American Benedictine Review* 30 (1979): 80–92.

Gabriel, Astrik L. "The Cathedral Schools of Notre-Dame and the Beginnings of the University of Paris." In *Garlandia: Studies in the History of the Medieval University.* Frankfurt: Joseph Knecht, 1969, pp. 39–64.

Gammersbach, Suitbert. *Gilbert von Poitiers und seine Prozesse im Urteil der Zeitgenossen.* Cologne: Böhlau Verlag, 1959.

Gandillac, Maurice de. "Intention et loi dans l'éthique d'Abelard. "In *Pierre Abélard, Pierre le Vénérable: Les courants philosophiques, littéraires et artistiques en occident au milieu du XIIe siècle.* Ed. René Louis, Jean Jolivet, and Jean Châtillon. Paris: CNRS, 1975, pp. 585–608.

———. "Le 'Dialogue' d'Abélard." In *Le "Dialogue," la philosophie de la logique.* Cahiers de la *Revue de théologie et de philosophie,* 6. Geneva, 1981, pp. 3–17.

———. "Notes préparatoires à un débat sur les Dialogues." In *Petrus Abaelardus (1079–1142): Person, Werk und Wirking.* Ed. Rudolf Thomas. Trier: Paulinus-Verlag, 1980, pp. 243–46.

———. "Sur quelques interprétations récentes d'Abélard" *Cahiers de civilisation médiévale* 4 (1961): 293–301.

Garrigues, Marie-Odile. "Quelques recherches sur l'oeuvre d'Honorius Augusto-dunensis." *Revue d'histoire ecclésiastique* 70 (1975): 388–425.

Gastaldelli, Ferruccio. "Le *Sententie* di Pietro Lombardo e l'*Expositio de symbolo apostolorum* di Uguccione da Pisa." *Salesianum* 39 (1977): 318–21.

Gaudel, Auguste. "La théologie de l'Assumptus Homo': Histoire et valeur doctrinale." *Revue des sciences religieuses* 17 (1937): 64–90, 214–34; 18 (1938): 45–71, 201–17.

Gaudemet, Jean. "La doctrine des sources du droit dans le Décret de Gratien." *Revue de droit canonique* 1 (1951): 5–31.

———. "le débat sur la confession dans la Distinction 1 du 'de penitentia' (Décret de Gratien, c. 33. q. 3)." *Zeitschrift der Savigny-Stiftung für Rechtsgeschichte*, kanonistische Abteilung 71 (1985): 52–75.

———. *Le mariage en occident: Les moeurs et le droit*. Paris: Éditions du Cerf, 1987.

———. "Sur trois 'Dicta Gratiani' relatifs au 'matrimonium ratum'." In *Études de droit et d'histoire: Mélanges Mgr. H. Wagnon*. Louvain: Faculté Internationale de Droit Canonique, 1976, pp. 543–55.

Gauss, Julia. "Das Religionsgespräch von Abaelard." *Theologische Zeitschrift* 27 (1971): 30–36.

Gaybba, Brian P. *Aspects of the Mediaeval History of Theology: 12th to 14th Century*. Pretoria: University of South Africa, 1988.

Geiselmann, Josef. *Die Eucharistielehre der Vorscholastik*. Paderborn: Ferdinand Schöningh, 1926.

Geyer, Bernhard. "Neues und Altes zu den *Sententie divinitatis*." In *Mélanges Joseph de Ghellinck, S.J.* Vol. 2. Gembloux: J. Duculot, 1951, pp. 617–30.

———. "Verfasser und Abfassungszeit der sog. Summa sententiarum." *Theologische Quartalschrift* 107 (1926): 89–107.

Ghellinck, Joseph de. "A propos de l'hypothèse des deux rédactions ou des deux éditions successives de la 'Somme des Sentences'." *Recherches de science religieuse* 15 (1925): 449–54.

———. "Dialectique et dogme aux Xe-XIIe siècles." In *Festgabe zum 60. Geburtstag Clemens Baeumker*. Beiträge zur Geschichte der Philosophie des Mittelalters, Supplementband 1. Münster: Aschendorff, 1913, pp. 79–99.

———. "Eucharistie au XIIe siècle en occident." In *Dictionnaire de théologie catholique*. Vol. 5. Paris: Letouzey et Ané, 1913, col. 1233–1302.

———. "La carrière de Pierre Lombard: Nouvelle précision chronologique." *Revue d'histoire ecclésiastique* 30 (1934): 95–100.

———. "La réviviscence des péchés pardonnés à l'époque de Pierre Lombard et de Gandulphe de Bologne." *Nouvelle Revue Théologique* 41 (1909): 400–08.

———. "La 'species quadriformis sacramentorum' des canonistes du XIIe siècle et Hugues de Saint-Victor." *Revue des sciences philosophiques et théologiques* 6 (1912): 527–37.

———. *Le Mouvement théologique du XIIe siècle*. 2nd ed. Bruges: De Tempel, 1948.

———. "L'Entrée d'essentia, substantia, et autres mots apparentés, dans le latin médiévale." *Archivum Latinitatis Medii Aevi* 16 (1941): 77–112; 17 (1942): 129–33.

———. "Les notes marginales du Liber sententiarum." *Revue d'histoire ecclésiastique* 14 (1913): 511–36, 705–19.

———. "Les 'opera dubia vel spuria' attribués à Pierre Lombard." *Revue d'histoire ecclésiastique* 28 (1932): 829–45.

———. *L'Essor de la littérature latine au XIIe siècle*. 2 vols. Brussels: l'Édition Universelle, 1946.

———. "Le traité de Pierre Lombard sur les sept ordres ecclésiastiques: Ses sources, ses copistes." *Revue d'histoire ecclésiastique* 10 (1909): 290–302, 720–28; 11 (1910): 29–46.

———. "L'histoire de 'persona' et d''hypostasis' dans un écrit anonyme porrétain du XIIe siècle." *Revue néo-scolastique de philosophie* 36 (1934): 111–27.

———. "Pierre Lombard." In *Dictionnaire de théologie catholique*. Vol. 12:2. Paris: Letouzey et Ané, 1935, col. 1941–2019.

———. "The Sentences of Anselm of Laon and Their Place in the Codification of Theology during the XIIth Century." *Irish Theological Quarterly* 6 (1911): 427–41.

———. "Un chapitre dans l'histoire de la définition des sacrements au XIIe siècle." In *Mélanges Mandonnet: Études d'histoire littéraire et doctrinale du moyen âge.* Vol. 2. Paris: J. Vrin, 1930, pp. 79–96.

Giacone, Roberto. "Masters, Books, and Library at Chartres according to the Cartularies of Notre-Dame and Saint-Pere." *Vivarium* 12 (1974): 30–51.

Giard, Luce. "Logique et système de savoir selon Hugues de Saint-Victor." *Thalès* 16 (1979–81): 3–32.

Gibson, Margaret T. *Lanfranc of Bec.* Oxford: Clarendon Press, 1978.

———. "Lanfranc's 'Commentary' on the Pauline Epistles." *Journal of Theological Studies*, n.s. 22 (1971): 86–112.

———. "The *Opuscula Sacra* in the Middle Ages." In *Boethius: His Life, Thought and Influence.* Ed. Margaret Gibson. Oxford: Basil Blackwell, 1981, pp. 214–34.

———. "The Place of the *Glossa ordinaria* in Medieval Exegesis." In *Ad litteram: Authoritative Texts and Their Medieval Readers.* Ed. Mark Jordan and Kent Emery, Jr. Notre Dame: University of Notre Dame Press, 1992, pp. 5–27.

———. "The Study of the *Timaeus* in the Eleventh and Twelfth Centuries." *Pensamiento* 25 (1969): 183–94.

Gilson, Étienne. "La cosmogonie de Bernardus Silvestris." *Archives d'histoire doctrinale et littéraire du moyen âge* 3 (1928): 5–24.

———. "Note sur les noms de la matière chez Gilbert de la Porrée." *Revue du moyen âge latin* 2 (1946): 173–76.

———. "Pierre Lombard et les théologies d'essence." *Revue du moyen âge latin* 1 (1945): 61–64.

———. "*Regio Dissimilitudinis* de Platon à Saint Bernard de Clairvaux." *Mediaeval Studies* 9 (1947): 108–30.

Giuli, G. de. "Abelardo e la morale." *Giornale critico della filosofia italiana* 12 (1931): 33–44.

Giuliano de Padova, Angela. "Alcuni rilievi sull'etica abelardiana." *Atti dell'Accademia delle scienze di Torino*, classe di scienze morali, storiche e filologiche 102 (1967–68): 437–60.

Giusberti, Franco. *Materials for a Study on Twelfth-Century Scholasticism.* Naples: Bibliopolis, 1982.

Glorieux, P. "Essai sur les 'Quaestiones in epistolas Pauli' du Ps.-Hugues de Saint-Victor." *Recherches de théologie ancienne et médiévale* 19 (1952): 48–59.

———. "Mauvaise action et mauvais travail: Le 'Contra quatuor labyrinthos Franciae'." *Recherches de théologie ancienne et médiévale* 21 (1954): 179–93.

Glunz, H. H. *History of the Vulgate in England from Alcuin to Roger Bacon: Being an Inquiry into the Text of Some English Manuscripts of the Vulgate Gospels.* Cambridge: Cambridge University Press, 1933.

Gneo, Corrado. "La dottrina del matrimonio nel 'De B. Mariae virginitate' di Ugo di S. Vittore." *Divinitas* 17 (1973): 374–94.

———. "L'Educazione morale di Pietro Abelardo 'ortodosso ribelle'." *Aquinas* 15 (1972): 562–75.

Gold, Penny S. "The Marriage of Mary and Joseph in the Twelfth-Century Ideology of Marriage." In *Sexual Practices and the Medieval Church.* Ed. Vern L. Bullogh and James Brundage. Buffalo: Prometheus Books, 1982, pp. 102–17.

Gössmann, Elisabeth. "'*Antiqui*' und '*moderni*' im 12. Jahrhundert." In *Antiqui und Moderni: Traditionsbewusstsein und Fortschrittsbewusstsein in späten Mittelalter.* Miscellanea mediaevalia, 9. Ed. Albert Zimmerman. Berlin: Walter de Gruyter, 1974, pp. 40–57.

———. "Zur Auseinandersetzung zwischen Abaelard und Bernhard von Clairvaux und die Gotteserkenntnis im Glaube." In *Petrus Abaelardus (1079–1142): Person, Werk und Wirkung.* Ed. Rudolf Thomas. Trier: Paulinus-Verlag, 1980, pp. 233–42.

Gössmann, W. E. "Die Bedeutung der Liebe in der Eheauffassung Hugos von St. Viktor und Wolframs von Eschenbach." *Münchener theologische Zeitschrift* 5 (1954): 205–13.

Gottschick, J. "Studien zur Versöhnungslehre des Mittelalters." *Zeitschrift für Kirchengeschichte* 22 (1901): 378–438; 23 (1902): 35–67.

Goy, Rudolf. *Die Überlieferung des Werke Hugos von St. Viktor.* Stuttgart: Hiersemann, 1976.

Grabmann, Martin. *Die Geschichte der katholischen Theologie seit dem Ausgang der Väterzeit.* Darmstadt: Wissenschaftliche Buchgesellschaft, 1961 [repr. of Freiburg im Breisgau, 1933 ed.].

———. *Die Geschichte der scholastischen Methode.* Vol. 2. Graz: Akademische Druck-u. Verlagsanstalt, 1957 [repr. of Freiburg im Breisgau, 1911 ed.].

———. "Hugo von St. Viktor (d. 1141) und Peter Abaelard (d. 1142): Ein Gedenkenblatt zum achthundertjährigen Todestag zweier Denkergestalten des Mittelalters." *Theologie und Glaube* 34 (1942): 241–49.

Grabois, Aryeh. "Un chapitre de tolérance intellectuelle dans la société occidentale au XIIe siècle: Le 'Dialogus' de Pierre Abélard et le 'Kuzari' d'Yehudah Halévi." In *Pierre Abélard, Pierre le Vénérable: Les courants philosophiques, littéraires et artistiques en occident au milieu du XIIe siècle.* Ed. René Louis, Jean Jolivet, and Jean Châtillon. Paris: CNRS, 1975, pp. 641–52.

Grane, Leif. *Peter Abelard: Philosophy and Christianity in the Middle Ages.* Trans. Frederick and Christine Crowley. New York: Harcourt, Brace & World, Inc., 1970.

Gregory, Tullio. "Abélard et Platon." In *Peter Abelard.* Ed. Eligius M. Buytaert. Leuven: Leuven University Press, 1974, pp. 38–64.

———. *Anima mundi: La filosofia di Guglielmo di Conches e la scuola di Chartres.* Florence: G. C. Sansoni, 1955.

———. "Considerazioni su 'ratio' e 'natura' in Abelardo." *Studi medievali,* 3ª ser. 14 (1973): 287–300.

———. "Il *Timeo* e i problemi del platonismo medievale." In *Platonismo medievale: Studi e ricerche.* Istituto storico italiano per il medioevo, studi storici, 26–27. Rome: Nella Sede dell'Istituto, 1958, pp. 53–150.

———. "L'*anima mundi* nella filosofia del XII secolo." *Giornale critico della filosofia italiana* 30 (1951): 494–508.

———. "L'Idea della natura nella scuola di Chartres." *Giornale critico della filosofia italiana* 31 (1952): 433–42.

Grillmeier, Aloys. "Fulgentius von Ruspe, De Fide ad Petrum und die Summa Sententiarum: Eine Studie zum Werden der frühscholastischen Systematik." *Scholastik* 34 (1959): 526–65.

Gross, Charlotte. "Twelfth-Century Concepts of Time: Three Reinterpretations of Augustine's Doctrine of Creation *Simul.*" *Journal of the History of Philosophy* 23 (1985): 325–38.

———. "William of Conches: A Curious Grammatical Argument against the Eternity of the World." In *Proceedings of the PMR Conference,* 11. Ed. Phillip Pulsiano. Villanova: Augustinian Historical Institute, 1986, pp. 127–33.

Gross, Julius. "Abälards Umdeutung des Erbsündendogmas." *Zeitschrift für Religions- und Geistesgeschichte* 15 (1963): 14–33.

———. "Die Ur- und Erbsündenlehre der Schule von Laon." *Zeitschrift für Kirchengeschichte* 76 (1965): 12–40.

———. "Ur- und Erbsünde bei Hugo von St. Viktor." *Zeitschrift für Kirchengeschichte* 73 (1962): 42–61.

Gross-Diaz, Theresa. "From *lectio divina* to the Lecture Room: The Psalms Commentary of Gilbert of Poitiers." In *The Place of the Psalms in the Intellectual Culture of the Middle Ages.* Ed. Nancy van Deusen. Binghamton: Center for Medieval and Early Renaissance Studies, forthcoming.

———. "Information Management in the Twelfth-Century Schools: The Psalm Commentary of Gilbert of Poitiers, or, 'Gilbert, We Hardly Knew Ye'." Unpublished.

———. "The Psalms Commentary of Gilbert of Poitiers: From *lectio divina* to the Lecture Room." Northwestern University Ph.D. diss., 1992.

Hadot, Pierre. "Forma essendi: Interprétation philologique et interprétation philosophique d'une formule de Boèce." *Les Études classiques* 38 (1970): 143–56.

Hallam, Elizabeth M. *Capetian France, 987–1328.* London: Longman, 1980.

Hamesse, Jacqueline. "Le traitement automatique du Livre des Sentences de Pierre Lombard." *Studies in Honour of Roberto Busa = Computazionale* 4–5 (1987): 71–77.

Hamesse, Jacqueline, ed. *Thesaurus Librorum Sententiarum Petri Lombardi.* Series A: Thesaurus Patrorum Latinorum. Corpus christianorum. Turnhout: Brepols, 1991.

Häring, Nikolaus M. "Abelard Yesterday and Today." In *Pierre Abélard, Pierre le Vénérable: Les courants philosophiques, littéraires et artistiques en occident au milieu du XII*ᵉ *siècle.* Ed. René Louis, Jean Jolivet, and Jean Châtillon. Paris: CNRS, 1975, pp. 31–43.

————. "A Hitherto Unkown Commentary on Boethius' *de Hebdomadibus* Written by Clarenbaldus of Arras." *Mediaeval Studies* 15 (1953): 212–21.

————. "A Latin Dialogue on the Doctrine of Gilbert of Poitiers." *Mediaeval Studies* 15 (1953): 243– 89.

————. "A Study of the Sacramentology of Alger of Liège." *Mediaeval Studies* 20 (1958): 41–78.

————. "Berengar's Definitions of *Sacramentum* and Their Influence on Mediaeval Sacramentology." *Mediaeval Studies* 10 (1948): 109–46.

————. "Character, Signum und Signaculum: Der Weg von Petrus Damiani bis zur eigentlichen Aufnahme in die Sakramentenlehre im 12. Jahrhundert." *Scholastik* 31 (1956): 41–69.

————. "Character, Signum und Signaculum: Die Einführung in die Sakramententheologie des 12. Jahrhunderts." *Scholastik* 31 (1956): 182–212.

————. "Das sogennante Glaubensbekenntnis des Reimser Konsistoriums von 1148." *Scholastik* 40 (1965): 55–90.

————. "Der Begriff der Natur bei Gilbert von Poitiers." In *La filosofia della natura nel medioevo.* Milan: Vita e Pensiero, 1966, pp. 279–85.

————. "Die theologische Sprachlogik der Schule von Chartres im zwölften Jahrhundert." In *Sprache und Erkenntnis im Mittelalter.* Miscellanea mediaevalia, 13:2. Ed. Albert Zimmerman. Berlin: Walter de Gruyter, 1981, pp. 930–36.

————. "Notes on the Council and the Consistory of Rheims (1148)." *Mediaeval Studies* 28 (1966): 39–59.

————. "Paris and Chartres Revisited." In *Essays in Honour of Anton Charles Pegis.* Ed. J. Reginald O'Donnell. Toronto: Pontifical Institute of Mediaeval Studies, 1974, pp. 268–329.

————. "San Bernardo e Gilberto vescovo di Poitiers." In *Studi su S. Bernardo di Chiaravalle nell'ottavo centenario della canonizzazione.* Rome: Editiones Cistercienses, 1975, pp. 75–91.

————. "Sprachlogik und philosophische Voraussetzungen zum Verständnis der Christologie Gilberts von Poitiers." *Scholastik* 32 (1957): 373–98.

————. "The Augustinian Axiom: *Nulli Sacramento Injuria Facienda Est.*" *Mediaeval Studies* 16 (1954): 87– 117.

————. "The Case of Gilbert de la Porrée, Bishop of Poitiers (1142–1154)." *Mediaeval Studies* 13 (1951): 1–40.

————. "The Character and Range of the Influence of St. Cyril of Alexandria on Latin Theology (430–1260)." *Mediaeval Studies* 12 (1950): 1–19.

————. "The Cistercian Everard of Ypres and His Appraisal of the Conflict between St. Bernard and Gilbert of Poitiers." *Mediaeval Studies* 17 (1955): 143–72.

————. "The Creation and Creator of the World according to Thierry of Chartres and Clarenbaldus of Arras." *Archives d'histoire doctrinale et littéraire du moyen âge* 22 (1958): 137–216.

————. "The Interaction between Canon Law and Sacramental Theology in the Twelfth Century." In *Proceedings of the Fourth International Congress of Medieval*

Canon Law. Ed. Stephan Kuttner. Vatican City: Biblioteca Apostolica Vaticana, 1976, pp. 483–93.

———. "The Porretans and the Greeks Fathers." *Mediaeval Studies* 24 (1966): 181–209.

———. "The *Sententiae Magistri A* (Vat. *MS lat.* 4361) and the School of Laon." *Mediaeval Studies* 17 (1955): 1–45.

———. "Two Catalogues of Mediaeval Authors." *Franciscan Studies* 26 (1966): 195–211.

Hartmann, Wilfried. "Manegold von Lautenbach und die Anfänge der Frühscholastik." *Deutsches Archiv für Erforschung des Mittelalters* 26 (1970): 47–149.

———. "Psalmenkommentare aus der Zeit der Reform und der Frühscholastik." *Studi Gregoriani* 9 (1972): 313–66.

Haskins, Charles Homer. *The Renaissance of the Twelfth Century*. New York: Meridian Books, 1957.

Hauréau, B. *Les oeuvres de Hugues de Saint-Victor: Essai critique*. Nouvelle éd. Frankfurt: Minerva GMBH, 1963 [repr. of Paris, 1886 ed.].

Hayen, A. "Le concile de Reims et l'erreur théologique de Gilbert de la Porrée." *Archives d'histoire doctrinale et littéraire du moyen âge* 11 (1936): 39–102.

Head, Thomas. "'Monastic' and 'Scholastic' Theology: A Change of Paradigm." In *Paradigms in Medieval Thought, Applications in Medieval Disciplines*. Ed. Nancy van Deusen and Alvin E. Ford. Lewiston, NY: Edwin Mellen Press, 1990, pp. 127–41.

Healy, Patrick Joseph. "The Mysticism of the School of Saint Victor." *Church History* 1 (1932): 211–21.

Heaney, Seamus P. *The Development of the Sacramentality of Marriage from Anselm of Laon to Thomas Aquinas*. Washington: Catholic University of America Press, 1963.

Heinzemann, Richard. *Die Unsterblichkeit der Seele und die Auferstehung des Leibes: Eine problemgeschichtliche Untersuchung der frühscholastischen Sentenzen- und Summenliteratur von Anselm von Laon bis Wilhelm von Auxerre*. Beiträge zur Geschichte der Philosophie und Theologie des Mittelalters, 40:3. Münster: Aschendorff, 1965.

Hödl, Ludwig. "Der Transsubstantiationsbegriff in der scholastischen Theologie des 12. Jahrhundert." *Recherches de théologie ancienne et médiévale* 31 (1964): 230–59.

———. "Die dialektische Theologie des 12. Jahrhunderts." In *Arts libéraux et philosophie au moyen âge*. Montreal: Institut d'Études Médiévales/Paris: J. Vrin, 1969, pp. 137–47.

———. *Die Geschichte der scholastischen Literatur und der Theologie der Schüsselgewalt*. Beiträge zur Geschichte der Philosophie und Theologie des Mittelalters, 37:4. Münster: Aschendorff, 1960.

———. "Die theologische Auseinandersetzung zwischen Petrus Lombardus und Odo von Ourscamp nach dem Zeugnis der frühen Quästion- und Glossenliteratur." *Scholastik* 33 (1958): 62–80.

———. "Logische Übungen zum christologischen Satz in der frühscholastischen Theologie des 12. Jahrhunderts." *Zeitschrift für Kirchengeschichte* 89 (1978): 291–306.

———. "Petrus Lombardus." In *Gestalten der Kirchengeschichte*. Vol. 3:1. Ed. Martin Greschat. Stuttgart: Kohlhammer, 1983, pp. 205–23.

———. "Sacramentum und res-Zeichen und Bezeichnetes: Eine begriffsgeschichtliche Arbeit zum frühscholastischen Eucharistietraktat." *Scholastik* 38 (1963): 161–82.

———. *Von der Wirklichkeit und Wirksamkeit des dreieinegen Gottes nach der appropriativen Trinitätstheologie des 12. Jahrhunderts*. Munich: Max Heueber Verlag, 1965.

Hofmeier, Johann. *Die Trinitätslehre des Hugo von St. Viktor dargestellt im Zusammenhang mit den trinitarischen Strömungen seiner Zeit*. Munich: Max Hueber Verlag, 1963.

Holmes, Urban T., Jr., "Transitions in European Education." In *Twelfth-Century Europe and the Foundations of Modern Society*. Ed. Marshall Clagett, Gaines Post, and Robert Reynolds. Madison: University of Wisconsin Press, 1961, pp. 15–38.

Horst, Ulrich. "Beiträge zum Einfluss Abaelards auf Robert von Melun." *Recherches de théologie ancienne et médiévale* 26 (1959): 314–26.

————. *Die Trinitäts- und Gotteslehre des Robert von Melun.* Mainz: Matthias-Grünewald Verlag, 1964.

————. *Gesetz und Evangelium: Das Alte Testament in der Theologie des Robert von Melun.* Munich: Ferdinand Schöningh, 1971.

Jansen, Wilhelm. *Der Kommentar des Clarenbaldus von Arras zu Boethius De Trinitate: Ein Werk aus der Schule von Chartres im 12. Jahrhundert.* Breslau: Müller & Sieffert, 1928.

Jeauneau, Édouard. *"Lectio philosophorum": Recherches sur l'école de Chartres.* Amsterdam: Adolf M. Hakkert, 1973.

Jocqué, Luc. "Les structures de la population claustrale dans l'ordre de Saint-Victor au XIIe siècle: Un essai d'analyse du 'Liber ordinis'." In *L'Abbaye parisienne de Saint-Victor au moyen âge.* Ed. Jean Longère. Paris: Brepols, 1991, pp. 53–95.

Jolivet, Jean. "Abélard entre chien et loup." *Cahiers de civilisation médiévale* 20 (1977): 307–22.

————. "Abélard et le philosophe: Occident et Islam au XIIe siècle." *Revue de l'histoire des religions* 164 (1963): 181–89.

————. *Abélard ou la philosophie dans le langage.* Paris: Éditions Seghers, 1969.

————. *Arts du langage et théologie chez Abélard.* 2nd ed. Paris: J. Vrin, 1982.

————. "Éléments du concept de nature chez Abélard." In *La filosofia della natura nel medioevo.* Milan: Vita e Pensiero, 1966, pp. 297–304.

————. "Le traitement des autorités contraires selon le *Sic et non* d'Abélard." In *Aspects de la pensée médiévale: Abélard. Doctrines du langage.* Paris: J. Vrin, 1987, pp. 79–92.

————. "Notes de lexicographie abélardienne." In *Aspects de la pensée médiévale: Abélard. Doctrines du langage.* Paris: J. Vrin, 1987, pp. 125–37.

————. "Sur quelques critiques de la théologie d'Abélard." *Archives d'histoire doctrinale et littéraire du moyen âge* 38 (1963): 7–51.

Jolivet, Jean, ed. *Abélard en son temps.* Paris: Les Belles Lettres, 1981.

Jorissen, Hans. *Die Entfaltung der Transsubstantiationslehre bis zum Beginn der Hochscholastik.* Münster: Aschendorff, 1965.

Jungmann, Joseph A. *The Mass of the Roman Rite: Its Origin and Development.* Vol. 2. Trans. Francis A. Brunner. New York: Benziger Brothers, Inc., 1955.

Kaufman, Peter Iver. "'Charitas non est nisi a Spiritui Sancto': Augustine and Peter Lombard on Grace and Personal Righteousness." *Augustiniana* 30 (1980): 209–20.

Kearney, Eileen. "Peter Abelard as Biblical Commentator: A Study of the Expositio in Hexaemeron." In *Petrus Abaelardus (1079–1142): Person, Werk und Wirkung.* Ed. Rudolf Thomas. Trier: Paulinus-Verlag, 1980, pp. 199–210.

Kern, Emmanuel. *Das Tugendsystem des heiligen Bernhard von Clairvaux.* Freiburg im Breisgau, Herder, 1934.

————. "Il sistema morale e della virtù nel pensiero di San Bernardo di Chiaravalle." *Rivista storica benedettina* 14 (1923): 7–44, 130–69, 217–51; 15 (1924): 16–37, 143–75, 230–47.

Kilgenstein, Jakob. *Die Gotteslehre des Hugo von St. Viktor.* Würzburg: Andreas Göbel, 1897.

Kleineidam, Erich. "De triplici libertate: Anselm von Laon oder Bernhard von Clairvaux?" *Cîteaux* 11 (1960): 55–62.

————. "Literargeschichtliche Bemerkungen zur Eucharistielehre Hugos von S. Viktor." *Scholastik* 20–24 (1949): 564–66.

————. "Wissen, Wissenschaft, Theologie bei Bernhard von Clairvaux." In *Bernhard von Clairvaux: Mönch und Mystiker.* Ed. Joseph Lortz. Wiesbaden: Franz Steiner Verlag GMBH, 1955, pp. 128–67.

Klibansky, Raymond. "L'Epître de Bérenger de Poitiers contre les Chartreux."

Revue du moyen âge latin 2 (1946): 314–16.

――――. "Peter Abelard and Bernard of Clairvaux: A Letter by Abelard." *Mediaeval and Renaissance Studies* 5 (1961): 1–27.

――――. "The School of Chartres." In *Twelfth-Century Europe and the Foundations of Modern Society*. Ed. Marshall Claggett, Gaines Post, and Robert Reynolds. Madison: University of Wisconsin Press, 1961, pp. 3–14.

Knapp, Fritz Peter. "Integumentum und Âventure: Nochmals zur Literaturtheorie bei Bernardus (Silvestris?) und Thomasin von Zerklaere." *Literaturwissenschaftliches Jahrbuch*, n.F. 28 (1987): 299–307.

Knoch, Wendelin. *Die Einsetzung der Sakramente durch Christus: Eine Untersuchung zur Sakramententheologie der Frühscholastik von Anselm von Laon bis zu Wilhelm von Auxerre*. Beiträge zur Geschichte der Philosophie und Theologie des Mittelalters, n.F. 24. Münster: Aschendorff, 1983.

Kögel, Julius. *Petrus Lombardus in seiner Stellung zur Philosophie des Mittelalter*. Greifswald: Julius Abel, 1897.

Korolec, J. B. and Palacz, R. "Commentaires sur les *Sentences*: Supplément au Répertoire de F. Stegmüller." *Mediaevalia Philosophica Polonorum* 11 (1963): 140–45.

Korolec, J. B., Póltawski, A., and Wlodek, Z. "Commentaires sur les *Sentences*: Supplément au Répertoire de F. Stegmüller." *Mediaevalia Philosophica Polonorum* 1 (1958): 28–30.

Köster, Heinrich. *Die Heilslehre des Hugo von Sankt-Viktor: Grundlagen und Grundzüge*. Emsdetten: Heinr. & J. Lechte, 1940.

Kritzeck, James. "L'Influence d'Abélard sur Pierre le Vénérable." In *Pierre Abélard, Pierre le Vénérable: Les courants philosophiques, littéraires et artistiques en occident au milieu du XIIe siècle*. Ed. René Louis, Jean Jolivet, and Jean Châtillon. Paris: CNRS, 1975, pp. 205–12.

――――. *Peter the Venerable and Islam*. Princeton: Princeton University Press, 1964.

Kryger, Henry S. *The Doctrine of the Effects of Extreme Unction in Its Historical Development*. Washington: Catholic University of America, 1949.

Kucia, Thaddeus. "Die Anthropologie bei Peter Abelard." In *Petrus Abaelardus (1079–1142): Person, Werk und Wirkung*. Ed. Rudolf Thomas. Trier: Paulinus-Verlag, 1980, pp. 233–42.

Kuksewicz, Zdzislaw. "Commentaires sur les *Sentences*: Supplément au Répertoire de F. Stegmüller," *Mediaevalia Philosophica Polonorum* 5 (1960): 45–49.

Kuttner, Stephan. "Graziano: L'uomo e l'opera." In *Gratian and the Schools of Law: 1140–1234*. London: Variorum, 1983, pp. 17–29.

――――. *Harmony from Dissonance: An Interpretation of Medieval Canon Law*. Latrobe, PA: The Archabbey Press, 1960.

――――. "Research on Gratian: Acta and Agenda." In *Proceedings of the Seventh International Congress of Medieval Canon Law*. Ed. Peter Linehan. Vatican City: Biblioteca Apostolica Vaticana, 1988, pp. 3–26.

――――. "Urban II and the Doctrine of Interpretation: A Turning Point?" *Studia Gratiana* 15 (1972): 53–85.

――――. "Zur Frage der theologische Vorlagen Gratians." In *Gratian and the Schools of Law: 1140–1234*. London: Variorum, 1983, pp. 243–68.

Landgraf, Artur Michael. "Abaelard und die Sentenzen des 'magister ignotus'." *Divus Thomas* 19 (1941): 75–80.

――――. "Bearbeitungen von Werken des Petrus Lombardus." *Collectanea Franciscana* 10 (1940): 321–37.

――――. "Beiträge zur Erkenntnis der Schule Abaelards." *Zeitschrift für katholische Theologie* 54 (1930): 360–405.

――――. "Das Problem *Utrum Christus fuerit homo in triduo mortis* in der Frühscholastik." In *Mélanges Auguste Pelzer*. Louvain: Bibliothèque de l'Université, 1947, pp. 109–58.

――――. "Der Einfluss des mündlichen Unterrichts auf theologische Werke der Frühscholastik." *Collectanea Franciscana* 23 (1953): 285–90.

————. "Der hl. Augustinus und der Bereich des Petrus Lombardus." *Scholastik* 29 (1954): 321–44.

————. "Der heilige Bernhard in seinem Verhältnis zur Theologie des zwölften Jahrhunderts." In *Bernhard von Clairvaux: Mönch und Mystiker*. Ed. Joseph Lortz. Wiesbaden: Franz Steiner Verlag GMBH, 1955, pp. 44–62.

————. "Der Magister Petrus episcopus." *Recherches de théologie ancienne et médiévale* 8 (1936): 198–203.

————. "Der Paulinenkommentar und der Psalmenkommentar des Petrus Cantor und die Glossa magna des Petrus Lombardus." *Biblica* 31 (1950): 379–89.

————. "Die Bestimmung des Verdienstgrades in der Frühscholastik." *Scholastik* 8 (1933): 1–40.

————. "Die Quaestiones super Epistolas S. Pauli und die Allegoriae." *Collectanea Franciscana* 16–17 (1946–47): 186–200.

————. "Die Stellungsnahme der Frühscholastik zur wissenschaftlichen Methode des Petrus Lombardus." *Collectanea Franciscana* 4 (1934): 513–21.

————. "Die Stellungsnahme der Scholastik des XII Jahrhunderts zum Adoptionismus." *Divus Thomas* 13 (1935): 257–89.

————. "Die *Summa Sententiarum* und die Summe des Cod. Vat. lat. 1345." *Recherches de théologie ancienne et médiévale* 11 (1939): 260–70.

————. "Diritto canonico e teologia nel secolo XII." *Studia Gratiana* 1 (1953): 371–413.

————. *Dogmengeschichte der Frühscolastik*. 4 vols. Regensburg: Friedrich Pustet, 1952–56.

————. "Ein neuer Fund zur Kommentierung des Paulinenkommentares des Petrus Lombardus." *Biblica* 25 (1944): 50–61.

————. "I Cor. 3, 10–17 bei den lateinischen Vätern und in der Frühscholastik." *Biblica* 5 (1924): 140–72.

————. "Familienbildung bei Paulinenkommentaren des 12. Jahrhunderts." *Biblica* 13 (1932): 61–72, 169–93.

————. *Introduction à l'histoire de la littérature théologique de la scolastique naissante*. Ed. Albert-M. Landry. Trans. Louis-B. Geiger. Montreal: Institut d'Études Médiévales, 1973.

————. "Kannte Langton das Original der Collectanea des Lombardus?" *Recherches de théologie ancienne et médiévale* 3 (1931): 72–75.

————. "Mitteilungen zur Schule Gilberts de la Porrée." *Collectanea Franciscana* 3 (1933): 182–208.

————. "Neu aufgefundene Handschriften mit Werken aus dem Bereich des Anselm von Laon." *Collectanea Franciscana* 15 (1945): 164–77.

————. "Nominalismus in den theologischen Werken der zweiten Hälfte des zwölften Jahrhunderts." *Traditio* 1 (1943): 183–210.

————. "Notes de critique textuelle sur les Sentences de Pierre Lombard." *Recherches de théologie ancienne et médiévale* 2 (1930): 80–99.

————. "Problèmes relatifs aux premières Gloses des Sentences." *Recherches de théologie ancienne et médiévale* 3 (1931): 140–57.

————. "Recherches sur les écrits de Pierre le Mangeur." *Recherches de théologie ancienne et médiévale* 3 (1931): 292–306, 341–72.

————. "Schwankungen in der Lehre des Petrus Lombardus." *Scholastik* 31 (1956): 533–44.

————. "Some Unknown Writings of the Early Scholastic Period." *New Scholasticism* 4 (1930): 1–22.

————. "Studien zur Theologie des zwölften Jahrhunderts." *Traditio* 1 (1943): 183–222.

————. "The First Sentence Commentary of Early Scholasticism." *New Scholasticism* 13 (1939): 101–33.

————. "Untersuchungen zu den Eigenlehre Gilberts de la Porrée." *Zeitschrift für katholische Theologie* 54 (1930): 180–213.

————. "Untersuchungen zu den Paulinenkommentaren des 12. Jahrhunderts."

Recherches de théologie ancienne et médiévale 8 (1936): 253–81, 345–68.

―――. "Werke aus dem Bereich der Summa Sententiarum und Anselms von Laon." *Divus Thomas* 14 (1936): 209–16.

―――. "Zum Werden der Theologie des 12. Jahrhunderts." *Zeitschrift für katholische Theologie* 79 (1957): 417–33.

―――. "Zur Lehre des Gilbert Porreta." *Zeitschrift für katholische Theologie* 77 (1955): 331–37.

―――. "Zur Lehre von der Gotteserkenntnis in der Frühscholastik." *New Scholasticism* 4 (1930): 261–88.

―――. "Zur Methode der biblischen Textkritik im 12. Jahrhundert." *Biblica* 10 (1929): 445–74.

―――. "Zwei Gelehrte aus der Umgebung des Petrus Lombardus." *Divus Thomas* 11 (1933): 157–82.

Landry, B. "Les Idées morales du XIIᵉ siècle: Les écrivains en Latin." *Revue des cours et conférences* 40 (1938–39): 385–98.

Le Bras, Gabriel. "Alger de Liège et Gratien." *Revue des sciences philosophiques et théologiques* 20 (1931): 5–26.

―――. "Inventaire théologique du Décret et de la Glose ordinaire: Êtres et monde invisibles. In *Mélanges Joseph de Ghellinck, S.J.* Vol. 2. Gembloux: J. Duculot, 1951, pp. 603–15.

―――. "La doctrine de mariage chez les théologiens et canonistes depuis l'an mille." In *Dictionnaire de théologie catholique.* Vol. 9:2. Paris: Letouzey et Ané, 1927, col. 2123–2317.

―――. "Le *Liber de misericordia et justicia* d'Alger de Liège." *Nouvelle Revue historique de droit française et étranger* 45 (1921): 80–118.

Le Bras, Gabriel, Lefebvre, Charles, and Rambaud, Jacqueline. *L'Âge classique, 1140–1378: Sources et théorie du droit.* Paris: Sirey, 1965.

Leclercq, Jean. "Écrits monastiques sur la Bible aux XIᵉ–XIIIᵉ siècle." *Mediaeval Studies* 15 (1953): 95–106.

―――. "Imitation of Christ and the Sacraments in the Teaching of St. Bernard." *Cistercian Studies* 9 (1974): 36–54.

―――. "Le commentaire du Cantique des cantiques attribué à Anselme de Laon." *Recherches de théologie ancienne et médiévale* 16 (1949): 29–39.

―――. "L'Éloge funèbre de Gilbert de la Porrée." *Archives d'histoire doctrinale et littéraire du moyen âge* 19 (1953): 183–85.

―――. "Origène au XIIᵉ siècle." *Irénikon* 24 (1951): 425–39.

―――. "S. Bernard et la confession des péchés." *Collectanea Cisterciensia* 46 (1984): 122–30.

―――. "S. Bernard et la théologie monastique du XIIᵉ siècle." In *Saint Bernard théologien.* Rome: Tipografia Pio X, 1953, pp. 7–23.

―――. "Textes sur Saint Bernard et Gilbert de la Porrée." *Mediaeval Studies* 14 (1952): 107–28.

―――. *The Love of Learning and the Desire for God: A Study of Monastic Culture.* 2nd. ed. rev. Trans. Catherine Misrahi. New York: Fordham University Press, 1974.

―――. "The Renewal of Theology." In *Renaissance and Renewal in the Twelfth Century.* Ed. Robert L. Benson and Giles Constable. Cambridge, MA: Harvard University Press, 1982, pp. 68–87.

Lee, Harold. "The Anti-Lombard Figures of Joachim of Fiore: A Reinterpretation." In *Prophesy and Millenarianism: Essays in Honour of Marjorie Reeves.* Ed. Ann Williams. London: Longman, 1980, pp. 129–42.

Lefebvre, Charles. "La notion d'équité chez Pierre Lombard." *Ephemerides Juris Canonici* 9 (1953): 291–304.

Lefèvre, Georges. *De Anselmo Laudunensi scholastico (1050–1117).* Evreux: C. Herissey, 1895.

Lefèvre, Yves. "Le *De Conditione angelica et humana* et les *Sententie Anselmi.*" *Archives d'histoire doctrinale et littéraire du moyen âge* 26 (1959): 249–75.

Le Goff, Jacques. *The Birth of Purgatory.* Trans. Arthur Goldhammer. Chicago:

Chicago University Press, 1984.

Leinsle, Ulrich Gottfried. *Vivianus von Prémontré: Ein Gegner Abaelards in der Lehre von der Freiheit*. Averbode: Praemonstratensia, 1975.

Lesne, Émile. *Histoire de la propriété ecclésiastique en France*. Vol. 5: *Les écoles de la fin du VIIIe siècle à la fin du XIIe*. Lille: Facultés Catholiques, 1940.

Liebeschütz, Hans. "Kosmologische Motive in der Bildungswelt des Frühscholastik." *Vorträge der Bibliothek Warburg* 3 (1923–24): 83–148.

———. "The Significance of Judaism in Peter Abaelard's *Dialogus*." *Journal of Jewish Studies* 12 (1961): 1–18.

Light, Laura. "Versions et révisions du texte biblique." In *Le moyen âge et la Bible*. Ed. Pierre Riché and Guy Lobrichon. Paris: Beauchesne, 1984, pp. 55–93.

Lilley, A. L. "A Christological Controversy of the Twelfth Century." *Journal of Theological Studies* 39 (1938): 225–38.

Lio, Hermenegildus. *Estne obligatio iustitiae subvenire miseris? Quaestionis positio et evolutio a Petro Lombardo ad S. Thomam ex tribus S. Augustini textibus*. Rome: Desclée & Socii, 1957.

Little, Edward Filene. "Bernard and Abelard at the Council of Sens, 1140." In *Bernard of Clairvaux: Studies Presented to Dom Jean Leclercq*. Washington: Cistercian Publications, 1973, pp. 55–71.

———. "The Heresies of Peter Abelard." University of Montreal Ph.D. diss., 1969.

Lobrichon, Guy. "Une nouveauté: Les gloses de la Bible." In *Le moyen âge et la Bible*. Ed. Pierre Riché and Guy Lobrichon. Paris: Beauchesne, 1984, pp. 93–114.

Löffler, Josef. *Die Störungen des geschlechtlichen Vermögens in der Literatur der autoritativen Theologie des Mittelalters: Ein Beitrag zur Geschichte der Impotenz und des medizinischen Sachverständigensbeweises im kanonischen Impotenzprocess*. Akademie der Wissenschaft und der Literatur in Mainz, Abhandlungen der geistes- und sozialwissenschaftlichen Klasse, 6. Wiesbaden: Franz Steiner Verlag GMBH, 1958.

Lohr, Charles H. "Peter Abälard und die scholastische Exegese." *Freiburger Zeitschrift für Philosophie und Theologie* 28 (1981): 95–110.

Lohrmann, Dietrich. "Ernis, abbé de Saint-Victor (1161– 1172): Rapports avec Rome, affaires financières." In *L'Abbaye parisienne de Saint-Victor au moyen âge*. Ed. Jean Longère. Paris: Brepols, 1991, pp. 180–93.

Longère, Jean. "La fonction pastorale de Saint-Victor à la fin du XIIe siècle et au début de XIIIe siècle." In *L'Abbaye parisienne de Saint-Victor au moyen âge*. Ed. Jean Longère. Paris: Brepols, 1991, pp. 291–313.

———. *Oeuvres oratoires des maîtres parisiens au XIIe siècle: Étude historique et doctrinale*. 2 vols. Paris: Études Augustiniennes, 1975.

Lorenzi, Giuseppi. "La filosofia di Pier Lombardo nei *Quattro libri delle Sentenze*." *Pier Lombardo* 4 (1960): 19–34.

Lottin, Odon. "A propos des sources de la 'Summa Sententiarum'." *Recherches de théologie ancienne et médiévale* 25 (1958): 42–58.

———. "Aux origines de l'école théologique d'Anselme de Laon." *Recherches de théologie ancienne et médiévale* 10 (1938): 101–22.

———. "Le concept de justice chez les théologiens du moyen âge avant l'introduction d'Aristote." *Revue thomiste* 44 (1938): 511–21.

———. "Le premier commentaire connu des Sentences de Pierre Lombard." *Recherches de théologie ancienne et médiévale* 11 (1939): 64–71.

———. "Les premiers linéaments du traité de la syndérèse au moyen âge." *Revue néo-scolastique de philosophie* 28 (1926): 422–59.

———. "Les théories du péché originel au XIIe siècle: I. L'école d'Anselme de Laon et de Guillaume de Champeaux." *Recherches de théologie ancienne et médiévale* 11 (1939): 17–32.

———. "Les théories du péché originel au XIIe siècle: II. La réaction abélardienne et porrétaine." *Recherches de théologie ancienne et médiévale* 12 (1940): 78–103.

———. "Les théories du péché originel au XIIe siècle: III. Tradition augustinienne." *Recherches de théologie ancienne et médiévale* 12 (1940): 236–74.

————. "Quelques recueils d'écrits attribués à Hugues de Saint-Victor." *Recherches de théologie ancienne et médiévale* 25 (1958): 248–84.

————. "Questions inédites de Hughes de Saint-Victor." *Recherches de théologie ancienne et médiévale* 26 (1959): 177–213.

Luchaire, Achille. *Louis VI le gros: Annales de sa vie et de son règne (1081–1137) avec une introduction historique.* Paris: Alphonse Picard, 1890.

————. "Remarques sur la succession des grands officiers de la Couronne qui ont souscrit les diplômes de Louis VI et de Louis VII (1108–1180)." *Annales de la Faculté des lettres de Bordeaux* 3 (1881): 63–77, 364–88.

Luscombe, David E. "Berengar, Defender of Peter Abelard." *Recherches de théologie ancienne et médiévale* 33 (1966): 319–37.

————. "Nature in the Thought of Peter Abelard." In *La filosofia della natura nel medioevo.* Milan: Vita e Pensiero, 1966, pp. 314–19.

————. "Peter Abelard: Some Recent Interpretations." *Journal of Religious History* 7 (1972): 69–75.

————. "Peter Comestor." In *The Bible in the Medieval World: Essays in Memory of Beryl Smalley.* Ed. Katherine Walsh and Diana Wood. Oxford: Basil Blackwell, 1985, pp. 109–29.

————. "St. Anselm and Abelard." *Anselm Studies,* 1. Ed. Gillian R. Evans. London: Kraus International, 1983, pp. 207–29.

————. "The Authorship of the *Ysagoge in theologiam.*" *Archives d'histoire doctrinale et littéraire du moyen âge* 43 (1968): 7–16.

————. "The *Ethics* of Abelard: Some Further Considerations." In *Peter Abelard.* Ed. Eligius M. Buytaert. Leuven: Leuven University Press, 1974, pp. 64–84.

————. *The School of Peter Abelard: The Influence of Abelard's Thought in the Early Scholastic Period.* Cambridge: Cambridge University Press, 1969.

McCallum, J. Ramsey. *Abelard's Christian Theology.* Oxford: Basil Blackwell, 1948.

McDannell, Colleen and Lang, Bernhard. *Heaven: A History.* New Haven: Yale University Press, 1988.

McGinn, Bernard. *The Calabrian Abbot: Joachim of Fiore in the History of Western Thought.* New York: Macmillan, 1985.

————. *Visions of the End: Apocalyptic Traditions in the Middle Ages.* New York: Columbia University Press, 1979.

McGrath, Alister E. *Iustitia dei: A History of the Christian Doctrine of Justification.* Vol. 1. Cambridge: Cambridge University Press, 1987.

McLaughlin, Mary Martin. "Abelard and the Dignity of Women." In *Pierre Abélard, Pierre le Vénérable: Les courants philosophiques, littéraires et artistiques en occident au milieu du XIIᵉ siècle.* Ed. René Louis, Jean Jolivet, and Jean Châtillon. Paris: CNRS, 1975, pp. 291–333.

————. "Abelard as Autobiographer: The Motives and Meaning of His 'Story of Calamities'." *Speculum* 42 (1967): 463–88.

McLaughlin, T. P. "The Formation of the Marriage Bond according to the *Summa Parisiensis.*" *Mediaeval Studies* 15 (1953): 208–12.

Maccagnolo, Enzo. *Rerum universitatis: Saggio sulla filosofia di Teodorico di Chartres.* Florence: Le Monnier, 1976.

Macy, Gary. "Berengar's Legacy as Heresiarch." In *Auctoritas und Ratio: Studien zu Berengar von Tours.* Ed. Peter Ganz et. al. Wiesbaden: Otto Harrassowitz, 1990, pp. 47–67.

————. "Of Mice and Manna: *Quid mus sumit* as a Pastoral Question." *Recherches de théologie ancienne et médiévale* 58 (1991): 157–66.

————. "Reception of the Eucharist according to the Theologians: A Case of Theological Diversity in the Thirteenth and Fourteenth Centuries." Unpublished.

————. *The Banquet's Wisdom: A Short History of the Theologies of the Lord's Supper.* New York: Paulist Press, 1992.

————. *The Theologies of the Eucharist in the Early Scholastic Period: A Study of the Salvific Function of the Sacrament according to the Theologians c. 1080–c. 1220.* Oxford: Clarendon Press, 1984.

Mahoney, John F. "The Premonstratensian Canons in the Renaissance Century." *Analecta Praemonstratensia* 23 (1957): 259–67.

Maioli, Bruno. *Gilberto Porretano: Dalla grammatica speculativa alla metafisica del concreto*. Rome: Bulzoni, 1979.

Makdisi, George. "The Scholastic Method in Medieval Education: An Inquiry into Its Origins in Law and Theology." *Speculum* 49 (1974): 640–61.

Malloy, Michael P. *Civil Authority in Medieval Philosophy: Lombard, Aquinas, and Bonaventure*. Lanham, MD: University Press of America, 1985.

Maréchaux, Bernard. "L'Oeuvre doctrinale de Saint Bernard." *La Vie Spirituelle* 16 (1927): 498–511, 634– 50; 17 (1927): 34–47, 196–207.

Marenbon, John. "A Note on the Porretani." In *A History of Twelfth-Century Western Philosophy*. Ed. Peter Dronke. Cambridge: Cambridge University Press, 1988, pp. 353–57.

———. *From the Circle of Alcuin to the School of Auxerre: Logic, Theology and Philosophy in the Early Middle Ages*. Cambridge: Cambridge University Press, 1981.

Martin, Christopher J. "The Compendium Logicae Porretanum: A Survey of Philosophical Logic from the School of Gilbert of Poitiers." Université de Copenhague, *Cahiers de l'Institut du moyen-âge grec et latin*, 46 (1983): xviii–xlvi.

Martin, Raymond-M. "El problema del influjo divino sobre las acciones humanas, un siglo antes de Santo Tomás de Aquino." *La Ciencia tomista* 5 (1915): 178–93.

———. "'Filia magistri': Un abregé des Sentences de Pierre Lombard." *Bulletin of the John Rylands Library* 2 (1914–15): 370–79.

———. "La necessité de croire le mystère de la très sainte trinité d'après Robert de Melun (d. 28 févr. 1167)." *Revue thomiste* 21 (1913): 572–78.

———. "Le péché originel d'après Gilbert de la Porrée (d. 1154) et son école." *Revue d'histoire ecclésiastique* 13 (1912): 674–91.

———. "Les idées de Robert de Melun sur le péché originel." *Revue des sciences philosophiques et théologiques* 7 (1913): 700–25; 8 (1914): 439–66; 9 (1920): 103–20; 11 (1922): 390–415.

———. "L'immortalité de l'âme d'après Robert de Melun (d. 1167)." *Revue néo-scolastique de Louvain* 36 (1934): 125–45.

———. "L'Oeuvre théologique de Robert de Melun." *Revue d'histoire ecclésiastique* 15 (1914): 456–89.

———. "Notes sur l'oeuvre littéraire de Pierre le Mangeur." *Recherches de théologie ancienne et médiévale* 3 (1931): 54–66.

———. "Pro Petro Abaelardo: Un plaidoyer de Robert de Melun contre S. Bernard." *Revue des sciences philosophiques et théologiques* 12 (1923): 308–33.

———. "Un texte intéressant de Robert de Melun." *Revue d'histoire ecclésiastique* 28 (1932): 313–29.

Martinet, Suzanne. *Montloon: Reflet fidèle de la montagne et des environs de Laon de 1100 à 1300*. Laon: Éditions de l'Imprimerie du Courrier de l'Aisne, 1972.

Massara, Antonio. "La leggenda di Pier Lombardo." In *Miscellanea storica Novarese a Raffaele Tarella*. Novara: G. Parzini, 1906, pp. 115–43.

———. *Pier Lombardo, il maestro delle Sentenze: Appunti per la storia della cultura e della filosofia medioevale*. Intra: Giuseppi Bertolotti, 1913.

Maxsein, Anton. *Die Philosophie des Gilbertus Porretanus unter besonderer Berücksichtigung seiner Wissenschaftslehre*. Münster: Westfälische Vereinsdruckerie, 1929.

Megivern, James J. *Concomitance and Communion: A Study in Eucharistic Doctrine and Practice*. Fribourg: The University Press, 1963.

Merlette, Bernard. "Écoles et bibliothèques à Laon, du déclin de l'antiquité au développement de l'Université." In *Enseignement et vie intellectuelle, IXe—XVIe siècle*. Vol. 1. Paris: Bibliothèque National, 1975, pp. 21–53.

Merzbacher, Friedrich. "Alger von Lüttich und das kanonische Recht." *Zeitschrift der Savigny-Stiftung für Rechtsgeschichte*, kanonistische Abteilung 66 (1980): 231–60.

Metz, René. "Regard critique sur la personne de Gratien, auteur du Décret (1130–40), d'après les résultats des dernières recherches." *Revue des sciences religieuses* 58 (1984): 64–76.

Mews, Constant J. "The List of Heresies Imputed to Peter Abelard." *Revue bénédictine* 95 (1985): 73–110.

———. "On Dating the Works of Peter Abelard." *Archives d'histoire doctrinale et littéraire du moyen âge* 52 (1985): 73–134.

———. "Peter Abelard's (Theologia Christiana) and (Theologia 'Scholarium') Re-examined." *Recherches de théologie ancienne et médiévale* 52 (1985): 109–58.

———. "The Development of the Theologia of Peter Abelard." In *Petrus Abaelardus (1079–1142): Person, Werk und Wirkung*. Ed. Rudolf Thomas. Trier: Paulinus-Verlag, 1980, pp. 183–98.

———. "The *Sententiae* of Peter Abelard." *Recherches de théologie ancienne et médiévale* 53 (1986): 130–84.

Miano, Vincenzo. "Il Commento alle Lettere di S. Paolo di Gilberto Porretano." In *Scholastica: Ratione historico-critica instauranda*. Rome: Pontificium Athenaeum Antonianum, 1951, pp. 171–99.

Micaelli, Claudio. "'Natura' e 'persona' nel *Contra Eutychen et Nestorium* di Boezio: Osservazioni su alcuni problemi filosofici e linguistici." In *Atti del Congresso internazionale di studi Boeziani*. Ed. Luca Obertello. Rome: Herder, 1981, pp. 327–36.

Michaud, E. *Guillaume de Champeaux et les écoles de Paris au XIIe siècle d'après des documents inédits*. Paris: Didier et Cie, 1867.

Miethke, Jürgen. "Theologenprozesse in der ersten Phase ihrer institutionellen Ausbildung: Die Verfahren gegen Peter Abaelard und Gilbert von Poitiers." *Viator* 6 (1975): 87–116.

Mignon, A. *Les origines de la scolastique et Hugues de Saint-Victor*. 2 vols. Paris: P. Lethielleux, 1895.

Minio-Paluello, Lorenzo. "The 'Ars disserendi' of Adam of Balsham (Parvipontanus)." *Mediaeval Studies* 3 (1954): 116–69.

Minnis, A. J. *Medieval Theory of Authorship: Scholastic Literary Attitudes in the Later Middle Ages*. London: Scolar Press, 1984.

Minnis, A. J. and Scott, A. B., ed. *Medieval Literary Theory and Criticism, c. 1100–c. 1375*. Oxford: Clarendon Press, 1988.

Miscellanea Lombardiana. Novara: Istituto Geografico de Agostini, 1957.

Moonan, Lawrence. "Abelard's Use of the *Timaeus*." *Archives d'histoire doctrinale et littéraire du moyen âge* 56 (1989): 7–90.

Moore, Philip S. "Peter of Poitiers." In *New Catholic Encyclopedia*. Vol. 9. New York: McGraw-Hill Book Company, 1969, pp. 227–28.

———. "Reason in the Theology of Peter Abelard." *Proceedings of the American Catholic Philosophical Association* 12 (1936): 148–60.

———. "The Authorship of the *Allegoriae super vetus et novum testamentum*." *New Scholasticism* 9 (1935): 209–25.

Moreau, Joseph. "'Opifex, id est Creator': Remarques sur le platonisme de Chartres." *Archiv für Geschichte der Philosophie* 56 (1974): 33–49.

Morin, G. "Le pseudo-Bède sur les Psaumes, et l'*Opus super Psalterium* de maître Manegold de Lautenbach." *Revue bénédictine* 28 (1911): 331–40.

Morrison, Karl F. *Tradition and Authority in the Western Church, 300–1140*. Princeton: Princeton University Press, 1969.

Müller, Michael. *Die Lehre des hl. Augustinus von der Paradiesesehe und ihre Auswirkung in der Sexualethik des 12. und 13. Jahrhunderts bis Thomas von Aquin*. Regensburg: Friedrich Pustet, 1954.

Munier, Charles. *Les sources patristiques du droit de l'église du VIIIe au XIIIe siècle*. Strasbourg: Salvator Mulhouse, 1957.

Murray, A. Victor. *Abelard and St. Bernard: A Study in Twelfth Century 'Modernism'*. Manchester: Manchester University Press, 1967.

Murray, John C. *The Infused Knowledge of Christ in the Theology of the 12th and 13th Centuries*. Windsor, Ontario, 1963.

Murray, Placid. "The Liturgical History of Extreme Unction." In *Studies in*

Pastoral Liturgy. Vol. 2. Ed. Vincent Ryan. Dublin: Gill & Son, 1963, pp. 18–38.

Nagari, Mario. "Giuseppe Regaldi e Pier Lombardo." *Bolletino storico per la provincia di Novara* 68 (1977): 78–94.

Nash, Peter W. "The Meaning of *Est* in the *Sentences* (1152–1160) of Robert of Melun." *Mediaeval Studies* 14 (1952): 129–42.

Nédoncelle, Maurice. "Les variations de Boèce sur la personne." *Revue des sciences religieuses* 29 (1955): 201–38.

Neunheuser, Burckhardt. *Eucharistie im Mittelalter und Neuzeit.* Freiburg im Breisgau: Herder, 1963.

Newell, John. "Rationalism at the School of Chartres." *Vivarium* 21 (1983): 108–26.

Nielsen, Lauge Olaf. "On the Doctrine of Logic and Language of Gilbert Porreta and His Followers." Université de Copenhague, *Cahiers de l'Institut du moyen-âge grec et latin* 17 (1976): 40–69.

———. *Theology and Philosophy in the Twelfth Century: A Study of Gilbert Porreta's Thinking and the Theological Expositions of the Doctrine of the Incarnation during the Period 1130–1180.* Acta theologica danica, 15. Leiden: E. J. Brill, 1982.

Nobile, Enrico. "Appunti sulla teologia dei *Quattro libri delle Sentenze* di Pier Lombardo." *Pier Lombardo* 4 (1960): 49–59.

Noonan, John T. *Contraception: A History of Its Treatment by the Catholic Theologians and Canonists.* Enlarged ed. Cambridge, MA: Harvard University Press, 1986.

———. "Gratian Slept Here: The Changing Identity of the Father of the Systematic Study of Canon Law." *Traditio* 35 (1979): 145–72.

———. "Marital Affection in the Canonists." *Studia Gratiana* 12 (1967): 479–509.

———. "Power to Choose." *Viator* 4 (1973): 419–34.

———. "Who Was Rolandus?" In *Law, Church, and Society: Essays in Honor of Stephan Kuttner.* Ed. Kenneth Pennington and Robert Somerville. Philadelphia: University of Pennsylvania Press, 1977, pp. 21–48.

Normore, Calvin. "Future Contingents." In *Cambridge History of Later Medieval Philosophy.* Ed. Norman Kretzman, Anthony Kenney, and Jan Pinborg. Cambridge: Cambridge University Press, 1982, pp. 358–81.

Olsen, Glenn. "The Idea of the *Ecclesia Primitiva* in the Writings of the Twelfth-Century Canonists." *Traditio* 25 (1969): 61–86.

Ostlender, Heinrich. "Die Sentenzenbücher der Schule Abaelards." *Theologische Quartalschrift* 117 (1936): 208–52.

———. "Die Theologia 'Scholarium' des Petrus Abaelard." In *Aus der Geisteswelt des Mittelalters: Studien und Texte Martin Grabmann zur Vollendung des 60. Lebensjahres von Freunden und Schülern gewidmet.* Vol. 1. Ed. Albert Lang, Joseph Lechner, and Michael Schmaus. Beiträge zur Geschichte der Philosophie des Mittelalters, Supplementband, 3:1. Münster: Aschendorff, 1935, pp. 263–81.

Ostler, Heinrich. *Die Psychologie des Hugo von St. Viktor.* Beiträge zur Geschichte der Philosophie des Mittelalters, 6:1. Münster: Aschendorff, 1906.

Ott, Ludwig. "Die platonische Weltseele in der Theologie der Frühscholastik." In *Parusia: Studien zur Philosophie Platons und zur Problemgeschichte des Platonismus. Festgabe für Johannes Hirschberger.* Ed. Kurt Flasch. Frankfurt: Minerva GMBH, 1965, pp. 307–31.

———. "Die Trinitätslehre der *Summa sententiarum* als Quelle des Petrus Lombardus." *Divus Thomas* 21 (1943): 159–86.

———. "Die Trinitätslehre Walters von Mortagne als Quelle der *Summa sententiarum.*" *Scholastik* 18 (1943): 78–90, 219–39.

———. "Hugo von St. Viktor und die Kirchenväter." *Divus Thomas,* 3rd ser. 27 (1949): 180–200, 293–332.

———. "Petrus Lombardus: Persönlichkeit und Werk." *Münchener theologische Zeitschrift* 5 (1954): 99–113.

———. *Untersuchung zur theologischen Briefliteratur der Frühscholastik.* Beiträge zur Geschichte der Philosophie und Theologie des Mittelalters, 34. Münster: Aschendorff, 1937.

————. "Walter von Mortagne und Petrus Lombardus in ihrem Verhältnis zueinander." In *Mélanges Joseph de Ghellinck, S.J.* Vol. 2. Gembloux: J. Duculot, 1951, pp. 646–97.

Otto, Stephan. "Augustinus und Boethius im 12. Jahrhundert." *Wissenschaft und Weisheit* 26 (1963): 15–26.

————. *Die Funktion des Bildbegriffes in der Theologie des 12. Jahrhunderts*. Beiträge zur Geschichte der Philosophie und Theologie des Mittelalters, 40:1. Münster: Aschendorff, 1963.

Oursel, Raymond. *La dispute et la grâce: Essai sur la rédemption d'Abélard*. Paris: Les Belles Lettres, 1959.

Pacaut, Marcel. *Louis VII et les élections épiscopales dans le royaume de France*. Paris: J. Vrin, 1957.

————. *Louis VII et son royaume*. Paris: SEVPEN, 1964.

Pagliari, Ada. "Il presunto commento ai Salmi di S. Lorenzo Giustiniani opera di Gilberto Porretano." *Aevum* 36 (1962): 416–29.

Paré, G., Brunet, A., and Tremblay, P. *La Renaissance du XIIe siècle: Les écoles et l'enseignement*. Paris: J. Vrin, 1933.

Parent, J. M. *La doctrine de la creation dans l'école de Chartres*. Paris: J. Vrin/Ottawa: Institut d'Études Médiévales, 1938.

Payen, Jean Charles. "La pénitence dans le contexte culturel des XIIe et XIIIe siècles: Des doctrines contritionistes aux pénitentiels vernaculaires." *Revue des sciences philosophiques et théologiques* 61 (1977): 399–428.

Pedersen, Jørgen. "La recherche de la sagesse d'après Hugues de Saint-Victor." *Classica et mediaevalia* 16 (1955): 91–133.

Pelikan, Jaroslav. *The Christian Tradition: A History of the Development of Doctrine*. Vol. 3. Chicago: University of Chicago Press, 1978.

Pelster, Franz. "Das vermeintliche Original der Sentenzen des Petrus Lombardus." *Scholastik* 5 (1930): 569–73.

————. "Der Brief Eugens III an Bischoff Heinrich von Beauvais und die Datierung der Libri IV Sententiarum." *Gregorianum* 15 (1934): 262–66.

————. "Die anonyme Verteidigungsschrift der Lehre Gilberts von Poitiers im Cod. Vat. 561 und ihr Verfasser Canonicus Adhemar von Saint-Ruf in Valence (um 1180)." In *Studia mediaevalia in honorem admodum reverendi patris Raymundi Josephi Martin*. Bruges: De Tempel, 1948, pp. 113–46.

————. "Einige Angaben über Leben und Schriften des Robertus Pullus, Kardinals und Kanzlers der römischen Kirche (d. 1146)." *Scholastik* 12 (1937): 239–47.

————. "Literaturgeschichtliche Beiträge zu Robert von Melun, Bischoff von Hereford (d. 1167)." *Zeitschrift für katholische Theologie* 53 (1929): 564–79.

————. "Wann hat Petrus Lombardus die 'Libri IV Sententiarum' vollendet?" *Gregorianum* 2 (1921): 387–92.

Peppermüller, Rolf. *Abaelards Auslegung des Römerbriefes*. Beiträge zur Geschichte der Philosophie und Theologie des Mittelalters, n.F. 10. Münster: Aschendorff, 1972.

————. "Exegetische Traditionen und theologische Neuansätze in Abaelards Kommentar zum Römerbrief." In *Peter Abelard*. Ed. Eligius M. Buytaert. Leuven: Leuven University Press, 1974, pp. 116–26.

Pession, Paulo M. "L'ordine sacro e i suoi gradi nel pensiero di Ugo di S. Vittore." *La Scuola Cattolica* 64 (1936): 124–49.

Peuchmaurd, M. "Le prêtre ministre de la parole dans la théologie du XIIe siècle: Canonistes, moines, et chanoines." *Recherches de théologie ancienne et médiévale* 29 (1962): 52–76.

Pinckaers, Servais. "Les origines de la définition de l'espérance dans les Sentences de Pierre Lombard." *Recherches de théologie ancienne et médiévale* 22 (1955): 306–12.

Pittenger, M. Norman. "The Incarnational Theology of Hugh of St. Victor." *Theology* 31 (1935): 274–78.

Poole, Reginald Lane. *Illustrations of the History of Medieval Thought and Learning*. London: SPCK, 1932.

————. "The Early Lives of Robert Pullen and Nicholas Breakspear, with Notes on Other Englishmen at the Papal Court about the Middle of the Twelfth Century." In *Essays in Medieval History Presented to Thomas F. Tout.* Ed. A. G. Little and F. M. Powicke. Manchester, 1925, pp. 61–70.

————. "The Masters of the Schools at Paris and Chartres in John of Salisbury's Time." In *Studies in Chronology and History.* Ed. Austin Lane Poole. Oxford: Clarendon Press, 1934, pp. 223–47.

Poppenberg, Everhard. *Die Christologie des Hugo von St. Viktor.* Herz: Jesu-Missionshaus Hiltrup, 1937.

Potts, Timothy C. "Conscience." In *Cambridge History of Later Medieval Philosophy.* Ed. Norman Kretzman, Anthony Kenny, and Jan Pinborg. Cambridge: Cambridge University Press, 1982, pp. 687–704.

————. *Conscience in Medieval Philosophy.* Cambridge: Cambridge University Press, 1980.

Principe, Walter H. *William of Auxerre's Theology of the Hypostatic Union.* Toronto: Pontifical Institute of Mediaeval Studies, 1963.

Protois, F. *Pierre Lombard, évêque de Paris dit le maître des Sentences: Son époque, sa vie, ses écrits, son influence.* Paris: Société Générale de Librairie Catholique, 1887.

Quain, Edwin A. "The Medieval *Accessus ad auctores.*" *Traditio* 3 (1945): 215–64.

Quinn, Philip L. "Abelard on Atonement: 'Nothing Unintelligible, Arbitrary, Illogical, or Immoral about It'." In *Reasoned Faith.* Ed. Eleonore Stump. Ithaca: Cornell University Press, 1993, pp. 281–300.

Ramponi, Carlo. "Leutaldo: Scuola teologica di Reims." *Pier Lombardo* 1 (1953): 14–15.

Rathbone, Eleanor. "John of Cornwall: A Brief Biography." *Recherches de théologie ancienne et médiévale* 17 (1950): 46–60.

————. "Note super Iohannem secundum magistrum Gilb[ertum]." *Recherches de théologie ancienne et médiévale* 18 (1951): 205–10.

Rauh, Horst Dieter. *Das Bild des Antichrist im Mittelalter: Von Tyconius zum deutschen Symbolismus.* Beiträge zur Geschichte der Philosophie und Theologie des Mittelalters, n.F. 9. Münster: Aschendorff, 1973.

Rebeta, Jerzy. "Commentaires sur les *Sentences*: Supplément au Répertoire de F. Stegmüller." *Mediaevalia Philosophica Polonorum* 12 (1967): 135–37.

Reinhardt, Heinrich J. F. *Die Ehelehre der Schule des Anselm von Laon: Eine theologie- und kirchenrechtsgeschichtliche Untersuchung zu den Ehetexten der frühen Pariser Schule des 12. Jahrhunderts.* Beiträge zur Geschichte der Philosophie und Theologie des Mittelalters, n.F. 14. Münster: Aschendorff, 1974.

————. "Literarkritische und Theologiegeschichtliche Studie zu den *Sententiae magistri A.* und deren Prolog 'Ad iustitiam credere debemus'." *Archives d'histoire doctrinale et littéraire du moyen âge* 36 (1969): 23–56.

Renna, Thomas J. "Bernard vs. Abelard: An Ecclesiological Conflict." In *Simplicity and Orderliness.* Ed. John R. Sommerfeldt. Kalamazoo: Cistercian Publications, 1980, pp, 94–138.

Riché, Pierre. "Jean de Salisbury et le monde scolaire du XIIᵉ siècle." In *The World of John of Salisbury.* Ed. Michael Wilks. Studies in Church History, Subsidia, 3. Oxford: Basil Blackwell, 1984, pp. 39–61.

Rigobello, Armando. *Linee per una antropologia prescolastica.* Padua: Antenore, 1972.

Rivière, Jean. *Le dogme de la rédemption au début du moyen âge.* Paris: J. Vrin, 1934.

————. "Le dogme de la rédemption au XIIᵉ siècle d'après les dernières publications." *Revue du moyen âge latin* 2 (1946): 101–12, 219–30.

————. "Le mérite du Christ d'après le magistère ordinaire de l'église, II: Époque médiévale." *Revue des sciences religieuses* 22 (1948): 213–39.

————. "Les 'capitula' d'Abélard condamnés au concile de Sens." *Recherches de théologie ancienne et médiévale* 5 (1933): 5–22.

Robinson, I. S. *The Papacy, 1073–1198: Continuity and Innovation.* Cambridge: Cambridge University Press, 1990.

Robson, C. A. *Maurice of Sully and the Medieval Vernacular Homily*. Oxford: Blackwell, 1952.

Rodnite, Helen [Lemay]. "Platonism in the Twelfth-Century School of Chartres." *Acta* 2 (1975): 42–52.

————. "The Doctrine of the Trinity in Guillaume de Conches' Glosses on Macrobius: Texts and Studies." Columbia University Ph.D. diss., 1972.

Rogers, Elizabeth Frances. *Peter Lombard and the Sacramental System*. New York, 1917.

Rohmer, Jean. *La finalité morale chez les théologiens de Saint Augustin à Duns Scot*. Paris: J. Vrin. 1939.

Rosier. Irène. "Les acceptations du terme 'substantia' chez Pierre Hélie." In *Gilbert de Poitiers et ses contemporains: Aux origines de la logica modernorum*. Ed. Jean Jolivet and Alain de Libera. Naples: Bibliopolis. 1987, pp. 299–324.

Rousset, Paul. "A propos de l''Elucidarium' d'Honorius Augustodunensis: Quelques problèmes d'histoire ecclésiastique." *Zeitschrift für schweizerische Kirchengeschichte* 52 (1958): 223–30.

Rozemond, Keetje. *La christologie de Saint Jean Damascène*. Ettal: Buch-Kunstverlag, 1959.

Ruiz Josué, Teodoro. "Los effectos jurídicos de la ignorancia en la doctrina matrimonial de Hugo de San Victor y Roberto Pulleyn." *Revista española de derecho canónico* 3 (1948): 61–105.

Russell, Jeffrey Burton. *Lucifer: The Devil in the Middle Ages*. Ithaca: Cornell University Press, 1984.

Russo, François. "Pénitence et excommunication: Étude historique sur les rapports entre la théologie et le droit canonique dans le domaine pénitentiel du XIe et XIIe siècle." *Recherches de science religieuse* 33 (1946): 257–79, 431–61.

Sanford, Eva Matthews. "Honorius, *Presbyter* and *Scholasticus*." *Speculum* 23 (1948): 397–425.

Santiago-Otero, Horacio. *El conocimiento de Cristo en cuanto hombre en la teología de la primera mitad del siglo XII*. Pamplona: Ediciones Universidad de Navarra, S.A., 1970.

————. "El conocimiento del alma de Cristo, según las enseñanzas de Anselmo de Laon y de su escuela." *Salmanticenses* 13 (1966): 61–79.

————. "El 'nihilianismo cristológico' y las tres opiniones." *Burgense* 10 (1969): 431–43.

————. "El término 'teología' en Pedro Abelardo." In *Sprache und Erkenntnis im Mittelalter*. Miscellanea mediaevalia, 13:2. Ed. Albert Zimmerman. Berlin: Walter de Gruyter, 1981, pp. 881–89.

————. "'Esse et habere' en Hugo de San Victor." In *L'Homme et son univers au moyen âge*. Vol. 1. Ed. Christian Wenin. Louvain-la-Neuve: Institut d'Études Médiévales, 1986, pp. 426–31.

————. "Gualterio de Mortagne (d. 1174) y las controversias cristológicas del siglo XII." *Revista española de teología* 27 (1967): 271–83.

————. "La actividad sapiencial de Cristo en cuanto hombre en la 'Suma de la sentencias'." *Revista española de teología* 28 (1968): 77–91.

————. "La sabiduría del alma de Cristo según Hugo de San Victor." *Recherches de théologie ancienne et médiévale* 34 (1967): 131–58.

————. "Pedro Lombardo: Su tesis acerca del saber de Cristo hombre." In *Miscelánea José Zunzunegui (1911–1974)*. Vol. 1. Vitoria: Editorial Eset, 1975, pp. 115–25.

Sartori, Luigi. "Natura e grazia nella dottrina di S. Bernardo." *Studia patavina* 1 (1954): 41–64.

Schlette, Heinz Robert. "Das unterschiedliche Personenverständnis im theologischen Denken Hugos und Richards von St. Viktor." In *Miscellanea Martin Grabmann: Gedenkenblatt zum 10. Todestag*. Munich: Max Hueber Verlag, 1959, pp. 55–72.

————. "Die Eucharistielehre Hugos von St. Viktor." *Zeitschrift für katholische Theologie* 81 (1959): 67–100, 163–210.

Schmidt, Margot. "*Regio dissimilitudinis*: Ein Grundbegriff mittelhochdeutscher Prosa im Lichte seiner lateinischen Bedeutungsgeschichte." *Freiburger Zeitschrift für Philosophie und Theologie* 15 (1968): 63–108.

Schmidt, Martin Anton. "Das Sentenzenwerk des Petrus Lombardus und sein Aufstieg zum Muster– und Textbuch der theologischen Ausbildung." In *Handbuch der Dogmen- und Theologiegeschichte.* Vol. 1. Göttingen: Vandenhoeck & Ruprecht, 1982, pp. 587–615.

————. *Gottheit und Trinitaet nach dem Kommentar des Gilbert Porreta zu Boethius, De Trinitate.* Studia Philosophica, Supplementum, 7. Basel: Verlag für Recht und Gesellschaft, 1956.

Schmoll, Polykarp. *Die Busslehre der Frühscholastik: Eine dogmengeschichtliche Untersuchung.* Munich: J. J. Lentnerschen Buchhandlung, 1909.

Schneider, Johannes. *Die Lehre vom dreieinigen Gott in der Schule des Petrus Lombardus.* Munich: Max Hueber Verlag, 1961.

Schneider, Karin. "Petrus Lombardus in mittelhochdeutscher Sprache." *Zeitschrift für deutsches Altertum und deutsche Literatur* 107 (1978): 151–64.

Schrimpf, Gangolf. *Die Axiomenschrift des Boethius (De hebdomadibus) als philosophisches Lehrbuch des Mittelalters.* Leiden: E. J. Brill, 1966.

Schultz, Janice L. "Honorius Augustodunensis." In *Dictionary of the Middle Ages.* Vol. 6. Ed. Joseph R. Strayer. New York: Charles Scribner's Sons, 1985, pp. 285–86.

Schupp, Johann. *Die Gnadenlehre des Petrus Lombardus.* Freiburg im Breisgau: Herder, 1932.

Schütz, Christian. *Deus absconditus, Deus manifestus: Die Lehre Hugos von St. Viktor über die Offenbarung Gottes.* Rome: Herder, 1967.

Siepl, Ignaz. "Die Lehre von der göttliche Tugend der Liebe in des Petrus Lombardus Büchern der Sentenzen und in der *Summa theologica* des hl. Thomas von Aquin." *Der Katholik,* ser. 3:34 (1906): 37–49, 189–201.

Sheehan, Michael M. "Choice of Marriage Partner in the Middle Ages." *Studies in Medieval and Renaissance History,* n.s. 1 (1978): 1–33.

————. "Theory and Practice: Marriage of the Unfree and the Poor in Medieval Society." *Mediaeval Studies* 50 (1988): 457–87.

Siegmund, P. Albert. *Die Überlieferung der griechischen christlichen Literatur in der lateinischen Kirche bis zum zwölften Jahrhundert.* Munich: Filser-Verlag, 1949.

Sikes, J. G. *Peter Abailard.* Cambridge: Cambridge University Press, 1932.

Silvain, René. "La tradition des Sentences d'Anselme de Laon." *Archives d'histoire doctrinale et littéraire du moyen âge* 22–23 (1947–48): 1–52.

Silverstein, Theodore. "The Fabulous Cosmogony of Bernardus Silvestris." *Modern Philology* 46 (1948): 92–116.

Silvestre, Hubert. "'Diversi sed non adversi'." *Recherches de théologie ancienne et médiévale* 31 (1964): 124–32.

————. "L'Idylle d'Abélard et Héloise: La part du roman." *Académie Royale de Belgique,* Bulletin de la classe des lettres et des sciences morales et politiques, 5:71 (1985): 157–200.

Simon, Maurice. "La Glose de l'épître aux Romains de Gilbert de la Porrée." *Revue d'histoire ecclésiastique* 52 (1957): 51–80.

Simonis, Walter, *Trinität und Vernunft: Untersuchungen zur Möglichkeit einer rationalen Trinitätslehre bei Anselm, Abaelard, den Viktorinern, A. Günther und J. Frohschammer.* Frankfurt: Josef Knecht, 1972.

Smalley, Beryl. "Gilbertus Universalis, Bishop of London (1128–34), and the Problem of the 'Glossa Ordinaria'." *Recherches de théologie ancienne et médiévale* 7 (1935): 235–62; 8 (1936): 24–60.

————. "Glossa ordinaria." In *Theologische Realenzyklopädie.* Vol. 13:3–4. Ed. Gerhard Müller et al. Berlin: Walter de Gruyter, 1984, pp. 452–57.

————. "La Glossa Ordinaria: Quelques prédécesseurs d'Anselme de Laon."

Recherches de théologie ancienne et médiévale 9 (1937): 365–400.

———. "L'Exégèse biblique dans la littérature latine." In *La Bibbia nell'alto medioevo*. Settimane di studio del Centro italiano di studi sull'alto medioevo, 10. Spoleto: Presso la Sede del Centro, 1963, pp. 631–55.

———. "L'Exégèse biblique du 12ᵉ siècle." In *Entretiens sur la renaissance du 12ᵉ siècle*. Ed. Maurice de Gandillac and Édouard Jeauneau. Paris: Mouton, 1968, pp. 273–83.

———. "Peter Comestor on the Gospels and His Sources." *Recherches de théologie ancienne et médiévale* 46 (1979): 84–129.

———. "*Prima clavis sapientiae*: Augustine and Abelard." In *Studies in Medieval Thought and Learning from Abelard to Wyclif*. London: Hambledon Press, 1981, pp. 1–8.

———. "Some Gospel Commentaries of the Early Twelfth Century." *Recherches de théologie ancienne et médiévale* 45 (1978): 147–80.

———. "The Bible in the Medieval Schools." In *Cambridge History of the Bible: The West from the Fathers to the Reformation*. Vol. 2. Ed. G. W. H. Lampe. Cambridge: Cambridge University Press, 1969, pp. 197–220.

———. *The Gospels in the Schools, c. 1100–c. 1280*. London: Hambledon Press, 1985.

———. *The Study of the Bible in the Middle Ages*. 2nd ed. New York: Philosophical Library, 1952.

Smalley, Beryl and Lacombe, George. "The Lombard's Commentary on Isaias and Other Fragments." *New Scholasticism* 5 (1931): 123–62.

Smiśniewicz, Leon M. *Die Lehre von den Ehehindernissen bei Petrus Lombardus und bei seinen Kommentatoren*. Posen: Drukarnia Katolicka, 1917.

Sommerfeldt, John R. "Bernard of Clairvaux and Scholasticism." *Papers of the Michigan Academy of Sciences, Arts, and Letters* 48 (1963): 265–77.

Southern Richard W. "Humanism and the School of Chartres." In *Medieval Humanism and Other Studies*. New York: Harper & Row, 1970, pp. 61–85.

———. *Platonism, Scholastic Method, and the School of Chartres*. Reading: University of Reading, 1979.

———. "The Schools of Paris and the School of Chartres." In *Renaissance and Renewal in the Twelfth Century*. Ed. Robert L. Benson and Giles Constable. Cambridge, MA: Harvard University Press, 1982, pp. 113–37.

Spagnolini, Pietro. "Cenni su l'esgesi nei *Libri delle Sentenze*." *Pier Lombardo* 4 (1960): 35–47.

Spicq, Ceslaus. *Esquisse d'une histoire de l'exégèse latine au moyen âge*. Paris: J. Vrin, 1944.

———. "Pourquoi le moyen-âge n'a-t-il pas davantage pratiqué l'exégèse littérale?" *Revue des sciences philosophiques et théologiques* 30 (1941–42): 169–79.

Spitzig, Joseph A. *Sacramental Penance in the Twelfth and Thirteenth Centuries*. Washington: Catholic University of America Press, 1947.

Sprandel, Rolf. *Ivo von Chartres und seine Stellung in der Kirchengeschichte*. Stuttgart: Anton Hiersemann, 1962.

Stegmüller, Friedrich. "Die Quellen der *Sententiae Varsavienses*." *Divus Thomas* 46 (1943): 375–84.

———. *Repertorium commentariorum in Sententias Petri Lombardi*. 2 vols. Würzburg: F. Schöningh, 1947.

Stickler, Alfonso M. "Teologia e diritto canonico nella storia." *Salesianum* 47 (1985): 691–706.

Stock, Brian. *Myth and Science in the Twelfth Century: A Study of Bernard Silvester*. Princeton: Princeton University Press, 1972.

Stollenwerk, Anneliese. "Der Genesiskommentar Thierrys von Chartres und die Thierry von Chartres zugeschreibenen Kommentar zu Boethius 'De Trinitate'." University of Cologne Ph.D. diss., 1971.

Studeny, Robert F. *John of Cornwall, an Opponent of Nihilianism: A Study in the Christological Controversy of the Twelfth Century*. Vienna: St. Gabriel's Mission Press, 1939.

―――. "Walter of St. Victor and the 'Apologia de Verbo Incarnato'." *Gregorianum* 18 (1937): 579–85.

Stufler, Johann. "Petrus Lombardus und Thomas von Aquin über die Natur der caritas." *Zeitschrift für katholische Theologie* 51 (1927): 399–408.

Synan, Edward A. "Brother Thomas, the Master, and the Masters." In *St. Thomas Aquinas, 1274-1974: Commemorative Studies*. Vol. 2. Ed. Armand A. Maurer et al. Toronto: Pontifical Institute of Mediaeval Studies, 1974, pp. 217–42.

Sweeney, Leo. "Lombard, Augustine and Infinity." *Manuscripta* 2 (1958): 24–40.

Teetaert, Amédée. *La Confession aux laïques dans l'église latine depuis le VIIIe jusqu'au XIVe siècle: Étude de théologie positive*. Wetteren: J. De Meester et Fils, 1926.

Theiner, Johann. "Gedanken zur Sündenlehre Abaelards in seinem Werk 'Ethica seu Scito teipsum'." In *Person im Kontext des Sittlichen: Beiträge zur Moraltheologie Josef Georg Ziegler zum sechzigsten Geburtstag gewidmet*. Ed. Joachim Piegsa and Hans Zeimentz. Düsseldorf: Patmos Verlag, 1979, pp. 110–29.

Thomas, Rudolf. *Der philosophisch-theologische Erkenntnisweg Peter Abaelards im Dialogus inter Philosophum, Judaeum et Christianum*. Bonn: Ludwig Röhrscheid Verlag, 1966.

―――. "Die Persönlichkeit Peter Abaelards im 'Dialogus inter philosophum, iudaeum et christianum' und in dem epistulae des Petrus Venerabilis: Widerspruch oder Übereinstimmung." In *Pierre Abélard, Pierre le Vénérable: Les courants philosophiques, littéraires et artistiques en occident au milieu du XIIe siècle*. Ed. René Louis, Jean Jolivet, and Jean Châtillon. Paris: CNRS, 1975, pp. 255–69.

Thompson, James Westfall, *The Development of the French Monarchy under Louis VI le Gros*. Chicago: University of Chicago Press, 1895.

Thompson, Richard J. "The Role of the Dialectical Reason in the Ethics of Abelard." *Proceedings of the American Catholic Philosophical Association* 12 (1936): 141–48.

Tříška, Josef, "Sententarii Pragensis." *Mediaevalia Philosophica Polonorum* 13 (1968): 100–10.

Tweedale, Martin M. *Abailard on Universals*. Amsterdam: North-Holland Publishing Company, 1976.

Urbani Ulivi, Lucia. *La psicologia di Abelardo e il "Tractatus de intellectibus"*. Rome: Storia e Letteratura, 1976.

Usener, Hermann. "Gislebert de la Porrée." In *Kleine Schriften*. Vol. 4. Leipzig: B. G. Teubner, 1913, pp. 154–62.

Van den Berge, Roger J. "La qualification morale de l'acte humain: Ébauche d'une reinterprétation de la pensée abélardienne." *Studia moralia* 13 (1975): 143–73.

Van den Eynde, Damien. "Autour des 'Enarrationes in Evangelium S. Matthaei' attribuées à Geoffroi Babion." *Recherches de théologie ancienne et médiévale* 26 (1959): 50–84.

―――. "Complementary Note on the Early Scholastic *Commentarii in Psalmos*." *Franciscan Studies* 17 (1957): 149–72.

―――. "De nouveau sur deux maîtres lombards contemporains du maître des Sentences." *Pier Lombardo* 1 (1953): 6–8.

―――. *Essai sur le succession et la date des écrits de Hugues de Saint-Victor*. Rome: Pontificium Athenaeum Antonianum, 1960.

―――. "La 'Theologia scholarium' de Pierre Abélard." *Recherches de théologie ancienne et médiévale* 28 (1961): 225–41.

―――. "Le recueil des Sermons de Pierre Abélard." *Antonianum* 37 (1962): 17–54.

―――. *Les définitions des sacrements pendant le première période de la théologie scolastique (1050-1240)*. Rome: Antonianum, 1950.

―――. "Les écrits perdus d'Abélard." *Antonianum* 37 (1962): 467–80.

―――. "Les 'Notulae in Genesim' de Hugues de Saint-Victor, source littéraire de la 'Summa Sententiarum'." *Antonianum* 35 (1960): 323–27.

―――. "Les rédactions de la 'Theologia Christiana' de Pierre Abélard." *Antonianum* 36 (1961): 273–99.

————. "Literary Note on the Earliest Scholastic *Commentarii in Psalmos.*" *Franciscan Studies* 14 (1954): 121–54.

————. *L'Oeuvre littéraire de Géroch de Reichersberg.* Rome: Antonianum, 1957.

————. "Nouvelles précisions sur quelques ouvrages théologiques du XIIe siècle." *Franciscan Studies* 13 (1953): 71–118.

————. "Précisions chronologiques sur quelques ouvrages théologiques du XIIe siècle." *Antonianum* 26 (1951): 223–46.

————. "The Terms 'Ius positivum' and 'Signum positivum' in Twelfth-Century Scholasticism." *Franciscan Studies* 9 (1949): 41–49.

————. "The Theory of the Composition of the Sacraments in Early Scholasticism, 1125–1240." *Franciscan Studies* 11 (1951): 1–20.

————. "William of Saint-Thierry and the Author of the *Summa Sententiarum.*" *Franciscan Studies* 10 (1950): 241–56.

Van den Hout, F. A. "Pensées de Saint Bernard sur l'être." *Cîteaux* 6 (1955): 233–40.

————. "Saint Bernard philosophe." *Cîteaux* 4 (1953): 187–205.

Van Dyk, John. "The Sentence Commentary: A Vehicle in the Intellectual Transition of the Fifteenth Century." In *Fifteenth-Century Studies*, 8. Ed. Guy R. Mermier and Edelgard E. DuBruck. Detroit: Fifteenth-Century Symposium, 1983, pp. 227–38.

————. "Thirty Years since Stegmüller: A Bibliographical Guide to the Study of Medieval Sentence Commentaries." *Franciscan Studies* 39 (1979): 255–315.

Van Engen, John. "Observations on the 'De consecratione'." In *Proceedings of the Sixth International Congress of Medieval Canon Law.* Ed. Stephan Kuttner and Kenneth Pennington. Vatican City: Biblioteca Apostolica Vaticana, 1985, pp. 309–20.

————. *Rupert of Deutz.* Berkeley: University of California Press, 1983.

————. "The 'Crisis of Cenobitism' Reconsidered: Benedictine Monasticism between the Years 1050–1150." *Speculum* 61 (1986): 269–304.

Van Hoecke, Willy and Welkenhuysen, Andries, ed. *Love and Marriage in the Twelfth Century.* Leuven: Leuven University Press, 1981.

Van Laarhoven, Jan. "Magisterium en Theologie in de 12e eeuw: De Processen te Soissons (1121), Sens (1140) en Reims (1148)." *Tijdschrift voor Theologie* 21 (1981): 108–31.

Vanneste, A. "Nature et grâce dans la théologie du douzième siècle." *Ephemerides Theologiae Lovanienses* 50 (1974): 181–214.

Vanni Rovighi, Sofia. "La filosofia di Gilberto Porretano." In *Studi di filosofia medioevale.* Vol. 1. Milan: Vita e Pensiero, 1978, pp. 176–247.

————. "S. Bernardo e la filosofia." In *S. Bernardo: Pubblicazione commemorativa nell'VII centenario della sua morte.* Milan: Vita e Pensiero, 1954, pp. 132–50.

Vaughan, Laurence S. *The Acquired Knowledge of Christ according to the Theologians of the 12th and 13th Centuries.* Rome: Pontificium Athenaeum Internationale "Angelicum," 1957.

Venuta, Goffredo. *Libero arbitrio e libertà della grazia nel pensiero di S. Bernardo.* Rome: F. Ferrari, 1953.

Vernet, A. "Un Remaniement de la *Philosophia* di Guillaume de Conches." *Scriptorium* 1 (1947): 243–59.

Viola, Coloman. "Jugements de Dieu et jugement dernier: Saint Augustin et la scolastique naissante (fin XIe-milieu XIIIe siècles)." In *The Use and Abuse of Eschatology in the Middle Ages.* Ed. Werner Verbeke, Daniel Verhelst, and Andries Welkenhuysen. Leuven: Leuven University Press, 1988, pp. 242–98.

————. "Manières personnelles et impersonnelles d'aborder un problème: Saint Augustin et le XIIe siècle. Contribution à l'histoire de la 'quaestio'." In *Les Genres littéraires dans les sources théologiques et philosophiques médiévales: Définition, critique et exploitation.* Louvain-la-Neuve: Institut d'Études Médiévales, 1982, pp. 11–30.

Volk, Ernst. "Das Gewissen bei Petrus Abaelardus, Petrus Lombardus, und

Martin Luther." In *Petrus Abaelardus (1079–1142): Person, Werk und Wirkung*. Ed. Rudolf Thomas. Trier: Paulinus-Verlag, 1980, pp. 297–330.

Wasselynck, René. "La présence des *Moralia* de saint Grégoire le Grand dans les ouvrages de morale du XIIᵉ siècle." *Recherches de théologie ancienne et médiévale* 35 (1968): 197–240.

Weigand, Rudolf. "Kanonistische Ehetraktate aus dem 12. Jahrhundert." In *Proceedings of the Third International Congress of Medieval Canon Law*. Ed. Stephan Kuttner. Vatican City: Biblioteca Apostolica Vaticana, 1971, pp. 59–79.

Weijers, Olga. "The Chronology of John of Salisbury's Studies in France (Metalogicon, II. 10)." In *The World of John of Salisbury*. Ed. Michael Wilks. Studies in Church History, Subsidia, 3. Oxford: Basil Blackwell, 1984, pp. 109–16.

Weijers, Olga, ed. *Terminologie des universités au XIIIᵉ siècle*. Rome: Edizioni dell'Ateneo, 1987.

Weingart, Richard E. "Peter Abailard's Contribution to Medieval Sacramentology." *Recherches de théologie ancienne et médiévale* 34 (1967): 159–78.

———. *The Logic of Divine Love: A Critical Analysis of the Soteriology of Peter Abailard*. Oxford: Clarendon Press, 1970.

Weisweiler, Heinrich. "Das Sakrament der Firmung in den systematischen Werken der ersten Frühscholastik." *Scholastik* 8 (1933): 481–523.

———. "Das Sakrament der Letzten Ölung in den systematischen Werken der ersten Frühscholastik." *Scholastik* 7 (1932): 321–53, 524–60.

———. "Die Arbeitsmethode Hugos von St. Viktor: Ein Beitrag zum Entstehen seines Hauptwerkes *De sacramentis*." *Scholastik* 20–24 (1949): 59–87, 232–67.

———. "Die Arbeitsweise der sogennanten *Sententiae Anselmi*: Ein Beitrag zum Entstehen der systematischen Werke der Theologie." *Scholastik* 34 (1959): 190–232.

———. "Die frühe Summe *Deus de cuius principio et fine tacetur*, eine neue Quelle der *Sententiae Anselmi*: Das Wachsen der scholastischen Angelologie und Anthropologie aus patristischen Denken." *Scholastik* 35 (1960): 209–43.

———. "Die Klagenfurter Sentenzen *Deus est sine principio*, die erste Vorlesung der Schule Anselms von Laon: Zum Werden der frühscholastischen Lehre von Schöpfung und Fall, Erlösung und christlicher Moraltheologie." *Scholastik* 36 (1961): 512–49, 37 (1962): 45–84.

———. "Die Ps.-Dionysiuskommentare 'In Coelestem Hierarchiam' des Skotus Eriugena und Hugos von St. Viktor." *Recherches de théologie ancienne et médiévale* 19 (1952): 26–47.

———. *Die Wirksamkeit der Sakramente nach Hugo von St. Viktor*. Freiburg im Breisgau, Herder & Co., 1932.

———. "Eine neue Bearbeitung von Abaelards 'Introductio' und der Summa sententiarum." *Scholastik* 9 (1934): 346–71.

———. "Eine neue frühe Glosse zum vierten Buch der Sentenzen des Petrus Lombardus." In *Aus der Geisteswelt des Mittelalters: Studien und Texte Martin Grabmann zur Vollendung des 60. Lebensjahres von Freunden und Schülern gewidmet*. Vol. 1. Ed. Albert Lang, Joseph Lechner, and Michael Schmaus. Beiträge zur Geschichte der Philosophie und Theologie des Mittelalters, Supplementband, 3:1. Münster: Aschendorff, 1935, pp. 360–400.

———. "Hugos von St. Viktor *Dialogus de sacramentis legis naturalis et scriptae* als frühscholastisches Quellenwerk." In *Miscellanea Giovanni Mercati*. Vol. 2. Vatican City: Biblioteca Apostolica Vaticana, 1946, pp. 179–219.

———. "La 'Summa Sententiarum' source de Pierre Lombard." *Recherches de théologie ancienne et médiévale* 6 (1934): 143–83.

———. "L'École d'Anselme de Laon et de Guillaume de Champeaux: Nouveaux documents." *Recherches de théologie ancienne et médiévale* 4 (1932): 237–69, 371–91.

———. "Sakrament als Symbol und Teilhabe: Der Einfluss des ps.-Dionysius auf die allgemeine Sakramentenlehre Hugos von St. Viktor." *Scholastik* 27 (1952): 321–43.

———. "*Sacramentum fidei*: Augustinische und ps.-dionysische Gedanken in der

Glaubensauffassung Hugos von St. Viktor." In *Theologie in Geschichte und Gegenwart: Michael Schmaus zum sechzigsten Geburtstag dargebracht von seiner Freunden und Schülern*. Ed. Johann Auer and Hermann Volk. Munich: Karl Zink, 1957, pp. 433–56.

———. "Wie entstanden die frühen Sententiae Berolinensis der Schule Anselms von Laon?" *Scholastik* 34 (1959): 321–69.

Westley, Richard J. "A Philosophy of the Concreted and the Concrete: The Constitution of Creatures according to Gilbert de la Porrée." *Modern Schoolman* 37 (1960): 257–86.

Wetherbee, Winthrop. *Platonism and Poetry in the Twelfth Century: The Literary Influence of the School of Chartres*. Princeton: Princeton University Press, 1972.

Wicki, Nikolaus. "Das 'Prognosticon futuri saeculi' Julians von Toledo als Quellenwerk der Sentenzen des Petrus Lombardus." *Divus Thomas* 31 (1953): 349–60.

———. *Die Lehre von der himmlischen Seligkeit in der mittelalterlichen Scholastik von Petrus Lombardus bis Thomas von Aquin*. Freiburg in der Schweiz: Universitätsverlag, 1954.

Wielocks, Robert. "La discussion scolastique sur l'amour d'Anselme de Laon à Pierre Lombard d'après les imprimés et les inédits." Katholieke Universiteit te Leuven, Hoger Instituut vor Wijsbegeerte Ph.D. diss., 1981.

Wielockx. R. "Autour de la *Glossa ordinaria*." *Recherches de théologie ancienne et médiévale* 49 (1982): 222–28.

———. "La sentence 'De caritate' et la discussion scolastique sur l'amour." *Ephemerides Theologicae Lovanienses* 58 (1982): 50–86, 334–56.

Williams, John R. "The Cathedral School of Reims in the Time of Master Alberic, 1118–1136." *Traditio* 20 (1964): 93–114.

Williams, Michael B. *The Teaching of Gilbert Porreta on the Trinity as Found in His Commentaries on Boethius*. Rome: Apud Aedes Universitatis Gregorianae, 1951.

Williams, Paul. *The Moral Philosophy of Peter Abelard*. Lanham, MD: University Press of America, 1980.

Wilmart, André. "Le commentaire sur les Psaumes imprimé sous le nom de Rufin." *Revue bénédictine* 31 (1914–19): 258–76.

———. "Un commentaire des Psaumes restitué à Anselme de Laon." *Recherches de théologie ancienne et médiévale* 8 (1936): 325–44.

Wlodek, Zofia. "Commentaires sur les *Sentences*: Supplément au Répertoire de F. Stegmüller." *Mediaevalia Philosophica Polonorum* 5 (1963): 144–46.

———. "Commentaires sur les *Sentences*: Supplément au Répertoire de F. Stegmüller d'après les MSS. de la Bibliothèque de Wrocław." *Bulletin de philosophie médiévale* 6 (1964): 100–04.

———. "Commentaires sur les *Sentences*: Supplément au Répertoire de F. Stegmüller d'après les MSS. de la Bibliothèque du Grand Séminaire de Pelplin." *Mediaevalia Philosophica Polonorum* 8 (1961): 33–38.

———. "Commentaires sur les *Sentences*: Supplément au Répertoire de F. Stegmüller d'après les MSS. des bibliothèques de Prague." *Bulletin de philosophie médiévale* 7 (1965): 91–95.

Wójciki, Kazimierz. "Commentaires sur les *Sentences*: Supplément au Répertoire de F. Stegmüller." *Mediaevalia Philosophica Polonorum* 13 (1968): 111–14.

Zedelghem, Amédée de. "Doctrine d'Abélard au sujet de la valeur morale de la crainte des peines." *Estudis Franciscans* 36 (1926): 108–25.

———. "L'Attritionisme d'Abélard." *Estudis Franciscans* 35 (1925): 178–94, 333–45.

Zeimentz, Hans. *Ehe nach der Lehre der Frühscholastik: Eine moralgeschichtliche Untersuchung zur Anthropologie und Theologie der Ehe in der Schule Anselms von Laon und Wilhelms von Champeaux, bei Hugo von St. Viktor, Walter von Mortagne und Petrus Lombardus*. Düsseldorf, Patmos-Verlag, 1973.

Zier, Mark A. "Peter Lombard." In *A Dictionary of the Middle Ages*. Vol. 9. Ed. Joseph R. Strayer. New York: Charles Scribner's Sons, 1987, pp. 516–17.

Zigon, Franz. "Der Begriff der Caritas beim Lombarden, und der hl. Thomas."

Divus Thomas 4 (1926): 404–24.

Zimara, C. "Quelques idées d'Abélard au sujet de l'espérance chrétienne." *Revue thomiste*, n.s. 18 (1935): 37–47.

Zinn, Grover A. "*Historia fundamentum est*: The Role of History in the Contemplative Life according to Hugh of St. Victor." In *Contemporary Reflections on the Medieval Christian Tradition: Essays in Honor of Ray C. Petry.* Ed. George H. Schriver. Durham: Duke University Press, 1974, pp. 135–58.

INDEX OF NAMES

Abel, 207
Abelard, Peter, v, ix, 5, 12, 17, 18, 44,
47–51, 52, 54–55, 66, 67, 72, 76,
85, 88, 90 n. 95, 96–104, 105, 106,
108, 109, 110, 113, 114, 115, 119,
120, 122, 128, 131, 136–37, 138 n.
129, 139, 141, 148, 150, 153, 154,
160, 189, 194–95, 198, 199, 200,
201, 202, 204, 212, 213, 219, 228,
230, 233, 234, 235, 236, 239, 241,
245, 247, 249, 253–60, 269–75, 276,
277, 281, 282, 284, 287, 288, 289,
290–302, 304, 311, 313, 314,
323–26, 328, 339, 345, 362, 365–66,
374, 388–89, 393, 394, 397, 400,
409, 411, 413, 431, 432, 438, 444,
453–55, 456–57, 458, 459, 463, 466,
467–68, 469, 477–78, 483–84, 487,
493–94, 495, 496, 497, 500, 505,
514, 534–35, 536, 540, 549, 566,
567, 595, 600, 601, 606, 639 n. 433,
640, 649, 650 n. 466, 774; as an
avant-garde thinker, 5, 48;
Aristotelianism in, 5, 48; Platonism
in, 57, 212, 213, 239, 245, 254–59,
493; doctrine of World Soul in, 51,
212–13, 239, 249, 253–60, 324, 493;
as a logician, 49, 50, 54–55, 67, 76,
83, 96, 98–100, 270–71, 274, 275,
276, 289, 290, 291–92, 294–95, 296,
496, 777; nominalist argument in,
85, 274, 285; *Logica "ingredientibus"*,
271, 274, 275; *Dialectica*, 259, 260;
Commentary on Romans, 48, 49 nn.
30–31, 33, 189, 194–95, 196, 198,
199, 200, 201, 202, 204, 290, 294,
295, 453; commentaries on
Apostles' and Athanasian Creeds,
409–10; sermons delivered as abbot
of St. Gildas, 49 n. 33, 409; *Sic et
non*, treatment of authorities in, 44,
50, 88, 253, 503; as a systematic
theologian, 47–51; *Theologia "summi
boni"*, 48, 49, 51, 254, 257; *Theologia
christiana*, 48, 49, 257, 290, 291, 292,
293, 295; *Theologia "scholarium"*, 48,
49, 257, 258, 259, 274–75, 290, 294,
295, 323, 324, 410, 492, 494;
schema of *theologiae*, 47–50; logical
inconsistencies in, 49–50; use of
authorities in, 50–51, 90 n. 95;

omissions in, 48, 52; theological
language in, 96–104, 105, 106, 108,
109, 110, 115, 119, 120, 126, 153,
154; doctrine of God in, 100, 122,
228, 229, 230, 269, 271–75, 276,
277, 281, 282, 290; God's
foreknowledge, predestination,
and providence in relation to
contingency, free will in, 269,
271–75, 276, 277, 281, 282, 290;
whether God can do better or different
than He does, 54–55, 85, 290–92,
293, 294–95, 296, 297; doctrine of
Trinity in, 100–04, 105, 106, 108,
109, 110, 113, 115, 120, 126, 131;
Hexaemeron, 48, 49 n. 33, 255, 323,
324, 325, 519, 641; creation in, 48,
255, 304, 323–26; fall of man in, 48,
49, 50, 325, 374, 388–89, 393, 394,
397; opposition to astral
determinism in, 325, 334;
Christology in, 139, 400, 409–10,
411, 412; as Peter Lombard's
alleged source for *habitus* theory of
hypostatic union, 431; Christ's
saving work in, 48, 219, 345, 449,
453–55, 456–57, 458, 459, 463, 469,
519, 641; *Ethics*, ix, 48 n. 29, 48;
intentionalism in, 49, 50, 301–02,
467, 477–78, 483–84, 487, 519,
534–35, 549, 595; definitions of sin
and virtue in, 301–02; faith in,
493–95, 496, 497, 749; charity in,
500; sacraments in, 519, 534–35,
536, 540, 549, 594–98; baptism in,
519, 534–35, 540, 549, 595; infant
baptism, 534–35, 549, 595; penance
in, 519, 595, 600, 601, 604, 606;
marriage in, 519, 639 n. 433,
640–41, 650 n. 466; as criticized by
Alberic of Rheims, 17; by Bruno
the Carthusian, 160; by Gilbert of
Poitiers, 128, 136–37, 139, 407–08,
409; by Hugh of St. Victor, 293,
294; by *Invisibilia dei*, 141; by
Porretans, 54–55, 85, 292; by
Robert of Melun, 296; by *Summa
sententiarum*, 113, 393–94; by
William of St. Thierry, 189; by
Peter Lombard, 85, 119–31, 148,
150, 154, 212–13, 239–41, 254–60,

372, 374–76, 378–80, 396, 733, 777; in *Sententie Anselmi*, 374; in Roland of Bologna, 374; in Porretans, 375, in Hugh of St. Victor, 375–76, 380; in *Summa sententiarum*, 374, 378, 380; in Peter Lombard, 378–80, 396, 733, 777. *See also* Eve; Man, nature of, original sin in

Adam, bishop of St. Asaph, 433–34

Adam du Petit-Pont, logician, 433; *Ars disserendi* of, 433

Adam of Balsham. *See* Adam du Petit-Pont

Adam of Wales. *See* Adam, bishop of St. Asaph

Adelard of Bath, 5

Alberic of Trois Fontaines, as testimonium of Peter Lombard, 31

Alberic, master at school of Rheims, opponent of Peter Abelard, later bishop of Bourges, 17

Alcuin, 173, 183, 184, 185, 340; as exegete of the Psalms, 173, 183, 184, 185; as an authority on creation, 340. *See also* Psalms, book of

Alexander III, pope, 65–66 n. 57, 429, 431, 432, 433, 434, 658; as not the same person as Roland of Bologna, 65–66 n. 57; as convenor of synod of Tours (1163), 429; consistory in Rome, 433, 434; Third Lateran council (1179), 429, 432; reform of St. Victor as ordered by, 431; support for principle of consent in marriage formation, 568. *See also* Adam of St. Asaph; Christology; John of Cornwall; Lateran council, Third; Sacraments, marriage; Tours, synod of; Victor, St.; Walter of St. Victor; William of the White Hands

Alexander of Hales, as adding distinction subdivisions to text of Peter Lombard's *Sentences*, 78 n. 75

Alger of Liège, 520–21, 522, 555, 561–62, 563, 564, 566, 591, 614; schema for organization of sacraments in, 520–21, 522; change of Eucharistic elements in, 555; differential effects of Eucharistic reception in, 561–62, 563, 564; spiritual benefits received by communicant in, 561–62, 563, 564, 566; defense of confessionism in penance in, 591; validity of sacraments administered by

unworthy priest in, 614. *See also* Sacraments, Eucharist, penance

Ambrose, 202, 322, 395, 462, 468, 481, 504, 536, 632, 637, 691, 747; his confusion with Ambrosiaster in twelfth century, 462; transmission of original sin in, 395, 462, 481; titles to be given to Christ in, 468; sin in, 481; cardinal virtues in, 504, 747; theological virtues in, 504; baptism by blood and by desire in, 536; defense of consent as principle of marriage formation in, 632, 637; remarriage, 691; on medicinal use of garlic, in *Commentarius Cantabridgensis*, 202; *De paradiso*, 322; *Hexaemeron*, 481. *See also* Christ; Ethics; Exegesis, biblical; Man, doctrine of; Sacraments, baptism, marriage

Ambrosiaster, 462. *See* Ambrose

Anonymous, Chartrain, commentator on Martianus Capella, 314–15; doctrine of Trinity in, 314–15; World Soul as a force of nature in, 315; as equatable with God or Holy Spirit, 315; incorporeals in, 315; creation *simul* in, 315. *See also* Chartrains; Creation

Anonymous of Arras, monk, on Peter Lombard as a biblical exegete, 157

Anselm, archbishop of Canterbury, 5, 6, 37, 38 n. 6, 42, 91, 218, 219, 220, 322, 344, 349, 449, 451–53, 454, 455, 457, 458, 459, 460, 461, 463, 464, 465, 466, 481, 486, 498, 742; as a Christian Aristotelian, 5; as a harbinger of scholasticism, 6; as a likely teacher of Honorius Augustodunensis, 37, 38 n. 6, 42; lack of interest in systematic theology in, 42; rationale for man's creation in, 322; Christ's saving work in, 218, 219, 220, 344, 449, 451–53, 454, 455, 457, 458, 459, 460, 461, 463, 464, 465, 466; on why fallen angels cannot be saved, 344, 349; evil as non-being in, 481; faith in, 498; *Cur deus homo*, 218, 344, 449, 451–53, 454, 457, 458. *See also* Angels; Christ; Ethics; Faith; Honorius Augustodunensis

Anselm of Laon, 6, 17, 42, 43, 44–47, 95, 164, 167, 180, 264, 276, 277, 278, 289, 328–29, 365, 373, 374, 376, 377, 475, 504, 508, 519, 533–34, 555, 570, 571, 592, 610, 670–71,

before the fall, in Porretans, 355; her motivation in original sin, in Anselm of Laon, 373, 377; in *Sententie Anselmi*, 373, 377; in William of Champeaux, 373; in Hugh of St. Victor, 373, 375, 378; in Peter Lombard, 372, 377, 378, 379, 488; on whether she sinned more seriously than Adam, 372–73, 374–76, 378–79; in Anselm of Laon, 374; in school of Laon, 374; in William of Champeaux, 375; in Peter Abelard, 374; in Robert Pullen, 374, 375; in Porretans, 375; in *Summa sententiarum*, 375; in Peter Lombard, 378–79, 380, 733, 777; view that primal parents were equally guilty, in Hugh of St. Victor, 375–76, 380; as a type of the church, in *Glossa ordinaria*, 165–66, Roland of Bologna, 331; in *Summa sententiarum*, 331, 367; in Peter Lombard, 367. *See also* Adam; Church, doctrine of; Man, doctrine of, original sin in

Exodus, book of, 28, 86, 335, 392, 396, 511

Ezechiel, prophet, 386, 504; virtues as analogized to figures in his vision, in Gregory the Great, 504; in *Sententie Anselmi*, 504. *See also* Ethics

Flint, Valerie I. J., 41

Florus of Lyon, 86, 88, 165, 193; his *catena* of Augustine, 86, 88; as model for abbreviated citation of authorities in *Glossa ordinaria*, 165, 193; in Robert of Melun's *Quaestiones de epistolas Pauli*, 193. *See also* Augustine; Exegesis, biblical, *Glossa ordinaria*, Robert of Melun

Fulgentius of Ruspe, 34 n. 2

Gabriel, archangel, 351

Galen, on human conception, 414, 415

Gandulph of Bologna, 435–36; as abbreviator of Peter Lombard and possible source for idea that he taught Christological nihilianism, 435–36; *habitus* theory in, 436. *See also* Christ

Genesis, book of, 1, 28, 56, 58–59, 62, 75, 81, 88, 231, 235, 255, 303–04, 308, 309–10, 316–18, 319, 320–21, 323, 325, 326–29, 331, 333, 336, 339, 340, 348, 367, 376, 380, 727, 728; creation account in, 56, 58–59,

62, 75, 88, 231, 235, 255, 303–04, 308, 309–10, 316–18, 319, 320–21, 323, 325, 326–27, 328, 329, 331, 333, 336, 339, 340, 348, 367, 727, 728; Augustine's interpretation of, 62, 88, 258, 317, 318, 321, 324, 326, 328, 333, 340; efforts, by Chartrains, to synthesize it with Platonic account of creation, 303–04, 309–10, 316, 320–21, 727; in Thierry of Chartres, 309–10; in Clarenbald of Arras, 316–18; account of original sin in, 376, 380. *See also* Augustine; Chartrains; Clarenbald of Arrras; Creation; Plato; Platonism; Thierry of Chartres

Gennadius, 34 n. 2, 581

Gerhoch of Reichersberg, 17, 31, 158, 161–62, 427–28; as testimonium of Peter Lombard, 31; his objections to Christology of Lotulph of Novara, 17; of Peter Lombard, 31, 427–28; whether human Christ should receive *dulia* or *latria* in, 427–28; as exegete of the Psalms, 158, 161–62; typology in, 161; use of authorities in, 161, 162; digressive style in, 161–62; contritionist-confessionist debate on penance in, 162; grace and free will in, 162. *See also* Christ; Exegesis, biblical; Grace, doctrine of; Free Will, doctrine of; Lotulph of Novara; Peter Lombard; Psalms, book of; Sacraments, penance

Geyer, Bernhard, 5

Ghellinck, Joseph de, 9, 10, 42

Gilbert of Poitiers, v, ix, 5, 12, 18, 24 n. 26, 52–53, 72, 96, 102, 104, 105, 119, 128, 129, 131, 132–48, 149, 150, 151, 152, 153, 154, 156, 162, 164, 167–70, 172, 173, 174, 187, 196, 215–17, 227, 229, 230, 245, 246, 249, 252, 304, 399–400, 404–07, 408, 409, 411, 418, 419–20, 422–25, 429–30, 432, 433, 437, 441, 448, 571, 598, 599, 610; as an avant-garde thinker in his day, 5; teaching career at Chartres, 53, 133, 304; at Paris, 24 n. 26, 53, 133, 168, 215 n. 155; trial at Council of Rheims (1148), 52; biblical exegesis of, 133, 156, 162, 164, 167–70, 172, 173, 174, 187, 196, 408, 448; *Media glossatura* as medieval name for, 156; commentary on the Psalms, 133, 162, 164, 167–70, 172, 173, 174,

592, 615, 663 n. 489, 664, 665, 666, 667, 669, 672–73, 677, 680, 683, 685, 687, 688, 689, 690, 693, 696, 763; validity of their administration by heretic, excommunicated, or immoral priest in, 521, 572, 592, 580; baptism in, 519, 521, 537, 543 n. 184, 545; infant baptism in, 537; time of baptism in, 543 n. 184; validity of if improper verbal formula is used in, 545; confirmation in, 521, 549; Eucharist in, 519, 521, 555–56, 566, 572, 579–80, 582, 757; real presence doctrine in, 555–56; spiritual benefits of reception in, 566; validity as affected by juridical status or morality of minister in, 572, 579, 580; defense of confessionism in penance in, 521, 589–90, 763; unction in, 521; holy orders in, 521, 615; accent on juridical and administrative rules pertaining to in, 615; ruling that monastic priest has same sacerdotal faculties as secular priest, 615; defense of consummation as principle of marriage formation, 521, 631, 763; change in rules governing marriage over time in, 663 n. 489; mutuality of spouses in rendering marriage debt in, 677, 696; marital impediments, grounds for nullification, separation in, 664, 665, 666, 667, 669, 672–73, 677, 679, 680, 683, 685, 687, 688, 689, 690, 691, 692, 693, 696; *De consecratione*, 519; *Decretum*, 28, 65, 89; *De penitentia*, 519. *See also* Charity; Ethics; Roland of Bologna; Paucapalea; Perjury, Peter Comestor; Peter Lombard; Sacraments

Gregory I, the Great, pope, 83, 89, 149, 165, 176, 199, 321, 329, 335, 340, 343, 346, 350, 374, 449, 475, 483, 485, 504, 511, 530, 541, 573, 584, 586, 587, 601, 659, 674, 699, 701–02, 703, 704, 705, 706, 708, 709, 712–13, 729, 715, 746, 747, 772; as an exegete of the Psalms, 165; misquotation in *Commentarius Cantabridgensis*, 199; *Moralia in Job*, 83, 485, 699, 704; as an authority on creation, 321, 335, 340, 729; on angelic hierarchy, 329, 343, 350, 729; on guardian angels, 346; on

"rights of the devil" view of atonement, 149; on cardinal and theological virtues, 504, 747; on etiology of seven deadly sins, 374, 485, 746; on salvation in the pre-Christian dispensation, 530; on pious fraud as an excuse for lying, 475, 483, 511; on administration of baptism, 55, 89, 541, 570; on repeatability of penance, 584, 586, 587; on definition of contrition, 601; on sexual relations and sexual dysfunction in marriage, 659, 674; on Last Things, 83, 176, 699, 701–02, 703, 704, 705, 706, 708, 709, 712–13, 715, 772; on the four states of souls in the resurrection, 176. *See also* Angels; Christ; Ethics; Last Things; Leander of Seville; Sacraments, baptism, penance, marriage

Gregory VII, pope, reform movement of, 35, 37, 428, 517, 520, 552, 59

Gregory Nazianzus, 706

Gross-Diaz, Theresa, 167

Guérin, abbot of St. Victor, 432

Häring, Nikolaus M., 19, 429

Haimo of Auxerre, as an exegete of the Psalms, 178, 179, 184; as an exegete of 1 and 2 Thessalonians, 206

Hauréau, Barthélemy, 5

Heloise, abbess of the Paraclete, 255, 323, 457, 641

Heman, as an author of Psalms, 171

Henry II, king of England, 433

Henry, bishop of Beauvais, 21

Herbert of Bosham, pupil of the Lombard, 23, 24; testimony that the master's Psalms commentary was written for his personal reflection, 23; as external witness to double redaction of Peter Lombard's commentary on Pauline epistles, 24; as putting finishing touches on his biblical exegesis, 24. *See also* Exegesis, biblical; Paul, St.; Peter Lombard; Psalms, book of

Hermannus, 51 n. 43, 52, 477, 505, 519 n. 113, 554, 566, 598, 598 n. 333, 611–12, 641–42, 644, 647, 655, 665, 666, 674, 683, 691; ethics in, 477, 505; intentionalism in, 477; natural virtue in, 505; definition of sacrament in, 519 n. 113; Eucharist in, 554, 566; which body Christ gave disciples at last supper in, 554; spiritual benefits of communion in, 566; inconsistent defense of contritionism in penance in, 598, 598 n. 333; unrepeatability of unction in, 611–12; defense of consent as principle of marriage formation in, 641–42; purely remedial conception of marriage in, 642, 647, 655, 674; change in rules governing marriage over time in, 664; marital impediments, grounds for nullification, separation in, 665, 666, 674, 683, 691. *See also* Abelard, Peter; Abelardians; Ethics; Sacraments, Eucharist, penance, marriage

Hervaeus of Bourg-Dieu, as an exegete of Romans, 188, 190–93; *accessus* to text in, 190–91; style and format in, 191, 193; use of authorities including Peter Abelard, Peter Lombard in, 190–91; moral emphasis in, 191–92; natural theology in, 191; anthropology in, 191; grace and free will in, 192

Hilary of Poitiers, 144, 163, 167, 251, 321, 444; as an authority favored by Gilbert of Poitiers, 144; as an exegete of the Psalms, 163, 167; as an authority on the Trinity, 251; on creation, 321; Peter Lombard's critique of his view that Christ was impassible, 444. *See also* Christ; Christ; Creation; Exegesis, biblical; Gilbert of Poitiers; Peter Lombard; Psalms, book of; Trinity, doctrine of

Hildebert of Lavardin, erroneous ascription to him of Peter Lombard's sermons in *Patrologia latina*, 26. *See also* Peter Lombard

Honorius Augustodunensis, 5, 35, 36, 37–42, 60, 69, 264–65, 279, 304, 321–23, 342, 344–45, 351, 372, 373, 376–77, 378, 380, 457–58, 381, 518, 520, 537, 565–66, 567, 589, 610, 614, 663 n. 489, 700–03, 704, 710, 712, 713; seen as an Aristotelian, 5; likelihood of his studies with Anselm and Eadmer of Canterbury, 37–38, 42; schema and use of authorities as a systematic theologian, 38–41, 321; intended audience of, 37–38; originality of, 42; popularity of his work, 41; doctrine of God in, 264–65, 279; God's ubiquity in, 264–65;

relationship of God's foreknowledge, predestination, providence to free will, contingency in, 279; creation in, 321–23, 342, 344–45, 351, 703; creation *simul* in, 321; rationale for creation of man in, 322; man as microcosm in, 322–23; rationale for creation of animals in, 322; Eden, its location and nature in, 322; angels in, 342, 344–35, 351; original sin in, 38, 39, 372, 373, 376–77, 378, 380; Christ's saving work in, 457–58; ethics in, 39, 89, 481; interweaving of ethics and sacraments in, 69; moral aptitudes and temptations of various occupational and age groups in, 39; evil as non-being in, 481; ecclesiology of, as context for treatment of sacraments, 518, 565–66; sacraments in, 518, 520, 537, 565–66, 567, 589, 610, 614; organization of treatise on sacraments in, 518, 520; baptism in, 537; spiritual benefits of communion in, 565–66, 567; penance in, 589; unction as *viaticum* in, 610; response of laity to immoral priests in, 614; Eucharistic ministry of priests in, 614; change in rules governing marriage over time in, 663 n. 489; Last Things in, 700–03, 704, 710, 712, 713; Antichrist in, 701; general resurrection in, 701, 703, 710, 712, 713; four states of souls in, 701, 712, 713; color-coded bodies of the resurrected in, 703, 710, 712; second coming of Christ in, 702; last judgment in, 702; new heavens, new earth in, 703; Hell in, 701, 702, 703; Purgatory in, 701, 703; Heaven in, 703; *Elucidarium*, 5, 35, 36, 37–42, 60, 69. *See also* Angels; Anselm of Canterbury; Christ; Church, doctrine of; Creation; Eadmer of Canterbury; Eden, garden of; Ethics; Free will, doctrine of; Hugh of St. Victor; Julian of Toledo; Last Things; Man, doctrine of; Robert Pullen; Sacraments, baptism, Eucharist, penance, unction, holy orders, marriage

Horace, as cited by Pseudo-Bede, 163

Hugh of St. Victor, v, 17, 18, 19, 20, 35, 57–63, 64, 65, 66, 67, 68, 69, 70, 72, 73, 74, 75, 76, 78, 80–81,

22–23, 30, 157, 428, 431; death, burial, and epitaph of, 23; obituary of, 28; last will and testament of, 28–29; library of, 28–29; personality of, as it emerges from his biography, 30, 32; medieval reputation and testimonia of, v, 11, 20, 22, 30–32, 157; works, v, 11, 15, 23–30; biblical exegesis of, 11, 15, 23, 26, 27–29, 31, 32, 83, 88, 149 n. 168, 152 n. 178, 156, 157, 160, 162, 170–88, 192–225, 238–39, 240, 242, 339, 272, 384, 403–04, 429, 460–61, 464, 466, 468, 487, 490, 499, 530, 625, 694, 711, 712, 714, 772; fragmentary or non-extant exegesis of, 27–28; *Magna glossatura* as medieval name of, 156; use of authorities in, 173, 174–75, 176–77, 178–79, 193, 207–12, 223, 224; use of classical authors in, 182; use of liberal arts in, 182, 173, 187, 211–12; rhetoric in, 170–74, 175, 183, 187, 194–95, 197, 200, 202, 211, 224; logic in, 182, 211–12; equipollent argumentation in, 182; reference to universals in, 211; commentary on the Psalms, 12, 23, 28, 156, 157, 170–88, 192, 194 n. 100, 208, 214, 372; influence of *Glossa ordinaria* on, 170, 173, 174, 184, 185; influence of Gilbert of Poitiers on, 167–70, 172–74; *accessus* to, 170–74, 175, 183, 187, 224; format of, 174, 187; on Psalms as a composite book, 171–72; key to Psalms on different themes in, 171–72, 187; accuracy of text in, 178–82, 187; awareness of variant texts of, 178–80; on authorship of, 170–71; typological and reading of, 170, 171, 172–74, 179, 182–83, 185, 187; anagogical interpretation in, 184; critique of Neoplatonic anthropology in, 174; concept of substance in, 177; problem of theological language in, 172; development of theological doctrine in, 173–78, 188, 712; hypostatic union in, 177, 188; whether human Christ should receive *dulia* or *latria* in, 175–76; ethics in, 173–74, 177–78, 185–86, 188; modes of fear in the moral life in, 177, 178; lying in, 185–86; sacraments in, 175, 186–87, 188; penance in, 175, 188; marriage in, 186–87; the four states

of souls in the resurrection in, 176–77, 712, 772; commentary on Pauline epistles, 12, 23–25, 149 n. 168, 152 n. 178; 156, 157, 186, 188, 192–225, 499, 530, 694, 711, 714, 772; format and mise-en-page of, 193, 224; *accessus* to St. Paul and to each epistle in, compared with Peter Abelard, *Commentarius Cantabridgensis*, Robert of Melun, *Quaestiones et decisiones in Epistolas divi Pauli*, 194–95, 197, 224; literal reading of text in, 195, 199–205; 2 Thessalonians as sole exception, 196, 205–07, 207 n. 136; historical contextualization and criticism of Paul in, 195, 196–98, 200–07, 212, 224; development of theological doctrine in, 196, 204–07, 403, 429, 487, 490, 498, 499, 530, 656, 694, 772; natural theology in, 212, 224, 238–39; critique of Peter Abelard's equation of Trinity with Platonic One, Nous, World Soul as accessible by natural reason in, 212–13, 239–40, 242, 294; his own countervailing appeal to Neoplatonic theology in, 212; predestination in, as a theological not logical problem, 213; Christology in, 215–17, 222–23, 403–04, 429, 460, 468; hypostatic union in, 222–23, 403–04, 429; Christ's saving work in, 217–20, 460–61, 464, 466; ethics in, 209, 213–14, 215, 298, 490, 499; intentionalism in, 213–14; psychogenesis of ethical acts in, 214; free will and grace in, 490; definition of faith in, 213–14, 298, hope in, 499, sin against the Holy Spirit in, 209, 215, 487; salvific power of Old Testament rites in, 530; sacraments in, 204–05, 220–22, 656, 694; Eucharist in, 220–22; marriage in, 204–05, 656, 694; Antichrist in, 196, 204, 205–07, 207 n. 136, 772; his teaching of exegesis, 23, 24, 25, 87; its use in his sermons, 26–27; reputation and influence as an exegete, 28, 30–32, 156–57, 170, 192, 193; *Sentences* of, 1, 2, 3, 4, 7, 8, 9, 10, 11, 23, 24, 25, 27, 28, 29, 30, 31–32, 34, 35, 77, 78–90, 92, 120, 122, 156, 157, 175, 176, 186, 204, 205 n. 132, 208, 214–15, 216, 217, 219, 221, 222,

729; view that angels influence men by their effects and not substantially in, 350; guardian angels, view that one angel can guard more than one human being simultaneously in, 351; role in Last Things in, 350, 711, 713, 729; creation and nature of man in, vi, 11, 78, 79, 81, 83, 84, 89, 123–26, 149–50, 204, 242–45, 260, 302, 331, 336, 338–39, 341, 350, 354–56, 366–72, 377, 379–86, 393, 396–97, 418, 421–22, 423, 443–44, 448, 472, 486–87, 489–90, 502, 515, 654, 657, 726, 727, 729, 727–28, 730–36, 737, 739, 740, 741, 742–43, 744, 745, 746, 747, 748, 750, 754–55, 773, 774, 775, 776–77; rationale for man's creation in, 336, 338–39, 351, 367, 444, 654, 727–28; creation of woman, her nature in comparison with that of man in, 366–68, 377, 657, 732–33, 776–77; rationale for creation of sub-human beings in, 338, 341, 728, 750; hylemorphic constitution of human nature in, 338–39, 341, 396–97, 418, 423; soul of prelapsarian man, its potential immortality in, 124–25, 366–71, 379–86, 731, 732–33, 745, 748, 773, 776–77; analogies of Trinity in, 123–26, 149–50, 242–45, 260, 421–22, 731; intellectual aptitudes of prelapsarian man in, 350, 731–32, 740, 741, 777; moral aptitudes of prelapsarian man, his free will, need for grace in order to advance in merit in, 370–72, 448, 472, 487, 489–90, 727, 729, 730, 731, 732, 741, 742, 744, 747, 777; body of prelapsarian man in, 204, 331, 354–55, 369, 731; freedom from pain, illness, exercising such natural functions as eating, 331, 369; sexual activity, 204, 354–55, 731; nature of children of Adam and Eve, had they been born before the fall in, 368–69; original sin in, 11, 81, 84, 186–87, 212, 214, 225, 370, 377–81, 382–85, 393–97, 421–22, 462, 464, 465, 487–88, 529, 555, 726, 732–36, 740, 741, 744, 745, 746, 747, 748, 754–55, 773, 776–77; psychogenesis of sin in, 378, 379–80, 732–33, 744, 776; as not excused by ignorance in, 378–79, 733, 745; Eve's motivation in fall in, 377, 378, 379, 488, 732–33, 744, 777; Adam's motivation in fall in, 379, 462, 469, 488, 733, 777; view that he sinned more seriously than she did in, 378, 380, 396, 733; effects of original sin in, 81, 187, 214, 383–85, 732, 733–34, 741, 754–55, 773; man's retention of conscience notwithstanding in, 385; transmission of original sin in, 81, 186–87, 393–97, 421–22, 734–36; Christology in, vi, vii, 11, 25, 81, 82, 83, 89, 125, 131, 150–53, 174, 175–78, 212, 215, 216–20, 222, 223, 247, 262, 266, 299–300, 302, 345, 383, 397, 403–04, 417–31, 433–38, 442–48, 449, 459, 461–70, 472, 477–78, 490, 492, 493, 499–504, 506, 508, 509, 514, 515, 516, 517, 533, 541, 558–60, 575–78, 579, 581, 582, 621, 622, 623–29, 650–51, 652, 657, 685–86, 702, 711, 712, 713, 714, 717, 723, 726, 730, 736–44, 748, 749, 750, 752, 753, 771, 773, 774, 776, 777–78; in sermons of, 27; influence of John Damascene on, 25, 151, 215, 217, 418–20, 423, 428, 437, 447; divinity of, as disclosed by Holy Spirit in, 533; incarnation of, in, 498, 736, 740, 774; exemption of Virgin Mary from original sin in, 421, 738; exemption of incarnate Christ from original sin in, 422, 443, 470, 738; His taking on of some of its effects in, 443–44, 446–47, 741; point in gestation process at which His human soul was infused into His body in, 420–21; hypostatic union in, 81, 150–53, 177, 216–17, 222, 223, 262, 266, 403–04, 417–31, 433–38, 448, 723, 736–40, 776; critique of *assumptus homo* theory in, 425, 426, 738–39; critique of *habitus* theory in *Sentences*, 425, 426, 429, 739; entertainment of *habitus* theory in gloss on Philippians, 223; critique of subsistence theory in, 425–26, 430, 739; attribution of Christological nihilianism to him, vi, 27 n. 36, 222, 223, 427–31, 433–36, 738, 739, 776, 777–78; Christ's human nature in, 81, 82, 83, 152–53, 215, 438, 442–48, 449, 461, 464, 466, 470, 472, 492, 499–500, 503–04, 506, 508, 509, 514, 515, 516, 736, 737, 740–41, 743, 749, 750, 752, 774,

Hugh of St. Victor on Trinity, 17; rejection of Boethian definition of *persona* in, 150; Christ's human knowledge in, 439, 440, 441; marriage in, 650 n. 466

Walter of St. Victor, allegation in his *Four Labyrinths of France* that Peter Lombard taught Christological nihilianism, 428, 431, 432–33, 434–35, 436

Weisweiler, Heinrich, 43

Willaim Andrensus, as testimonium of Peter Lombard, 31 n. 52

William, archbishop of Tyre, 28, 30–31; as pupil of Peter Lombard, 28; as source for his wider work as a biblical exegete, 28; as testimonium of Peter Lombard, 30–31

William of Champeaux, 6, 276, 289, 357, 360, 371, 373, 375, 378, 383, 386, 411, 417, 420, 437, 445, 446, 485–86, 504, 508, 534, 536, 553–54, 555; as a theological conservative in his day, 6; God's providence and predestination in, 276; Peter Lombard's critique of his view that God chooses elect because of their *praevisa merita*, 289; human psychology in, 357, 360, 371; original sin in, 373, 375, 378, 386; hypostatic union in, 411, 417, 420, 437; Christ's moral capacities in, 445, 446; deadly sins in, 486; modes of fear of the Lord in moral life in, 508; sacraments in, 534, 536, 553–54, 555; baptism in, 534, 536; Eucharist in, 553–54, 555; which body Christ gave His disciples at last supper in, 553–54; change of Eucharistic elements in, 555. *See also* Laon, school of

William of Conches, 101, 102, 104 n. 34, 256, 310–14, 315, 316, 317, 319; theological language in, 313; definition of substance in, 104 n. 34; doctrine of Trinity in, 311, 313, 314; as criticized by William of St. Thierry, 256, 311, 313, 316, 319; critique of Trinitarian theology of Peter Abelard, 101, 102; creation in, 310–14; primordial causes in, 311; *formae nativae* in, 312; primordial matter in, 311, as created *simul* in, 312; seminal reasons in, 312; World Soul as force of nature in, 312; whether to equate it with Holy Spirit in, 312, 313,

314; *Dragmaticon*, 311; *Elementorum philosophiae*, 313; *Glosae super Platonem*, 311, 313; *Philosophia mundi*, 311. *See also* Chartrains; Creation; Platonism; World Soul

William of St. Thierry, 188–90, 191, 212, 253, 256, 304, 311, 313, 316, 534; as commentator on Romans, 188–90, 191; critique of philosophy in, 189, 190; critique of natural theology in, 190; critique of Peter Abelard in, 189, 190, 212; use of authorities in, 189, 190; use of Augustine in, 189, 190; style and aim in, 189, 190; moral, hortatory emphasis in, 189–90; critique of theology of Peter Abelard in other works, 253, 256; critique of William of Conches on Trinity, 256, 311, 313, 316, 319; critique of Chartrains in general, 304; infant baptism in, 534. *See also* Abelard, Peter; Augustine; Chartrains; Exegesis, biblical; Paul, St.; William of Conches

William of the White Hands, archbishop of Sens and, from 1176, archbishop of Rheims, 429, 431–32, 434; as charged by pope Alexander III with reform of St. Victor, 431–32; with being alert to teaching of Christological nihilianism within his see, 434

Wisdom, book of, 28

Wodeham, Adam, commentary on *Sentences* of Peter Lombard, 1

Ysagoge in theologiam, 52, 345, 478, 485, 505, 515, 520, 526, 535, 538, 549, 556, 568, 576, 588 n. 310, 598, 598 n. 333, 642, 647, 655, 663 n. 489, 674 n. 523, 679; schema as a sentence collection, 52; confirmation of angels in fallen or unfallen states in, 345; departure from Peter Abelard on Christ's saving work in, 345; ethics in, 478, 485; intentionalism in, 478, 485; natural virtue in, 505, 515; cardinal virtues in, 505; seven deadly sins in, 485; sacraments in, 52, 520, 526, 535, 538, 549, 556, 558 n. 310, 598, 598 n. 33, 644, 647, 655, 663 n. 489, 674, 679; baptism in, 52, 535, 538; confirmation in, 520, 526, condition of minister in, 549; Eucharist in, 556, 558, 568; 576; change of

INDEX OF SUBJECTS

requiring grace in order to activate free will toward the good, in Augustine, 343, 348; as a twelfth-century consensus position, 343, 349–50, 353, 729–30, 745, 777; in Peter Lombard, 345, 348, 349–50, 353, 729–30, 745, 777; his use of Origen as an authority on this point, 345; their fall, 38, 66, 320, 322, 329, 335, 338, 343–44, 348, 349, 378, 729–30; in Honorius Augustodunensis, 38, 322, 343–44; in Hugh of St. Victor, 329; in *Summa sententiarum*, 334–44; in Robert Pullen, 335; in Peter Lombard, 338, 349, 378, 729–30; timing of fall, in Honorius Augustodunensis, *Sententie Anselmi*, *Summa sententiarum*, 343–44; as being partially limited in their free will after their fall, in Honorius Augustodunensis, 344; in Hugh of St. Victor, 345; in *Summa sententiarum*, 345–46, 349; as retaining free will after fall, in Peter Lombard, 347, 349–50, 353, 730, 772, 777; their confirmation in their fallen or unfallen state, as a consensus position vs. Origen, 320, 344–46, 349–51, 378, 445, 729–30, 742, 772, 773; in Anselm of Canterbury, 344, 348; in Honorius Augustodunensis, 344–45, 351; in school of Laon, 344–45, 346, 348; in Porretans, 345; in *Ysagoge in theologiam*, 345; in Hugh of St. Victor, 345; in *Summa sententiarum*, 345–36, 349; in Robert Pullen, 346, 349, 350; in Peter Lombard, 349–50, 378, 445, 772, 773; fallen angels, 69, 70, 170, 343, 344, 345–46, 348–50, 616, 617, 620, 703, 704; number of, in Hugh of St. Victor, 346; as lacking in gradations, in *Summa sententiarum*, 343, 350; as having gradations, in Peter Lombard, 350; their assignment to Hell or upper air and function as tempters of men, in Honorius Augustodunensis, 40, 344; in Hugh of St. Victor, 346; in *Summa sententiarum*, 345; in Peter Lombard, 350; their role in Last Things, in Peter Lombard, 350, 703, 704, 713; good angels, their hierarchy, 69, 74, 329, 342–43, 350–53, 703, 729, 742; in Gregory the Great, 329, 343,

350; in Pseudo-Dionysius, 69, 343, 350; in Honorius Augustodunensis, 703; in Anselm of Laon and his school, 329, 342; in Robert of Melun, 74; in Peter Lombard, as related to gradations of angels before fall, 348, 351, subsets of three within nine orders of, 351; gradations within each angelic rank, 351; perfection in their contemplation of God, in quality of their love and merit, but growth in knowledge of events occurring in time and in quantity of virtue, their capacity for growth a means of distinguishing them from God, in Peter Lombard, 352–53, 742; missions of, 40, 69, 70, 74, 170, 320, 343, 346, 350, 351, 376–77, 383 n. 36, 702, 703, 711, 713, 729; whether all ranks of angels are sent, in Hugh of St. Victor, 346, 351; in *Summa sententiarum*, 346, 352; in Robert of Melun, 74, in Peter Lombard, 351, 729; their assumption of bodies on such missions, 343, 346, 350, 729, metaphysical status of these bodies and bodies of offspring angels may engender while using them, in church fathers, 343; in Augustine, 343; in Porretans, 343; unwillingness of Peter Lombard to rule on this question, 350; his view that angels interact with men by their effects, not substantially, 350, 729, role of angels as guardians of Eden after fall, 376–77; as guardians of men, 40, 69, 70, 170, 346, 351, 483 n. 36, 703, 729; in Gregory the Great, 356; in Honorius Augustodunensis, 40, 703; in Gilbert of Poitiers, 170; in Hugh of St. Victor, along with view that number of good angels is identical at any given moment with number of human beings on earth, 346; in *Summa sententiarum*, 346, in Peter Lombard, with critique of Hugh and view that one angel can guard more than one human being at the same time, 351, 729; role of, in Last Things, in Honorius Augustodunensis, 702, 703, in Porretans, 704; in Peter Lombard, 711, 713, 729

Animals, rationale for their creation,

66; in Hugh of St. Victor, 56, 142;
in *Summa sententiarum*, 62, 64, 65,
117–19; in *Sententiae divinitatis*, 56,
142; in Robert Pullen, 68–69, 71,
106, 107; in Robert of Melun, 74,
75, 110; in Peter Lombard, 11,
25, 27, 31, 79, 81, 82, 84, 86, 88,
150–53, 171, 208 n. 138, 215, 217,
222–23, 253, 443, 444, 503–04, 515,
516, 576, 730, 736–44, 752;
influence of John Damascene on,
25, 151, 215, 217, 418–20, 423, 428,
437, 447; allegation that he taught
Christological nihilianism by John
of Cornwall, 27 n. 36; 428–31, 434,
435, 436; by Walter of St. Victor,
428, 431, 432–33, 434–35, 436;
testimony that he did not teach this
doctrine by pupils Adam of St.
Asaph, 434; Odo of Ourscamp, 424
n. 49; Peter Comestor, 424 n. 49.
See also Christ
Church, doctrine of, 39, 40, 60, 61,
64, 69, 82, 158, 164, 165–66, 167,
172, 182–83, 185, 188, 203, 204,
206–07, 518, 525, 527, 532, 561–62,
565–66, 567, 574, 576, 577–78,
582–83, 591, 618–19, 622, 625, 631,
636, 642, 644, 646, 647, 650–51,
652, 665–66, 686, 700, 715, 757,
762, 764; in Ivo of Chartres, 566;
in Honorius Augustodunensis, 39,
40, 518, 565–66, 700; in Letbert
of Lille, 158; in *Glossa ordinaria*,
165–66; in Hugh of St. Victor, 56,
60, 61, 518, 525, 565–66, 618–19,
622, 625; in Robert Pullen, 69, 70,
574, 625; in Peter Lombard, 182–83,
188, 206–07, 532, 576, 577, 578,
582–83, 622, 651, 715, 757; as
persons bonded by Eucharistic
communion, in Honorius
Augustodunensis, 565–66; in Hugh
of St. Victor, 565–56; in *Summa
sententiarum*, 561–62, 578; in Robert
Pullen, 578; in Peter Lombard, 576,
577, 578, 582–83, 757; marriage as
signifying its union with Christ, as
a consensus position, 172, 631, 636,
642, 644, 646, 647, 650–51, 652,
665–66, 685–86, 764; in
Commentarius Cantabridgensis, 204;
in Peter Lombard, 650–51, 652,
685–86, 764; argument, by
confessionists, that church must be
satisfied by penitential satisfaction
imposed by confessor, 591;

communion of saints in church, in
connection with Purgatory, in Peter
Lombard, 715. *See also* Last Things;
Sacraments, Eucharist, penance,
holy orders, marriage
Church, fathers of, 7, 8, 10, 55, 58,
62, 63, 71, 72, 76, 81, 86, 89, 95,
146, 149, 159, 162, 163, 165, 166,
182, 189, 191, 193, 202, 207, 233,
287, 303, 321, 322, 323, 329, 333,
336, 343, 344, 374, 385, 400, 401,
491, 494, 504, 505, 508, 509, 517,
541, 542, 594, 666, 667, 669, 700,
711, 727, 736, 748, 769, 772; Greek
fathers on grace and free will, 385,
491. *See also* Ambrose; Augustine;
Authorities; Basil the Great;
Cyprian; Hilary of Poitiers; Jerome;
Gregory the Great; Origen; Pseudo-
Chrysostom; Theodore
Church, Gallican, its rules on
penance, 584, 585; on marriage,
629, 631, 674–75, 676–77, 679–80,
692
Church, Roman, its rules on penance,
584; on marriage, 674–75, 679, 692
Church, primitive, idea of, 44–90,
202, 204, 205–07, 467, 532–34, 537,
541–44, 546, 550, 570, 583, 584–88,
589, 590, 601–02, 607, 608, 611,
666–68, 684, 690, 698, 754, 758,
761; general attitude to, in
canonists, 46, 532, 584–85, 667–68;
in Gratian, 584–85, 667–68, 691,
692; in scholastic theologians,
44–90, 202, 204, 205–07, 532, 537,
542–44, 546, 550, 570, 584–88, 589,
608, 666–68, 684, 690, 698, 754,
758, 761; in school of Laon, 46–47,
543–44, 570, 586, 589, 602; in
Hugh of St. Victor, 586–87, 601,
602, 666, 667; in *Summa sententiarum*,
588; in Porretans, 542–43, 570, 588
n. 310, in Hermannus, 566, 666; in
Commentarius Cantabridgensis, 204; in
Sententiae Parisiensis I, 666; in *Ysagoge
in theologiam*, 588 n. 310; in Roland
of Bologna, 537, 550, 585; in
Sententiae divinitatis, 546, 587–88,
589, 590; in Master Simon, 667; in
Robert Pullen, 588 n. 310; in Peter
Lombard, 202, 205–07, 601–02,
608, 684, 690, 698, 754, 758, 762; in
twelfth-century debates on baptism,
46–47, 537, 542, 546, 570; on
confirmation, 550; on Eucharist,
570; on penance, 583, 584–88, 589,

676, 677, 678, 685, 768. *See also* Sacraments, marriage

Women, their perceived inequality to men, in twelfth-century theologians, 365–66, 731; in Peter Lombard, 366–68, 377, 731, 733, 776–77; their salvation, in the Old Testament dispensation, in Gregory the Great, 530; in Hugh of St. Victor, 525; in Peter Lombard, 530; their role in the church, in St. Paul, 203–24; as interpreted by Peter Lombard, 203–04; by *Commentarius Cantabridgensis*, 204

Work, as a natural good present in Eden, in Robert of Melun, 356; in Roland of Bologna, 356

Works, good, in William of St. Thierry, 190; in Hugh of St. Victor, 60, 522, 525; in *Summa sententiarum*, 526; in Peter Lombard, 530–31. *See also* Ethics

World Soul, in Plato, 308; in Vergil, 308; twelfth-century debates over, 51, 74, 75, 80, 85, 212–13, 234, 236, 239, 249, 253–60, 308, 309, 310, 315, 317, 318, 319, 324, 326, 349–50, 493, 775; in Peter Abelard, 51, 212–13, 234, 239, 249, 253–60, 324, 493; in Abelardians, 51, 249; in Bernard Silvestris, 308; in William of Conches, 102, 312, 317; in Thierry of Chartres, 309, 310, 317; in Chartrain Anonymous, 315; in Clarenbald of Arras, 317, 318, 319; in Hugh of St. Victor, 326; in Robert Pullen, 360; in Robert of Melun, 74, 75, 236; equation of, with Holy Spirit, as criticized by Peter Lombard, 212–13, 349–50, 775. *See also* Creation; Trinity, doctrine of

BRILL'S STUDIES IN INTELLECTUAL HISTORY

1. POPKIN, R.H. *Isaac la Peyrère (1596-1676)*. His Life, Work and Influence. 1987. ISBN 90 04 08157 7
2. THOMSON, A. *Barbary and Enlightenment*. European Attitudes towards the Maghreb in the 18th Century. 1987. ISBN 90 04 08273 5
3. DUHEM, P. *Prémices Philosophiques*. With an Introduction in English by S.L. Jaki. 1987. ISBN 90 04 08117 8
4. OUDEMANS, TH.C.W. & A.P.M.H. LARDINOIS. *Tragic Ambiguity*. Anthropology, Philosophy and Sophocles' *Antigone*. 1987. ISBN 90 04 08417 7
5. FRIEDMAN, J.B. (ed.). *John de Foxton's Liber Cosmographiae (1408)*. An Edition and Codicological Study. 1988. ISBN 90 04 08528 9
6. AKKERMAN, F. & A.J. VANDERJAGT (eds.). *Rodolphus Agricola Phrisius, 1444-1485*. Proceedings of the International Conference at the University of Groningen, 28-30 October 1985. 1988. ISBN 90 04 08599 8
7. CRAIG, W.L. *The Problem of Divine Foreknowledge and Future Contingents from Aristotle to Suarez*. 1988. ISBN 90 04 08516 5
8. STROLL, M. *The Jewish Pope*. Ideology and Politics in the Papal Schism of 1130. 1987. ISBN 90 04 08590 4
9. STANESCO, M. *Jeux d'errance du chevalier médiéval*. Aspects ludiques de la fonction guerrière dans la littérature du Moyen Age flamboyant. 1988. ISBN 90 04 08684 6
10. KATZ, D. *Sabbath and Sectarianism in Seventeenth-Century England*. 1988. ISBN 90 04 08754 0
11. LERMOND, L. *The Form of Man*. Human Essence in Spinoza's *Ethic*. 1988. ISBN 90 04 08829 6
12. JONG, M. DE. *In Samuel's Image*. Early Medieval Child Oblation. (in preparation)
13. PYENSON, L. *Empire of Reason*. Exact Sciences in Indonesia, 1840-1940. 1989. ISBN 90 04 08984 5
14. CURLEY, E. & P.-F. MOREAU (eds.). *Spinoza. Issues and Directions*. The Proceedings of the Chicago Spinoza Conference. 1990. ISBN 90 04 09334 6
15. KAPLAN, Y., H. MÉCHOULAN & R.H. POPKIN (eds.). *Menasseh Ben Israel and His World*. 1989. ISBN 90 04 09114 9
16. BOS, A.P. *Cosmic and Meta-Cosmic Theology in Aristotle's Lost Dialogues*. 1989. ISBN 90 04 09155 6
17. KATZ, D.S. & J.I. ISRAEL (eds.). *Sceptics, Millenarians and Jews*. 1990. ISBN 90 04 09160 2
18. DALES, R.C. *Medieval Discussions of the Eternity of the World*. 1990. ISBN 90 04 09215 3
19. CRAIG, W.L. *Divine Foreknowledge and Human Freedom*. The Coherence of Theism: Omniscience. 1991. ISBN 90 04 09250 1
20. OTTEN, W. *The Anthropology of Johannes Scottus Eriugena*. 1991. ISBN 90 04 09302 8
21. ÅKERMAN, S. *Queen Christina of Sweden and Her Circle*. The Transformation of a Seventeenth-Century Philosophical Libertine. 1991. ISBN 90 04 09310 9
22. POPKIN, R.H. *The Third Force in Seventeenth-Century Thought*. 1992. ISBN 90 04 09324 9
23. DALES, R.C & O. ARGERAMI (eds.). *Medieval Latin Texts on the Eternity of the World*. 1990. ISBN 90 04 09376 1
24. STROLL, M. *Symbols as Power*. The Papacy Following the Investiture Contest. 1991. ISBN 90 04 09374 5

25. FARAGO, C.J. *Leonardo da Vinci's 'Paragone'*. A Critical Interpretation with a New Edition of the Text in the *Codex Urbinas*. 1992. ISBN 90 04 09415 6
26. JONES, R. *Learning Arabic in Renaissance Europe*. Forthcoming. ISBN 90 04 09451 2
27. DRIJVERS, J.W. *Helena Augusta*. The Mother of Constantine the Great and the Legend of Her Finding of the True Cross. 1992. ISBN 90 04 09435 0
28. BOUCHER, W.I. *Spinoza in English*. A Bibliography from the Seventeenth-Century to the Present. 1991. ISBN 90 04 09499 7
29. McINTOSH, C. *The Rose Cross and the Age of Reason*. Eighteenth-Century Rosicrucianism in Central Europe and its Relationship to the Enlightenment. 1992. ISBN 90 04 09502 0
30. CRAVEN, K. *Jonathan Swift and the Millennium of Madness*. The Information Age in Swift's *A Tale of a Tub*. 1992. ISBN 90 04 09524 1
31. BERKVENS-STEVELINCK, C., H. BOTS, P.G. HOFTIJZER & O.S. LANKHORST (eds.). *Le Magasin de l'Univers. The Dutch Republic as the Centre of the European Book Trade*. Papers Presented at the International Colloquium, held at Wassenaar, 5-7 July 1990. 1992. ISBN 90 04 09493 8
32. GRIFFIN, JR., M.I.J. *Latitudinarianism in the Seventeenth-Century Church of England*. Annoted by R.H. Popkin. Edited by L. Freedman. 1992. ISBN 90 04 09653 1
33. WES, M.A. *Classics in Russia 1700-1855*. Between two Bronze Horsemen. 1992. ISBN 90 04 09664 7
34. BULHOF, I.N. *The Language of Science*. A Study in the Relationship between Literature and Science in the Perspective of a Hermeneutical Ontology. With a Case Study in Darwin's *The Origin of Species*. 1992. ISBN 90 04 09644 2
35. LAURSEN, J.C. *The Politics of Skepticism in the Ancients, Montaigne, Hume and Kant*. 1992. ISBN 90 04 09459 8
36. COHEN, E. *The Crossroads of Justice*. Law and Culture in Late Medieval France. 1993. ISBN 90 04 09569 1
37. POPKIN, R.H. & A.J. VANDERJAGT (eds.). *Scepticism and Irreligion in the Seventeenth and Eighteenth Centuries*. 1993. ISBN 90 04 09596 9
38. MAZZOCCO, A. *Linguistic Theories in Dante and the Humanists*. Studies of Language and Intellectual History in Late Medieval and Early Renaissance Italy. 1993. ISBN 90 04 09702 3
39. KROOK, D. *John Sergeant and His Circle*. A Study of Three Seventeenth-Century English Aristotelians. Edited with an Introduction by B.C. Southgate. 1993. ISBN 90 04 09756 2
40. AKKERMAN, F., G.C. HUISMAN & A.J. VANDERJAGT (eds.). *Wessel Gansfort (1419-1489) and Northern Humanism*. 1993. ISBN 90 04 09857 7
41. COLISH, M.L. *Peter Lombard*. 2 volumes. 1993. ISBN 90 04 09859 3 (Vol. 1), ISBN 90 04 09860 7 (Vol. 2), ISBN 90 04 09861 5 (Set)
42. VAN STRIEN, C.D. *British Travellers in Holland During the Stuart Period*. Edward Browne and John Locke as Tourists in the United Provinces. 1993. ISBN 90 04 09482 2
43. MACK, P. *Renaissance Argument*. Valla and Agricola in the Traditions of Rhetoric and Dialectic. 1993. ISBN 90 04 09879 8
44. DA COSTA, U. *Examination of Pharisaic Traditions*. Supplemented by SEMUEL DA SILVA's *Treatise on the Immortality of the Soul*. Tratado da immortalidade da alma. Translation, Notes and Introduction by H.P. Salomon & I.S.D. Sassoon. 1993. ISBN 90 04 09923 9
45. MANNS, J.W. *Reid and His French Disciples*. Aesthetics and Metaphysics. 1994. ISBN 90 04 09942 5
46. SPRUNGER, K.L. *Trumpets from the Tower*. English Puritan Printing in the Netherlands, 1600-1640. 1994. ISBN 90 04 09935 2
47. RUSSELL, G.A. (ed.). *The 'Arabick' Interest of the Natural Philosophers in Seventeenth-Century England*. 1994. ISBN 90 04 09888 7
48. SPRUIT, L. Species intelligibilis: *From Perception to Knowledge*. Volume I: Classical Roots and Medieval Discussions. 1994. ISBN 90 04 09883 6